Research on the Dai Fertility Culture in China

Guo Shan

Research on the Dai Fertility Culture in China

Translated by Chi Xiao Qiu Xin

PETER LANG
Lausanne • Berlin • Bruxelles • Chennai • New York • Oxford

Library of Congress Cataloging-in-Publication Data

Names: Guo Shan, author.
Title: Research on the Dai fertility culture in China /
Guo Shan.
Description: New York: Peter Lang, [2023] | Includes bibliographical
references.
Identifiers: LCCN 2022060744 (print) | LCCN 2022060745 (ebook) |
ISBN 9781433181474 (hardback) | ISBN 9781433181481 (ebook) |
ISBN 9781433181498 (epub)
Subjects: LCSH: Fertility, Human—China. | Tai (Southeast Asian
people)—Population.
Classification: LCC HB1064.A3 S53 2023 (print) | LCC HB1064.A3 (ebook) |
DDC 304.6/320951—dc23/eng/20230105
LC record available at https://lccn.loc.gov/2022060744
LC ebook record available at https://lccn.loc.gov/2022060745
DOI 10.3726/b17188

Bibliographic information published by the **Deutsche Nationalbibliothek.**
The **German National Library** lists this publication in the German
National Bibliography; detailed bibliographic data is available
on the Internet at http://dnb.d-nb.de.

Cover design by Peter Lang Group AG

ISBN 9781433181474 (hardback)
ISBN 9781433181481 (ebook)
ISBN 9781433181498 (epub)
DOI 10.3726/b17188

Published by Peter Lang Publishing Inc., New York, USA
info@peterlang.com - www.peterlang.com

This publication has been peer reviewed.

Contents

List of Figures

List of Tables

1 Introduction

To fully review and summarize the course and research achievements of the China Population Association (CPA) over the past three decades, the 30th Anniversary Celebration & 2011 Annual Conference of CPA was held this year in Beijing. In his keynote speech at the event, Mr. Zhang Weiqing, CPA President, said, "... over the past three decades, CPA and all the experts, scholars and practitioners have been part of and witnesses to the history of demographic transition in China. Today, we can proudly declare to the world that China has successfully completed its demographic transition and blazed a new trail of demographic transition with Chinese characteristics" (Zhang, 2011).

His remarks sent a message: It is such a proud thing for China to achieve demographic transition within 30 years of time! However, while taking pride in our historical achievements, we also must be aware that such low growth rates of the total population, as well as low fertility rates, have been attributed to the strict family planning policy the Chinese government has adopted since the 1970s, efficient institutional arrangements and effective administrative organization. In other words, today's decline in the fertility rate has, in fact, been driven more by exogenous forces rather than the Chinese populace, and a strong desire to have more children still seems to be an irresistible pursuit of the general public. The *Decision on Effectively Strengthening Population and Family Planning Efforts to*

Address Population Issues in a Coordinated Manner issued in 2006 by the State Council made it clear that,

> More than 400 million births have been averted nationwide since the introduction of family planning in China, not only effectively alleviating the pressure of population on resources and environment but also boosting economic development and social progress. But we must be keenly aware that China is now confronted with unprecedented complex dynamics of population development and the real risk of the low fertility rate rebounding . . . During the Eleventh Five-year Plan period (2006–2010), our population and family planning work should focus on keeping the fertility rate at a lower level, solving population-related issues in a coordinated manner, and promoting the all-round development of human beings. Making every endeavor to stabilize a lower fertility rate will remain among the priorities during this period . . . as a result, the focus and difficulty of our population and family planning work still lie in rural areas, that is, keeping the fertility rate in rural areas at a lower level should be the top priority in our effort to comprehensively address the population-related issues.

Hence, stabilizing a lower fertility rate is the goal of population and family planning in China in the upcoming period. To this end, we must make sense of the driving mechanisms behind a declining fertility rate.

The demographic transition doctrine, a Western theory of macro-demography, analyzes the trends of population development based on the natural variation of population induced by changes in fertility and mortality rates. Its basic tenets are as follows: (1) The human fertility pattern evolves following the Primitive-Traditional – Modern trajectory; (2) The process of population development is closely related to that of social/economic development, and demographic transitions are premised on fundamental changes in social/economic conditions; (3) Demographic transitions are achieved mainly through changes in birth rate (fertility rate) and mortality rate and their long-term equilibrium; (4) In the early stages of the evolution from the traditional agrarian society to the modern industrial society, the decline in fertility rate lagged behind that in mortality rate, and there was a "time lag" between them. Therefore, accelerating social/economic modernization and shortening the "time lag" of fertility rate decline are the key driving factors behind demographic transitions.

In a nutshell, the key to demographic transitions lies in fertility decline, which in turn depends upon social and economic modernization. The micro-population theories, especially "Rational Choice of Marginal Offspring, Tradeoff Between Quantity and Quality of Offspring", "Wealth Flow and Supply-Demand for

Offspring Determined by Fertility Rate", attribute the gap between the theoretical and actual fertility of human beings to our economic rationality, holding that the driving force behind restrained fertility is the trade-off between fertility utility and fertility payoffs. These theories, though providing different perspectives, all have come down to a basic proposition: economic forces have a strong and significant leverage effect on changes in the population size. That is to say, the fertility behavior of human beings are decisions based on rational economic considerations. Hence, "agrarian society", "poverty" and "economical underdevelopment" are arguably the root causes of "more births", and so, it follows that to change from "more births" to "fewer births", the optimal approach is to replace the agrarian society with the industrial society.

The above-mentioned research provides a theoretical explanation of the actual processes of the mortality rate and fertility rate changing from a high level to a low one and the resulting slowing or even negative population growths as agrarian societies transformed into industrialized ones in modern developed countries, especially in Europe, and convincingly demonstrates why Malthus's theory of population, i.e., the idea that the population necessarily increases as long as means of subsistence are available, has not been borne out by reality. Meanwhile, it also opens to us a macro-historical narrative of human fertility patterns: in terms of space, developed countries tend to have lower fertility rates and underdeveloped countries have higher fertility rates. Yet, in temporal terms, fertility rates in developed countries used to be higher, and the current low fertility rates are simply the outcome of a fertility transition from high to low in modern times. In other words, in the past, people in underdeveloped countries (regions) all chose to have more offspring, whereas nowadays, people in developed countries (regions) tend to have fewer offspring, while people in less developed countries (regions) still prefer to have more. This suggests that as less developed countries (regions) become more developed, their fertility pattern will also transition from having more offspring to having fewer one. Just for this reason, "this doctrine of human reproduction was among the hottest topics of contention at the 1974 World Population Conference in Bucharest, coming out with a compelling and thought-provoking argument that development is the most effective birth control pill" (Gu, 1992).

Chinese demographers represented by Mr. Fei Xiaotong characterized the traditional procreation customs in China as "having as many offspring as possible, preferably male". Based on his empirical research in rural China in the 1930s, Fei Xiaotong revised Thomas Malthus's "double-checks" doctrine, pointing out that "to meet the need for laborers in farming, it is necessary to maintain a large population in the countryside. In an economic structure like this where people mean productive forces, a large population over a small land is inevitable." Due to high infant mortality rates, "to maintain the capacity of such a social structure, it is imperative to have as many children as possible", "only when farming becomes less labor-intensive can China see a gradual decline in its population" (Fei, 1998).

To ensure the integrity of an existing social structure, not only does having children enable generational succession (passing-down) but it is also instrumental for parent care (reciprocating for child-rearing). Within the parameters of this longstanding and stable social structure both respect for and support of the elderly have become customary. This analytical framework featuring a parent care by adult children model in which parents take care of their young children, and are supported in old age by their adult children offers a good explanation for the underlying cause and practical rationality of the customary "preference for more, especially male offspring" in rural China at that time. As for the contemporary era, Li Yinhe has built a "Village Society of Acquaintances" model in her work: *Procreation and Village Cultures* to expound on the reasons why women in the countryside "have many children, start having children early, and prefer sons to daughters". Proceeding from Li's critical inquiry into the inapplicability of Becker's Quantity-Quality Tradeoff theory to China and her modification of Fei Xiaotong's parent care by adult children model in the traditional Chinese fertility institutions, Li Yinhe commented that "fertility cultures in various Chinese regions don't seem to originate from the cultural tradition of the entire Chinese nation, but rather are rooted in particular living environments of various regions" (Li, 1994a) and defined the cultural atmospheres derived from their particular living environments as village cultures. Largely characterized by information sharing, a village culture (including ethics and behavioral norms) is shared by a small group of folks and has at least the following distinct features: first, the village scale is limited to the extent to which ordinary village members have gotten acquainted with one another; second, there is a low mobility of village members; third, fellow villagers tend to compete with each other (irrational comparison with others, keeping up with the Joneses); and fourth, fellow villagers are pressured to converge in all aspects of life (pursuits). Living in such a context, individuals' fertility behavior are inevitably governed by and manifested in the logic that "a greater say comes from more voices, namely more offspring", thus encouraging more offspring and extended families. On one hand, the "competition" rule motivates village members to go all out in the fertility competition, while on the other, the "convergence" rule and the strong demand for fairness among village members combine to form a force constraining each other (Li,

1994b). Hence, more births and earlier parenthood are, of course, the common goal for all families in a village.

When it comes to the fundamental causes of the longstanding intention to have more children in the Chinese society and the driving mechanism behind the shift of intention away from a higher fertility rate to a lower one, a basic consensus has recently been reached in the domestic academia: nowadays, though the fertility pattern in China has been in the critical period when the traditional exogenous pattern is quickly giving way to the modern endogenous one, the shift in the desire to bear children has rather lagged. Much research on the endogenous factors of the shift in fertility concepts and behaviors has been done so far and many researchers hold economic determinism, but the similar effort on diverse fertility cultures has been rather limited, which, as a result, has seriously inhibited us from making science-based judgments on the working mechanisms and conditions of transitions in fertility behavior in various cultural patterns and contexts.

Indeed, the negative correlation between the level of economic development and the fertility rate as explained in the demographic transition theory has already been verified by the actual historical processes of population changes in industrialized countries, especially in Europe, and therefore, the argument that development is the most effective birth control pill has also been accepted by most scholars both at home and abroad. However, any assumption, inspired by the relation between "economic development and population", that all the issues and problems concerning population will disappear or be solved as an economy develops, is sure to be a misunderstanding of the issue of population, neither objective nor comprehensive or thorough.

In fact, under the influence of cultural factors, folks in a traditional agrarian society could also foster the desire to bear fewer children, and thus experience lower fertility rates. These realities have recently captured attention and interest from scholars both at home and abroad. For example, in his paper to the International Union for the Scientific Study of Population, Ansley J. Coale noted that a closer examination of the objective conditions for the declining marital fertility rates in more than 700 European provinces/regions revealed that differences in the demographic transition process in various countries and regions could not be explained in terms of socio-economic features alone (Coale, 1992). Research by Ronald Freedman shows that fertility rates are falling almost simultaneously in countries at radically different levels of industrialization and urbanization, and even some less-developed regions experienced much sharper declines in fertility rates than their developed peers did.

Studies have shown that fertility patterns in regions with similar cultures exhibit similar profiles and are largely irrelevant to the critical socioeconomic development indicators underlying the Population Transition Theory (Freedman, 1992). From the perspective of human fertility customs, any qualitative changes in fertility rates are driven by changes in fertility concepts. Without changes in fertility concepts, fertility rates may slide sharply under the influence of external forces but will rebound quickly once the external forces weaken or disappear (Zhai and Liu, 2000). In fact, we have seen cases with lower fertility rates in Chinese agrarian societies, and cultural factors are, obviously in most cases, a significant part of the stories (Guo and Lyu, 2007). And so on.

From their perspectives, these studies have demonstrated that cultural factors play a crucial role in the formation of ideas about fertility, and once formed and established, these ideas become deeply entrenched and difficult to dislodge.

Low fertility rates derive from the reproductive behavior of fewer births. Proceeding from the revisit to some established population theories on human fertility behavior and customs, this research expounds on the formation mechanism of the traditional behavior of fewer births in Dai people in traditional agrarian societies and reaches the following conclusions: (1) The fertility behavior of human beings are rational choices made based on their living environments and don't necessarily have some decisive correspondence with the developmental levels of social productivity, namely, there is, all the same, the pattern of lower fertility rates even in an agrarian society; (2) fertility concepts and birth behaviors are governed by social values. In a society with basic living needs met (namely, with sufficient availability of foods, clothing and shelter), fertility behavior are more regulated by its culture and values, namely, culture is a decisive influencing factor of its fertility behavior and customs; (3) with fertility cultures having diverse cultural structures, intensive efforts integrating ethnological and sociological research should be made to build up and enrich our in-depth understanding of fertility cultures of various nationalities.

It is our sincere hope that this research will serve as a case through which we can get a more comprehensive and profound understanding of human fertility behavior in various cultural contexts in the world we live in, and contribute to accomplishing the goal of having and maintaining a stable and lower endogenous fertility rate amid the ongoing Chinese population development.

References

Coale, Ansley J. "Rethinking on Population Transition Theory". In *Sociodemographic Perspective,* edited by Gu Baochang, 142–143. Beijing: The Commercial Press, 1992.

Fei, Xiaotong. *Reproduction Institutions in Rural China*, 227–229. Beijing: Peking University Press, 1998.

Freedman, Ronald. *Sociodemographic Perspective*, 265–266. Edited by Gu Baochang. Beijing: The Commercial Press, 1992.

Gu, Baochang. *Sociodemographic Perspective.* Beijing: The Commercial Press, 1992, 143

Guo, Shan, and Lyu Zhaohe. "Modernization of Dai Traditional Culture and Fertility Behavior". *Thinking*, no. 6 (2007): 82–87.

Li, Yinhe. *Procreation and Village Cultures.* Beijing: China Social Sciences Press, 1994a, 3

Li, Yinhe. *Procreation and Village Cultures.* Beijing: China Social Sciences Press, 1994b, 69.

Zhai, Zhenwu, and Liu Shuang, et al. "Stabilizing Lower Fertility Rates: Concepts. Theory and Tactics". *Population Research*, no. 3 (2000): 1–17.

Zhang, Weiqing. "Approach to Population Transition with Chinese Characteristics". *Population Research*, no. 5 (2011): 3.

2 Theoretical Research on Fertility Behavior in Demography

In Western demography, theoretical research on fertility behavior and fertility rates has, at both the macro and the micro levels, laid out a self-contained theoretical framework and developed two theoretical models, respectively known as "Total Population Theory" and "Population Variables Theory". The former focuses on the development process and the growth limit of the total population from the perspective of the interrelation between population growth and economic development, and the latter on changes in the population size from the perspective of internal variables, such as birth rates (fertility rates) and mortality rates, and their interrelations. Comprehensive research, represented by the "Theory of Demographic Transition", illustrates the process of demographic transitions mainly by examining the relationships between social and economic development and population development stages marked by changes in fertility and mortality rates (Li, 2004a). Comparatively speaking, for some widely acknowledged reasons, the research by Chinese scholars has no such clear-cut classifications and has not established a unique and complete theoretical framework.

Section 1 Theories Abroad on Fertility Behavior

Double Check Theory

In his *An Essay on the Principle of Population* (1803), Thomas Robert Malthus (1766–1834) observed that,

> I think I may fairly make two postulata. First, That food is necessary to the existence of man. Secondly, That the passion between the sexes is necessary and will remain nearly in its present state. These two laws, ever since we have had any knowledge of mankind, appear to have been fixed laws of our nature ... Assuming then my postulata as granted, I say, that the power of population is indefinitely greater than the power in the earth to produce subsistence for man" (Malthus, 1992b). According to this assertion, known among demographers as Thomas Malthus's Population Proliferation Doctrine, human beings have a natural propensity to produce more offspring. Proceeding along the train of thought, he continued, "In a state therefore of great equality and virtue, where pure and simple manners prevailed, and where the means of subsistence were so abundant that no part of the society could have any fears about providing amply for a family, the power of population being left to exert itself unchecked, the increase of the human species would evidently be much greater than any increase that has been hitherto known." A strong case in support of this view is that "in the United States of America, where the means of subsistence have been more ample, the manners of the people more pure, and consequently the checks to early marriages fewer, than in any of the modern states of Europe, the population has been found to double itself in twenty-five years (Malthus, 1992c).

Having further expounded on the aforementioned view, he concluded,

> The theory on which the truth of this position depends appears to me so extremely clear that I feel at a loss to conjecture what part of it can be denied. That population cannot increase without the means of subsistence is a proposition so evident that it needs no illustration. That population does invariably increase where there are the means of subsistence, the history of every people that have ever existed will abundantly prove. And that the superior power of population cannot be checked without producing misery or vice, the ample portion of these too bitter ingredients in the cup of human life and the continuance of the physical causes that seem to have produced them bear too convincing a testimony (Malthus, 1992a).

The different ratios at which population and food increase, where population increases at a geometrical ratio while food increases at an arithmetical one, means that the increase in food can never answer the demands of an increasing population. In response to this "incontrovertible proposition of truth", Malthus provided a solution: Only through double checks – "preventive check" and "positive check" – can any society control its population growth. The former is implemented by imposing restrictions on marriages in the form of delayed marriage and premarital sexual restraint; and the latter allows population growth to run its natural course, which, in turn, leads to overpopulation, exacerbated poverty, widespread famines, and eventually rising deaths, thus curbing further population growth. The presence of preventive checks in the Western world has prevented overpopulation and maintained economic prosperity, while in the non-Western world, it is exactly the lack of preventive checks that has led to overpopulation, poverty, and backwardness. In Malthus's dichotomized system of population development for the East and West, China was viewed as a typical representative of the non-Western world. He noted particularly, "China is the prime example of a society dominated by the positive check and virtually devoid of any preventive check", "On the population growth in China, famines were the most powerful and frequent of all the positive checks" (Li, 2000a). In Thomas Malthus' view, family planning required a uniquely modern Western ability to calcaulate consciously the costs and benefits of having children and to decide to delay or curtail marriage. This idea of his doctrine has a profound influence even in the postmodern world[1]. In an extension to this idea, "Individual Choice" is construed as the top prerequisite for demographic transition, that is, only in a society where individuals are free to make their own choices can people fully realize the prices and consequences of their actions, weigh the costs and benefits of their choices against other opportunities, and extend their careful calculations into their decision- making on having children. Hence, this idea of "Individual Choice" has since dominated the explanations among Western academics for declining fertility rates. In the meantime, "Where capitalism flourishes, so does delayed marriage and individual choice "

1 Hajnal (1982) and Schofield (1989) claimed that if the Western family system might be deemed as at one end of the social system, the one represented by China and India at the other. In the History of Population and Social Structure published in 1997, Cambridge scholars Wrigley and Schofield came up with the conclusion: "Hade Thomas Malthus been a person of foresight, he might have classified a society with preventive checks, i.e., the one with marriage serving as the controller to changes in the population, as the "British society", whereas the one with positive checks, i.e. the one with the death rate serving as the controller to changes in the population, the "Chinese society". See also James Z. Lee et al., *One Quarter of Humanity: Malthusian Mythology and Chinese Realities (1700–2000)* (Beijing: Sanlian Bookstore, 2000), 6, 16.

(Li, 2000b). In their view, a declining fertility rate entails three conditions: it has to be part of conscious calculations and choices made by individuals, beneficial and technically feasible.

The above-mentioned theoretical framework of systematic analysis of the relationship between the population growth and the increase in means of subsistence put forward by Thomas Malthus had lasting and far-reaching reverberations in the Western population world, having long influenced later scholars' understanding of the relationship between the change of the total population and the accumulation of the means of livelihood. The worry had since lingered that Thomas Malthus's prediction that rapid population growth will be a drag on economic growth and social welfare improvement would come true, making the "Total Population Theory" mainly represented by the Malthusian Theory of Population the mainstream doctrine in Western demography until the late 1930s." (Li, 2004a).

Demographic Transition Theory

In the second half of the 20th century, the economic boom that started in Europe significantly enriched people's means of livelihood. Yet, the total population didn't grow with the increase in means of livelihood as Thomas Malthus had predicted, and instead, fertility rates declined. This phenomenon that ran against Thomas Malthus's proposition of population proliferation rose to be a hot topic in the Western demography community, thus shifting the focus of population research to the causes and consequences of declining fertility rates as the economy developed. In the 20th century, there emerged a variety of population theories trying to explain the phenomenon of declining fertility rates in the context of increasing means of livelihood. Based on comprehensive observations on the relationship between the total population development and the social and economic development and the relationship between the fertility rate and the mortality rate, as part of the internal factors driving population changes, the Demographic Transition Theory that came into being after the World War II classified per the criteria corresponding to different levels of social productivity all the fertility patterns of human society hitherto into three types: The primitive one (characterized by high birth rates, extremely high mortality rates and extremely low natural growth rates), the traditional one (by high birth rates, high mortality rates and low natural growth rates) and the modern one (by low birth rates, low mortality rates and low natural growth rates). Among them, the primitive one existed in the primitive society with extremely low productivity, corresponding to the times of hunting and gathering economy, the traditional one existed in traditional agrarian society in the slavery, feudal and earlier capitalist periods, corresponding to the manual labor-dominated farming economy, and the modern one existed in the post-industrial revolution capitalist society, corresponding to the modern economy based on modern technology and socialized mass production, forming the so-called "3/4-stage" theoretical model in the change of population reproduction patterns. Its basic viewpoints are: (1) The demographic transition is closely related to the social and economic development; (2) The demographic transition is achieved mainly through changes in the birth (fertility) and mortality rates and the equilibrium between them; and (3) in the early days of industrialization, the decline in the birth rate lagged behind that in the mortality rate, thus, there is a "time lag" between them. "In short, the key to demographic transitions lies in the decline in fertility rates, which in turn depends upon social and economic modernization" (Li, 2001a).

Drawing on his predecessors' reflections on the Demographic Transition Theory, Ansley J. Coale, in his paper published at the 1973 plenary session of the International Union for the Scientific Study of Population, put forward a five-period theoretical model of demographic transitions, i.e., the human fertility pattern evolves along a five-stage trajectory: The stable high-rate stage in the pre-industrial society, the premodern stage, the transitional stage, the modern stage, and the stable low-rate stage in modern society. This model is the early expression of the three-stage pattern featuring "High-High-Low, High-Low-High and Low-Low-Low" describing the relationship among birth rates, mortality rates and natural growth rates widely used in today's demographic community. In the meantime, based on the historical reality of declining fertility rates in Western European countries, he also put forward the two-stage demographic transition doctrine: The Malthusian shift of earlier and prevalent marriage losing ground to later marriage and prevalent celibacy and the Neo-Malthusian shift of the marital fertility rate going down. Thus, he concluded that, "Two shifts tend to happen in a traditional society as it modernizes, and each shift greatly contributes to an overall decline in the fertility rate provided that it has two features: a higher marital fertility rate and a larger earlier marriage rate in its early stages of such modernization" (Coale, 1992). In short, a glance back at the histories of demographic transitions in the most modernized countries suggests that the theory of demographic transition tells the right story to us that all developing countries had fairly high fertility and mortality rates before their modernization. A high degree of modernization is a sufficient condition for a decline in fertility rates.

Theory of Net Intergenerational Wealth Flows

Inspired by the perception of "economic change alone doesn't suffice to explain declining fertility rates and demographic transitions", John C. Caldwell put forward the Wealth Flows Theory on fertility decline in 1976, aiming to explain the root cause of changes in the fertility rate by looking into the intergenerational flows of wealth from parents to offspring. In this theory, Caldwell defined the term "wealth flows" as the transfer of wealth, including money, goods, properties, services, guarantees, etc., from one individual to another, and further illustrated that the choice of the word "wealth" instead of other phrases, such as income, is to highlight that wealth is not limited to money since wealth is not in a tangible form all the times.

This theory holds that the fundamental condition for a decline in fertility rates is a radical transformation in family relationships, especially the one in wealth flows within families, to be more specific, the direction and the net difference of wealth flows across generations. In many developing countries, the reason why parents disapprove of birth controls is the one-way flow of incomes from children to parents. Only when the direction of wealth flows is reversed to a downward flow from parents to children will parents start to restrict their fertility rates. The former scenario is largely seen in a household production-dominated traditional society whereas the latter is often found in a labor market (non household production)-dominated modern society, which means a shift in fertility rates is impossible in traditional societies.

In an agrarian society (as in most developing countries), having children can benefit the parents in six ways:

(1)They are income earners; (2) They are laborers on the farm and in the house; (3) They can help the parents with a range of tasks, including farm work; (4) Adult children can provide help for the parents unrelated to farming, such as attending community events on behalf of parents; (5) Running farms and businesses or doing housework for the elderly parents; and (6) Parental investment into children's development, especially in education and training, will generate return in the form of an increased ability of the children to support parents in the future. Therefore, people have an incentive to have more children.

Generally speaking, whenever rational fertility behavior prevail in any stage of society, fertility rates, either high or low, are the outcomes of individuals, couples and households weighing economic benefits. The fertility rate is determined by economic drivers, and which in turn by social conditions. For example, the fundamental social condition for changes in the fertility rate is the changed direction of net intergenerational flows of wealth, which in turn depends on radical transformations in family relationships. However, a reverse flow of net wealth between parents and children won't, obviously, take place until strong emotional and financial ties in most families completely wear off, and thus, there won't be fundamental changes in the fertility rate.

Leibenstein's Rational Choice Theory of Fertility Decisions

In the 1950s, based on his examination into family planning decisions, Harvey Leibenstein was the first to conduct a benefit-cost analysis of having children with Western microeconomic theories and built this theoretical model of micro population economics, a research model on fertility rates. "Rational Choice" means that people's actions are not necessarily motivated by the desire to maximize utility or to minimize cost, as they would be for an economic man ("homo economicus") would. They can also be an expression of a rational choice. It is a behavior mode relative to and transcends *homo economicus* (Li, 2004b). The basic meaning of this theory is that due to different social, economic and cultural factors, families have different expectations in terms of the number of children, and make their decisions on the acceptance of the Nth child based on the comparison of and trade-off between the costs and benefits (utility) from the Nth child, and this theory has multiple implications: (1) The analysis is limited to a micro one exclusively at the family level; (2) The family size can be determined by parents' choice of the the number of children; (3) Parents' decision on the acceptance of their children is based on their analysis and comparison of costs and benefits from children; (4) Parents' decision on the acceptance of children is only specific to the marginal children (the children that a family can go with or without), i.e., they need to make a rational decision on the acceptance of the marginal children only; and (5) Parents' decision follows the law of diminishing marginal utility, that is, the Nth child delivers a less marginal utility than the (N-1)th one (Li, 2004c).

The costs of having a child break down into direct and indirect components, with the former covering parents' expenses on child-raising, education, medical care and others during the period from the pregnancy of the mother to the delivery of the child up till the time when the child can live independently, and the latter, also known as the opportunity cost, covering parents' educational and income-generating opportunities lost from having the additional child, for example, the loss of the mother's work pays during the pregnancy and the child feeding, the reduced consumption and loss of time of the other family members due to the nursing of the additional child, etc.

The benefits (utility) from an additional child is classified into six categories: (1) Consumption utility: A child is regarded as a "consumer good", i.e., serving as a source of happiness for parents; (2) Labor/economic utility: A child can be expected to be a laborer in a family, providing incomes for the family; (3) Old-age security utility: A child is regarded as the "potential source of security" in a family, serving as the life support for aging parents; (4) Anti-financial-risk utility: A child is a bearer of a family's future financial risks; (5) The utility in maintaining the family status; and (6) The utility in contributing to the expansion and development of a family.

The analysis shows that except for the utility in (1) and (6), all the other utilities from an additional child in a family with multiple children tend to diminish as the financial status of the family improves.

The decision on having marginal children is, Harvey Leibenstein believed, made mainly through two approaches: The cost-benefit analysis of marginal children production and the judgment on the potential contribution of marginal children to a family's social and economic status.

Based on his analysis of the fertility rate choice by families in the context of rising family incomes, Harvey Leibenstein came to the following conclusions: First, as the cost of having children rises with the rising per capita incomes, families' desire to have children declines; second, in the context of rising per capita incomes, even if the direct cost of having children stay the same, families' desire to have children still declines when the indirect cost of having children rises sharply due to an increase in the value of unit time; third, with increased per capita incomes, parents have more financial means in maintaining and improving the living standards for their families and a greater financial strength for supporting themselves in their advanced ages, hence a reduced need of children as the source of their future security, so families' desire to have children declines; and fourth, the income increase is negatively correlated with all the utilities from having children except the consumption one (which has no significant correlation with the former).

In a market economy, families with higher incomes have higher social status and correspondingly a higher target consumption level and a greater preference for consumer goods over children, and thus are more likely to have fewer or no children. Meanwhile, eager to improve their social status and achieve a higher target consumption level, low-income families will follow the example of high-income families and tend to have fewer children. In short, a prerequisite for a decline in fertility rates is an increase in per capita household incomes.

Becker's Quantity-Quality Trade-off Hypothesis

In the 1960s, based on his analysis of fertility behavior and decisions at the family level with consumer behavior theories in Western economics, Gary Becker put forward the quantity-quality trade-off of children theory. Treating children as analogous to"consumer durables" and thus the demand for children as to that for consumer durables, the theory analyzes a family's demand for children and fertility decision-making, from the perspectives of the diversity, complementarity and substitutability of commodities (Li, 2001b). He argued that commodities have the following attributes: Diversity, complementarity and substitutability, and the demand for any type of commodities is negatively correlated with their value. In economists' terms, a child can be regarded as either a consumer good or a productive one for a family. When the cost of raising a child exceeds the utility that it delivers, the child can be seen as a durable consumer good, which, though, is not purchased but produced by the family itself, and the gain it brings to the parents is the psychological benefit. When the utility exceeds the cost, a child can be seen as a durable productive good. As fertility behavior depend on not only the demand for children but also the ability to support them, fertility choices are related to various factors, including income levels, the elasticity of income effects and price changes. Raising children costs parents not only their money but also their time and energy, so children are a "time-intensive commodity". Becker divided the time for a family into two parts: work time and leisure time, proposed the valuation of a child as a commodity at the "shadow price" of time, conducted a comparative analysis of its demand with that for other consumer goods, and came to the conclusion that there exists a trade-off relation between the declining number and the improving quality of children in modern societies, which means, parents are supposed to prefer fewer but better children over more but worse ones, and this explained why families chose to have fewer children since the mid-19th century. Later, R. J. Willis enriched Becker's theoretical model to establish the "household utility function": V=u (N, Q, and S). Wherein, V is the household utility function; u the household utility; N the family satisfaction from the child number; Q the family satisfaction from the child quality; S the family satisfaction from other commodities other than children. According to the formula, the household utility maximization depends on the distribution of N, Q and S in a family, and the three factors are mutually substitutive (Li, 2001c).

In the 1980s, Niloff revised Becker's theoretical model for family gain and child utility maximization by proposing that the family gain or the family utility should be extended to cover the family benefits. As thus, the fertility choice in a family depends on the optimization of the family benefits instead of the maximization of the family utility.

Supply-Demand Theory of Fertility Determination

In his 1969 article "Toward a Socioeconomic Theory of Fertility: A Survey of Recent Research on Economic Factors in American Fertility," Richard A. Easterlin first described the supply-demand theory of fertility, and taking into account demographic transition and social modernization, he provided a more systematic discussion on this theory in his 1985 book *The Fertility Revolution: A Supply-Demand Analysis.*

According to Easterlin, three key variables affect fertility behavior at the family level: Cd, a family's demand for children, i.e.,.the number of surviving children desired by a couple when birth control is almost costless; Cn, the possible number of children (child supply), i.e., the number of surviving children that a couple would likely to have if they didn't intentionally control birth; and the cost of birth control (Easterlin, 1992), including both objective material cost and subjective psychological cost, and the time and money spent learning and using certain birth control methods. The direct determinant for the demand for children in a family include the family income, the price of children against other goods and the couple's preference; and the possible number of children in a family depends on the natural fertility rate and the expected survival rate of babies. The relationship among the three factors can lead to options and trade-offs centered around them: The motivation to use birth control is determined by the gap between Cd and Cn. If Cn is less than Cd, there is no motivation to use birth control, as is the case with most agrarian societies; if Cn is greater than Cd, the motivation to use birth control with arise, and further, the larger the gap between the two, the stronger the motivation to use birth control. Moreover, the comparison between the Cn-Cd gap and the cost spent on birth control should also be factored in: The actual motivation to use birth control will be weaker when the Cn-Cd gap is narrower and the cost of birth control larger, and will be stronger only when there is a larger Cn-Cd gap and a higher cost of birth control. The sharper the contrast between the motivation and the cost spent, the more active a couple will be in controlling birth, and the lower the fertility rate in a family, as is the case in modern developed countries. Easterlin also believed that the basic determinants behind the three variables are modernization as well as social and cultural factors.

This theory looks into child production not from the single perspective of demand but from the perspectives of both supply and demand, and changes in the fertility rate not only from the micro perspective of fertility behavior at the family level but also the macro perspective of demographic transition. It regards the fertility revolution as the essence and key element of demographic transition, delves into its significance from the perspective of social modernization, raise it to the level of the social change theory, and emphasizes that it is a reflection of not only changes in fertility levels but also the radical transformation of the fertility desire, ideas of childbearing and fertility behavior (Li, 2001d).

Freedman's Theory of Multiple Motivations

In 1979, Ronald Freedman published the article *Theories of Fertility Declines: A Reappraisal*, in which he argued that the classical demographic theories are inadequate in trying to interpret the motivation to have fewer children based on economic variables alone. Detailed empirical research no longer suffices to establish at particular levels a synthesis of systemic development variables associated with the European fertility declines. Detailed research on fertility shifts in Europe has shown that fertility rates began to decline almost simultaneously in countries with radically different levels of industrialization and urbanization, and some less developed areas even experienced such decline earlier than their more developed peers. Moreover, researchers have found that many culturally similar areas, such as those of linguistic or ethnic similarities, exhibit similar similar fertility patterns, which is basically unrelated to the indicators of social and economic development that are critical to the transition theory. Even with different levels of development, subregions with a common culture tend to show a similar pattern of declining fertility rates, and the distinguishing factor among them may be cultural differences in the family structure, for example, traditional practices and women's status. This evidence seems to suggest that different cultural categories are often associated with birth rates in ways that can't be explained by general social structural factors at the heart of the transition theory, thus posing a challenge to the classical economic determinism on demographic transition (Freedman, 1992a).

Based on his reappraisal of the classical demographic transition theories and examination into a number of cases of fertility decline in underdeveloped countries, Ronald Freedman came out with the following findings: First, under the current circumstances, the highly-developed Western modernization is not a necessary condition for a fertility decline; second, the motivation to lower fertility stems from the parents' perception that it is better to have fewer children – a perception that has arisen in response to changes in living conditions, and there is proof that this motivation predates the modern industrial age and led to lower fertility rates; third, in the West, the basic feature of the modern demographic shift from high to low fertility lies in the family functions transitioning to those of larger non-family organizations, which in turn are an integral part of increasingly interdependent national and international production networks. At present, what changes have led to changes in lifestyle and thus created the motivation to have fewer children is not yet known; fourth, cultural factors – those that don't easily translate into common development variables – seem to influence the demand for children and the willingness to accept birth control; and fifth, the idea and practice of limiting family sizes seem to have other intrinsic causal forces that help determine when and at what rate the motivation to reduce fertility arises (Freedman, 1992b).

Based on these findings, he concluded that there exists multiple pathways to reducing fertility rates. In other words, there may be a diversity of driving forces other than financial considerations that contribute to fertility decline.

It is obvious that the different explanations of fertility decline in these Western theories all start logically from the "Malthusian Concern", i.e., while embracing the Malthusian "doctrine of the human instinct for more births", they all tried to demystify the "Malthusian Paradox" of fewer, rather than more, births amid economic development in the West. Except for the theory proposed by Ronald Freedman, all these theories shared one basic understanding that the leverage of economic forces on changes in the population size is strong and significant. In other words, the fertility behavior of human beings of having more or fewer children is a decision made through rational economic calculations; hence, "agrarian society", "poverty" and "economical backwardness" are arguably the root causes of "more births", and so, it follows that to transit from "more births" to "fewer births", the optimal approach is to replace the agrarian society with the industrial society. The mantra "Modernization is the most effective birth control pill" is the most pertinent and vivid description of such views. However, with economic growth and income increase as the main explanatory variables, these classical analyses reduced the reproductive instinct of human beings to an indirect means of survival and ignored the effects of factors other than economic ones on human fertility behavior. They touched less on non-economic factors, particularly the effects of culture on changes in the population size, to say the least.

In fact, since the second half of the 20th century, some scholars have already observed the effects of non-economic factors on fertility rates and propounded various doctrines (Kingsley Davis and Judith Blake, 1956; John Bongaarts, 1982), including the Theory of "Intermediate Fertility Variables", asserting that social and economic factors have indirect rather than direct influences on the fertility process and fertility rates, and must necessarily work only through intermediate fertility variables. In 1992, the United Nations Population Fund also pointed out emphatically in its *Report on Population Growth and Economic Development* that economic factors have a secondary influence on population growth. However, the foregoing economic determinism has remained the mainstream theory of reproductive economics in the contemporary Western world (Li, 1998). As for the causes of the contemporary fertility decline in China, it is generally understood that the decline in fertility rates in China since the 1980s is largely the result of the vigorous implementation of the national family planning policy rather than the rational decisions made by individual citizens.

Section 2 Research in China on Fertility Behavior

Generational Succession – Parent Care by Adult Children Model

In 1946, Mr. Fei Xiaotong applied the anthropological functionalism theory to his research on fertility behavior of human beings, concluding in his writings: *The Institutions for Reproduction* that for their survival, human beings have to maintain the integrity of their social structures and that the function of the institutions for reproduction is to maintain the integrity of their social structures. He said,

> For a sound personal life, individuals have to maintain the integrity of the social structures they live in. Human beings are creatures and will eventually die. Yet, death threatens the integrity of the social structures they have lived in, and, therefore, the soundness of the living's personal life. Therefore, any community has to prepare for its next institutions for replacing the old with the new to protect its population from extinction. As biological functions alone cannot fully guarantee the continuity of human races, these institutions are created by man instead of coming into being out of their own accord. Human beings have to resort to the force of social sanction to keep on producing babies and ensure the babies have a chance to grow up into adults as future replacements for the dying or the dead in such social structures (Fei, 1998a).

This self-imposed social sanction by human beings is the institutions for reproduction.

By introducing some revisions to Thomas Malthus's "Two Types of Checks" Theory, Fei Xiaotong took a step forward to assert that population growth or shrinkage is neither a natural biological phenomenon nor the result of the changing availability of foods but depends on the nature of social structures Fei added,

> The size of the population is determined by the need from a specific social structure then and there. If a big population is needed by a specific social structure, the people therein can even lie in a quasi-dormant state, doing without an adequate supply of food; on the contrary, if only a small population is needed to sustain a structure, the people therein won't produce children at a geometric rate even if there is an abundant supply of foods.

Based on his analysis of the living conditions in rural China in the 1930s, he inferred that "in order to satisfy the demand for farming laborers, a large population had to be maintained in the countryside. In such an economic structure where the (working) population constitutes the main driving force for production, a higher population density is inevitably a common phenomenon." Due to a higher infant mortality rate, "it is impossible to maintain the capacity of a social structure without more births." In China, "the rural population won't decline over time before other alternative forces to manual labor are employed in the farming sector" (Fei, 1998b).

To ensure the integrity of an existing social structure, childbearing is not only an act of generational succession (continuing lineage) but also an imperative to realize the social function of younger generations supporting their elders (reciprocating for parental care for their young children), and this longstanding and stable institution of maintaining social structures people live in has given rise to the tradition of showing respect for and supporting one's aging parents.

However, a larger population is not always better. The field investigation at Jiang village found that, "despite the perceived significance of raising children among villagers, there are also practical factors at work, mandating that the population growth must be checked, as the arable land has already been hard-pressed to sustain a larger population." Check on excessive population growth is meant to prevent poverty, and only those "with ample wealth had the financial luxury of raising more children and are proud of their larger families, a symbol of affluence in rural China" (Fei, 2001). Hence, the desire to have more children and the aversion to infanticides and abortions have always coexisted in rural China.

Village Society of Acquaintances Model

In her book *Procreation and Chinese Village Culture* published in 1994, Ms. Li Yinhe describes her research approach: Sociologically, to delve into the issue of human fertility, one can't avoid the issue of fertility motivation, i.e., why people want to have children. The issue of fertility motivation has direct relations with their beliefs about life, their way of life and their living environments, which are all part of their culture. Therefore, if you explore the fertility behavior of human beings, you must deem their fertility behavior as a kind of culture, and examine them as a kind of culture (Li, 1994a).

Proceeding from her critical inquiry into the inapplicability of Becker's Quantity-Quality Trade-off theory to China and her modification of Fei Xiaotong's Generational Succession-Parent Care by Adult Children model in the traditional Chinese fertility institutions, Li Yinhe commented that, "Fertility cultures in various Chinese regions don't seem to originate from the cultural tradition of the whole Chinese nation, but rather are rooted in particular living environments of various regions" (Li, 1994b). She defined the cultural atmospheres derived from their particular living environments as village cultures. Characterized largely by shared information, a village culture (including ethical ideas and behavioral norms) is shared by a small group of folks and has at least the following distinct features: First, the village scale is limited to the extent to which ordinary village members have gotten acquainted with one another; second, there is limited migration of village members; third, village members tend to compete with each other; and fourth, village members are pressured to converge in all aspects of life. Living in such a context, individuals' fertility behavior are inevitably governed by and manifested in the logic that "a greater say comes from more voices, i.e., more offspring", thus encouraging more offspring and extended families. On one hand, the "competition" rule motivates village members to go all out in the fertility competition, while on the other, the "convergence" rule and the strong demand for fairness among village members combine to form a force constraining each other (Li, 1994c). Hence, more births and earlier parenthood are, of course, the common goal for all families in a village.

Ms. Li Yinhe believes that since the family-centered culture cares more about family expansion through reproduction, it is inevitable that people prefer having more children, while the people in an individual-centered culture certainly prefer fewer children since they are more concerned about their own happiness. As a result, some seemingly senseless behaviors are still commonplaces in rural China. For example, some fairly wealthy rural households are willing to spend lavishly on ancestral tombs and their sons' wedding ceremonies. These local customs suggest that in the context with a strong village culture, affluence itself does not lead to a new way of life, and it means a better life for individuals only in urban settings. Therefore, there are only two ways to control population growth in China: Mandatory family planning, or to bring more people out of the village culture and into the urban culture. There is no other way out of this (Li, 1994d).

Fertility Culture Model

Based on their research on the ideology reflecting the Chinese fertility changes and development (i.e., ideas, beliefs, ethics, morals and behavioral norms developed in the fertility practice) and its physical forms, Tian Xueyuan, Chen Shengli, et al. published in 2006 a book *Research on Fertility Culture*, holding that a fertility culture consists of four logical dimensions: quantity, quality, structure and form. A fertility culture is the outcome of the interaction between a culture and a fertility practice, and its essence lies in the intrinsic link between fertility changes and development and cultural changes and development, i.e., the cultural essence of fertility changes and development, a relatively stable ideology established amid the interplay between the cultural development and fertility changes and development. Recurring amid the fertility changes and development, this ideology evolves into a regular movement, from which the essence of things are abstracted and concentrated into an idea, i.e., an ideology that suffices to govern fertility behavior and exert sufficient influence on fertility changes and development (Tian, 2006a). While affirming the non-economic nature of a fertility culture, they also have made their clear value judgment from their analysis of the evolution process of a fertility culture: A fertility culture can be divided into two categories: traditional and modern fertility culture. The traditional fertility culture goes usually with traditional production modes, the pro-childbearing policies, ideas of childbearing with preference for more births, for earlier parenthood and for boys over girls, backward fertility practices and unscientific fertility knowledge (so, the fertility culture in an agrarian society may be as well boiled down into one sentence: The more sons, the more blessings). The modern fertility culture, also known as a new type of fertility culture, is a product of modern methods of production, or a product in the industrialized era (Tian, 2006b). Regardless of economic, political, or institutional and policy factors, demographic transition works through the changes in fertility cultures. That is, the completion of demographic transition ultimately depends on the formation of a modern fertility culture, which is a guarantee for entrenching the progress in the demographic transition.

In her 2006 book *Research on the Fertility Cultures of Ethnic Groups in Southwest China,* based on her systematic observation and research on the fertility cultures of ethnic minorities in southwest China, Yang Zhuhui argues that there had historically been few systematic concepts and measures of family planning among ethnic minorities in southwest China, and generally speaking, there is also no self-consciousness of family planning in a scientific sense among most ethnic minorities in southwest China except Dong and Yao in some regions (Yang, 2006). She added that under new historical circumstances, all ethnic peoples in southwest China are facing the transformation from traditional fertility cultures to modern ones, and with the effective implementation of the national family planning policy over years, a new fertility culture, as a new cultural phenomenon, has taken shape among ethnic people in southwest regions but still has a long way to go to entrench itself due to the grip traditional cultures continue to have on these people.

In addition, more prominent views among recent academic papers on fertility behavior include: In terms of either the values or the reality, "having a boy" remains the core pursuit of most families in vast rural areas (Chen, 1998); "having more children, especially more boys" responds to the psychological need of most farmers in China's rural areas. Besides being related to the objective conditions in rural areas where the mode of livelihood still relies mainly on manual labor, such fertility demand is more of an outcome of the influence and restriction by cultural concepts. In fact, it is the reflection of cultural concepts at the behavioral level and thus a demand with internalized social and cultural values. Both the traditional ideas of Confucianism and traditional concepts in specific cultural circumstances in rural China influence the fertility behavior of farmers and so on (Ji, 2001).

To sum up, studies by Chinese scholars share the following features: (1) in terms of research objects, the focus is mainly on the Han society steeped in Confucianism; (2) in terms of time, the research focus is largely limited to the periods since the founding of the People's Republic of China, especially the 30 years since the reform and opening-up; (3) in terms of the points of view, it is widely understood that the fertility pattern of "more births, earlier parenthood and preference for boys" is an outdated one (both in the economic and cultural dimensions) that matches traditional societies and won't transform into a new one featuring "fewer births, later parenthood and no gender preference" without social modernization; (4) in terms of the analysis of the causes behind the fertility behavior pattern, it is unanimously held that: steeped in traditional concepts, such as "Of the three things children can do to breach their filial duty, being childless is the most egregious", "The more offspring, the more blessings" and "the continuation of the family line", Chinese families, especially in rural areas, have a strong desire to have more offspring, which is the root cause behind the intense conflict between the micro fertility demand at the family level and the macro fertility policy at the state level; and (5) in terms of the measures for controlling population growth, it is held that the shift in farmers' concepts of birth control mentioned above is subject to the modernization of the rural economy. However, given a large farmer base, a high ratio of the rural population to the national total, a poor economic foundation and a lower level of development in rural areas, we have no luxury of sitting idle for further economic development before controlling population growth, which means, we can't wait long for a natural decline in the fertility rate. Therefore, family planning will still be forcibly implemented through policy measures and government actions for a certain period of time (Li, 2001e). In comparison with their foreign peers, Chinese scholars, while drawing on Western theories of fertility behavior in exploring China-specific issues, seem to have been more focused on the influences of non-economic factors, such as regional cultures, on human fertility behavior, and tried to interpret the causes of the formation of the Chinese traditional fertility behavior from various perspectives.

In the preface to *The Origin of the Family, Private Property and the State* (first edition), Engels pointed out that, "According to Materialism, the decisive factor of history comes down to the production and reproduction of direct life. Yet there are two kinds of production itself: The production of means of livelihood, including food, clothing, housing and tools necessary for the purposes thereof, and the production of human beings themselves, that is, the reproduction of the human race." (Compilation & Bureau, 1972). This explains the foundational and decisive role of fertility behavior in the development of human society because except isolated achievements of modern science and technology (such as test-tube babies), all human population has been, either in the past or at the present, the result of human reproductive behaviors. As thus, fertility behavior have been an inevitable topic in demography since its inception, and have naturally been an integral part of any population theory. The incomplete and sketchy look-back at the theories and views of human fertility behavior in this Chapter aims to provide a theoretical framework for the analysis of traditional fertility behavior in Dai people in the subsequent Chapters.

References

Central Compilation & Translation Bureau. *Selected Works of Marx and Engels*, Vol. 4. Beijing: People's Publishing House, 1972, 2.

Chen, Zhen. "Externality and Cultural Marginality of Peasants' Fertility Behavior". *Population & Economics*, no. 1 (1998): 39.

Coale, Ansley J. "Rethinking on Population Transition Theory". In *Sociodemographic Perspective*, 141–142. Translated by Gu Baochang. Beijing: The Commercial Press, 1992.

Easterlin, Richard A. "An Economic Framework for Fertility Analysis". In *Sociodemographic Perspective*. Translated by Gu Baochang. Beijing: The Commercial Press, 1992, 225.

Fei, Xiaotong. *Reproduction Institutions in Rural China*. Beijing: Peking University Press, 1998a, 116.

Fei, Xiaotong. *Reproduction Institutions in Rural China*. Peking University Press, 1998b, 227–229.

Fei, Xiaotong. *The Economy of Jiang Village: The Life of Chinese Peasants*. Beijing: the Commercial Press, 2001, 46–47.

Freedman, Ronald. "Doctrine on Fertility Declines: Reappraisal". In *Sociodemographic Perspective*, 250–251. Translated by Gu Baochang. Beijing: The Commercial Press, 1992a.

Freedman, Ronald. "Doctrine on Fertility Declines: Reappraisal". In *Sociodemographic Perspective*, 265–266. Translated by Gu Baochang. Beijing: The Commercial Press, 1992b.

Ji, Pingping. "Effects of Traditional Culture on Fertility Behavior of Peasants". *Population & Economics*, no. S1 (2001): 15.

Li, Jingneng. *Modern Population Theories in the West*. Shanghai: Fudan University Press, 2004a, 5.

Li, Jingneng. *Modern Population Theories in the West*. Shanghai: Fudan University Press, 2004b, 34.

Li, Jingneng. *Modern Population Theories in the West*. Shanghai: Fudan University Press, 2004c, 35.

Li, Jingneng. *New Selection of Population Theories*. Beijing: China Population Publishing House, 2001a, 477.

Li, Jingneng. *New Selection of Population Theories*. Beijing: China Population Publishing House, 2001b, 459.

Li, Jingneng. *New Selection of Population Theories*. Beijing: China Population Publishing House, 2001c, 460–461.

Li, Jingneng. *New Selection of Population Theories*. Beijing: China Population Publishing House, 2001d, 462–463.

Li, Jingneng. *New Selection of Population Theories*. Beijing: China Population Publishing House, 2001e, 525–526.

Li, Jingneng. *Research on Population and Economy in Current China*. Beijing: China Population Publishing House, 1998, 87.

Li, Yinhe. *Procreation and Village Cultures*. Beijing: China Social Sciences Press, 1994a, 1.

Li, Yinhe. *Procreation and Village Cultures*. Beijing: China Social Sciences Press, 1994b, 3.

Li, Yinhe. *Procreation and Village Cultures*. Beijing: China Social Sciences Press, 1994c, 69.

Li, Yinhe. *Procreation and Village Cultures*. Beijing: China Social Sciences Press, 1994d, 221–223.

Li, Zhongqing. *One Fourth of Human Beings: Thomas Malthus's Myth and the Realities in China (1700–2000).* Translated by Wang Feng, Chen Wei and Yao Yuan. Beijing: Joint Publishing Press, 2000a, 5–8.

Li, Zhongqing. *One Fourth of Human Beings: Thomas Malthus's Myth and the Realities in China (1700–2000).* Translated by Wang Feng, Chen Wei and Yao Yuan. Beijing: Joint Publishing Press, 2000b, 25.

Malthus, Thomas. *An Essay on the Principle of Population.* Translated by Zhu Yang, Hu Qilin and Zhu Hezhong. Beijing: The Commercial Press, 1992a, 16.

Malthus, Thomas. *An Essay on the Principle of Population.* Translated by Zhu Yang, Hu Qilin and Zhu Hezhong. Beijing: The Commercial Press, 1992b, 6–7.

Malthus, Thomas, *An Essay on the Principle of Population.* Translated by Zhu Yang, Hu Qilin and Zhu Hezhong. Beijing: The Commercial Press, 1992c, 11.

Tian, Xueyuan, and Chen Shengli, eds. *Research on Reproductive Culture.* Beijing: Chinese Financial & Economic Publishing House, 2006a, 6–7.

Tian, Xueyuan, and Chen Shengli, eds. *Research on Reproductive Culture.* Beijing: Chinese Financial & Economic Publishing House, 2006b, 341, 11.

Yang, Zhuhui. *Research on the Fertility Cultures of Ethnic Groups in Southwest China.* Beijing: China Minzu University Press, 2006, 288.

3

Historical Overview of the Dai Traditional Fertility Behavior

Dai people are distributed in southwest Yunnan of China. Most of them are clustered in the Xishuangbanna Dai Autonomous Prefecture and the the Dehong Dai and Jingpo Autonomous Prefecture bordering Myanmar and Laos. The remaining are distributed in Gengma Dai and Wa Autonomous County, Menglian Dai, Lahu and Wa Autonomous County, Jinggu Dai and Wa Autonomous County, and Xinping Yi and Dai Autonomous County. In addition, there are also small settlements or scattered distribution of Dai people in more than 30 cities and counties such as Jingdong, Pu'er, Simao, Tengchong, Longling, Shuangjiang, Ximeng, Yuanyang and Hekou. Before the founding of the People's Republic of China, governments had conducted no censuses of any demographic significance in these areas. There are also only very limited records in the historical literature of the overall demographic situation in Xishuangbanna and Dehong, the two major settlement regions for Dai people, with no demographic data specific to them, albeit they are the predominant ethnic group in these areas. Take Xishuangbanna as an example, the *Development Plan for the Border Area in Sipu* prepared in the third year of the R.O.C. Period (1944) by the Civil Affairs Department of Yunnan Province contained the following records of the composition of ethnic people in the three counties under Xishuangbanna – Cheli County (today's Jinghong Municipality), Fohai County and Nanqiao County (today's Menghai County): "The total population of Twelve Bannas is about 180,000, with the Baiyi (now Dai) people being the predominent aborigines. According to the latest accurate demographic statistics for the three Counties . . . the Baiyi people in Cheli account for over 80 percent of the total population, and in Fohai and Nanqiao over 60 percent of their respective total populations, while the Hans in these counties only five percent" (Compilation Committee of Local Chronicles of Xishuangbanna Dai Autonomous Prefecture, 2002a). In his *The Chronicles of the Twelve Bannas*, Mr. Li Fuyi recorded that, "In the period from the 12th year to the second year of the R.O.C. Period (1923–1933), the Baiyi people made up 60.40 percent of the total population in Twelve Bannas (including Cheli County, Fohai County, Nanqiao County, Liushun County, Zhenyue County, Ningjiang Provisional Administrative Area, the old Puwen County and Zhengdong District)." (As shown in Table 3.1).

In *The Life and Culture of the Baiyi People*, Mr. Jiang Yingliang summed up that, "There are as many as 28 ethnic groups in Twelve Bannas, and their designations and populations are listed in the following Table 3.2. Among the inhabitants in the region, the Baiyi people make up 62.00 percent of the total population, representing an absolute majority, the Han 7.30 percent, and the other ethnic people combined 30.70 percent" (Jiang, 1950).

The Baiyi (now Dai) residents accounted for 54.17% of the total population in the region when the Xishuangbanna Dai Autonomous Prefecture was established in 1953 (Compilation Committee of Local Chronicles of Xishuangbanna Dai Autonomous Prefecture, 2002b). Therefore, we can still glean relevant information from these scattered accounts of local conditions and customs in historical documents, and get a rough picture of the traditional fertility behavior of the Dai families based on their population and average household size in this period.

Section 1 General Picture of the Dai Population in the Late Qing Dynasty and the R.O.C. Period

With frequent changes in the administrative division to the Dai settlement areas during the R.O.C. Period,[2] the same geographical name in different periods was often associated with different territorial areas. Thus, the indicator "Total Population"

2 Today's Xishuangbanna, known as "Twelve Bannas" in the later Qing Dynasty, covered an area of about 25,000 square kilometers, and consisted of six counties/administrative areas (Cheli, Fohai, Nanqiao, Zhenyue, Liushun, Ningjiang) and parts of Simao and Jiangcheng counties. In the First Year of the R.O.C. Period (1912), the Government established the General Administration Bureau of Pusi Frontiers under the Cheli Pacification Superintendent, which was composed of eight administrative divisions. In the 18th year

Table 3.1: The Ethnic Composition of the Xishuangbanna Population, 1923–1933

Ranking by size	Ethnicity	Population	Percentage	Remarks
1	Baiyi (Now Dai)	104,820	60.40	Including Han (Dry) Baiyi, Shui (Water) Baiyi and Huayao (Colorful-belt) Baiyi
2	Han	31,029	17.88	Including Islamists
3	Aka	12,418	7.16	Including Sanda
4	Puman	10,671	6.15	aka Pu Man
5	Luohei	4,446	2.57	Including Major Luohei and Yellow Luohei
6	Youle	2,338	1.34	
7	Xiangtan	1,560	0.90	aka Xiangtan
8	Laoben	1,180	0.68	
9	Yao	1,142	0.66	Including Dingji Yao and Blue Yao
10	Buxia	930	0.54	aka Busha or Bu Sha
11	Luoluo	505	0.30	aka Datou
12	Ake	492	0.28	aka A Ke
13	Woni	292	0.17	aka Wo Ni, including Black Woni and White Wonii
14	Miaozi	291	0.17	Including Sumiao and Baimiao
15	Yimang	246	0.14	aka Chaman
16	Kuanka	230	0.13	
17	Kawa	215	0.12	aka Ka Wa (known as the Wa ethnic group since the founding of the People's Republic of China)
18	Sha	170	0.10	
19	Buyuan	152	0.08	
20	Kakang	110	0.06	aka Ka Kang, including Lang, Xidong and Caiwa
21	Kamo	94	0.05	
22	Laopin	82	0.05	
23	Kalao	76	0.04	aka Ka Lao
24	Lisu	52	0.03	aka Li Su
Total		178,539	100	

Source: Li Fuyi, The Annals of Twelve Bannas – Ethnic People, pp. 417–419.

Table 3.2: The Ethnic Composition of the Xishuangbanna Population, 1945–1946

Designation	Population	Designation	Population	Designation	Population	Designation	Population
Baiyi (Now Dai)	71,621	Aka	8,765	Puman	8,583	Han	8,420
Luohei	5,340	Yao	2,108	Ben	1,677	Xiangtan	1,546
Woni	1,416	Qidi	1,349	Youle	1,300	Ximole	601
Hoululaoka	348	Lami	306	Kucong	270	Ake	257
Sanda	200	Mahei	151	Bujiao	150	Miao	146
Bulong	130	Chaman	100	Buxia	100	Sha	80
Datou	55	Kang	36	Kawa	25	Laopin	24

Source: Jiang Yingliang, The Life and Culture of the Baiyi People, p. 69.

Table 3.3: Households, Population and Average Household Size in Pu'er Prefecture in the First Year of the Emperor Xuantong Reign in the Qing Dynasty (1909)

Region	Number of Households	Total Population (Persons)	Average Household Size (Persons)
Ninger County	12,264	60,688	4.95
Simao Department	3,158	13,322	4.22
Weiyuan Department	6,764	23,614	3.49
Talang Department	8,424	37,564	4.46
Total	30,610	135,188	4.42

Source: Calculations from data in the *Archival Documents of Population Data of Modern Yunnan* (Deng, 1996).

in demographic data usually couldn't truly reflect the natural changes in population in the same geographical area during different periods. However, according to

of the R.O.C. Period (1929), adjustments were made to the jurisdictions and names of various administrative areas. In the 21st year of the R.O.C. Period (1932), adjustments were made once again and the General Administration Bureau of Pusi Frontiers was left to have only four counties. See also Rui Yifu, *Preface to The Annals of Twelves Bannas by Li Fuyi* (Taiwan: Chiang Kai-shek Publishing Company, 1955).

Table 3.4: Populations in Western Dai Settlement Areas in the 26th Year of the R.O.C. Period (1937) (Jiang and Jiang, 2003)

Region	Number of Households	Total Population	Average Household Size (Persons)
Mangshi	5,461	27,000	4.94
Zhefang	1,260	3,300	2.62
Mengmao	1,500	2,930	1.95
Longchuan	2,162	7,860	3.64
Zhanda	3,000	12,000	4.00
Ganya	5,000	20,000	4.00
Nandian	8,000	30,000	3.75
Total	26,383	103,090	3.91

demographic statistics, the changes in the administrative division generally do not lead to the regional migration of population, therefore, the indicator "Average Household Size", to a certain extent, can reflect the demographic situation within a region.

The census data of Pu'er Prefecture during the reign of Xuantong Emperor in the Qing Dynasty (as shown in Table 3.3) is the earliest statistical information on the population of the Dai people in this region available to the author. The scope of jurisdiction for the three prefectures and one county in the following table covers most of the administrative area of the present Xishuangbanna.

In the late Qing dynasty and the R.O.C. Period, there were no well-demarcated administrative jurisdictions for the vast area where today's Dai-Jingpo Autonomous Prefecture of Dehong commands, and the Dai people then were mainly distributed over seven regions administered by various chieftains: Mangshi, Zhefang, Mengmao, Longchuan, Zhanda, Ganya and Nandian. According to the data for the 26th year of the R.O.C. Period (1937) gleaned by Mr. Jiang Yingliang, the total population in these chieftain regions stood at 103,090 persons in 26,383 households (as shown in Table 3.4),[3] and thus the average household size was supposed to stand at 3.91 persons per household.

3 Mr. Jiang questioned the accuracy of the data, suspecting it was "very incorrect The reasons are 1. Except for approximate estimates, no reasonable surveys were made on the populations in various areas. 2. Chieftains were reluctant to make public true population figures. Generally speaking, they were prone to underreporting their numbers. However, the more accurate population figures of the Dai people in the Dehong region in the Republic of China or earlier are no longer available for examination, and the 103,000 people recorded in the book are the only reference numbers". Also seen in Jiang Yingliang, *The Real Life of the Baiyi (Dai) People in Western Yunnan* (Dehong Ethnic Publishing House, 2003), 57.

Table 3.5: Populations in Cheli and Mengla in Selected Years of the R.O.C. Period

Year	Cheli County (Precinct 1)			Mengla County (Precincts 5 and 6)		
	Number of Households	Total Population	Average Household Size	Number of Households	Total Population	Average Household Size
The 2nd of the R.O.C. Period (1913)	11,735	54,375	4.63	7,728	30,498	3.95
The 12th Year of the R.O.C. Period (1923)	9,556	46,481	4.86	7,203	26,717	3.71
The 16th Year of the R.O.C. Period (1927)				4,840	15,939	3.29
The 21st Year of the R.O.C. Period (1932)	7,559	41,159	5.45	5,150	17,604	3.42
The 22nd Year of the R.O.C. Period (1933)	7,559	43,300	5.73			
The 23rd Year of the R.O.C. Period (1934)	7,559	41,159	5.45			
The 25th Year of the R.O.C. Period (1936)				5,460	19,269	3.53
The 27th Year of the R.O.C. Period (1938)	8,775	32,917	3.75	4,907	15,980	3.26
The 28th Year of the R.O.C. Period (1939)	7,839	31,978	4.08	4,948	16,269	3.29
The 29th Year of the R.O.C. Period (1940)	8,907	33,655	3.78	4,943	16,669	3.37
The 30th Year of the R.O.C. Period (1941)	8,907	38,214	4.29	4,944	17,038	3.45

Table 3.5: Continued

Year	Cheli County (Precinct 1)			Mengla County (Precincts 5 and 6)		
	Number of Households	Total Population	Average Household Size	Number of Households	Total Population	Average Household Size
The 31st Year of the R.O.C. Period (1942)				4,048	14,416	3.56
The 32nd Year of the R.O.C. Period (1943)	8,907	33,655	3.78	5,730	16,270	2.84
The 33rd Year of the R.O.C. Period (1944)				4,662	19,010	4.08
The 34th Year of the R.O.C. Period (1945)				5,532	22,128	4.00
The 35th Year of the R.O.C. Period (1946)				4,662	19,641	4.21
The 36th Year of the R.O.C. Period (1947)	8,065	4,7841	5.93			

Source: *The Annals of Jinghong County,* Yunnan People's Publishing House, 2000; *The Annals of Mengla County,* Yunnan People's Publishing House, 1994.

In contrast, there were relatively complete and accurate demographics for the area where today's Xishuangbanna commands. The demographic data in selected years of this period by the district in Cheli (toady's Jinghong Municipality), Mengla and Menghai are respectively shown in Table 3.5 and 3.6.

According to the *Brief Annals of Frontier Regions in Pusi,* Mr. Li Fuyi sorted out the data on the households by district and incorporated it in *The Chronicles of the 12 Bannas* (as shown in Table 3.7).

Table 3.8 represents the overall data in the R.O.C. Period for the administrative jurisdiction of today's Xishuangbanna.

Table 3.6: Populations in Menghai County in Selected Years of the R.O.C. Period

Year	Region	Number of Households	Total Population (Persons)	Average Household Size(Persons)
The 1st Year of the R.O.C. Period (1912)	Precinct 2 (Mengzhe) Precinct 3 (Menghai)	6,255 5,445	50,840	4.35
The 12th Year of the R.O.C. Period (1923)	Precinct 2 Precinct 3 Precinct 4	6,255 5,539 3,230	61,952	4.13
The 22nd Year of the R.O.C. Period (1933) Fohai County	Nanqiao County Fohai County Linjiang Provisional Administrative Area	7,166 5,513 2,072	56,307	3.82
The 27th Year of the R.O.C. Period (1938)	Nanqiao County Fohai County Jiangning Provisional Administrative Area	6,338 5,495 2,009	55,671	4.08
The 32nd Year of the R.O.C. Period (1943)	Nanqiao County Fohai County Jiangning Provisional Administrative Area	6,338 5,495 2,009	56,849	4.11

Source: *The Annals of Menghai County*, Yunnan People's Publishing House, 1997.

According to the six sets of data, both the statistical figures for Pu'er Prefecture in the first year of Emperor Xuantong's Reign in the Qing dynasty (1909) and those for Dehong and Xishuangbanna in the R.O.C. Period suggest that there has been no significant change in the average household size in today's Dai settlement areas. The average household size in Pu'er Prefecture in 1909 stood at 4.42, that in Cheli in 11 selected years during the period from 1913 to 1947 at 4.66, that in Mengla in 14 selected years during the period from 1913 to 1946 at 3.58, that in Menghai in five selected years during the period from 1912 to 1943 at 4.08, and that in Dehong in 1937 at 3.91.

Table 3.7: Households by District in the R.O.C. Period

Year	Precincts and Seats	Number of Households	Total (Households)	Total Population	Total (Households)	Average Household Size (Persons)	Average (Persons)
The 2nd Year of the R.O.C. Period (1913)	Precinct 1 (Seat: Cheli)	6,952		35,838		5.16	
	Precinct 2 (Seat: Mengzhe)	5,899		23,235		3.94	
	Precinct 3 (Seat: Menghai)	5,445	25185	27,605	112,731	5.07	4.48
	Precinct 4 (Seat: Damenglong)	3,077		10,858		3.53	
	Precinct 5 (Seat: Mengla)	3,812		15,195		3.99	
The 12th Year of the R.O.C. Period (1923)	Precinct 1 (Seat: Cheli)	9,556		46,481		4.87	
	Precinct 2 (Seat: Mengzhe)	6,255		27,472		4.39	
	Precinct 3 (Seat: Menghai)	5,539	28243	27,663	122,901	4.99	4.35
	Precinct 4 (Seat: Mengzhu)	3,230		6,817		2.11	
	Precinct 5 (Seat: Mengpeng)	3,663		14,468		3.95	
The 22nd Year of the R.O.C. Period (1933)	Cheli County (Seat: Jingde)	7,559		41,159		5.45	
	Wufu County (Seat: Mengzhe)	7,166		25,108		3.50	
	Fohai County (Seat: Menghai)	5,513	27460	22,314	115,070	4.08	4.19
	Linjiang Provisional Administrative Area (Seat: Mengwang)	2,072		8,885		4.29	

(*Continued*)

Table 3.7: Continued

Year	Precincts and Seats	Number of Households	Total (Households)	Total Population	Total (Households)	Average Household Size (Persons)	Average (Persons)
	Zhenyue County (Seat: Yiwu)	5,150		17,604		3.42	
The 27th Year of the R.O.C. Period (1938)	Cheli County (Seat: Jingde)	8,775		32,917		3.75	
	Nanqiao County (Seat: Mengzhe)	6,107		23,260		3.81	
	Fuhai County (Seat: Menghai)	5,465	27326	23,526	104,568	4.30	3.83
	Ningjiang Provisional Administrative Area (Seat: Mengwang)	2,072		8,885		4.29	
	Zhenyue County (Seat: Yiwu)	4,907		15,980		3.26	
The 30th Year of the R.O.C. Period (1943)	Cheli County (Seat: Jingde)			27,831			
	Nanqiao County (Seat: Mengzhe)			26,180			
	Fohai County (Seat: Menghai)			23,536	103,449		
	Ningjiang Provisional Administrative Area (Seat: Mengzhu)			8,885			
	Zhenyue County (Seat: Yiwu)			17,017			

Source: Author's compilation based on Li Fuyi's *The Chronicles of the 12 Bannas.*

Table 3.8: Populations, Households and Average Household Size in Xishuangbanna in the R.O.C. Period

Year	Number of Households	Population(Persons)	Average Household Size (Persons)
1913	38,256	168,547	4.41
1923	39,681	168,391	4.24
1932	34,094	152,243	3.89
1933	27,460	115,070	4.19
1935	32,022	137,423	4.29
1938	39,179	154,854	3.95
1939	28,600	119,715	4.19
1940	32,472	128,842	3.97
1948	28,552	119,549	4.19

Source: The data for 1913, 1932, 1935, 1939, 1940 and 1948 is extracted from *The Chronicles of Dai Autonomous Prefecture of Xishuangbanna*, and that for 1923, 1933 and 1938 from *The Annals of 12 Bannas.*

"Baiyi people have lower fertility rates and smaller populations" (Yao, 2003) is the general demographic picture of Xishuangbanna in the early 20th century (1939) painted by Mr. Yao Hesheng. Mr. Jiang Yingliang's findings from his survey among 100 healthy couples in the three-fourth year of the R.O.C. Period (1945) in today's Jinghong Municipality (the then Cheli) was the earliest data about the Dai family fertility behavior(as shown in Table 3.9).

Through comparison between the "Average Household Size" figures in the preceding Table and Mr. Jiang's survey findings, combined with a pictorial description about these abstract data, we can get a sweeping view of reproduction and population at that time of Dai people: Families in the Dai settlement areas at that time had, on average, no more than five members, which means that there were typically no more than three children in a family.

Due to various historical causes, such as adjustments to administrative divisions, these statistical data couldn't, admittedly, reflect the demographic realities in these regions; perfunctory performance by officials and erroneous clerical work by unskilled investigators might also result in inconsistent survey statistics. In

Table 3.9: Childbirth among Dai Families in Jinghong

Number of Couples Interviewed		100
Age of the Couple		29–45 Years Old
Duration of Marriage		10–29 Years
Number of Children	4 Survived to aduldhood	6 Couples
	3 Survived to Adulthood	24 Couples
	2 Survived to Adulthood	38 Couples
	1 Survived to Adulthood	17 Couples
	None Survived to Adulthood	10 Couples
	Never gave Birth (s)	5 Couples
	Average number of Children/ Couple	1.89

Source: Jiang Yingliang: *The Cultural Life of the Baiyi People*, Shanghai: Zhonghua Book Company, 1950, p. 188.

addition, "underreported data" filed by local authorities also would lead to some deviations from the historical realities.[4] However, despite various imperfections

4 In The Annals of Twelve Bannas, Mr. Li Fuyi noted that, "we found during the survey that all the administrative funds of the counties and bureaus had been apportioned by households since the First Year of the R. O. C. period. The mounting call for reduced burdens on households and the rampant official corruption of collectors inevitably led to underreporting"; "The figures reported by townships to counties were usually about 80 percent of their true statistical figures, and counties, in turn, underreported them by 10 percent to the province, and then, the figures finally reported to the province were only about 70 percent of the true statistical figures."... "I had conducted a survey on my own in Cheli County, and found that a lot of households were missing in the official data". See also Li Fuyi, *The Annals of Twelve Bannas* (Taiwan: Chiang Kai-shek Publishing Company, 1955), 38. 52. Mr. Jiang Yingliang gave a detailed description in The Life and Culture of the Baiyi People, "I personally believe that the census figure from this survey (the Yunnan border resident distribution survey conducted by Mr. Jiang in the 32th -3fourth Year of the R. O. C. Period) was necessarily smaller than the actual population for three reasons: (1) Given the taxes were collected based on households in the Dai regions, the reported numbers of households were fewer than the actual figures; (2) The underreported numbers of households in some counties or regions were not necessarily attributable to intentional but rather unknown acts, as most of border residents were sparsely located in hilly areas inaccessible to census officials, and would not have the chance of meeting with them throughout their lifetime; (3) Some counties and districts reported apparently unreliable estimates and others even did not reported their figures, so the populations in these counties and districts were not included in the total figures. The author (Jiang himself) had made a door-to-door survey of the populations of two townships in Cheli County, and found that the actual numbers of residents in the two townships were nearly one third larger than the figures reported by the survey officials. Therefore, the author could conclude that a 30% amplification

mentioned above, these data are still important information about the overall population size in the Dai settlement areas during that period.

Section 2 Dai People's Demographic Situation from the Founding of the People's Republic of China to the Initial Phase of Reform and Opening-up

With the constant improvement in people's living standards and medical conditions after the founding of the People's Republic of China in 1949, the mortality rate saw a rapid drop. Meanwhile, "with the war times gone, land reforms completed and the resulting peaceful and worry-free life, the first baby boom came in 1950–1957, with the natural growth rate of the population reaching as high as 20–25 per thousand persons". "Later, as the 'Great Leap Forward' campaign caused severe hardship for the national economy and people's lives, resulting in a 'low ebb' of natural population growth with a declining fertility rate and a rising mortality rate from 1958 to 1961. However, with national economic adjustments, the national population rallied soon and returned to former levels with a high fertility rate, a low mortality rate and a high natural growth rate. In the early post-disaster decade from 1962 to 1972, the compensatory reproduction pushed the fertility rate to over 40‰, and the mortality rate fell far below the 1957 figure of 10‰ to 7.0‰, leading to a surge in the natural growth rate to 30‰. Thus the second baby boom after the founding of the People's Republic of China (Yuan, 1991a)." As thus, the national population increased by nearly 105 million – one-fifth (Li, 1998a) within eight years from nearly 542 million in 1949 to nearly 603 million in 1954 and further nearly 647 million in 1957. During this period, Chinese demographers represented by Ma Yinchu called for more attention to the problem of an imbalance between population and economic development and the need to control excessive population growth; the then Premier Zhou Enlai also proposed that "some measure of birth control should be in place" to better protect women and children and focus more on raising offspring well to benefit the national health and prosperity. Despite all of the this, the mainstream conception that "A large population is an advantage" prevailed over all the dissenting voices amid the "Great Leap Forward" fever, exerting a decisive influence on China's population development at that time (Li, 1998b). Later, the "Four

of the reported official figures might be closer to the actual populations. See also Jiang Yingliang, *The Life and Culture of the Baiyi (Dai) People* (Shanghai: Zhonghua Book Company, 1950), 87–88.

Clean-ups Movement" in full swing in 1964 and the "Cultural Revolution" initiated in 1966 led to increasingly intense "class struggle", putting scientific research on the economics of population to a grinding halt. Although the first family planning institutions were established in 1964, population growth still ran its natural course. As a result, China's population grew to 705 million in 1964, 807 million in 1969 and 909 million in 1974, with the amount of time it took for the population to grow by 100 million people decreasing from ten years to five years during the period (Yuan, 1991b).

As an integral part of the national population, the population of ethnic minorities also saw significant increases during the same period. At the macro level, the four national census data from 1953 to 1990 shows that the population of ethnic minorities on the Chinese mainland increased from 35.32 million in 1953 to 39.884 million in 1964, to 67.239 million in 1982 and further to 91.3231 million in 1990, posting an increase of 158.6% in the 37 years and seeing its proportion in the national population rise from 6.06% in 1953 to 8.08% in 1990. By 1990, the Zhuang people, the largest minority people in China, had a population of 15.5558 million, the Manchus had a population of nearly 10.00 million (exactly 9.8468 million), the Luobas, the smallest minority people, expanded to 2,322 persons, and the Hezhens also increased to 4,254 persons in 1990 from a tiny group of 300 in the early days of the People's Republic of China (Zhang, 1993).

Yet, in sharp contrast with other minority people in frontier regions, the Dai population extended a relatively steady trend amid the "soaring national population", which is reflected in the macro data comparison in Table 3.10.

The data in the Table 3.10 shows that either in the 1950s and 60s when there was no birth control at all, the 1970s when family planning was under preparation, or the 1980s when the family planning was implemented nationwide, the growth rate of the Dai population had always been at a low level relative to other minority people. It seems that Dai people were "going their own way" on fertility issues and didn't follow the national demographic trends.

At the micro-level, the investigation on the social and historical situations of minority people by the joint team composed of the Frontier Working Committee and the Ethnic Affairs Commission of Yunnan Province in 1954 provided us with a valuable glimpse of the population data on the minority people. Taking Xishuangbanna as an example, the statistical figures in Table 3.11 are derived from the feudal hierarchy-specific statistical findings in the Dai villages in the surveyed areas. Given the politically charged investigation was mainly aimed at finding out the true situation of the feudal hierarchy in Xishuangbanna, so, the households and residents in the villages without distinct class identities were

Table 3.10: Comparison of Population Changes of seven Ethnic Minorities in Frontier Regions in Yunnan as per the three National Censuses (10,000 persons)[5]

Ethnic Group	Population (1953)	Population (1964)	Population (1982)	Population Growth, 1953–1982	
				Margin of Population Growth	Growth Rate (%)
Provincial Total	1,713.27	2,050.95	3,255.36	1,540.11	90.00
Han	1,149.81	1,410.89	2,223.16	1,073.35	93.35
Ethnic Minorities	563.46	640.06	1,032.20	468.74	83.19
Dai	47.88	53.43	83.57	35.69	74.54
Hani	48.12	62.86	105.84	57.72	119.94
Lahu	13.91	19.12	30.41	16.51	118.71
Bulang	3.21	3.94	5.83	2.62	81.43
Jingpo	10.18	5.72	9.28	−0.89	−8.80
Achang	1.77	1.20	2.04	0.26	15.02
Demao	1.15	0.72	1.22	0.07	6.73

Source: Chen Xuguang and Li Guangcan (Edited), *An Introduction to the Population of Ethnic Minorities in Yunnan,* Yunnan People's Publishing House, 1990, pp. 3–4.

not incorporated in the statistical results (Editorial Committee of Five Series of Books on Ethnic Issues, 1983) (for example, some tiny villages in Menghai, such as Yiwu and Xiangming; some residential blocks in Jinghong, such as Jinglan, Jiasa, Jiadong and Manlong; and some villages for lepers in Jinghong, such as Manyan and Manlongxiang), leaving the survey data incomplete. However, thanks to its relatively extensive coverage (involving 113,216 residents in 23,153 households from 696 Dai villages in 26 administrative districts), this set of very detailed survey data still presents a rather clear picture of the Dai families in Xishuangbanna at that time. For example, there were, on average, 4.89 persons in a household.

Since the 1970s, with the approach to monitoring national population dynamics becoming more science-based and standardized, more science-based and

5 The unusual changes in the populations of minority groups in the Table, such as Jingpo, Achang and Demao, during the period 1953–1962, were due to various factors, including inaccurate censuses, ethnic identification and integration of clans, changes in ethnic compositions, political factors and natural migrations of populations. See also Chen Xuguang and Li Guangcan, eds, *An Introduction to the Population of Ethnic Minority Groups in Yunnan* (Yunnan People's Publishing House, 1990), 8–12.

Table 3.11: Households, Population and Average Household Size of Dai Villages In Xishuangbanna, 1954–1955

Serial No.	Township	Villages	Households	Population	Average Household Size	Serial No.	Township	Villages	Households	Population (persons)	Average Household Size (persons)
1	Jinghong	93	2,848	14,369	5.05	14	Menghan	54	1,440	8,761	6.08
2	Menghai	44	1,330	6,426	4.83	15	Jingha	4	226	1,193	5.28
3	Menghun	34	1,434	6,928	4.83	16	Mengkuan	4	137	731	5.34
4	Daluo	9	269	463	1.72	17	Mengyang	23	642	2,903	4.52
5	Mengban	6	247	1,303	5.28	18	Mengwang	7	109	491	4.50
6	Mengsong	12	507	2,395	4.72	19	Jingnuo	28	674	3,171	4.70
7	Mengwang	15	587	3,154	5.37	20	Puwen	11	321	1,569	4.89
8	Mengkang	4	90	361	4.01	21	Jingdong	12	255	1,344	5.27
9	Meng'a	8	306	1,252	4.09	22	Menglun	21	541	2,746	5.08
10	Mengzhe	95	2,573	12,716	4.94	23	Mengyuan	5	275	1,559	5.67
11	Jingzhen	37	1,046	4,272	4.08	24	Mengxing	3	99	576	5.82
12	Mengman	8	426	1,793	4.21	25	Mengla	51	2,296	8,684	6.36
13	Menglong	63	2,838	15,963	5.62	26	Mengpeng	45	1,637	8,093	4.94

Source: A compilation from *A Survey of the Dai Ethnic Society and History -Vol. 2, 5, 7 and 9.*

effective statistical data, including the total fertility rates (TFR), the order-specific fertility rates, are available to us, so we can get a more comprehensive understanding of the fertility situations in various regions and among minority people.

Table 3.12 shows that, throughout the 1970s, Dai women had the lowest TFR among the three minority groups in the frontier regions (with the average rate standing at 4.14 for the Dai people, 5.86 for the Was, and 6.30 for the Bulangs). The TFR of the Dai people dropped below 4.0 in the late 1970s, and further below 3.0 in the early 1980s.

Table 3.12: The TFRs of Three Minority Groups in the Frontier Region, 1971–1981

Year	Dai	Wa	Bulang	Year	Dai	Wa	Bulang
1971	4.66	5.28	6.14	1977	3.42	5.67	5.91
1972	5.55	6.47	6.24	1978	3.61	5.40	5.28
1973	4.91	6.39	5.78	1979	3.38	5.23	7.30
1974	5.32	6.66	7.09	1980	3.03	5.30	6.51
1975	4.21	6.56	7.28	1981	2.94	4.90	5.79
1976	4.46	6.65	6.02				

Source: The sample survey data on women's marriage and reproduction status of eight minority groups, *Population and Development Review,* 1989, p. 21.

The Table shows that the average number of births of a Dai woman throughout her lifetime was four in the 1970s and less than three after the 1980s. But this change in the fertility rate among Dai women was not a result from the government's policy interventions. In fact, the Central Government still adopted very loose family planning policies on minority groups across the Province of Yunnan in this period, with the provision for counties inhabited by minority people set forth as: no more than two births for an urban ethnic minority family and no more than three for an ethnic minority family in rural or chilly hilly areas. In frontier townships in the Province, only the publicity on family planning were carried out among rural ethnic minority families but no fertility restrictions were imposed (Chen and Li, 1990a). The above realities show that the uniqueness in fertility behavior of the Dai families had already shown up before the implementation of the national family planning policy in Xishuangbanna.

Section 3 Dai Fertility Behavior Since the Reform and Opening-up

In response to severe population pressure, China began in the early 1970s to roll out the family planning policy in both urban and rural areas to strictly control population growth. In 1971, the State Council approved and forwarded the *Report on Doing a Good Job in Family Planning,* with the indicators for population growth control incorporated in the national economic development plan for the first time. In 1975, in his comments on the *Report on the 1975 National Economic Development Plan* filed by the State Development Planning Commission, Mao

Zedong pointed out that population growth must be brought under control. Henceforth, the general policy orientation for family planning in China has taken shape: "later births, fewer births and larger birth intervals" and "Only one child for any couple is best, no more than two". The CPC Central Committee issued on September 25, 1980 the mobilization order: *An Open Letter to All Members of the CPC and the Youth League on the Issue of Controlling Population Growth* and launched a nationwide publicity campaign themed "One Child per Couple". On March 6, 1981, the 17th Meeting of the Party Committee of the Fifth National People's Congress decided to set up the National Family Planning Commission and appointed Chen Muhua, then Vice Premier of the State Council, to be its Director. In November 1981, the Fourth Session of the Fifth National People's Congress articulated the population policy for China: "To Keep the Population Growth under Control and Improve the Population Quality". Soon later in February 1982, the State Council issued the *Directive on Further Improving Family Planning*, requiring that

> except when special approval has been granted, all couples, including cadres, workers and urban residents, are required to have only one child. Couples in rural areas are encouraged in principle to have only one child; for rural couples in real need of more than one child, a second birth may be permitted and arranged in a planned manner; and in no circumstance is a third birth permitted. Ethnic minorities are encouraged to practice family planning also although the rules can be somewhat relaxed,

and stressing that, "necessary rewards and restrictions should be put in place to ensure a smooth development of family planning work" (Peng, 1997).

At the 12th National Congress of the CPC in September 1982, family planning became a national basic policy and was enshrined in the newly revised Constitution in November the same year, demonstrating the government's determination to carry out the policy of family planning and population growth control.

The decision was met with backlash across the country, especially in the vast rural areas, making implementation particularly challenging. The reason was that the policy requirement of "having only one child or at most two for a couple" deviates far from the fertility desire of the masses, resulting in tension between family planning workers and the masses and even leading to tense confrontations in some places during its actual implementation. In this most serious cases, it posed a threat to the relationship between the government and social stability. In response to these developments and based on the reports by the Party Committee at the National Family Planning Commission, the CPC Central Committee made some targeted adjustments to the national implementation measures of the policy in its CPC No. 7 Document in 1984, effectively mitigating the tensions between family planning workers and the masses of childbearing age.

The following quote provides a true and accurate description of the family planning work during that special historical period:

> Since the founding of the People's Republic of China, the work of population and family planning has met with twists and turns. It was a tortuous course as the Party experienced repeated back-and-forth movements and deviations in its understanding of population issues; meanwhile, it was also a heroic journey as the public, especially the women of childbearing age, have made great contributions and sacrifices for its implementation (Zhang, 2007).

In sharp contrast to the above situation, the implementation of this policy in the Dai areas didn't encounter any resistance, and birth control techniques were also readily accepted and well promoted among the Dai people. In fact, shortly after contraception methods were applied in the clinical practice in China, Ms. Dao Meiying, a Dai woman and the then Director at Women's Federation of Jinghong Municipality, took the initiative to go through a tubal ligation surgery in April 1957 at the First People's Hospital of Yunnan Province (Kunhua Hospital). In July the same year, the first female contraceptive operation in Xishuangbanna was also successfully performed on Ms. Dao Meili, another Dai woman, at the People's Hospital of Jinghong Municipality, marking that the tubal ligation birth control technology was successfully introduced and mastered at the People's Hospital of Xishuangbanna. Our fieldwork findings show that at the back of their mind, the Dai people were not at all averse to various contraception and birth control measures.

In Table 3.12 in the preceding Section, we have already found that the Dai people had a rather low fertility rate even before the implementation of the national family planning policy (The TFR for the Dai people was 2.94 in 1981). When the policy was rolled out across the nation, the Dai masses gave a favorable response with an even more positive attitude and actions. All Dai women of childbearing age took contraceptive measures as required by related birth control regulations, and once having their second child, some Dai women eligible for a third birth as per related policy requirements even volunteered to prevent further pregnancy by using the most reliable birth control measure – the fallopian ligation surgery. In 1985, only 1.52% of Dai women had four children or more, and as many as 329 villages in total saw no cases of giving more than two births across the county of Jinghong. In particular, the Dai village in Mangajian Township in Menghan district had seen no case of giving a third birth for seven consecutive years and was cited and rewarded by both the National and Provincial Family Planning Commissions (Chen and Li, 1990b). From the following Table 3.13, we can see that the Dai people had the lowest population growth rate among the seven ethnic groups in the frontier areas in Yunnan.

According to Table 3.14, the synchronic comparison showed that at the time of the third, fourth and fifth censuses, the Dai people had the lowest figures among the eight ethnic minority groups in the frontier regions in Yunnan in three main indicators: the TFRTFR, the average number of survived births of women of childbearing age and the rate of multiple births. To be specific, in 1982, all of the three indicators of the Dai people were below those of the Han people and the provincial average; in 1990, despite being a little higher than that of the Han people, the TFRTFR of the Dai people was largely on par with the provincial average, and despite being higher than that of the Han people, the average number of survived births of Dai women of childbearing age was lower than the provincial average; and in 2000, the TFR of the Dai people slid once again below that of the Han people and the provincial average; despite being higher than that of the Han people, the average number of survived births of women of childbearing age was on par with the provincial average; and the rate of multiple births was below both that of the Han people and the provincial average. The diachronic study showed that the TFR of the Dai people dropped from 3.39 in 1982 to 2.63 in 1990, and then to 1.70 in 2000, and the rate of multiple births (three births or more) from 38.01% in 1982 to 23.49% in 1990, and then to 4.96% in 2000. Besides, the general fertility rate of the Dai people was also on the decline, dropping from 105.20 per mill during the third national census to 99.56 per mill during the fourth national census, and then to 53.44 per mill during the fifth national census. The Dai people ranked 18th among all of the 26 ethnic minority groups in the Province in the general fertility rate both during the third and fourth national censuses, and slid sharply to 26th during the fifth census, becoming the one with the lowest fertility rate among the 26 ethnic minority groups in Yunnan (Luo, 2004).

These figures showed that all of the demographic indicators of Dai people had constantly been sliding during the 18 years since the national implementation of the family planning policy: Their TFR had fallen below the critical level of population replacement, their average number of survived births of women of childbearing age below three in 1990, and their rate of multiple births also at

Table 3.13: Comparison of the Population Changes of seven Ethnic Minorities in Yunnan Frontier Region in the Six Censuses (10,000 Persons)[6]

Ethnic people	Population (1953)	Population (1964)	Population (1982)	Population (1990)	Population (2000)	Population (2010)	Population Growth (1982–2010)	
							Margin of Population Growth	Growth Rate (%)
Provincial Total	1,713.27	2,050.95	3,255.36	3,697.25	4,236.0	4,601.6	1,346.24	41.35
The Hans	1,149.81	1,410.69	2,223.15	2,461.45	2,820.13	3,066.2	843.05	37.92
Ethnic Minorities	563.46	640.26	1,032.20	1,235.8	1,415.87	1,535.4	503.2	48.75
Dai	**47.88**	**53.43**	**83.57**	**101.46**	**114.21**	**122.4**	**38.83**	**46.46**
Hani	48.12	62.86	105.84	124.92	142.50	163.1	57.26	54.10
Lahu	13.91	19.12	30.41	40.83	44.76	47.6	17.19	56.53
Bulang	3.21	3.94	5.83	8.18	9.04	11.7	5.87	100.69
Jingpo	10.18	5.72	9.28	11.84	13.02	14.2	4.92	53.02
Achang	1.77	1.20	2.04	2.76	3.35	3.8	1.73	84.80
Demao	1.15	0.72	1.22	1.54	1.78	2.0	0.78	63.93

Source: *An Introduction to the Population of Ethnic Minorities in Yunnan,* Chen Xuguang and Li Guangcan (Edited), Yunnan People's Publishing House, 1990; *Yunnan Province 1990 census data (electronically aggregated data),* Census Office of Yunnan Province, China Statistical Publishing House, 1992; *Yunnan Province 2000 Census Data, Census Office of Yunnan Province,* Yunnan Science and Technology Press Co., Ltd., 2002; *Yunnan Statistical Yearbook – 2011,* Statistical Bureau of Yunnan Province (Edited), China Statistical Publishing House, 2011.

a rather low level. The above facts suggest that there existed virtually no cases of multiple births. Meanwhile, the third national census data also showed that the gender ratio in the Dai population was lower than 101, reflecting that Dai people not only have no desire to have more children but also no preference for males to females in their fertility culture.

6 The unusual changes in the populations of ethnic groups in the Table, such as Jingpo, Achang and Demao, during the period 1953–1962, were due to various factors, including inaccurate censuses, ethnic identification and integration of clans, changes in ethnic compositions, political factors and natural migrations of populations. See also Chen Xuguang and Li Guangcan, eds., *An Introduction to the Population of Ethnic Minorities in Yunnan* (Yunnan People's Publishing House, 1990), 8–12.

Table 3.14: Demographic Dynamics of Major Ethnic People in the Dai Ethnic Settlement Areas according to the third, fourth and fifth Censuses

	1982: the third Census				1990: the fourth Census				2000: the fifth Census			
Ethnic Group	Total Fertility Rate (TFR)	Average Number of Survived Births for Women of 15–64 Years Old	Gender Ratio (F=100)	Rate of Multiple Births (%)	Total Fertility Rate (TFR)	Average Number of Survived Births for Women of 15–50 Years Old	Gender Ratio (F=100)	Rate of Multiple Births (%)	Total Fertility Rate (TFR)	Average Number of Survived Births for Women of 15–64 Years Old	Gender Ratio (F=100)	Rate of Multiple Births (%)
Yunnan Province	3.79	3.18	102.7	49.44	2.61	2.67	105.7	21.89	2.09	1.56	110.1	6.00
Han People	3.37	3.13	103.5	45.88	2.42	2.44	106.8	20.00	2.03	1.51	112.0	9.26
Hani	5.59	3.46	102.2	59.56	3.36	2.96	105.0	35.36	2.16	1.82	110.8	16.18
Dai	**3.35**	**3.05**	**98.6**	**38.01**	**2.63**	**2.56**	**100.3**	**23.49**	**1.70**	**1.57**	**100.9**	**4.96**
Lahu	5.64	3.57	101.7	56.76	3.67	3.15	105.1	43.74	2.10	1.87	109.1	12.25
Wa	5.53	3.53	100.7	59.52	6.64	3.23	103.7	47.51	2.30	2.05	109.1	20.37
Jingpo	4.86	3.34	92.8	57.64	4.21	2.99	95.8	46.86	2.18	1.79	98.8	14.41
Bulang	6.35	3.37	101.3	61.58	4.19	3.03	105.1	49.26	2.34	1.92	109.7	21.64
Achang	4.70	3.15	98.4	55.83	3.71	2.74	100.1	42.14	2.32	1.79	103.9	14.55
Demao	5.88	3.40	100.1	57.25	4.96	3.09	99.9	49.11	2.50	1.88	102.1	15.63

Source: *Compilation of the Third Census in Yunnan Province,* Census Office of Yunnan Province, October 1984; *Yunnan Province 1990census data (electronically aggregated data),* Census Office of Yunnan Province, China Statistical Publishing House, 1992; *Yunnan Province 2000 census data,* Census Office of Yunnan Province, Yunnan Science and Technology Press Co., Ltd., 2002; *Yunnan Province 2000 Census Data (Volume-Ethnic people),* Census Office of Yunnan Province, The Nationalities Publishing House of Yunnan, 2003.

Since population data of demographic significance concerning the fertility behavior of the Dai people for the period from the late Qing Dynasty, the R.O.C. Period and to the early days of the People's Republic of China was virtually unavailable, this author could only gather data scattered in voluminous historical literature, such as "total population", "average household size" and "the proportion of Dai people in the population", and cross-reference related cultural, literary and historical descriptions to piece together a rough picture of their fertility behavior, and thus these data could only be seen as "fuzzy data" of the fertility status of the Dai people.

Due to incomplete indicators in the demographic data from national censuses during the period from the 1950s to the 1970s, we again had to rely on such data as "Dai population" and "average size of Dai households" to extrapolate the fertility situations of the Dai communities. With the presence of various influencing factors, for example, deaths and migrations, such data items cannot, in technical terms, accurately reflect the true fertility situations, so, the author classified these data as "indirect data", which mens, they can only indirectly reflect the fertility behavior of the Dai people.

It was not until 1982 when the third national census was carried out that more accurate and science-based data items, such as the TFR, rate of multiple births, the average number of survived births of women of childbearing age and gender ratio, could be available for us to get a more comprehensive understanding of the fertility situation of the Dai people. Hence, the author classified these data as "direct data", through which, we have come out with the following judgments on the real historical scenarios of the Dai fertility behavior in the 20th century:

1. During the period from the late Qing dynasty and the R.O.C. Period to the early days of the People's Republic of China, the fertility behavior of the Dai people were in a state of "total freedom", i.e., being independent of any policy interventions from their feudal lords and the state. But they had a not-so-high fertility rate, and had, on average, no more than three children in a family. This proves that the description "foreign groups have low fertility rates and smaller populations" is accurate and credible;
2. After the founding of the People's Republic of China, the population policy went through three phases: "population boom" (Zhang, 1999) was promoted from the 1950s to the early 1970s; family planning was deliberated and prepared from 1971 to 1981; and family planning was formally implemented from 1982 onwards. Along with the three policy changes, the national population underwent significant transformations largely following a trend of "growing sharply before sliding slowly". Overall, this

national trend was also true of the Dai population, but the difference was that the latter changed at a moderate and steady pace and saw no "outstanding performance", i.e. "growing slowly before sliding sharply". This indicates that the fertility behavior of the Dai people were less swayed by external policies, basically maintaining their "going my own way" reproductive pattern.;

3. The Dai people had the lowest figures among the eight ethnic minority groups in the frontier regions in Yunnan in three main indicators: the TFR, the average number of survived births of women of childbearing age and the rate of multiple births at the time of the third, fourth and fifth censuses, respectively. Their TFR and rate of multiple births were below the provincial averages of Yunnan and these for the Han people both at the time of the third and fifth national censuses; their average number of survived births for women of childbearing age was at the lowest level at the time of the third national census, higher than that for the Han people but below the provincial average of Yunnan at the time of the fourth national census, and on par with the provincial average of Yunnan at the time of the fifth national census. All of these data shows that their fertility behavior were free of the propensity of "having more births" with other ethnic people;
4. The gender ratio among the Dai people at the time of the third, fourth and fifth national censuses respectively was below the provincial average of Yunnan, that of the Han people and the stable value range of 103–106, indicating that the Dai people Dai people showed no "male preference".

The non-existence among the Dai people of a preference for more children and for sons over daughters makes their fertility behavior patterns different from both what Chinese scholars have argued is the norm in rural China and what classical Western population theory has claimed regarding traditional agrarian society. Why is this? Why, as a traditional agrarian society, do they choose the pattern of a low fertility rate instead of striving for a high fertility rate? Why don't they have a "male preference" in relation to the sex of their children?

With these questions in mind, this author entered their lives, hoping to get to know and understand the lives of Dai people through close contact.

References

Calculations from the related data from Zhang Tianlu, ed. *The Evolution of the Chinese Ethnic Populations.* Beijing: China Ocean Press, 1993, 1, and China Census Data in 2000. China Statistical Publishing House, 2002.

Chen, Xuguang, and Guangcan Li, eds. *An Introduction to the Population of Ethnic Minorities Minority Groups in Yunnan.* Kunming: Yunnan People's Publishing House, 1990a, 11.

Chen, Xuguang, and Guangcan Li, eds. *An Introduction to the Population of Ethnic Minorities in Yunnan.* Kunming: Yunnan People's Publishing House, 1990b, 360.

Compilation Committee of Local Chronicles of Xishuangbanna Dai Autonomous Prefecture. *Chronicles of Xishuangbanna Dai Autonomous Prefecture.* Beijing: Xinhua Publishing House, 2002a, 371–372.

Compilation Committee of Local Chronicles of Xishuangbanna Dai Autonomous Prefecture. *Chronicles of Xishuangbanna Dai Autonomous Prefecture.* Beijing: Xinhua Publishing House, 2002b, 372.

Deng, Yongjin. Immigration and development [A], Lin Chaomin. *New Pine Collection* [C]. Yunnan University Press, 1996, 223.

Editorial Committee of Five Series of Books on Ethnic Issues. *A Survey of the Dai Ethnic Society and History* (Xishuangbanna-Vol. 2). Kunming: The Nationalities Publishing House of Yunnan, 1983, 86.

Jiang, Yingliang. *The Culture and Life of the Baiyi (Dai) People.* Shanghai: Zhonghua Book Company, 1950, 69–70.

Jiang, Yingliang, and Xiaolin Jiang. *The Real Life of the Dai Ethnic People in Western Yunnan.* Yunnan: Dehong. The Ethnic Publishing House, 2003, 57.

Li, Jingneng. *Research on Population and Economy in Current China.* Beijing: China Population Publishing House, 1998a, 1–3.

Li, Jingneng. *Research on Population and Economy in Current China.* Beijing: China Population Publishing House, 1998b, 5.

Luo, Chun et al. Comparative Research on Women's Fertility Rates and Patterns of Ethnic People in Yunnan. *Journal of Yunnan Nationalities University*, no. 6 (2004): 44.

Peng, Peiyun, ed. *Encyclopedia of Family Planning in China.* Beijing: China Population Publishing House, 1997, 19.

Yao, Hesheng. *The Folklore of Shui Clan of the Dai Ethnic Group.* Kunming: Yunnan People's Publishing House, 2003, 141.

Yuan, Yongxi, ed. *China's Population (General Introduction).* Beijing: Chinese Financial & Economic Publishing House, 1991a, 84.

Yuan, Yongxi, ed. *China's Population (General Introduction).* Beijing: Chinese Financial & Economic Publishing House, 1991b, 22.

Zhang, Tianlu. *Fifty Years of Research on Chinese Ethnic Minority Populations.* Ethno-National Studies, no. 5 (1999): 34–35.

Zhang, Weiqing, ed. *Readings on Coordinated Efforts in Solving Population Issues.* Beijing: China Population Publishing House, 2007, 31.

4 Empirical Study of the Dai Traditional Fertility Behavior

Based on the consolidated demographic data of the Dai people scattered in the above-mentioned historical documents and the incomplete census data cross-referenced from the early days of the People's Republic of China, we got a rough knowledge of the changes of population and traditional fertility behavior of the Dai minority before the 1980s. After 1982, with access to more sufficient and improved demographic indicators in the national censuses, such as the TFR, the general fertility rate, the sex ratio, etc., we could see a clearer picture of some features of their fertility behavior. However, given the national family planning policy interventions that somewhat influenced the traditional fertility behavior of the Dai people during this period, to "recreate" the history of the Dai traditional fertility behavior in a more authentic way, it is necessary to conduct an empirical investigation of the fertility history of the Dai families following the ethnologic fieldwork methodology, so that we can understand the philosophies governing the birth control and fertility desires and behaviors of the Dai people from a micro perspective.

Section 1 Survey Design

Survey Site Selection

In his book *Jiangcun Economy*, Mr. Fei Xiaotong wrote that,

> To investigate people's lives in a deeper and detailed manner, it is necessary for researchers to limit their investigations to a smaller social unit. This is a practical consideration as investigators must get easier access to the interviewees to be able to conduct close observation in person on them. But on the other hand, the social unit to be studied should not be too small so that it can provide a complete slice of people's social life (Fei, 2001).

This passage sheds light on how to make site selection for ethnologic fieldwork.

According to the sixth National Census in 2010, 54.5% of the 1.224 million Dai people in China lived in two autonomous prefectures (316,000 in Xishuangbanna Autonomous Prefecture and 350,000 in Dehong Dai and Jingpo Autonomous Prefecture), and 25.7% were distributed in three counties (114,300 in Gengma, 144,200 in Menglian and 55,600 in Jinggu). So, we selected Xishuangbanna Dai Autonomous Prefecture and Dehong Dai and Jingpo Autonomous Prefecture as our main investigation sites. Various methods, including data collection, meetings and talks and in-home interviews, were adopted to collect primary fieldwork data of fertility behavior of the Dai families in the selected villages in the two prefectures. For other Dai settlement areas, the participant observation, meetings and talks and other methods were adopted to get the basic information. As the Dai residents were distributed relatively evenly across the three administrative regions under Xishuangbanna (Jinghong Municipality, Menghai County and Mengla County), we selected one village each from the three regions. Similarly, as the Dai residents in Dehong Dai and Jingpo Autonomous Prefecture were predominately clustered in two cities: Mangshi and Ruili, we also selected one village each from them. In fact, the author had already started the survey and research as early as 2007.

Interviewee Selection

The survey was to reflect the voluntary fertility behavior in history of the Dai families in these villages, to understand the "productive freedom" situation of rural Dai families before the the national family planning policy was fully implemented in 1984 among the frontier ethnic minority groups. Since Dai women in these selected villages generally get married at around 20 years old, we defined the timeframe of 20 years as a generation, and mainly chose Dai women born in or before 1950 to be our interviewees. The purpose for such design was to obtain as many intergenerational fertility samples as possible that would best reflect their actual traditional fertility behavior.

Paradigm for Recording Survey Results

Fertility behavior are not only a practical manifestation of fertility desire, but also an objective behavioral expression of the fertility concepts, values and views of life in an individual's real life, involving his/her complex psychological activities. To better understand such psychological activities of the interviewees, it is necessary to capture as comprehensively as possible the original language expressions of interviewees in the local area and at the time of interview, during our fieldwork survey. So, we set a unified paradigm for recording their expressions as follows:

1. According to the Dai terminology, the Chinese phrase "rural areas" was transcribed as "village" or "hamlet";
2. For the sake of authenticity, we recorded interviewees' own words as much as possible;
3. The female head of household was the main narrator of the family's reproductive history and family members supplied additional information when necessary;
4. Response of the interviewee herself was recorded in the Section "Current Generation", that of her mother in the Section "Parents' Generation", that of her children in the Section "Children's Generation", that of her grandchildren in the Section "Grandchildren's Generation", that of her great-grandchildren in the Section "Great-grandchildren's Generation", and so on.
5. The children born to a family were separately listed according to their sex and in the following order, following local conventions: first son and first daughter; second son and second daughter; third son and third daughter; and so on;
6. In addition to the written records for each household surveyed, a schematic family tree diagram: A genogram was also drawn. The genogram and the written records for the same household had a consistent serial number for the convenience of information search and statistics; and
7. The icons used in the following Genogram are as follows:

(1) ▲: male interviewee; ●: female interviewee;
(2) △: male; ○: female;
(3) ■: male who died before turning 15; ★: female who died before turning 15;
(4) □: a pregnancy with unknown sex of the fetus;
(5) The sex of those born within each generation are listed in descending order of age, from left to right.

Section 2 Written Records of Interviews

Special Survey in Xishuangbanna Dai Autonomous Prefecture

Village M in Gasa Township of Jinghong Municipality[7]

General Information of the Village and Surveyed Households Village M, administered by the Villagers' Committee of Manmian in Gasa Township, is located a few kilometers on the left side, to the southeast along the highway leading from Gasa Town to Dongfeng Farm and Damenglong Township. Not far from the village is Manfeilong reservoir, a pleasant site for townsfolks in Jinghong Municipality to enjoy the cool in hot weather and also an ideal venue for youths to spend their romantic time.

By December 2007, it had been home to 461 residents (228 males and 233 females) in 103 households, and except for the five matrilocal sons-in-law who are Han and one man who is Bulang, all the rest were Dai.

In July 2009, when we surveyed the village, 40 households met the above–mentioned criteria, accounting for 38.83% of the total. The basic information of the surveyed households is listed below in Table 4.1.

Written Records of the Reproductive Histories of the Surveyed Households For expository ease, only one household with a relatively complete intergenerational population out of all the valid samples was selected as the model for describing the reproductive history and drawing family trees in the text. The rest of the survey samples would be presented in the Appendix "Written Records of the Reproductive History Survey of the Dai Families".

1. Household No. 5; Interviewee: Yu Xiang; Figure 4.1

7 All villages and individuals in our surveys have been anonymized to protect privacy as required by related regulations.

Table 4.1: Basic Information of the Interviewees (Born in or before 1950) in Village M

Serial No.	Household No.	Name	Date of Birth	Number of Lifetime Births	Surviving Births	Time of Last Childbirth	Age at Last Childbirth (Years Old)	Sex of Children in Descending Order of Birth
1	5	Yu Xiang	1940.4	4	4	1967	27	F – M – F – F
2	8	Yu Bian	1931.2	3	2	1969	38	M – F – F
3	11	Yu Tao	1924.8	4	4	1966	32	F – F – F – M
4	15	Yu Enzai	1938.11	5	3	1967	29	M – F – M – F – M
5	19	Yu Lameng	1944.1	3	3	1973	29	M – M – F
6	20	Yu Nan	1940.3.8	4	4	1969	29	F – M – M – M
7	21	Yu Yan	1926.2	2	1	1950	24	F – M
8	26	Yu Ban	1926.10	5	5	1966	40	M – M – M – M – F
9	28	Yu Xiang	1940.2	4	4	1968	28	M – M – F – M
10	34	Yu Yang	1932.5	5	5	1963	31	F – F – M – M – M
11	35	Yan La	1950.3	0	-	-	-	
12	36	Mi Meng	1923.9	5	5	1964	44	F – M – M – F – M
13	37	Yu Yinghan	1949.8	4	4	1978	29	M – M – M – F
14	38	Yu Jing	1939.1	5	5	1971	28	M – M – F – M – F
15	43	Yu Han	1922.3	1	1	1941	19	M
16	44	Yu Pengban	1932.5	5	4	1969	37	M – F – M – F – F
17	45	Yu Nanlong	1946.6	3	3	1973.11	27	F – F – M
18	47	Yu Yingbie	1931.1	4	4	1965	34	M – F – M – F
19	49	Yu Bingbian	1921.1	4	3	1966	45	F – F – F – F

(*Continued*)

Table 4.1: Continued

20	52	Yu Ta	1928.11	3	3	1966	38	M – F – M
21	53	Yan Xiangzai	1925.8	4	4	-	-	M – M – F – M
22	55	Yu Lalun	1938.2	3	3	1966	28	M – M – F
23	56	Yu Wangsa	1938.11	4	3	1968.	30	M – M – F – M
24	58	Yu Taoda	1940.10	4	4	1966.	26	F – F – M – F
25	62	Kang Nanbing	1926.4	6	6	-	-	M – M – F – F – M –(M – F)
26	63	Yu Zhuang	1925.10	7	6	1968	43	M – M – F – F – M – F – F
27	65	Yu Yian	1946.8	3	3	1974	28	M – F – F
28	66	Yu Lun	1921.9	5	3	1960	39	M – F – M – F – F
29	67	Yu Shuailong	1944.6	3	2	1973	29	M – M – F
30	68	Yu Lao	1918.5	5	5	1966	48	M – M –(M – F) – F – F
31	71	Yu Hanxiang	1923.7	8	8	1973	50	F – F – F – M – M – F – M – F
32	75	Yu Yan	1939.4	3	3	1964	25	F – M – M
33	77	Yu Haner	1937.2	5	5	1968.	31	F – M – M – F – F
34	78	Yu Lilong	1946.7	3	3	1971	25	F – F – M
35	82	Yu Jianxiang	1932.1	5	5	1968	36	F – M – M – F – M
36	83	Yu Ying	1929.3	5	5	1965	42	F – M – M – F – F
37	88	Yu Ernan	1946.12	2	2	1969	23	F – F
38	90	Yan Wenxiang	1950.4	3	3	-	-	M – M – M
39	92	Yan Dunhan	1927.2	2	2	1961	34	F – M
40	98	Yan Hannan	1943.3	8	8	1981	38	M – M – F – M – M – F – M – M

Source: Field Survey Statistics by the Research Team (2).

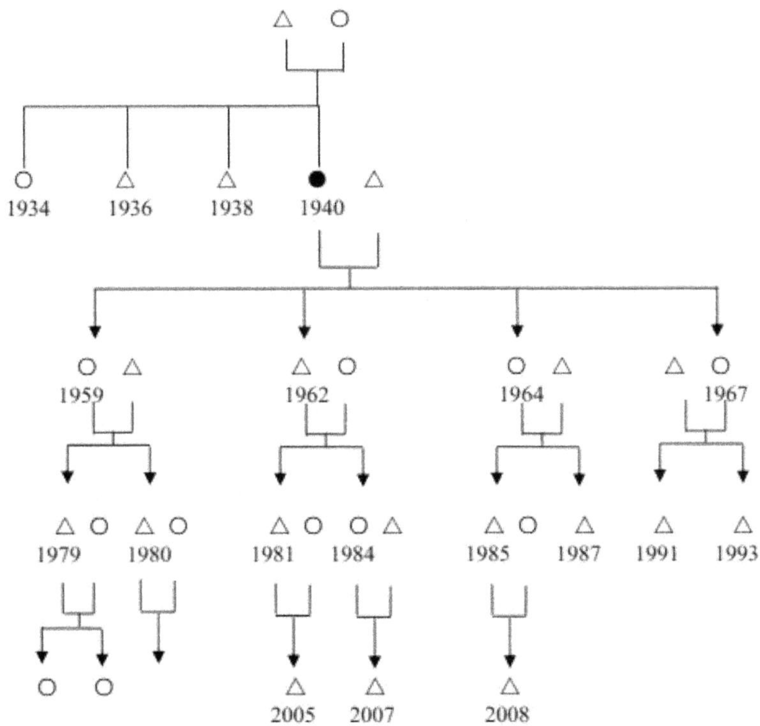

Figure 4.1 Genogram for Yu Xiang's Family
▲: male interviewee; ●: female interviewee;
△: male; ○: female;
■: male who died before turning 15; ★: female who died before turning 15;
□: a pregnancy with unknown sex of the fetus;
The sex of those born within each generation are listed in descending order of age, from left to right.

Yu Xiang was born in April 1940 and is the fourth child in the family. Her elder sister never married and is living with their mother.

Parents' Generation:

Yu Xiang's mother had four children, two males and two females; sex of the children in descending order: F (1934) – M (1936) – M (1938) – F (1940). Yu Xiang is the youngest daughter.

Current Generation:

Yu Xiang was born in April 1940 and had four children, three females and one male; sex of the children in descending order of births: F (1959) – M (1962) – F (1964) – F (1967).

Children's Generation:

The first daughter got married in 1978 and had two children; sex of the children in descending order of births: M (1979) – M (1980).

The first son got married in 1981 and had two children; sex of the children in descending order of births: M (November 1981) – F (February 1984).

The second daughter got married in 1984 and had two children; sex of the children in descending order of births: M (May 1985) – M (July 1987).

The third daughter got married in 1990 and had two children; sex of the children in descending order of births: M (September 1991) – M (August 1993).

Grandchildren's Generation:

The first daughter's first child got married in 1997 and had two children, both females.

The first daughter's second child got married and divorced, had no children.

The first son's first child got married in 2003 and had one child, male (April 2005).

The first son's second child got married in 2006 and had one child, male (June 2007).

The second daughter's first child got married in 2006 and had one child, male (January 2008).

The second daughter's second child was unmarried.

The third daughter's two children were still unmarried.

Great-grandchildren's Generation:

Five great-grandchildren, two females and three males.

Summary The oldest interviewee in the 40 households was Yu Lao, born in May 1918 (92 years old), and the youngest Yan Wenxiang, born in April 1950 (61 years old). The reproductive statistics by age cohort (five-year interval) are shown in the following Tables 4.2–4.5.

Statistics of Births and Surviving Births in Surveyed Households by Generational Cohort:

The Statistics of Births and Surviving Births in Surveyed Households by Generational Cohort:

The Statistics of the Timeframes and Proportions of Births by Generational Cohort in the Surveyed Households:

Table 4.2: Reproductive Statistics of the Interviewees (Born in or before 1950) in Village M

Number of Households	Age Cohort (Year of Birth)	Number of Lifetime Births (Persons)			Number of Children Who Survived till the Age of 15 or above (Persons)			Average Births/ Household	Average Surviving Births/ Household
		Total Births	M	F	Total Births	M	F		
7	1946—1950	18	9	9	18	9	9	2.57	2.57
3	1941–1945	14	10	4	13	9	4	4.67	4.33
10	1936–1940	41	23	18	38	22	16	4.1	3.8
5	1931–1935	22	11	11	20	9	11	4.4	4.0
6	1926–1930	24	14	10	23	14	9	4.0	3.83
8	1921–1925	38	16	22	34	14	20	4.75	4.25
1	1916–1920	6	3	3	6	3	3	6	6
In total: 40 Households		163	86	77	152	80	72	4.08	3.8

Source: Field Survey Statistics by the Research Team.

The retrospective reproductive statistics presented above showed that by July 2009:

1. The households of 40 interviewees (36 females and four males) born in or before 1950 (59 years old or above) in village M had given birth to a total of 163 children, each giving birth to 4.08 children on average, and 152 children had survived till the age of 15 or above, 3.8 per household. The overall survival rate of the births stood at 93.25%;
2. The interviewees had throughout their lifetime given birth to 86 boys and 77 girls, with the boys slightly outnumbering the girls, and 80 boys and 72 girls had survived till the age of 15 or above, with the survival rate of the boys and the girls standing at 93.02% and 93.51% respectively, with the rate for boys slightly lower than that for girls;
3. The interviewees (except for one who had never given births) had given births anywhere between once and eight time throughout their lifetime,

Table 4.3: Lifetime and Surviving Births of the Interviewees (born in or before 1950) in Village M

Sample Size		40 Interviewees (Households)			
Age of Interviewee		61–84 Years Old			
	8 Lifetime Births	2		8 Surviving Births	2
	7 Lifetime Births	1		7 Surviving Births	0
	6 Lifetime Births	1		6 Surviving Births	2
Number of Lifetime Births	5 Lifetime Births	11	Number of Children Who Survived till the Age of 15 or above	5 Surviving Births	8
	4 Lifetime Births	10		4 Surviving Births	9
	3 Lifetime Births	10		3 Surviving Births	11
	2 Lifetime Births	3		2 Surviving Births	4
	1 Lifetime Birth	1		1 Surviving Birth	2
	0 Lifetime Birth	1		0 Surviving Birth	1

Source: Field Survey Statistics by the Research Team.

4.03 per person on average, and the number of surviving births was in the 1–8 range;

4. The ages when the interviewees gave birth to their last child were between 50 years old (Yu Hanxiang in household No. 71, who gave birth 8 times) to 19 years old (Yu Han in household No. 43 had only one child), with the average age of final birth being 32.86 years old;
5. The time of final birth was from 1941 (Yu Han in household No. 43 at her first childbirth) to 1981 (Yan Hannan in household No. 98 at her 8th childbirth);
6. The interviewees who had given birth five times throughout their lifetime made up the largest share of the total at 27.5%, and those who had had three surviving children made up the largest share of the total at 27.5%;
7. The interviewees who had given births five or fewer time and four or fewer time respectively made up 89.74% and 61.54% of the total, and those who had had five or fewer surviving births and four or fewer surviving births respectively made up 87.18% and 66.67% of the total;

Table 4.4: Reproductive Statistics of the Surveyed Households by Generational Cohort (Interviewees Born in or before 1950) in Village M (No. 1)[8,9]

Generational Cohort	Number of Households	Number of Lifetime Births (Persons)			Number of Children Who Survived till the Age of 15 or above (Persons)			Average Number of Births	Average Number of Surviving Births
		Total Births	M	F	**Total Births**	M	F		
Parents' Generation	30	-	-	-	106	39	67	-	3.53
Current Generation	40	163	86	77	152	80	72	4.08	3.8
Children's Generation	139	263	139	124	258	136	122	1.89	1.85
Grandchildren's Generation	105	126	66	60	124	66	58	1.2	1.18

Source: Field Survey Statistics by the Research Team.

Table 4.5: Reproductive Statistics of the Surveyed Households by Generational Cohort (Interviewee Born in or before 1950) in Village M (No. 2)

Generation/ Decade/Percent (%)	1940s	1950s	1960s	1970s	1980s	1990s	2000s	Percent (%)
Current Generation	6.40	29.07	53.50	10.40	0.63			100.00
Children's Generation			2.35	29.01	50.98	15.68	1.98	100.00
Grandchildren's Generation					3.30	22.31	74.39	100.00

Source: Field Survey Statistics by the Research Team.

8 Many older interviewees in the village couldn't recall the exact information about their mothers' children dying young, so this statistical item was not included herein.

9 When the parents of an interviewee were in the same household, there would be inconsistency in the number of households between "Current Generation" and "Parents' Generation". The same below.

8. Each generation tends to have fewer births but more surviving ones on average than the preceding one. The survival rate of the births by Current Generation, Children's Generation and Grandchildren's Generation was respectively 93.25%, 98.10% and 98.41%;
9. Those of Current Generation (except for one who had never given births) gave birth was from the 1940s to the 1980s, with most of the births taking place in the 1950s and the 1960s, or 82.57% of the total number of births;
10. Those of the Children's Generation gave birth from the 1960s to the 2000s, with most of the births taking place from the 1970s to the 1980s, making up 79.99% of the total the births by Children's Generation; and;
11. Those of the Grandchildren's Generation gave birth from the 1980s to the 2000s, with most of the births taking place in the 2000s.

Village G in Mengzhe Township of Menghai County

General Information of the Village and Surveyed Households In the southeastern of Mengzhe Township, eight natural villages fall under the administration of Jingzhen Villagers' Committee: Jingmai, Jingdai-I, Jingdai-II, Manhai, Mansai, Manhelong, Manhui and Manyang. To the east of the National Highway No. 214 connecting Menghai County and Laku Ethnic Autonomous County, one would find village G administered by Jingzhen Villagers' Committee. As of April 2010, the village had been home to 339 residents (162 males and 177 females) in 65 households. Besides two Han ethnic villagers and one Bulang ethnic villager, all the rest were the Dai residents.

By the time of the survey (April 2010), there had been 14 households meeting the survey criteria, making up 21.53% of the total. The basic information of the surveyed households is listed below in Table 4.6.

The Written Records

For the Written Records of the Reproductive Histories of the Surveyed Households, Please Refer to the Appendix.

Summary Among the interviewees from the 14 households in the village, the oldest was born on March 10, 1926 (84 years old), and the youngest on April 6, 1949 (61 years old). The reproductive statistics by age cohort (five-year interval) are shown in the following Tables 4.7–4.10.

Table 4.6: Basic Information of the Female Interviewees (Born in or before 1950) in Village G

Serial No.	Household No.	Name	Date of Birth	Time of First Marriage	Age at First Marriage (Years Old)	Marital Status	Time at Last Childbirth (Year)	Age at Last Childbirth (Years Old)	Contraception Methods
1	6	Yu Duan	1939.4.5	1956.2	17	First Marriage	1976	37	Tubal ligation
2	7	Yu Yingjiao	1931.9.12	1950.3	19	Remarriage	1971	40	Abortion-induced Infertility
3	8	Yu Shuo	1938.6.5	1957.6	19	Widowhood	No Birth		Toxic Birth[10]
4	13	Yi Yingkan	1942.4.28	1960.6	18	Restored Marriage	1980	38	Tubal ligation
5	14	Yu Xiangnuo	1948.4.16	1964.6	16	First Marriage	1970	28	Estrangement
6	15	Yu Wanjiao	1926.3.10	1945.5	19	Widowhood	1961	35	Tubal ligation
7	20	Yu Kan	1938.10.12	1957.2	19	Widowhood	1967	29	Tubal ligation
8	21	Yu Liu	1929.11.13	1949.2	20	Widowhood	1968	41	Toxic Birth
9	22	Yu Yan	1947.8.13	1964.1	17	First Marriage	1968	21	Tubal ligation
10	34	Yu Shuai	1938.8.17	1960.4	22	First Marriage	1972	34	IUD
11	35	Yu Xiang	1949.4.6	1968.10	19	First Marriage	1972	33	Tubal ligation
12	36	Yu Xiangdi	1937.4.11	1955.4	18	Remarriage	1971	34	Tubal ligation
13	42	Yu Yinger	1945.4.21	1961.2	16	Widowhood	1968	23	Tuba ligation
14	44	Yu Hansai	1947.6.1	1967.2	20	Remarriage	1973	26	Tubal ligation

Source: Field Survey Statistics by the Research Team.

10 Toxic birth is a folkloric interpretation among the Dai people of the birth that will lead to infertility in the future.

Table 4.7: Reproductive Statistics of the Female Interviewees (Born in or before 1950) in Village G

Number of Households	Age Cohort (Year)	Number of Lifetime Births (Persons)			Number of Children Who Survived till the Age of 15 or above (Persons)			Average Births/ Household	Average Surviving Births/ Household
		Total Births	M	F	Total Births	M	F		
4	1946–1950	15	9	6	14	8	6	3.75	3.5
2	1941–1945	10	4	6	9	4	5	5.0	4.5
5	1936–1940	18	11	7	16	9	7	3.6	3.2
1	1931–1935	8	4	4	7	3	4	8.0	7.0
2	1926–1930	16	8	8	11	3	8	8.0	5.5
In total: 14 Households		67	36	31	57	27	30	4.79	4.07

Source: Field Survey Statistics by the Research Team.

Statistics of Birth and Surving Births of the Surveyed Households by Generational Cohort:

Statistics of Birth and Surving Births of the Surveyed Households by Generational Cohort:

The Statistics of the Timespans and Proportions of Births in the Surveyed Households by Generational Cohort:

The retrospective reproductive statistics presented above showed that:

1. By April 2010, 14 female interviewees born in or before 1950 (60 years old or above) in village G had given birth to 67 children, on average 4.79 children per person, and 57 children had survived till 15 years old or above, on average 4.07 per person. The overall survival rate of the births stood at 85.07%.
2. The reproductive statistics of births by five-year interval showed, with a declining average age of the mothers, the average number of children in a household also declined, i.e., younger mothers gave birth to fewer children.
3. The interviewees had throughout their lifetime given birth to 36 boys and 31 girls, with the boys slightly outnumbering the girls, and 27

Table 4.8: Reproductive Statistics of the Female Interviewees (Born in or before 1950) in Village G

Female Interviewees		14 Interviewees (Households)			
Age of Female Interviewee		61–84 Years Old (1926–1949)			
Number of Lifetime Births	8 Births	3	Number of Children Who Survived till the Age of 15 or above	8 Surviving Births	0
	7 Births	1		7 Surviving Births	2
	6 Births	1		6 Surviving Births	1
	5 Births	1		5 Surviving Births	3
	4 Births	4		4 Surviving Births	2
	3 Births	3		3 Surviving Births	5
	2 Births	0		2 Surviving Births	0
	1 Birth	0		1 Surviving Birth	0
	0 Birth	1		0 Birth	1

Source: Field Survey Statistics by the Research Team.

boys and 30 girls had survived till the age of 15 or above, with the survival rate of the boys and the girls standing respectively at 75.00% and 96.77% and the survival rate of the boys being slightly lower than that of the girls.

4. The interviewees who had given birth four times throughout their lifetime made up the largest share of the total at 28.57% and those who had had three surviving births made up the largest share of the total at 35.71%.
5. The interviewees who had given four or fewer births made up 57.14% of the total, and those who had had four or fewer surviving births made up 57.14%.

Table 4.9: Reproductive Statistics of the Surveyed Households by Generational Cohort (Interviewees Born in or before 1950) in Village G (No. 1)

Generational Cohort	Number of Households	Number of Lifetime Births (Persons)			Number of Children Who Survived till the Age of 15 or above (Persons)			Average Average Total Births per Household/ Household	Average Average Total Surviving Births per Household/ Household
		Total Births	M	F	Total Births	M	F		
Parents' Generation	12	74	36	38	53	23	30	6.17	4.41
Current Generation	14	67	36	31	57	27	30	4.79	4.07
Children's Generation	51	118	56	62	107	48	59	2.31	2.09
Grand-children's Generation	49	64	37	27	62	35	27	1.31	1.27
Great-grandchildren's Generation	3	3	3	0	3	3	0	1.00	1.00

Source: Field Survey Statistics by the Research Team.

Table 4.10: Reproductive Statistics of the Surveyed Households by Generational Cohort (Interviewees Born in or before 1950) in Village G (Table 4.7)

Generation/ Decade/Percent (%)	The 1940s	The 1950s	The 1960s	The 1970s	The 1980s	The 1990s	The 2000s	Percent (%)
Current Generation	6.30	15.80	55.80	20.60	1.5			100.00
Children's Generation			1.80	12.85	57.80	22.02	5.53	100.00
Grandchildren's Generation					5.97	34.33	59.70	100.00

Source: Field Survey Statistics by the Research Team.

6. The interviewees got married for the first time in the age range from 16 to 22 years old, and those who had got married for the first time at 19 years old made up 35.71% of the total, the average age at which people got married for the first time was 18.5.
7. The interviewees (except for one who had never given birth) gave birth to their last child between the ages of 21 and 41, at 32.46 years old on average.
8. The interviewees (except for three who became infertile) of childbearing age took contraceptive measures. Nine had gone through tubal ligation surgeries and one had used an IUD, accounting for 90.91% of the total.
9. Each generation tends to have fewer births than the preceding one but more surviving ones on average. The survival rate of the births given by Parents' generation, Current Generation, Children's Generation, Grandchildren's Generation and Great-grandchildren's Generation was 71.62%, 85.07%, 90.68%, 96.88% and 100%, respectively.
10. The period of time during which those of the Current Generation (except for one having never given birth) gave birth extended from the 1940s to the 1980s, with most of the births taking place from the 1950s to the 1960s, accounting for 76.40% of the total.
11. The period of time during which those of the Children's Generation gave birth extended from the 1960s to the 2000s, with most of the births taking place from the 1980s to 1990s, accounting for 79.82% of the total.
12. The period of time during which those of the Grandchildren's Generation gave birth extended from the 1980s to the 2000s, with most of the births taking place after 2000.

Village H in Mengpeng Township of Mengla County

General Information of the Village and Surveyed Households In the southwestern of Mengla County, Mengpeng Township is located approximately 34 kilometers away from the seat of the county government. Administered by Mengpeng Township, village H is approximately seven kilometers from the seat of the township government. This village was every inch an "authentic" Dai village. By October 2008, the village had been home to 383 residents in 93 households (186 males and 197 females), and all the others (except for one Han ethnic matrilocal son-in-law) were Dai.

When we surveyed the village (in January 2009), 27 households met our survey criteria, accounting for 29.03% of the total. The basic information of the surveyed households is listed below in Table 4.11.

The Written Records

For the Written Records of the Reproductive Histories of the Surveyed Households Please Refer to the Appendix.

Summary Among the interviewees in the village, the oldest was Nan La, born on January 2, 1906 (103 years old), and the youngest was Yi Guanghai, born on July 3, 1950 (59 years old). The reproductive statistics of these interviewees by age cohort (five-year interval) are shown in the following Tables 4.12–4.14.

The Statistics Births and Surviving Births of the Surveyed Households by Generational Cohort:

Statistics of Birth and Surving Births of the Surveyed Households by Generational Cohort:

The retrospective reproductive statistics presented above showed that:

1. By 2009 January, 27 interviewees born in or before 1950 (59 years old or above) in village H had given birth to 95 children, each giving birth to 3.52 children on average, and 88 children had survived till the age of 15 or above, or 3.26 on average per household. The overall survival rate of the births was 92.63%.
2. The interviewees had throughout their lifetime given birth to 55 boys and 40 girls, with the boys slightly outnumbering the girls; and 52 boys and 36 girls had survived till the age of 15 or above, with the survival rate of the boys and the girls standing respectively at 94.55% and 90.00% and the survival rate of the boys being slightly higher than that of the girls.
3. The interviewees had given births 2–6 times throughout their lifetime, with each interviewee having given 3.51 births on average, and had surviving births in the 1–6 range;

4. The interviewees who had given birth four times throughout their lifetime made up the largest share of the total at 33.33%, and those who had had four surviving births made up the largest share of the total at 33.33%;
5. The interviewees who had given birth five times or fewer and four or fewer births throughout their lifetime respectively made up 96.30% and 85.19% of the total, and those who had had five or fewer surviving births and four or fewer surviving births throughout their lifetime respectively made up 96.30% and 92.59% of the total.
6. Each generation tends to have few births but more surviving ones on average. The survival rate of the births for Parents' generation, Current Generation, Children's Generation and Grandchildren's Generation was respectively 97.26%, 92.63%, 98.51% and 100.00%.

Special Report on Dehong Dai and Jingpo Autonomous Prefecture

Village N in Fengping Township of Luxi City

General Information of the Village and Surveyed Households Located in the middle of the Mangshi Intermontane Basin and approximately 10 kilometers away from the seat of the municipal government of Mangshi, Fengping Township is cut through by the National Highway 320 and the Luxi-Yingjiang Expressway, and thus it is the only route from Mangshi to Ruili and an important transportation hub in the City and even the entire Prefecture. Under its administration are 11 villagers' committees, one neighborhood committee, 99 villagers' groups and 191 cooperatives, and its farming population accounts for 94.11% of the total. The famous Fengping Pagoda, right beside the National Highway 320, is located approximately 1.5 kilometers away from the seat of the Township Government. Historical records show that the Pagoda was built more than 200 years ago and has the typical style of pagoda architecture in the later period of Theravada Buddhism.

In southern Fengping Township, village N is administered by the Villagers' Committee of Fengping, and is located approximately four kilometers away from the seat of the township government of Fengping. According to the statistics of the Villagers' Committee, as of December 2009, the village had been home to 358 residents in 74 households, including 180 males and 178 females. Except for eight Han and three Deang residents, all the others were Dai.

Table 4.11: Basic Information of the Interviewees (Born in or before 1950) in Village H

Serial No.	Household No.	Name	Date of Birth	Number of Lifetime Births	Surviving Births	Sex of children in descending order of birth
1	11	Yan Xiangyong	1941.7.6	2	2	M – F
2	13	Yi Yingjiao	1931.12.4	4	4	M – M – F – F
3	14	Yi Luo	1936.8.7	3	3	M – F – F
4	18	Yan Hanjiao	1947.7.2	3	3	M – F – M
5	21	Yu Ernan	1935.3.17	4	4	M – M – M – M
6	22	Nan La	1906.1.2	4	2	M – F – F – F
7	23	Yi Yingdi	1923.7.11	6	6	F – F – M – M – M – F
8	28	Yi Xiangshuai	1940.8.13	5	4	M – F – M – F – F
9	29	Yi Erweng	1931.4.9	4	3	F – M – F – M
10	31	Yan Honglong	1942.5.2	4	4	M – M – M – F
11	38	Yan Wenbing	1943.10.20	3	3	M – M – M
12	41	Yan Zaibao	1929.6.6	4	4	M – M – M – M
13	42	Yi Kangnan	1943.4.6	3	3	M – F – M
14	43	Yi Jinzhang	1934.3.2	4	4	M – M – M – F
15	53	Yan Wenbang	1938.8.4	2	2	F – M
16	56	Yi Jianla	1949.11.3	3	3	F – F – F
17	57	Yi Nannen	1949.5.18	2	1	M – F
18	59	Yi Tila	1937.7.2	5	4	M – M – M – F – M
19	61	Yan Labing	1934.2.11	4	4	F – M – F – M
20	65	Yan Dila	1949.2.16	3	3	M – M – F
21	67	Yan Ruan	1936.1.3	5	5	F – M – F – F – M
22	69	Yan Ta	1944.6.4	2	2	M – F
23	74	Yan Lahong	1940.1.4	4	4	F – M – M – M
24	77	Yan Wenxing	1943.1.13	3	3	F – M – M
25	78	Yi Guangsao	1947.11.12	2	2	M – M
26	79	Yan Honghe	1944.6.9	2	2	M – F
27	81	Yi Guanghai	1950.7.3	2	2	F – F

Source: Field Survey Statistics by the Research Team.

Table 4.12: Reproductive Statistics of the Female Interviewees (Born in or before 1950) in Village H

Number of Households	Age Cohort (Year)	Number of Lifetime Births (Persons)			Number 3of Children Who Survived till the Age of 15 or above (Persons)			Average Births/ Household	Average Surviving Births/ Household
		Total Births	**M**	**F**	**Total Births**	**M**	**F**		
6	1946–1950	15	7	8	14	7	7	2.5	2.33
7	1941–1945	19	13	6	19	13	6	2.71	2.71
6	1936–1940	24	13	11	22	11	11	4.00	3.67
5	1931–1935	20	13	7	19	13	6	4.00	3.80
1	1926–1930	4	4	0	4	4	0	4.00	4.00
1	1921–1925	6	3	3	6	3	3	6.00	6.00
0	1916–1920	-	-	-	-	-	-	-	-
	1911–1915	-	-	-	-	-	-	-	-
1	1906–1910	4	1	3	2	0	2	4	2
In total: 27 Households		92	38		86	51	35	3.41	3.19

Source: Field Survey Statistics by the Research Team.

Table 4.13: Lifetime and Surviving Births of the Interviewees (Born in or before 1950) in Village H

Interviewees		27 Interviewees (Households)			
Age of Interviewee		50–103 Years Old			
Number of Lifetime Births	6 Births	1	Number of Children Who Survived till the Age of 15 or above	6 Surviving Births	1
	5 Births	3		5 Surviving Births	1
	4 Births	9		4 Surviving Births	9
	3 Births	7		3 Surviving Births	8
	2 Births	7		2 Surviving Births	7
	1 Birth	0		1 Surviving Birth	1

Source: Field Survey Statistics by the Research Team.

Table 4.14: Reproductive Statistics of the Surveyed Households by Generational Cohort (Interviewees born in or before 1950) in Village H

Generational Cohort	Number of Households	Number of Lifetime Births (Persons)			Number of Children Who Survived till the Age of 15 or above (Persons)			Average Total Births per Household	Average Total Surviving Births per Household
		Total Births	M	F	Total Births	M	F		
Parents' Generation	17	73	43	30	71	42	29	4.29	4.18
Current Generation	27	95	55	40	88	52	36	3.52	3.26
Children's Generation	71	134	67	67	132	66	66	1.89	1.86
Grandchildren's Generation	41	54	22	32	54	22	32	1.32	1.32

Source: Field Survey Statistics by the Research Team.

When the survey was conducted in April 2010, 29 households met the survey criteria in the village, making up 39.19% of the total population. The basic information of the surveyed households is listed below in Table 4.15.

The Written Records

For the Written Records of the Reproductive Histories of the Surveyed Households, Please Refer to the Appendix.

Summary Among the interviewees from the 29 households, the oldest was born on October 8, 1921 (89 years old), and the youngest in July 1950 (60 years old). The reproductive statistics by age cohort (five-year interval) are shown in the following Tables 4.16–4.19.

Statistics of Birth and Surviving Births of the Surveyed Households by Generational Cohort:

Table 4.15: Basic Information of the Interviewees (Born in or before 1950) in Village N

Serial No.	Household No.	Name	Date of Birth	Age at First Marriage	Number of Lifetime Births	Surviving Births	Time at Last Childbirth	Age at Last Childbirth (Years Old)	Sex of Children in Descending Order of Birth
1	3	Jiaomie Suowang	1921.10.8	1950.10	7	7	-	-	F – F – M – M – F – M – M
2	4	Xiangmie Yantuanwa	1941.3.12	1961.10	4	3	1971	30	M – F – F – M
3	5	Caimie Xiangya	1936.11.24	1960.10	3	3	1966	30	F – M – M
4	7	Xianmie Pin	1934.8.10	1953.10	5	4	1967	33	F – F – F – F – M
5	8	Daomie Yanhanguo	1942.10	1961.	3	3	1972	30	M – F – F
6	9	Jinmie Yanxiangzuo	1945.	1961.	4	4	1979	34	M – M – F – F
7	10	Daomie Yanfangbao	1940.8.	1962.7	4	4	1973	33	M – M – M – M
8	13	Xiangmie Pin	1944.11.	1965.10	4	4	1973	29	F – F – M – M
9	15	Xianmie Guobao	1949.12.12	1973.	2	2	1981	32	M – M
10	16	Mie Yuefeng	1943.12.	1964.10	4	4	1975	32	F – M – F – M-
11	17	Yuemie Hanjin	1949.11.7	1970.	3	3	1975	26	F – F – F
12	18	Xiangmie Yuebaowang	1943.3.8	1969.10	4	4	1985	42	F – F – F – F
13	21	Xiangmie Wanpa	1942.10.	1962.10	4	4	1973	31	F – M – F – F
14	22	XiangmieTuanhuang	1936.4.	1958.10	4	4	1967	31	– F – M – M – M-
15	24	Jinmie Hannuo	1937.5.	1955.12.	6	5	1969	32	F – F – F – F (F – F) – M
16	25	Jinmie Yanhantuan	1946.2.	1966.1.	4	4	1975	29	M – F – M – F

(*Continued*)

Table 4.15: Continued

Serial No.	Household No.	Name	Date of Birth	Age at First Marriage	Number of Lifetime Births	Surviving Births	Time at Last Childbirth	Age at Last Childbirth (Years Old)	Sex of Children in Descending Order of Birth
17	27	Mie Yuexiang	1941.10.	1961.7.	5	4	1973	32	M – F – M – F – M
18	33	Jinmie Yantuanguo	1940.5.	1960.	4	3	-	-	M – M – F – F
19	36	Jinmie Yuebaowan	1950.7.	1972.10.	3	3	1978	28	F – F – F
20	40	Jiaomie Suoban	1942.10.	1962.	1	1	1983	41	M
21	44	Caibo Yanwan	1950.5.	1970.1.	5	4	-	-	M – F – M – M – F
22	47	Jiaomie Yuehansuo	1946.9.	1965.10.	2	2	1969	23	F – F
23	52	Daomie Xianghuang	1949.9.	1975.	1	1	1975	26	F
24	54	Jiaomie Yanhanya	1933.4.	1954.11.	5	4	1965	32	M – F – F – M – F
25	55	Xiangmie Yanxiangbao	1948.10.5	-	1	1	1968	20	M
26	57	Limie Genwa	1942.11.	1962.10.	5	5	1975	33	F – M – M – F – F
27	61	Daomie Yuehanwa	1943.1.9	1961.11	6	6	1976	33	F – F – F – F – F – M
28	63	Daomie Yuepaguo	1948	1969	4	4	1976	28	F – F – F – M
29	67	Xiangmie Yuewangbao	1939	1957	6	6	1970	31	F – M – M – F – F – F

Source: Field Survey Statistics by the Research Team.

Table 4.16: Reproductive Statistics of the Interviewees (Born in or before 1950) in Village N

Households	Age Cohort (Year)	Number of Lifetime Births (Persons)			Number of Children Who Survived till the Age of 15 or above (Persons)			Average Births/ Household	Average Surviving Births/ Household
		Total Births	M	F	Total Births	M	F		
9	1946—1950	25	9	16	24	9	15	2.78	2.67
11	1941—1945	44	17	27	42	16	26	4.00	3.82
6	1936—1940	27	14	13	25	14	11	4.50	4.17
2	1931—1935	10	3	7	8	3	5	5.00	4.00
0	1926—1930	-	-	-	-	-	-	-	-
1	1921—1925	7	4	3	7	4	3	7	7
In total: 29 Households		113	47	66	106	46	60	3.90	3.66

Source: Field Survey Statistics by the Research Team.

Table 4.17: Lifetime and Surviving Births of the Female Interviewees (Born in or before 1950) in Village N

Number of The Female Interviewees		29 Interviewees (Households)			
Age Cohort		60–89 Years Old (1921–1950)			
	7 Births	1		7 Surviving Births	1
	6 Births	3		6 Surviving Births	2
Number of Lifetime Births	5 Births	5	Number of Children Who Survived till the Age of 15 or above	5 Surviving Births	2
	4 Births	11		4 Surviving Births	12
	3 Births	4		3 Surviving Births	6
	2 Births	2		2 Surviving Births	3
	1 Birth	3		1 Surviving Birth	3

Source: Field Survey Statistics by the Research Team.

Statistics of Birth and Surviving Births of the Surveyed Households by Generational Cohort:

The Statistics of the Timespans and Proportions of Births in the Surveyed Households by Generational Cohort:

The retrospective reproductive statistics presented above showed that:

1. By 2010 April, 29 interviewees born in or before 1950 (59 years old or above) in village N had given birth to 113 children, each giving birth to 3.09 children on average, and 106 children had survived till the age of 15 or above, with a household having had 3.66 surviving children on average. The overall survival rate of the births was 93.81%;
2. The interviewees had throughout their lifetime given birth to 47 boys and 66 girls, with the boys being slightly outnumbered by the girls, and 46 boys and 60 girls had survived till the age of 15 or above, with the survival rate of the boys and the girls standing respectively at 97.87% and

Table 4.18: Reproductive Statistics of the Surveyed Households by Generational Cohort (Interviewees Born in or before 1950) in Village N (No. 1)

Generation	Households	Number of Lifetime Births (Persons)			Number of Children Who Survived till the Age of 15 or above (Persons)			Average Total Births per Household	Average Total Surviving Births per Household
		Total Births	M	F	Total Births	M	F		
Parents' Generation	29	194	89	105	140	59	81	6.69	4.83
Current Generation	29	115	48	67	107	47	60	3.97	3.67
Children's Generation	105	200	92	108	195	90	105	1.90	1.86
Grandchildren's Generation	29	31	12	19	31	12	19	1.07	1.07

Source: Field Survey Statistics by the Research Team.

Table 4.19: Reproductive Statistics of the Surveyed Households by Generational Cohort (Interviewees Born in or before 1950) in Village N (Table 4.16)[11]

Generation/ Decade/Percent (%)	1950s	1960s	1970s	1980s	1990s	2000s	Percent (%)
Current Generation	4.76	52.38	39.05	3.81	–	–	100.00
Children's Generation	–	–	–	36.67	40.00	23.33	100.00
Grandchildren's Generation	–	–	–	–	–	–	–

Source: Field Survey Statistics by the Research Team.

90.91% and the survival rate of the boys being slightly higher than that of the girls;

3. The interviewees had given birth 1–7 times throughout their lifetime, an average of 3.90 births per person, and the number of surviving births was in the 1–7 range;
4. The interviewees got married for the first time in the age range from 16 (interviewee No. 9: Jinmie Yanxiangzuo) to 29 years old (interviewee No. 3: Jiaomie Suowang), and gave birth to their last child in the age range from 42 (interviewee No. 18: Xiangmie Yuebaowang, who had given birth four times) to 23 years old (interviewee No. 47: Jiaomie Yuehansuo, who had given birth twice), at 30.81 years old on average;
5. The interviewees gave birth to their last child in the period from 1966 (interviewee No. 5: Caimie Xiangya, giving her third birth) to 1985 (interviewee No. 18: Xiangmie Yuebaowang, giving her fourth birth);
6. The interviewees who had given birth four times throughout their lifetime made up the largest share of the total at 37.93% and those who had given four surviving births made up the largest share of the total at 41.38%;
7. The interviewees who had given birth five times or fewer and four times or fewer throughout their lifetime made up 86.21% and 68.97% of the

11 Given the information of the time of birth of most Grandchildren's Generation children was unavailable, so, this data item was statistically insignificant and omitted in our survey statistics.

total respectively, and those who had had five or fewer surviving births and four or fewer surviving births throughout their lifetime respectively made up 89.66% and 82.76% of the total;

8. Each generation tends to have few births but more surviving ones on average. The survival rate of the births by Current Generation, Children's Generation and Grandchildren's Generation was respectively 92.44%, 97.89% and 100.00%; and
9. Those of the Current Generation gave birth from the 1950s to the 1980s, with most of the births taking place from the 1960s to the 1970s, accounting for 91.43% of the total the newborns in this period;
10. Those of the Children's Generation gave birth from the 1970s to the 2000s, with most of the births taking place from the 1970s to the 1980s, accounting for 76.67% of the total the births in this period;
11. Those of the Grandchildren's Generation gave birth from the 1980s to the 2000s, with most of the births taking place in the 2000s;
12. With the exception of one interviewee who never married and one who never gave birth, the other 27 interviewees had had their final birth by the end of 1980s, with seven, 16 and three interviewees giving birth to their last child respectively in 1960s, 1970s and 1980s.

Village Z in Jiexiang Township of Ruili City

General Information of the Village and Surveyed Households Situated in the southwest of Ruili City, Jiexiang Township is bordered by Huyu Township on the north, Longdao Township on the west and Myanmar on the south and southeast; Located approximately 20 kilometers away from the seat of government of Ruili City, the Township is cut through by the Gazhong-Leiyun Highway. Under its administration are 13 villages, including Eluo, Longxiang and Hejie, and is a border town with close contacts with Myanmar.

Village Z is in southwest Jiexiang Township and is approximately six kilometers away from the seat of the township government. According to the statistics of the villagers' committee, as of December 2010, the village had been home to 714 residents (367 males and 347 females) in 163 households in the village. Except for 13 Han ethnic villagers, all the others are Dai people.

When the survey was conducted in the village in October 2011, there were 29 households (43 persons) meeting the survey criteria, making up 17.79% of the total households. The basic information of the surveyed households is listed below in the following Table 4.20.

The Written Records For the Written Records of the Reproductive Histories of the Surveyed Households, Please Refer to the Appendix.

Summary The oldest interviewee in 29 households, Yuehen Tuanwang, was born in 1927 (84 years old), and the youngest, Hanshuai Yanxin and Ruiban Ruiliang, 1951 (60 years old). The reproductive statistics by age cohort (five-year interval) are shown in the following Tables 4.21–4.24.

Statistics of Birth and Surving Births of the Surveyed Households by Generational Cohort:

Statistics of Birth and Surviving Births of the Surveyed Households by Generational Cohort:

The Statistics of the Timespans and Proportions of Intergenerational Births in the Surveyed Households:

The retrospective reproductive statistics presented above showed that:

1. By October 2011, 29 interviewees born in or before 1951 (60 years old or above) in village Z had given birth to 154 children, each giving birth to 5.31 children on average, and 136 children had survived till the age of 15 or above, with each household having had 4.69 surviving children on average. The overall survival rate of the births was 88.31%;
2. The interviewees had throughout their lifetime given birth to 81 boys and 73 girls, with the boys being slightly outnumbered by the girls, and 71 boys and 65 girls had survived till the age of 15 or above, with the survival rate of the boys and the girls standing respectively at 87.65% and 89.04% and the survival rate of the boys being slightly lower than that of the girls;
3. The interviewees (except for one having never given births and another having never married) had given births between once and 11 times throughout their lifetime, with each interviewee having given 5.17 births on average, and had surviving births in the 1–10 range;
4. The interviewees got married for the first time in the age range from 16 to 30 years old (respectively Interviewee No. 5: Yue En and Interviewee No. 10: Moen Shuaimeng and Interviewee No. 12: Shuai Ensan), and gave birth to their last child in the age range from 24 to 46 years old (Interviewee No. 10: Moen Shuaimeng, giving her fourth birth, interviewee No. 16: Shuai Enna, giving her second birth, and Interviewee No. 75: Yuehen Tuanwang, giving her 10th birth), at 31.79 years old on average;

Table 4.20: Basic Information of the Interviewees (Born in or before 1950) in Village Z

Serial No.	Household No.	Name	Time of Birth	Age at First Marriage	Number of Lifetime Births	Surviving Births	Time at Last Childbirth	Age at Last Childbirth (Years Old)	Sex of Children in Descending Order of Birth (Adoptees)
1	2	Shuaien Miewang	1946	18	0	2	-	-	F – M
2	5	Yue En	1936	16	11	6	1975	39	F-(F) -(M) - (M) – M-(F) – F – M – F-(M) – M
3	6	Yue Hantuan	1949	18	3	3	1978	29	M – M – M
4	8	Mei Hantuan	1947	18	7	7	1981	34	F – M – M – F – F – M – M
5	10	Moen Shuaimeng	1947	16	4	4	1971	24	M – M – F – F
6	12	Shuai Ensan	1950	30	2	2	-	-	F – F
7	14	Yue Enzhan	1937	17	10	10	1978	41	M – F – M – M – F – M – M – F – M – M
8	15	Xiang Henyan	1943	22	3	3	-	-	M – M – M
9	16	Shuai Enna	1941	20	1	2	1965	24	F – M
10	18	Mai Hanleng	1947	18	3	3	1973	26	F – F-(M) – M
11	19	Mo Enshuai	1943	17	5	4	1975	32	F – F – F – F-(M)
12	20	Han Shuai	1947	23	3	3	1978	31	F – F – F
13	21	Shuai Enpin	1949	17	4	4	1978	29	F – M – M – F
14	30	Shuai Henhan	1948	20	4	4	1978	30	M – M – F – M
15	43	Shuai Hanlun	1939	19	5	4	1971	32	(F) – F – M – M – F
16	51	Mo Hanmen	1940	18	9	9	1977	37	M – F – M – M – M – F – F – M – M
17	60	Man Xianghuang	1941	19	6	4	1971	30	F – F-(F) -(F) – M – M

Table 4.20: Continued

Serial No.	House-hold No.	Name	Time of Birth	Age at First Mar-riage	Num-ber of Life-time Births	Sur-viving Births	Time at Last Child-birth	Age at Last Child-birth (Years Old)	Sex of Children in Descending Order of Birth (Adoptees)
18	61	Ruiban Ruiliang	1951	-	0	0	-	-	-
19	62	Shuai Enlai	1947	16	9	9	1981	33	M – F – M – M – F – F – F – M – M
20	65	Ruiban	1946	18	4	4	1973	27	M – F – F – M
21	67	Yue Enman	1942	20	6	6	1973	31	F – M – M – M – M – M
22	68	Shuai Xiangbao	1941	17	7	6	1976	35	(F) – M – F – M – F – FF
23	69	Yu Hanwang	1929	18	9	8	1967	38	M-(F) – M – F – F – F – F – M – M
24	70	Yuehan Xiangsha	1946	17	5	3	1966	20	(M) -(M) – F – F – M
25	74	Mo Hanleng	1936	17	8	6	1967	31	(M) – M – M – M – F – M – F-(M)
26	75	Yuehen Tuanwang	1927	19	10	8	1973	46	F – F – F-(F) – F – F – M-(M) – M – M
27	78	Shuai Xiangjing	1946	18	5	5	1976	28	F – M – F – F – F
28	90	Hanshuai Yanxin	1951	19	3	3	-	-	M – M – M
29	96	Yue Xiangyan	1948	19	4	4	1979	31	M – F – F – F

Source: Field Survey Statistics by the Research Team.

Table 4.21: Reproductive Statistics of the Female Interviewees (Born in or before 1951) in Village Z

Households	Age Cohort	Number of Lifetime Births (Persons)			Number of Children Who Survived till the Age of 15 or above (Persons)			Average Births/ Household	Average Surviving Births/ Household
		Total Births	M	F	Total Births	M	F		
2	1951—1955	3	3	0	3	3	0	1.50	1.50
14	1946—1950	57	27	30	54	24	30	4.07	3.86
6	1941—1945	28	13	15	24	12	12	4.67	4.00
5	1936—1940	43	27	16	35	22	13	8.60	7.00
0	1931—1935	-	-	-	-	-	-	-	-
2	1926—1930	19	8	11	16	7	9	9.50	8.00
In total: 29 Households		150	78	72	132	68	64	5.17	4.55

Source: Field Survey Statistics by the Research Team.

5. The interviewees gave birth to their last child in the period from 1965 (Interviewee No. 16: Shuai Enna, giving her second birth) to 1981(Interviewee No. 8: Mei Hantuan, giving her 7th birth; Interviewee No. 62: Shuai Enlai, giving her 9th birth);
6. The interviewees who had given three or four births made up the largest share of the total at 34.48% and those who had had four surviving births made up the largest share of the total at 27.59%;
7. The interviewees who had given birth five times or fewer and four or fewer births respectively made up 62.07% and 48.28% of the total, and those who had had five or fewer surviving births and four or fewer surviving births respectively made up 65.51% and 62.07% of the total;
8. Each generation tends to have few births but more surviving ones on average. The survival rate of the births by Current Generation, Children's Generation and Grandchildren's Generation was respectively 88.31%, 95.74% and 98.10%;

Table 4.22: Lifetime and Surviving Births of the Interviewees (Born in or before 1951) in Z Village

Number of Interviewees		29 Interviewees (Households)			
Age of Interviewees		60–84 Years Old			
Number of Lifetime Births	11 Births	1	Number of Children Who Survived till the Age of 15 or above	11 Surviving Births	0
	10 Births	2		10 Surviving Birth	1
	9 Births	3		9 Surviving Births	2
	8 Births	1		8 Surviving Births	2
	7 Births	2		7 Surviving Births	1
	6 Births	2		6 Surviving Births	4
	5 Births	4		5 Surviving Births	1
	4 Births	5		4 Surviving Births	8
	3 Births	5		3 Surviving Births	5
	2 Births	1		2 Surviving Births	2
	1 Birth	1		1 Surviving Birth	1
	0 Birth	2		0 Surviving Birth	1

Source: Field Survey Statistics by the Research Team.

9. The period of time during which those of the Current Generation gave birth extended from the 1940s to the 1980s, with most of the births taking place from the 1960s to the 1970s, accounting for 82.76% of the total the births in this period;
10. The period of time during which those of the Children's Generation gave birth extended from the 1970s to the 2000s, with most of the births taking place from the 1980s to 1990s, accounting for 77.04% of the total the births in this period;
11. Those of the Grandchildren's Generation gave birth from the 1990s to the 2000s, with most of the births taking place in the 2000s;
12. Except for one who never married and another who never gave birth, the 27 interviewees had had their final birth by the end of 1980s, with four, 18 and two interviewees giving birth to their last child respectively in 1960s, 1970s and 1980s.

Table 4.23: Reproductive Statistics of the Surveyed Households by Generational Cohort (Interviewees Born in or before 1951) in Village Z

Generation	Households	Number of Lifetime Births (Persons)			Number of Children Who Survived till the Age of 15 or above (Persons)			Average Total Births per Household	Average Total Surviving Births per Household
		Total Births	M	F	Total Births	M	F		
Current Generation	29	154	81	73	136	71	65	5.31	4.69
Children's Generation	128	258	140	118	247	134	113	2.02	1.93
Grandchildren's Generation	84	105	55	50	103	53	50	1.25	1.23

Source: Field Survey Statistics by the Research Team.

Table 4.24: Reproductive Statistics of the Surveyed Households by Generational Cohort (Interviewees Born in or before 1950) in Village Z (Table 4.21)

Generation/Decade/Percent (%)	1940s	1950s	1960s	1970s	1980s	1990s	2000s	Percent (%)
Current Generation	2.07	13.10	38.62	44.14	2.07			100.00
Children's Generation				6.57	38.52	38.52	16.39	100.00
Grandchildren's Generation						9.00	91.00	100.00

Source: Field Survey Statistics by the Research Team.

Section 3 Integrated Data Information

According to the above survey design, the research team conducted a comprehensive retrospective survey on the fertility history of the Dai families in the five villages in two prefectural regions from January 2009 to October 2011 and extracted the following integrated information from the surveyed data(as shown in Tables 4.25–4.27):

The above statistics provided the following information:

1. By October 2011, the 139 interviewees (Current Generation) had given birth to a total of 585 children, an average of 4.21 children per person, and 533 children had survived till the age of 15 or above, an average of 3.83 surviving children per household. The overall survival rate of the births was 91.11%;
2. The interviewees had throughout their lifetime given birth to 301 boys and 284 girls, with the boys slightly outnumbering the girls, and 272 boys and 261girls had survived till the age of 15 or above, with the survival rate of the boys and the girls standing respectively at 90.37% and 91.90%; and the survival rate of the boys was slightly lower than that of the girls;
3. The interviewees (except for four who never gave birth) had given 1– 11 births throughout their lifetime, and had 0–10 surviving births;
4. The interviewees who had given three or four births made up the largest share of the total at 48.92% and those who had three or four surviving births made up the largest share of the total at 53.96%;
5. The interviewees who had given birth five times or fewer and four or fewer births respectively made up 82.01% and 64.75% of the total, and those who had given five or fewer surviving births and four or fewer surviving births respectively made up 83.45% and 72.66% of the total;
6. The interviewees got married for the first time in the age range from 16 to 30 years old, at 19.57 years old on average, and gave birth to their last child in the age range from 19 to 50 years old (respectively giving the first birth and the 8th birth), at 31.93 years old on average;
7. The interviewees gave birth to their last child in the period from 1950 (total of two births) to 1985 (total of four births);
8. Each generation tends to have few births but more surviving ones on average. The survival rate of the births by Current Generation, Children's Generation and Grandchildren's Generation was 90.91%, 96.51% and 98.42%, respectively;
9. Those of the Current Generation gave birth from the 1940s to the 1980s, with most of the births taking place from the 1960s to the 1970s, accounting for 83.29% of the total number of births in this period;

Table 4.25: Reproductive Statistics of the Interviewees (Born in or before 1951) in Five Villages

Households	Age Cohort (Year)	Number of Lifetime Births (Persons)			Number of Children Who Survived till the Age of 15 or above (Persons)			Average Births/ Household	Average Surviving Births/ Household
		Total	M	F	Total	M	F		
2	1951–1955	3	3	0	3	3	0	1.50	1.50
40	1946–1950	130	61	69	124	57	67	3.25	3.10
29	1941–1945	115	57	58	107	54	53	3.97	3.69
32	1936–1940	153	88	65	136	78	58	4.78	4.25
13	1931–1935	60	31	29	54	28	26	4.62	4.15
11	1926–1930	63	34	29	54	28	26	5.73	4.91
10	1921–1925	51	23	28	47	21	26	5.10	4.70
1	1916–1920	6	3	3	6	3	3	6.00	6.00
0	1911–1915	-		-	-	-	-	-	-
1	1906–1910	4	1	3	2	0	2	4	2
In total: 139 Households		585	301	284	533	272	261	4.21	3.83

Source: Field Survey Statistics by the Research Team.

10. Those of the Children's Generation gave birth from the 1970s to the 2000s, with most of the births taking place from the 1980s to 1990s, accounting for 78.38% of the total the births in this period;
11. Those of the Grandchildren's Generation gave birth from the 1990s to the 2000s, with most of the births taking place in the 2000s;
12. Except for four interviewees who never gave birth, the length of time separating the time of their first marriage and the time of their last birth ranged from 1 (one lifetime birth, female) to 27 years (10 lifetimes births, four males and six females), in 12.36 years on average.

Table 4.26: Reproductive Statistics of the Female Interviewees (Born in or before 1951) in Five Villages

Age Cohort (At the interview time)		60–103 Years Old (1906–1951)			
Number of Lifetime Births	11 Births	1	Number of Children Who Survived till the Age of 15 or above	11 Surviving Births	0
	10 Births	2		10 Surviving Births	1
	9 Births	3		9 Surviving Births	2
	8 Births	4		8 Surviving Births	4
	7 Birth	5		7 Surviving Births	4
	6 Births	8		6 Surviving Births	10
	5 Births	24		5 Surviving Births	15
	4 Births	39		4 Surviving Births	40
	3 Births	29		3 Surviving Births	35
	2 Births	13		2 Surviving Births	16
	1 Birth	5		1 Surviving Birth	7
	0 Birth	4		0 Surviving Birth	3

Source: Field Survey Statistics by the Research Team.

Table 4.27: Generational Reproductive Statistics of the Households of the Interviewees (Born in or before 1951) in Five Villages

Generation	Households	Number of Lifetime Births (Persons)			Number of Children Who Survived till the Age of 15 or above (Persons)			Average Average Total Births per Household/ Household	Average Total Surviving Births per Household/ Household
		Total Births	M	F	Total Births	M	F		
Parents' generation	58/88	341	168	173	370	163	207	5.88	4.20
Current Generation	139	594	306	288	540	277	263	4.27	3.88
Children's Generation	494	973	494	479	939	474	465	1.97	1.90
Grandchildren's Generation	308	380	192	188	374	188	186	1.23	1.21
Great-grandchildren's Generation	3	3	3	0	3	3	0	1.00	1.00

Source: Field Survey Statistics by the Research Team.

Section 4 External Expression of the Dai Ethnic Traditional Fertility Behavior

Most of the Dai people live in low-lying flat areas near hills and rivers (intermontane basins), known as Bazi[12] in Yunnan. As a result of repeated floods from rivers and brooks over thousands of years, these broad valleys and low hills generally are covered by dense forest vegetation due to fertile soils and a pleasant climate at low latitudes. It can be known from historical literature and field interviews

12 Bazi, a common name for an intermountain basin among local residents in Yunnan, means, in geological terms, a small/medium basin of an internal slope of 8–12 degrees, which features a lower and flat trough and higher edges. Typical examples include the alluvial plains in small valleys, valley terraces, river shoals, alluvial diluvial sections, gentle plateaus, tiny hills in broad valleys and larger valleys. The internal areas and edge areas of all Bazis have been developed to varying degrees by humans. See also Research on Intermontane Basins in Yunnan, Tong Shaoyu. Chen Yongsen (Kunming: Yunnan University Press, 2007), 20–21.

that until the end of the 20th century, most Dai people had still lived the typical farming life. They live in a hamlet and make their livelihood by farming. Rice is the main crop in their paddy fields, and corn and sugar canes are the main crops in their mountainous fields. They usually plant vegetables and fruits around their houses, and keep the bulk of their harvests for themselves and sell the remaining in local fairs. Their life is almost completely tied to their farming fields. Put it in their own words, "Having your farming fields well tendered, and you will be free of worry about your food, clothing, housing and daily necessities".

They usually get married before the age of 20, and plan their life by a traditional rule of "a person should get married on coming of age". As long as their conditions allow, both men and women have to get married. It is abnormal for a person to remain single all his/her life. Being unmarried is simply a helpless alternative as a result of undesirable causes, such as physical diseases. It is also abnormal for couples not to have children. Dai families unable to have their own children usually adopt instead of remaining childless and treat adopted children as their biological children. Whether it is in a family or a village, adopted children are treated equally with biological ones.

In Dai society, there is no differentiation between the two forms of marriage: a man taking a wife and a woman taking a husband, and either of them is known as "joining the family". When getting married, either the husband can join and live with the wife's family or the wife can do the husband's family, totally depending on their circumstances. But in the past, it was mostly the case that the husband lived with the wife's family. Therefore, the Dai marriage institution is usually classified as the mode of "matrilineal family" (living with wife's family) in historical literature.

The fertility pattern of Dai people has four features: Early, Dense, Short and Excessive. "Early" means that they not only get married early but also have their first birth early. They usually get married before the age of 20 and then have their first birth within one year; "Dense" refers to a short interval between births. They usually have their first birth within one year of marriage and then have one birth every two years or two births every three years until giving birth to their last child; "Short" refers to a short reproductive cycle for women of childbearing age. They have only a reproductive period of fewer than 13 years on average, i.e., less than 12 years on average available for a Dai woman to complete her lifetime fertility behavior if she has her first birth one year after getting married. Their mantra is "An earlier parenthood leads to an earlier life of easiness". The phrase "an earlier life of easiness" contains two meanings: For one thing, if you get married and have children earlier, you will get help earlier with household chores and on the farms from your children, and relax earlier, which is a kind of happiness; for another, if you get married and have children earlier, you will still be relatively young when your children grow up and move away, and have more free time to yourself; and "Excessive" means that Dai women tend to give birth more times (three or more).[13]

"Endogenous self-control" is another external feature of the fertility behavior of Dai women. Throughout their reproductive period, the surveyed women gave birth 4.21 times (including unwanted ones) on average, completing their fertility behavior in less than 13 years (12.36 years) after getting married. Calculated based on the best reproductive age, they had spent 34 years from 15 to 49 years old on average giving birth, just 36.32% of the standard fertility cycle. This indicates that even though they were not subject to the national family planning policy interventions, this group ("Current Generation" herein) exercised nonetheless voluntarily exercised control over their fertility behavior during most of their fertility years. The vast majority of the interviewees having given birth in our fieldwork samples explicitly or tacitly acknowledged that they had taken some measures to prevent pregnancy. In fact, there are some popular techniques for preventing pregnancy and birth among Dai women. Here's an example cited by the staff at the Family Planning Office of Menghai County,

> Dai people have herbal medicines for both contraception and pregnancy. Dai women take some herbal medicines to avoid unwanted pregnancy, and other herbal medicines to help get pregnant if they wish to have a baby. These recipes in the Dai medicine are generally handed down over the ages and kept secret to outsiders. Dao Zhenggang, the former deputy head of Menghai County, was a Dai doctor skilled at these techniques, and his herbal medicines were very efficacious in controlling birth spacing. Newly married couples not wishing to get pregnant right away often go to see him for help. Some couples wish to give birth every two years or so, while others every three years or so. Couples not wishing to have additional babies also go to see him, and will get sterilized after taking two or three doses of his medicines. But generally speaking, Dai women prefer physical means of birth control (for example, sleeping alone or rhythm method) over medical therapies.

13 In the author's view, prior to the 1960s, having three to four children for life should be classified as "moderate birth" rather than "excess births", especially for residents in rural areas. However, given the established thinking in the academic community and based on the national family planning policy evaluation criteria, giving three or more births remained collectively classified as "more births".

Dai women have no desire to have too many children and disapprove of the idea of "The more offspring, the more blessings", which can be corroborated by the fertility behavior of both Children's Generation and Grandchildren's Generation. The 494 households of Children's Generation interviewed during this survey had 1.97 births each on average, and 308 ones of Grandchildren's Generation had 1.23 births. When asked why they didn't have more children as Current Generation did, they gave such comments as "The more kids, the heavier the burden on parents" and "With too many kids on hand, the dad will have less time entertaining, and the mum less time dressing up. It doesn't pay." An old saying has been popular among Dai people, "As too many fruits bend a tree, too many children make life harder for parents." Take as an example Current Generation. Most of local Dai women very soon learned how to use various birth control instruments during local campaigns of promoting reproductive health and disseminating contraception knowledge and techniques, and almost all of them had the tubal ligation surgery as soon as it was successfully introduced at local county-level people's hospitals in the mid/late 1970s and the 1980s. All the families of Children's Generation and Grandchildren's Generation had full knowledge of various contraceptive techniques, and most of them chose to exercise birth control through the tubal ligation technique after two births. They said so themselves, "Getting this done saves so much trouble in the future!"

Dai people attach great importance to the quality of life, and the quality of sex life is, of course, part of it. For couples with children, having tubal ligation surgery will free them from any worries later and enable them to pursue happiness in a better way and enjoy a happy and harmonious sex life.

In terms of the sex of their children, Dai people show no "Male Preference". The sex ratio of the lifetime births given by the interviewed women in our survey stood at 105.9. Their ideal sex composition for their children was "having both boys and girls". They largely didn't appreciate, and even felt baffled by such concepts as "Male Sex Preference" and "Continuation of Family Lines". The common reply to such questions given by most interviewees was that, "These are the ideas held by you the Han people. We Dai people don't have such ideas". As a matter of fact, it is generally believed in the Dai society that it is better to have daughters as they can help mothers with household chores and are emotionally closer to their mothers.

In terms of the family structure of the Dai society, the nuclear family has increasingly replaced the extended family as the dominant family type. Often, the one child who gets along the best with the parents (regardless of sex or age), is expected to continue to live with them, while the other children would be allowed to move away after getting married. The child who stays in the original family inherits all the properties left by the parents but also assumes the responsibility of supporting the parents in their advanced age.

As a result of the fertility behavior, fertility willingness and preference with respect to the sex of the children mentioned above, the size of a Dai family is usually rather small. There are usually five members in most families of Current Generation and four members in most families of Children's Generation.

Dai people are more obedient and adaptive to state policies. If any disagreement with governmental policies, they tend to live with them and say, "Policy is a stone, and we are eggs. It is no use dashing an egg against a stone", which well exposes their softness and cowardliness.[14]

Dai people also have a different attitude towards marriage, families and fertility from other ethnic minority groups. Especially in the number of births, the selection preference for baby sexes, the choice of contraceptive measures, etc., Dai people show a distinct difference from these of the Han ethnic majority living in inland regions on the Chinese mainland. While the Han people endorse the fertility concept of "the more offspring, the more blessings" and have the preference for male offspring, the Dai parents want to have a balanced sex composition for their births: "Having both boys and girls, and either sex being fine". Based on their birth control motivation and value judgment on fertility issues and stemming from profound influences of the traditional Dai culture, the orientation and practice of the Dai people having fewer births have maintained long-term stability.

Reference

Fei, Xiaotong. *The Economy of Jiang Village*. Beijing: the Commercial Press, 2001, 24.

14 Jiang Yingliang used the two Chinese characters to describe the leading personality trait of the Dai people. Also seen in Jiang Yingliang, *The Real Life of the Dai people in Western Yunnan* (Dehong: Dehong Ethnic Publishing House, 2003), 223.

5

Factors in Traditional Low Fertility Rates among the Dai

A review of the classical population theories in the West and domestic research on human fertility behavior suggests that the mainstream views hold that in a traditional agrarian society, people tend to have many children. This can only change with economic development and social modernization. Easterlin, a U.S. population economist, went so far as to describe the change in human fertility behavior as "one of the most dramatic upheavals in human history, or rather, a fertility revolution." He added that the fertility revolution is part of the "modernization" originating in Northwest Europe in the mid-18th century and then spread across Europe and even the whole globe. It was marked by two shifts: The shift in the fertility rate from a high level to a low one (The average number of lifetime births for a woman declined from six or more to about two) and the shift in the fertility concept from the "natural fertility rate" to the "conscious birth control at the family level" (Li, 2009).

An examination into the fertility behavioral features of the Dai people described in the previous Chapter by Easterlin's indicator shows that the representations of the "fertility revolution" had emerged before the 1950s in the Dai society, though it remained a traditional agrarian one at that time with no relation to modernization. So why could they develop this fertility pattern featuring low fertility rates in a traditional agrarian society? Anthropological research shows that "human behavior in any primitive tribe or in any nation in the forefront of civilization is learned in daily living. No matter how bizarre his act or his opinion, the way a man feels and thinks has some relation to his experience. If the search took one into trivial details of daily intercourse, so much the better. That was where people learned" (Benedict and Ruth, 1990). To shed light on the fertility behavior of the Dai society, which deviate way far from the "classic fertility behavior" summarized by domestic and foreign demographers, we have to start with an understanding of their daily lives. The Dai people live in a distinct cultural context from that of their Han peers, which leads to a far cry in almost all aspects of their life, from the basic necessities of life, family structures, marriage customs, land system to even the entire way of life, from those of the Han society familiar to us. Given those facts, the author will give a panoramic description of the living conditions of the Dai people in the current Chapter based on his own fieldwork at Jing village in Menghai County in Xishuangbanna[15] as well as the records of investigation of ethnic villages in the 1950s, the survey in 2000 at Mangang village in Mengzhe Township of Menghai County by the Ethnic Village Investigation Team of Yunnan University and other historical literature. All the work has provided necessary background information for delving into the formation mechanism of and a theoretical explanation of, the traditional fertility behavior of the Dai people in the next chapter.

According to the historical literature, in 1914, the General Border Administration Bureau of Pusi started to recruit construction teams to build the Simao – Cheli via Puwen and Mengyang courier route suitable for both passengers and postal carriages. In December 1930, the Second Border Administration Office of Pu'er dispatched technicians to survey the route from Cheli to Myanmar via Fohai, started the road construction in the spring of 1940 and completed the Cheli-Daluo section of the low-grade road in May 1949. When the task forces of the Fourth Field Army of the People's Liberation Army of China advanced to Xishuangbanna from Kunming in 1953, the road section suitable for automobile traffic ended at Pu'er, and the remaining section leading to Cheli (now Jinghong) was still the courier road. Hence, it could be inferred that as a result of poor accessibility, the whole Xishuangbanna had had a rather weak connection with inland regions on the Chinese mainland until the founding of the People's Republic of China. In the case of Menghai, before the extension of the Kunming-Daluo Highway to Menghai in 1954, there had been no roads at all

15 The village is among the ones in which that the author has been doing fieldwork since the 1990s.

in the County, and all the transportation was done by manual and animal haulage (cattle and horses) and people went around on foot. The poor transportation infrastructure led to limited and stable intercourse spaces for local residents. Most of the ordinary residents in *Bazi* (intermontane basin) areas went around in a radius of three to five kilometers, having never venturing farther than their own or surrounding villages, which was verified by the author's inquiry into the original hometowns of those married to native Jing villagers. Living in the same natural environment, residents from all villages in *Bazi* areas in the County shared a very similar way of living, and there was hardly any fundamental difference between the living standards of the villagers in the same stratum. Therefore, the descriptions of the daily life of people in Menghai Dai villages in the R.O.C. Period in various categories of literature are, to a certain extent, the portrayals of the daily life in Jing village. Based on the author's investigation and personal experience, the descriptions of the life of the Dai villages in Xishuangbanna in historical documents are largely the same except for natural produces[16] as a result of the elevation differences among Menghai, Jinghong and Mengla. That is to say, there are few differences in the behaviors, the ways of thinking and the habits of emotional expression among residents. Therefore, it is arguably believed that the real situation captured during the survey in Jing village is also, to a considerable extent, that of the entire Dai population in Xishuangbanna. It means that there exists a mutually corroborating relationship between the two. In addition, the fieldwork in 2000 at Mangang village in Mengzhe Township of Menghai County by the Ethnic Village Investigation Team of Yunnan University also verified the mentioned-above belief.

The following sections present more detailed descriptions of their life in the three dimensions: economic life, family structure and social environment.

Section 1 Traditional Economic Life of the Dai People

> Mankind must first of all eat, drink, have shelter and clothing, before it can pursue politics, science, art, religion, etc.; that therefore the production of the immediate material means of subsistence and consequently the degree of

16 Menghai County has a higher elevation (with its average elevation at 1,176 meters above sea level and the elevation of Jing village – which is near the seat of Menghai county – at 1,196 meters above sea level) than that of Jinghong Municipality (at 552.7 meters above sea level) and the seat of Mengla County (at 639 meters above sea level) and has traditionally been known for its tea trees rather than other tropical cash crops, such as watermelons, bananas and rubber trees.

> economic development attained by a given people or during a given epoch form the foundation upon which the state institutions, the legal conceptions, art, and even the ideas on religion, of the people concerned have been evolved, and in the light of which they must, therefore, be explained, instead of vice versa, as had hitherto been the case (Foreign Languages Publishing and Distribution Administration, 1955).

The material motivations of fertility have an important influence on the implementation of specific fertility behavior. By understanding their traditional economic life, we can learn about the economic basis underlying the fertility behavior of the Dai people living in a traditional agrarian society and the effects of child-rearing on their material life.

Daily Consumption of the Dai People

A glimpse into people's daily consumption, including food, clothing, housing and expenses, helps shed light on their living standards. Certain material conditions are necessitated for any family to live a normal life, and their satisfaction is the fundamental motivation for family members to engage in production. The same is true of the conduct of giving birth.

Housing

According to the historical records of the Dai people, the Burmese tile-making technique spread to Menghai during the reign of Menghai Chieftain Zhaoguang Meng from 927 to 959, leading to the emergence of tile-roofed houses in the Town of Menghai. However, only chieftains, town councilors and their relatives, tribal chiefs and Burmese temples at that time were allowed to build tile-roofed houses, while the common people continued to live in small and lowrise thatched cottages featuring a bamboo-wood structure until the 1950s (Local Chronicle Compilation Committee of Menghai County in Yunnan Province, 1997a). Compared with a multitude of accounts in historical literature, the book by Mr. Jiang Yingliang, *The Cultural Life of the Dai Ethnic Group,* gave a more comprehensive and detailed description of the structures and building methods of housing of ordinary families in the Dai villages in Xishuangbanna before 1950s: At that time, a Dai family didn't need to spend any financial resources or physical effort by itself on housing as this issue for a new Dai family was solved through the joint efforts of the whole village. Hence, "living in a decent house" had never been a problem for the Dai people in rural areas.

Baiyi (Dai) villages are on streams, rivers and lakes in extensive plains, and are, in most cases, surrounded by woods and bamboos. So, we have the saying: where there are vivid jungles, there are Dai villages. These villages consist of varying numbers of families from 300 or 200 to just a few dozens, and every family lives in a separate compound featuring detached buildings and large clearings. In the border areas in Sipu, dwellings are built completely from bamboo and wood, with the upper storey for residents and the ground one for domestic animals, and are similar in style to large tents, exactly consistent with the description in the ancient Chinese Work *The Masters of Huainan*: 'People in southern frontiers live on trees'. These bamboo-wood dwellings specific to the Dai families have a typical layout: The ground storey runs seven to eight *chi* (*chi*: a unit of length in ancient China) in height, has no enclosures, and is reserved for domestic animals, such as horses and oxen. Stepping up along the stairway to the upper storey, you will first land on an open terrace and then farther into a large rectangle living room, which is divided further by a bamboo fence into two functional sections: the bed-chamber and depository for valuable articles and an open and spacious bay. The rooftop stays not very high from the floor, and the slopping roof boards are fixed in a tilted way on each side of the upper storey to meet with and be supported by the floor slabs at the eaves, so there are no windows for the upper storey (there may be one small window on each side of the upper storey and/or a small door on one side of the upper storey if the eaves stay high above the floor). In the center of the upper floor is a fire pit where the fire is kept alive for the cooking or tea brewing all year round, whether in the day or at night and in summer or winter. Both the host and guests have small talks, squatting or sitting around the fire pit. The roof is fully covered with thatch, and all the beams, pillars, doors, windows, ceilings and floors are made of bamboo. It is very easy to build such a residence: You just need bamboo poles, together with some help from neighbors, to complete it in a few days. However, it is also very perishable and needs to be repaired every year after the rainy season, so the residences of chieftains and tribal heads, despite being unchanged in the building style, are built usually from wood instead of bamboo and are also larger and taller. Moreover, their residences are roofed with tiles instead of thatches.

The Dai people in the twelve bannas bake tiles by themselves. Looking like fish scales, the tiles take the shape of a square with four three-*cun*-long sides, and are approximately two or three *fen* in thickness (both *cun* and *fen* are units of length in China). Every tile has a hook on one side for fixing with the bamboo strips nailed in advance on the roof rafters at the two-*cun* interval, and no reinforced mortar is needed. So, the tiled roofs look like the clouds of fish scales and can't withstand excessive external forces, such as climbing. When doing the roof repairing, one just need to remove a broken tile from under a corresponding rafter to replace it with a new one hooked. Only richer families

> in a village could, in most cases, afford such luxury dwellings, and even Cheli Pacification Superintendent's official residence also took such a style except for being much more spacious: Its upper storey is enclosed with railed corridors, usually partitioned into various rooms of different sizes and has poor lighting as a result of no windows for all the rooms, whereas the ground storey, unfenced in all sides, consists of neatly-arranged 120 pillars and serves as the free-ranging venue for domestic animals, including cattle, horses, pigs and chickens. Such building serves as both the private dwelling and the governmental office of the supreme leader of local Dai communities (Jiang, *The Life and Culture of the Dai Ethnic Group,* 1950b).

When the author first visited Jing village in the 1990s, its family compounds largely retained the layout described above except that the former "wattled walls" of some compounds had been replaced by brick walls and the traditional bamboo pole-supported and thatch-roofed "stilt houses" (also known as traditional bamboo houses or the first-generation bamboo houses) by the wood-framed and tile-roofed ones (also known as the second-generation bamboo houses), which only richer men, such as chieftains or village headmen, could have afforded. A few families even lived in brick-wood or steel-concrete framed "stilt houses" (also known as the third-generation bamboo houses). As some elders recalled, there were not so many households in the R.O.C. Period in Jing village, and the residence of every household was then enclosed with bamboo/batten fences to form an independent compound, with the clearings between fences serving as aisles for walkers and animals. Bamboo houses are the typical "stilt house" buildings with a bamboo-wooden structure for the Dai families: They take the shape of a square, and sit high about two meters above the ground on more than 20 woodpiles as the supporting pillars, with the upper storey for family living and the unfenced lower storey for domestic livestock and household sundries. Their double-beveled roofs are covered with thatch or hooked tiles (namely the Burmese tiles known to the Dai people). Stepping up along the stairway to the upper storey, one will find a corridor leading onto a bamboo/batten-paved balcony, which is named "Zhan" by the Dai people and serves as the venue for washing and drying up household articles. Indoor space is partitioned lengthways by bamboo fences or wooden boards into two zones: The one near the balcony is for the guest room, and the other is for the bedroom, which is accessed through two doors on the partition, with the one near the stairway for ladies and the other for men. There are no more partitions in the bedroom and all family members sleep in the same bedroom. There are no beds in the bedroom, and everyone lies on a "pa mat" directly spread on the floor. The couples are separated from their children with a cloth curtain and non-family members are not allowed to get in the bedroom. The guest room is the place for doing daily activities and welcoming visitors and has a fire pit near the door. Live-in visitors sleep at night beside the fire pit. Given there are no windows or just a small opening on the walls, the fire pit and the interstices between bamboo strips and wooden boards provide the main avenue for lighting and ventilation in the upper storey.

Yan Kang, an old carpenter in the village, said that no matter who wanted to build a house, adults all over the village would come over with their own tools to help: men hauling the raw timber out of mountains to the construction site, grading the construction site, erecting the frames and pillars, setting up the roof, laying out the boards and so on, while women doing the cooking and tea brewing. It usually took one to three days to build a house depending on the size of the house. According to the literature, there were various procedures and expenses for building houses as shown in the following Table 5.1.

Table 5.1: House-building Procedures and Expenditures for the Dai Families

Sequence	Procedures	Activities and Expenses
1	Select the raw timber for the central pillars in mountains	Two pairs of wax sticks ("Dings" in the Dai language), a bunch of betel nuts and a bowl of wine are sacrificed to the two trees chosen to be the central pillars
2	Present gifts to the village headman for help in hauling the raw materials	Offer a bunch of betel nuts and a jar of wine to the village headman "Naiman", who would call for villagers to help haul the raw timber out of the mountains to the construction site.
3	Offer gifts to the carpenter	Offer four pairs of wax sticks, one bowl of millet and rice each, a piece of 20 *chi*-long white cloth, a piece of five *chi*-long red cloth (or three Yunnan-minted silver coins)[17] to the carpenter for house designing. If the carpenter is a local villager, just a bunch of betel nuts and a bottle of wine will suffice. If a house is designed by the would-be house owner himself, no such procedure is needed.

17 One Yunnan-minted Silver Dollar coin was equivalent to half of one Chinese Silver Dollar coin at the time.

Sequence	Procedures	Activities and Expenses
4	Pay tribute to a new seat of a house	If the house is built on a new seat, a "Bozhang" (a minister in temple management) or a Buddha will be invited to recite sutras, and the gifts include a bowl of rice, a pair of wax sticks, and dozens of copper coins or a couple of silver coins
5	Offer gifts to the village headman for help in building the house	With the construction site leveled, pay tribute and report once again to the Naiman, requesting him to call for villagers to help with the construction. The gifts include a bunch of betel nuts and a bottle of wine
6	Offer gifts to Zhaopianling (local feudal ruler) for the purchased land plot for the house	The gifts are three Yunnan-minted silver coins for a small house, five ones for a large house, or nineteen or thirty-three ones for a tile-roofed stone-foundation house. Besides, the house owner also should purchase the footprints and handprints of Zhaopianling for sticking on the central beam of a new house, demonstrating the new house owner complies with the regulation: "being a taxpayer once the house is completed" and has since been officially an obedient subject of the Zhaopianling.
7	Celebrate the new house	On the evening of the new house completion, the owner and villagers have a celebration party. On the second day, the owner officially moves into the new house and throws a thanking banquet for villagers. One pig (or ox for a richer owner), fifty to sixty *jin* (a unit of weight in China) of wine and about one hundred *jin* of rice are consumed for the banquet, with the head of the pig or the ox offered to the carpenter, and the tenderloin to the village headman. A poorer house owner at least should reward his villagers with chickens for their help.

Source: Local Chronicle Compilation Committee of Yunnan Province, *A Comprehensive Survey of the Dai Ethnic Society in Xishuangbanna (2)*. The Nationalities Publishing House of Yunnan, 1983, pp. 74–76.

When I told the elderly in Jing village what I had read in the above literature, they said,

> The situations in all villages are basically the same. Building a new house is a big thing, and everyone will do what needs to be done (referring to offering sacrifices to the trees and offering gifts to the Naiman, the Bozhon, etc.). In the case of house building in a village, the house owners do not need to pay any wages, just some wine and dinners will suffice. Of course, you have to kill a pig when you celebrate the completion of your new house. This is because every family has to build a house sooner or later, it is only a matter of time. If you help others today, others will help you in the future.

Dressing Customs

Dressing matters much in the daily life of the Dai people. Throughout history, Dai women can do both the spinning and weaving, and cotton is also produced locally. Therefore, it is easy for locals to solve this important issue in their daily life. In fact, what they are concerned about is not whether they have clothes to wear, but how to dress smart and beautiful. Mr. Jiang Yingliang summarized the dress characteristics of the Dai people in the 1940s as follows: "The Dai clothes are characterized by simpleness, cleanliness, beautiful styles and balanced color tones" (Jiang, *The Life and Culture of the Dai Ethnic Group,* 1950c).

Indeed, the dressing customs for the Dai people are known for simpleness and distinctiveness: Men wear black or dark-colored jackets and trousers, while young women wear brightly-colored straight skirts and elderly ladies wear a lightly-colored tight jacket and a dark-colored straight skirt. According to the elderly, since cotton was locally produced, they used to spin and weave their own fabric for making clothes or other domestic purposes. During the period from the late Qing Dynasty to the early R. O. C. Period, as more trade caravans were coming here in regular seasons every year in dealing in tea, prettier cloth came here with them. In addition, businessmen from inland regions on the Chinese mainland and even from Myanmar also traded all kinds of exquisite fabrics here, so local women couldn't help buying them for making clothes. Spinning, weaving and sewing are among the basic skills for the Dai woman, and as a matter of fact, they usually sew by themselves for their families, which has not changed much to date. During the period of the fieldwork, the author stayed with Mr. Dao's family, and his elder daughter-in-law, Yu Langdun, had been sewing Dai clothes by herself till then. Highly skilled at sewing, she made more beautiful clothes than others, and so had a lot of customers. She operated a tiny workshop nearby, and fellow women about the same age in this village would gather here on holidays or special occasions, chatting and sewing Dai clothes. It is really a very lively scene.

Dai women are very fond of bedecking themselves with accessories and often say that, "We are always dolling up ourselves with all kinds of gems and ornaments, every inch from head to toe" (meaning the ornaments are indispensable). According to what the author had seen and heard by himself, when it comes to dressing-up and making-up, women are never stingy: It can never do without ornaments with them, such as hairpins, earrings, necklaces, bracelets, girdles; the dressing-up would reach a climax during holidays and festivals, with all sorts of accessories showcased in a imaginative fashion, the gold, silver and jade being the mainstay material. As a matter of fact, a love of beauty, the hallmark of Dai women, has become a signature highlight of the tourism industry in Dehong and other Da settlement areas. Those brightly dressed Dai women, with a slim graceful figure, wears straight skirts and fresh flowers in their hair, and are always smiling to welcome tourists, making them unwilling to leave.

Diets

Food is a major item of household consumption. In contrast with housing and clothing, this consumption happens every day, and storing the right amount of food for maintaining a normal life is a constant in household consumption. To feed themselves, humans have to work hard, and that is the biggest source of material motive for procreation. But historically, Dai people have never had to face food scarcity. In fact, they have been able to enjoy a diversity of foods that provide all the nutrition the human body needs. Mr. Yao Hesheng's writing on this bears it out:.

Skillful at rice-growing, Dai people have rice as their staple food. They prefer glutinous rice at dinner for its softness and stickiness in quality and have indica rice (the long-grained non-glutinous rice) only at breakfast (processed in the form of dried rice, or rather, rice noodles). In the old days, Dai families stored paddy rice instead of polished rice, and in the early morning every day, every family in a village had to pestle the paddy rice into husked rice grains before the cooking. So, together with the bird singing, the rooster crowing and the dog barking, the paddy rice-pestling sounded like a pleasant symphony to the ear of tourists, and was a unique sight in the Dai settlement areas. Dai people prefer pork, beef, chicken, fish and a variety of wild species, including frogs and insects in farming fields, lakes, rivers and mountains, and also consume a variety of vegetables, for example, green vegetables, melons, beans and others. But these vegetables widely familiar and available to them nowadays had not been introduced to the predominantly Dai localities till as late as during the R.O. C. period, and before then, all varieties of vegetables on their dinner table came from mountains and plains. In addition, they also have various cooking methods, including burning, roasting, frying, boiling, steaming, marinating and chopping.[18] Of course, rice wine is a regular drink on the dinner table in the Dai settlement areas. Thanks to its unique taste and cooking methods, the Dai flavored cuisine has been one of the most distinctive varieties in Yunnan's catering industry.

In his work, *The Folklore of Shui Clan of the Dai Ethnic Group*, Mr. Yao Hesheng gives a detailed account of what he saw and heard in Xishuangbanna from 1939 to 1940, especially providing us with a nuanced panoramic view of the Dai cuisine and bringing to life their diverse and unique food culture.

> The most interesting thing is that they only have glutinous rice rather than indica rice and have no definite number and time of meals in a day. In the early morning, when the meal is cooked, every family member fills his/her flat-round bamboo-woven lunch box with food, takes the box to their workplaces, or keeps it by the stove (if staying at home). Whenever hungry, they grab a few handfuls and eat them.
>
> As for their dishes, it is, indeed, pitiful. There are almost no vegetables or meats, but just a few betel nuts, a spoonful of honey, or a few wild fruits. These are all they have for a meal.
>
> In terms of the food materials, in most cases, the meats are pork, chicken and buffalo meat, and on very few occasions, there are also fish and meats of wild games, such as muntjac, deer, birds and others. But except wild plants (such as treetops, etc.), vegetables are hard to come by, to say nothing of green dishes, melons or beans.
>
> Here is a list of famous delicious cuisines. (1) Nasha (or Jinsha): To put boiled ox intestines (and entrails) together with chopped raw beef, add some seasonings (for example, salt, pepper, onion and others), mix them well, and then,

18 Chopping is a meat cooking technique in Dai cuisine, also known as "raw meat chopping", and the most common courses in the Dai families processed using this technique are "live fish chopping" and "raw beef chopping". The cooking method is to mix up minced raw meat with various seasonings, including chili, salt and coriander, to form pastes, and then is served directly at the dinner. The chopping courses are renowned for their unique features: sweet, spicy and delicious.

serve on the dinner table; (2) Bageluoli: To cut pork into fine pieces and cook them, add ox intestines (and entrails), vegetables and seasonings, cook the mixture once again, and then, serve on the dinner table; (3) Nami: To keep cooked vegetables in a sealed jar to let them ferment, take out the fermented vegetables (when they smell terrible), dry them up under the sun, mix them up with salt and pepper, and then, serve on the dinner table; (4) Nala: To keep bamboo shoots in a sealed jar, take them out (when they turn sour), and then, serve on the dinner table; (5) Shale: To cut a pig lung into fine pieces, slightly fry the pieces in a wok, take out the half-boiled pig blood, mix the blood with cold water, keep the mixture in a cool place to let it condense into lumps, and then, serve on the dinner table; (6) Nabo: To smash unshelled crabs in a bamboo tube into bits, mix them up with seasonings (salt, pepper, etc.) when they turn blackish and smelly, and then, serve on the dinner table; (7) Jinwubo: To smash a chicken with a knife blade into a floppy meat pie, mix up the pie with seasonings (salt, pepper and others), wrap tightly the mixture in green vegetables, roast it over a fire, pour oil on it, and then, serve on the dinner table; (8) Gai: To make very thin round cakes of five *cun* or so in diameter out of some freshwater algae growing on rocks in a river, dry up the cakes under the sun. Cut the dried cakes into bits, fry the bits in lard, and then, serve on the dinner table. This dish tastes very delicious and crispy.

They are very fond of various kinds of edible insects, especially (1) baby cicadas; (2) bamboo insects; and (3) queen termites.

Another expensive and delicious dish is the chicken-shaped brown fungus.

Besides staple foods and dishes, there are a wide variety of snacks in the Dai cuisines. These snacks are especially popular with young women and girls, and most of them are made of rice flour.

The Dai people are very fond of drinking, and even young girls drink heavily. Made from rice, their wines taste strong but not so mellow, and have no strong aroma.

Though tea bushes grow everywhere in the twelve bannas, they do not like tea very much. Instead, they like to dip a ladle of cold water from a pitcher to quench their thirst (Yao, 2003a).

As recounted by the elderly in Jing village,

The daily diets in ordinary Dai families at that time consisted mainly of glutinous rice and common vegetables. There was nothing fancy. But on some

> special occasions,[19] such as the Dai New Year, the Door-opening Festival and the Door-closing Festival, things were very different: We had a more abundant variety of foods, including pork, beef, chicken, fish and insects. But all of them were home-grown or collected in mountains. No money was spent on them and there were no farmers' markets at all at that time.

Based on the author's investigation, many of the "expensive and delicious dishes" that Mr. Yao had mentioned are still on the dinner table of the Dai people today, but have become standing dishes and have also taken their Chinese names. For example, Nasha is known as Raw Meat Chopping, Shale as Prosperity, Nala as Sour Bamboo Shoots, Nabo as Crab Sauces, Nami as a generic term for all the sauces made of tomatoes, peppers, etc. (such as vegetable sauces, tomato sauces, and chili sauces), Jinwubo as Wrapped Roasted Chicken, Gai as Fried Green Moss and so on. Therefore, it is apparent that there are no significant changes in their diet culture.

Today, the Dai people still live on rice (mainly glutinous rice) as their staple food and have three meals a day. For breakfast, they usually have cooked glutinous rice, fermented black beans, dried rice pies, or rice noodles. They still have their lunch by the fields during busy farming seasons. They have a sumptuous dinner, but generally, do it after dark. Their cooking method of glutinous rice remains the same as in the past: Steamed rice is kept in round bamboo boxes or small earthen jars, or repackaged with small plastic bags and kept in insulation buckets. They just take out some bags of it at a time for a meal. Indica rice is cooked in an aluminum pot or an electric cooker. Their meat dishes mainly include fish, pork, beef, buffalo meat and chicken, while their vegetarian dishes are mainly made of wild vegetables and bamboo shoots. Nowadays, the chicken-shaped brown fungus hasn't been so easy to come by as in the past, but other vegetables, such as cabbages, green vegetables, cucumbers, eggplants, tomatoes, turnips and so on, have not been uncommon on their dinner table. Usually, they have only a limited variety and quantity of dishes, and still do not use chopsticks or bowls for their meals. They just knead cooked glutinous rice into balls and eat them along with Nami. In their own words, "The tighter the balls are kneaded, the better they taste". But chopsticks and bowls are used for indica rice and dishes. Some women

19 The Dai Ethnic Calendar Year, i.e. the Water-Sprinkling Festival observed by the Dai and other ethnic minorities, falls in the middle or later third lunar month (before the Grain Rain solar term) every year, while the Door Opening Festival and the Door Closing Festival fall respectively on the first and last day in the mentioned-above "Retreat for the Rainy Season". The three occasions are the most important Buddhist festivals in a year observed by the Dai people.

also prefer to have indica rice soaked in tea. Most Dai men like to drink. Even without decent dishes to go with the wine, they can drink until midnight or even all night long. They often chitchat while drinking.

Daily-use Articles

Living tropical regions with abundant water resources, rivers and streams, Dai people have easy access to all kinds of plants, especially bamboos, trees and bushes, so they have bamboos as their main material for various daily purposes, and many of their daily articles are made of bamboo and wood. Their tables, chairs, boxes, cabinets, cabas, food baskets, crates, buckets and so on are all made of bamboo, and their water-storing earthen jars, cooking pots, cooking shovels, kitchen knives and so on are also produced usually by local craftsmen in their villages. They buy and sell these homemade daily articles in local fairs, or trade them off with husked rice or something. Even today, these handmade daily articles are still commonly used in the Dai families.

During his fieldwork at Jing village, the author found that though many families have already moved into reinforced concrete structured Dai-style buildings (might as well be known as the fourth-generation Dai-style buildings), their dining tables, chairs, stools and others are still made of bamboo in their traditional styles and patterns, and the elder still prefers bamboo-made boxes or cabinets.

When Mr. Dao's family rebuilt their house in 1999, they just retrofitted the "bedroom" component of the original bamboo house into a two-storeyed concrete structure, leaving the kitchen unchanged in the structural style of the Dai buildings, and continued to use bamboo-made cooking utensils. When asked why they still kept the kitchen unchanged, the Mietao (the popular term for middle-aged and elder Dai ladies) replied, "My son proposed to change it, saying it would look nicer. But I was afraid that I would not get used to it, so I asked the carpenter to leave this part alone (referring to the kitchen)." Mr. Dao added, "The kitchen was rebuilt with the wood materials recovered from the demolished old house. It, indeed, took a lot of doing, but she insisted on it in this way, so we had to do so as she liked to." It seems that the kitchen is the main place in the daily life of a Dai woman in China. Either for the convenience of use or life habits, they retain their unique preference for wooden "stilt houses" and their traditional bamboo utensils.

Ceremonial Offerings

The Dai people is a religious ethnic group. Most of them believe in Buddhism, while the minority in Natural Religion.[20] The activities related to Buddhism play a very important role in their daily life, and the "making offerings" event as a special ritual usually takes huge inputs in time, financial resources, materials and effort, which is unimaginable in the eye of a stranger to the Dai areas. We will make a specific discussion of the religious life of the Dai people later. In this section, we limit our topic to the subject matter of "household consumption" in their daily consumption. In terms of this subject matter, the Dai people have rather modest physical demands but "much richer spiritual pursuits".

"Dan" in the Dai language (meaning sacrifices, offering, or giving) is a unique phrase in Southern Buddhist areas, and usually refers to the offering of properties or money to a Buddhist temple to pray for good fortunes and avert disasters. Of course, the offering events the Dai people hold in a year are not just limited to Buddhist activities, but also include the rituals related to Natural Religion, for example, the Offerings for the Village's Prosperity, Offerings to the Village Deity, Offerings to the Spirit of Grains, Offerings to the Deity of Waters, and so on. Having varying intervals, duration and scales, these offering events are unevenly spaced in all the months over a year, with some lasting simply a very short period and others several days. The offering events can be roughly classified into three categories: Regular, Irregular and Discretionary. The regular offering events take place on certain fixed dates in the Dai calendar every year, such as the Offerings at the New Dai Ethnic Year, the Offerings at the Door-closing Festival and the Offerings at the Door-opening Festival, while irregular offering events take place in certain preset time ranges in a year based on the actual situation, such as the Tower Offerings and the Cassock Offerings. Discretionary offering events refer to the ones that families may choose to hold based on their realities on meaningful occasions, such as death of a family member, birth of a baby, completion of a new house, departure for a long journey and so on. Table 5.2 is the Schedule of Major Dai Ethnic Offering Events in a year that was summed up by the author during his fieldwork.

Glutinous rice, wax sticks,[21] towels (handkerchiefs or small pieces of handmade coarse cloth) and a few small-denomination coins, and in most cases,

20 The Dai people in Jinping, Yuanjiang, Xinping, Huaping and other scattered/mixed ethnic communities in the basins of the Red River and the Jinsha River believe in Natural Religion, making up less than 15% of the national Dai population.

21 Home-made wax candles were commonly used for lighting in the Dai families. Being made of beeswax-coated cotton threads, they are yellow in color, very thin in diameter and slightly soft in quality, and are easy to be fixed vertically on a wall ("Ding" in the Dai language).

Table 5.2: Dates of Buddhist Ceremonial Offerings by the Dai People

Month (Lunar Calendar)	Month (Dai Calendar)	Month (Gregorian Calendar)	Major Rites and Events
1	4	2	
2	5	3	
3	6	4	Offerings to the Buddha, Offering at the New Dai Ethnic Year (the Water Sprinkling Festival). Offering at the Sandcastle Festival
4	7	5	
5	8	6	
6	9	7	Offering at the Door-closing Festival (the event held every seven days after the Door-closing Festival) Haohuaihe Offering, Galawa Offering, Gunbaibeng Offering, Gunbaibo Offering and Haogan Offering Tanmu Offering, Sala Offering, Salashuai Offering, Tower Offering, Offering at the Door-opening Festival
7	10	8	
8	11	9	
9	12	10	
10	1	11	Handkerchief Offering
11	2	12	Offering at the White Wood Burning Festival, Offering at the White Elephant Festival
12	3	1	

Source: Results from the Author's Fieldwork.

together with Haonuosuo,[22] Henen[23] and other dishes, are the must-have offerings on each offering event. On major events, such as the Water Sprinkling Festival, the Door-opening Festival, the Door-closing Festival, the Buddhist Scripture Offerings Day, the Sala Offerings Day and other festivals, flower baskets must be offered, banquets thrown, spark displays (also known as firework displays) staged in the evening, sky lanterns flew, and so on. Despite the excessive costs of all these activities in a year, no one cares about it. They are happy to make these offerings, and they are never tired of talking about it. For them, every additional offering they made is equal to an additional piece of "blessing field"[24] they reclaimed, not only bringing happiness and benefits to themselves and their offspring but also making a contribution to their village. In *The Economic Life of the Dai Group*, Mr. Jiang Yingliang described as follows:

> The material life of the Dai people cannot be separated from their religion for one basic reason: They believe that all the gains throughout their life they earned through their hard work should be attributed to the Revered Buddha. In addition, there is a Buddhist world in their minds, which, they believe, is the permanent home of life, and only in the Buddha's world can a person truly enjoy all the desires and pleasures of life. Therefore, they are willing to commit all their spirit and money to religion and lead a simple or even ascetic life in reality to have compensation in their afterlife in the future. In the view of the Dai people, it (offering) is a kind of savings with higher interest rates. With this controlling idea in their minds, of course, the religious consumption of the Dai people has been the top consumption item in their expenditures (Jiang, *The Economic Life of the Dai Ethnic Group* 1950a).

Here and now, we do not want to go further into what the top consumption item in their expenditures is exactly meant for. Just looking into the preceding schedule of the Dai major offering events, you can get the sense of the description from Mr. Jiang and realize the important role of offerings in the life of a Dai family.

22 Mix up powered glutinous rice with brown sugar, peanuts and other seasonings, wrap it up with banana leaves and steam it in a cooking pan. It looks like the Zongzi (a traditional Chinese rice pudding popular among the Han ethnic majority) and tastes like the Ciba (a Chinese-style glutinous rice cake).

23 Mix up chopped beef with seasonings, wrap up it with banana leaves and then steam it in a cooking pan. It has a similar cooking technique to Haonuosuo, and is known as beef dumplings.

24 Giving alms to monks in temples is believed as the act of doing the good in a Buddhist culture, and is known as cultivating one's blessing field, meaning that today's act of doing the good will be rewarded with the harvest of blessings in the afterlife.

What we saw and heard during the fieldwork also shows that Dai families don't care much about the articles and utensils for daily use in craftsmanship. But when it comes to offerings at a Buddhist temple, they care very much: All the offerings are made elaborately and exquisitely, showing their rich imagination both in the content and the decoration. These donated articles are nothing short of the top achievement in their folk arts. The excessive consumption of the Dai families in this aspect shows that they have sufficient "financial resources" to meet not only their material needs but also their spiritual pursuits.

Tributes

In addition to the money and properties for their daily life, such as food, clothing and shelter, and for the spiritual needs, such as offerings, the Dai families also used to pay tribute to the rulers.

Among the materials obtained in the fieldwork in various Mengs (an administrative division unit in the Dai settlement areas in Yunnan) and villages in Xishuangbanna just before the Movement of Democratic Reforms in 1954, there are the *Taxation Load Books of Financial and Physical Contributions to the Royal Treasury in the Qing Dynasty* from *Each Meng*, the *Pacification Superintendent's Decree on Collecting Entertainment Expenses for Royal Officials*, the *Pacification Superintendent's Books on the Office Expenses from the Twelve Bannas*, the *Pacification Superintendent's Provisions on Marriage and Funeral Rites, Gift Offerings and Service Provision* issued in February 1921, and other related documents. These historical records show that the tribute was paid not only in the form of labor corvee but also in the forms of physical materials and financial means. For example, the *Mengzhe Chieftain's Labor Assignment Records* (Local Chronicle Compilation Committee of Yunnan Province, 1983a) stated that:

> On the occasions where the Chieftain builds new houses, marries his daughters, or makes an inspection tour of villages, every village must contribute one pig and three *liang* (a unit of weight in China, equal to 50 grams) of silver. Manleis must carry a fishing net with them and accompany the Chieftain to new houses.

> Each village must pay tribute to the Chieftain in the form of millet, which will be distributed to "Bolangs" in charge of villages. The amount of millet given to a Bolang depends on the number of households in the villages he is in charge of.

> The guards of honor on the Door-closing Festival and the Door-opening Festival: Jingkangs and Yunlongs raise a pair of red flags, walking in front of

> the Chieftain, while others raise a pair of colored leopard head flags, walking behind the Chieftain . . . Zailongs carry a pair of long knives, walking side by side with the Chieftain. In addition, there is also a sedan . . . The villagers living on mountains serve as the cook of the Chieftain, taking care of his luggage and cooking furniture, and Hanas are responsible for carrying cooking oil and salt for the Chieftain.
>
> Every village on mountains contributes five bowls of beans, five bowls of sesame, 10 *jin* (a unit of weight in China) of flower seeds . . . Manmaiduis play the role of Saolongs, contributing one piece of woven bed mats and two loads of elephant grass. Xidings play the role of Shaonans, carrying two loads of water for the Chieftain and the Pacification Superintendent for their bath every day during the period from March to the end of April of the Dai calendar.

A taxation notice (Local Chronicle Compilation Committee of Yunnan Province, 1983b) put out by a town council in 1938 stated as follows:

Notice

According to the Supreme Decree from the Pacification Superintendent, the Town Council declares herein that, regardless of being produced or traded by either men or women, all the articles for sales on markets, including meats, fish, cigaretts, liquor, tea, chili pepper, ginger, salt, vegetables, tobacco, areca nuts, rice noodles, dried rice pies, green bean jellies, fruits and tuber, are subject to taxes from the date of notice herein as required by the Decree, and no non-compliance shall be permitted.

The tax rates are:

One *jin* of buffalo meat for one buffalo; one *jin* of cattle meat for one cattle; eight *liang* of pork for one hog; one bowl of liquor for one trader/producer; one bowl of rice noodles (dried rice pies) for one trader/producer; one *liang* of salt for one trader/producer; one *liang* of tobacco for one trader/producer; and areca nuts, fruits and vegetables are taxed at rates deemed appropriate.

June 1, 1300 (the Dai Calendar)

To sum up, there were two levels of tribute in the R.O.C. Period: The tribute by Chieftains to the imperial court and the one by common people to Chieftains, with the former paid mainly in the form of money, while the latter in the forms of money, physical materials (in-kind) and/or labor corvee. At the village level, tributes are paid only to chieftains, including office expenses, alimony, grain, labor corvee, supply and fees levied for special events, which include those for marriages, funerals, childbirth, hereditary succession, birthday celebration, festivals and construction and renovation of chieftain family's residence (Jiang, 1983a).

Though the above-mentioned historical records on tributes were not specific to Jing village, under a unified political system, there impossibly existed marked variations both in the form and quantity of tributes undertaken by various villages. The main daily expenses represented by the Dai families in Jing village before 1950 showed that the daily consumption of the Dai families at that time had the following features:

Source: They are mostly homemade physical products and only a very small proportion of them are bought from the market, such as clothing decorations and some offerings and tributes at offering events.

Contents: They had an abundant supply of foods but preferred simple dressing, housing and daily use, thus spending less in their daily life.

Accessibility of consumer goods: Their houses were jointly built by villagers while clothes and domestic supplies were mainly homemade. Thus, it is not difficult for them to get access to their daily consumer goods.

The ratio of incomes to expenses: Their compulsory tribute expenses and daily expenses didn't account for much, but the voluntary religious expenses made up the bulk of their expenses.

The mentioned-above breakdown of their expenses showed that at least until the earlier 20th century, the Dai society was still a self-production-centered and self-consumption-oriented agrarian society, almost having no attributes of a commodity economy. The supply of local produces sufficed to meet their basic needs of life. By the traditional rural standards of living, they were rather rich in their basic life, having no need to worry about their food and clothing. Therefore, there was no basis for such ideas as "to increase family incomes by having more children" in their life.

Farming Products and Techniques in the Dai Communities

The special natural geographical environment and climate contribute to the distinct difference in the daily life between the Dai people and their peers in inland regions on the Chinese mainland, especially in farming products and farming technology.

Due to the advantageous environmental conditions and the fertile intermontane basins they live in, they can easily get access to rich local natural resources, which had been much discussed in the historical writings. "The frontiers have been reported to be barren lands, but the Dai regions in Yunnan are different. They are rich and beautiful lands. These plain areas, generally speaking, are covered by the abundant vegetation of various plants" (Jiang, *The Life and Culture of the Dai Ethnic Group,* 1950d). While talking about the local farming products in Cheli, a frontier area of primitive farming, Mr. Zhang Fengqi described,

> The main produce here is rice: there are white glutinous rice, purple glutinous rice, flagrant glutinous rice and . . .. Menghai, Nannuo, Yibang, Yiwu and Youle are all known for their tea leaves, while Damenglong for its cotton, Menglong and Ganlanba for their lac encrusted twigs and Mengzhe and Menghai for their camphor. In addition, there are borneol and vegetable glues across the region. So, in terms of farming plants alone, the entire Cheli (in Xishuangbanna) might as well be an inexhaustible treasure trove.

"Another valuable resource is camphor, mainly produced in Menghai, Mengzhe, Dingzhen, Meng'a and Mengsong. On my journey from the Town of Cheli to Mengsong, I saw all the hills and mountains along the entire route were thickly covered by tea bushes and camphor trees."

"Another plant, the purple root, also grows in various counties like Cheli, Liushun and Zhenyue. The Bo ethnic people use it for producing dried indigo, a dying agent."

"They also grow citruses, and their harvest not only suffices to meet local consumption but also sells in the Sipu region."

"Cheli also grows tea bushes and is famous nationwide for its Pu'er-branded tea leaves" (Zhang, 1938).

When it comes to the technical state of farming in the region, citing Menghui Intermontane Basin as an example, Mr. Zhang said that,

> Generally speaking, the farming here is 'single cropping agriculture': They plow fields in the lunar March and April with their plows and harrows; loosen the soil in their farming fields in the lunar April and May; breed seedlings in the lunar April, which takes about two months and two days; and transplant the seedlings in the lunar April. The crops bloom in the lunar July and are ripe for harvest in the lunar September. With too many rivers and brooks, there is no problem with their farming irrigation, and also no risk of flooding and drought disasters. But sometimes, damage by insects may take place. Some red-headed black insects or yellow insects often ruin seedlings. They never manure or weed out as the entire region is scarcely populated, namely, there are too few laborers for so many fields across the region. Even in this primitive farming way, they can have a satisfying harvest in the end, sufficing to meet living needs.

Based on his more detailed investigation of local produces and farming technology, Mr. Jiang Yingliang made a summarized description of the farming techniques and said,

> in terms of the living culture, Dai people are, as it were, one of the most advanced among all the ethnic groups in the southwest frontiers, not only having gone beyond the stage of hunting and animal husbandry completely into the farming one but also having grown out of the slash-and-burn primitive cultivation into the plowing-and-gardening farming technology. However, on the other hand, their today's living culture remains completely in the agrarian society, having not yet fully developed their industry and commerce along the way . . .
>
> The main farming products in the Dai areas include:
>
> Rice: Rice is the main produce in the Dai rural areas, and thus the centerpiece in the Dai economy. They measured and priced anything and matter of economic significance with rice. The staffers at Chieftain Offices were compensated with rice instead of money, hired laborers were paid with rice and the wealth of a family was measured by harvested rice. Generally speaking, rice is oversupplied in the Dai areas, and there were even cases of taking excess rice as firewood. Though there are almost no such cases any longer nowadays, rice has not been as valuable in the regions as it is in the predominately Han regions . . . Except for Xiangyun, Baoshan and Midu in the West and Yuxi and Yuanjiang in the South, in the expansive Southwestern frontiers from Kunming to the Dai areas, there aren't any longer large plains extending twenty to thirty *li* in sight, and most of the residents here live on oat, tartary buckwheat and corns. A meal of rice is a rare thing here, and some dwellers in hilly areas even have never had a taste of rice throughout their life. Yet, in the Dai areas, not only all families have rice as their staple food all the year round, but all domestic animals, such as cattle and horses, are also fed with rice instead of beans, which is an envy to the Han people in the adjacent frontier areas . . .
>
> 2. Beans: In terms of side crops, the Dai farmers grow mainly beans, especially broad beans and peas . . . They also grow peanuts, not using them as food materials but for cooking oil extraction or for sale on the market.
> 3. Cotton: cotton is mostly grown across the twelve bannas . . . Each family grows relatively small patches of cotton here, and there aren't large pieces of cotton fields.
> 4. Sugar canes: Sugar canes are grown in almost all the Dai villages. These sugar canes are mainly used for producing sugar with local techniques and are largely sufficient to meet local demand.

5. Tea: Many counties, especially Cheli, Fohai and Nanqiao, grow a variety of tea leaves, including the world-famous Pu'er-branded tea. . . . It is very easy to plant tea bushes. Once planted, tea bushes need no additional management. When they have matured, you just pick up the leaves off the tea bushes with a basket in spring and sell them to tea-processing mills operated by Han people or Han traders. In autumn and winter every year, long trains of horse caravans flow the Dai farming areas, especially Fohai and Cheli, to purchase tea leaves. These caravans come from all parts of the entire country, including from as far as about 100 days' journey away in Tibet, signifying a booming tea trade.
   Fruits: The Dai areas are rich in fruits . . . large swatches of fields everywhere in Cheli and Fohai are devoted to growing pineapples, the most important cash crops for the areas.

In the Dai areas, the main agricultural produce is rice. With fertile soils and a warm climate, rice could have been grown and harvested twice every year in most of the areas. However, due to extensive fields and excess harvest relative to sparsely populated residents, local farmers, in fact, prefer to grow grains once a year, leaving their cultivated lands to stay idle for the remaining half of a year. The farming state and techniques in the Dai areas are briefly described as follows:

1. They divide up large plain areas into small plots of farming fields. These plots border each other and have fixed scopes. But they don't define the scopes of their farming plots by the dimensions of the fields (length or width) but by the quantity of seeds to be sown in a plot. For example, if a bamboo basket of seeds can be sown in a plot of land, they name the surface of this plot as a bamboo basket.
2. They have established related systems and institutions for water conservancy construction and river and ditch management. They are skilled at making use of natural rivers and have built relatively full-fledged networks of ditches, not only for farming irrigation but also for mitigating flooding and drought.
3. They never manure.[25] In their eye, less yield means the farming fields have become less fertile. So, they turn to new plots, leaving the unfertile plots to

25 In his work: the Economic Life of The Dai Group, Mr. Jiang Yingliang said: the techniques of sowing, transplanting and harvesting in the Dai areas are different from inland regions on the Chinese mainland in that the Dai farmers neither use manures nor weed out. They just plow in spring but never bother to control weeds in their fields in summer. Not only do they never use any manures in their paddy rice fields, but also never for their vegetables, beans, sugar canes and cotton at all. They are even

stay idle for several years before recultivating them. Therefore, manures are not essential to the farming production in the Dai areas.

4. They don't plant new crops anymore in late autumn. After rice planted in this spring grows ripe and has been harvested, they leave the plots idle until the sowing season in the next year. Only by this time will they start to irrigate and plow their plots.
5. Their farming tools include plows, harrows, hoes, sickles and others. All of them are mainly made of iron, have bamboo or wooden handles, and are similar in shape and function to the ones used in other regions in the Chinese mainland. Oxen are also used to plow the fields. They usually harness two buffaloes to haul a single plow, and sometimes also harness oxen for the farming work.
6. They sow seeds around the lunar April every year, plant seedlings in the lunar May and June, and harvest in the lunar September and October. During the period from the seedling planting until crop harvesting, there is no need for management on the farming fields: They neither do the manuring nor the weeding. They even don't bother to make a trip to inspect their farming plots far away from their residences once the seeds are sown or the seedlings planted therein, and straightly go with relatives and friends to harvest their crops based on their expected harvest time or the kindly messages from someone who happens to pass by their fields on his trip to the market . . .

. . .

9. While harvesting their ripe rice, the Dai farmers are even reluctant to lower their waists to cut off the stalks near the roots, leaving the residual stumps of more than one *chi* (a unit of length in China, approximately equal to 1.09 foot) long on the fields. The reason why they do so is that rice straws are of no use to them (their cattle and horses live mainly on freshly collected green grass instead of dried rice straws, and usually lose weight in winter when living in the Han areas due to no fresh grass).

The case of rice cultivation and harvest is also true of other crops. The process is also very simple and casual: There is no need to manure, weed out, loosen soils, select seedlings/seeds and kill insects. They just sow the seeds or plant the seedlings, and all things are done. Even so, they remain able to have a big harvest. All this has much to do with their advantageous natural conditions: fertile

very confused and amazed at hearing the practice of using feces as manure for the crops and vegetables in other parts of the Chinese mainland, exclaiming that how people can have the crops grow in the fields with so filthy things, and how people can eat the crops grown out of so filthy soils. See also Jiang Yingliang, *The Economic Life of the Dai Group* (Guangzhou: Tsinghua Press, 1950), 45.

soils and favorable climate (Jiang, *The Life and Culture of the Dai Ethnic Group,* 1950e).

During his investigation in Jing village, the author also found that glutinous rice, the staple food for the Dai people, accounted for 80–90% of the paddy fields. Yes, they also grew non-glutinous rice and purple rice. But the former was only used for making dried rice pies, rice noodles and some snacks, and the latter for making purple rice cakes as offerings during their offering events. They grew corns, peanuts, beans and potatoes on dry fields. Corn was mainly used for making liquors or feeding pigs, and peanuts for making daily snacks. The beans were largely soybeans, but some families also grew broad beans, peas, cowpeas and other varieties of beans. They used soybeans mainly as the raw ingredients for making bean curds or soy sauces. Tea leaves were the main cash crop in Menghai. Almost every family in Jing village had a tea bush plantation. Besides tea bushes, they grew camphor trees and cotton on the hilly areas, and tobacco plants on small land plots mainly for their own use. They grew a wide variety of fruits, including pineapples, pears, oranges and grapefruits. They grew few types of green vegetables (mainly cabbages) and various seasoning plants in their vegetable gardens, including fennel, coriander, peppermint, onion, ginger and other condiments, and got their wild vegetables mainly in the fields, by the ditches and on the mountains.

The seasons, techniques, manners and tools of planting in the Dai areas were just the same as what Mr. Jiang had described, and the practice of not being reluctant to stoop to cut off the rice stalks near the roots and leaving long stumps on the fields has remained unchanged until today. Yan Lao, a 78-year-old man, gave me a detailed account of the farming here. First of all, they never used any manures either in their paddy fields or dry fields, and maintained and restored their soil fertility mainly using the crop rotation and fallow system. They planted rice in paddy fields only once a year in spring to have them stay fallow after the harvest until the next year, and staggered their planting on dry fields to have them stay fallow in alternative seasons. They thought that the grains grown out of farmyard manures were unsuitable for consumption, especially for offerings at their offering events, which would be a great disrespect. Secondly, their cultivation and field management was simpler: They tilled the fields, cultivated seedlings, transplanted seedlings, and once all this was done, they just sit idle to wait for the harvest. The field tillage roughly included five steps: plowing, ridge-building, soil-turning-up, harrowing and land-leveling. They prepared for field tillage in late April every year and began to plow waterlogged fields around

May when the rainy season set in. About 10–15 days later, they built ridges in the fields: With wooden shovels, they amassed freshly-plowed soil into lines and rows of ribs, and buried the weeds and stalks deeply in the mud, leaving them to rot slowly into manures. Ridge-building is helpful to soil-ripening. Another 10–15 days later, they harrowed the fields: With paddy field harrows, they turned up the soil in the fields. This process was to quicken the rotting of the weeds and stalks deeply buried in the mud, produce smaller soil blocks and make the soil looser. Harrowing usually took place about 10 days later after ridge-building. With ridge-building and harrowing completed, they ran the harrow with a long bamboo pole back and forth in the fields to level the fields. Once the fields had been leveled, they stopped the water supply to the fields. By this time, all were gotten ready for transplanting seedlings (the process is commonly known as the white water seedling transplanting). The rice seedling cultivation in the Dai areas was usually done in wet rice beds. The wet beds might not be required to be very standardized but the seeds should be densely sown. In addition, the practice of transplanting seedlings, i.e. seedling replanting, was also popular: A large cluster of 10–20 seedlings was raised in new wet beds for about 30 days before being planted in the paddy fields. Despite one additional step, the practice was reported to help increase the yield by 10%-20%. Once seedlings were planted, paddy fields were encircled with wooden stakes and bamboo fences to keep cattle or horses away. From then on, they needed to do nothing but irrigate and sit idle until the harvest. The harvest process was divided into four steps: crop collection, drying-up, heaping-up and threshing. With a jagged scythe, the Dai people stood to cut off the rice ears only, leaving the residual stalks of nearly 30 centimeters long on the fields, kept the freshly-harvested rice ears stay spread out on the fields for drying up for around three days, and then stacked the dried-up rice ears in heaps before threshing them three to five days later. While threshing, they first spread a large bamboo mat on the threshing ground and set a whipped plate in the center of the mat, then flung the rice ears hard against the whipped plate to get most of the rice grains off, and finally beat the rice ears with a bent stick to get off the remaining rice grains. They screened out the immature grains and imperfections with bamboo-woven baskets, packed the finished rice grains in bags and carried them home. After harvest, they often had their cattle and horses graze in paddy fields. The rice stalks left in paddy fields would have been largely rotted by the planting season of the next year, and be plowed and buried deep in the mud as good manure.

To sum up, the farming products and farming techniques in the Dai areas were generally characterized by "abundant resources, simple technology and low productivity". Due to advantageous conditions, such as excess arable fields, a smaller population, easy access to foods and abundant natural resources, residents had the luxury of doing the single cropping a year rather than the double cropping and could still have a good harvest even without good field management. Therefore, it was unlikely for them to develop the idea of having more children to help with household chores and on the farming fields.

Handicraft, Business and Home Farming in the Dai Ethnic Areas

Handicraft

Before the founding of the People's Republic of China, the local handicraft industry covered a wide variety of craftsmanship, such as house-building, Burmese tile-making, iron and wood farming tool making, hardware and pottery making, bamboo and rattan ware weaving, spinning and sewing, paper- making, umbrella -making, sugaring, brewing, and entertainment products and religious article making. On the whole, there were a lot of craftsmen in every village, and their levels of skill were also rather high, which is exactly the common character of any agrarian society. Generally speaking, most men in a village mastered the skill of making daily necessities, and their products were mainly made by themselves and for their own use. Even though some finished products had to be made through cooperation, for example, a craftsman skilled at knife-making might cooperate with a craftsman skilled at scabbard-making in making knives. Such cooperation between them was also a mutually beneficial way of production, with no money being paid to each other. That is to say, their craftsmanship had not developed into a specialized profession. Another example is house-building. No one in a village specialized in house designing for others, and no one took house-building as his profession. Every man in a village served both as an architect and a clay carpenter. If a family in a village wanted to build a house, they just needed to get the materials ready, and then asked villagers for help through Bozhang. Within three or five days, a house could be built. You didn't need to pay the helpers but should also lend a helping hand when your fellow villagers built their houses. In their eye, mutual help was a kind of reward. With this kind of mutual help, no one had to spend money, but the houses were built. Furniture-making provides another good example. Most families made their bamboo tables and wooden stools by themselves and for themselves. Of course,

> some handicrafts are mastered by only a few people among the Dai people, but none of them live on their special skills or rely on their handicrafts as a means

of livelihood. Therefore, in technical terms, the handicraft industry in the Dai areas is nothing but a sideline in the countryside. The handicrafts the Dai people 7 are skilled at are listed as follows:

1. Bamboo craft: Bamboo craft, the representative of the Dai craftsmanship, are far more widespread in the use and exquisite in the craftsmanship than those of their Han peers. Their houses are made almost entirely of bamboo, including beams, pillars, walls, floors, stairways, doors and windows, and their furniture and daily utensils are also all made of bamboo, including kitchen kits, tables, chairs, stools, cases, baskets and food boxes. In particular, their buckets are made of natural bamboo poles directly cut off in the fields, and even their bridges over rivers are also made of large bamboo.
2. Weaving craft: By the time they turn eleven or twelve, Dai girls must begin to learn how to weave and embroider, skills that render a female desirable to men. For this reason, Dai women are all highly skilled weavers and embroiderers and can weave convex-concave patterns even on a piece of white coarse cloth. Brocade, one of their most exquisite embroidery products, has been cited as their representative art and is usually used as offerings during offering events.
3. Pottery-making craft: Dai people in the southern region are skilled at making tiles and bricks, evidenced by the fact that all the Buddhist temples and residences for chieftains and headmen are built with their bricks and tiles.

In addition, there are also Dai silversmiths and blacksmiths. However, though rather developed, these handicraft industries are usually dismissed as sidelines in rural areas, affirming that there is no working class in the Dai society. The reason is that these handicraft industries and exquisite works are all secondary to farming, and no one depends on them for a living, so the handicrafts produced in this way could only be dismissed as the by-products of farming (Jiang, *The Life and Culture of the Dai Ethnic Group,* 1950f).

According to the author's investigation, among the current 415 households in the village, there were back then six blacksmiths highly skilled at making iron tools, five time-honored pottery families, including Yu Guangjiao, Yu Han and Yu Lajuan, and three best cotton-weaving families including Yu La, Yuwandi and Yu Han.

Commercial Business

According to *The Annals of the Twelve Bannas* ,

The twelve bannas sell a wide variety of commodities, mainly tea leaves, both internationally and domestically . . . Fohai exported about 500 pack-loads

> of camphor every year to Myanmar, worth 130,000 Yunnan-minted silver coins ... Cheli and Fohai have exported about 2,000 pack-loads of purple stems every year since many years ago to Myanmar and Siam, worth 36,000 Yunnan-minted silver coins, about 1,000 pack-loads of citruses every year to Myanmar and via Yibang to Chinese hinterlands: Simao and Ninger, worth 24,000 Yunnan-minted silver coins, and about 2,000 pieces of Solo-branded clothing every year to Chinese hinterlands: Simao and Ninger, worth 12,000 Yunnan-minted silver coins. Fohai exported about 300 pack-loads of brown sugar every year to border towns in Myanmar and via Liushun to Chinese hinterlands: Simao, worth 6,000 Yunnan-minted silver coins (Li, 1955a).

It is apparent that the main products to be sold at home and abroad at that time were camphor, purple stems, citruses, Solo-branded clothing and brown sugar in Menghai County. But as far as Jing village is concerned, only two produces: tea leaves and camphor and a regular bazaar (known locally as the Turf Fair and held every five days) might be deemed to have something to do with commercial trades in nature. Every year, villagers could have a relatively steady flow of monetary incomes from selling tea leaves and camphor oil. Mr. Dao Shuren, the last chieftain of Menghai County, said,

> In the past, merchants would come here to purchase camphor in winter, which was an income source for us. Camphor is a good raw material for medicines. In the time of wars, due to a huge demand for it, camphor was once more expensive than tea leaves. Before, camphor trees were interplanted with tea bushes, which contributed to the high quality of tea leaves in Menghai. But nowadays, with no demand, camphor is useless any longer to farmers. So, they cut down all the camphor trees in tea plantations. It is really a pity.

In the R.O.C. Period, the tea plantation area in Xishuangbanna was customarily demarcated by the Lancang River into two sections: Jiangnei and Jiangwai. The tea plantations to the west of the Lancang River, including Fohai, Nanqiao, Jiangning Provisional Administrative Area, Nannuoshan (part of Cheli) and Menghai, were collectively referred to as the "Jiangwai Section". Menghai (the former Fohai), the tea production stronghold in Jiangwai Section, grew tea bushes everywhere, including the hilly regions near intermontane basins and on the mountains 1,000 meters above sea level, and led the entire section both in the acreage and the output of tea plantation. As described above by Mr. Li Fuyi, the exported commodities in the Dai areas were mainly the raw tea leaves collected in due seasons, which were transported in bulk to Simao to be processed into finished tea products before they were sold in Tibet. But the trading volume every year was limited and there were no stable commercial markets. In the second year of the Reign of the Xuantong Emperor in the late Qing Dynasty (1910), Zhang Tangjie, a Shiping businessman, opened the first-ever tea house in downtown Menghai – Hengchun Teahouse, hiring Han tea kneaders from Simao for processing local tea leaves. In turn, those tea kneaders taught a large group of Dai and Bulang ethnic apprentices. From then on, tea houses mushroomed in Menghai, and by 1930, there had been 10 tea houses in downtown Menghai, producing a stable tea leaf market and providing a relatively stable marketing channel for fresh and raw tea leaves for tea farmers in villages(as shown in Table 5.3).

In the R.O.C. Period, Mr. Li Fuyi also had a tea house in Menghai. In his book *The Annals of the Twelve Bannas*, he talked about the picking, processing and marketing techniques of tea leaves:

> Tea production season begins about half a month before the Tomb-sweeping Day and ends on the Frost's Descent Day, lasting seven months from June to December on the lunar calendar. Except for brief breaks during the period, tea leaves can be harvested at any time. The tea leaves harvested in the range of half a month around the Tomb-sweeping Day are commonly known as Spring Tea. The tea leaves ripening before the Tomb-sweeping Day are, in fact, the fluff-covered buds, and thus known as White Tippy Tea (Baimaojian in Chinese), namely Tippy Tea in short (Maojian in Chinese) or nicknamed as Spring Tippy Tea. The tea leaves ripening after Spring Tea are blackish in the leaf color and brightly brown in the juice color, and thus known as the Brown Stripy Tea (Heitiaocha in Chinese). As a result of the more rapid growth in a more abundant rain season, the tea leaves ripening after Brown Stripy Tea are usually light in the leaf texture, larger and thicker in the leaf shape and yellowish in the leaf color, and thus known as Second Rainfall Tea (Ershuicha in Chinese). The tea leaves ripening after Second Rainfall Tea are all classified as Coarse Tea, featuring dark yellow leaves, the thinnest texture and the lowest quality. After the Coarse Tea harvest, there is a brief break for tea bushes to recover their vitality. Tea bushes won't sprout out till the time when rice blossoms. The tea buds given out during this period are similar to the spring ones, but lighter in the tea texture and larger and thicker in the tea shape. Sprouting out while rice is in full bloom, they are also known as Rice Flower Tea (Guhuacha in Chinese). Tea farmers can harvest another crop of tea leaves before winter sets in, and then turn to make their preparations for the rice

Table 5.3: Tea Houses in Downtown Menghai in 1930

Trade Name	Business Owner		Date of Establishment	Number of Tea Stoves
	Name	Birthplace		
Hengchuan	Zhang Tangjie	Shiping, Yunnan	1910	2
Hongji	Dong Yaoting	Tengchong, Yunnan	1924	7
Keyixing	Zhou Piru	Yuxi, Yunnan	1925	2
Hengshenggong	Zhang Jingbo	Heqing, Yunnan	1928	4
	Su Xingyuan	Yunnan	1928	1
Shan Tealeaf Cooperative	Dao Zonghan	Menghai, Yunnan	1928	2
Yun Sheng Xiang	Li Yunsheng	Tengchong, Yunnan	1930	2
Fuxing	Li Fuyi	Liuzhou, Guangxi	1930	2
Shilihe	Wang Qiushi	Shiping, Yunnan	1930	2
Lili	Han Rongbang	Jinggu, Yunnan	1930	2
Dingxing	Ma Dingchen	Mengzi, Yunnan	1930	2

Source: Local Chronicle Compilation Committee of Menghai County in Yunnan Province, *The Annals of Menghai County*, Yunnan People's Publishing House, 1997, p. 210.

harvest. It might be said that tea cultivation is simply a sideline for farmers in the twelve bannas.

They roast freshly-picked tea leaves in a caldron, roll the half-withered tea leaves into strips by hand, and then dry them up in the sun on a spread bamboo mat before selling them at once in a city or keeping them in bamboo baskets for sale in future. Two baskets of tea leaves usually weigh 30 kilograms or so (equal to 100 *jin*), a load suitable for a horse to carry (known as a pack-load). The tea leaves to be packed and sold in this manner are known as Tea Leaves in Bulk (Li, 1955b).

Yan Hanying (born in 1936) recalled,

At that time, all families in the village dried up their greenish down-covered tea leaves by themselves. We just roasted the freshly-picked tea leaves in a pot to get the moisture off, kneaded them with hands into strips in bamboo wattles or dustpans, and then dried them up under the sun. In the end, we kept the dried tea leaves in bags and waited for peddlers in this village to pick them up. From the lunar March, when Spring Tea – the first crop of tea leaves- is ripe, we could harvest several crops of tea leaves up till the lunar October, when rice is ripe for harvest. Spring Tea leaves are generally harvested during the period from the lunar March to the lunar June. The tea leaves harvested around the Tomb-sweeping Day are known as Spring Tippy Tea (Chunjian in Chinese) and fetch the highest prices. The tea leaves harvested during the period from the Grain Rain (the sixth solar term in the Chinese calendar) to the Start of Summer (the seventh solar term in the Chinese calendar) is called Mid-spring Tea (Chunzhongcha in Chinese), also known as Brown Stripy Tea or Second Rainfall Tea. With a tropical rain climate, the tea leaves ripening during the period from the lunar June to the lunar August have a relatively light taste. Immediately after the lunar August, we had the Autumn Tea (Qiucha in Chinese). Once into the lunar October, we had Rice Flower Tea. Despite a smaller output, Rice Flower Tea leaves usually fetch a better price than that of Second Rainfall Tea leaves.

There is also such a passage of description in historical literature,

Take the case in 1939 as an example. The current market price for a picul of tea leaves (picul: a unit of weight in China) was 10 Yunnan-minted silver coins. This price was the purchase price paid by tea houses, which purchased tea leaves in bulk (including freshly-harvested green tea leaves) through local intermediaries. With agreed purchase prices every year, the trade guild would designate

> a purchase zone for a tea house, which would, in turn, entertain village headmen (known as Laoba in local term) with dinner and gifts, such as salt, bean vermicellis and felt hats. Following that, the tea house would entrust Laoba to purchase tea leaves at the set prices. Local tea farmers were also ready to sell their tea leaves via Laoba to teahouses (Editorial Committee of Five Series of Books on Ethnic Issues, 1983a).

In addition to tea leaves, camphor was another source of commercial income for families in the village. Yan Bingyue (born in 1940) told the author,

> Camphor earned less than tea, but a family still could, much or less, benefit from it. There were two main categories of camphor trees here: sassafras and tenuipilum. The latter grows in this region only (Tenuipilum, a unique tree species in Menghai, has later been designated as a nationally protected species), and is cultivated either in tea plantations or on specialized plots of land. It is very simple and easy to extract camphor from trees: Just a pair of cauldrons would suffice (meaning the distillation technique among local folks: By distilling camphor woodblocks, they got crude camphor powder with larger moisture and then sold it directly on the market). They just kept the dried camphor powder at home, waiting for some peddlers to purchase it. A chunk of camphor powder (weighing three *jin*) could sell 2.5 Yunnan-minted silver coins.

Jing village was very close to the Town of Menghai County, so some older villagers proudly said that this village was the earliest street across Menghai and also exactly the downtown in the good old days. According to *The Annals of Menghai County*,

> During the reign of the Chongzhen Emperor in the Ming Dynasty, a makeshift open market developed for barter trade among local Dai people in front of the Jinglong Buddhist Temple in Menghai. During the reign of the Tongzhi Emperor of the Qing Dynasty, Bayakezhang, a Dai native in Jinggu Prefecture, migrated to today's Xiangshan Town, doing the catering business. Since then, many businessmen in Chinese hinterlands had come here in a throng to do business. Eventually, a business block – Manga Street (that is, today's Old Street) came into existence. In the late Qing Dynasty, dozens of the shops and stalls run by Zhang Tangjie, Wang Xianzhi, Li Runting, Zhou Piru and others formed the first-ever commercial market across the county. During the R. O. C. Period, with the rise of the tea-making industry, the commercial trade in Menghai saw rapid growth. For example, the Xiangshan market in Menghai had grown to be the main commercial center in the entire border region and

> was even nicknamed 'Mini Shanghai' and 'Mini Kunming'. Later, with the Japanese occupation of Myanmar, the export channels for Chinese goods were cut off, and the tea leaves also encountered poor sales. In addition, repeated Japanese air bombings also played havoc with the local commercial activities: manufacturers and shops shut down and evacuated, leaving the market in the doldrums. Despite some recovery after the Anti-Japanese War, the sector had never come back to its former boom (Local Chronicle Compilation Committee of Menghai County in Yunnan Province, 1997b).

Jinglong Buddhist Temple mentioned above was one of the Buddhist temples in the village. On each open day, both the Dai people and people from other ethnic groups in nearby villages and mountainous areas would come over with a torch, gathering and trading at the Turf Fair in the early morning. Most of the Han businessmen here were regular shopkeepers from inland regions on the Chinese mainland. They had stationary shopfronts and would start their business even before dawn. Transactions were made amid the hustle and bustle. The Dai villagers peddled their produces freshly from their fields and home -made handicrafts, such as rice, clothing, bamboo utensils, silver ornaments, wine, sugar, vegetables and fruits; other minorities from surrounding mountainous areas brought with them mountain products, including firewood, herbal medicines, mountain fruits, cotton and linen products, tea leaves, games and wild birds; and the Han traders sold a wide variety of exotic articles shipped from inland regions on the Chinese mainland and even foreign countries, including silk, satin, muslin, woolen clothing, cosmetics, cigarettes, toothpaste, matches and other gadgets. After sunrise, the traders began to trickle out of the ground, and by noon, all the trading activity would have almost been over. The author found that, when recalling the scene at that time, some old people would fall deep into their memory, with their faces brimming with apparent pleasure. These moments in the good old days might be, perhaps, their sweetest memorable past.

According to the description from the local fairgoers, the turf fair here was not much different by the commodities from farmers' markets in many other county towns today, but the nature was quite different as

> going to the turf fair was not a commercial activity for two reasons: 1. The goods traded on the turf fairs were mostly the raw produces grown in their own farmlands, or the articles collected in the open fields or the handicrafts made by their own skills, and the money from the sale was at once spent for the goods needed for their life. In essence, such a kind of trade retained the features of 'barter

> exchange', or rather 'exchange what one has for what one has not' in primitive society. Buyers and sellers, rather than being intermediaries for making a profit, directly did their exchanges, which was in essence the exchange between producers and consumers. 2. There was, indeed, another class of fairgoers who invest their fixed funds in trading in goods for earning profits, which, however, only sufficed to maintain their basic living. The Han businessmen on the turf fair largely fell within this category. This shows that though performing acts of purchase and sale, the Dai fairgoers were, in technical terms, not businessmen (Jiang, *The Life and Culture of the Dai Ethnic Group,* 1950g).

In fact, the Dai families at that time still just sold what they produced by themselves and for themselves. Hence, for villagers, turf fairs were more of the venue of entertainments and small talks than of the floors for commercial transactions. Other facilities with similar functions included water wells in every village, which doubled as a social place for women.

Household Husbandry

According to *A Brief History of the Dai Ethnic Group*, harnessing animal power for farming in the area dated back to the Eastern Han Dynasty more than one thousand years ago: Buffalos were raised mainly for farming, while oxen were raised mainly as beef cattle and pack cattle. Farming cattle were the main means of production in the area. According to historical records, during the R.O.C Period, renting out farming cattle could earn a decent amount of income. The ethnic survey data collected in the 1950s also showed that by renting farming cattle during the spring plowing, some wealthy families in the village could get as many as 30–50 piculs of rice in the autumn harvest (Editorial Committee of Five Series of Books on Ethnic Issues, 1983b). Cattle were raised by natural grazing. When the harvest season came to an end, some families had their cattle graze on the mountains, while others had their cattle run around and graze in intermontane basins. But cows were raised by 'being hung for grazing', i.e., a long bamboo pole is attached to a fixed wooden stake in the fields with abundant water sources and grass. One end of the bamboo pole is tied to the nose of a cow via a rope, but the other end is kept down with a stone counterweight. As a result, the rope tied to the nose of the cow is always hung in the air. In this way, on one hand, the cow is confined to a limited area centered on the stake, and on the other, this method avoids the possible winding of the rope with the stake while the cow is grazing back and forth around the stake and eventually prevents the cow from being unable to move on due to the shortened rope. According to the author's observation, "hung grazing" is a unique approach to cattle raising in Xishuangbanna.

Pig raising was the main sideline in household-based production, and almost all families in Jing village raised pigs. But usually, they didn't raise their pigs in pigsties. Perhaps at night, few families would confine their pigs downstairs within a makeshift enclosure made of bamboo fencing, but during the daytime, all the pigs were set free to range around and graze in the open fields. Their pig feeds were mainly mixtures of rice husks and green forages, such as wild vegetables or plantain stems. Having been boiled, the mixtures would be watered down with cold water before being given to pigs. The pigs were fed simply twice a day respectively in the morning and evening, and no much labor input was needed.

Every family had chickens and ducks. Camellia chickens, the most common species of small poultry in Menghai, were domesticated red jungle-fowls or hybridized creatures of good stock from pheasants and domestic chickens and were among the most popular dishes in the local cuisine. In addition to meeting their own family consumption, Dai women also sold their cooked chickens in the turf fair. Hence, camellia chickens were the most common and convenient source for Dai housewives to earn their pocket money.

Most families had dogs. Villagers kept dogs for home security, entertainment and hunting. With the plethora of rivers, streams and ditches around, fishing was, of course, also a common activity for men in Jing village. Before the founding of the People's Republic of China in 1949, no family did fish farming in the village. They simply went to catch wild fish. They made various fishing tools by themselves with bamboo strips, such as spindle cages, conical cages, cover pots and triangle-shaped fishing pockets. Besides their own consumption, women also processed the spare fish into a variety of finished foods for sale on the fair. For example, lemongrass-seasoned grilled fish cooked by Dai women has been a unique flavored dish in the Dai cuisine culture.

Thus, we can see that with an underdeveloped handicraft industry and commerce, all trades other than farming could only serve as "sidelines". Handcraft industry and household husbandry mainly satisfied the purpose of self-use, and to a lesser extent, sales for pocket money. Therefore, the Dai families didn't have any "business" for their children to carry forward, and their top "business" was farming, and this business didn't entail too much labor input.

Through the aforementioned panoramic scan based on both the historical literature revisit and anthropological fieldwork, we could make a summary of the economic life of the Dai people before 1950:

1. In terms of production mode, they were still in the typical stage of farming mainly based on manual labor, and acquired all their means of production and livelihood almost entirely from their lands, and applied extensive farming techniques. The handicraft industry, commerce and cultivation industry, in technical terms, had not yet taken shape. They sold excess produces, cash crops, handmade items, poultry and others to earn incomes, which were further exchanged for a small variety of living necessities and production instruments they couldn't produce by themselves, such as salt, iron pots, colored cloth, choppers, plows and plowshares. With fertile soils and a favorable climate, a small amount of labor input in the fields could earn them an abundant harvest of grains and other food sources, such as vegetables and fruits. They made clothes with coarse cloth spun and woven by themselves, built their houses through coordinated efforts from fellow villagers, and produced almost all their living utensils for self-use. By the living standards of a traditional agrarian society, they could be described as "enjoying ample food and clothing".
2. In terms of lifestyle, they lived a traditional farming life and no one could survive without agriculture. As the means of livelihood were easy to come by and sufficient to meet the needs of daily consumption and tribute payment, they had the blessing of leading a worry-free life in material terms. On the other hand, being devout believers in Southern Buddhism, they didn't crave for wealth, so their principal purpose of production is the "being sufficient is best", that is, they took the satisfaction of use-value as their only goal, and thus were willing to devote their spare time and wealth to offerings for the pursuit of their spiritual fulfillment.

By the living standards of a traditional agrarian society, the economic life described above had freed Dai families of the subsistence pressure from insufficient material goods. Therefore, when it came to the issue of fertility, they did not need to produce more children to help them obtain more subsistence materials or raise boys to supplement domestic labor, nor had they amassed a decent amount of wealth for their children to inherit. It is exactly in this sense that the author inferred that Dai people in a traditional agrarian society led a life "free of worry about feeding, clothing and sheltering themselves". They lived a relatively closed, simple and relaxing rural life on their land of abundance, and were content with their leisure, slow pace of life, and tranquility.

Let's get a clue about the fertility desires among the elderly in Jing village living in the mentioned-above living environment again from the face-to – face interviews with them.

By October 2008, there were 148 women born in or before 1950 in 417 households in Jing village, accounting for 35.49% of the total households in the village. The oldest interviewee was born in January 1906 (102 years old) and the youngest was born in September 1950 (58 years old). The retrospective statistics of lifetime births by age cohort (five-year interval) are shown in the following Table 5.4.

The only 11 women born before 1925 (in three age cohorts) had their births per capita of 4.5, 7.5 and 0. This sample was too small, failing to produce a statistically significant result, and thus was treated as individual cases. After excluding this factor, the average number of "natural births" and surviving births for the rest interviewees in Jing village stood respectively at 3.5 and 3.34, consistent with the statistical results of the survey in this village shown in the previous Chapter.

Now, let's look at the lifetime and surviving births of these female interviewees in these households(as shown in Table 5.5).

The fertility history statistics above showed that the women with three lifetime births in Jing village made up the largest proportion of all the interviewees at 72.97%, and the women with three surviving births also made up the largest proportion at 30.41%. The women with one to four lifetime births made up 72.97% of the total the interviewees, and the women with one to four surviving births made up 76.36%.

The statistical results for the women who have given birth to only girls (three or fewer) in their lifetime by the age cohort are listed as follows:

1. Twenty-two interviewees (households) gave birth to three or fewer girls during their lifetime, with a 100% girl's survival rate.
2. Six interviewees (households) gave birth to three girls during their lifetime, with four in the age cohort of 58–62 years old (1946–1950), one in the age cohort of 68–72 years old (1936–1940) and one in the age cohort of 73–77 years old (1931–1935).
3. Nine interviewees (households) give birth to two girls during their lifetime, with seven in the age cohort of 58–62 years old (1946–1950) and two in the age cohort of 73–77 years old (1931–1935).

Table 5.4: Fertility History Questionnaire for the Female Interviewees (Born in or before 1950) in Jing Village

Households	Age Cohort (Year)	Number of Lifetime Births (Persons)			Children who Survived till the Age of 15 (Persons)			Average Number of Births in a Household	Average Number of Surviving Births in a Household
		Total Births	M	F	Total Births	M	F		
33	1946–1950	81	29	52	78	27	51	2.45	2.36
21	1941–1945	64	35	29	62	34	28	3.05	2.95
25	1936–1940	92	47	45	89	46	43	3.68	3.56
29	1931–1935	120	61	59	117	59	58	4.14	4.03
29	1926–1930	122	54	68	112	48	64	4.21	3.86
6	1921–1925	27	15	12	24	13	11	4.5	4.0
2	1916–1920	15	7	8	10	5	5	7.5	5.0
2	1911–1915	9	2	7	9	2	7	4.5	4.5
1	1906–1910	4	1	3	2	0	2		
In total: 148 Households		534	251	283	503	234	269	3.61	3.39

Source: Results from the Author's Fieldwork.

4. Seven interviewees (households) gave birth to one girl during their lifetime with two in the age cohort of 58–62 years old (1946–1950), two in the age cohort of 68–72 years old (1936) -1940) and three in the age cohort of 78–82 years old (1926–1930).

These 22 interviewees (households) accounted for 15% of the total number of the surveyed households.

Interviews with the interviewees with three lifetime births in the age cohort of 58–62 years old (1946–1950) showed that the time of birth of the youngest among the last births was June 1977. When asked if they ever wanted a boy and whether it was the state family planning policy that led to their not having one more birth, they all gave a negative reply. The reply from Yu Fang (born 1937) among them was most representative: "Why do we have to have a boy? We

Table 5.5: Lifetime and Surviving Birth Statistics of the Female Interviewees (Born in or before 1950) in Jing Village

Female Interview-ees		148 Interviewees (Households)			
Age Cohort		58–102 Years Old			
Number of Lifetime Births	10 Births	1	Number of Children Who SurvivedTill the Age of 15 and Above		
	9 Births				
	8 Births	1		8 Surviving Births	1
	7 Births	6		7 Surviving Births	3
	6 Births	8		6 Surviving Births	7
	5 Births	22		5 Surviving Births	22
	4 Births	34		4 Surviving Births	31
	3 Births	41		3 Surviving Births	45
	2 Births	24		2 Surviving Births	26
	1 Birth	9		1 Surviving Birth	11
	0 birth	2		0 Surviving Birth	2

Source: Results from the Author's Fieldwork.

the Dai peoplehave never preferred sons. In our mind, having a daughter is better than having a son. Three kids are good enough. Why should we bother to have one more?" The doctrine that sons are to carry on the family line seems inconceivable and generally even ridiculous in the mind of the local people.

There were 10 interviewees with 0 lifetime birth or seven or more lifetime births in the village. I interviewed seven of them: two having 0 lifetime birth, three having seven lifetime births, one having eight lifetime births and one having 10 lifetime births, and gained the following results:

The two female interviewees (Yu Da, born in March 1927 and Yu Nen, born in February 1950) with 0 lifetime birth were infertile throughout their lifetime. Yu Da couldn't recall the exact time of marriage but only knew that she still had not got pregnant into about five years of her marriage. With no result from treatment, she finally adopted a boy. Yu Nen got married in 1969 and recalled, "I got pregnant once, but miscarried. After an illness, I had never got pregnant anymore. During that period, all things seemed to be in a hubbub: City dwellers had meetings all day long, and the same in our village, so I was in no mood to see a doctor and the days went on like this." According to the records in *The Annals of Menghai County* and recalls from elder people in the village, the period from late 1968 to the entire 1970s was an eventful age in Menghai: In the beginning, the Revolutionary Committee of Menghai County composed of soldiers, cadres and representatives of the masses was set up in September 1968; next, there were various campaigns: the "taking sides" in January 1969, the "fighting (selfishness), "repudiating (revisionism) and reforming (feudalism)", the "purifying the class ranks", the "four clampdowns" (combating counter-revolutionary sabotage, corruption, profiteering and extravagance) in governmental agencies, and the "political border defense" in rural areas, the "rural reeducation" for junior high school graduates in 1966, 1967 and 1968, the "witch-hunting" campaign across the county (clamping down on landlords, richer farmers, reactionaries, evil-doers and rightists). In addition, there were also various natural disasters: The earthquake, storms and frost respectively in March, April and December 1973 played huge havoc with the county, with hundreds of cattle frozen to death, early rice seedlings seriously damaged, all the 4,873 *mu* of cinchuna seedlings ruined, and tea bushes, bamboo forests, fruit trees and other crops damaged to varying degrees, the county-wide epidemic in March 1975 led to 11 deaths in 11,496 cases, and the continuous rains in July the same year caused a flood disaster, with more than 24,000 *mu* of paddy fields and roads in intermontane basins inundated and many bridges and culverts destroyed. The "anti-rightist overturning movement" was launched in February 1976, and the "Gang of Four" was crushed in October the same year. Later, wrong or false convictions were reexamined in 1978, and a large number of educated youths "sent down to rural areas for reeducation" returned to their home cities in 1979 such as Beijing, Shanghai, Sichuan and Kunming. In early 1980, the epidemics of porcine streptococcal disease and swine fever as a result of imported commodities led to the death of more than 30,000 pigs across the county and also huge losses to all the families in the village. All these events described above were consistent with Yu Nen's account. The questions we raised and the answers Yu Da and Yu Nen gave were listed as follows:

The question: "Were there any gossips about you not having children?" The reply: "No. To have or not have a child is your own business. No one else cares. Of course, as far as myself is concerned, I still wanted to have a child. Yet for such a thing, there was nothing I can do about it." The question: "Did you ever think about what to do with the farming fields without children when you are too old?" The reply: "To be sure, I had thought of that, but it doesn't matter. When I am too old to work in the fields, I will quit. This situation is also true for many others." Yu Da's husband had passed away and she then lived with her adopted son. Her life was no different from that of others. Leaving Yu Da's house, I turned to ask Yu Nen, who was accompanying me to the interview, whether or not Yu Da's adopted son treated her as well as her biological son would. Having replied "He treated the old lady very well!", Yu Nen immediately asked me, "Why did you ask such a question? Is there, do you think, any difference between an adopted son and a biological one?" Hearing my explanations about the purpose of my question and the concepts of "raising sons as source of support in old age" and "the continuation of the family line" popular among the Han people, Yu Nen said, "We the Dai people don't have such ideas as these. You the Han people have too many considerations."

Three interviewees had given seven births throughout their lifetime. The specific situation of each interviewee is described as below.

Yu Nan was born in February 1930, got married at the age of 23, and suffered some hearing impairment in both ears at the time of the interview. According to the recollections of herself and her grandson, she had given birth to four sons and three daughters, and her first and third children died young. Due to the lack of experience in taking care of babies when she was young, her first child died before turning one, and her third child died from an illness at three years old.

Yu Meng was born in January 1930 and married at the age of 21. She was a very optimistic old lady. When asked why she had more children than others, she joked with a smile, "I saw nothing bad about it (having more kids). When I got it (got pregnant), I had to give birth. Besides, since you got it in there (being pregnant), you had to find a place out for it (meaning that once a woman was pregnant, she had no other choice but to give birth to the baby since there were no way to terminate a pregnancy, such as induced abortion, at that time)."

Yu Guanghan was born in September 1940, and her husband Yan Xiang, three years older than her, was born in February 1937. He is a very joke-loving

"Botao". The couple gave birth to three sons and four daughters, all surviving and grown-up. When asked about their experience of raising children, they answered, "The main feeling is the more kids you have, the more tired you feel. It is not that you couldn't afford to feed and clothe them, but that it eats into your free time for attending some events, for example, Doing-the-Dan (religious offerings)[26] or Ganbai (meaning 'going to a fair', the biggest event during the Water-splashing Festival where people buy and sell goods). And you will also have less time for doing the farming in the fields." While looking back at the situation of his wife taking care of their children, Yan Xiang said that whenever seeing other men playing around, he also very much wanted to, but looking back to see his wife so busy with the kids, he would feel a little embarrassed to utter out his attempt but could only give it up. It was, indeed, an itching experience!"

I asked Yan Xiang teasingly, "Did you regret having too many kids and having less free time to fool around?" He whispered with a sly smile, "Yes. It's all my own fault. I hadn't controlled myself. Now that it is so (having too many kids), there's no way out of it (to escape from the trouble of taking care of them)! I have to close my eyes and stay at home!" (Without effective contraception measures, he has too many children and thus has less free time and missed the chance to fool around with pretty girls. He has to be confined at home!).

Yujin was born in October 1939 and had eight children from her two marriages. She first got married at 20 years old and gave birth to two sons and two daughters with her former husband. Later, she married Yan Han, and also had two sons and two daughters with him. Yan Han, her current husband, was three years younger than her and was born in January 1942.

Yu Xiang, born in December 1917, had given birth to 10 children all her life, but only six children survived. When I interviewed her, I found that she had no clear memory of her past. It was not easy to dialogue with her directly, and the interview was completed with the help of her husband and granddaughter, who happened to be at home at the time. In addition, my guide, a native in Jing village, also knew something about her family. Based on their stories, I learned that Yu Xiang had given birth to four sons and six daughters all her life, but only three sons and three females survived. The old lady lived with her youngest son and her other children often came over to visit her. She seemed to be in good health and was said to often help her children with some housework in the kitchen. She

26 Doing the Dan is a special term for any Southern Buddhism-related religious events among the Dai people, also see the detailed description later.

also made a stroll and attended religious events at the Buddhist temple during the Vassa (the Yuanjiu period).[27] In the morning the author met her at her house – it happened to be a day of Ganbai (meaning "going to a fair", the biggest event during the Water-splashing Festival where people buy and sell goods) in the village, the old lady was getting charcoal ready for sale on the fair downstairs. It seemed to us that she lived a very comfortable life.

The fertility history of Mr. Dao's family, with which the author lived during his fieldwork, was described as follows:

The First Generation:

Mr. Dao's parents gave birth to five children, and Mr. Dao himself, the third child in the family, was born in 1933. He enrolled at a Han school in Menghai at eight years old and dropped out two years later (1943) when the school was shut down amid the bombing of Menghai by Japanese planes. Later, he stayed at a Buddhist temple as a monk until the Great Leap Forward Campaign in 1957, when he was forced to resume secular life. Further later, he had worked at the Cultural Center of Menghai County from October 1958 until his retirement in 1993. His wife Yu Xiangye was born in 1940 and was the youngest of four siblings.

The Second Generation:

Mr. Dao and Yu Xiangye gave birth to five children throughout their lifetime and four of them survived. The first child, born in 1960, was a boy and the others were all girls. Their youngest daughter was born in 1973, and Yu Xiangye went through the tubal ligation surgery in 1975.

It was well into the era of family planning when their four children got married. Since getting married in 1982, their son had lived with their daughter-in-law in Manguan village, four kilometers away from Jing village. Their second daughter settled down in Jing village with her husband and lived less than 200 meters away from Mr. Dao's house. Their third daughter married a Han soldier

27 Vassa (the Yuanjiu Period) is the tropical rainy season when the Indian Ocean monsoon blows, and falls within the three-month period from April 16 to July 15 in the Chinese lunar calendar (September 15 to December 15 in the Dai calendar) in Xishuangbanna in southern China. According to the Buddhist sutras: Vinaya and Mahavagga, monks and nuns must stay in peace at temples during the period so as to sit in meditation, practice Buddhism and avoid going out and trampling on life. No monks and nuns should venture out of their temples except for special reasons. Villagers as laymen also attend preaching sessions at Buddhist temples during the rainy season unsuitable for travel. Hence, Vassa is an important season in southern Buddhism. See also Song Lidao, *Tradition and Modernity: The Changing World of Southern Buddhism [M]* (Beijing: China Social Sciences Press, 2002), 51.

and then lived in Wenshan County, Yunnan Province, and their fourth daughter married and lived with her husband three kilometers away from Jing village.

The Third Generation:

Mr. Dao's first son and daughter-in-law had given birth twice but only one child survived. Their first child was a daughter, born in 1983, and their second was a son, born in 1986. Mr. Dao's daughter-in-law received the tubal ligation surgery one week after the birth of her son, who died of illness a full month after he was born. Mr. Dao's second daughter and son-in-law gave birth to one boy. Mr. Dao's third daughter and fourth daughter each gave birth to one girl.

The Fourth Generation:

Mr. Dao's granddaughter married a local Han lad in 2003 and gave birth to a girl in 2004, and received the tubal ligation surgery just one week after the girl was born. Mr. Dao's grandson got married in 2007 and hadn't yet given birth to any child. Mr. Dao's third and fourth granddaughters both have not got married.

The Fifth Generation:

Mr. Dao had only one great-granddaughter by the time of the interview.

In 2004, Mr. Dao's first son died of illness, and the daughter-in-law moved from Manguan village to Jing village to live with Mr. Dao. On various occasions, the author lived with Mr. Dao's family, celebrating Dai festivals with them. On these public holidays, Mr. Dao's children and grandchildren would come over to see him and his wife.

Whenever grandchildren and great-grandchildren came back, there would be a big dinner. It was a very lively scene. When the night was in, they all went back to their respective homes, never staying at Mr. Dao's house, albeit there was enough room for them.

Figure 5.1 is the "family tree" showing the reproductive history of the Dao family.

During the stay at Mr. Dao's family, I (the author) asked him if he ever thought having more children would be better for him in the future. He replied, "It wouldn't be better. It is too tiring to have more children. So, Mietao (Yu Xiangye)[28] didn't wish to have too many kids." I also asked Mietao on a separate occasion, "Did Yujin (her fourth daughter) wish to have another child?" She stared at me and said, "Nonsense. Why did she wish to have one more?" (implying that she got pregnant unexpectedly, and didn't wish to have any more). I asked again, "Why did she receive the tubal ligation surgery as late as in 1975?" (Yu

28 Mietao and Botao are respectively the popular terms for middle-aged and elder Dai ladies and men.

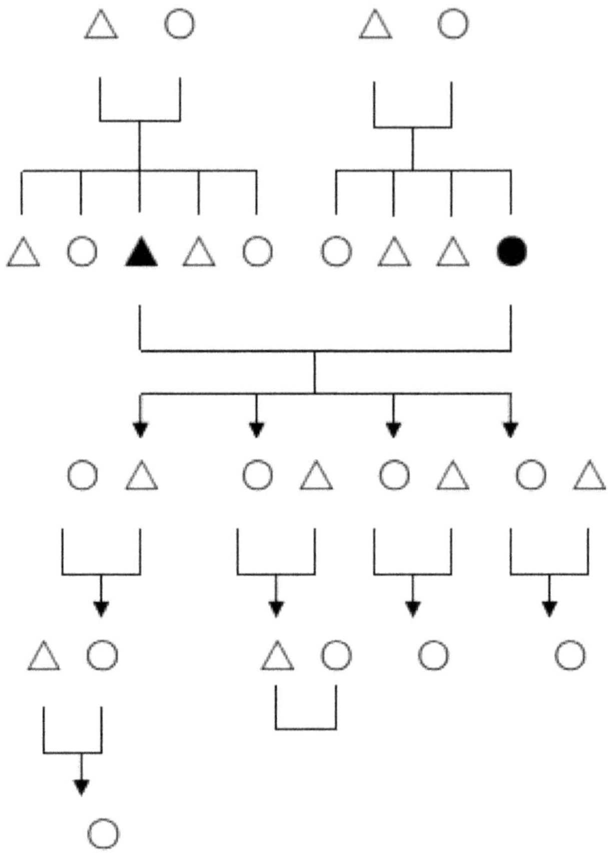

Figure 5.1 Genogram of Mr. Dao's family
△: Male ○: Female ▲: Male Interviewee ●: Female Interviewee
▲: male interviewee; ●: female interviewee;
△: male; ○: female;
■: male who died before turning 15; ★: female who died before turning 15;
□: a pregnancy with unknown sex of the fetus;
The sex of those born within each generation are listed in descending order of age, from left to right.

Xiangye went through the surgery at 35 years old). She answered, "They asked her to receive the surgery, so she didn't think too much about it. And she herself also held that once ligated, she would no longer be worried about unplanned pregnancy once again in future." I asked, "Were the 'they' that you just referred to the family planning officials?" She replied, "No. I meant that 'they' were a cohort.[29] Someone in the cohort suggested the surgery. So, all the people in the cohort went through it". I asked, "How many people are there in a cohort?" She replied: "Six." I asked, "Did all the people in the cohort do anything together?" She replied, "Yes. It is supposed to be so. But they couldn't do it for all of them (implying that the hospital couldn't do the surgical ligation for all the women in a cohort at the same time), so they went through the surgery separately".

As for the inquiry about how many children there are usually in a Dai family, she said,

> Most of our families have three or four children, but there are also a few women having seven or eight babies in her lifetime. No one will gossip about such a thing as we believe that she is meant to have so many children. There are some folk methods of controlling birth for women if they already have two to three kids and don't wish to have more. For example, they can take some herbal medicines. But only a few women engage in proactive birth control, and most people choose to not intervene in nature. So how did they manage to let nature take its course and have fewer children during nearly 30 years of reproductive history? Generally speaking, couples who already have kids choose to abstain, for example, by sleeping separately, especially when their children are old enough to help with housework. So, though there is much love and respect for each other, it is commonplace for the Dai couples above the age of 40 years old to sleep at night on separate beds. It is bad to succumb to one's carnal desires, which is, in their minds, part of their belief in Buddhism and observance of Buddhist teaching. They are content with having had children, and don't care much about such things as whether their children are boys or girls or whether a man should consolidate his family status in a village by having more children.

The facts cited by the old lady were also validated in Mangang village in Menghai County:

> When talking about the marriage of their children, the Dai villagers never use such expressions as "Qu" (a man taking in a wife) or "Jia" (a woman being given to a husband) but always use the phrase "Shangmen" (joining a family) to cover both the cases. This variation in the expression is less about their language habits, but more about their psychological tendency: The Dai people have no significant preference for males to females. Hence, some tragic incidents in

29 The cohort is a quantifier commonly used by locals, meaning a team or a group of peers. The Dai people would form various cohorts by the age cohort for various daily events. Members in a cohort would do things together, for example, going to a fair, doing religious donations and doing some shopping.

> other regions or ethnic groups, such as aborting, drowning, or abandoning female infants, had never happened in Mangang village and were also incomprehensible to the Dai communities here.
>
> Most women in Mangang village gave only two births. In 1998, out of the 127 married women of childbearing age, 34 had one child, 81 had two children, and three had multiple children (three children and above). The birth control methods for the women were mostly tubal ligation and medication. According to 1998 statistics, 80 out of the 81 women with two children had gone through the tubal ligation surgery, two out of the three women with multiple children had done it, and 16 out of the 34 women with only one child had even also done it (Zhang, 2001a).

According to historical records and surveys, the Dai infants had suffered a higher mortality rate (Jiang, 1983b), so the saying "a smaller population" didn't indicate Dai people had a lower birth rate of infants. According to the author's survey, the fact that the interviewees had multiple births didn't indicate that the Dai people preferred to have multiple births in their fertility behavior. The true cause behind their multiple births was generally that without reliable and convenient guidance on birth control techniques, they had to give more births in the case of an unplanned pregnancy. In their words, "There is no way of avoiding it (giving birth). Get it, and then you have to accept it (once being conceived with a baby, you will have no other choice but to give birth to it." This case could be verified by their attitude towards the availability of contraceptives: Soon after the government's promotion campaigns on health and contraception were launched and the technology supports provided, most of them learned how to use various birth control devices. In the mid to late 1970s, when the tubal ligation surgery was successfully introduced at the People's Hospital of Menghai County, a considerable number of women of child bearing age, including Yu Xiangye of 35 years old at the time, underwent the surgery. This fact might as well be convincing evidence that historically, the Dai people had no desire to have excess births.

Section 2 Traditional Family Structure in Dai Society

The family structure is directly related to fertility behavior. It is the bond between various relationships among family members, including family relationships, marital relations, property relations, etc., and it usually plays a vital role in realizing various functions, such as carrying on the family line, rearing the young and supporting the old. In addition, it is also an outward expression of different lifestyles. But in the organizational structure of the Dai families, there are no surnames or clans. This unique pattern of family structure has a strong influence on the fertility behavior of the Dai people.

Family Population Composition

The Dai family structure features small monogamous families. In this family system, once having come of age and got married, children will move out of their original families and set up their own ones. Mr. Li Fuyi said, "Dai parents are very laissez-faire with their children, seldom punishing them, and usually live separately from their grown-up children" (Li, 1955c). It is very rare for married children to live in the same bamboo house with their parents, and brothers and sisters-in-law from one family also never share a household. If a family has several children, all the older children, once married, will usually move out of their original family and set up their own ones, and the youngest son or daughter will stay to live with the parents and is responsible for supporting them in their advanced years. There are also cases where all the grown-up children set up their own families, live separately from their parents and lead their own life. So, it is also very common for elderly widows or widowers to live alone, but there is not the case of "multiple generations living under one roof" as popular in inland regions on the Chinese mainland.

According to Tao Yunkui, "Baiyi (Dai) families are the so-called nuclear families known to us today, usually consisting of one couple and their unmarried children."

> Ordinary persons are mostly monogamous, but polygamy was not prohibited. It was not uncommon for an ordinary man to join his bride's family. But joining one's bride's family doesn't mean living in his father-in-law's house. Instead, the son-in-law would live in a separate house near his father-in-law's and farm the land acquired in the name of his father-in-law's family from the local chieftain.
>
> Some men stay throughout their lifetime with their brides' families, while others do so just some years, and then go back with their wives to live near their own parents' houses. The Dai people are prone to having an independent family, living near either their parents' houses or their parents-in-laws' houses. What makes Dai's 'joining the bride's family' special is that the groom plows his parents-in-law's land to serve the bride's original family (Tao, 1948).

And according to Mr. Li Jinghan,

> Though polygamy or concubinage is allowed in the Baiyi (Dai) society, most ordinary people are monogamous and have a small family system. Apart from Mangshi with a strong Han cultural exposure, where some married children still live with their parents and brothers, in the Dai society, children usually leave their parents' families and live elsewhere after marriage, and there are few cases of mothers-in-law, daughters-in-law and sisters-in-law living under the same roof. However, men living with their mothers-in-law are more common than with their own parents, and widows are also more likely to live on their own than to live with their parents-in-law (Li, 1940a).

To sum up, the Dai families have the following three features in the population structure:

1. The monogamous small family system is adopted. Usually, there are only two generations consisting of parents and unmarried children in a family. Married children leave their parents and set up independent families and live separately from their parents. Parents, grown-up children, grown-up siblings (and sisters/brothers-in-law) rarely live together.
2. When childless married children live with their parents, it is usually the case where husbands live with their parents-in-law, i.e. being matrilocal sons-in-law commonly known to the Han society. Once having their own children, they will move out of their parents-in-law's houses, and set up their own families or live separately near their parents-in-law's houses. The concept "living with" in the Dai society is linked to "bearing the burden of living", and is not the same as that in the Han society on inland regions on the Chinese mainland.
3. The widows either remarry or set up their new families but never live with the siblings of their deceased spouses.

According to the surveys by the author, in Jing village, there were several registered households with widowed elderly men or women. Most of them lived in and were taken care of by Buddhist temples, while others chose to live at home. In the latter case, their children, relatives or neighbors would regularly pay them a visit, bringing necessities, helping with housework or just having small talks with them. During the day, these widowed persons chatted, cooked and dined with their visitors just like a family, and also made a stroll in the village or paid a visit to their children or relatives at their home, but in the evening, they usually stayed alone in their own houses. In a word, the Dai families had simpler population compositions. Parents and their children both lived independently, and they also preferred a quiet life. Even nowadays, even though their grown-up children have larger tile-roofed houses and enough room for them to live in, it is very common for old couples to live separately in their own Dai houses.

This nuclear family-centered pattern of living has low correlations with the number of children in a family. Living a relatively independent life, parents neither will be lonely with fewer children nor lively with more children. The custom of having a matrilocal son or a daughter to support old-age parents prevents a preference for boys over girls and the conception that only sons are the life support in parents' advanced years.

The survey in Mangang village also showed that in the families either with matrilocal sons-in-law or with uxirolocal daughters-in-law and in either mixed or independent families, the elderly parents could have a decent life, which means, "the elderly were supported and looked after properly". In their mind, both sons and daughters may stay behind to take care of their parents, and matrical sons-in-law have almost the same status as that of sons. The children living at home with their parents are caregivers for the elderly. Parents know who is taking care of them, and children also know who is responsible for taking care of their parents (Zhang, 2001b).

Marriage Customs

The marriage customs of the Dai people were recorded in historical documents as follows:

> The *Legends of Ethnic Minorities in China* says,
>
> They don't care much about virginity, and it is also very rare to get engaged and married through matchmakers. Mature girls (14–16 years old) sing in antiphonal style with boys (16–18 years old), finding out and getting engaged as husband and wife with their loves. Girls are often led into the boys' families, having their feet washed by the boys' mothers, and then sent back a few days later. Only by this time do boys propose to girls through matchmakers, offering sheep, wine, gem and silky cloth as the betrothal gifts to girls' parents (Jiang, 1983c).

The Annals of the Twelve Bannas show the following descriptions: "The Baiyi (Dai) people marry young, largely at 15 or 16 years old. A Baiyi (Dai) man may take in a wife ('Qu' in Chinese), and a woman also may take in a husband. Besides, their marriage is not constrained by seniority in the family or clan hierarchy and blood lineage". "The nobles may have more than one wife, but ordinary people can't." "Husbands (after marriage) more often than join and live with their brides' families, and girls are more valued than boys" "The Baiyi (Dai) people (except the nobles) enjoy absolute freedom in marriage and see much more divorces. Whenever unsatisfied with their relationship, either husband or wife may ask for estrangement or divorcement and is fairly treated by the society, and vice versa (as the result, divorcement, reunion, or remarriage are commonplaces to them)" (Li, 1955d).

Mr. Yao Hesheng gave another description:

> The marriage of the common people is completely the result of free love . . . The ball-throwing game (choose a husband) during the New Year festival and the yarn-spinning sessions on winter nights are usually the triggers behind many happy marriages. Even local fairs also serve as the venues for romantic affairs. On market days, a majority of fair-goers are young women. They take advantage of these occasions to meet more people and perhaps meet their desirable loves by chance. Here, the Platonic love is unknown to them.

"The Dai people are strictly monogamous. Ordinary people are not legally forbidden to take concubines. That is, as long as having sufficient conditions and money, they may have as many women as they like. But in reality, there are many restrictions, and divorcement is also easy and simple."

"In many ethnic groups, most people have their sex life since the time of marriage and are restricted by marriage. But the sex life of the Dai people is not constrained by marriage. They have had a rich sexual experience even before marriage. In fact, they have already been 'married' persons by their first marriage, and often have their own romantic lives in secret" (Yao, 1990).

According to historical documents, the Dai society was divided based on its social and political structure into two classes: civilians and aristocrats represented by chieftains. In terms of marriage, it was also divided into two intermarriage groups. In the civilian class, the monogamous small family system was adopted, in which young men and women had the freedom to fall in love and choose their spouses, but have to get engaged through a matchmaker. In the aristocratic class, polygamy was acceptable and a man may have more than one wife. However, his principal wife (first legal wife) must be from his own intermarriage group, while his concubines were not subject to this restriction.

To sum up, the Dai marriage customs have the following features:

1. Free love and no interference from parents: Aristocrats like chieftains, who had to take into account the social status of their potential spouses,

usually had to marry the partners chosen by their parents. But common persons enjoyed a high degree of freedom in love and marriage. Young men and women could love each other freely and establish their relationships. Just as the saying goes, "Marriage is not arranged by parents, and proposals not made through matchmakers. As long as loving each other, they may marry freely". Mr. Jiang Yingliang said,

> Being lively by nature and living in a free social climate, young men and women interact without restraint, and various events, such as religious gatherings, festivals, weddings, funerals, public/private banquets and others, present desirable occasions for them to meet and fall in love with each other. Once having got acquainted with each other on such occasions, they will walk arm in arm and sing together after sunset, murmuring their mutual love (Jiang, *The Life and Culture of the Dai Ethnic Group,* 1950h).

2. Early marriage and childbearing and no gender preference. Most young men and women marry at the age of 16 years old or so and become parents around 18 years old. They have no gender preference and are welcome to have either boys or girls. They always rear their kids on a loose rein, and never force them to do what they do not want to do.
3. Freedom of marriage and high popularity of men living with parents-in-law. If they decide to get married, men and women from the common class in free love will consult with their parents about marriage issues, such as betrothal gifts and ceremonies, and are, in most cases, approved by their parents. Then, a bride's family throws a wedding banquet, and friends and relatives will come over, congratulating the bride on taking in the matrilocal son-in-law. In individual cases, wedding banquets are prepared by a bridegroom's family, and the bride is escorted to live in the groom's family.
4. Freedom of divorce and freedom from social discrimination. Like the freedom of marriage, they also enjoy the freedom of divorce. Not unsatisfied with the relationship, either party may ask for a divorce and will get divorced only with approval from the village chief. All the issues, such as children's upbringing and family property division, are decided by the spouses through consultation. Divorcees are free of any criticism or discrimination and any barrier to remarriage.
5. Most marriages are in the Dai people, i.e. the intra-ethnic marriages, but there are also a few marriages with the Han people.

6. Social class-based marriage institution and concubinage. Aristocrats, like chieftains, only marry each other, and civilians also only marry civilians. However, this marriage institution is limited to the marriages between aristocrats and their first legal wives and doesn't extend to the concubinage. For example, chieftains are allowed to take in concubines or assistant wives, whose social class is not subject to these restrictions.

Polygamy is commonplace in the aristocratic class while sporadic among the civilian class.

The survey results in Jing village and Mangang village were roughly consistent with the mentioned-above descriptions except for the absence of conspicuous early marriage and parentage of women in Jing village. Regarding this phenomenon, Mr. Dao Shuren, the last chieftain of Menghai (taking office in 1944) explained to me, "Early marriage and parentage were just the latest developments over the recent five to six decades among the Dai people. Going back as recently as in the generations of my parents or grandparents, they all got married after 20 years old." Out of the five women I surveyed who gave no fewer than seven births throughout their lifetime, the earliest one married at 18 years old, while the latest at 24.

As for the polygamy among the aristocratic class, Mr. Dao said,

> My father Dao Liangchen was born in 1903 and inherited the title of nobility as Menghai Chieftain at 16 years old. He was in office for 24 years and died at 41 years old (1944). He married four Dai wives and had six children: three boys and three girls. But he was a special case as he happened to be in times of radical social changes. Having had been to Japan and Yangon, Myanmar as a young man, he had been too much exposed to foreign cultures, and so he was just a special case. But my grandparents were monogamous. In fact, most of the Dai people are monogamous, and only a very few men have multiple wives, which are just exceptions. Yet, we also have no explicit regulations against polygamy. Whether a man has one or more than one wife depends completely on his own situation, and has not much to do with his financial position. Many wealthy men have only one wife. This reality, in general, might have something to do with Buddhism. Buddhism preaches that a man should be in peace. Monogamy is conducive to peace while having two wives in your family is hard for you to lead a peaceful life. That is common sense to us all. The men who marry several wives are usually the fun-loving ones, absent often from home, or on the go all the time. When I was a kid, polygamous men would be made fun of as an example of troublesome family relationships.

When it comes to the number of children in Mr. Dao Shuren's family, he said, in the paternal line, his father was one of six children (three males and three females) born of the same parents, while in the maternal line, his mother was among the four siblings (two males and two females) born of the same parents. Mr. Dao himself was one of six children (three males and three females) from the same father and different mothers.

In the view of the author, the distinct features of the marriage customs among the Dai people\ might be summed up as follows: freedom of love, marriage, divorce and remarriage; gender equality; popularity of monogamy together with sporadic cases of polygamy.

These "liberal" marriage customs led to "liberal" fertility behavior, such as early marriage, early childbearing, multiple marriages, and multiple births (as was the case with Yujin in Jing village, who had eight children) but not gender preference (boys or girls are equally welcome), freedom of divorce and remarriage led to more single-parent or mixed families, and the customs of the husband living with the wife's family discouraged the wife from cementing her own position in the family by giving birth to a son, and thus contributed to a harmonious relationship between mother-in-law and daughter-in-law.

Surnames and Names

According to historical records, before the Yuan Dynasty, the Dai persons had no surnames (family names) but only names (personal names), and a person often had more than one personal name. In most cases, with the change in his/her status, a person's personal name is also changed based on certain rules. A man has at least four personal names in his life: infant name, monastic name, secularized name and fatherhood name, and some even have an official name. A woman has at least two personal names in her life: infant name and motherhood name. The rules for name changes in various periods of a man's life are introduced as follows:

1. Infant name: A newborn baby must be named by the chief monk from a Buddhist temple or a secularized monk: "Kanglang", and he will use this infant name until being enrolled at a Buddhist temple as a young monk.
2. Monastic name: At the age of six or seven or at latest ten years old, a Dai boy must be sent to a Buddhist temple to be a young monk for several years and is given a monastic name by the chief monk at the Buddhist temple. At this time, his infant name is replaced by the monastic name.

3. Secularized name: After a few years as a monk at a Buddhist temple, while few boys choose to remain as monks throughout their lifetime at the temple, most of them are secularized to be a layman. As a layman, they can marry and have children. Once secularized, they use their secularized names instead of their monastic names.
4. Fatherhood name: Once becoming a father, a man doesn't use his secularized name any longer. Instead, he is called by a unique fatherhood name. For example, if a child is called "Yan Kang", he is accordingly called Bo Yankang, meaning Yan Kang's father.
5. Official name: A man with strong ability and authority in a village may be a headman or village leader, and even hold a position at Pacification Superintendent's Office. He takes the title of his official position as his personal name: his official name. His official name changes with his official position.

Unable to be a young monk at a Buddhist temple or a headman or a village leader in her village, and also unlikely to hold a position at Pacification Superintendent's Office, a Dai woman has no monastic name, secularized name, or official name but just two names all her life: the infant name and then the motherhood name after her marriage and motherhood.

Mr. Li Fuyi described surnames and names of the Dai people in Xishuangbanna as follows:

> The Dai people in the twelve bannas have only names but no surnames. Their names change with their life stages as an infant, a monk, a layman, a father and an official. That is to say, they have different names for different life stages and always change their names into the next ones as shifting into the next life stage. Once having children, they are named after their first child, regardless of being a son or daughter, born by the principal wife instead of a concubine. For example, if the first child is a son named Aijin, the father is accordingly named Bo Aijin and the mother Mie Aijin; and if the first child is a daughter named Yujiao, the father is accordingly named Bo Yujiao and the mother Mie Yujiao. The word Bo or Mie in their names means respectively the father or mother. Once becoming an official, a man is named after his official title, namely taking the official name as his personal name (Li, 1955e).

This naming method gives rise to the case of the same name for various men. Therefore, a man differentiates from his namesakes by adding his village name before his name. The namesakes in the same village add their respective features before their names for identification. Hence, there are such names as "Tall Yan Zhen" and "Fat Yan Kang". Mr. Li Fuyi also said, "The Dai people have no surname and many persons have the same or similar names. So, they differentiate from their namesakes by adding their residential places or individual features such as age and body shape" (Li, 1955f).

This practice has died hard up till today, the author himself knew two men named Yan Xiangzai in Jinghong, one the current Director at the Bureau of Ethnic & Religious Affairs of Xishuangbanna Prefecture, who lives in downtown Jinghong Municipality and the other the boss of a township enterprise, who lives in Gasa Township. The two men are on good terms, keep in touch with each other, and are called by locals "Jinghong Yan Xiangzai" and "Gasa Yan Xiangzai" respectively. Another example is that the mentioned-above last Chieftain of Menghai (his Han ethnic name was Dao Shuren) had the same name Zhao Xiangmeng as Mr. Shixun (the last Chieftain of Xishuangbanna)'s father (his Han name was Dao Dongting), and was addressed by locals as Zhao Xiangmeng Menghai to show the difference.

In the Yuan Dynasty, the Imperial Court (the Central Government) of China began to tighten control over Xishuangbanna by granting the surname "Dao" (the Chinese character刀) to local leaders, and the aristocrats represented by chieftains had since taken "Dao" as their surname. According to the genealogy book of the Pacification Superintendent of Cheli in Xishuangbanna,

> His ancestors of earlier four generations all had no surname but only their names: Bazhen, Taokangleng, Taoping and Taolongjianzai. His ancestor of the earlier fifth generation was called Dao Liangnong, and a note specially attached under the name Dao Liangnong reads, 'The surname Dao was granted by the Imperial Court'. In terms of the time sequence, Dao Liangnong succeeded to the hereditary title in the 619th year in the Dai Calendar, namely, the fifth year of the Reign of Emperor Lizong in the Southern Song Dynasty (also the 1257 AD). By that time, Kublai Khan, the first emperor of the Yuan Dynasty, had already conquered the Kingdom of Dali and ruled the Yunnan region. The 'Imperial Court' in the note attached under Dao Liangnong could be deduced to be some emperor of the Yuan Dynasty. Therefore, the surname should be granted by the Imperial Court of the Yuan Dynasty. Historical records also showed that surname-granting to people in the southwest border areas in China began in the Yuan Dynasty. As thus, it could be inferred that the Dai people began to have surnames in the early Yuan Dynasty (Jiang, *The Life and Culture of the Dai Ethnic Group,* 1950i).

However, the author found during his survey at Jing village that locals didn't agree with this viewpoint. For this reason, the author paid a special visit to Mr. Dao Shuren and was given the following explanations:

> It was said in historical literature that the surname Dao was granted to the Dai people by the Imperial Court of the Yuan Dynasty. But we the Dai people didn't believe in such rumors. The folklore goes that a Dai man paid his tribute to the emperor and was inquired of his (full) name. He replied, 'My name is Dao ××'. The minute-taker couldn't figure out the right Chinese character for the pronunciation 'Dao', and thus recorded his name down as 'Dao X X'. This episode was later rumored to be the surname granting by the monarch. In some books from the Ming Dynasty, the surname for Dai people was also recorded as 'Dao ××'. In fact, the surname 'Dao' was truly derived in the phonetic transcription from the voice 'Dao' (the second tone in Pinyin – the Chinese phonetic system) and is also written as 陶 or 匋 in the Zhuang ethnic dialects. Dao means an aristocrat in Laos, and an elderly man or an aristocrat across Xishuangbanna, China, to both the Dai and Zhuang ethnic peoples. In modern Chinese, Dao is written as 陶 and means an elderly or a senior. In ancient ages, when there were no official titles, elderly or senior men were principals and had the greatest authority and prestige, and thus were known as Taogai (陶丐). The surname Dao first appeared in the genealogy book of the Pacification Superintendent but didn't have a very long history. Around that time, the Bureaucratizing-Native-Officers movement was in full swing across ethnic minority regions adjacent to the Han communities on the Chinese mainland, so it could be inferred that the emergence of the surname Dao might be the result of increased exposure to the Han culture. Anyway, in the Dai folklore, there is no legend that the emperor granted the surname Dao to them. As for the word Zhao, it didn't refer to officials but owners. For example, if you were the owner of a stall selling goods, you would be known as Zhaohuang, and if you were the owner of a house, you would be known as Zhaolun. Therefore, 'Zhao' isn't an official but a 'master', meaning the man whose words count for something, i.e. the one who has the final say.

Even so, the tale of "Imperial Court Granting the Surname Dao" mentioned in historical literature might be of more or less significance to the aristocratic class represented by chieftains, but everything remained business as usual with the man in the street still having no surname.

Even nowadays, this is still the case in Jing village and Mangang village. As for the reason why Dai people have no surname, the following interpretation from Mr. Dao Shuren might shed some light:

> Not just in bannas in China, it was also true of Dai people in Thailand, who as well used to have no surname. The concept of surnames didn't exist in Thailand until the Fifth King, who reigned not more than 200 years ago and sent a lot of people to study in the West. It was under the influence of a Western culture that surnames had emerged and had been gradually embraced. Unlike the Han ethnic majority who take the first word in their father's name as their surnames, for example, in the cases of Zhang's or Li's, the Thai people added the last word in their grandfather's or father's name to their names to get their full names, and this naming method was simply exclusive to aristocrats with genealogies. Even nowadays, common people in Thailand still have no surnames just as they did in the past. The case is the same here in our bannas in China, also in Laos, Myanmar and the Assam state of India. In all these regions, it is irrelevant to talking about surnames.

As the practice of "just names but no surnames" has gone on and on, Dai people have no concept of "continuing their family lines" or "extending their genealogical books". They are at a loss about such ideas in the Han society as male descendants carrying on family lineages and contributing to booming clans, and naturally won't be swayed by the propensity of the male preference in their fertility behavior.

Family and Kinship Relationship

Dai people have very harmonious family relationships, and such cases as quarrels between husband and wife, punishments of children, and ill-treatments with the elderly rarely happen. Family members are also economically equal and enjoy greater freedom. Parents, siblings, or older children all have their own pocket money. Unmarried women earn their incomes by keeping poultry, cultivating gardens, etc., and are free from any interference or control of their incomes from other family members. Married women are usually responsible for managing the financial affairs of their families, and have the final say in buying or selling their family's domestic animals. The properties accumulated through their joint labor (e.g., cattle or farming tools) are jointly owned by couples. Husbands keep and freely dispose of the small money from his small business or handcrafts and are free of interference from their wives, and wives also do the same with the incomes from their family sideline production.

> On market days or during festivals or religious events, wives usually run business stalls, selling freshly-picked fruits or finished foods, and earn extra incomes for themselves. The individual savings gained from these occasions by wives are often way more than these of their husbands. In addition, women are usually thriftier, spending less than men. Therefore, there is a saying in the Dai communities, 'Without a wife, a husband will be reduced to begging in a couple of years; whereas, without a husband, a wife will be rich enough to hold a Baizi' The messages are: husband and wife should make coordinated efforts in managing their family financial affairs, making and spending their money together, and only in this way can a family make its ends meet. If living alone, a husband is prone to overspending and thus will be poorer. Conversely, if living alone, a wife is prone to amassing huge savings and thus will be so rich as to be able to hold a great Baizi (doing religious donations to build up one's religious merits). This saying exactly sheds light on the delicate family relationships in financial cooperation between the Dai couples (Jiang, *The Life and Culture of the Dai Ethnic Group,* 1950j).

Mr. Li Jinghan commented,

> Most Dai families are small families with four or five members. Both husband and wife have the capability of economic production. Being usually more skillful at earning money than husband, the Dai wives enjoy a higher actual family status than their Han peers. They enjoy greater freedom in divorce, remarriage, or singlehood to get out of unsatisfactory relationships. But the husband is still ostensibly the head of a family in handling housework duties. When the husband is dead, the widowed wife is the head of the family. In an extended family without parents, the eldest son is the head of the family. If the eldest son is dead, the second son is the head of the family, but the widowed sister-in-law also has a high say in the family affairs (Li, 1940a).

However, a rural Han wife in the Chinese mainland cannot receive these treatments. As for the causes behind the difference between the Dai and Han wives, Mr. Jiang Yingliang concluded that,

> Husband and wife have the balanced responsibility and burden in production and consumption of a family. The fact that women can live independently from men in the Baiyi (Dai) society also has its inevitable causes: First, the

> production pattern is simple, where women can just do anything a man can do; second, there are not social discrimination or oppression against women, and few religious taboos against or constraints over women; and third, a simpler family life liberates wives from family chores, leaving them with spare time and effort to engage in economic production. Thanks to these three factors, women can have economic productivity in a family not lower than that of their husbands, and thus have an equal family status to their husbands and the same voice as their husbands in controlling domestic affairs and disposing of family properties (Jiang, *The Life and Culture of the Dai Ethnic Group,* 1950k).

The survey at Jing village shows that the equality between men and women in Dai people isn't limited to economic abilities but in almost all aspects of social life. While doing the farming either in paddy fields or on the mountains, men and women have a relatively reasonable division of labor, with men responsible for heavier physical labor in the fields and family sideline production, including plowing, harrowing, irrigation, fencing, planting seedlings, pulling up seedlings, separating seedlings (dividing bunches of seedlings into smaller ones for easier transplanting), gathering stalks, threshing crops, collecting firewood, cutting hays, building houses, grazing cattle, planting vegetables, fishing, weaving bamboo baskets, processing wood furniture and so on. Women are mainly responsible for house chores and part of the farming work, mainly including fetching water, pounding rice, cooking, raising pigs, feeding chickens, washing clothes, taking care of babies, going shopping, trading in small articles on fairs, spinning, weaving, sorting out firewood (after men cut it down), carrying firewood home (after men cut it down), carrying grains home (after men threshed them), transplanting rice seedlings, gathering grain stalks, drying up fresh grains and so on. In most cases, most of the shoulder-carrying labor is done by women, while the field works, like harvesting grains, are jointly done by men and women. Whether working at home or in the fields, they cooperate, talking and joking. They help each other and go ahead in no hurry. In the Dai families, they take everything easy, and everything also takes their natural pace. There are never such scenes as quarrels or debates over something. They all talk in soft voices. Young couples always have smiles on their faces, and Botaos and Mietaos treat each other with respect. Of course, such working paces won't lead to high working efficiency. According to older people, they used to work about five to six hours a day even during the busy farming seasons. Take grain-threshing as an example. They threshed grains in the morning, went back for a break by noon, simply leaving the unhusked grains in the field dry up under the sun, and came back to carry them home in the later afternoon. During light seasons, they did the Dan (religious offerings), had chats, and strolled around. A 1958 survey recorded the labor efficiency of Dai people as follows:

> Feudal relations of production constrained the peasants' enthusiasm for production, resulting in low labor efficiency. Peasants worked for relatively short periods a year: Men engaged in farming and sideline production for about 120 days a year and 4–5 hours a day and spent the remaining time of the year mostly on chitchatting with friends, going to fairs, Doing-the-Dan (religious offerings) and taking strolls, while women worked in agriculture for just 50 days or so a year. A laborer could carry only three pack-loads (about 150 *jin*) of crop stalks a day during the busy farming season. In addition, the mentality of sharing the burden gave rise to serious egalitarianism among peasants. Any public work for the entire village, even if could be done by individuals, was to be done by all the villagers together, resulting in the idling of the labor force, low efficiency and poor working performance (Editorial Committee of Five Series of Books on Ethnic Issues, 1983c).

Despite being a highly politically charged twist, this description truly mirrored the normalcy of their life.

In contrast with the Han ethnic majority, who treat a surname as a representation of family bloodlines and an identifier of clan kinships, the Dai minority had never cared much about it and had never approved of such representation since ancient time. Even if there were, indeed, surnames from the Yuan Dynasty onwards, they were simply exclusive to the aristocratic class represented by chieftains and few families with high exposure to the Han culture. They were only limited to the Chieftain aristocracy and some families with a deep degree of Chinese civilization and had nothing to do with common people. Moreover, either being reportedly granted by the Imperial Court or created by imitating the practice of the Han ethnic majority, these surnames also could not serve as the identifiers of the lineages of clans as persons from different clans might be granted the same surname, persons with the same surname were not necessarily from the same clan, and fellow clansmen and even siblings in the same family might have different surnames.

> Though chieftains in this Banna were not of the same clan, they all had the same surname Dao as the Pacification Superintendent of Cheli. Therefore, those surnamed Dao didn't necessarily have clan relationships. Conversely,

> persons having blood relations with each other didn't necessarily have the same surname. For example, now that the Cheli Pacification Superintendent of the earlier fifth generation was granted the surname Dao by the Imperial Court, generations of his offspring should have always had Dao as their surname. However, among them, the Cheli Pacification Superintendent of the 13th generation was named Sanbaolidai; of the 1st generation Sankaileng; of the 15th generation Zhaokan; of the 16th generation Shilisongban; of the 18th generation Shilisusheda; of the 21st generation Shilisutanma; of the 22nd generation Zhaokangle; and of the 25th generation Zhaobianmeng: They all were not surnamed Dao. Additionally, Mr. Dao Dongliang, the recently deceased senior Cheli Pacification Superintendent, had a brother named Zhao Menggang, who was a former President of Cheli County Council and also was not surnamed Dao. So, it could be concluded from these examples that persons with the same surname Dao aren't necessarily of the same clan, and the reverse is also true: Those surnamed Dao and those not surnamed Dao may be full brothers (Jiang, *The Life and Culture of the Dai Ethnic Group,* 1950i).

In civil life, there were cases that surnames have nothing to do with clans. According to some elderly people, during the Republic of China period, the Han teachers at the schools in Xishuangbanna run by the Nationalist Government of China would arbitrarily assign Han names (which contain surnames) to the Dai pupils (who had names but no surnames) for identification. As a result, the pupils from the same family had different surnames: A pupil might be surnamed Zhang while his brother surnamed Li. Fortunately, the Dai people didn't care much about it, accepting happily the surnames assigned to them, and had used them since.

Common people in the Dai society had neither ancestral halls or clan groups nor genealogical books. Though chieftains had their genealogical books, their genealogical books were just the records on the succession of their hereditary titles rather than the meaningful records of their family trees or clan lineages. For example, though beginning as far back as in the Song Dynasty, Cheli Pacification Superintendent's genealogy only contained the records of the branch clan that inherited the position of Pacification Superintendent and ignored all the other branch clans. As a result, it is impossible to trace back to other branch clans by this genealogy. As thus, we can fairly say that in the cultural context of the Dai people, there has never been the concept of clans.

Yet, despite an absence of the concept of clans, the Dai people have a sense of kinship, and, in fact, attach great importance to it. They just address their relatives in different ways from these of the Han ethnic majority in inland regions on the Chinese mainland. In their kinship terms, they do not distinguish the relatives of their father's clan from the ones of their mother's clan or their wife's clan. That is, they have no different treatment with their patrilineal and matrilineal relatives.

Mr. Dao Shuren explained it to the author, saying that,

> The Dai people don't define kinship by the surname but by the direct blood relationship. Everyone recognizes their relatives within the consanguinity distance of up to three generations. There is no problem with that. But when the distance is extended to the fourth, or even fifth, generation, they usually are not sure of it. So, on some occasions such as the New Lunar Year festival, common people without family tree records would get together, introduce themselves (their family lines), and find unknown relatives—"count relatives" in their own words. Such folk customs have come down from generation to generation. We the Dai people "count" both our unknown patrilineal and matrilineal relatives in this way and figuratively likened it to the split bamboo pole: The interior of the split bamboo pole (Biba in the Dai dialect) is likened to the patrilineal relatives while the exterior of the split bamboo pole (Bibu in the Dai dialect) the matrilineal relatives. If you want to know who's whose relative, you would always, first of all, ask the question: 'A Biba or a Bibu?' meaning that: Are you a patrilineal relative or a matrilineal one? The reason is, many kinship terms refer to both patrilineal and matrilineal relatives.

This explanation shows that not only in the past but even today, the Dai society has still been one of the acquaintances. The term of address to a man must correspond to the man in person, or you can't tell different men apart from each other just by the term of address.

Conjugal harmony in a relationship, sex equality in a family, light work in farming fields, and mutual assistance between partners, together with the custom of valuing immediate relatives and neglecting clans, make it neither likely for them to have the view that boys are superior to girls in their fertility behavior nor be motivated to "have more children, especially more sons" to help their families on the farming fields, and eliminate the hotbed for such ideology as "carry on the family line". In their living context, children, relatives and the villagers they live with and rely on are of the most significance to their real life and serve as the support they can fall back on when needed.

Family Property and Inheritance

Family Property

For an average rural family in inland regions on the Chinese mainland, the biggest pieces of family property are farmlands and houses. But in the Dai areas, "lands were owned by Zhao, and farmlands by the village", families only had the right of use of rather than ownership of the farmlands they worked on and the houses they lived in. When migrating out of a village, the family must hand over their farmlands and houses back to the village. Except for these two items, the remaining properties left in a Dai family were the self-produced foods, cash crops, livestock, and production and living utensils. During his fieldwork, the author took note of the main categories of production and living utensils in a Dai family, which are listed in the Table 5.6 below.

As can be seen from the above table, except for a very few iron wares, most of their instruments and articles were made of bamboo and wood and had simpler structures. As a local saying puts it, "The mobile properties of a Baiyi (Dai) family are not enough for three pack-loads", meaning that a Dai family has so few properties that all their furniture and personal articles can't even fill up three pack-loads.

> Various families cultivated their farmlands of similar sizes, lived in their houses with a similar number of rooms, and led a largely similar life: There was almost no significant difference between them. Except for a few nobles, there were neither extremely rich or well-off families nor absolutely poor ones surviving on begging. Equality here might be said to be the most obvious feature among common persons. If you said a family was richer than others, it just means that it had a couple of cows, horses, and pigs, chickens, or fruit trees more than others did. Most families had several pigs, about half of them had cattle, and very few of them had horses. Almost every family had cats and dogs. Locals were not good at saving, or rather had nothing to save. With the underdeveloped industry and commerce, they could only earn meager incomes mostly in freshly-harvested farming produces. They were pious believers in Buddhism, and spent most of their spare money (if any) on religious events (Li, 1940b).

Mr. Jiang Yingliang also said,

> In the Dai society, we could say that there were no extremely rich and extremely poor among common people. More practically, there were two contrasting

Table 5.6: List of Production Instruments and Daily-use Articles for the Dai Families

Serial No.	Production Instruments			Daily-use Articles	
	Designation	Materials	Purposes	Designation	Materials
1	Plow	Plowshare was made of iron and handle of bamboo or wood	Plowing	Rice steamer, rice mortar, salt crusher, rice wood basin	Wood wares
2	Harrow	Frame was made of wood, and teeth made of bamboo	Crushing soil blocks and leveling the ground	Spoon, lunch box, rice cylinder, stool, table, box, dustpan, sieve, water bamboo tube	Bamboo wares
3	Burmese hoe	Handle was made of wood and iron	Hoeing	Wonk, tripod, poker (made of iron or bamboo), kitchen knife	Iron wares
4	Burmese sickle	Handle was made of wood	Harvesting crops	Earthen pot, teapot and pot lid	Pottery wares
5	Trimmer knife	Handle was made of wood	Making wood/bamboo items, cutting down trees		
6	Bamboo mat	Made of bamboo slips	Spreading, threshing and drying up crops.		
7	Threshing bed	Made of wood	Threshing crops		
8	Threshing stick	Made of bamboo	Threshing crops		
9	Fan	Made of bamboo and bamboo leaf	Winnowing grains		

Table 5.1: Continued

Serial No.	Production Instruments			Daily-use Articles	
	Designation	Materials	Purposes	Designation	Materials
10	Bamboo basket	Made of bamboo	Serving as a container and measuring vessel, and used for carrying goods.		
11	Bamboo steamer	Made of bamboo	Storing goods		
12	Spinning wheel	Made of wood	Spinning a yarn		
13	Loom	Made of wood	Weaving fabric		

Source: Results from the Author's Fieldwork.

classes by the financial position: chieftains, who were extremely rich, and ordinary folks, who were moderately well-off. In a society where all folks are small peasants or rather in a single farming society where all folks are tenant farmers of a similar position, it is, indeed, impossible to give rise to an extreme disparity between the rich and the poor among them. The so-called "who is rich" or "who is poor" in the eye of the locals were simply the difference by a few cows or horses or a few pack-loads of freshly harvested grains. All the families in a village were similar in almost all aspects of daily life: foods, clothing and housing. There was no significant difference between them (Jiang, *The Life and Culture of the Dai Ethnic Group,* 1950l).

Family Consumption

We have given a qualitative description of family consumption in Section 1 of this Chapter. Here, we go on to take a look at a quantitative survey conducted in the 27th year of the R.O.C. Period (1938) by Mr. Li Jinghan on the incomes and consumption of an ordinary Dai family within one year to get a more comprehensive glimpse of the consumption of the Dai families. In his survey, Mr. Li Jinghan said,

> Suppose a farming family in Mangshi had five members: two parents in the prime of life, one 15-year-old girl, one 10-year-old boy and one five-year-old girl. Their life was generally as follows:
>
> They consumed 5–6 'baskets' of seeds for the cultivation (in the Dai regions, the cultivating land area is measured by the weight of consumed seeds rather than the area unit: *mu*) and harvested over 400 baskets of grain in Major Spring Harvest season. Deducting the farming land rent in grain to the chieftain, they had about 300 baskets of grain left, approximately 200 silver coins worth of finished rice. In addition, they could harvest more than 20 baskets of peas, broad beans and wheat each in Minor Spring Harvest season, approximately 100 silver coins worth of finished rice. In total, they got incomes in grains of more than 300 silver coinss all the year round. Together with their gains from cattle, pigs, poultry, chickens, ducks, vegetables, fruit trees and handicrafts, the family's annual incomes could be approximately 400 silver coins.

Then, based on his detailed records of 10 life fields: foods, clothes, bedding, housing, firewood, health-care, decoration, worships, entertainments and education, Mr. Li Jinghan concluded that,

> From the above simple descriptions, you could know a little about the daily life of ordinary Dai families and folks. They produced (rather than purchased) most of their daily necessaries, such as grains, vegetables, fruits, housing materials and some household articles, wove their clothing, bartered other items (for example, exchanging a pig for the equivalent value of pork at a fair), and purchased only a very few of non-essentials. Not good at saving, they were largely break-even between incomes and expenses. Except for a spendthrift life, a family usually could make their ends meet: neither in deep debt nor in excessive surplus. In currency terms, their net incomes stood at 300 silver coins a year, or nearly 400 silver coins if farming land rents and taxes were added in. Measured by a sound life for human beings, the life of the Dai families was nothing less than decent, but by the creature comfort and ease of living, the Dai families had a life way more abundant than that for their rural peers in inland regions on the Chinese mainland.

The breakdowns of their other incomes and uses of surpluses (if any) were as follows:

> Most Dai women are skilled in embroidery. They weave colorful ridged designs or embroider assorts of exquisite patterns on clothing. These handmade articles are very suitable for quilt coverings, pillowcases, cloth bags and interior decorations, fetch a good price in the range of several, tens, or even well more than one hundred silver coins a piece, and sell as souvenirs like hot dogs to travelers and tourists. Dai women also run vending stalls in markets, at fairs, or on main religious occasions, selling their homemade items and earning money to supplement their family incomes. Besides, there is much-unclaimed wasteland outside their village, where they can graze domestic animals and raise poultry. So, they have various options to make money.
>
> They spent most of their spare money on holding the Baizi (Baizi: a religious offering event). They often readily forked out all their spare money of 100 silver coins or so, together with another 100 silver coins or so borrowed from fellow folks, to hold the Baizi as such an act would win the holder high respect and the reputation of "Well-doer". For holding the Baizi, you have to buy Buddhist statues and Buddhist sutras, invite monks to recite sutras at home, and feast on relatives and friends. The cost is large, ranging from one hundred to several hundred silver coins. The Dai people believe that those who have held the Baizi in the present life will become a Buddha in the next life. This practice is among the main reasons why the Dai people have not much in savings (Li, 1940c).

In *The Life and Culture of the Dai Ethnic Group*, Mr. Jiang Yingliang gave a common consumption breakdown in an ordinary Dai family, covering the consumption items from both their own production and outsourcing.

(a) Self-produced consumption items

1. Grains: self-produced, with a part of them for family consumption and livestock feeds, a part for rent/tax contributions to chieftains and the government, and the remaining for selling for or bartering for other daily necessities.
2. Vegetables: self-produced and mainly self-consumed, with the remaining for sale at the market.
3. Meat: each family raised livestock: chickens or ducks were self-produced and self-consumed, and pigs or cows were slaughtered for doling out or selling to fellow villagers.

4. Lamp oil: extracted from wild pine seeds or purchased at the market.
5. Sugar: mainly extracted from home-grown sugarcanes.
6. Tobacco leaf: self-cultivated and self-consumed.
7. Farming implements: self-made except iron devices.
8. Household utensils: mostly made of bamboo or wood and self-made.
9. Clothing: cotton was grown, yarns spun, clothing woven, and dresses sewn on their own. But in most cases, they sold home-grown cotton for yarns, wove the clothing with the purchased yarns and made their dresses on their own.

(b) Outsourced consumption items

1. Salt: except for nearby residents of Moxie salt mines, most of the Dai people in the twelve bannas relied on imported salt from inland regions on the Chinese mainland.
2. Yarns: mainly from Han traders. In recent years, Sipu Enterprise Bureau also purchased locally-grown cotton, and span yarns to meet a partial demand from the Dai people.
3. Iron articles: iron wares for family life included pots, knives, needles, plows, nails, hoes and so on. The Dai families made their plows, hoes and knives on their own, and purchased other iron wares from Han ethnic importers.
4. Pottery wares: Some Dai families made some pottery wares, others purchased from Han ethnic traders. In addition, all the ceramic wares were purchased.

The four categories of daily necessities mentioned above were limited to ordinary families. Aristocrats, such as chieftains, purchased much more assorts of consumption items, such as silk, satin, clothing, blankets, cigarettes, leather shoes, luxury goods and cosmetics. These items were available in the market and in brisk demand but didn't fall in the category of daily necessaries for all families.

As thus, the Dai families lived so simple a life that they even could go without any money expenses. Therefore, it was virtually impossible to investigate and measure the annual consumption expenditure in the Dai families in terms of money. The creature comfort in a family was completely defined by hard work. A few more acres of farmlands cultivated, a few more trees planted and a few more pigs or chickens raised could lead to a much richer life. Lazy men just

> sowing seeds and leaving things run their natural course wouldn't have a rich life except for freedom from want. In short, in the Dai society, not all were necessarily related to money (Jiang, *The Life and Culture of the Dai Ethnic Group*, 1950m).

This paragraph also confirmed Mr. Li Jinghan's claim that: "The Dai people were not good at saving. They were largely break-even between incomes and expenses. Except for a spendthrift life, a family usually could make their ends meet: neither in deep debt nor in excessive surplus". It could be seen that though having very advantageous natural conditions, the Dai people are simply content with "sufficiency" as the production goal for their family life. That is, they took the satisfaction of use-value as their ultimate goal, and spent most of their spare time on "enjoying life". Once having a surplus, they would devote it to Doing-the-Dan (religious offerings). Therefore, they had not much wealth left to be inherited by their offspring.

Property Inheritance

They have no surnames, no clans and little family property. Unmarried children have their own private money and livestock to live on, and married children live separately. When it comes to property inheritance, there exist no strict "institutional" norms and rules in the Dai minority. In the talks during the fieldwork, some old people said, "The children who got married earlier all migrated out to live separately, so the properties of original families were given to the ones who stayed behind (continuing to live in original families). But in fact, there was nothing to be inherited in a Dai family." Others echoed that, "Getting married, children took away their personal things, and parents also gave out their valuables in advance and no one would wait until getting old to deal with their properties. The remaining things left would naturally go to whoever stayed behind and lived with their parents. No one would have the face to ask for the remaining things." Based on the author's observations, when getting old enough, the Dai elderly would quit the farming work, leaving all the jobs like tendering to crops and tea leaf picking to the live-in children. Mietaos might help out in the kitchen, while Botaos almost didn't do any housework, just attending preaching sessions at a Buddhist temple or chitchatting with like-minded villagers, which, awesome, they say, was their business. Live-in adult children shared all the production instruments and living utensils with their elderly parents and assumed most of the responsibility of taking care of their elderly parents. Thus, it seemed that there was no case of siblings dividing up their deceased parents' properties. The adult children who live with elderly parents might be either their natural or adopted sons (daughters) or matrical sons-in-law or daughters-in-law. Whoever lived with them would be the heir to their properties. This mode of property inheritance has also been confirmed by the fieldwork of other scholars[30]

These remarks are rather similar to accounts made in the R.O.C. Period by Mr. Yao Hesheng. In his *The Folklore of Shui Clan of the Dai Ethnic Group*, he noted:

> The ownership of movable properties in a family is often based on the effort of individuals: Each member of a family – either men or women or even children – all has their own private properties. In addition to money savings, women had their own weaving apparatus, and children had their own chickens, ducks and so on. For example, we once approached the head of a family to buy chickens, and his concubine, his daughter-in-law and his daughter all offered their own chickens to us. The money had to be paid to whoever sold the chickens. Before leaving, we paid one additional silver coin to his daughter-in-law and his daughter each as our clothes were washed by his daughter-in-law and the drinking water for the day was fetched by his daughter.
>
> Since land were collectively owned by a village, the land a person acquired, of course, couldn't be passed on as his private properties directly to his children and grandchildren and had to be recovered by the collective and be reallocated by the leader in a village. There were no standardized inheritance rules here. They neither necessarily gave all their properties only to the eldest son born of the legal wife nor necessarily distributed them equally among all the children. Fortunately, all adult children could make a living on their own and didn't necessarily live on assets left by parents. Moreover, their inheritance was too meager to fill a single sheet of typing paper even if everything from clothes

30 Researcher Zheng Xiaoyun witnessed in 2003 the full process of the property inheritance in Yan Yang's family in Manfeilong village in Xishuangbanna. Turning 50 years old in 2003 and believing he had reached the age of "retirement", Yan Yang handed over to his youngest daughter's husband (namely his matrilocal son-in-law), who lived with him, all the assets and their management and control rights, including all his rubber trees, land, savings in cash, livestock and houses. The couple of his youngest daughter since managed and disposed of exclusively all the incomes from the rubber tree plantation and land, and funded Yan Yang's pocket money. Parting with all the properties from his hard work all the life, Yan Yang didn't worry about his life in the future as the institution of supporting elderly parents remained well in place in the Dai society nowadays. See also Zheng Xiaoyun, *The Value of Private Funds in the Development of Modern Rural Frontier Areas, Pattra leaf Culture and Ethnic and Social Development* (Kunming: Yunnan University Press, 2007), 91. Similar observations were also made by Zhang Xiaohui and Xu Zhongqi et al during their on-site survey in Mangang village in 2000. See also Zhang Xiaohui, ed., *Survey on Ethnic Villages in Yunnan·Dai Ethnic Group in Mangang Village, Mengzhe Township, Menghai County* (Kunming: Yunnan University Press, 2001), 31. 130.

> and kitchenware to dishcloths was counted in. Money savings were nothing to speak of, a man with a couple of hundreds of silver coins would be deemed as an extremely rich man. So, no children would go so farther as to fight for a tiny piece of the meager property, and their ancestors had never bothered to have made something like inheritance laws (Yao, 2003b).

A prominent feature of the Dai families is the small-family structure, where both parents and children have their own relatively independent life. Equal and harmonious family relationships, relatively liberal marriage customs, non-existence of surnames but personal names, no distinct clan affiliation, the firm belief in Southern Buddhism, meager family assets, the low-level consumption habit and the natural family property inheritance . . . all these factors lead to the non-existence of such concepts and thoughts as "continuing the family lines", "extending genealogical books" and "superiority of boys to girls". They are very permissive and liberal with children's cultivation and have no demanding requirements for children's support. Therefore, there is no possibiliy for them to develop the propensity for a pursuit of "more births" and the "preference for male offspring" in their fertility behavior.

Section 3 Traditional Social Environment for the Dai families

Given the research focus of this paper, we limit the scope of the traditional social environment herein to land systems and village environments, which are closely related to fertility behavior and ignore all the other aspects, such as political institutions, taxation regimes, education systems, etc.

Land Systems

In regards to the land system in Xishuangbanna before the founding of the People's Republic of China, both the literature during the R.O.C Period and social historical investigations show that the land system of "being owned by lords, collectively held by villages and possessed by cultivators" was implemented in this region. According to Mr. Ma Yao, till the Democratic Reform, the Dai society in Xishuangbanna was still roughly in the historical stage of feudal lord society in the Western Zhou Dynasty, and the remains of the rural commune remained relatively intact.

In the book *Cheli* by Li Fuyi published in 1933, there is a passage presenting the following descriptions:

> The fields were owned by the public and thus could not be traded. All of them belonged to the people, who must cultivate the land to feed themselves. Whoever cultivated the land would possess the fields. Therefore, this was a communist society in real sense . . . For an emigrant who settled in the village, the whole village would come over to build a house for him, which took three to five days for completion, with no pay asked for. If it were a family emigrant, the owner just had to treat the villagers and helpers several meals to show their gratitude . . . The Pacification Superintendents and Chieftains had their dedicated fields, which were to be cultivated and sowed by the common people after they finished the mass faring work. It was much like the Nine-square system of land ownership in ancient China (Li, *Cheli*).

In his book *The Annals of the Twelve Bannas*, Mr. Li also gave similar descriptions about the allocation of resources such as paddy fields, cultivated lands, forests, rivers in the Dai communities.

As for lotment lands around this period, Mr. Li Wenlin wrote in his book *Immigration to Pusi Border Region* that,

> Here, the public ownership of land, no grain levies from the government and the measurement of crops by pack-load instead of *dou* or *sheng* (both *dou* and *sheng* are units of dry measure for grains in ancient China). Populace laborers tilled official lands (referred to the dedicated land for chieftains) for chieftains and would be paid with a pack-load of grains out of the autumn yield for each land plot. With some tea leaves or snacks as gifts, immigrants just paid a visit to the village leader ("Dapa" in the Dai language), who would hold public discussions with his fellow villagers on the allocation of lands to the newcomers for their new life. Gross violators who had aroused public anger would be deprived of their farmlands and driven out of the village. This kind of land system was similar to the Nine-Square system of land ownership in the times of Mencius (an ancient Chinese thinker). To put it in a word, it was undoubtedly a primitive communist society. It came out a little surprise to us that we found a living fossil of social evolution in it (Li, 1933).

In the foreword to the Section: A Land of Happiness Free of Wealth Difference and Exploitation of *The Folklore of Shui Clan of the Dai Ethnic Group*, which was written and published in the 1940s, Mr. Yao Hesheng quoted Mencius's statements, "Either stayed behind or migrated out, people are still within a narrow reach from each other, and all families in the same Nine-Squares block are loving each other, helping each other and taking care of each other. Thus, that is a harmonious society!" And commented that,

> Either in the social organization or people's lifestyle, it seemed to me that the current pattern of the Dai people is very much like the model during the Three Dynasties (Xia, Shang and Zou) in our history. Their land system was exactly the Nine-Square system of land ownership during the Three Dynasties widely known to Confucianists. Though it might be very suspicious that their farming land could be neatly divided up into numerous land plots of regular square blocks, I do believe the fact that their farming land was divided into official and private land plots, and that official land plots were tilled by the populace for their owners (Yao, 2003c).

Mr. Yao Hesheng observed that, in 1948, the "official lands" in Xishuangbanna were the land plots tilled by peasants,who paid the labor rent mainly in the form of service, for the local lords. This proved these claims that the land was collectively owned and roughly evenly distributed among villagers at that time and there were not sharp class divisions within the Dai communities.

In his book *The Land Tenure System in Xishuangbanna before the Founding of the People's Republic of China*, Mr. Chen Hansheng classified the land relation there as "pre-feudalism land relation", referring to the Feudal Lord Economy which goes before the Feudal Landlord Economy in Chinese history, that is, the Feudal Lord System before the Warring States Period in the central Chinese mainland, which is characterized by "land is owned by Lords", and held that "Rural communes featuring 'collective ownership and private possession of land' played a very important role in the society in Xishuangbanna" (Chen, 1984). This is Mr. Chen's understanding of the Xishuangbanna land system in the 1940s.

In July 1935, Mr. Jiang Yingliang served as the magistrate of Cheli County (now Jinghong Municipality) and made a summary of the land system at that time based on his systemic and comprehensive inspection tour of the Dai villages across his jurisdiction.

1. In the Baiyi (Dai) areas, peasants didn't own the land they farmed, so they could not trade, transfer, or handle it as they wished, even though they could farm the same land generation after generation, with little risk of it being taken away from them.

2. Village headman managed all the land in a village, chieftains had the final say in what is to be done with the land within his jurisdiction, and he had to follow local customs and conventions.
3. Headmen assigned land in a village to cultivators at their request, and the land so acquired would be cultivated hereditarily except for emigrations, and couldn't be arbitrarily revoked or deprived by either headmen or chieftains. Cultivators could request to be given additional land when their families grew, or return their land to headmen if their families shrank.
4. Emigrants abandoned and returned their land and homesteads unconditionally to their villages under the management of headmen, and reclaimed them when moving back (unless they had already been allocated to others). Village headmen allocated land and homesteads to new immigrants and neighbors would help with building new bamboo and wood houses for newcomers in villages. Each family in villages would lend grains to newcomers for starting a new livelihood or as farming seeds, which might be repaid in installments over harvest seasons in the future. The preferential treatments, including three-year rent exemption, would be given to immigrants from jurisdictions of other chieftains.
5. Villagers were obligated to make contributions and turn in taxes in grains or labor services to their chieftains in proportion to their respective acreages of land.

> Generally speaking, taxes and rents were collected based on the number of households in a village in the twelve bannas, and chieftains would take into account the suggestions of headmen and common opinions of villagers on the allocation and disposal of land. As thus, the land ownership system in the twelve bannas was substantially similar to the one collectively owned by villages (Jiang, *The Life and Culture of the Dai Ethnic Group,* 1950n).

In a survey tour of the Dai areas in the 1950s, the ethnic work investigation team under Mr. Ma Yao made an in-depth investigation into the economy and society in Xishuangbanna before the founding of the People's Republic of China in various dimensions, especially the form of land ownership, the village community system, the form of land rents and the status of immediate cultivators, and came up with the following conclusions:

First, political "sovereignty" and economic "land ownership" were unified: A feudal lord in a region was the owner of all the land in the whole region, and there were no "landlords of private lands" other than the feudal lord. Therefore, any free trade in the land was not allowed, which was much like the institutions of "lands were owned by kings" and "land trade was prohibited" in the Western

Zhou Dynasty. Within the whole hereditary territories, "the lands owned directly by feudal lords" and "the lotments possessed by serfs" were separated, much like the division between "official lands" and "private lands" in the Western Zhou Dynasty.

Second, the feudal system was anchored on rural communes: The rural commune herein was a unique pattern of "collective ownership and private possession of the land" in the ancient Orient. Feudal lords usurped the lands owned collectively by village communes and, in turn, allocated them to serfs by taking advantage of the institution of regularly redistributing the lands owned collectively by village communes. In essence, feudal lords forcibly rented their feudal fiefs out to serfs, thus establishing a special type of feudal relations of production similar to the one under the Nine-Square system of land ownership in China's slave society.

Third, the main form of exploitation was "labor corvee", which is equivalent to the "surplus value": For local lords, "land rents" and "taxes" were combined. In the Dai areas, the distinct clue of shifting from "tribute" to "labor corvee" and "rent in kind" was found, greatly contributing to the understanding of expressions such as 贡, 助 and 彻 in ancient Chinese literature.

Fourth, there were three categories of immediate producers: free-peasant-turned serfs, who were much like 众 (the populace), 庶人 (common people) and 民 (civilians) in the Western Zhou Dynasty; privately-owned slave-turned coloni (tenant peasants) and serfs, who were very similar to the 臣 (servants or ministers), 妾 (female slaves) and 鬲 (criminal-turned slaves) to kings in the Western Zhou Dynasty; and few yeomen peasants, who were spun off from the aristocratic class and much like the 士 (intelligentsia, a social stratum in ancient China between officials and civilians) in the Western Zhou Dynasty (Ma, 1998).

The investigations on the land system in the Dai society conducted separately from the 1930s to the early 1950s by the above scholars and others were unrelated to each other but came up with basically the same conclusions, convincingly proved the objectivity and authenticity of these investigations themselves.

The survey of the author in Menghai was also consistent with the above descriptions. The lands under the direct control of chieftains and headmen at all levels were classified into two categories: official lands and lotments. Official lands were divided further into various types by the owners and beneficiaries of all the yields therefrom: Pacification Superintendent lands, Chieftain lands, Zhaoguan lands, Bolang lands, Balong lands, Buddhist Monastery lands and so on; while lotments into Nahagun lands, Naman lands and Natang lands (also known as Nawei lands). Nakhakun lands referred to clan lands, which could be transferred and inherited only within a clan, and were "possessed collectively and cultivated collectively" or "possessed collectively and cultivated privately". These lands were not incorporated into the lands in a village for reallocation and returned to the clan rather than the village by their emigrating possessors. Naman lands were the village lands (also known as the common lands of a village), namely the lands of being "collectively owned and privately possessed" in a rural commune. These lands were derived from the Nahagun lands of defunct clan communes, made up the largest share of the lands in a village, and were equally distributed among all the villagers. Natang lands (Nawei lands), namely taxable lands, were the lands that feudal lords offered to villagers to cultivate on the condition of paying the taxes of land, also known as "lotments". In addition, there were also a small amount of Naxin lands, namely private lands, which were reclaimed by peasants around their "lotments", or private lands owned by Zhaozhuang in a village. In Menghai, the official lands accounted for about 11% of the total cultivated area, Nahagun lands about 7%, and Naman lands and Natang lands combined about 80%.

Residents in Jing village fell within the "Gunhenzhao" rank in the social hierarchy, meaning "official people", which consisted of four types of identities: "Lingnan", "Maozai", "Gunnai" and "Zhaozhuang"; "Lingnan" was responsible for Zhaomeng's security; "Maozai" for cooking, shoe-embroidering, affairs attending, etc.; "Gunnai" for firewood-cutting, water-fetching, rice-pounding and other domestic services. By the form of land rents, the former three identities were taxpayers mainly in labor corvee, with their labor corvee making up more than 90% of their taxable amounts. "Zhaozhuang" was a special identity and had a small population, which mostly were distant relatives of the lord and only served as guards for Zhaomeng. They needed to pay no land rent and could inherit their hereditary lands, being similar in the social status to free peasants.

According to old people's memories, "At that time, all the families had largely the same amount of land, not less than 10 *mu* or even more (mu: a unit of area in ancient China and equal to 0.0667 hectares). Having no sufficient laborers to take care of so much land, a family of three to five members usually would rent out all or part of it or hire workers to do the farming during the busy season".

The land system of "being owned by lords, collectively held by villages and possessed by cultivators" grants families only the right to use the lands but not the right to trade in, transfer or rent the lands and descendants' right to inherit families' land. This system also ensures that all villagers can have plots of land, thus eliminating the basis for the idea of inheriting family properties through male offspring.

Families and Villages

In a Dai village, every family seemed to be a unit embedded in the village framework. Whatever its size, a village always had a full-fledged internal organizational structure and a clear-cut division of roles. In short, there were typically the following roles in a village:

> 1. Boman and Mieman: namely the Village Father and Village Mother; 2. Kunhan: warriors or sergeant; 3. Taoge: elderly villagers; 4. Boban; 5. Kunqian: clerks; 6. Bozhang; 7. Bomo; 8. Naimao and Naishao; 9. Zhangha; and 10. Banmen.

Boman and Mieman were the main principals in a village and similar to the leaders in a village today. They were mainly responsible for managing the migration of village residents, including accepting newcomers on behalf of the village and approving the emigration of villagers; managing the land of a village; collecting taxes and levies on behalf of lords; managing the Buddhist temple-related funds and all religious affairs of a village; managing marriages; settling civil disputes in a village, etc.

Kunhan assisted Boman and Mieman in defending the common boundaries of a village, maintaining the public order in a village, and punishing violators or breakers of the public order, good customs and feudal laws and regulations laid out by chieftains.

Taoge was responsible for mediating civil or family disputes in a village and adjudicating civil conflicts. The role was similar to a member of a neighborhood committee in the Han ethnic settlement regions. They were usually eloquent and good at communicating with neighbors. In a village without Naimao, they also were responsible for youth's dating and love activities in a village, much like the functionaries of women's federations and trade unions in the Han ethnic settlement regions.

Boba's job was to communicate messages, call on villagers for meetings, entertain village guests, arrange business trips and oversee fire prevention, anti-floods and other duties in a village.

Kunqian was the village clerk, assisting Boman and Mieman in managing and registering the land in a village and managing the public funds, grains and properties of a village. This role was not a full-time one except for in a larger village.

Bozhang played an important role in religious activities in a village and had to be a highly respected secularized Buddhist who was well versed in Buddhist scriptures. He was responsible for all religious activities, conducting religious rites, reciting Buddhist scriptures for the masses, chose the right dates for marriages, funerals, housing groundbreaking ceremonies and other events in a village.

Bomo was in charge of honoring deities in a village as well as protecting "Diula" (namely the Village Deity). He also offered sacrifices to ghosts and drove the demons away for villagers. In short, he was the man in charge of natural religious activities in a village.

Naimao and Naishao were respectively the ringleader or convener of young men and women in a village and usually were held by influential married men and women among the village youth. They were responsible for organizing young men and women for a variety of entertaining and gaming activities, for example, dancing, duetting, fireworks-displaying, and lantern-flying, on major occasions (fairs, annual festival holidays and religious events). They were also responsible for managing the romantic affairs of young men and women and stopping them from violating the village rules and regulations. They approved boys from other villages to visit and date girls in this village and expelled them out of the village without permission.

Zhangha was a folk singer and poet in the Dai society and was invited to stage performances on major occasions such as marriages, religious events, housing groundbreaking ceremonies, movement into a new house. Listening to duets by Zhangha was one of the most popular activities during the festival holidays.

Banmen was the water resource manager in a village, and whose duty was to manage the irrigation of the village's paddy fields, diverting water in public main irrigation channels into branch channels in the fields to meet irrigation needs of paddy fields in a village during the transplanting season each year.

In this organizational structure, most of the public affairs in a village were decided and implemented collectively by the village council ("Guan" in the Dai language). Folk proverbs, such as "爬细敦兵桑，滚细敦兵贯" (The collective wisdom of four monks is equal to the knowledge of the Buddha, and four villagers are also smart enough to decide the affairs in a village), "缀甘格，把甘崩" (collective decision and collective implementation) and "娃滚课，情滚甘" (everyone contributed his inputs and made concerted efforts), exactly illustrated the collectivism of the Dai people. Even today, public works in the Dai villages, including digging irrigation channels, building embankment dams, digging fish ponds, planting bamboo fences around a village and building a road, still are completed by all the villagers following the approach of each household contributing a laborer.

With this basic village structure, many affairs for individual families (such as marriages, house building, plowing, seedling planting, harvesting, grain threshing, vigil keeping and funerals) were not done completely by the particular families but by a reciprocal network of villages and communities in the Dai society.

In their opinion, "Just as a single village can't make a Meng, a single family also can't make a village." (Meng: a unit of administrative division in the Dai settlement regions in Yunnan). Therefore, they believed in the convention: "Fields should be farmed collectively by all, and the deceased should be buried collectively by all". No matter who was to build a new house, adults all over the village would come over with their tools to help: Men would haul the raw timber out of mountains to the construction site, erect the frames and pillars, set up the roof, fix the boards, install windows and doors and so on, while women would help do the cooking and tea brewing. It usually took one to three days to build a new house. When someone died, every family in the village would send one man to keep vigil at the deceased's family for a couple of nights, and the whole village would suspend working until the deceased's funeral had been over (Editorial Committee of Five Series of Books on Ethnic Issues, 1984a).

Seasonal farming work, such as plowing and harvesting, was done in small groups of villagers, and preferential treatments, such as one to three years of rent exemption and other subsidies, would be granted to new residents in a village. In addition, there is the custom of making "Laogengs": Regardless of gender, people born in the same year were "Laogeng" to one another, which meant the peers of similar age who have played and grown up together. They often had a deep friendship, took care of each other, and helped each other out. Therefore, the number or presence of farming laborers in a Dai family didn't necessarily affect the survival of the family.

This social network of reciprocity seemed to provide every family with a village-based external labor supply security system, and the customs of "living with bride's family" and "adopted children" in the Dai society also provided families with the guarantee mechanism for labor force replenishment and parental support. Moreover, villagers' rules and conventions also embraced filial piety to the elderly. For example, the Dai villagers' rules and conventions of Meng (a unit of administrative division) before the Movement of Democratic Reforms in 1954 in Xishuangbanna had the following provisions: common persons have three parents: the first is their natural parents, the second their elder siblings, and the third the elderly men and headmen in their villages. They should respect and show filial piety to all the three parents, and the failure to do so is ungracious. Grown-up children should share their parents' burden and labor, and show filial piety to their parents. Loitering about or showing no filial piety to parents is ungracious and guilty. Children may not beat or scold their elderly parents, and any failure to support their elderly parents is ungracious and guilty (Editorial Committee of Five Series of Books on Ethnic Issues, 1984b). The Dai sayings were going like this, "Just as red soil is necessitated in harnessing intermontane basins, so old men are relied on in community governance", "Ridges are the soul of grains, and old men the treasures of a village", "Emulating the better and respecting the elderly", and so on.

Villagers provided support for widowers, widows, orphans, or the childless elderly, assuming the same responsibilities as the normal families did. Historical literature recorded, "The homeless, the elderly and the disabled are supported collectively by their villages and communities", "Their shelter is provided through public houses built by villages and communities, and their food and clothing are provided by villagers in turn, so that there is no shortage of daily necessaries for them". "Therefore, having or not having children makes no big difference in the Dai society" (Li, 1955g).

The Dai villagers had the responsibility to support the elderly incapable of supporting themselves, and otherwise would be despised and condemned by other villages. The village security system of "providing for the elderly" rendered it impossible for them to have the concept of "raising sons as support in advanced years" ingrained in the Han ethnic majority society, and in their discourse, we also could not find out a word that has the same meaning.

This land-use system and family-village relationship enabled a sharp contrast in the family property inheritance and elderly parental support between the Dai families and the Han ethnic majority society: The strong awareness of inheriting family properties by male offspring and ensuring parental support by having male offspring, which influences and reflects the fertility behavior of the Han ethnic families, can't find the soil for its generation, survival, or continuation in the Dai families. Therefore, they were unlikely to show a preference for male births in their fertility behavior.

To conclude, the attitude of the Dai people toward childbirth is "just having children is good". They simply wanted to have children but didn't particularly ask for more children. They wished to have both sons and daughers but didn't have any gender preference. At the level of either the family or the society, the Dai people had no motivation to "have more offspring, especially more male offspring" in their fertility behavior.

References

Benedict, Ruth. *The Chrysanthemum and the Sword*. Translated by Lyu Wanhe et al. Beijing: the Commercial Press, 1990, 8.

Chen, Hansheng. *Land Tenure in Xishuangbanna before the Founding of People's Republic of China*. China Social Sciences Press, 1984 Edition, 16. Extracted from Ma Yao's A Collection of Academic Treatises by Ma Yao, 27.

Editorial Committee of Five Series of Books on Ethnic Issues. *A Comprehensive Survey of the Dai Society in Xishuangbanna* (1). Kunming: Yunnan People's Publishing House, 1983a, 49.

Editorial Committee of Five Series of Books on Ethnic Issues. *A Comprehensive Survey of the Dai Society in Xishuangbanna* (1). Kunming: Yunnan People's Publishing House, 1983b, 54.

Editorial Committee of Five Series of Books on Ethnic Issues. *A Comprehensive Survey of the Dai Society in Xishuangbanna* (1). Kunming: Yunnan People's Publishing House, 1983c, 15.

Editorial Committee of Five Series of Books on Ethnic Issues. *A Comprehensive Survey of the Dai Ethnic Society in Xishuangbanna* (2). Kunming: The Nationalities Publishing House of Yunnan, 1984a, 74–75. *A Survey of the Dai Ethnic Society and History* (Xishuangbanna-Vol. 2), Yunnan People's Publishing House, 1983, 34–35.

Editorial Committee of Five Series of Books on Ethnic Issues, *A Comprehensive Survey of the Dai Ethnic Society in Xishuangbanna* (2). Kunming: The Nationalities Publishing House of Yunnan, 1984b, 21.

Friedrich Engels's Speech on Karl Marx's Funeral. *Selected Works of Mark and Engels*, Vol. II. Beijing: Foreign Languages Publishing and Distribution Administration, 1955, 166.

Jiang, Yingliang. *The Economic Life of the Dai Ethnic Group*. Guangzhou: Social and Economic Research Institute of Southwest in Lingnan University, 1950a, 72.

Jiang, Yingliang. *The Life and Culture of the Dai Ethnic Group*. Shanghai: Zhonghua Book Company, 1950b, 164–166.

Jiang Yingliang. *The Life and Culture of the Dai Ethnic Group*. Shanghai: Zhonghua Book Company, 1950c, 176.

Jiang, Yingliang. *The Life and Culture of the Dai Ethnic Group*. Shanghai: Zhonghua Book Company, 1950d, 67.

Jiang, Yingliang. *The Life and Culture of the Dai Ethnic Group*. Shanghai: Zhonghua Book Company, 1950e, 137–140.

Jiang, Yingliang. *The Life and Culture of the Dai Ethnic Group*. Shanghai: Zhonghua Book Company, 1950f, 146–149.

Jiang, Yingliang. *The Life and Culture of the Dai Ethnic Group*. Shanghai: Zhonghua Book Company, 1950g, 150–151.

Jiang, Yingliang. *The Life and Culture of the Dai Ethnic Group*. Shanghai: Zhonghua Book Company, 1950h, 179.

Jiang, Yingliang. *The Life and Culture of the Dai Ethnic Group*. Shanghai: Zhonghua Book Company, 1950i, 212.

Jiang, Yingliang. *The Life and Culture of the Dai Ethnic Group*. Shanghai: Zhonghua Book Company, 1950j, 210.

Jiang, Yingliang. *The Life and Culture of the Dai Ethnic Group*. Shanghai: Zhonghua Book Company, 1950k, 209–210.

Jiang, Yingliang. *The Life and Culture of the Dai Ethnic Group*. Shanghai: Zhonghua Book Company, 1950l, 154–155.

Jiang, Yingliang. *The Life and Culture of the Dai Ethnic Group*. Shanghai: Zhonghua Book Company, 1950m, 157–158.

Jiang, Yingliang. *The Life and Culture of the Dai Ethnic Group*. Shanghai: Zhonghua Book Company, 1950n, 129–131.

Jiang, Yingliang. *The History of the Dai Ethnic Group*. Chengdu: People's Publishing House of Sichuan, 1983a, 486–489.

Jiang, Yingliang. *The History of the Dai Ethnic Group*. Chengdu: People's Publishing House of Sichuan, 1983b, 596.

Jiang, Yingliang. *The History of the Dai Ethnic Group*. Chengdu: People's Publishing House of Sichuan, 1983c, 591.

Li, Fuyi. *Cheli*. Commercial Press Universal Library Book Series of History and Geography, 140–141. Extracted from Ma Yao's A Collection of Academic Treatises by Ma Yao, 25.

Li, Fuyi. *The Annals of the Twelve Bannas*. Taiwan: Chiang Kai-shek Publishing Company, 1955a, 99–100.

Li, Fuyi. *The Annals of the Twelve Bannas*. Taiwan: Chiang Kai-shek Publishing Company, 1955b, 107.

Li, Fuyi. *The Annals of the Twelve Bannas*. Taiwan: Chiang Kai-shek Publishing Company, 1955c, 118.

Li, Fuyi. *The Annals of the Twelve Bannas*. Taiwan: Chiang Kai-shek Publishing Company, 1955d, 119.

Li, Fuyi. *The Annals of the Twelve Bannas*. Taiwan: Chiang Kai-shek Publishing Company, 1955e, 140.

Li, Fuyi. *The Annals of the Twelve Bannas*. Taiwan: Chiang Kai-shek Publishing Company, 1955f, 141.

Li, Fuyi. *The Annals of the Twelve Bannas*. Taiwan: Chiang Kai-shek Publishing Company, 1955g, 118.

Li, Jianmin. "China's Fertility Revolution". *Population Research*, 1 (2009).

Li, Jinghan. "The Living Conditions and Social Organizations of Dai People". *The Southwest Frontiers*, no. 11 (1940a, September), The Southwest Frontiers Monthly of Kunming.

Li, Jinghan. "The Living Conditions and Social Organizations of Dai People". *The Southwest Frontiers*, no. 11 (1940b, September): 1, The Southwest Frontiers Monthly of Kunming.

Li, Jinghan. "The Living Conditions and Social Organizations of Dai People". *The Southwest Frontiers*, no. 11 (1940c, September): 3–5, The Southwest Frontiers Monthly of Kunming.

Li, Wenlin. *Research on Issues in Yunnan Border Regions*. Kunming: Yunnan Provincial Kunhua Public Education Museum, 1933 edition, 93–94. Extracted from Ma Yao's A Collection of Academic Treatises by Ma Yao, 26.

Local Chronicle Compilation Committee of Menghai County in Yunnan Province. *The Annals of Menghai County*. Kunming: Yunnan People's Publishing House, 1997a, 478.

Local Chronicle Compilation Committee of Menghai County in Yunnan Province. *The Annals of Menghai County*. Kunming: Yunnan People's Publishing House, 1997b, 354.

Local Chronicle Compilation Committee of Yunnan Province. *A Survey of the Dai Ethnic Society and History* (Xishuangbanna-Vol. 3). Kunming: The Nationalities Publishing House of Yunnan, 1983a, 72.

Local Chronicle Compilation Committee of Yunnan Province. *A Survey of the Dai Ethnic Society and History* (Xishuangbanna-Vol. 3). The Nationalities Publishing House of Yunnan, 1983b, 75, 76.

Ma, Yao. *A Collection of Academic Treatises by Ma Yao*. Kunming: Yunnan People's Publishing House, 1998, 38–39.

Tao, Yunkui. "The Circle of Life of Dai People in Cheli County". *Frontier Research Series*, Vol. 1945–1948, 209.

Yao, Hesheng. *The Folklore of Shui Clan of the Dai Ethnic Group* (photocopy). Shanghai: Shanghai Literature & Art Publishing House, 1990, 104–108.

Yao, Hesheng. *The Folklore of Shui Clan of the Dai Ethnic Group*. Kunming: Yunnan People's Publishing House, 2003a, 144–147.

Yao, Hesheng. *The Folklore of Shui Clan of the Dai Ethnic Group*. Kunming: Yunnan People's Publishing House, 2003b, 112–113.

Yao, Hesheng. *The Folklore of Shui Clan of the Dai Ethnic Group*. Kunming: Yunnan People's Publishing House, 2003c, 109–111.

Zhang, Fengqi. "A Frontier Area of Primitive Agricultural Production – Cheli". *The Southwest Frontiers*, no. 2 (1938, November): 15–21.

Zhang, Xiaohui, ed. *Survey on Ethnic Villages in Yunnan•Dai Ethnic Group in Mangang Village, Mengzhe Township, Menghai County*. Kunming: Yunnan University Press, 2001a, 26, 31.

Zhang, Xiaohui, ed. *Survey on Ethnic Villages in Yunnan Dai Ethnic Group in Mangang Village, Mengzhe Township, Menghai County*. Kunming: Yunnan University Press, 2001b, 66–69.

6

Theoretical Analyses and Interpretations of the Traditional Low Fertility Behavior of the Dai

Section 1 Analysis of the Applicability of Classical Population Theories to the Dai Ethnic Traditional Low Fertility Behavior

Thomas Malthus pointed out in *An Essay on the Principle of Population*: "That population does invariably increase where there are the means of subsistence, the history of every people that have ever existed will abundantly prove" (Zhu, 1992a). "In a state therefore of great equality and virtue, where pure and simple manners prevailed, and where the means of subsistence were so abundant that no part of the society could have any fears about providing amply for a family, the power of population being left to exert itself unchecked, the increase of the human species would evidently be much greater than any increase that has been hitherto known." A strong case in support of this view is that "In the United States of America, where the means of subsistence have been more ample, the manners of the people more pure, and consequently the checks to early marriages fewer, than in any of the modern states of Europe, the population has been found to double itself in twenty-five years" (Zhu, 1992b). Taking a further step forward, he proposed his renowned proposition that "The power of population multiplication is infinitely greater than the capacity of land to provide the means of subsistence for human production and living." However, this proposition was not only denied by the fact of "declining populations in growing economies" in modern western industrialized countries, represented by Europe, but also has failed to account for the fertility behavior of the Dai people living in a traditional agrarian society. The description in the preceding Chapter has shown us that in the Dai society, means of subsistence is in a sufficient supply, shelter for any family is provided through collective efforts from the whole village, clothing is home-spun and woven, daily-use articles are home-made, and just a small input of individual labor can satisfy family members' daily needs for grains, chickens, ducks, vegetables and meat. All fellow villagers offer a helping hand to families in need, disputes and maltreatment rarely happen in a village, and both families and family members are on harmonious and equal terms. Therefore, the social climate here might as well be simple and pure, and the means of subsistence were so abundant that no part of the society could have any fears about providing for a family. However, the population here didn't see an unchecked proliferation to the extent beyond the capacity of their land to provide the means of subsistence. Hence, Thomas Malthus's theory of exponential population doesn't stand water here.

By factoring in explanatory variables, such as fertility cost, fertility utility, the number and quality of children, some Western demographers represented by Harvey Leibenstein and Becker developed the theories such as the Rational Choice of Marginal Children and the Quantity-Quality Trade-off of Children, reasonably explaining the "Malthusian Paradox" of "declining populations in growing economies" in industrialized countries in modern West, especially in Europe. However, these theories turned out to have an insufficient interpretive force for traditional fertility behavior of the Dai people here. Let's first take a look at the theory of the Rational Choice of Marginal Children.

First, to make a rational choice for a marginal child, the fertility cost and utility that such a child will bring to a family must be, first of all, compared and balanced to determine the rationality of giving birth to such a child. However, the Dai people said, "It is the duty of a person to have and raise children". "One should do what he or she should do during his/her lifetime. My grandparents gave birth to my father, and my parents gave birth to me, so I should also give birth to and raise my children. This is the way we've come down from generation to generation, and this is just one of the right things you're supposed to do in life." When it comes to having children, that's the belief of the Dai families. Why should they do that? They don't bother to think about it. The idea of deciding whether or not to raise a child by evaluating whether it makes financial sense to do so is unthinkable in the cultural context of the Dai society. Therefore, they don't make such a "seemingly rational choice".

Second, according to Harvey Leibenstein's cost-utility concept, the sum of the parental expenses for upbringing, education, medical care and other expenses incurred during the period from the mother's pregnancy and birth until the child is able to live on his/her own is the direct cost of raising a child; the indirect costs (opportunity costs) refer to the loss of education and income opportunities for parents to raise an additional child, the reduction in the consumption level and the loss of time of other family members due to the care and upbringing of the additional child, etc. The utilities that this child brings to a family include consumer utility, labor-based financial utility, old-age security utility, economic risk utility, the utility of maintaining family status and the utility of contributing to the expansion and development of the family. For a Dai child, the "direct costs" in daily consumption, education and health care are usually low. The "indirect costs", such as lost education and income opportunities of his parents and reduced consumption of the other family members, almost do not exist. But the "consumer utility" of the child bringing happiness to his parents, the "financial utility" of the child expected to bring income to the family after growing up and the "old-age security utility" of the child supporting his elderly parents are really there.

In other words, to Dai parents, the utilities of raising a child far outweigh the costs they have invested. Should they make their financial calculations following Harvey Leibenstein's train of thoughts, namely act on the cost-utility theory, they would, without doubt, choose to have "more births". But the reality is that they do not make such a choice. Instead, they hold that "excessive children make life harder for parents". In their eye, having more children means less leisure time and entertainment chances. That is not worth it. Therefore, the theory of the Rational Choice of Marginal Children cannot explain the Dai people's traditional fertility behavior of choosing fewer children when the costs of raising children are less than the utilities.

Now let's look at how Becker's Quantity-Quality Trade-off theory applies here.

First of all, under the historical conditions at that time, a Dai boy at six to seven years old had to live at a Buddhist temple as a monk for a period of time to learn necessary knowledge, which was a required course, while a girl stayed at home and learned needlework skills. Any family made largely the same input in raising each of its children, and thus all the children also had largely the same quality. There were no convincing reasons for Dai parents to reduce the number of their births in expectation of improved quality of their births, that is, to trade off the number of children against the quality of their children. Therefore, Becker's logic of quantity-quality trade-off of children is not tenable here.

Next, as described above, from the perspective of the Dai daily life, families generally didn't contribute much to raising their children. Usually, parents were laissez-faire with their children and had no special expectation for them, but were likely to get significant financial returns from their grown-up children. That is to say, parents would surely get greater rewards than inputs from raising more children. As thus, according to Becker's theory, parents would inevitably try to have as many children as possible, but this is not the case here. Therefore, Becker's theory doesn't apply here, either.

In the opinion of the author, the reason why classical population theories in the West doesn't apply here is that their logic is based on the assumption of "economic man", that is, a man always tries to get the maximum return with the least input. But the Dai people in the traditional agrarian society harbored the mindset of "enough is the best" about the means of subsistence, i.e., they were stoic and indifferent to the pursuit of material goods. This attitude toward life mandated that the Dai people in the traditional agrarian society didn't act as an "economic man". Therefore, it is fundamentally inevitable that these western theories are not applicable in analyzing the behaviors of the Dai people living in the traditional agrarian society.

The Chinese population research community represented by Mr. Fei Xiaotong encapsulated the traditional fertility behavior in China into "having more offspring, especially more male offspring". Based on his analysis of the situation in rural China in the 1930s, Fei Xiaotong pointed out that, "To maintain the laborers needed for farming, the countryside has to support a large population. In an economic structure where people mean productive forces, it is inevitable to have a big population in small areas." Due to high infant mortality rates, "to maintain the capacity of such a social structure, it is imperative to have as more children as possible", "China's population will decline only if its agriculture can be driven by other forces than manual labor" (Fei, 1998).

To ensure the integrity of an existing social structure, raising children not only functions as the generational succession (family line continuing from parents to children) but also meets the demand for generational support (parent care by adult children, i.e., the later generations supporting their previous ones). This theoretical framework of generational succession (the son inheriting his father's properties and business) and generational support (raising sons as support in advanced years) well explains the underlying cause and practical rationality of "having more offspring and preference for male offspring" prevalent in rural China at that time.

The Dai people in rural areas also relied on manual labor to sustain the family survival and harnessed men as the driving force for production, but they did not face challenge of "too little land for too many people" as their Han ethnic peers did; they also needed to ensure the integrity of their existing social structure, but their situation only fell under a "modified" "parent care by adult children" model, which is reflected only in the "generational support" (the next generation supports the previous generation) but no "generational succession" (the son inheriting his father's properties and business). This model is referred to as "modified parent care by adult children" model because the Dai people in China don't depend exlusively on their children for their livelihood in their advanced ages. While children are their first choice, for the elderly without children, they can turn to relatives, friends, Buddhist temples for support. In their traditional customs, fellow villagers provided for those who have no kin and cannot support themselves, assuming the same responsibilities as the normal family members did. Just as recorded in the historical literature, "The elderly, the disabled and those who have nobody to depend on are supported collectively by their village communities", "Their shelter is provided through public houses built by village communities, and their food and clothing are provided by villagers in turn, so they do not suffer from shortages", and "whether one has children or not, therefore, makes little difference in the Dai society" (Li, 1955a).

In comparison, the structure of the Dai traditional society in Jing village was more similar to that of the Village Society of Acquaintances constructed by Ms. Li Yinhe, but the conclusions from her interpretation of the fertility behavior by the Han ethnic majority in Chinese rural regions with this interpretative framework deviated far from the traditional fertility behavior of the Dai people in Jing village.

In her interpretative framework, the Village Society of Acquaintances must have the following five characteristics:

1. The information inside the village is shared;
2. The scale of a village is limited to the extent to which ordinary village members have got acquainted with one another;
3. The mobility of fellow villagers is low;
4. Fellow villagers tend to compete with each other (irrational comparison with others, keeping up with the Joneses);
5. Fellow villagers are under pressure to converge in all aspects of life (pursuits).

The situation of Jing village was, so to speak, completely consistent with the above characteristics. There were 417 households in Jing village. I found during my fertility history survey that villagers knew pretty well about each other, for example, the specific sites of a fellow villager's house, the number of siblings in the family, and even the primary or secondary schools his kids attend. If you could describe just one feature of the person you are looking for, either a young man or an elderly man, they could pinpoint the exact location of his family house, which made it much easier for my survey.

As for migration, old people said: Once settled down here, newcomers are our people in the village. People here seldom move out or in except for something extraordinary. We all families and villagers here got along very well, why would we bother to move around? Therefore, there was little mobility in the villagers.

As for the (irrational) comparison and convergence among peers, that is a time-honored tradition for the Dai people. That was true then, and it remains true today. It has been mentioned in the preceding Chapter that a village is composed of various small groups, which are known locally as "cohorts". As long as being part of some "cohort", women are consistent in their dress and accessories, the consistency reflected not only in grade and style but also in color and even brand; and this is also true for men, for example, men tend to be consistent in their cigarettes, their motorcycles and even their mobile phones. Take the strait skirts for women as an example: As long as in the same "cohort", all the ladies wear the same line of straight skirts, which are the same in almost all aspects, including style, color and texture. On major occasions, such as the religious offering events, the parade of five to six or seven to eight peers in the same cohort is, without doubt, an eye-catching scene. These customs, especially having been demonstrated by Dai women, remain to be, as they have always been, among the most beautiful unique spots on the tourism landscape of Xishuangbanna to visiting strangers.

Solar water heater adoption is yet another compelling example of the psychological tendency of peer comparison and convergence. In 2004, Yan Peng equipped his rebuilt house with a solar water heater-the first-ever in Jing village. In the same year, five out of the seven families in his cohort followed suit, buying their own heaters of the same brand, and soon later, almost all families across the village had solar water heaters. In the back of their mind, a failure to catch up with their neighbors is inferior to others, which is a disgrace. Xiao Tong, a businessman from Zhejiang who is now in charge of selling water heaters here, said to me,

> It is really a weird experience to do business with the Dai families – It never rains but pours. When it comes to product promotion here, it is hard in the beginning: Everyone just takes a wait-and-see attitude, refraining from clinching a deal. Yet, one sheep leaps over the ditch, all the rest will follow. Whenever one deal is clinched, you will see no end of a constant stream of deals. All the families will vie with each other to buy your products, and these of the same make.

Yet, in this typical context that "enables herd behaviors" and in this Village Society of Acquaintances that "enables anything related to you to be amplified", the actual fertility behavior of the Dai people didn't dovetail with the argument from Li Yinhe:

> Living in such a context, individuals' fertility behavior are inevitably governed by and manifested in the logic that 'a greater say comes from more voices, namely more offspring', thus encouraging more offspring and extended families. On one hand, the 'competition' rule motivates village members to go all out in the fertility competition, while on the other, the 'convergence' rule and the strong demand for fairness among village members combine to form a force constraining each other. Hence, more births and earlier parenthood are, of course, the common goal for all families in a village (Li, 1994a),

and of course, they couldn't lead to her corollary: "Therefore, to control its population growth, there are only two options for China: compulsory family planning and the integration of more people away from their village culture into the urban one, and there are no other alternatives" (Li, 1994b).

According to the author's observation, in the Dai villages, it seemed that in almost all aspects, villagers tended to keep up with the Joneses, but never did so in one thing: Who has more children, as in their mind, has nothing to do with an individual's capability, but it is the manifest destiny or "karma" that determines how many children he can have. A family without children could adopt ones to realize its wish of having children, and in their mind, it makes no difference "having or not having children" or "having how many children". In other words, it's not something that the Dai people think you can compare with others.

Though Mr. Fei Xiaotong's Generational Succession and Parent Care by Adult Children model and Ms. Li Yinhe's Village Society of Acquaintances model satisfactorily explain the fertility behavior of the Han ethnic farming families in inland regions on the Chinese mainland, they both fail to fully shed light on the traditional fertility behavior of the Dai families in most rural families. As the author believed, the cause of this difference lies in neither the farming environment where physical force in the form of manual laborers (men) is essential nor in the village environment where acquaintances gather and interact, but in the cultural environment that constitutes the contents of people's lives.

In fact, whether it is Mr. Fei Xiaotong's analysis of the Generational Succession-Parent Care by Adult Children model or Ms. Li Yinhe's interpretation of the Village Society of Acquaintances model, they have touched on the regulating power of a cultural environment over human behaviors. Mr. Fei Xiaotong pointed out in his model that the generational succession (children inheriting parents' properties and business) and the generational support (later generations supporting previous ones) are the products of Chinese society; he attributed them to the traditional Chinese culture. It is exactly the traditional Chinese culture of "carrying on family lines" and "raising sons as support in advanced years" that has fostered the cultural climate of "to maintain the capacity of such a social structure, it is imperative to have as more children as possible" and has sufficiently justified the fertility behavior of "having more offspring and preference for male offspring" in the traditional agrarian society, so that such "traditional fertility behavior" can continue. With regard to her model, Li noted that "fertility cultures are rooted in particular living environments".

In this typical context that "enables herd behaviors" like the Village Society of Acquaintances, all members in rural families have to live following the same life logic. When it comes to specific issues like fertility behavior, giving birth to at least one boy is a widely recognized standard, and failing to reach this standard, you are incapable, inferior to other men, debased as "the last one of your family line" (without issue) in the eye of others, and live a meaningless life in your own eye. That's why it is very important to pursue "having more offspring, especially more male offspring" to secure "a greater say based on more voices" and ease the pressure of being looked down upon as the "peculiar creature" by fellow villagers.

Such life logic is mandated by a traditional village culture but also is an embodiment of the outlooks on life and values of persons living in such a culture. The value standard lying beneath these outlooks on life and values functions like a strong invisible rope, regulating the behaviors of all persons "born and living in such a culture" and thus forcibly turning the fertility behavior, which would otherwise be individual behaviors freely chosen by individual families, into the herding behaviors. That's the power of the cultural environment in shaping human behaviors.

As we have seen, fertility behavior is governed by the logic of life, which in turn is rooted in the value standard recognized by the persons living in a cultural environment. Farther down the road, the value standard is an embodiment of outlooks on life and values in terms of individual persons, and an embodiment of a culture in terms of cultural anthropology. It is exactly in the dimension of different values of fertility in Eastern and Western cultures that Mr. Fei Xiaotong demonstrated the root causes behind the significant difference in the attitude towards fertility between Chinese farmers and Westerners.

However, on the grounds that "persons in the village culture find it hard to get off from the much heavier pressure of childbirth, and will be haunted by a heavy sense of failure – even in throughout their lifetime – from failure to comply with the rules. In contrast with their rural peers, urban dwellers suffer lighter conformity pressure due to a freer cultural environment" (Li, 1994c), Ms. Li Yinhe attributed different attitudes towards childbirth between urban and rural areas to the different living environments. In fact, different living environments result in different lifestyles, which in essence constitute different cultures. But in Li Yinhe's case, different cultures happen to exist between rural and urban China.

In a nutshell, different fertility behavior stem from different concepts of birth control, which, in turn, stem from different lifestyles, that is, different cultures. Therefore, the author believes that the inapplicability of Mr. Fei Xiaotong's Relay-Support model and Ms. Li Yinhe's Village Society of Acquaintances model in explaining the traditional fertility behavior of the Dai people lies neither in the farming environment where physical force in the form of manual laborers (men) is essential nor in the village environment where acquaintances gather and interact, but in the cultural environment that constitutes the contents of people's lives.

Section 2 Formation of the Traditional Fertility Concept in the Dai Ethnic Society

Given the cultural context is the source of the fertility concept, which, in turn, governs fertility behavior, so, to decipher the fertility behavior of the Dai people in the traditional agrarian society, we have to start with their traditional culture and cultural life.

Southern Buddhist Culture and Its Role in the Dai Traditional Cultural Life

In general, the Cultural Life of the Dai Group living in the traditional agrarian society is one centered on Buddhist culture. As Mr. Jiang Yingliang put it, "The cultural atmosphere full of Buddhist thoughts constitutes their whole living space" (Jiang, 1950a). In *The Annals of the Twelve Bannas*, Mr. Li Fuyi documented:

> Buddhism is the 'state religion' in the twelve bannas. In any village or town with the Dai people, there is at least one Buddhist temple. Functioning like the school for the Dai people, Buddhist temples are the only educational institutions for civilizing people and training talents ... Given a majority of border persons read in the Dai language only, all the official announcements had to be made in the Dai language to reach out to a wider audience. Even in a remote hamlet, it was not hard to find someone who can read in the Dai language (Li, 1955b).

Though the specific time when Southern Buddhism came in the Dai areas remains an open issue in academic circles, the genealogical books of Cheli Pacification Superintendent recorded that the ancestor of the first generation:

Bazhen became the reign of Xishuangbanna in the 54 second Year in the Dai calendar (the 7th Year of the Chunxi Era during the Reign of Emperor Xiaozong in the Southern Song Dynasty, i.e., 1180 A.D.) and was entitled the "Supreme Lord Buddha in the Golden Palace Kingdom of Jinglong", suggesting that Southern Buddhism had already had established a relationship with the rulers in Xishuangbanna at that time. The records of the enthronement of the 13th generation Lord Sanboledai in the *Histories of the Region of Le* say: "With the Lord elected, crowds poured into the Buddhist temple. Standing in front of the Buddha statue and holding Sutras in hand, the Lord took the oath in the presence of the Abbot and three representatives of Buddhists, and the oath was later inscribed in the temple." Sanboledai was enthroned in 1457 A.D., that is, the 819th Year in the Dai calendar (Liu, 1993). Therefore, it should be an indisputable fact that by then, Southern Buddhism had already been introduced into Xishuangbanna.

There were also descriptions in some sutras of the scenes of Buddhism dissemination: "Together with his disciples, the Buddha preached for years in various places, and was welcomed and revered by locals. He was offered food, water and goods. His hair and footprints were collected for establishing Buddhism, and the Hair of Buddha Pagoda, the Footprints of Buddha Pagoda and Buddhist temples were built as the worship venues for his believers" (Editorial Board of the Complete Works of Chinese Pattra leaf Scriptures, 2006). Thus, there is the saying that "Every village has Buddhist temples and monks" in Xishuangbanna. With the ubiquitous presence of the Buddha in their life, the Dai people have been known as an ethnic group of all believers in Southern Buddhism. Mr. Li Fuyi said that, "the Dai people believe in Buddhism. Towering Buddhist temples and Buddhist pagodas are everywhere. Men must be tonsured to be monks once in their life" (Li, 1955c). Mr. Yao Hesheng said, "Here is every inch a world of Buddhism in the twelve bannas. Every man has been a monk, and every woman is a devout Buddhism believer. So, there are a lot of temples here. Almost every village has at least one Buddhist temple" (Yao, 2003). Mr. Jiang Yingliang also said that, "the Dai people have a very unified and simple religion. They all believe in Buddhism. In the Dai area, there are no other religious beliefs except Buddhism" (Jiang, 1950b). These accounts reflected the close relationship between Southern Buddhism and the life of the Dai people.

In real life, a Dai Buddhist has been deeply immersed in the expansive Southern Buddhist culture throughout his entire life cycle. Southern Buddhism has been an integral part of their social life. A Dai boy at birth is named by a monk, lives in a Buddhist temple as a monk at six to seven years old, and is secularized when coming of age and gets married. Yet, secularization doesn't mean he parts forever with his religion: He has to live a religious life on a regular basis as a monk at a Buddhist temple. He is a monk in a Buddhist temple and a believer outside it. Everyone has a lifetime obligation to provide for monks and devote their savings to funding Buddhist temples or Buddhist pagodas and Buddhist events. Every man begins to amass their learning and cultural attainments from being a monk and reading Buddhist sutras, and every woman begins to do so from listening to Buddhist stories. They observe various Buddhist festivals in a year, and invite monks to chant sutras and pray for good fortune for their ill family members or at the funerals of their deceased family members.

All this shows the lofty and dominant position that Southern Buddhism holds in the heart of the Dai people. They have always shown high respect to anything associated with Southern Buddhism, which could be evidenced by their attitude and their words and behaviors toward Buddhist temples, monks, Buddhist scriptures and Buddhist rituals.

1. Buddhist temples: Where there is a Dai village, there are Buddhist temples. In larger villages, there is more than one Buddhist temple. Even in a tiny hamlet of just a dozen of families, there is also a plain Buddhist temple. Even when a village was relocated to a temporary place under unusual circumstances, such as floods, warfare and banditry, makeshift Buddhist temples also had to be built, and before the village and its villagers came

back, the original Buddhist temples had to be refurnished and monks invited to move back.

In contrast with bamboo stilt-houses, Buddhist temples are the most imposing buildings in a village.

> Not only local villagers, but also residents from neighboring areas, are ready to contribute their inputs in the form of labor service, funds and donated materials in the construction or repairing of Buddhist temples. Hence, Buddhist temples are usually the most magnificent buildings in a Dai village, and the spectacle of a brightly-colored red-tiled grand palace towering over a tiny hamlet of dozens of fenced hay-thatched cottages is also the unique scenery on the local landscapes in the Dai settlement regions . . . The Dai communities have very low living standards and ordinary villagers all live in rather simple residences, but only Buddhist temples and pagodas are very magnificent. One temple or pagoda may cost tens of thousands of silver coins, but it doesn't seem to be difficult to fund it as the Dai people have never been stingy with these religious projects. Some Buddhist temples or pagodas were even funded completely with the private savings of chieftains or their mothers . . . Of course, ordinary people would be sure to vie with each other to make such munificent acts if they couldn't afford . . . but such inputs are enough to demonstrate the fanaticism of Buddhism among the Dai communities (Jiang, 1950c).

2. Monks and nuns: Dai men have to go through monastic life. The monk class consists of Junior Monks, Senior Monks, Buddhas, Senior Buddhas and Great Buddhas by seniority and referred to in the Dai language as 帕 (Bha), 帕竜 (Bhalhung), 都 (Du), 都竜 (Dulhung) and 都比竜 (Dubilhung), respectively. Boys usually enroll into a Buddhist temple as a monk at six to seven years old, and most of them get secularized at 20 years old or so to get married and have children. What a Buddhist temple was to young men in the Dai society in the past is like what a primary school is to them nowadays. A Buddhist temple serves as a place to impart knowledge and those few who choose to be a monk throughout their lifetime may climb up the ladder to the rank of Great Buddha. Being a monk, "At his audience, even his parents also would worship him, covering their faces with cassock to show their reverence" (Li, 1955d). The etiquettes of this kind shed light on the lofty status of being a monk.

To be promoted to a Great Buddha, a Senior Buddha must have the following qualifications: First of all, having great religious accomplishments, firm religious faith and high creditworthiness among common believers; second, having a high familiarity with the sutras and in-depth understanding of the Buddhist principles; third, having the ability to deal with various affairs and strong leadership; and fourth, having the longest experience in being a monk among his peers.

Not only ranking highest in a temple, Great Buddhas are also the most venerated persons in their village, and are highly respected even outside their village. Great Buddhas can talk on an equal footing with chieftains in political domains, are respected by chieftains on all religious occasions, and are leaders or rulers in the minds of the local population.

3. Buddhist scriptures: Buddhist scriptures are roughly classified by medium into pattra-leaf and paper-printed scriptures: The former are usually inscribed on processed pattra-leaves with a pin-shaped iron pen and having gilded titles, and the latter written on stencil tissue paper, protected with exquisitely embroidered satin or figured cloth covers, and usually bound into scrolls. Buddhist scriptures may also be classified by content into two categories: the original Sanskrit texts of Buddhism and the Jakata Tales.

Many scriptures are the wishes or promises made by common believers, recorded by Buddhas or secularized "Kanglangs", and donated to Buddhist temples on religious offering events. On annual major religious offering events like the Door-opening Festival and the Door-closing Festival, either in the name of individuals or families, believers donate their scriptures. Several families may also pool their financial funds to donate larger volumes of scriptures. The author participated in the Ceremony of Donating Scriptures on September 13, 2008 in Manfeilong Village, Jinghong Gasa Township: By pooling RMB 1,200, 14 families donated a hardbound two-volume book of the Jakata Tales: Weixiandala (维先达腊 in Chinese) published by the People's Publishing House of China to a local Buddhist temple, making a big splash in the village. It was reportedly the grandest event of the kind in their village since the Cultural Revolution. The 14 donating families were rewarded with rapturous applause and some families planned to follow their suit to make a bigger donation next year.

4. Buddhist rituals: the religious rituals of paying tributes to the Buddha are termed as "performing offerings" among the Dai believers, i.e. making donations. Many events of this kind take place in a year or even a month. On these occasions, "Villagers offer their flowers, wines and

> meals, kowtowing and worshipping to the Buddha. Especially during major events, many believers even stay at Buddhist temples for several days in a row. Throughout the rituals, the lamp in the wooden niche by the side of the Buddha statue is burning, and there is always a monk sitting in the niche chanting day and night." During the Door-closing Festival [the Vassa (the Yuanjiu Season) in the preceding Chapter 3], the religious offering events take place every seven days.

> In the three months from lunar mid-June to lunar mid-September every year (the exact period is subject to the Dai calendar), the Dai people go have a longer-term monastic experience. It falls exactly in a unique tropic rainy season in border regions and all outdoor activities have to be suspended or delayed due to heavy rain and hot weather. Crops are growing freely, needing neither manuring nor weeding, so the Dai farmers who are left idle turn to devote their time to religion, having a brief monastic life at Buddhist temples. Beginning on the first day of this season, every person and every family quit their work on hand, meditating, worshipping and attending preach sessions at Buddhist temples, and even the governmental affairs have to be suspended. The middle-aged and senior men must stay at Buddhist temples for at least three days every seven days. During their stay at temples, they live the same life as monks: no stepping out and refraining from lunch (fasting from noon to the dawn of the next day). On the last day of the 90-day season, all villagers, both men and women, worship the Buddha and pray at Buddhist temples, repenting their sins over the past year. This day is the day of 'opening the door', meaning the brief monastic life at temples comes to an end and everything begins to return to normal. Only by this day will people turn their attention to the farming work and government affairs (Jiang, 1950d).

Going through centuries of vicissitudes, Southern Buddhism emerged as the mainstream culture in this piece of land and its rational elements have been deeply integrated into the cultural life of the Dai people. Buddhist scriptures featuring the Jakata Tales have been going around in the folks in visualized forms such as murals, pictures and sculptures, and the vivid accounts of the "Buddha attaining enlightenment" ordeal, which are usually illustrated with various character images of kings, farmers, ladies and villains, have become cautionary tales in civilizing the masses and provide beneficial value guidance and spiritual consolation to the Dai people in their daily life. Not only being the venue for monks to gain learning and expound on scriptures, but Buddhist temples also are the classrooms of moral education for the masses and the exchange hubs for folk arts: They encapsulate the spiritual life, moral education, entertainment and emotional exchanges into one spatio-temporal sphere, where everyone can find their role models of personal behaviors, get their inspirations for their life goals, and recognize their own values.

Core Values of Southern Buddhism and Their Impact on Fertility Behavior

According to Buddhist scriptures, Sakyamuni's enlightenment went through a process from "awakening to sufferings" to "realizing sufferings" and "getting extricated from sufferings", i.e. the upgrading and sublimation of his mental status and ideology from first being aware of "sufferings", next to trying to recognize them, then to trying to transcend over them, and finally to getting extricated from them. So, it might as well be concluded that what he cared about were the issues about the value of life and spiritual extrication of human beings, and his "Enlightenment" theory was also developed around philosophical issues of life, and he envisioned the ideal goal: the harmonious life of mutual understanding, help and support among human beings. To have this thought acceptable to all living creatures, the Buddha used his own ordeal of realizing the truth of life as the educational materials and expounded on his thoughts on the value of life and spiritual extrication as a human being to monks by describing his spiritual experience throughout the course of getting enlightened, establishing the thought system of the Primitive Buddhism anchored on the basic doctrines of the Four Noble Truths, the Dependent Origination of Things, the Four Essentials of the Dharma and the Noble Eightfold Path. To sum up, Sakyamuni's Buddhist thought system embodies at least the following core values (Wang, 2003a):

1. Recognizing Equality: This thought was promoted throughout Sakyamuni's preaching to all living creatures since he got enlightened and became a Buddha. It was both a reaction to the then-dominant Brahmin caste system and new development in the Sramana ideology. In the eyes of The Buddha, the fate and situation of a person are mandated neither by Brahma (Brahmin teachings) or will of Deity nor by the destiny of his previous lives (as preached by predestinarians), and they also don't occur without cause as preached by Fortuitist, or rather they are incidental but are determined by a person's actions. For example, in *Dighanikara Vol. 27: Agganna Sutta is the Dharma*, the Buddha explained to two Brahmins: Vasistha and Brahmaputra. By expounding upon the origins of nations and castes, the Buddha refuted the superiority of Brahmin's

caste doctrine (Guo, 1997a). In *Dighanikara Vol.3: Ambatthasuttam*, the Buddha answered the questions raised by Ambattha, a visiting young Brahmin, admonishing that those who are bound by class origin, surnames, arrogance and marriage are far from great attainments in virtue and wisdom (Guo, 1997b). In addition, *Suttanipata Vol. 2: Cullavagga – Brahmin Dharma Sutra, Tatiya Vagga, Mahaa Vagga and Vasaṭṭha Sutta*, and *Majjhima Nikaya Vol. 84: Madara Sutta*, there are also expositions by the Buddha against Brahmin's caste superiority. In *Majjhima Nikaya Vol. 93: Assalāyana Sutta*, the Buddha commented: The four castes – Brahmin, Kshatriya, Vaisya and Shudras- are not universal eternal existences. Persons from each caste can get good retribution by doing the good, and all the four castes are pure and completely equal (Guo, 1997c). By refuting the theory of caste superiority, Sakyamuni put a person's behaviors in the first place, highly affirming the subjective initiative of a person, and pointed out that a person's life and destiny are shaped by the interaction of various causes and conditions, which are mainly "karmas", namely the acts that a person conducts in the course of his life. The fates of all living creatures in the present life and the consequences in their next life are determined by the "karmas" in the previous life or in the present life, that is to say, "a person reaps the consequences of his own acts". In this way, persons are encouraged to do good rather than evil through their own efforts. That is to say, "Never do any evil and do all good"

Self-restraint and No Greed: The Four Essentials of the Dharma says that, "All desires are sufferings". The desire therein is the meaning of worry or suffering. There are many kinds of worry. Among them, greed, hatred and ignorance are known collectively as the three poisons. Besides, there are arrogance, suspicion and wrong view. These six types of desires are collectively known as six fundamental worries (Wang, 2003b). The "right thought" in the Noble Eightfold Path teaches people that they should correct their thoughts and resolve, reflect on the Buddhist principles correctly, and refrain from greed, hatred and harm, while the "right mindfulness" suggests that people should concentrate their mind, observe and reflect on the four objects: physical body, sensation, mind and Dharma (basic principles of the cosmos) with a high degree of Buddhist wisdom, and keep away from greed and ignorance (Li, 2000).

3. Peace in the Present Life: the Four Essentials of the Dharma says that, "Whatever is phenomenal is ephemeral". This is just the thought that

the Buddha emphasized in his specific elaboration of the "right view" in the Noble Eightfold Path. In *Anguttaranikara: Tikanipaata*, the Buddha said that, "Whether or not the Tathagata is present, the Dharma of the Realms is always there. That is to say, whatever is phenomenal is ephemeral" (Guo, 1997d). The meaning is, all things and all phenomena in the universe are interrelated with one another. The birth and death of one always have something to do with these of others, and there is no constancy and immutability. So, any phenomenon is impermanent in its nature, and can "emerge", "exist", "change" and "perish" in an instant. The "in the snap of a finger" in Buddhist scriptures is the period of time lasting 60 instants, and within one instant, the entire process of "emerge, exist, change and perish" can be completed. The whole life of a person is composed of "birth, senility, illness and death" happenings in the continuum of countless instants. From the perspective of individual happenings, it is that "emerge", "exist", "change" and "perish" can take place within an instant, thus highlighting the thought that persons should place more premium on peace and stability in the present life. In addition, karma says that the idea of "one's own work and one's own consequences" also encourages people to do good deeds in this life in order to achieve earthly peace. Besides, the thought: "a person reaps the consequences of his own acts" as preached by the Karma Doctrine also advocates that a person should do the good in the present life to get peace in the present life.

4. Optimism and Open-mindedness. In *Sayuttanikāya Vol. 56: Satyas* and *Vinaya Pitaka: Mahaa-Vagga*, the Buddha explained the Four Noble Truths and defined his own style of practice as "Majjhima Patipada" or moderation. He said,

> Attentions, all the Buddhist monks! As a monk, you should avoid two extremes. What are the two extremes? One is the indulgence in sensual pleasures, which would be degraded, vulgar, secular, indecent and meaningless, and the other is the aspiration for ascetic practices, which would be painful, indecent and meaningless. Attentions, all the Buddhist monks! Tathagata had refrained from the two extremes and got the essence of moderation. Moderation engenders views and perceptions and leads to tranquility, wisdom, equal enlightenment and nirvana. All the Buddhist monks! What is moderation? That is the Noble Eightfold Path: right view, right judgment, right speech, right action, right livelihood, right effort, right mindfulness and right concentration (Guo, 1997e).

The Noble Eightfold Path doctrine founded by the Buddha epitomizes the proposition of neither being ascetic nor indulgent, pointing out that only by avoiding the two extremes: the ascetic practices advocated by Jainism and the indulgence in sensual pleasures advocated by Lokayatika and Fortuitism and leading a moderate life can a person truly get extricated from sufferings in life and reach the ideal state of nirvana. Therefore, a person should be content with what he has and be optimistic about life.

5. Reconciling with natural courses. The Interdependence doctrine is among the basic teachings in Buddhism, also known as the "Interactions of Causes and Conditions" theory. Interdependence refers to "all dharmas are from the combination of elements". That is to say, all things or phenomena in the world are interrelated with and conditional on each other. Without interrelations and conditions, nothing can come into being and exist. Sakyamuni defined the "Interdependence" as follows: "As this emerges and exists, so that emerges and exists; and as this perishes and is gone, so that perishes and is gone." To give an example in popular language, there would be no forest without trees, and trees are from seeds, so there would be no trees without seeds. Trees depend on soil, sunlight, air and water, so there would be no tree seeds without soil, sunshine, air, water and other conditions. So, forests, trees, soil, air, sunlight and water are interrelated to and conditional on each other. Without the others, one couldn't exist independently. Thus, without these conditions, there would be no seeds; without seeds, there would be no trees; and without trees, there would be no forest (Wang, 2003c). A certain result in the world arises from the preexisting conditions for producing such a result, and these conditions and the result are in the interdependent relationship, therefore, a person should not make deliberate pursuits in doing everything and should reconcile with the fate and the present situation.

The thought system of the Primitive Buddhism established and disseminated by Sakyamuni marked the formation of the Primitive Buddhist culture. With the preaching of the Buddha, believers increased and the Buddhist thought also gained traction, spreading out from India to Sri Lanka and then to Southeast Asian countries across the Indian Ocean and it was later known as Southern Buddhism due to its geographical orientation of dissemination. Having used the Tipitaka in Pali language as its main scriptures during its dissemination,

Southern Buddhism has perfectly retained the teachings and doctrines in the original Buddhist thought system of the Buddha when he was alive. Therefore, the Southern Buddhist culture with the Tipitaka in Pali language at its core well reflects the cultural thought of Primitive Buddhism created by Sakyamuni, and has maintained its core values: Recognizing Equality, Self-restraint and No greed, Peace in the Present Life, Optimism and Open-mindedness, and Reconciling with natural courses. In the value of life system constructed by Sakyamuni, "getting extricated from sufferings" is the supreme goal. If a man is the one of intelligence, all his "acts" should be conducted for the purpose of realizing this goal. To "get extricated from sufferings", he must, first of all, "recognize sufferings". What is "suffering"? "Suffering" is "desire", and is "worry". The greatest worry in life is rooted in greed, hatred, ignorance, arrogance, suspicion and evil. Having recognized "sufferings", a man should strive to improve himself, avoid extremes and live a "moderate" life. In this way, he would be able to extinguish his "desire" and enter the ideal status of nirvana, achieving the highest goal of "getting extricated from sufferings".

With this goal of values, all acts of a man should be trained to the aim of "Recognizing Equality, Self-restraint and No greed, Peace in the Present Life, Optimism and Open-mindedness, and Reconciling with natural courses".

As thus, this principle is also true with fertility behavior, so, a man should be "optimistic", should "reconcile with his current situation" and should be "equal". Children are born of their parents. Whether to have a boy or a girl, the relationship between parents and their children is "Whatever is phenomenal is ephemeral". From pregnancy to delivery, the safety of both the mother and the child is a blessing. Meanwhile, when to get pregnant, when to give birth, whether to give birth or not, and to give birth to a boy or a girl are all related to fate, and parents should not make a deliberate choice or try to control it on their own wishes. Any deliberate choice or control is rooted in "desire". Moreover, no matter the child is a boy or a girl, they are all born equal, have no distinction of being superior or inferior, and should be treated equally instead of a preference for one over the other.

In a word, a man shouldn't be greedy with anything. "Neither fate nor retribution, everything has its natural course". When it comes to fertility behavior, this concept is "moderation" and the Buddhist idea of reproduction. In contrast, the concepts of birth control, like the deliberate pursuit of "more births" or "preference for male offspring", run counter to the fundamental intentions advocated by the Buddha.

Formation of Religious Outlook on Life, Values and Traditional Fertility Concept in the Dai Society

From the perspective of cultural anthropology, the embracement of the Southern Buddhism culture by the Dai people is essentially a process where they became increasingly identified with it. The Southern Buddhism culture was an alien culture in the Dai settlement regions, and its dissemination and embracement by locals suggested that the value orientation, attitudes and ways of life advocated by Sakyamuni were accepted by the Dai people.

Through persistent, diverse, flexible and open dissemination accessible to the common masses in the Dai settlement regions, the Primitive Buddhist thoughts advocated by the Buddha had over time become the values of life and spiritual sustenance, taking root in the minds and hearts of the Dai people and becoming entrenched in all the aspects of their production and life.

1. Believers: All Dai boys at seven to eight years old enroll in a Buddhist temple to be monks. It is the duty of parents to send their boys to a Buddhist temple as monks. Being a monk at a Buddhist temple means that a boy can understanding things around him, learn writing and arithmetic skills, and become an intellectual in the Dai society. Therefore, he is more respected by others and can find a wife more easily. Otherwise, he is still an uncivilized savage and is looked down upon by others (Editorial Committee of Five Series of Books on Ethnic Issues, 1983). This common understanding in the Dai society prompts every man to choose to learn Buddhism directly at a Buddhist temple. Through religious offerings, Vassa and other events as well as through imperceptible influence from male family members, girls are taught Buddhist teaching indirectly. Therefore, the universal education of Southern Buddhism gained traction in the Dai society.
2. Duration: In addition to the long-term education of the Buddhist culture at Buddhist temples as monks, men, even being secularized, have to attend preaching sessions back at temples with their fellow villagers during the Vassa Period (the rainy season) every year. Such rituals are like annual training sessions on the entire population including men and women. Besides, there are many religious offering events every year, and at least seven major events must be held. Each event is equivalent to a re-education session on Buddhist culture in a Buddhist temple. The long-term learning as monks at Buddhist temples, regular training sessions

during the Vassa period and frequent offering events combine to provide the continued education.

3. Contents: Buddhist temples provide standardized, strict and systematic education in three fields to monks: The Dai language, systematic Buddhist contents such as Tipitaka, and scientific knowledge including history, literature, medicine, arts, ethics, law and philosophy. With no Dai writing before the introduction of Buddhism into China, most Buddhist scriptures at Buddhist temples are written and cited in the Dai language. In most cases, only those who have been monks at Buddhist temples can read the Dai language. Therefore, being a monk at a temple is the main way for the Dai people to learn the Dai language. In Tipitaka, Vinaya-Pitaka is the collection of Buddhist canons and precepts, Sutta Pitaka the collection of scriptures propagating the teachings, and Abhidhamma the collection of scriptures summarizing or interpreting various Buddhist teachings or concepts. Meanwhile, Buddhist temples teach monks how to behave and work right. Only industrious, virtuous and honest monks can be promoted to be Buddha, Great Buddha and then Kuba. To be a respected man by learning the Dai language, Tipitaka and scientific knowledge at Buddhist temples is the ideal of the Dai people. The learning of believers at home is nonacademic and their main contents are lighthearted Buddhist stories. In the rainy season, villagers gather on the upper floor of the village temple to listen attentively to humorous Buddhist stories like Aesop's fables. These education contents integrating religious rules, doctrines and stories are popular among believers, showing the popularity, or the folk nature, of Buddhist culture education.
4. Forms: Buddhist temples provide systematic and formal education to monks, with daily routines (mendicancy, morning/afternoon sessions, labor, meals, bedtime, etc.) going on as scheduled at temples. Preaches are made for believers at home during the Vassa period, on the offering events, during festival holidays or on major family occasions (house-building, marriage, child-naming, funerals and so on). The chanting of sutras is like informal education, benefiting both monks and believers at home, and diversifying the forms of enlightenment.
5. Methods: While attending preaches at Buddhist temples during the Vassa period is a kind of systematic cultural learning for villagers, the daily enlightenment is a relatively liberal and informal approach of education, which can be represented by junior monks begging for meals in villages every morning, villagers holding the offering events at temples,

and monks' Parinama[31] to the Buddha's preaches during various festivals. The combination of systematic learning and informal learning reflects the flexibility in educational methods.

6. Venues: Inside Buddhist temples, Buddhas give preaches to both incumbent and secularized monks (taking Buddhas as their teachers), while outside Buddhist temples, "Bozhangs" in charge of Buddhist affairs engage and dialogue with the masses (taking Bozhangs as their teachers). Therefore, either inside or outside Buddhist temples, believers are exposed to the Buddhist culture. The combination of enlightenment inside and outside temples enhances the diversity in educational venues. The extensive and persistent enlightenment has integrated the core values of Southern Buddhism culture deeply into the value system of the Dai community.

The Dai people set "recognizing sufferings and getting extricated from sufferings" through their right effort of self-cultivation and improvement as their goal of life, and regard the "worry-free" and "moderate" life as their pursuit of value. In short, their ideal life is the Buddhist life, and their outlook on life and values are also the Buddhist ones. Herein, the author took their funeral ceremony as an example to substantiate this claim.

In the eyes of the Dai believers in Theravada Buddhism, death marks the end of a person's suffering in his present life and the beginning of his fate in his afterlife. If he has amassed enough merits and virtues in his present life, not only will he himself enjoy affluence in his afterlife but also his soul will be able to bless posterity from suffering and hardship. The final thing his surviving family members should do for him is to set him smoothly on the path paved with his amassed merits and virtues to Heaven, so that his soul can be the ancestral deity putting his surviving family members under his protection. So, funeral services are the opportunities of spiritual baptism for surviving family members to reflect on themselves against the deceased and reaffirm the convention that they should not only create and amass sufficient wealth in their present life, but more importantly, they should also set aside enough wealth for their afterlife. This convention has been constantly strengthened over ages in the Dai society that it has become the life motto and the principle and logic of their behaviors.

31 Parinama, a Buddhist term, means Buddhists sum up all the virtues they amassed and devoted themselves to the goal of wishing all living creatures would become the Buddha. See also Xia Zhengneng, ed., *Comprehensive Dictionary* (abridged edition) (Shanghai: Shanghai Lexicographical Publishing House, 1979), 764.

Edmund Leach, the British anthropologist, believed that in using symbols to distinguish between different categories of things, they are drawing a man-made boundary in a naturally continuous domain. This boundary divides the social space and time into two spheres: One segment is normal, temporal, specific and thus is centrally-located and worldly, while the other, the symbol of the bounded space and time, is abnormal, timeless and fuzzy and thus is located in the margin and sacred; and crossing the boundary and "threshold" has always been associated with some ceremonies (Guo and Zuo, 2000a).

The Dai funeral ceremonies consist of two processes: the sacrifice during the burial and the post-burial sacrifice to Buddhist temples. Going through the whole ceremony from sacrificing, burial, scripture chanting, water dropping and Buddhist offerings, all the surviving participants can clearly feel that the world of mankind is divided into two spheres: This sphere is a finite worldly world, where humans (the surviving participants) are limited both in their life and their ability, and will surely get old over time and eventually die; while that sphere is the realm of immortal and omnipotent Buddhas and deities, where they exist forever in the infinite time and space covering the past, the present and the future.[32] Through the funeral ceremony, the surviving participants can cross the threshold separating humans from deities and Buddhas, have the opportunity to communicate with them, and give out their sacrifices or perform the religious offerings – signifying that their gifts presented to deities and Buddhas have been accepted, and will be rewarded with blessings to themselves in their next life. Just as Leach said, funeral ceremonies allow "the offerors to set up a bridge between the divine world and the human world, and through this bridge, the offerors can get access to the power of the divine" (Guo and Zuo, 2000b).

Villagers well knew that how much divine power they would be rewarded in their next life (that is blessings) depends on the quality and quantity of offerors' offerings (i.e., the merits and virtues). When asked why they perform offerings, villagers replied, "It's good for the next life." When asked the extent to which they should perform religious offerings, the answer is, "It is up to yourself. Anyway, the more you offer, the more you will be rewarded; the less you offer, the less you will be rewarded; and if you don't offer at all, you will not be rewarded at all."

32 In the Dai concept and belief system, the deities consist of Family Deities, Village Deities and Meng Deities, respectively the ancestral deities of families, villages and Mengs; while the Buddha is specifically referred to as Sakyamuni Buddha. Both the deities and the Buddhas are sacred forces that control the worldly life of humans, and therefore should be respected.

When further asked "Why do you spend so much on the offerings since you're not rich now?" they explained,

> A person has both his present life and his next life. He can control how his present life fares (that is, he can shape his present life through his actual behaviors) but can't control how things will go in his next life (that is, he can't control his next life) and will only bank on the protection from deities and Buddhas. The protection from deities and Buddhas in his next life depends on the offerings he performs in his present life. So, if he doesn't take the offerings seriously in his present life, he will suffer much in his next life.

Hence, the "wealth" in their life not only contains the properties that they actually own but also the properties that they have offered to the deities and the Buddhas through the offerings. And the latter are more significant to their life as it relates to their reputation and social status. Thus, the role of the religious offerings in funeral ceremonies is very important.

In Claude Levi-Strauss's view, the communication between humans and deities is the exchange of information via a medium between different status levels. The medium is the offerings that humans sacrifice to deities in the ceremonies.

> Sacrifices are necessary because the two 'information receivers' on different status levels are placed in advance in the sessions of exchange of information, therefore, sacrifices are absolute or extreme activities, and involve a medium. The sacrificial rituals are the attempts to establish necessary connections between two separated spheres, as it has been aptly described, so as to realize the prayers and wishes of humans through distant deities. It is believed that the two separated spheres can be connected through the means of consecrated offerings to achieve the aim (realizing the prayers and wishes of humans through distant deities) (Li, 1987).

Deities enjoy higher statuses than of humans, so they should be respected and revered through considerate sacrifice rituals. Therefore, in funeral ceremonies, either sacrifice during the burial or the post-burial sacrifice to Buddhist temples, participants must make prayers on their bent knees, and their offerings must be clean and fresh, and must contain all categories of articles in their daily life. They must offer 12 portions of each sacrifice, symbolizing the deities can enjoy their offerings each month of the year, etc. In addition, in order for the "communication medium" to be received securely and quickly, participants during their sacrificing events should light candles to create light for the deities in the sky to see the medium, drip water to create moisture for the deities under the ground to feel the medium, and chant scriptures for the deities to hear the scene. Through funeral ceremonies, be it the notion of the "abnormal, timeless, fuzzy, marginal and sacred sphere" as framed by Leach, or what Claude Levi-Strauss described as the other "information receivers" on different status levels, they are both actualized into some sanctified and personified beings, and are truly integrated into the real life of local folks and influence the latter's behaviors.

Furthermore, in the eyes of the Dai people, to show their respect, considerateness, piety and obedience to the other "information receivers" on different status levels as described by Claude Levi-Strauss, the offerors must follow the requirements as below while performing the offerings:

(1) All the money, foods and other goods used as the offerings must have been obtained through legitimate means. In local villagers' eyes, manual labor, especially growing rice, is the most legitimate and moral route to get "clean" wealth, while the gains from engaging in commerce are not clean as they are earned by buying at lower prices and selling at higher prices, which goes against the prohibition against lying; (2) All the efforts must be voluntary, sincere and not motivated by the pursuit of economic gains; (3) Offerors must have a bath and change into clean clothes to keep their bodies clean; (4) Offerors must be discreet in their behaviors, speak softly and politely and refrain from talking nonsense. In the language of Buddhist teaching, offerors must keep their things, minds, bodies and mouths clean, and only then would the deities and the Buddhas be willing to accept their offerings, and can the offerors earn blessings and protection. While explaining that the "spiritual qualities" of offerors are more valuable than the physical wealth they offered, locals cited a tale as an example to the author: An overnight rich man flaunted his wealth by performing offerings, and was very arrogant for lavishly funding a magnificent Pagoda and temple. Having no valuable items as offerings, a devout but poor widow had to perform the offerings at a Buddhist temple by piling up a tiny Buddhist pagoda with river sands she carried over. While she was dropping clean water on wax strips, the deities, earth deities and the Buddhas were moved by her piety and sincerity and accepted the widow's offering – the sand-built pagoda instead of the Buddhist Pagodas and Temples by the arrogant rich man. Soon then, the pagodas and monasteries built by the rich man crashed, but the sand-built pagoda by the widow continued to stand on. Later, the rich man did not get the blessing and protection from the deities and the Buddhas and died of illness before the natural end of his life in a foreign land, while the widow died a natural death at home, getting her deserved blessings. This story's message is that offerors don't feel uneasy with their humble offerings, the most important thing is their sincerity. There are many stories of

such "offering-return" between humans and the deities and the Buddhas in the pattra-leaf scriptures in the Dai language, and elder men could tell them off the reel if you would like to hear. They believed that the deities and the Buddhas are beings of high morality and extraordinary capability, and their own prayers and actions during the rituals are efficacious and effective. The mantra: "What can't be seen through by humans but by the Heaven" has been the words on their lips, which is the popular expression of their convention: the Reward of the Wicked and the Good.

While trying to get some insights into the significance of the offering performance in funeral ceremonies in the local Dai context, we found that they have a very clear understanding of the logical relationship between the offering in their present life and the blessings in their next life and the whereabouts of their offerings. This can be evidenced by the saying: "The more you perform the offerings, the more you will be rewarded; the less you perform the offerings, the less you will be rewarded; and if you don't perform offerings, you will not be rewarded at all." Though any man well knows how their physical offerings to the Buddhist temples are dealt with in reality and where they land, in their mind, these factual aspects are of little importance as what they have offered is their sincerity, and what the Buddhas have known and valued is exactly their sincerity.[33] To put it in Leach's words[34], what the Buddhas want are the gifts that the heart holds rather than the gifts hands hold. When the Buddhas accept the gifts held by the heart from a man (or rather the soul of the man), the gifts in his hands will become meaningless, and thus he can be completely indifferent about the offerings are dealt with in reality.

33 After the post-burial sacrifice, all the offerings were divided into three shares: respectively for Great Buddha, the Buddhist temple (Pazhao – also representing the Bodhisattva) and Bozhang. The shares for Great Buddha and Bozhang were respectively handled by themselves, while the share for the Bodhisattva went to Buddhist Management Team, which was responsible for the management of the Bodhisattva's shares, and, in the case of Man Village, consisted of three members: Yan La, Yan Jiaolong and Yan Bin. All the offerings may put up for sale in Buddhist temples. For example, before a religious offering event, a family may buy the offerings sacrificed by other believers from either Great Buddha, Bozhang or Buddhist Management Team. The resale of the offerings by a Buddhist temple is "uzha" in the Dai language. The "uzha" offerings are cheaper than the similar items at a shop, and the proceeds from the "uzha" offerings go to their owners. The proceeds from the "uzha" offerings under the management of Buddhist Management Team would be used for the operation and management of a Buddhist temple. In most cases, all the offerings would be fully "uzha" by believers nearby.

34 In studying the social structure in the Kachin highlands, Myanmar, Leach found that when it comes to properties and their ownerships, Kachins have a clear distinction between the "gifts of the heart" and the "gifts of the hands". Though the former is economically valueless, their receivers remain obliged to their givers. See also [The U.K.] Edmund·Leach, *Political Systems in the Highlands of Burma*, trans. Yang Chunyu and Zhou Xinhong (The Commercial Press, 2010), 139.

If we made an economic analysis of their mantra: "The more you perform the offerings, the more you will be rewarded; the less you perform the offerings, the less you will be rewarded; and if you don't perform offerings, you will not be rewarded at all.", its logic is that they give the properties of their present life to the Buddhas, and the Buddhas will return these properties to them in their next life. The sacred Buddhas seem to be the custodians who only keep humans' properties under their custody in their present life and will return these properties to them in their next life. In other words, the Buddhas do not change the ownership of the objects offered during the offering ceremony, so, the wealth they have offered remain in their own hands. the Buddhist idiom – "You get what you deserve" – speaks to the truth of wealth. According to this thinking logic, they believed that the wealth they have now on their hands is from the merits and virtues they had amassed from their wholehearted tribute to the Buddhas in their previous life. If they do not sincerely donate part of their wealth in their present life under the custody of the Buddhas, they will have nothing in their afterlife, and then will not be able to have a decent life in their next life. Only by devoting themselves to the Buddhas can the Buddhas help them keep their wealth in their present life, and can they still have wealth in their next life. For the Dai people, only the wealth having been accepted and kept by the Buddhas can be one's real wealth. Thus, they had a rather different notion of wealth from that of "modern men" who measure their wealth by the money they own.

> The concept of the wealth of the Dai people is obviously tinged with a distinct hint of mystery and sacredness, or rather, it represents all the information of wealth, including the implications about the relative relationship between a wealth owner and the Buddhas: Wealth only belongs to its owner and can neither be exchanged nor be borrowed or lent as it is the donor who will eventually be rewarded with blessings and still own the same wealth in his next life. All these are mandated by the Buddhas, who are the omnipotent and just masters of humans (Chu, 2005).

In the back of the mind of the Dai people, as Durkheim put it, "The deities are the protectors of property owners, who ensure by holding regular ceremonies that the deities continue to bring benefits to them" (Qu and Fu, 2001).

There is no denying that today's people are living in the present world, and of course, what they pay attention to is the situation in real life. But just as we live in a world guided by historical materialism, we have developed ideas about the past, the present and the future. Apart from looking into the life in the past and the life in the present, we also think about the life in the future. In terms of thinking logic, the Dai people are living in a world of deities and Buddhas, they also have to not only look into their present life but also think about their next life. In their mind, their next life is actually the future form of their present life, and their present life the present form of their previous life. In other words, the present life is the future form of the previous life, and the next life the future form of the present life. In the logic of time, the relationships between the previous life, the next life and the present life are only the relationships between the past form of the present life and the future form of the present life. The previous life, the present life and the next life are connected, continuous and selfsame. In the logic of life, the previous life and the next life are the same as the present life, having exactly the same conditions as the present life does. The living conditions in the present life are rooted in the previous life, and the living conditions in the next life depend on the behaviors in the present life. This thought about life likewise shows the Buddhist thinking logic of "you get what you deserve".[35] Therefore, the "blessings" in the next life are not fantasies in the air. Instead, they are very real matters of life but must be realized through realistic behaviors of humans. That is to say, they must be realized only through "communications" between deities and Buddhas and humans in the form of ceremonies.

It is under the influence of this religious outlook on life and values that the Dai minority has developed their unique behavioral patterns: "refraining from lust and greed, valuing equality, staying indifferent to fame and fortune, keeping mutually respectful and being ready to do the giving", and fostered their traditional fertility concepts: having no sex preference (recognizing equality) and refraining from deliberately pursuing more births (reconciling with natural courses, exercising moderation and refraining from greed). Such a religious outlook has provided the ideological basis for low fertility behavior in the Dai families.

Section 3 Formation Mechanism of Traditional Low Fertility Behavior in the Dai Society

Amid influences from various factors, fertility concepts are eventually translated into concrete fertility behavior, which is a top-down inevitable law. There are

35 Due to historical reasons, "you get what you deserve"("自作自受") has taken on strongly negative connotations, and become a derogatory phrase. But in the Buddhist sense, it is a neutral phrase, meaning that nobody else but ourselves will have to face the consequences of whatever we have done, good or bad.

various factors at work in the concrete traditional low fertility behavior formation in the Dai society. For example, it is guided by fertility concepts, sustained by natural environments, constrained by traditional social and economic levels, guaranteed by property and power systems, and regulated by social customs.

At the society level: The existing land system, on one hand, guarantees sufficient arable lands for families,in the Dai society, while on the other, also suppresses the embezzlement by families of the lands owned by village communities, thus providing a relatively fair resource distribution platform and establishing the working mechanism for the property-power relations in families and the society. This system

> restricted the resource use by specific men to specific purposes and within specific scopes, thus establishing the authority over specific men and enabling the compulsory distribution of economic gains by specific men by the means of institutionalized property-power relations, and eventually leading to the supply ways and distribution rules of various resources and the resulting resource allocation models in a society (Chen, 2001).

In addition, the basic characteristics of a society with no strong obsession with surnames and clans lead to a loose community bond of family properties and powers that stems from family property inheritance. Consequently, an expansion of a family community won't necessarily lead to an expansion of family powers, so as to mitigate or even eliminate the financial relevance of offspring to a family community and social pressure on childless families, and eventually ensure the stable continuation of a relatively fair resource allocation pattern at the village community level.

The systems and features mentioned above are among the important causes that there exist no such thoughts and ideas as "the continuation of the family line", "the more offspring, the more blessings" and "a greater say comes from more voices, namely more offspring" in the Dai society.

With advantaged natural conditions, even without full effort in economic activities, the Dai people could easily obtain sufficient means of subsistence from the resources allocated by their village communities, and their families were free of the survival pressure from a lack of materials. From the perspective of an "economic man", they could have obtained more wealth through more input in economic activities. However, given basic conditions in a traditional agrarian society, there were no market and technological infrastructure for the circulation of goods. Excess land availability to smaller populations and an equal farming land distribution system, indeed, could ensure that there is enough material to which any additional labor can be applied. However, there were no channels or receivers for the added properties along with the added inputs and efforts by laborers. Therefore, the surplus labor in families could only be left idle. It was impossible that families would realize the desire of expanding their labor forces by having more children.

As Southern Buddhism culture entered and gained a foothold over time in the Dai society, the Buddhist core values become incorporated into the Dai value system. Maybe, it is the easy access to means of subsistence that has enabled the Dai people to have enough time to experience and enjoy a Buddhist lifestyle, or perhaps it is the desire to enjoy a more Buddhist lifestyle that has made them relatively indifferent to material wealth. In short, a set of behavioral patterns imbued with strong religious commitment and sentiment has been cemented through institutionalized practices among the Dai people. These institutionalized behavioral patterns mandate the order of survival and ensure the maintenance of the interests of the village community, and the codes of conduct featuring "mutual respect" and "giving" and the social networks endorsing the practices of helping each other and supporting and respecting the elderly are exactly realistic expressions of these institutionalized Buddhist norms. In such a social framework, supporting the elderly is a common obligation in the Dai society, and families, family communities and village communities provide the three-level guarantee for the fulfillment of this obligation, as a result, eliminating the hotbed for the idea of having children as parents' support in their advanced ages.

Meanwhile, the belief in Southern Buddhism has enabled the Dai people to get their own value interpretations to happiness, pleasure, accomplishment and other concepts. They worship the Buddha with all their hearts, and regard the religious events, including the offering events and attending the preaches, as representational expressions of their self-cultivation and improvement, and are willing to make more inputs into them piously. In their eyes, having more births does not necessarily mean more blessings, while having no children does not necessarily mean a miserable life in advanced ages as being "the last one of your family line" (or without issue). In addition, women having fewer births to keep fit and stay in shape is also a widely accepted value for them.

At the family level, the abundant labor force and a sound old-age security system has reduced utilitarian incentives to these fertility behavior that are aimed at producing more harvests (and income) by adding laborers to the family and securing support in old age by having more children. The system in which both husband and wife contribute to household income, have equal right to spend their joint earnings, and everybody in the household gets to keep whatever they earn through their "side job" makes sex equality an inevitability. Both parents and children prefer to live separately and be independent of one another. Due to these living arrangements and small family structures, having more children is no more a source of pride for a couple than having few children is a source of shame and disdain. Adoption not only shields couples who cannot have biological children from the societal pressure often put on those who are childless but also give them the joy of parenthood; the practice of the son-in-law moving into his wife's house allows her parents to enjoy the psychological satisfaction associated with a feeling of having both a son and a daughter, and given the absence of a system of male primogeniture, there is no basis for the preference for sons over daughters. All these factors have had direct or indirect effects on the fertility behavior of the Dai people.

In short, with favorable natural environments and institutionalized farmland-centered property-power relations, the Dai people in the traditional agrarian society were free from economic considerations in their fertility motivation and had very low utilitarian need of having births. The less parent-child interdependence and the independent habit of different generations living separately consolidated the small family-centered structure and reduced the emotional need of having children. In addition, the simple folk customs (mutual assistance among neighbors and fellow villagers, helping the poor and respecting the elderly), the firm belief in the Buddhist life view and the life goal benchmarked against "recognizing equality", "reconciling with natural courses", "exercising self-restraint" and "staying indifferent to fame and fortune" also helped to temper their desire for material things in life and enrich their spiritual pursuits. It's exactly the combined influence of multiple factors in material life, spiritual pursuits and institutions that has shaped the fertility concept among the Dai minority of "sex equality" and "the more kids, the heavier the burden on parents" and led to the fertility behavior of "no deliberate pursuit of more births" or "no preference for male offspring".

Section 4 Theoretical Interpretation of Traditional Low Fertility Behavior in the Dai Ethnic Society

Maslow classified the behavioral motivations of human beings into two categories: deficiency motivations and transcnedence-motivations (growth motivations), with the former "the common motivations of humans below the self-actualization

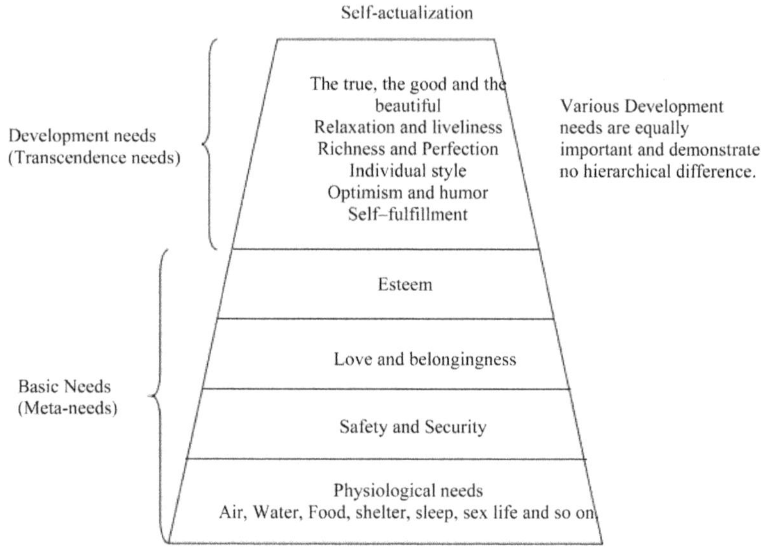

Figure 6.1: Abraham Maslow's Hierarchy of Needs (Feng, 2002a)

level, that is, the motivations driven by basic needs (deficiency needs) of human organisms, and the latter the motivations driven primarily by transcendence needs in higher levels instead of basic needs" (see Figure 6.1) (Liu, 2005).

In this theory of motivations, human needs are classified into two categories: basic needs (deficiency needs) and transcendence needs in ascending order. Basic needs, forming a hierarchical system by advantage or strength in the ascending order, consist of physiological needs (air, water, food, shelter, sleep, sex, and so on), and need for safety and security, for love and belongingness and for mutual respect, while transcendence needs cover self-fulfillment, optimism and humor, individual style, richness and perfection, relaxation and liveliness, the true, the good and the beautiful, self-actualization, etc. Maslow asserted that,

> We say that the basic needs of humans constitute a relatively advantageous level, we mean that certain lower needs (for example, physiological hunger) have to be satisfied before higher needs can be addressed. By now, these higher needs (no longer physiological hunger) step over to control the human organisms, and then, when these higher needs are satisfied once again, some even higher needs will come out and step over to control the human organisms, and so on. Therefore, the obvious emergence of self-actualization-oriented transcendence needs usually depends on the satisfaction of deficiency needs such as physiological ones, need for safety and security, and for love and esteem (Feng, 2002b).

> More importantly, it is human nature to have endless needs. Yet, not all needs can be satisfied, and only a very few can be completely satisfied. Whenever one desire is satisfied, another will quickly emerge to take place of the former, and when this latter one is satisfied, another new one will stand out. Humans are always hoping for something, which is simply an attribute throughout the life of humans (Feng, 2002c).

The analysis of the Dai fertility motivation with this classification approach of behavioral motivations led to the conclusion that, due to favorable living environments, the Dai people in the traditional agrarian society had already shaken off the constraints of deficiency needs, and proceeded on to pursue self-satisfaction and self-actualization driven by transcendence motivations. Therefore, the author constructed a "Survival Pursuit" hierarchy-based analytical framework to interpret the traditional fertility behavior of the Dai people.

The Figure 6.2 implies the following: the Dai people lived in a favorable living environment. Multiple factors, such as advantageous natural conditions, small family structure, social institutions and customs, enabled them to be free of wants (sufficient food, clothing and shelter) with only a small input of individual labor, satisfying their need for living in peace and contentment. They had good social customs and simple lifestyles, got along with each other, cared and respected each other. By the living standards of a traditional agrarian society, such a life sufficed to satisfy their basic survival needs. In other words, all the basic needs in the four levels in Abraham Maslow's Hierarchy of Needs were

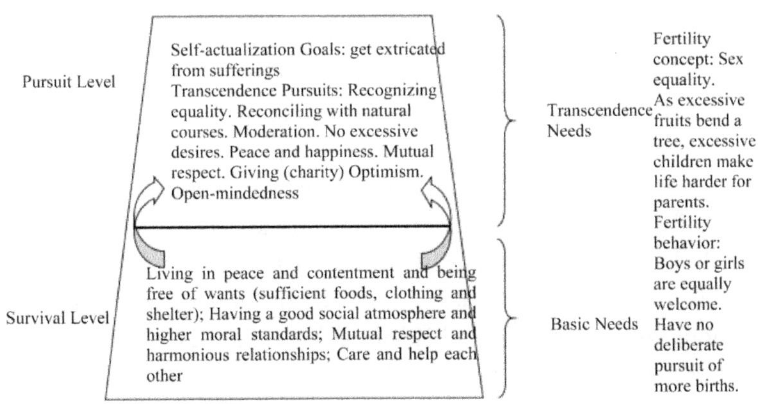

Figure 6.2: The "Survival Pursuit" hierarchy-based analytical framework for the traditional fertility behavior in the Dai society

satisfied. Therefore, transcendence needs naturally rose to be their pursuits, and they were also well positioned to "step over" the threshold to strive for their transcendence pursuits. In the Dai people's transcendence motivations, their goal of self-actualization, that is, their ultimate goal, is to hit the summit of their recognized values of life: To have a Buddhist life (get extricated from sufferings). Their ideal status of life was "equality", "mutual respect" and "giving (charity)", their behavioral pattern was: "reconciling with natural courses", "exercising moderation", "refraining from excessive desire" and "living in peace", and their mindset was to achieve "happiness", "optimism" and "open-mindedness". They might have a humble material life but must have a rich spiritual life. With such transcendence-need-oriented motivation, they were unlikely to have the fertility motivation in expectation of obtaining material satisfaction and living security from their children but only to be content with their hope that children can bring happiness to them. However, raising too many children would distract them from their devotion to the Buddha, performing offerings and their leisure life. Raising children just provided fleeting pleasure, but devotion to the Buddha and performing offerings to the deities generates lasting happiness throughout one's lifetime, that is to say, the latter could deliver greater and longer spiritual satisfaction, so they didn't want to squander their time and effort on raising too many children. "Having children in itself is enough. The more children you have, the more time and effort you need to spend on them, and this will distract you from your devotion to the Buddha. It's not worth it" was their answer. So the desire for more children and the preference for sons over daughters was never part of the Dai fertility culture.

To verify the applicability of the "Survival Pursuit" hierarchy-based analytical framework to explaining fertility behavior, the author, based on the life logic of the Han people in the countryside as described by Mr. Fei Xiaotong and Ms. Li Yinhe, applied the analytical framework in Figure 6.3 to explain the fertility behavior of the Han people both in well-off and poor rural regions.

In poor rural regions, the living needs of the Han people were still to meet the basic needs of the organism, that is, the lower basic needs – the level: Relatively Deficient Basic Needs. The material supply in this level could only maintain their humblest life – food, clothes, houses, daily supplies and so on. Such living conditions could only satisfy their physiological needs: the lowest-level basic needs in Abraham Maslow's Hierarchy of Needs, and what people most cared about in their real life was how to acquire safety, security, love, esteem and so on: the survival-level basic needs, and they had not much expectation for the pursuit-level transcendence needs, such as self-fulfillment, individual style, a rich

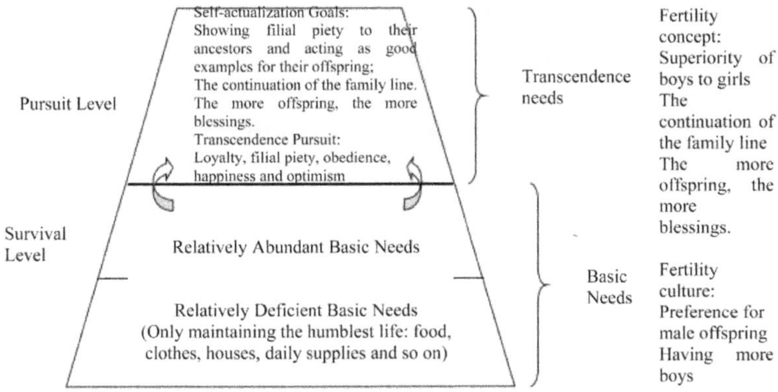

Figure 6.3: The "Survival Pursuit" hierarchy-based analytical framework for the rural fertility behavior in the Han society

and consummate life. Thus, their behavioral motivation was developed more around the survival- needs, and their main aim of life was to raise the material needs of their families from a relatively deficiency status to a relatively abundant one. Figure 6.3 shows this group of people were trying to move up the motivation ladder from the level of relatively deficient basic needs satisfied to that of relatively abundant basic needs satisfied. Therefore, people have stronger utilitarian fertility motivations, i.e. a stronger desire to add family laborers, bring more incomes to families and provide living security to their old-age parents by having more births, albeit of course they retain other motivations and pursue other goals, such as obtaining spiritual enjoyments (intimate family relationships, a sense of achievement, mutual care and so on), "showing obedience and filial piety to their parents", "living a happy and optimist life", and even "showing filial piety to their ancestors and acting as good examples for their offspring", "extending and carrying on their family lines" and "obtaining more blessings by having more offspring". However, since they are still struggling with their basic survival needs, which is in a relatively deficient status, this much or less constrains them from striving for more pursuit-needs. Their life has not risen to the status that enables them to "leap" over the survival level to the pursuit level. In other words, their fertility behavior are not only driven by both stronger utilitarian and emotional motivations but also mandated by the heavy task of continuing their family lines. Hence, with such deficiency-need-oriented motivation, their fertility motivation is inevitably the tendency to "have more offspring, especially more male offspring", otherwise it would be humiliating to their ancestors and families.

In well-off rural regions, the Han people had higher material standard of living. Not only were their physiological needs met, the lowest basic needs in Abraham Maslow's Hierarchy of Needs, but some of their higher-level basic needs, such as the need for safety and security, love and belongingness, esteem and so on were also met. Figure 6.3 shows they had satisfied all the relatively deficient basic needs and relatively abundant basic needs. Therefore, their life ideal was over "the demarcation line of Survival-Pursuit" and more hopefully to satisfy the transcendence needs in the pursuit level. These well-off families no longer expected to add family laborers and increase family incomes by banking on children, but more expected to continue their family lines, inherit parents' properties and business, and acquire greater family happiness from their children. In other words, they had a weakened utilitarian fertility need but a strengthened emotional fertility need. Since this group of people held similar ideas to those of their peers in poor regions in terms of the life values, their pursuit-level transcendence needs remained "showing obedience and filial piety to their parents" and "living a happy and optimist life", and their ultimate wishes in life were "showing filial piety to their ancestors and acting as good examples for their offspring", "extending and carrying on their family lines" and "obtaining more blessings by having more offspring". Hence, with such transcendence-need-oriented motivation, their fertility motivation also remained "having more offspring, especially more male offspring".

As Maslow put it, "A subsistence state might be satisfying for some but far from so for others, depending on the desire for existence. Generally speaking, as long as the most basic subsistence needs are met, average persons can survive, but won't be content with such needs satisfied. It is in this way that human beings develop" (Feng, 2002d). Yet, different men have different desires for existence. Different desires for existence imply different value goals, and then further, different life logics, which in turn are the core components of their meaning of life, that is, the constituent contents of their transcendence needs. In the "pursuit" level, different values of life (i.e., diversity of life values) or life goals give rise to different behavioral motivations, which result in different behavioral outcomes. The traditional fertility behavior of the Dai minority are the logical outcomes of their unique pursuit for a Buddhist life.

References

Chen, Qingde. *Resources Allocation and Institutional Change*. Kunming: Yunnan University Press, 2001, 45.

Chu, Jianfang. *Between People and Gods*. Beijing: Social Sciences Academic Press 2005, 327.
Claude Levi-Strauss. *La Persée Sauvage*. Translated by Li Youzheng. Beijing: The Commercial Press, 1987, 256–257.
Editorial Board of the Complete Works of Chinese Pattra leaf Scriptures. *The Complete Works of Chinese Pattra leaf Scriptures-Volume 1 – The Buddha's Tour*. Beijing: People's Publishing House, 2006, 1.
Editorial Committee of Five Series of Books on Ethnic Issues. *A Survey of the Dai Ethnic Society and History* (Xishuangbanna-Vol. 3). Kunming: Yunnan People's Publishing House, 1983, 105.
Emile Durkheim. *Leçons de Sociologie: Physique des Moeurs et du Droit*. Translated by Qu Dong and Fu Degen. Shanghai: Shanghai People's Publishing House, 2001, 176.
Fei, Xiaotong. *Reproduction Institutions in Rural China*. Beijing: Peking University Press, 1998, 227–229.
Guo, Liangyun. *Buddhas and Primitive Buddhist Thoughts*. Beijing: China Social Sciences Press, 1997a, 149.
Guo, Liangyun. *Buddhas and Primitive Buddhist Thoughts*. Beijing: China Social Sciences Press, 1997b, 153.
Guo, Liangyun. *Buddhas and Primitive Buddhist Thoughts*. Beijing: China Social Sciences Press, 1997c, 153–155.
Guo, Liangyun. *Buddhas and Primitive Buddhist Thoughts*. Beijing: China Social Sciences Press, 1997d, 139.
Guo, Liangyun. *Buddhas and Primitive Buddhist Thoughts*. Beijing: China Social Sciences Press, 1997e, 58.
Jiang, Yingliang. *The Economic Life of the Dai People*. Guangzhou: Tsinghua Press, 1950a, 80.
Jiang, Yingliang. *The Life and Culture of the Dai Ethnic Group*. Shanghai: Zhonghua Book Company, 1950b, 227.
Jiang, Yingliang. *The Life and Culture of the Dai Ethnic Group*. Shanghai: Zhonghua Book Company, 1950c, 227–229.
Jiang, Yingliang. *The Life and Culture of the Dai Ethnic Group*. Shanghai: Zhonghua Book Company, 1950d, 229–246.
Leach, Edmund Ronald. *Culture & Communication*. Translated by Guofan and Zou He. Shanghai People's Publishing House, 2000a, 33–36.
Leach, Edmund Ronald. *Culture & Communication*. Translated by Guofan and Zou He. Shanghai People's Publishing House, 2000b, 83–86.
Li, Fuhua et al. *The Encyclopedia of Modern Science in China: Religions – Buddhism*. Beijing: Contemporary World Press, 2000, 176.
Li, Fuyi. *The Annals of 12 Bannas*. Taiwan: Chiang Kai-shek Publishing Company, 1955a, 118.
Li, Fuyi. *The Annals of 12 Bannas*. Taiwan: Chiang Kai-shek Publishing Company, 1955b, 178–179.
Li, Fuyi. *The Annals of 12 Bannas*. Taiwan: Chiang Kai-shek Publishing Company, 1955c, 114.
Li, Fuyi. *The Annals of 12 Bannas*. Taiwan: Chiang Kai-shek Publishing Company, 1955d, 115.
Li, Yinhe. *Procreation and Village Cultures*. Beijing: China Social Sciences Press, 1994a, 69.
Li, Yinhe. *Procreation and Village Cultures*. Beijing: China Social Sciences Press, 1994b, 221–223.
Li, Yinhe. *Procreation and Village Cultures*. Beijing: China Social Sciences Press, 1994c, 82.

Liu, Yan. *Southern Buddhism and Dai Ethnic Culture*. Kunming: Yunnan People's Publishing House, 1993, 91.

Maslow. *Realize the Value of Life*. Translated by Feng Huaping. Hohhot: People's Publishing House of Inner Mongolia, 2002a, 26.

Maslow. *Realize the Value of Life*. Translated by Feng Huaping. Hohhot: People's Publishing House of Inner Mongolia, 2002b, 29.

Maslow. *Realize the Value of Life*. Translated by Feng Huaping. Hohhot: People's Publishing House of Inner Mongolia, 2002c, 49.

Maslow. *Realize the Value of Life*. Translated by Feng Huaping. Hohhot: People's Publishing House of Inner Mongolia, 2002d, 25.

Maslow. *Maslow's Wisdom*. Translated by Liu Ye. Beijing: China Film Press, 2005, 48.

Malthus, Thomas. *An Essay on the Principle of Population*. Translated by Zhu Yang, Hu Qilin and Zhu Hezhong. Beijing: the Commercial Press, 1992a, 16.

Malthus, Thomas. *An Essay on the Principle of Population*. Translated by Zhu Yang, Hu Qilin and Zhu Hezhong. Beijing: the Commercial Press, 1992b, 11.

Wang, Xiaochao. *15 Lectures on the Essentials of Religion*. Beijing: Peking University Press, 2003a, 120.

Wang, Xiaochao. *15 Lectures on the Essentials of Religion*. Beijing: Peking University Press, 2003b, 120–122.

Wang, Xiaochao. *15 Lectures on the Essentials of Religion*. Beijing: Peking University Press, 2003c, 120–122.

Yao, Hesheng. *The Folklore of Shui Clan of the Dai Ethnic Group*. Kunming: Yunnan People's Publishing House, 2003, 178.

7

Rethinking of the Interpretation Paradigm of Human Fertility Behavior

Section 1 Commonalities and Differences of Human Fertility Behavior

As noted in the preceding research summary of fertility behavior theories, in the understanding of human fertility behavior, the view on economic determinism has long been a mainstream one. Various theories in the West, including John C. Caldwell's Wealth Flow, Harvey Leibenstein's Rational Choice of Marginal Children, Becker's Quantity-Quality Trade-off Theory, Easterlin's Supply-Demand for Offspring and Population Transition Theory, shared one fundamental view that human fertility behavior (fertility rates) are determined by the level of economic life (economic development). In societies at lower economic development levels, such as traditional agrarian societies, human fertility behavior are all orientated to a common goal – having more births (higher fertility rates), and only when the economic standard of living of humans has improved to a specific level will human fertility behavior shift to fewer births (lower fertility rates). This argument has been at the heart of the Population Transition Theory, and also is the origin of the phrase "development is the most effective birth control pill". Chinese demographic researchers, represented by Fei Xiaotong and Li Yinhe, also hold that in an agrarian (village) society, where the productivity is typically at a low level, to maintain the labor demand of farming, fertility behavior inevitably tend to have more births. Based on this view, they've built the Relay Support – Back Feeding Model and the Village Society of Acquaintances model to explain the excess fertility behavior in agrarian societies in China. These studies show that many of the above-mentioned theories or conclusions are based on a common theoretical assumption: There are some commonalities with human fertility behavior. To put it in more precise technical terms, it should be: There are some commonalities with human fertility behavior across the societies at the same level of economic development. In traditional agrarian societies, humans tend to have more births (or higher fertility rates), while in modern industrialized societies, humans tend to have fewer births (lower fertility rates). The applicability in the real world of these theories and their acceptance by the majority of demographic researchers suggest that this assumption is fairly consistent with the true human fertility behavior that have been already known to us. Up till today, we haven't got sufficient factual evidence to refute them. Such a result, to a certain degree, confirms the assumption underlying these theories.

However, it is not enough to go just so far in understanding human fertility behavior as, besides commonalities, there are also differences in human fertility behavior in the real world, and this research is an example of such differences.

Based on an exploration into the traditional fertility behavior of the Dai people in a traditional agrarian society, we find that, due to the sociality of humans, any individual in a society is inevitably subject to the traditional culture of the society where he/she is living. This traditional culture is the product of an objective historical process, and it has come into being over the long-term course of communities of humans in a society engaging in production, striving for survival and livelihood and adapting to the relationships between man and nature and those between individuals and the society. Under the guide of specific value orientations, the traditional culture has gradually evolved into a standardized, institutionalized and relatively stable form, also known as the cultural pattern in cultural anthropology. It plays an important role in regulating the behaviors of communities of humans living in a particular society.

Given the regulating function of the value orientation of a community toward the behaviors of individuals, individuals from different community value systems will respond differently to the same issues and act in different ways due to their different values, that is, there are some differences in their behaviors. This is exactly the power of culture in modeling human behaviors and it can lead to different behaviors among individuals from different cultures. Hence, sometimes, the same behaviors may be deemed to be a matter of course and perfectly justified by individuals in one community but weir and shocking by individuals in another community, and may be accepted as essential elements by some but dismissed as trivialities by others. Behavioral differences arising from cultural differences have already been verified by empirical facts, and they have led to differences in human fertility behavior. Under the influence of multiple factors, including natural environments, religious culture, family structures and social institutions, the Dai people in a traditional agrarian society gradually forged a unique set of cultural values over their long-term course of production and life. Tempered by this traditional culture, their view of life, values and fertility idea took on some distinct attributes following Buddhist rationality: Setting a life goal of "getting extricated from sufferings", following the life principles of "equality, mutual respect, charity, reconciling with natural courses, exercising moderation, refraining from excessive desires, peace, happiness, optimism and open-mindedness", and, to be specific in their fertility behavior, forming such ideas as "boys or girls are equally welcome and refraining from deliberately pursuing more births" as the rules guiding their behaviors. Thus, their fertility behavior emerged as a sharp contrast to those of other ethnic groups which pursue "having more offspring, especially more male offspring".

Anthropological research shows that: "Each cultural group has its own unique history, characteristics and laws of development"[36], "Every culture has its value of existence and unique merits, and every nation has its own dignity and values", and "The culture of every nation can only be construed as a product of its history and has the characteristics determined by its social and geographical environments" (Xia, 1997). In this sense, there should be as many cultural groups and fertility behavior patterns as many nations in the world. Cultural relativism gives the most convincing interpretation of the inevitability of differences in human fertility behavior.

However, on the other hand, we also have to admit an empirical fact that human beings, as the same species, do have many commonalities in their behaviors. Otherwise, our world would be unthinkable. Though representing different value systems, different cultures are not poles apart from each other. Some value orientations are universal in human society. For example, we all have the need for family affection and friendship, have the desire to love and be loved, and seek after equality and justice. Bentham held that the pursuit of pleasure is the ultimate

36 Franz Boas defined the concept "Cultural Group" to be a community of individuals with a common history and common culture, where all individuals follow the same and common logic of thinking and make their value judgments. An ethnic group is a typical Cultural Group.

uniform principle governing human behaviors. He asserted that: "Nature has placed mankind under the governance of two sovereign masters, pain and pleasure., which implies that how we should do and what we will do. They (pleasure and pain) govern our behaviors, our words and our thinking" (Chen, 2003). When it comes to fertility behavior, no nation or cultural pattern would deny the emotional satisfaction that children bring to their parents. Yes, it is a hard task to raise children, but all the same, it is more fun. In the process, humans indeed experience both pain and pleasure. It is more of the fundamental driving force than an instinct for the reproduction of human beings and the common pursuit of human beings.

The duality of commonality and differentiation with human fertility behavior is an important theoretical premise for our interpretative framework of human fertility behavior.

Section 2 Theoretical Interpretation of Human Fertility Behavior

Following the idea of building an interpretative framework of the Dai traditional fertility behavior and in the light of an understanding of the duality of commonalities and differences, the author tried at a higher level and from a broader perspective to come up with a broader and more general interpretative framework of human fertility behavior based on the existing anthropological and psychological theories.

In the previous section, we have discussed the influences of culture on human fertility behavior and concluded that values are the "hard core" of a culture; values have come into being over the long course of a people's community engaging in production, striving for survival and livelihood, and adapting to the relationships between man and nature and those between man and society; they have evolved into a stable cultural form, also known as the cultural pattern in cultural anthropology. Values play an important role in regulating the behaviors of a people's community living in a particular society, and every individual in a society is inevitably subject to the culture of the society where he/she is living. This is the power of culture in modeling human behaviors and an external expression of the sociality of humans. The differences in human fertility behavior are exactly the inevitable result of such cultural differences.

Meanwhile, as biological existences of a kind, humans have to cope with the reality of life. First of all, their behaviors are subject to the need for survival as it is the prerequisite for all human behaviors. In general, the things of the most importance and most immediate relevance to keeping life alive are always the most urgent needs guiding the human actions. On this issue, Maslow's Hierarchy of Needs Theory has provided an important methodology for us to study human behaviors. His research showed that man is a unified and organized whole, and the vast majority of his desires and impulses are interrelated, therefore, "There is no such thing as the needs from the belly, the mouth or the genitals but only the needs from a man. It is John Smith who needs to eat rather than his stomach needs to eat, and it is the whole organism that is satisfied, not just a part of it. It is John Smith's hunger instead of his is stomach's hunger that is quelled by food" (Feng, 2002a). "What drive humans to act are a cluster of hereditary and instinct constant needs, which are truly the intrinsic essences of the nature of humans, and cannot be eliminated but only suppressed by culture. Thus, the actions of humans are governed by the necessity of life, which is the instinctive need of life and existence, and only when this need is satisfied can there be the life and existence of humans" (Feng, 2002b). This suggests that instinctive drive comes first and in the primary layer, while the non-instinct drive, also known as the "cultural drive", comes second and in the secondary layer, and is at a different grade from the biological "primal drive" that can be perceived by any human being. According to this hierarchy of needs, when the living standard of humans is still in the layer of basic needs, satisfying basic material needs (such as food, clothing, housing and use) will be their top consideration in life. Young children can help parents with house chores at home and some light work on farming fields, and grown-up children can help parents do all work at home, in farming fields and business, increasing incomes to families and becoming the "breadwinners" for the entire families when parents get older. This expectation will encourage parents to have more children. If the motivations behind fertility behavior are classified into material and emotional ones, we might as well infer that when the living standard is still in the layer of focusing on basic needs, material motivations play a greater role in determining fertility behavior than emotional ones, and families are likely driven more by material motivations than emotional ones to have more children. This inference is consistent with the above-mentioned theories and views of the economic determinism of human fertility behavior proposed in the demographical research both at home and abroad, which shows that when the living standard of humans is still in the layer of basic needs, in other words, when the level of social and economic development is low, the fertility behavior of humans have a common tendency – to have more births.

From this, we can get a corollary that the commonalities and differences in fertility behavior are much correlated to the biological and societal duality of the existence of humans.

The Hierarchy of Human Survival Needs theory points out that when the lowest-layer basic needs (deficiency-needs, for example, physiological hunger and others) are satisfied, higher-layer needs (no longer physiological hunger) will step over to control the human organisms, and then, when these higher-layer needs are satisfied once again, some even higher-layer needs will come out and step over to control the human organisms, and so on. Eventually, the self-actualization-oriented meta-needs will emerge. "The basic needs come out according to the law of relative potentials in a largely definite order in the hierarchy: physiological needs (in a lower layer) come first before the need for safety, love and esteem in order, and then further is followed by individual-specific needs, also called self-actualization-oriented transcendence needs" (Lin, 1987a). "Various self-actualization-oriented transcendence needs are equally important and demonstrate no hierarchical difference." But whether or not that some transcendence needs become the ones of a particular human completely depends upon his values and only "the satisfaction of these higher needs conforming to the self-value judgments of a human can deliver more desirable subjective effects to such human, namely a greater happiness, a deeper peace and a richer inner feeling" (Lin, 1987b).

> The pursuit of self-actualization-oriented value life (in the spiritual, religious, philosophical, axiological and so on aspects) is one of the biological attributes of humans, which falls within the same continuum as, rather than absolutely distinctive from, even contradictory or mutually exclusive to, that of 'lower' animals, and thus may be universal with all human races and go beyond cultures, albeit its realization can't be independent of particular cultures (Lin, 1987c).

It seems to us that there is a long "flight of stairs" of satisfying human needs, where human behaviors are mandated by two main categories of motivations – physical and psychological ones. Located in the lower part of the "flight of stairs" are basic needs, including physical needs, the need for safety, the need for love, the need for esteem, etc., and are mainly governed by physical motivations, while in the upper part are development needs, including self-fulfillment, relaxation, optimism, humor, justice, order, individual style, truth, goodness and virtue, etc., and are more governed by psychological motivation. It is exactly the synergistic dynamics of these two categories of motivations that lead to a wide variety of life.

In the synergistic dynamics of these two categories of motivations, human behaviors demonstrate a wide diversity: both commonalities and differences. In the previous analysis, we have found from the perspective of material and emotional motivations that, when the living standard is still in the layer of focusing on basic needs, material motivations will play a greater role in determining fertility behavior than emotional motivations, and families will be driven more by material motivations than emotional motivations to have more children. This reflects the commonalities in fertility behavior of humans. As basic material needs for survival are gradually satisfied, and material motivations weaken accordingly, family fertility behavior will be driven more by emotional motivations. In other words, under these circumstance, emotional motivations play a greater role in determining fertility behavior than material ones. Yet, unlike material needs among the human survival needs, emotional needs are relatively elastic and can be satisfied by alternative approaches. Hence, choosing to have more or fewer births depends upon the values of communities of humans where families are living. This is an embodiment of the differences in fertility behavior of humans. For example, the Han people may prefer to get happiness from extended families by having more children, while the Dai people may choose to have fewer children so as to have more spare time and effort devoted to the religious offerings to achieve more self-fulfillment. Here, there is no conflict between the consistency in the goal of achieving self-actualization and the diversity in the choices arising from different values because what types of goals should be deemed as self-actualization ones is determined by values.

Modeling the logical thinking of the Hierarchy of Human Survival Needs, we integrated the biological and societal duality of human survival and the duality of commonalities and differences in fertility behavior of humans and came up with an interpretative framework of human fertility behavior under various cultural patterns.

Basic Meanings of Figure 7.1

1. In the hierarchy of human needs, the decent life layer, where only basic needs (including food, cloth, housing and use) can be satisfied, is the lowest part, providing the basis for the survival of humans, and the affluent life layer, where basic needs have already been satisfied, and people live in peace and contentment, lead a relatively well-off and secure life in food, cloth, housing and use, and have a stable social climate, is the upper part. Over the affluent life layer is an infinite space, where humans can realize their self-pursuits, for example, striving for self-fulfillment, optimism,

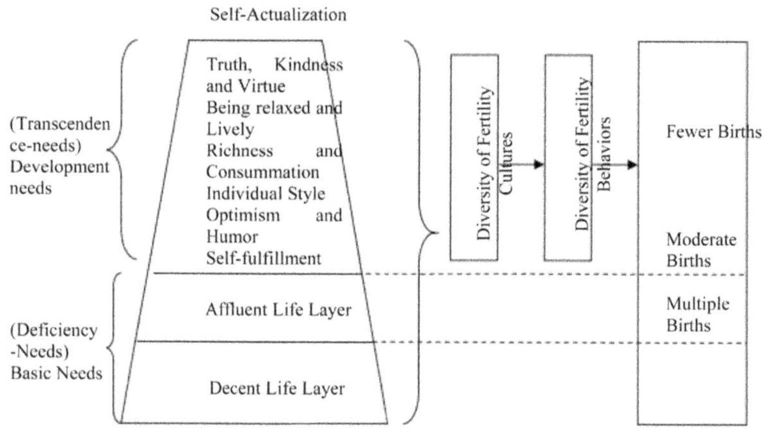

Figure 7.1. The interpretative framework of human fertility behavior

humor, individual style, richness, consummation, being relaxed and lively, being true, kindly and virtuous and so on. Yet, the needs in both the decent life layer and affluent life layer still belong to the basic needs of human life.

2. When the basic needs in the decent life layer (i.e. only basic food, cloth, housing and use can be guaranteed) have been satisfied, the higher-level basic needs in the affluent life layer (a relatively well-off and secure life, a stable social climate, a satisfying sex life, reciprocal support, reciprocal affection, care and mutual respect, etc.) will follow immediately. When these basic needs in the affluent life layer are satisfied, the development needs (pursuit of happiness of a variety of self-actualization, for example, striving for self-fulfillment, optimism, humor, individual style, richness, consummation, being relaxed and lively, being true, kindly and virtuous and so on) will follow immediately. Therefore, humans are always pursuing the goal of self-actualization.
3. The desire of humans always evolves from the needs in the decent life layer to ones in the affluent life layer, and thus the sequence of pursuits is the basic needs before development needs. That is, humans, first of all, strive for their basic needs, and then for their development needs: starting with the basic needs in the decent life layer, next, satisfying the basic needs in the affluent life layer, and finally proceeding to realize self-values and seek more happiness only when the basic needs in the affluent life layer have been satisfied.

4. The cultural diversity of humans does not vary with the layers in the hierarchy of human needs where humans are living. In other words, the diversity of fertility cultures runs through all the layers in the hierarchy of human needs, and inevitably leads to the diversity of fertility behavior, thus forming different behavioral results.
5. When in the decent life layer of basic needs (more common in rural China nowadays), due to a larger pressure from survival, material needs are the primary ones for families. Since the labor force is the main means for families to obtain survival materials, families of course like to have more children so as to have more labor force, earn more survival materials, help parents do more housework, provide life security for elderly parents, and resist the risk of the potential early death of their children, etc. Driven by satisfying basic material needs, families develop the motivation to have multiple births, which demonstrates a consistent phenomenon of excess births in fertility behavior. This motivation is common to all humans, regardless of nations. In other words, this need goes beyond cultures (The relative consistency in the fertility motivation among various cultures leads to a strong commonality in fertility behavior).
6. When in the affluent life layer of basic needs (more common in urban regions nowadays), material needs have already been fully satisfied. Being free of wants (i.e., with sufficient availability of food, clothing, shelter and use), humans have self-actualization-oriented pursuits at the center of their life. Under the dominance of different values, the diversity of self-actualization-oriented goals is more pronounced and leads to the diversity of fertility motivations and, then further, the diversity of fertility behavior. However, the general trend is that humans tend to have moderate births (As the consistency of fertility motivations weakens, the difference stands out relatively obvious. As a result, fertility behavior demonstrate a weakening commonality and rising difference).
7. When in the layer of development needs (more common in developed countries, or advanced urban and rural regions in some developing countries), humans have more diverse aspirations and pursue the needs in the development layer: self-fulfillment, optimism, humor, individual style, richness and consummation, truth, goodness and virtue, etc., to achieve their higher spiritual satisfaction. As a result, humans have further diversified fertility motivations and, generally speaking, tend to have fewer births but better rearing in terms of fertility behavior (Lower fertility rates are more common with this class of humans).

8. The living standards in the decent life layer mean the need of the bare necessities of life (the minimum levels for food, cloth, shelter and use) for survival and the simplest life and is relatively rigid. This layer breaks down into two parts: the lower part and the upper part. The lower part is in the bottom position in the hierarchy of human needs, which means people are living in poverty and have the highest living pressure. Moving up the "flight of stairs" of the hierarchy, poverty decreases. In contrast, the living standards in the affluent life layer are more flexible as depending on the values governing a human's desire for life, the same living status that is satisfying for someone might be far from being enough for others.
9. Judging from the history and current situation of human development, the majority of humans are still in the decent life layer at the present stage and also have higher fertility rates.[37] They have to make great efforts to rise from the decent life layer to the affluent life layer. Therefore, it is unlikely that there will be a great change in fertility behavior in the short term. Only when the living levels rise to reach the affluent life layer will fertility behavior be more diverse with the improved life. Of course, with different regions, populations and historical phases, there are different evaluation criteria for what can be defined as an affluent life.

To verify the above-mentioned arguments, we applied this interpretative framework to the fertility behavior analysis of both the Dai people in the traditional agrarian society and the Han people in poor and affluent rural China.

1. By the living standards of a traditional agrarian society and their requirements of material needs, the Dai people should be deemed as leading an easy and bountiful life: ample food and clothing, simple folk customs and harmonious neighborhoods, and should be in the affluent life layer. Everyone had the luxury of striving for their development needs. In the process, driven by their value orientation, their ultimate goal was to lead a Buddhist life, their fertility concepts featured "sex equality" and "the more kids, the heavier the burden on parents", and their fertility

37 According to the United Nations 2000–2005 Global Fertility Survey, most countries and regions have a total fertility rate above the population replacement level of 2.1, with the fertility rate in European countries roughly in the 1.0–2.5 range; that in most Asian countries above 2.1; that in most countries in Americas in the 2.1–4.0 range; that in the vast majority of countries in Africa above 4.0; and that in most Oceanian countries mostly above 2.1. See also: Population Division of Department of Economic and Social Affairs of United Nation: World Population 2004, United Nations Publication.

behavior, as the real embodiment of fertility concepts, demonstrated the attributes of moderate births: "having no preference for male offspring" and "refraining from deliberately pursuing more births".

2. The living standards of Han people in rich rural areas have already been in the affluent life layer, and those in eastern China are even at higher levels in the affluent life layer. Besides the secure availability of ample food and clothing and peaceful life, they also have the luxury of fully pursuing their self-development and much weaker utilitarian fertility needs. Influenced by traditional Confucian culture, their core values in life are "loyalty and filial piety" and "obedience" to their parents, their fertility concepts are "continuing their family lines", "more sons, more blessings" and "the consummate happiness coming from extended families". Driven by these emotional fertility motivations, their family fertility behavior take on the distinct feature of "having more offspring, especially more male offspring".
3. The living standards of the Han people in impoverished rural areas are at lower levels in the decent life layer, i.e. they are still stuck at the level of how to survive and improve their life. As a result, they tend to secure their family labor supply and increase their family incomes by having more births as children can deliver significant and direct economic effects on the families, and are expected to provide living security to their old-age parents. In other words, they have stronger material motivations behind their fertility behavior. Their life goal is to rise from the decent life layer to the affluent life layer, and under the influence of traditional Confucian culture, their core values in life are "continuing their family lines" and "more sons, more blessings", and their spiritual expectation is "raising sons as support in advanced years". Driven by utilitarian and emotional motivations, their fertility behavior inevitably have the feature of "having more offspring, especially more male offspring".

Section 3 Rethinking of the Interpretation Paradigm of Human Fertility Behavior

While designing the aforementioned interpretative framework of fertility behavior, we, first, interpreted the differences in fertility behavior of humans under different cultural contexts by means of the cultural relativism of anthropology, and then, the fertility behavior of humans in different layers of survival needs in a hierarchical manner in the light of the findings of psychological research: (1) When living standards have not yet reached the layer in which basic needs have been satisfied, fertility behavior are driven more by utilitarian needs and show a common tendency to have more births; (2) when living standards have risen over the layer in which basic needs have been satisfied, guided by the pursuit of development needs, fertility behavior of humans will demonstrate more differences, i.e. having a higher diversity. In addition, having more or fewer births depends on individuals' value judgments which define their self-actualization-oriented goals. Hence, this framework may be as well-known as an integrated framework built on the theories of two disciplines. The overall interpretation of human fertility behavior based on this integrated framework is generally consistent with the historical reality that we have already known by now, and in particular, dovetails with the changes in fertility behavior since the 20th century.[38] But among the most complex behaviors of humans, fertility behavior are influenced by too many factors. Focusing on the number of births and not factoring in many other variables, such as the quality of children and the timing of birth, this interpretative framework can't cover all fertility behavior. That is, there remain some "blind sections" in the fertility behavior range unaccounted for by this interpretative framework. Therefore, in technical terms, it can only serve as a general overall conceptual framework before its rationality and effectiveness are further tested.

The biological and societal duality of humans as social beings inevitably manifests itself in their behaviors. Except for instinct reactions and emergency responses, human behaviors are mostly driven by motivations and needs. Objectively, though being rooted in natural instinct, fertility behavior of humans are not purely instinctive, but more often than not motivational, and in most cases are swayed by psychological, social and financial needs. That is to say, all these factors play their role throughout the long journey from the formation of fertility concepts to the initiation of fertility motivations and the fulfillment of fertility behavior. Hence, there remains too much unknown space to be explored to get a full understanding of fertility behavior.

38 In their works: the Fertility Revolution, Easterlin and Crimmins contended that with a growing global economy and modernized societies, the decline in fertility rates is an irreversible global trend. The author believes that this trend is exactly the result of the convergence of values amid the global economic integration triggered by market-oriented economic development. As the convergence of values rises, cultural differences objectively reduce. This "degrading" cultural diversity also leads to a "degrading" fertility behavior diversity, which objectively translates into the outcome of fewer births, but the underlying mechanism doesn't work exclusively to economic factors.

First of all, given this research limited its scope of focus to analyzing the voluntary fertility behavior at the family level, various variables, such as state policy, public health and medical technology, were not incorporated as dominant factors in this interpretative framework, but that does not mean that these variables play no important roles in fertility behavior. In fact, state population policies have inflicted significant influences on family fertility behavior, as evidenced by the rapid decline in the fertility rate in China since the 1970s. The popularization of public health and medical technology plays a crucial role in reducing the mortality rate. With a reduced mortality rate, the fertility motivation to resist the risk of the potential early death of children and to have sufficient surviving children is greatly weakened, and the desire to have additional children changes accordingly, resulting in changes in fertility behavior. Therefore, modifications will have to be introduced to this framework if these variables are factored in.

Next, the "low fertility rate" has become a global commonplace, especially in developed countries and regions. Research has shown that "After the population transitions, fertility rates in almost all countries have not stabilized as predicted by Population Transition Theory, but has moved further towards very low and even extremely low levels" (Li, 2009). This framework would only lead to such a conclusion: This phenomenon is attributable to the pursuit of development needs and is a result of cultural values. However, this overall interpretation can neither provide clarity to the micro – mechanism of its occurrence nor shed light on the differences among countries and regions to give clear judgments on the trends in the future. That is, it can only provide a sketchy overall analysis at the macroscopic level, and the analysis of issues of this kind is one of the "blind sections" of this interpretative framework. Therefore, new interpretative frameworks are still needed to explore the causes, formation mechanisms and non-cultural influencing factors of such special happenings.

Third, this framework analyzes human fertility behavior only at the "class population" level, analyzes the differences in fertility behavior in the dimension of the cultural relativism of anthropology, and interprets the differences in fertility behavior by means of the differences in the value orientation of communities of humans. However, it is also important to note that, regardless of the community value systems, fertility behavior in real life vary with individuals' circumstances. During his survey of the reproductive history of Jing village, the author found that there were those who never had any children and those who gave birth to as many as 10 children. Mr. Fei Xiaotong also found in his survey in Jiang village that "wealthier families were less constrained in having more children" (Fei, 2001). These findings confirmed the preceding argument and suggested that differences in fertility behavior exist not only among communities but also within them. Besides the overall knowledge of fertility behavior at the macro level, we must also analyze them at the micro-level to get a true picture of fertility behavior in real life.

Finally, in general, fertility behavior of humans are rational actions with specific purposes, especially nowadays when birth control and contraceptive technologies have been well-developed and widely available. As the main components of human life and basic cells for acquiring means of subsistence, families have always played an important role in fertility behavior, and all the preexisting discussions and insights into fertility behavior, either utilitarian or emotional needs, were based and centered on families. However, with the change of society, concepts about marriages and families also change quietly: The function that families act as basic cells to organize economic activities (production, consumption and labor distribution) has been weakening with increasing industrialization and urbanization, and new lifestyles and emerging forms of the division of labor between men and women have brought fundamental impacts on fertility behavior of humans. This latest development in fertility behavior needs to be delved into and understood from new perspectives.

In terms of either biological or societal attributes of humans, fertility behavior is one of the most basic human behaviors, and thus its motivations, means and results are sure to produce profound effects on humans per se. On the causes behind the "intention for more births" entrenched among the broad masses and the drive mechanisms of facilitating a shift to the "intention for less births", a basic consensus has been achieved in the light of the current situation: The fertility pattern in China is now in the critical period when the traditional exogenous pattern is quickly giving way to the modern endogenous one, but the shift in fertility desire is lagging behind. Much research on the endogenous factors of the shift in fertility concepts and behaviors has been done so far, which advocates economic determinism, but the similar effort on diverse fertility cultures has been rather scarce, which has inhibited us from making scientific judgments on the working mechanisms and conditions of transitions in fertility behavior under different cultural patterns. This research provides a typical case of the "traditional low fertility pattern" in an agrarian society, demonstrating that fertility behavior as a rational choice made by humans based on their living environments don't necessarily have deterministic correlations with the level of social productivity, which reputes the economic determinism to some extent. In addition, this research also shows that the formation of family-level fertility ideas and the realization of fertility behavior are governed by social values. In particular, in a society where the most basic needs (food, clothing, shelter and so on) have been satisfied, family-level fertility behavior are more regulated by cultural value orientations. That is, culture is a vital determinant of fertility behavior, providing a typical sample for understanding the fertility behavior of humans in this world of diverse cultures.

References

Chen, Huixiong. *The Principle of Pleasure: An Analysis of Human Economic Behaviors*. Beijing: Economic Sciences Press, 2003, 134.

Fei, Xiaotong. *On Economy of Jiang Village*. Beijing: the Commercial Press, 2001, 47.

Li, Jianmin. "China's Fertility Revolution". *Population Research*, no. 1 (2009): 1–9.

Lin, Fang, ed. *Human Potential and Value*. Beijing: Huaxia Publishing House, 1987a, 200.

Lin, Fang, ed. *Human Potential and Value*. Beijing: Huaxia Publishing House, 1987b, 202.

Lin, Fang, ed. *Human Potential and Value*. Beijing: Huaxia Publishing House, 1987c, 223.

Maslow. *Realize the Value of Life*. Translated by Feng Huaping. Hohhot: People's Publishing House of Inner Mongolia, 2002a, 3.

Maslow. *Realize the Value of Life*. Translated by Feng Huaping. Hohhot: People's Publishing House of Inner Mongolia, 2002b, 1.

Xia, Jianzhong. *Theories of Cultural Anthropology*. Beijing: China Renmin University Press, 1997, 68, 72, 73.

8

China Adapts to Low Fertility Rates

Section 1 Current Situation and Issues of Population Development in China

According to the data of the 6th National Census released in April 2011 by the National Bureau of Statistics (The 6th Census), China has a total population of 1.339.7 billion, increasing by 739 million or 5.84% over the figure of 12.658 billion in the fifth Census and posting an average annual growth rate of 0.57%. This means China has fully achieved the national strategic goal of keeping its total population under 1.36 billion by the end of the 11th Five-Year Plan period.

While the total population has been kept under effective control, the following changes have also taken place: (1) sex composition: the male population stands at 686.8 million, accounting for 51.27%, and the female population stands at 652.9 million, accounting for 48.73%, with the sex ratio in the total population declining to 105.20 from 106.74 in the fifth Census in 2000. (2) age composition: the age cohort of 0–14 years old has a total population of 222.5 million, accounting for 16.6% of the total population and seeing its proportion slide by 6.29 percentage points from that in 2000; the age cohort of 15–59 years old has a total population of 939 million, accounting for 70.1% and seeing its proportion increase by 3.36 percentage points; and the age cohort of 60 years old or above has a total population of 1.776 million, accounting for 13.3% and seeing its proportion increase by 2.93 percentage points (esp., the age cohort of 65 years old or above has a total population of 1.7188 million, accounting for 8.87% and seeing its proportion increase by 1.91 percentage points). (3) Education level: having risen to a varying degree for all segments from that in the fifth Census. To be specific, the population with college education grows to 8,930 per 100,000 persons from 3,611; that with high school education grows to 14,032 from 11,146; that with junior middle school education grows to 38,788 from 33,961; and that with primary school education shrinks to 26,779 from 35,701. (4) significant changes in urban/rural and migrant populations: the urban population stands at 665.6 million, accounting for 49.68% of the total population and increasing by 207.1 million or 13.46 percentage points over that in the fifth Census in 2000; the rural population stands at 674.1 million, accounting for 50.32% and decreasing by 133.2 million; and the migrant population increases by 81.03%.

China has become the world's second-largest economy. According to the data released by the National Bureau of Statistics, China's GDP in 2010 grew to RMB 3.97983 trillion (USD 6.04 trillion or more than USD 4,500 per capita). However, it is important to note that, while having a slowing growth, China's population also experienced marked structural changes: The proportion of persons under 14 years old has slid sharply and that of persons over 60 years old has risen sharply, indicating that China is, undoubtedly, moving into an aging society. Cai Fang commented that over the past decade or so, though China has created world-class miracles in economic growth and per capita income increase, its population has also experienced an even more rapid transition rarely seen in human history, resulting in a widening gap between the population transition and the per capita income increase and sliding into what is described as the predicament of "getting old before getting rich". In response to this premature aging, we will have to face up to challenges posed by the confluence of the early waning tide of demographic dividends, the belated next wave of demographic dividends and the insufficient old-aged supporting resources. Based on his research, Guo Zhigang said that most national census data showed the total fertility rate in China over the past 20 years has been in the 1.3–1.5 range, but relevant authorities have maintained it is 1.8. As a result, population planning by governmental agencies and most population projections, including the research on the national population development strategy, have been largely based on this assumption of the total fertility rate being around 1.8, significantly underestimating the severity of the sub-replacement fertility and aging population. Based on the "6th Census" demographic data, Guo Zhigang obtained the simulated total fertility rates during the period from 1990 to 2010, which are all below 1.5 and even below 1.4 for multiple years, and called for the government to seriously reexamine its future population decisions. Facts showed that the ongoing low fertility rates in China are largely attributable to two main factors: The forcible implementation of the one-child policy and the synthetic fallout from increased life pressure, a higher level of social and economic development, a higher overall education level, delayed marriages and others.

Some scholars pointed out that following "excessively rapid growth" over centuries, China's population dynamics are experiencing a historic turnaround, and the ongoing debate over birth policies is, in essence, from different judgments on the population situation. All in all, China is stepping into a new population landscape marked by a falling fertility rate, a severely aging population, accelerated urbanization and mass mobility. These features will mark not only China's population but also its society. In fact, this is simply the reality "the 6th Census" data revealed to us all.

Section 2 Thoughts and Recommendations on Stabilizing Low Fertility Rates in China

Following the release of "the 6th Census" main data, in its latest analysis and forecast of the world population: *World Population Prospects: 2010 Revision* published in May 2011, the Population Division of United Nations made major adjustments in its assessment and forecast on China's population: revising down China's total population and modifying its judgment on China's population trend. The UN Publication forecasts that Chin"s population will peak at 1.396 billion in 2026 before sliding sharply to 1.295 billion in 2050 (Cai, 2012). The six national census data over the 60 decades following the founding of the People's Republic of China shows that China's population growth process could be divided into three phases: rapid expansion, sharp decline and steady downtrend.

From 1965 to 1970, the average annual growth rate of China's population soared to 2.74%, recording a 0.7 percentage point higher than the global average, and slowed sharply down to 1.44% by the end of the 1970s before a brief fluctuation in growth in the 1980s. Since 1990, the population growth has shown a continuing slowdown to 0.5% now, less than half the global average and even below that of Britain, Sweden, the United States, Canada and other developed countries. The slowing population growth in China mainly stems from falling fertility rates. Should the fertility rate stay below the replacement level for too long, the population pyramid would transform into an inverted one (in a situation where children and young men are outnumbered by the elderly), and inflict huge impacts on the distribution of resources, economic development and social and political stability.

An analysis of the latest *World Population Policy 2009* released by the United Nations shows that since the 1970s, the growth rate of the world population has slowed sharply with a declining total fertility rate. In 1976, 36.7% of countries considered its current fertility level to be higher, which were mainly in East Africa, West Africa and South Asia; this proportion peaked at 45.3% in 1996 and has since declined to 37.4% in 2009. But the proportion of countries considering their current fertility rates at a too low level, which were mainly concentrated in Europe, such as Finland and France, increased every year from a mere 10.7% in 1976 over the past three decades and doubled to 24.1% in 2009; such countries were mainly distributed in East Asia and Oceania, such as Japan, South Korea and Australia. Nowadays, a growing number of countries no longer regard high fertility rates as scourges but instead are struggling with their persistently low fertility rates. In addition, some governments have even started to make some adjustments to their population-related policies.

In East Asia, the fertility rate in Japan began to take a turn in the early 20th century and has dropped below the replacement rate since the mid-1960s. Singapore, South Korea and Taiwan once had a total fertility rate as high as six births per woman, but later saw a rapid decline due to their social and economic reforms and family planning measures, with Singapore seeing its total fertility rate drop to its replacement rate in 1976, Taiwan in 1983, and South Korea in 1984. In sharp contrast with Western countries such as Britain, France and Italy, the decline in fertility rates in the three East Asian regions progressed at a much more hurried pace and within a much short period. For example, the UK and the US saw their fertility rates hovering around their replacement rates for almost three-quarters of a century before falling further, Japan did the same for almost two decades, but Singapore, South Korea and Taiwan saw their fertility rates continue to drop immediately after hitting their replacement rates. Terrified by such continued slides, the three governments moved to implement some adjustment policies, including direct financial allowances to moderate the inhibiting effects of rising childrearing costs for more births, improving conditions and facilities for childrearing (for example, implementing maternity leave policies and building additional childcare centers) to balance labor participation and childbirth and reduce the opportunity costs of childbirth (as shown in the following Table 8.1). However, these policy measures have not worked as expected, and all

Table 8.1: Policy Measures in Some East Asian Economies to Boost Birth Rates

	Providing direct financial allowances to childbirth and childrearing		Improving conditions and facilities for childrearing	
Japan	1990	Significant increases in child care allowances	1991	Unpaid parental leave for full-time workers
	1999	An extended period of child care allowances	1994	More child care institutions and partially paid parental leave
	2006	A further extended period of child care allowances	1999	More government-subsidized child care centers and after-school childcare services
	2006	The monthly child-care allowance for kids up to three years old was increased from 5,000 yen to 10,000 yen	2001	Partially-paid parental leave pay was increased from 25% to 40%. Parental leave was also available to some part-time workers
Korea	2006	Tax breaks for families with more than one child		Parental leave and shorter working hours during the childcare period
	2006	Lower health insurance contributions for families with more than one child		Daycare and pre-school education allowances for children under four years based on family incomes
	2006	Reduced or no testing fees for IVF babies		More childcare facilities run by government and working units
Singapore	1987	Tax breaks for families with three or more children		Allowances for children daycare
	2000	Allowances for families with two and three children		Paid maternity leave was extended from eight weeks to 12 weeks
	2004	Allowances for families with 1–4 children		More allowances for children daycare

(*Continued*)

Table 5.1: Continued

	Providing direct financial allowances to childbirth and childrearing		Improving conditions and facilities for childrearing	
Taiwan Region (China)	2008	Lower threshold for zero-interest home purchase/rental allowances for newly married couples buying or changing homes for childbirth or renting homes with children		NT$3,000 monthly allowance for parents having a third child or more children under two years old in the care of the community nanny system

Source: Shen Ke et al., "The Global Population Policy Shifts and Lessons for China", *International Economic Review*, 2012, Issue No. 1, p. 119.

four regions remain among the ones with the lowest fertility rates in the world. According to the statistics, the total fertility rate in 2010 in Japan, South Korea, Singapore and Taiwan was respectively 1.39, 1.22, 1.1 and 0.9 (Shen, Wang and Cai, 2012).

Within the same cultural circle, the four East Asian economies and China share similar cultural contexts, and certainly share more commonality in such highly culturally relevant issues as the population and fertility. Therefore, their population dynamics and policy intervention results are of great referential value to China.

Just as it is hard to reduce fertility rates quickly when humans desire more children, it is also hard, and even more challenging, to rekindle the passion for children when humans, badly strained by economic, demographic and cultural pressures amid deepening globalization, prefer fewer children. This is just what Viennese demographer Wolfgang Lutz et al. described as the "Low Fertility Trap": Once dropping below a certain level (TFR=1.5), fertility rates will continue to decline and are unlikely or even impossible to reverse due to a confluence of various factors, including changed values and increased survival pressures (Shi, 2010). As findings from this research have shown, the formation of family fertility ideas and the realization of fertility behavior are governed by social values. In a society where the most basic needs (food, clothing, shelter and so on) have been satisfied, culture is a vital determinant of fertility behavior.

Based on the preceding thinking, the author believes that with deepening urbanization and irreversible global integration, the family planning policy in China has completed its historical mission after 30 years of implementation, and suggests that the Chinese government should phase out its restriction of having only one child for couples at appropriate times: while adjusting the current old-age insurance system, it is necessary to allow "double one-child" couples (both spouses are the only child in their respective family before getting married), "single one-child" couples (one spouse is the only child in his/her family before getting married) and "non-one-child" couples (both spouses have siblings before getting married) in sequence to have no more than two children. In short, the focus of the Chinese family planning policy should shift from "stabilizing the low fertility rates at any cost" to "forestalling the faster and deeper population aging", "better harnessing population dividends" and "avoiding the Low Fertility Trap", which is the key to ensuring the long-term and stable development of China's population, economy and society.

References

Cai, Yong. "UN Forecasts: China Is Rapidly Aging". *International Economic Review*, no. 1 (2012): 73–75.

Shen, Ke, Feng Wang, and Yong Cai. "The Global Population Policy Shifts and Lessons for China". *International Economic Review*, no. 2 (2012): 113–118.

Shi, Renbing. "Low Fertility Trap: Truth or Myth?". *Population Research*, no. 2 (2010): 108.

Appendix

Survey Records of the Reproductive Histories of Surveyed Dai Households

Xishuangbanna Dai Autonomous Prefecture

Village M in Gasa Township of Jinghong Municipality[39]

General Information of the Village and Surveyed Households

Village M was administered by the Villagers' Committee of Manmian in Gasa Township. Starting at the seat of Gasa Town, walking southeast along the highway connecting Dongfeng Farm and Damenglong Township a few kilometers, and then veering off to the left, you will be there. Not far from the village is Manfeilong reservoir, a pleasant site for townfolks in Jinghong Municipality to enjoy the cool in hot weather and also an ideal venue for youths to spend their romantic time.

By December 2007, it was home to 461 residents (228 males and 233 females) in 103 households, and except for the five matrical sons-in-law who are Han and one man who is Bulang, all the rest were of the Dai minority. In July 2009, when we surveyed the village, 40 households met the above-mentioned criteria, accounting for 38.83% of the total. Its basic information is listed below in Table A.1.

39 All villages and individuals in our surveys have been anonymized to protect privacy as required by related regulations.

Table A.1: Basic Information of the Interviewees (born in or before 1950) in Village M

Serial No.	Household No.	Name	Date of Birth	Number of Lifetime Births	Surviving Births	Time at Last Childbirth	Age at Last Childbirth (Years Old)	Sex of children in descending order of birth
1	5	Yu Xiang	1940.4	4	4	1967	27	F – M – F – F
2	8	Yu Bian	1931.2	3	2	1969	38	M – F – F
3	11	Yu Tao	1924.8	4	4	1966	32	F – F – F – M
4	15	Yu Enzai	1938.11	5	3	1967	29	M – F – M – F – M
5	19	Yu Lameng	1944.1	3	3	1973	29	M – M – F
6	20	Yu Nan	1940.3.8	4	4	1969	29	F – M – M – M
7	21	Yu Yan	1926.2.	2	1	1950	24	F – M
8	26	Yu Ban	1926.10.	5	5	1966	40	M – M – M – M – F
9	28	Yu Xiang	1940.2	4	4	1968	28	M – M – F – M
10	34	Yu Yang	1932.5	5	5	1963	31	F – F – M – M – M
11	35	Yan La	1950.3	0	–	–	–	–
12	36	Mi Meng	1923.9	5	5	1964	44	F – M – M – F – M
13	37	Yu Yinghan	1949.8	4	4	1978	29	M – M – M – F
14	38	Yu Jing	1939.1	5	5	1971	28	M – M – F – M – F
15	43	Yu Han	1922.3	1	1	1941	19	M
16	44	Yu Pengban	1932.5	5	4	1969	37	M – F – M – F – F

17	45	Yu Nanlong	1946.6	3	3	1973.11	27	F – F – M
18	47	Yu Yingbie	1931.1	4	4	1965	34	M – F – M – F
19	49	Yu Bingbian	1921.1	4	3	1966	45	F – F – F – F
20	52	Yu Ta	1928.11	3	3	1966.	38	M – F – M
21	53	Yan Xiangzai	1925.8	4	4	–	–	M – M – F – M
22	55	Yu Lalun	1938.2	3	3	1966	28	M – M – F
23	56	Yu Wangsa	1938.11	4	3	1968	30	M – M – F – M
24	58	Yu Taoda	1940.10	4	4	1966.	26	F – F – M – F
25	62	Kang Nanbing	1926.4	6	6	–	–	M – M – F – F – M (M – F)
26	63	Yu Zhuang	1925.10	7	6	1968	43	M – M – F – F – M – F – F
27	65	Yu Yan	1946.8	3	3	1974	28	M – F – F
28	66	Yu Lun	1921.9	5	3	1960	39	M – F – M – F – F
29	67	Yu Shuailong	1944.6	3	2	1973	29	M – M – F
30	68	Yu Lao	1918.5	5	5	1966	48	M – M (M – F) – F – F
31	71	Yu Hanxiang	1923.7	8	8	1973	50	F – F – F – M – M – F – M – F
32	75	Yu Yan	1939.4	3	3	1964	25	F – M – M
33	77	Yu Han’er	1937.2	5	5	1968	31	F – M – M – F – F

(Continued)

Table A.1: Continued

34	78	Yu Lilong	1946.7	3	3	1971	25	F – F – M
35	82	Yu Jianxiang	1932.1	5	5	1968	36	F – M – M – F – M
36	83	Yu Ying	1929.3	5	5	1965	42	F – M – M – F – F
37	88	Yu Ernan	1946.12	2	2	1969	23	F – F
38	90	Yan Wenxiang	1950.4	3	3	–	–	M – M – M
39	92	Yan Dunhan	1927.2	2	2	1961	34	F – M
40	98	Yan Hannan	1943.3	8	8	1981	38	M – M – F – M – M – F – M – M

Source: Field Survey Statistics by the Research Team.

Records of the Reproductive Histories of the Surveyed Households

Household No.: 5; **Interviewee: Yu Xiang; Figure A.1**

Yu Xiang, the fourth child in the family, was born in April 1940. Her elder sister remained single all her life and lived with their mother.

Parents' Generation:

Yu Xiang's mother gave birth to four children, two males and two females. Sex of the children in descending order: F (1934) – M (1936) – M (1938) – F (1940). Yu Xiang was the youngest daughter.

Current Generation:

Yu Xiang was born in April 1940 and gave birth to four children, three females and one male. Sex of the children in descending order: F (1959) – M (1962) – F (1964) – F (1967).

Children's Generation:

The first daughter got married in 1978 and gave birth to two children. Sex of the children in descending order: M (1979) – M (1980).

The first son got married in 1981 and gave birth to two children. Sex of the children in descending order: M (November 1981) – F (February 1984).

The second daughter got married in 1984 and gave birth to two children. Sex of the children in descending order: M (May 1985) – M (July 1987).

The third daughter got married in 1990 and gave birth to two children. Sex of the children in descending order: M (September 1991) – M (August 1993).

Grandchildren's Generation:

The first daughter's first child got married in 1997 and gave birth to two children, both females.

The first daughter's second child got married, divorced and had no children.

The first son's first child got married in 2003 and gave birth to one child, M (April 2005).

The first son's second child got married in 2006 and gave birth to one child, M (June 2007).

The second daughter's first child got married in 2006 and gave birth to one child, M (January 2008).

The second daughter's second child were unmarried.

The third daughter's two children were unmarried.

Great-grandchildren's Generation:

Five great-grandchildren, two females and three males.

Household No.: 8; Interviewee: Yu Bian; Figure A.2

Parents' Generation:

Yu Bian's mother gave birth to five children. Sex of the children in descending order: F – F – F – F – M. Yu Bian is the oldest child in the family.

Current Generation:

Yu Bian was born in February 1931 and gave birth to three children and two children survived. Sex of the children in descending order: M – F (1966) – F (1969). The boy died in infancy.

Children's Generation:

The first daughter got married in 1983 and gave birth to two children. Sex of the children in descending order: F (September 1983) – M (April 1987).

Grandchildren's Generation:

The first daughter's first child got married in 2006 and gave birth to one child, F (November 2007).

The first daughter's second child was 22 years old and was still unmarried.

The second daughter's two children were young and remained single.

Great-grandchildren's Generation:

One great-grandchild, F.

When asked about having children, Yu Bian told us: "At that time (when she was young), we were fun-loving young people. We were always together with mates in our cohort. Even when we fell in love, we also fell in love with mates in our cohort. Neither of us wanted to get married until we felt it was time for family life."

Household No.: 11; Interviewee: Yu Tao; Figure A.3

Parents' Generation:

Yu Tao's mother gave birth to five children all her life, two males and three females. Sex of the children in descending order: F – M – M – F – F. Yu Tao was the fourth child in the family. Yu Tao's husband Yan Mai's mother gave birth to two children, Yan Mai and his younger sister.

Current Generation:

Yu Tao was born in August 1924 and gave birth to four children. Four children survived. Sex of the children in descending order: F (June 1946) – F (1957) – F (1962) – M (March 1966).

Children's Generation:

The first daughter got married in 1964 and gave birth to three children. Sex of the children in descending order: F (1966) – F (August 1972) – M (November 1973).

The third daughter got married in 1979 and gave birth to two children, all males (October 1983 and February 1985).

The fourth daughter got married in 1980 and gave birth to two children. Sex of the children in descending order: F (July 1983) – M (March 1985). She later remarried her second husband, namely the first son of Yu Nan from Household No. 20 in this village.

The second son got married in 1988 and gave birth to two children, both males (the first kid was born in October 1990; the second child was born in 1992 and died in 2000).

Grandchildren's Generation:

The first daughter's first child gave birth to two children. Sex of the children in descending order: M (1986) – F (1988).

The first daughter's second child got married in 2001 and gave birth to one child, M (2005).

The first daughter's third child got married in 2000 and gave birth to one child, M (December 2001).

The third daughter's first child got married in 2008 and was four months into her pregnancy.

The third daughter's second child got married in 2004, had never got pregnant, and was being treated with infertility.

The fourth daughter's first child gave birth to two children, both males (respectively in 2003 and 2008).

The fourth daughter's second child gave birth to one child, F (March 2008).

Great-grandchildren's Generation:

Seven great-grandchildren, five males and two females.

The second son's second child died at the age of eight (2000). According to local regulations, a birth that didn't survive 14 years old (inc. 14 years old) didn't be counted in. According to state regulations, Yu Tao's second son was eligible for a second child but chose not to do so. Therefore, he got the only-child certificate and enjoyed the corresponding treatment.

Household No.: 15; Interviewee: Yu Enzai; Figure A.4

Yu Enzai's maternal grandmother Yu Guangzai is the elder sister of Yu Tao from Household No. 11 in this village.

Parents' Generation:

Yu Enzai's mother gave birth to four children, two males and two females. Sex of the children in descending order: F – F (1938) – M – M. Yu Enzai was the second child in the family.

Current Generation:

Yu Enzai was born in November 1938, and her husband was Yan Maizai, the younger brother of Yu Bian from Household No. 8 in this village. Yu Enzai gave birth to five children, but four children survived (one baby boy died). The first daughter also died shortly after graduating from primary school. Sex of the children in descending order: M – F (1959) – M (April 1962) – F (October 1965) – M (November 1967).

Children's Generation:

The first son died soon after his birth.

The first daughter also died shortly after graduating from primary school in 1973.

The second son got married in 1980 and gave birth to two children. Sex of the children in descending order: M (December 1981) – F (July 1983), and his wife was the second daughter of Yu Taoda from Household No. 58 in this village.

The second daughter got married in 1983 and gave birth to two children. Sex of the children in descending order: M (1983) – F (August 1985).

The third son got married in 1985 and gave birth to two children. Sex of the children in descending order: F (January 1985) – F (October 1986).

Grandchildren's Generation:

The second son's first child got married in 2002 and gave birth to one child, F (June 2005).

The second son's second child got married in 2001 and gave birth to one child, M (May 2003).

The second daughter's first child got married in 2003 and gave birth to one child, M (July 2004).

The second daughter's second child got married in 2007 and gave birth to one child, M (August 2008).

The third son's first child got married in 2002 and gave birth to one child, F (2005).

The third son's second child got married in 2002 and still had no children.

Great-grandchildren's Generation:

Five great-grandchildren, three males and two females.

Household No.: 19; Interviewee: Yu Lameng; Figure A.5

Parents' Generation:

Yu Lameng's mother adopted Yu Lameng (due to failure to get pregnant in her first year into marriage), and later gave birth to six children, three males and three females. Her husband Mai Shuai was the youngest boy in his family of five siblings. Mai Shuai had two sisters and two brothers.

Current Generation:

Yu Lameng was born in January 1944, and her husband was born in August 1940. Yu Lameng gave birth to three children. Sex of the children in descending order: M (1966 December) – M (1970) – F (1973).

Children's Generation:

The first son got married in 1983 and gave birth to one child, F (1986).

The second son got married in 1990 and gave birth to two children. Sex of the children in descending order: M (April 1991) – F (May 1993).

The first daughter gave birth to one child, F.

Grandchildren's Generation:

The first son's daughter got married in 2007 and gave birth to one child, F (2008).

All the other grandchildren were unmarried.

Great-grandchildren's Generation:

One great-grandchild, F.

As for child adoption in the Dai society, Yu Wen, Director at the Family Planning Office of Gasa Township of Jinghong Municipality, said: "The Dai families prefer a girl over a boy. Girls always have a better relationship with their adopted parents. Boys are naughtier and not easy to rear."

Household No.: 20; Interviewee: Yu Nan; Figure A.6

Parents' Generation:

Yu Nan's mother gave birth to two children. Sex of the children in descending order: F – M. Yu Nan's husband Yan Ying's mother gave birth to three children. Yan Ying was the first child in her family and had two younger sisters.

Current Generation:

Yu Nan was born in August 1940 and gave birth to four children. Four children survived. Sex of the children in descending order: F (1961) – M (1963) – M (May 1966) – M (September 1969).

Children's Generation:

The first daughter got married in 1978 and gave birth to two children. Sex of the children in descending order: F (1979) – M (1981). Her husband was the second son of Yan Xiangzai from Household No. 53 in this village.

The first son married the fourth daughter of Yu Tao from Household No. 11 in this village and had no children. But the fourth daughter of Yu Tao had one boy and one daughter with her first husband.

The second son got married in 1986 and gave birth to two children, both males (respectively in November 1988 and July 1990).

The third son married in 1990 the little daughter of Yu Xiang from Household No. 05 in this village, and gave birth to two children, both males (respectively in September 1991 and August 1993).

Grandchildren's Generation:

The first daughter's first child got married in 1996 and gave birth to one child, M (2000 January).

The first daughter's second child got married in May 2002 and adopted a girl born in May 2007 as his wife had never got pregnant.

The first son's stepson and stepdaughter both were married. The stepdaughter gave birth to two children, both males (respectively in 2003 and 2008) and the stepson gave birth to one child, F (March 2008).

The second son's first child got married in 2009 and still had no children.

All the other grandchildren were unmarried.

Great-grandchildren's Generation:

Five grandchildren, three males and two females.

Household No.: 21; Interviewee: Yu Yan; Figure A.7

Parents' Generation:

Yu Yan's mother gave birth to six children. All six children survived. Yu Yan was the first child in the family and had four younger sisters and one younger brother.

Current Generation:

Yu Yan was born in February 1926 and gave birth to two children. One child survived. Her first daughter died at three years old and her son was born in 1950. Yu Yan were unmarried after her husband was executed as a Kuomintang member in 1953.

Children's Generation:

Her son married twice. He gave birth to one child with his first wife (the third daughter of Yu Hanxiang from Household. No 71 in this village), F (1973), and gave birth to two children with his second wife, all males (respectively in 1976 and 1979).

Grandchildren's Generation:

The first daughter lived with his first wife, married in 1991 with the third son of Yu Xiang from Household No. 28 in this village, and gave birth to a girl (died three days after her birth) in 1992. She had never got pregnant later and adopted a girl in September 1996.

The first son remained single.

The second son got married in 2000 and gave birth to two children. Sex of the children in descending order: M (2002) – F (2009).

Great-grandchildren's Generation:

Two great-grandchildren, one male and one female.

Household No.: 26; Interviewee: Yu Ban; Figure A.8

Yu Ban was the younger sister of Yu Tao from Household No. 11 in this village and the youngest daughter in the family.

Parents' Generation:

Yu Ban's mother gave birth to five children. Five children survived. Sex of the children in descending order: F – M – M – F – F. Her first elder sister Yu Guangzai (born in December 1914) was the maternal grandmother of Yu Enzai from Household No. 15 in this village, and her second elder sister was Yu Tao (born in August 1924) from Household No. 11 in this village. Yu Ban herself was the youngest daughter in the family.

Current Generation:

Yu Ban was born in October 1926 and gave birth to five children, four males and one female. Five children survived. Sex of the children in descending order: M (1952) – M (1955) – M (1959) – M (1962) – F (1966).

Children's Generation:

The first son married twice. He gave birth to one child with his first wife, M (1974) and had no children with his second wife.

The second son gave birth to two children, both females.

The third son got married in 1981 and gave birth to two children, both males (respectively in June 1984 and March 1987).

The fourth son married twice. He gave birth to one child with his first wife, F (1986), and gave birth to two children with his second wife. Sex of the children in descending order: F (1991) – M (1993).

The first daughter got married in 1985 and gave birth to two children, both males (respectively in March 1986 and October 1988).

Grandchildren's Generation:

The first son's second wife didn't discipline her stepson, who left the village after being released from prison in the 1990s and his marriage was unknown to villagers.

The second son emigrated far away to live in his wife's village and had almost no connections with this village. Therefore, there was no information about the marriage and births of the two granddaughters.

The third son's first child got married in 2006 and gave birth to one child, M (January 2007).

The third son's second child was married but had no children.

The fourth son's first child got married in 2008 and still had no children.

The first daughter's first child got married in 2007 and gave birth to one child, M (2008).

All the other grandchildren were unmarried.

Great-grandchildren's Generation:

Two great-grandchildren, all males.

The fourth son remarried and lived with the children from his two wives, and his family of five got along very well.

Household No.: 28; Interviewee: Yu Xiang; Figure A.9

Yu Xiang was the second younger sister of Yu Bian from Household No. 8 in this village.

Parents' Generation:

Yu Xiang's mother gave birth to five children. Sex of the children in descending order: F – F – F – F – M. Yu Xiang was the third child in the family. Yu Xiang's husband Kang Nanlang was born in September 1936, had one younger brother and one younger sister. The Chinese character 喃 in her husband's name indicates that he was of aristocratic descent, namely having some kind of kinship with Zhaopianling (local feudal rulers).

Current Generation:

Yu Xiang was born in February 1940 and gave birth to four children. Sex of the children in descending order: M (1960) – M (January 1962) – F (1966) – M (April 1968).

Children's Generation:

The first son got married in 1983 and gave birth to two children, both females (respectively in 1985 and 1991).

The second son got married in 1980 and gave birth to two children. Sex of the children in descending order: M (1982) – F (April 1985).

The first daughter got married in 1986 and gave birth to two children, both females (respectively in 1987 and 1989).

The third son married in 1991 the oldest granddaughter (1973) of Yu Yan from Household No. 21 in this village, and gave birth in 1992 to a girl (died three days after her birth). His wife had never got pregnant later and the couple adopted a girl in September 1996.

Grandchildren's Generation:

All the grandchildren were still young and unmarried.

Household No.: 34; Interviewee: Yu Yang; Figure A.10

Yu Yang's husband was Kang Langzai, who was the second child in his family and had an elder sister and a younger brother. The character Kang Lang in the name of Yu Yang's husband indicated that he had been once a Buddha before being secularized.

Parents' Generation:

Yu Yang's mother gave birth to two children, and her brother was the husband of Yu Tao from Household No. 11 in this village.

Current Generation:

Yu Yang was born in May 1932 and gave birth to five children, two females and three males. Sex of the children in descending order: F (1954) – F (1956) – M (1958) – M (1961) – M (1963). Her husband was the first younger brother of Yu Lao from Household No. 68 in this village.

Children's Generation:

The first daughter married twice. She didn't give birth to any children with her first husband and got divorced. Later, she remarried her second husband and gave birth to two children. Sex of the children in descending order: M (1976) – F (1979).

The second daughter also married twice. She got married in 1973 and gave birth to two children with her first husband. Sex of the children in descending order: F (1974) – M (1976). In 1986, she remarried and didn't have a child with her second husband.

The first son got married in 1977 and gave birth to two children. Sex of the children in descending order: F (1979) – M (1981).

The second son got married in 1984 and gave birth to one child, M (1985).

The third son got married in 1982 and gave birth to two children. Sex of the children in descending order: F (July 1983) – M (May 1985).

Grandchildren's Generation:

The first daughter's first child emigrated to his wife's village and gave birth to two children. Sex of the children in descending order: F – M. His reproductive history was unknown.

The first daughter's second child got married in 1998 and gave birth to two children. Sex of the children in descending order: F (1999) – M (2002).

The second daughter's first child married twice. She had no children with her first husband, a farmer divorced. In 1997, she remarried her second husband and gave birth to one child, M (1999). They had received the only-child certificate.

The second daughter's second child got married in 1998 and gave birth to one child, F (2004). Now, they were expecting their second child.

The first son and second son were both unmarried.

The third son's first child got married in 2003 and gave birth to one child, M (April 2005). Her husband was the second daughter of the first son of Yu Ta from Household No. 52 in this village.

The third son's second child got married in 2007 and gave birth to one child, M (2008).

Great-grandchildren's Generation:

Eight great-grandchildren, three females and five males.

Household No.: 35; Interviewee: Yan La

Yan La was born in March 1950, got married in 1986, and his wife was the second daughter of Yu Yang from Household No. 34 in this village. Yan La had no children with Yu Yang's second daughter and had lived with his wife next to his parents-in-law.

Household No.: 36; Interviewee: Mi Meng; Figure A.11

Mi Meng's husband Yan Meng had one brother and three sisters. Sex of the children in descending order: M – M – F – F – F. He was the first child in the family.

Parents' Generation:

Mi Meng's mother gave birth to five children. Sex of the children in descending order: F – F – F – F – M. Mi Meng was the second daughter in the family.

Current Generation:

Mi Meng was born in February 1923, got married in 1940, and gave birth to five children. Sex of the children in descending order: F (1944) – M (1949) – M (1951) – F (1957) – M (1964). The youngest boy died in 1985 of an accident shortly after marriage (killed by an ox) and had no children.

Children's Generation:

The first daughter got married in 1968 and gave birth to three children. Sex of the children in descending order: M (1968) – M (1969) – F (1973). Her first son died young.

The first son got married in 1969 and gave birth to two children. Sex of the children in descending order: F (1973) – F (1975).

The second son got married in 1969 and gave birth to two children. Sex of the children in descending order: F (December 1971) – M (December 1974).

The second daughter got married in 1977 and gave birth to two children. Sex of the children in descending order: M (August 1978) – F (March 1980).

Grandchildren's Generation:

The first daughter's second child got married in 1989 and gave birth to one child, M (June 1989).

The first daughter's third child got married in 1992 and gave birth to one child, M (December 1993).

The first son's first child got married in 1989 and gave birth to two children. Sex of the children in descending order: F (April 1990) – M (May 1992).

The first son's second child got married in 1992 and gave birth to one child, M (July 1994).

The second son's first child got married in 1990 and gave birth to two children. Sex of the children in descending order: M (1991 April) – F (September 1994).

The second son's second child got married in 2005 and gave birth to one child, F (December 2007).

The second daughter's first child got married in 2006 and gave birth to one child, F (May 2007).

The second daughter's second child got married in 2000 and gave birth to one child, M (2002).

Mi Meng said, before family planning knowledge was popularized, women in this village more often gave birth to two children in three years rather than in four years.

Household No.: 37; Interviewee: Yu Yinghan; Figure A.12

Parents' Generation:

Yu Yinghan's mother married twice. She had Yu Yinghan (August 1949) with her first husband, and after remarrying her second husband, she gave birth to Yu Yinghan's younger brother (December 1957).

Current Generation:

Yu Yinghan was born in August 1949 and gave birth to four children, three males and one female. Sex of the children in descending order: M (August 1968) – M (1971) – M (1975) – F (1978).

Children's Generation:

The first son got married in 1987 and gave birth to one child, M (1987).

The second son got married in 1992 and gave birth to one child, M (July 1994).

The third son got married in 1996 and gave birth to one child, M (January 2001). His wife was the first daughter of the second son from Yan Xiangzai, Household No. 53 in this village.

The youngest daughter got married in 2005 and gave birth to one child, F (2007).

Grandchildren's Generation:

The first son's child got married in 2005 and gave birth to one child, F (2005). All the other grandchildren were unmarried.

Great-grandchildren's Generation:

One great-grandchild, F (2005).

Household No.: 38; Interviewee: Yu Jing; Figure A.13

Yu Jing was the youngest sister of Mi Meng's husband Yan Meng from Household No. 36 in this village.

Parents' Generation:

Yu Jing's mother gave birth to five children, two males and three females. Five children survived. Sex of the children in descending order: M – M – F – F – F.

The oldest child was Mi Meng's husband from Household No. 36 in this village and Yu Jing was the youngest daughter in the family.

Current Generation:

Yu Jing was born in January 1939 and gave birth to five children, three males and two females. Sex of the children in descending order: M (1962) – M (1964) – F (1966) – M (1968) – F (1971).

Children's Generation:

The first son got married in 1982 and gave birth to two children. Sex of the children in descending order: F (1983) – M (1987).

The second son got married in 1994 and gave birth to two children, both females (respectively in 1995 and 1999).

The first daughter got married in 1984 and gave birth to two children. Sex of the children in descending order: M (1986) – F (1988). She divorced her first husband and remarried her second husband, who had a girl with his former wife (July 1988).

The third son died at 25 years old (1993).

The youngest daughter got married in 1990 and gave birth to one child, F (1991).

Grandchildren's Generation:

The first son's first child got married in 2008 and gave birth to one child, F (December 2008).

All the other grandchildren were unmarried.

Great-grandchildren's Generation:

One great-grandchild, F (December 2008).

Household No.: 43; Interviewee: Yu Han; Figure A.14

Parents' Generation:

Yu Han's mother gave birth to her: a one-child.

Current Generation:

Yu Han was born in March 1922 and got married in 1940. She gave birth to one child, M (1941). Her husband was classified as a landlord at the beginning of liberation and died in the 1960s.

Children's Generation:

Yu Han's son got married in 1967 and gave birth to two children. Sex of the children in descending order: F (1968) – M (1971).

Grandchildren's Generation:

All the grandchildren were unmarried.

Household No.: 44; Interviewee: Yu Pengban; Figure A.15

Parents' Generation:

Yu Pengban was her mother's only child.

Current Generation:

Yu Pengban was born in May 1932 and gave birth to five children. Four children survived. Sex of the children in descending order: M (1952) – F (December 1955) – M (1960) – F (1965) – F (1969). The second son died in infancy.

Children's Generation:

The first son got married in 1971 and gave birth to two children, both males (respectively in 1973 and 1979).

The first daughter got married in 1973 and gave birth to two children, both males (respectively in January 1974. August 1978).

The second daughter got married in 1982 and gave birth to two children, both females (respectively in 1983 and 1985).

The third daughter got married in 1986 and gave birth to two children, both males (respectively in November 1988 and July 1990). Her husband was the third son of Yu Nan from Household No. 20 in this village.

Grandchildren's Generation:

The first son's first child got married in 1995 and gave birth to a boy in 1996.

The first so"s second child gave birth to one child, F.

The first daughter's first child got married in 2001 and gave birth to two children. Sex of the children in descending order: M (2003) – F (2008).

The first daughter's second child got married in 2002 and gave birth to one child, F (2003).

The second daughter's first child got married in 2005 and gave birth to one child, F (2007).

The second daughter's second child got married in 2007 and still had no children.

The third daughter's first child got married in 2009 and still had no children.

All the other grandchildren were unmarried.

Great-grandchildren's Generation:

Six great-grandchildren, two males and four females.

Household No.: 45; Interviewee: Yu Nanlong; Figure A.16

Yu Nanlong was the first daughter of Yu Tao from Household No. 11 in this village.

Parents' Generation:

Yu Nanlong's mother was born in August 1924 and gave birth to four children. Four children survived. Sex of the children in descending order: F (1946) – F (1957) – F (1962) – M (March 1966).

Current Generation:

Yu Nanlong was born in June 1946, got married in 1964, and gave birth to three children. Sex of the children in descending order: F (1966) – F (August 1972) – M (November 1973).

Children's Generation:

The first daughter got married in 1985 and gave birth to two children. Sex of the children in descending order: M (1986) – F (1988).

The second daughter got married in 2001 and gave birth to one child, M (2005).

The first son got married in 2000 and gave birth to one child, M (December 2001).

Grandchildren's Generation:

Four grandchildren (3 males and one female) were all still unmarried.

Household No.: 47; Interviewee: Yu Yingbie; Figure A.17

Yu Yingbie was the elder sister of Yu Enzai from Household No. 15 in this village.

Parents' Generation:

Yu Yingbie's mother gave birth to four children, two males and two females. Sex of the children in descending order: F (1931) – F (1938) – M – M. Yu Yingbie was the eldest child in the family and her husband had one elder sister and two younger sisters, and was the second child in his family.

Current Generation:

Yu Yingbie was born in January 1931 and gave birth to four children. Four children survived. Sex of the children in descending order: M (1952) – F (1957) – M (1961) – F (1965).

Children's Generation:

The first son emigrated 1972 to Mandou, got married, and gave birth to two children, both females (respectively in 1973 and 1975).

The first daughter got married in 1974 and gave birth to three children, all males (respectively in 1975, 1976 and 1979). Her husband was the first son of Kang Nanbing from Household No. 62 in this village.

The second son got married in 1981 and gave birth to two children, both females (respectively in April 1982 and 1986).

The second daughter got married in 1986 and gave birth to two children, both males (respectively in May 1987 and November 1988).

Grandchildren's Generation:

The two grandchildren's reproductive history was unknown as the first son was in Mandou.

The first daughter's first child got married in 1995 and gave birth to one child, M (1997).

The first daughter's second child got married in 1996 and gave birth to one child, F (1997).

The first daughter's third child got married in 1999 and gave birth to one child, M (March 2000).

The second son's first child got married in 2002 and gave birth to one child, F (June 2004).

The second son's second child got married in 2009 and still had no children.

The second daughter's two children both still had no children.

Great-grandchildren's Generation:

Five great-grandchildren, two males and three females.

Household No.: 49; Interviewee: Yu Bingbian; Figure A.18

Parents' Generation:

Yu Bingbian's mother gave birth to two children, both females. Yu Bingbian was the second child in the family, and her husband was the eldest among the five siblings in his family. Sex of the children in descending order: M – F – M – F – M.

Current Generation:

Yu Bingbian was born in January 1921 and gave birth to four children, all females. Three children survived (1957, 1962 and 1966). The first child died in infancy.

Children's Generation:

The second daughter got married in 1975 and gave birth to two children, both males (respectively in February 1975 and August 1979).

The third daughter got married in 1981 and gave birth to two children. Sex of the children in descending order: F (January 1982) – M (October 1983).

The fourth daughter got married in 1984 and gave birth to two children. Sex of the children in descending order: M (October 1986) – F (September 1989).

Grandchildren's Generation:

The second daughter's first child got married in 1996 and gave birth to one child, M (January 1997).

The second daughter's second child got married in 2002 and gave birth to one child, F (2003).

The third daughter's first child got married in 2000 and gave birth to one child, F (August 2003).

The third daughter's second child got married, divorced, and had no childrens.

The fourth daughter's first child got married in 2006 and gave birth to one child, F (November 2007).

The fourth daughter's second child were unmarried.

Great-grandchildren's Generation:

Four great-grandchildren, one male and three females.

Household No.: 52; Interviewee: Yu Ta; Figure A.19

Parents' Generation:

Yu Ta's mother gave birth to three children, one male and two females. Sex of the children in descending order: M – F (1928) – F. Yu Ta was the second child in the family, and her husband was of Aini ethnic descent.

Current Generation:

Yu Ta was born in November 1928 and gave birth to three children. Three children survived. Sex of the children in descending order: M (1959) – F (1962) – M (1966).

Children's Generation:

The first son married twice. He had no children with his first wife. He married his second wife in 1980 and gave birth to two children. Sex of the children in descending order: M (January 1981) – F (December 1982).

The first daughter got married in 1981 and gave birth to two children. Sex of the children in descending order: M (November 1981) – F (February 1984).

The second son got married in 1986 and gave birth to two children, both males (respectively in January 1987 and February 1989).

Grandchildren's Generation:

The first son's first child got married in March 2001 and gave birth to one child, M (May 2003).

The first son's second child worked in Shanghai and were unmarried.

The first daughter's first child got married in January 2003 and gave birth to one child, M (April 2005). His wife was the first daughter of the third son of Yu Yang from Household No. 34 in this village.

The first daughter's second child got married in 2005 and gave birth to one child, M (June 2007).

The second son's two children were unmarried.

Great-grandchildren's Generation:

Three great-grandchildren, all males.

Household No.: 53; Interviewee: Yan Xiangzai; Figure A.20

Parents' Generation:

Yan Xiangzai's mother gave birth to two children, both males. His wife was the youngest of the five siblings in her family.

Current Generation:

Yan Xiangzai was born in August 1925 and gave birth to four children. Four children survived. Sex of the children in descending order: M (1954) – M (1959) – F (1962) – M (1968).

Children's Generation:

The first son got married in 1977 and gave birth to one child, M (1979).

The second son got married in 1978 and gave birth to two children. Sex of the children in descending order: F (1979) – M (1981). His wife was the first daughter of Yu Nan from Household No. 20 in this village.

The first daughter got married in 1983 and gave birth to two children, both females (respectively in February 1984 and January 1986).

The third son got married in 2003 and chose to have no children.

Grandchildren's Generation:

The first son's child worked in the provincial capital and were unmarried.

The second son's first child got married in 1996 and gave birth to one child, M (January 2000). Her husband was the third son of Yu Yinghan from Household No. 37 in this village.

The second son's second child were unmarried.

The first daughter's first child got married in 2002 and gave birth to one child, F (June 2005).

The first daughter's second child got married in 2007 and gave birth to one child, M (2008).

Great-grandchildren's Generation:

Three great-grandchildren, two males and one female.

Household No.: 55; Interviewee: Yu Lalun; Figure A.21

Parents' Generation:

Yu Lalun's mother gave birth to four children, one male and three females. Sex of the children in descending order: F – M – F – F (1938). Yu Lalun was the youngest in her family and her brother was the husband of Yu Yingbie from Household No. 47 in this village.

Current Generation:

Yu Lalun was born in February 1938 and gave birth to three children. Three children survived. Sex of the children in descending order: M (1957) – M (1962) – F (1966).

Children's Generation:

The first son got married in 1975 and gave birth to three children. Sex of the children in descending order: M (1976) – M (1978) – F (1981).

The second son got married in 1982 and gave birth to two children. Sex of the children in descending order: M (1983) – F (1985).

The first daughter got married in 1982 and gave birth to two children, both males (respectively in March 1983 and March 1985).

Grandchildren's Generation:

The first son's first child got married in 1995 and gave birth to one child, M (1997).

The first son's second child got married in 2000 and gave birth to one child, M (September 2001).

The first son's third child got married in 2003 and gave birth to one child, F (November 2005).

The second son's children were unmarried.

The first daughter's first child got married in 2003 and gave birth to one child, F (July 2005).

The first daughter's second child got married in 2008 and still had no children.

Great-grandchildren's Generation:

Four great-grandchildren, two males and two females.

Household No.: 56; Interviewee: Yu Wangsa; Figure A. 22

Parents' Generation:

Yu Wangsa's mother gave birth to two children, one male and one female. Sex of the children in descending order: F (1938) – M. Yu Wangsa was the eldest in the family and her husband Kang Langzhong was the younger brother of Yu Pengban's husband Yan Dan from Household No. 44 in this village.

Current Generation:

Yu Wangsa was born in November 1938 and gave birth to four children. Three children survived. Sex of the children in descending order: M

(1961) – M (1964) – F (1966) – M (1968). The only daughter died of a heart attack at 11 years old.

Children's Generation:

The first son got married in 1980 and gave birth to two children, both females (respectively in November 1982 and May 1983).

The second son got married in 1984 and gave birth to two children. Sex of the children in descending order: F (May 1985) – M (March 1987). His wife was the second daughter of Yu Zhuang from Household No. 63 in this village.

The third son got married in 1989 and gave birth to two children, both females (respectively in January 1991 and December 1992).

Grandchildren's Generation:

The first son's first child got married in December 2001 and gave birth to one child, F (2003), and received a one-child certificate.

The first son's second child got married in 2006 and gave birth to one child, M (2008).

The second son's first child got married in 2007 and still had no children.

All the other grandchildren were unmarried.

Great-grandchildren's Generation:

Two great-grandchildren, one male and one female.

Household No.: 58; Interviewee: Yu Taoda; Figure A.23

Parents' Generation:

Yu Taoda's mother gave birth to six children, one male and five females. Sex of the children in descending order: F – M – F – F – F (1940) – F. Yu Taoda was the fifth child in her family and her husband was the third child of five siblings in his family. Sex of the children in descending order: M – M – M – F – M.

Current Generation:

Yu Taoda was born in October 1940 and gave birth to four children. Four children survived. Sex of the children in descending order: F (1959) – F (March 1962) – M (August 1964) – F (1966).

Children's Generation:

The first daughter got married in 1981 and gave birth to two children. Sex of the children in descending order: F (1984) – M (1990).

The second daughter got married in 1980 and gave birth to two children. Sex of the children in descending order: M (December 1981) – F (July 1983). Her husband was the second son of Yu Enzai from Household No. 15 in this village.

The first son got married in 1990 and gave birth to one child, M (1995).

The third daughter got married in 1986 and gave birth to two children. Sex of the children in descending order: M (1987) – F (1989).

Grandchildren's Generation:

The first daughter's children were unmarried.

The second daughter's first child got married in 2002 and gave birth to one child, F (June 2005).

The second daughter's second child got married in 2001 and gave birth to one child, M (May 2003).

The first son's children were unmarried.

The third daughter's first child were unmarried.

The third daughter's second child got married in 2008 and gave birth to one child, M (August 3, 2008).

Great-grandchildren's Generation:

Three great-grandchildren, two males and one female.

Household No.: 62; Interviewee: Kang Nanbing; Figure A. 24

Parents' Generation:

Kang Nanbing's mother gave birth to four children, two males and two females. Sex of the children in descending order: M – F – M – F. He was the first child in his family and his wife was the first child of three siblings in her family. Sex of the children in descending order: F – M – F.

Current Generation:

Kang Nanbing was born in April 1926 and gave birth to six children. Six children survived. Sex of the children in descending order: M (1950) – M (1956) – F (1959) – F (1963) – M (1965) – Fraternal twins (1968).

Children's Generation:

The first son got married in 1974 and gave birth to three children. Sex of the children in descending order: M (1975) – M (1976) – M (1979). His wife was the first daughter of Yu Yingbie from Household No. 47 in this village.

The second son got married in 1979 and gave birth to one child, M (1981). His wife was a remarried mother with a one-year-old boy (1978).
The first daughter got married in 1978 and gave birth to two children. Sex of the children in descending order: F (March 1979) – M (March 1981).
The second daughter married twice. Her first husband was the third son of Mi Meng from Household No. 36 in this village. She had no child with her first husband (who was killed by an ox). She married her second husband and gave birth to two children. Sex of the children in descending order: M – F.
The third son got married in 1986 and gave birth to two children, both males (respectively in February 1987 and June 1989).
Twins were born in the prefecture hospital. Yu Dashuang, one of the twins, was adopted by the prefecture hospital. The other twin: Yu Xiaoshuang got married in 1990 and gave birth to one child, F (July 1991). Yu Xiaoshuang died of leukemia in 1997.

Grandchildren's Generation:

The first son's first child got married in 1995 and gave birth to one child, M (1997).
The first son's second child got married in 1996 and gave birth to one child, F (1997).
The first son's third child got married in 1999 and gave birth to one child, M (March 2000).
The second son's first child (a stepson from his wife) got married in 2003 and gave birth to one child, F (2004).
The second son's second child got married in February 2002 and gave birth to two children, both females (respectively in 2004 and 2009).
The first daughter's first child got married in 2001 and gave birth to one child, F (June 2002).
The first daughter's second child got married in 2003 and gave birth to one child, M (November 2005).
The second daughter was married out of this village and her children's marriage was unknown.
The third son's first child got married in 2007 and still had no children.
The third son's second child got married in 2008 and still had no children.
Yu Xiaoshuang's daughter were unmarried.

Great-grandchildren's Generation:

Eight great-grandchildren, three males and five females.

Household No.: 63; Interviewee: Yu Zhuang; Figure A.25

Parents' Generation:

Yu Zhuang's mother gave birth to five children, three males and two females. Sex of the children in descending order: M – F (1925) – M – F – M.

Yu Zhuang was the second child in her family and her brother was the husband of Yu Bingbian from Household No. 49 in this village.

Current Generation:

Yu Zhuang was born in October 1925 and gave birth to seven children. Six children survived. Sex of the children in descending order: M (February 1943) – M (1949) – F (1953) – F (1958) – M (1961) – F (1964) – F (1968). Her first daughter died in infancy.

Children's Generation:

The first son suffered from a congenital mental illness and never married.

The second son emigrated to Mandou village, got married in 1969, and gave birth to two children, both females (respectively in 1971 and 1976).

The second daughter got married in 1974 and gave birth to two children, both females (respectively in July 1976 and February 1979).

The third son got married in 1979 and gave birth to two children. Sex of the children in descending order: F (August 1980) – M (September 1983).

The third daughter got married in 1984 and gave birth to two children. Sex of the children in descending order: F (May 1985) – M (March 1987).

The fourth daughter married twice. She got married the first time in 1989 and gave birth to one child, M (1990). Having divorced her first husband for his habit of petty theft, she married her second husband in 1998 and gave birth to one child, F (September 1999).

Grandchildren's Generation:

The second son emigrated out of this village to live in his wife's family and the marriage and birth information about his two children was unknown.

The second daughter's first child got married in 1996 and gave birth to two children. Sex of the children in descending order: M (July 1997) – F (February 2001). Her husband was the first child of Yu Lun's second daughter from Household No. 66 in this village.

The second daughter's second child got married in 2007 and still had no children.

The third son's first child married twice. She got married in 1998 with her first husband and had no children. She remarried her second husband in 2007 and still had no children.

The third son's second child got married in 2006 and still had no children.

The third daughter's first child got married in 2007 and still had no children.

All the other grandchildren were unmarried.

Great-grandchildren's Generation:

Two great-grandchildren, one male and one female.

Household No.: 65; Interviewee: Yu Yan; Figure A.26

Parents' Generation:

Yu Yan's mother gave birth to six children, one male and five females. Sex of the children in descending order: F – M – F – F – F – F (1946). Yu Yan was the youngest daughter in her family and her husband was the fourth of 10 siblings in his family. Sex of the children in descending order: M – F – F – M (May 1943) – M – F – M – F – M – M.

Current Generation:

Yu Yan was born in August 1946, got married in 1965 and gave birth to three children. Three children survived. Sex of the children in descending order: M (March 1967) – F (September 1972) – F (1974).

Children's Generation:

The first son got married in 1988 and gave birth to two children. Sex of the children in descending order: F (January 1989) – M (November 1991).

The first daughter got married in 1986 and gave birth to one child, F (May 1987).

The second daughter got married in 2001 and gave birth to one child, F (2002).

Grandchildren's Generation:

The first son's first child got married in 2009 and still had no children.

All the other grandchildren were unmarried.

Household No.: 66; Interviewee: Yu Lun; Figure A.27

Parents' Generation:

Yu Lun's mother gave birth to only one child. Yu Lun was the only child in her family and her husband had only one younger brother in his family.

Current Generation:

Yu Lun was born in September 1921 and gave birth to five children. Three children survived. Sex of the children in descending order: M – F (1946) – M – F (1957) – F (1960). Her two boys died in infancy.

Children's Generation:

The first daughter got married in 1967 and gave birth to three children. Sex of the children in descending order: F (1968) – M (1970) – M (1974).

The second daughter got married in 1973 and gave birth to two children, both males (respectively in December 1975 and 1977).

The third daughter got married in 1978 and gave birth to two children, both males (respectively in 1979 and July 1981).

Grandchildren's Generation:

The first daughter's first child was married in 1988 to Ganlanba village and gave birth to one child, F (1989).

The first daughter's second child got married in 1990 and gave birth to one child, M (October 1991).

The first daughter's third child got married in 2006 and still had no children.

The second daughter's first child got married in 1996 and gave birth to two children. Sex of the children in descending order: M (July 1997) – F (February 2001). His wife was the first child of Yu Zhuang's second daughter from Household No. 63 in this village.

The second daughter's second child got married in 2008 and still had no children.

The third daughter's first child got married in 2001 and gave birth to one child, M (2001).

The third daughter's second child got married in 2002 and gave birth to one child, F (2003).

Great-grandchildren's Generation:

Six great-grandchildren, three males and three females.

Household No.: 67; Interviewee: Yu Shuailong; Figure A.28

Parents' Generation:

Yu Shuailong's mother was Mi Meng from Household No. 36 in this village and gave birth to five children, three males and two females. Sex of the children in descending order: F (1944) – M (1949) – M (1951) – F (1957) – M (1964). Yu Shuailong was the eldest daughter in her family.

Current Generation:

Yu Shuailong was born in June 1944, got married in 1968, and gave birth to three children. Sex of the children in descending order: M (1968) – M (1969) – F (1973). Her first son died young.

Children's Generation:

The second son got married in 1989 and gave birth to one child, M (June 1989).

The first daughter got married in 1992 and gave birth to one child, M (December 1993).

Grandchildren's Generation:

Two grandchildren, all males.

Household No.: 68; Interviewee: Yu Lao; Figure A.29

Parents' Generation:

Yu Lao's mother gave birth to three children, two males and one female. Yu Lao was the eldest girl in her family and had two younger brothers. Her first younger brother was the husband of Yu Yang from Household No. 34 in this village, and her husband was the one child in his family.

Current Generation:

Yu Lao was born in May 1918, got married in 1937 and adopted her first daughter Yu Lameng in 1944, the householder of Household No. 19 in this village. Later, Yu Lao gave birth to five children (twins in the third birth). Sex of the children in descending order: M (1950) – M (1956) – M – F (1957) – F (1962) – F (1966).

Children's Generation:

The first daughter Yu Lameng's reproductive history as described above.

The first son got married in 1973 and gave birth to two children, both females (respectively in 1974 and 1976).

The second son got married in 1985 and gave birth to two children, both males (respectively in 1986 and 1989).

Yu Dashuang (third son) got married in 1978 and gave birth to two children. Sex of the children in descending order: F (March 1979) – M (1981).

Yu Xiaoshuang (second daughter) got married in 1975 and gave birth to two children, both males (respectively in 1976 and 1982).

The third daughter got married in 1980 and gave birth to two children. Sex of the children in descending order: M (February 1982) – F (April 1985).

The fourth daughter got married in 1984 and gave birth to two children. Sex of the children in descending order: F (September 1985) – M (August 1989).

Grandchildren's Generation:

The first son's first child got married in 1997 and gave birth to one child, M (March 1998).

The first son's second child got married in February 2003 and gave birth to one child, F (2004).

Yu Dashuang's first child got married in 2001 and gave birth to one child, F (June 2002).

Yu Dashuang's second child got married in February 2003 and gave birth to one child, M (November 2005).

Yu Xiaoshuang's first child got married in 2008 and still had no children.

The fourth daughter's first child got married in 2007 and still had no children.

All the other grandchildren were unmarried.

Great-grandchildren's Generation:

Five great-grandchildren, two males and three females.

Household No.: 71; Interviewee: Yu Hanxiang; Figure A.30

Yu Hanxiang married four husbands and gave birth to eight children. She didn't know much about her mother's births.

Current Generation:

Yu Hanxiang was born in July 1923, got married first time in the 1940s, and gave birth to one child with her first husband, F (1953). She married her second husband and gave birth to two children, both females (respectively in 1955 and 1957). She married her third husband and gave birth to four children. Sex of the children in descending order: M (1962) – M (1964) – F (1966) – M (1968). She married her fourth husband and gave birth to one child, F (1973).

Children's Generation:

The first daughter got married in 1973 and gave birth to two children. Sex of the children in descending order: M (1976) – F (1974). She adopted one girl in January 1997 after her natural daughter died at eight years old.

The second daughter got married in 1970 and gave birth to two children. Sex of the children in descending order: M (1972) – F (1974).

The third daughter married twice. Her first husband was the son of Yu Yan from Household No. 21 in this village. She got married in 1972 and gave birth to one child, F (1973). She later married once again and gave birth to two children with her second husband, all females (respectively in 1979 and 1981).

The first son got married in 1981 and gave birth to two children. Sex of the children in descending order: F (1983) – M (1985).

The second son got married in 1986 and gave birth to two children, both females (respectively in August 1987 and November 1989).

The fourth daughter was married out of this village to Chuxiong City and there was no information about her childbirth.

The third son got married in May 1990 and gave birth to two children, both males (respectively in November 1991 and September 1993).

The fifth daughter got married in 1989 and gave birth to two children. Sex of the children in descending order: M (August 1991) – F (February 1993).

Grandchildren's Generation:

The first daughter's first child married twice. He got married in 1998 and had no children with his first wife, and remarried in 2003 and gave birth to one child, M (June 2005).

The second daughter's reproductive history was unknown.

The third daughter's first child (the eldest granddaughter of Yu Yan from Household No. 21 in this village) got married in 1991. Her husband was the third son of Yu Xiang from Household No. 28 in this village. The couple gave birth to one child (The baby girl died three days after her birth in 1992), and adopted one girl in September 1996.

The third daughter's second child got married in 2006 and gave birth to one child, F (2007).

The third daughter's third child got married in 2002 and gave birth to one child, M (2003).

The first son's first child got married in 2002 and gave birth to one child, F (June 2003).

The first son's second child got married in 2007 and gave birth to one child, M (August 2008).

The second son's first child got married in June 2009 and still had no children.

The second son's second child got married in 2007 and still had no children.

All the other grandchildren were unmarried.

Great-grandchildren's Generation:

Five great-grandchildren, three males and two females.

Household No.: 75; Interviewee: Yu Yan; Figure A.31
Yu Yan didn't know much about her mother's childbirth.

Current Generation:

Yu Yan was born in April 1939, got married in January 1955 and gave birth to three children, all of whom survived. Sex of the children in descending order: F (1960) – M (1962) – M (1964). Her husband was Yan Langnan, the youngest brother of Yu Yang's husband Kang Naozai from Household No. 34 in this village.

Children's Generation:

The first daughter got married in 1980 and gave birth to two children. Sex of the children in descending order: M (1981) – F (1983).

The first son got married in 1981 and gave birth to two children. Sex of the children in descending order: M (January 1983) – F (February 1985).

The second son emigrated out of this village after marriage and gave birth to two children. Sex of the children in descending order: M – F.

Grandchildren's Generation:

The first daughter's first child were unmarried.

The first daughter's second child got married in 2003 and gave birth to one child, F (2004).

The first son's first child got married in 2005 and gave birth to one child, M (June 2007).

The first son's second child got married in 2003 and gave birth to one child, F (2007).

The reproductive history about the second son's children was unknown.

Great-grandchildren's Generation:

Three great-grandchildren, two females and one male.

Household No.: 77; Interviewee: Yu Han'er; Figure A.32

Parents' Generation:

Yu Han'er's mother gave birth to three children, all females. Yu Han'er was the eldest child in her family. Her husband was also the eldest in his family and had two younger brothers. Her husband's first younger brother was Kang Nanzhong, the husband of Yu Wangsa from Household No. 56 in this village, and the second younger brother was Yan Dan, the husband of Yu Pengban from Household No. 44 in this village.

Current Generation:

Yu Haner was born in February 1937, got married in March 1955, and gave birth to five children. Five children survived. Sex of the children in descending order: F (1955) – M (1957) – M (1962) – F (1964) – F (1968).

Children's Generation:

The first daughter got married in 1975 and gave birth to two children, both females (respectively in 1976 and 1978).

The first son got married in 1978 and gave birth to two children. Sex of the children in descending order: M (1979) – M (1980). His wife was the first daughter of Yu Xiang from Household No. 5 in this village.

The second son got married in 1982 and gave birth to two children, both males (respectively in March 1983 and March 1985). His wife was the first daughter of Yu Lalun from Household No. 55 in this village.

The second daughter got married in 1987 and gave birth to two children. Sex of the children in descending order: F (April 1988) – M (December 1989).

The third daughter got married in 1993 and chose to have no children.

Grandchildren's Generation:

The first daughter's first child got married in 1998 and gave birth to one child, F (1999).

The first daughter's second child were unmarried.

The first son's first child got married in 1997 and gave birth to two children, both females.

The first son's second child got married and divorced, and had no children.

The second son's first child got married in 2003 and gave birth to one child, F (July 2005).

The second son's second child got married in 2008 and still had no children.

The second daughter's first child got married in 2009 and still had no children.

The second daughter's second child were unmarried.

Great-grandchildren's Generation:

Four great-grandchildren, all females.

Household No.: 78; Interviewee: Yu Lilong; Figure A.33

Parents' Generation:

Yu Lilong's mother gave birth to three children, all females. Yu Lilong was the youngest daughter in her family and her elder sister was Yu Han'er from Household No. 77 in this village.

Current Generation:

Yu Lilong was born in July 1946, got married in February 1964, and gave birth to three children. Three children survived. Sex of the children in descending order: F (1966) – F (1969) – M (1971).

Children's Generation:

The first daughter got married in 1982 and gave birth to two children, both females (respectively in 1983 and 1987).

The second daughter married twice. She married her first husband in 1988 and gave birth to one child, F (April 1989), divorced, remarried her second husband in 1993 and gave birth to one child, F (December 1994).

The first son got married in 1991 and lived in Mandou village. His reproductive history was unknown.

Grandchildren's Generation:

Four grandchildren were all girls.

Household No.: 82; Interviewee: Yu Jianxiang; Figure A.34

Parents' Generation:

Yu Jianxiang's mother gave birth to five children. Sex of the children in descending order: M – F – M – F – M. She was the fourth child in her family, and her eldest brother was the husband of Yu Bingbian from Household No. 49 in this village.

Current Generation:

Yu Jianxiang was born in January 1932 and gave birth to five children. Five children survived. Sex of the children in descending order: F (1955) – M (1960) – M (1964) – F (1966) – M (1968).

Children's Generation:

The first daughter got married in 1975 and gave birth to two children, both females (respectively in 1976 and 1978).

The first son got married in 1982 and gave birth to two children. Sex of the children in descending order: F (1983) – M (1985).

The second son got married in 1984 and gave birth to two children. Sex of the children in descending order: F (September 1985) – M (August 1989). His wife was the fourth daughter of Yu Lao from Household No. 68 in this village.

The second daughter got married in 1984 and gave birth to two children, both females (respectively in 1985 and 1987).

The third son got married in 1989 and gave birth to two children. Sex of the children in descending order: F (April 1990) – M (May 1992). His wife was the first son's first child of Mi Meng from Household No. 36 in this village.

Grandchildren's Generation:

The first daughter's first child got married in 2004 and gave birth to one child, F (2005).

The first daughter's second child got married in 2007, got pregnant once but miscarried, and still had no children.

The first son's first child got married in 2004 and gave birth to two children. Sex of the children in descending order: M (2005) – M (2008).

The first son's second child were unmarried.

The second son's first child got married in 2007 and still had no children.

The second son's second child were unmarried.

The second daughter's first child got married in 2002 and gave birth to one child, F (2003).

The second daughter's second child got married in 2009 and still had no children.

The third son's two children were unmarried.

Great-grandchildren's Generation:

Four great-grandchildren, three females and one male.

Household No.: 83; Interviewee: Yu Ying; Figure A.35

Parents' Generation: Yu Ying's mother gave birth to two children. Sex of the children in descending order: M – F. Yu Ying was the second child in her family.

Current Generation:

Yu Ying was born in March 1929 and gave birth to five children. Five children survived. Sex of the children in descending order: F (1949) – M (1953) – M (1959) – F (1962) – F (1965).

Children's Generation:

The first daughter got married in 1968 and gave birth to three children. Sex of the children in descending order: M (1969) – M (1972) – F (1975).

The second son got married in 1973 and gave birth to two children, both males (respectively in January 1974 and August 1978).

The third son got married in 1978 and gave birth to two children, both males (respectively in 1979 and 1981).

The second daughter got married in 1982 and gave birth to two children. Sex of the children in descending order: F (July 1983) – M (May 1985). Her husband was the third son of Yu Yang from Household No. 34 in this village.

The third daughter got married in 1983 and gave birth to two children, both females (respectively in 1984 and 1986). The first daughter died in infancy.

Grandchildren's Generation:

The first daughter was married out of this village to live with her husband and her children's reproductive history was unknown.

The first son's first child got married in 2000 and gave birth to two children. Sex of the children in descending order: M (2003 January) – F (December 2008).

The first son's second child got married in 2002 and gave birth to one child, M (2003).

The third son's first child got married in 2000 and gave birth to one child, F (2003).

The third son's second child got married in 2002 and gave birth to one child, M (December 2004).

The second daughter's first child got married in 2003 and gave birth to one child, M (April 2005).

The second daughter's second child got married in 2007 and gave birth to one child, M (2008).

The third daughter's second child got married in 2007 and gave birth to one child, F (January 2008).

Great-grandchildren's Generation:

Eight great-grandchildren, five males and three females.

Household No.: 88; Interviewee: Yu Ernan; Figure A.36

Parents' Generation:

Yu Ernan's mother gave birth to six children. Sex of the children in descending order: M – F – M – F – F – M. She was the second child in her family and her mother was the elder sister of Mi Meng from Household No. 36 in this village.

Current Generation:

Yu Ernan was born in December 1946 and gave birth to two children. Two births survived, all females (respectively in 1966 and 1969).

Children's Generation:

The first daughter got married in 1983 and gave birth to two children. Sex of the children in descending order: M (April 1984) – F (February 1986).

The second daughter got married in 1991 and gave birth to one child, M (1992).

Grandchildren's Generation:

The first daughter's first child got married in 2006 and still had no children.

The first daughter's second child got married in 2007 and had no children and was divorced.

The second daughter's child were unmarried.

Household No.: 90; Interviewee: Yan Wenxiang; Figure A.37

Yan Wenxiang was the first son of Kang Nanbing from Household No. 62 in this village.

Parents' Generation:

Yan Wenxiang's mother gave birth to six children. Six children survived. Sex of the children in descending order: M (1950) – M (1956) – F (1959) – F (1963) – M (1965) – Fraternal twins (1968).

Current Generation:

Yan Wenxiang was born in April 1950, got married in 1974 and gave birth to three children, all males (respectively in 1975, 1976 and 1979). His wife was the first daughter of Yu Yingbie from Household No. 47 in this village.

Children's Generation:

The first son got married in 1995 and gave birth to one child, M (1997).

The second son got married in 1996 and gave birth to one child, F (1997).

The third son got married in 1999 and gave birth to one child, M (March 2000).

Grandchildren's Generation:

Three grandchildren, two males and one female.

Household No.: 92; Interviewee: Yan Dunhan; Figure A.38

Parents' Generation:

Yan Dunhan didn't know much about her mother's reproductive history.

Current Generation:

Yan Dunhan was born in February 1927 and gave birth to two children. Two births survived. Sex of the children in descending order: F (1950) – M (1961).

Children's Generation:

The first daughter got married in 1969 and gave birth to two children. Sex of the children in descending order: F (1970) – M (1974).

The first son married twice. He got married first in 1980 and had no children with his first wife. In 1989, he married his second wife (who had already two girls) and also had no children with his second wife.

Grandchildren's Generation:

The first daughter's first child got married in 1988 and gave birth to two children, both males (respectively in October 1990 and 1992). Her second child died in infancy in 2000, and her husband was the second son of Yu Tao from Household No. 11 in this village.

The first daughter's second child got married in 1995 and gave birth to one child (twins), all males (1996).

The first son's two children were unmarried.

Great-grandchildren's Generation:

Two great-grandchildren, all males.

The second child of the first daughter (Yu Tao)'s second son died at the age of eight (2000). According to local regulations, a birth that didn't survive 14 years old (inc. 14 years old) didn't be counted in. According to prefecture regulations, Yu Tao's second son was eligible for a second child but chose not to do so. Therefore, he got the only-child certificate and enjoyed the corresponding treatment.

Household No.: 98; Interviewee: Yan Hannan; Figure A.39

Yan Hannan emigrated in the 1970s from Myanmar to this village.

Parents' Generation:

Yan Hannan didn't know much about her mother's reproductive history.

Current Generation:

Yan Hannan was born in March 1943, got married in 1960 and gave birth to eight children. Eight births survived. Sex of the children in descending order: M (1960) – M (1963) – F (1967) – M (1971) – M (1973) – F (1975) – M (1976) – M (1981).

Children's Generation:

The first son got married in 1982 and gave birth to two children. Sex of the children in descending order: M (May 1983) – F (May 1984).

The second son got married in 1984 and gave birth to two children. Sex of the children in descending order: M (1985) – F (1987).

The first daughter lived in Myanmar and her reproductive history was unknown.

The third son got married in 1990 and gave birth to two children, both females (respectively in 1992 and 1995).

The fourth son married a divorced mother with two children and had no children with his wife.

The second daughter got married in 1997 and gave birth to one child, F (1998).

The fifth son were unmarried.

The sixth son got married in 2003 and gave birth to one child, M (2005).

Grandchildren's Generation:

The first son's first child got married in 2007 and still had no children.

The first son's second child got married in 2005 and gave birth to one child, F (2006).

The second son's first child got married in 2007 and gave birth to one child, F (August 2008).

The second son's second child got married in 2005 and gave birth to one child, M (2007).

All the other grandchildren were unmarried.

Great-grandchildren's Generation:

Three great-grandchildren, one male and two females.

Summary

Among the interviewees from the surveyed 40 households, the oldest was Yu Lao, born in May 1918 (92 years old) and the youngest was Yan Wenxiang, born in April 1950 (61 years old). The reproductive statistics by age cohort (five-year interval) are shown in the following Table A.2.

The Births and Surviving Births of the Households are shown in the following Table A.3.

The statistics of average total births per household and surviving births and surviving children of surveyed households are shown in the following Table A.4.

Table A.2: Reproductive Statistics of the Interviewees (Born in or before 1950) in Village M

Households	Age Cohort (Year)	Number of Lifetime Births (Persons)			Births Surviving till the Age of 15 or above (Persons)			Average Births / Household	Average Surviving Births / Household
		Total Births	M	F	Total Births	M	F		
7	1946–1950	18	9	9	18	9	9	2.57	2.57
3	1941–1945	14	10	4	13	9	4	4.67	4.33
10	1936–1940	41	23	18	38	22	16	4.1	3.8
5	1931–1935	22	11	11	20	9	11	4.4	4.0
6	1926–1930	24	14	10	23	14	9	4.0	3.83
8	1921–1925	38	16	22	34	14	20	4.75	4.25
1	1916–1920	6	3	3	6	3	3	6	6
In total: 40 Households	163	86	77	152	80	72	4.08	3.8	

Source: Field Survey Statistics by the Research Team.

Table A.3: Lifetime and Surviving Births of the Interviewees (Born in or before 1950) in Village M

Sample Size		40 Interviewees (Households)			
Age of Interviewee		61–84 Years Old			
Number of Lifetime Births	8 Births	2	Births Surviving till the Age of 15 or above	8 Surviving Births	2
	7 Births	1		7 Surviving Births	0
	6 Births	1		6 Surviving Births	2
	5 Births	11		5 Surviving Births	8
	4 Births	10		4 Surviving Births	9
	3 Births	10		3 Surviving Births	11
	2 Births	3		2 Surviving Births	4
	1 Birth	1		1 Surviving Birth	2
	0 Birth	1		0 Surviving Birth	1

Source: Field Survey Statistics by the Research Team.

The statistics of the timespans and proportions of average total births per household in the surveyed households are shown in the following Table A.5.

The retrospective Reproductive Statistics mentioned above showed that:

1. By 2009 July, 40 interviewees (36 females and four males) born in or before 1950 (59 years old or above) in village M had given birth to 163 children, each giving birth to 4.08 children on average, and had 152 children that had survived till the age of 15 or above, with one household having 3.8 surviving children on average. The overall survival rate of the births was 93.25%.
2. The interviewees had throughout their lifetime given birth to 86 boys and 77 girls, with the boys slightly outnumbering the girls, and 80 boys and 72 girls had survived till the age of 15 or above, with the survival rate of the boys and the girls standing respectively at 93.02% and 93.51% and the survival rate of the boys being slightly lower than that of the girls.
3. The interviewees (except for one having never had any children) had given births between once and eight time throughout their lifetime, an average of 4.03 children per person, and had 1–8 surviving births;

Table A.4: Reproductive Statistics of the Interviewed Households by Generational Cohort (Interviewees Born in or before 1950) in Village M (No. 1)[40,41]

Generation	Households	Number of Lifetime Births (Persons)			Births Surviving till the Age of 15 or above (Persons)			Average Total Births per Household	Average Total Surviving Births per Household
		Total Births	M	F	Total Births	M	F		
Parent generation	30	-	-	-	106	39	67	-	3.53
Current Generation	40	163	86	77	152	80	72	4.08	3.8
Children's Generation	139	263	139	124	258	136	122	1.89	1.85
Grandchildren's Generation	105	126	66	60	124	66	58	1.2	1.18

Source: Field Survey Statistics by the Research Team.

40 Many older interviewees in the village couldn't recall the exact information about their mothers' children dying young, so this statistical item was not included herein.

41 When the parents of an interviewee were in the same household, there would be inconsistency in the number of households between "Current Generation" and "Parents' Generation". The same below.

Table A.5: Reproductive Statistics by Generational Cohort of the Surveyed Households (Interviwees Born in or before 1950) in Village M (No. 2)

Generation\Decade\ Percent (%)	1940s	1950s	1960s	1970s	1980s	1990s	2000s	Percent (%)
Current Generation	6.40	29.07	53.50	10.40	0.63			100.00
Children's Generation			2.35	29.01	50.98	15.68	1.98	100.00
Grandchildren's Generation					3.30	22.31	74.39	100.00

Source: Field Survey Statistics by the Research Team.

4. The interviewees gave birth to their last child in the age range from 19 to 50 (Interviewee No. 43 Yu Han, gave birth to her first and only child and Interviewee No. 71 Yu Hanxiang gave birth to her 8th child), at 32.86 years old on average.
5. The interviewees gave birth to their last child in the period from 1941(Interviewee No. 43 Yu Han who had only one child) to 1981(Interviewee No. 98 Yu Hannan, who had given birth to eight children).
6. The interviewees who had given birth to five children throughout their lifetime made up the largest share of the total at 27.5%, and those who had had three surviving births made up the largest share of the total at 27.5%.
7. The interviewees who had given birth to five or fewer children and four or fewer children respectively made up 89.74% and 61.54% of all, and those who had had five or fewer surviving births and four or fewer surviving births respectively made up 87.18% and 66.67% of all;
8. Each generation tends to have few births but more surviving ones on average. The survival rate of the births by Current Generation, Children's Generation and Grandchildren's Generation was respectively 93.25%, 98.10% and 98.41%.
9. The reproductive lifespan for Current Generation (except for one who had never had children) extended from the 1940s to the 1980s, but most of the births were from the 1950s to the 1960s, accounting for 82.57% of all the newborns in this period.
10. The reproductive lifespan for Children's Generation extended from the 1960s to the 2000s, but most of the births were from the 1970s to the 1980s, accounting for 79.99% of all the newborns in this period.
11. The reproductive lifespan for Grandchildren's Generation extended from the 1980s to the 2000s, but most of the births were in the 2000s.

Genograms

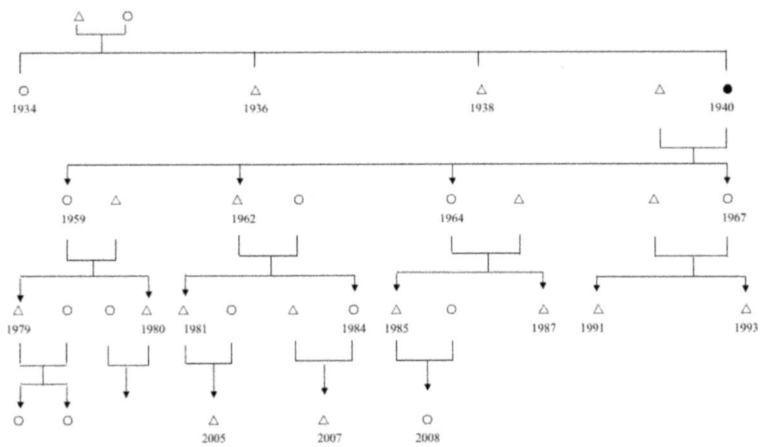

Figure A.1 Genogram for Yu Xiang's family
▲: male interviewee; ●: female interviewee;
△: male; ○: female;
■: male who died before turning 15; ★: female who died before turning 15;
□: a pregnancy with unknown sex of the fetus;
The sex of those born within each generation are listed in descending order of age, from left to right.

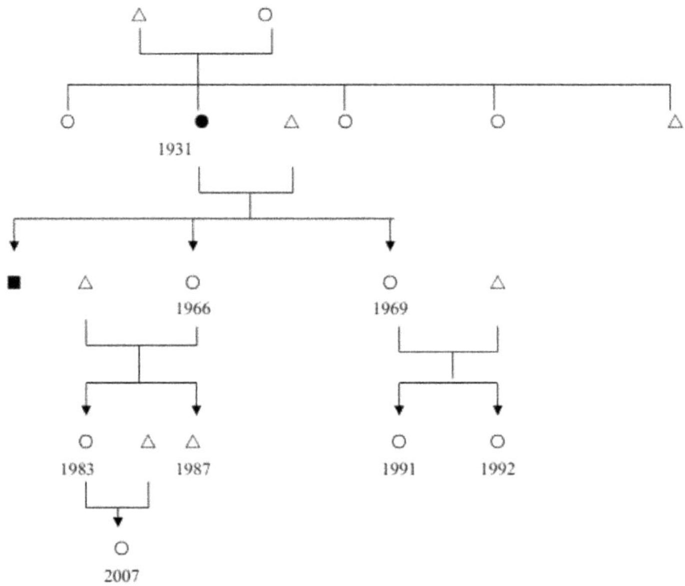

Figure A.2 Genogram for Yu Bian's family
▲: male interviewee; ●: female interviewee;
△: male; ○: female;
■: male who died before turning 15; ★: female who died before turning 15;
□: a pregnancy with unknown sex of the fetus;
The sex of those born within each generation are listed in descending order of age, from left to right.

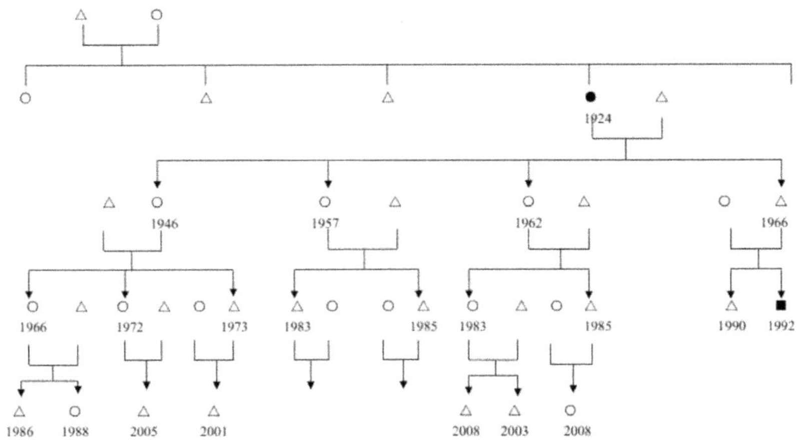

Figure A.3 Genogram for Yu Tao's family
▲: male interviewee; ●: female interviewee;
△: male; ○: female;
■: male who died before turning 15; ★: female who died before turning 15;
□: a pregnancy with unknown sex of the fetus;
The sex of those born within each generation are listed in descending order of age, from left to right.

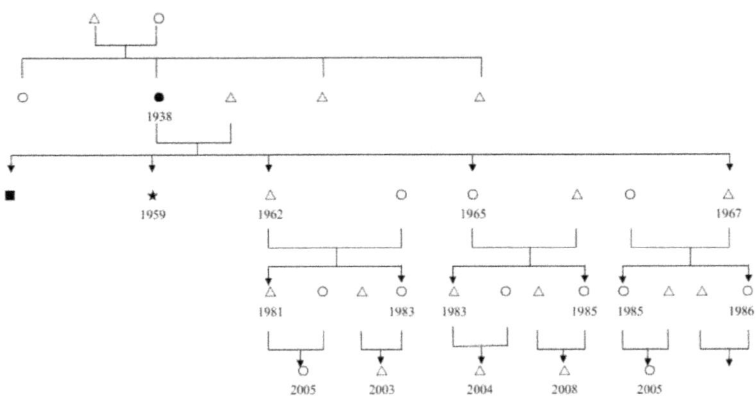

Figure A.4 Genogram for Yu Enzai's family
▲: male interviewee; ●: female interviewee;
△: male; ○: female;
■: male who died before turning 15; ★: female who died before turning 15;
□: a pregnancy with unknown sex of the fetus;
The sex of those born within each generation are listed in descending order of age, from left to right.

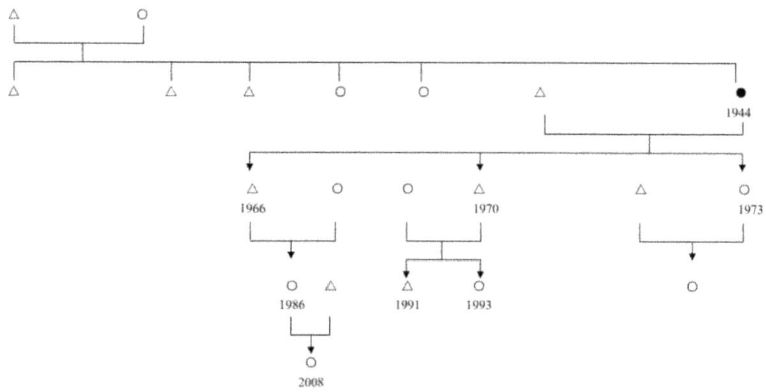

Figure A.5 Genogram for Yu Lameng's family
▲: male interviewee; ●: female interviewee;
△: male; ○: female;
■: male who died before turning 15; ★: female who died before turning 15;
□: a pregnancy with unknown sex of the fetus;

The sex of those born within each generation are listed in descending order of age, from left to right.

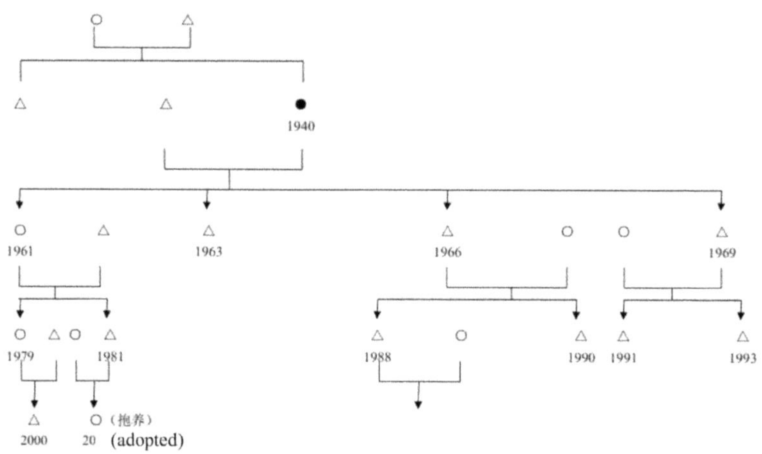

Figure A.6 Genogram for Yu Nan's family
▲: male interviewee; ●: female interviewee;
△: male; ○: female;
■: male who died before turning 15; ★: female who died before turning 15;
□: a pregnancy with unknown sex of the fetus;

The sex of those born within each generation are listed in descending order of age, from left to right.

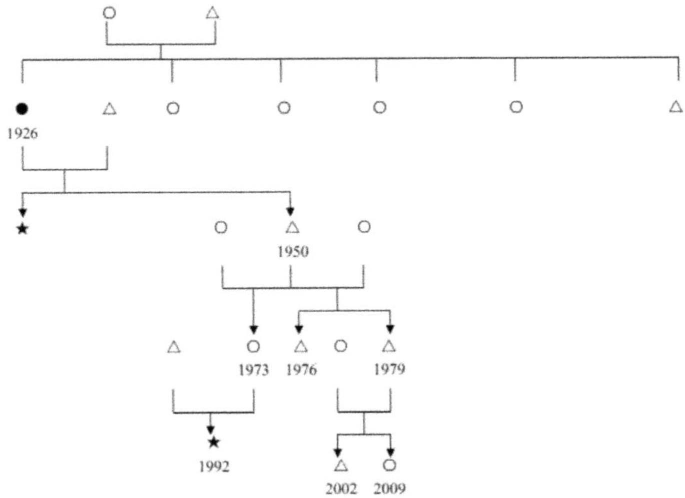

Figure A.7 Genogram for Yu Yan's family
▲: male interviewee; ●: female interviewee;
△: male; ○: female;
■: male who died before turning 15; ★: female who died before turning 15;
□: a pregnancy with unknown sex of the fetus;
Genogram No. 1–8 Yu Ban
The sex of those born within each generation are listed in descending order of age, from left to right.

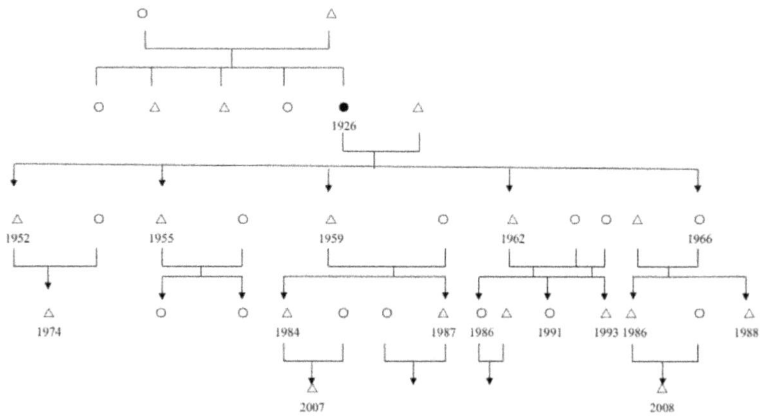

Figure A.8 Genogram for Yu Ban's family
▲: male interviewee; ●: female interviewee;
△: male; ○: female;
■: male who died before turning 15; ★: female who died before turning 15;
□: a pregnancy with unknown sex of the fetus;
The sex of those born within each generation are listed in descending order of age, from left to right.

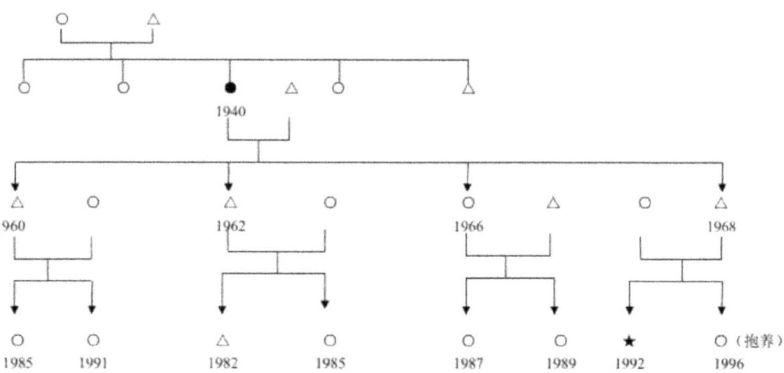

Figure A.9 Genogram for Yu Xiang's family
▲: male interviewee; ●: female interviewee;
△: male; ○: female;
■: male who died before turning 15; ★: female who died before turning 15;
□: a pregnancy with unknown sex of the fetus;
The sex of those born within each generation are listed in descending order of age, from left to right.

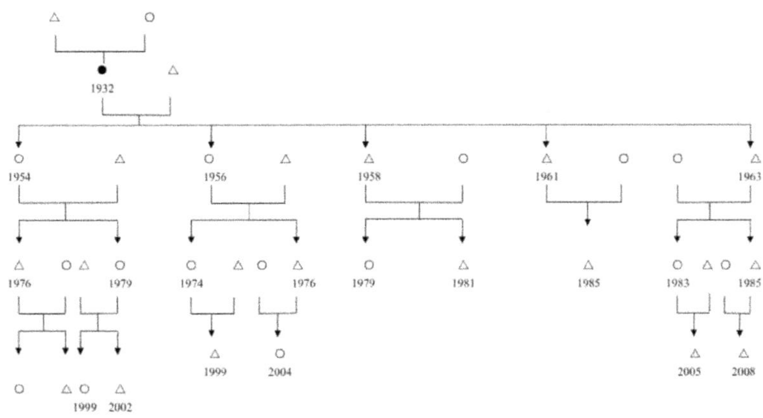

Figure A.10 Genogram for Yu Yang's family
▲: male interviewee; ●: female interviewee;
△: male; ○: female;
■: male who died before turning 15; ★: female who died before turning 15;
□: a pregnancy with unknown sex of the fetus;

The sex of those born within each generation are listed in descending order of age, from left to right.

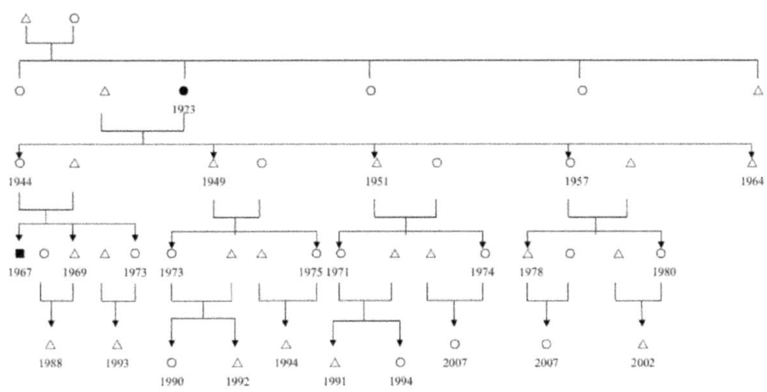

Figure A.11 Genogram for Mi Meng's family
▲: male interviewee; ●: female interviewee;
△: male; ○: female;
■: male who died before turning 15; ★: female who died before turning 15;
□: a pregnancy with unknown sex of the fetus;

The sex of those born within each generation are listed in descending order of age, from left to right.

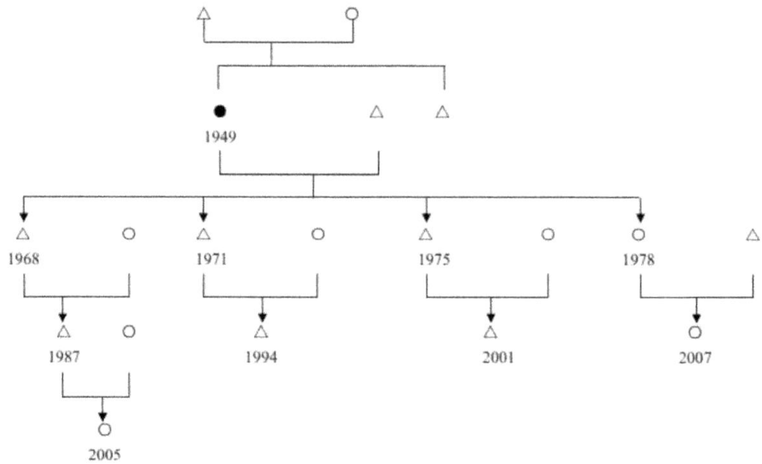

Figure A.12 Genogram for Yu Yinghan's family
▲: male interviewee; ●: female interviewee;
△: male; ○: female;
■: male who died before turning 15; ★: female who died before turning 15;
□: a pregnancy with unknown sex of the fetus;
The sex of those born within each generation are listed in descending order of age, from left to right.

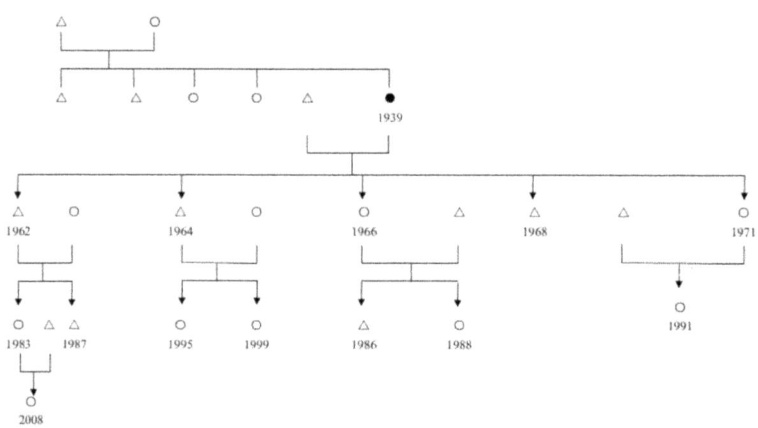

Figure A.13 Genogram for Yu Jing's family
▲: male interviewee; ●: female interviewee;
△: male; ○: female;
■: male who died before turning 15; ★: female who died before turning 15;
□: a pregnancy with unknown sex of the fetus;
The sex of those born within each generation are listed in descending order of age, from left to right.

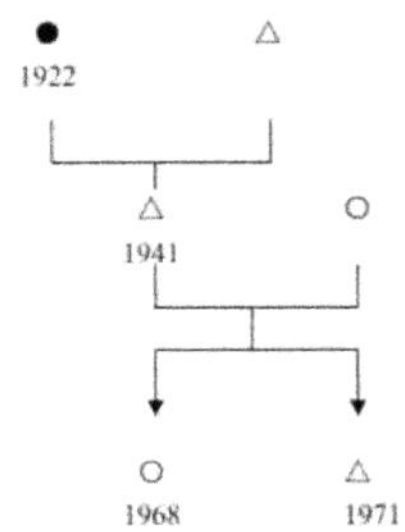

Figure A.14 Genogram for Yu Han's family
▲: male interviewee; ●: female interviewee;
△: male; ○: female;
■: male who died before turning 15; ★: female who died before turning 15;
□: a pregnancy with unknown sex of the fetus;
The sex of those born within each generation are listed in descending order of age, from left to right .
The sex of those born within each generation are listed in descending order of age, from left to right.

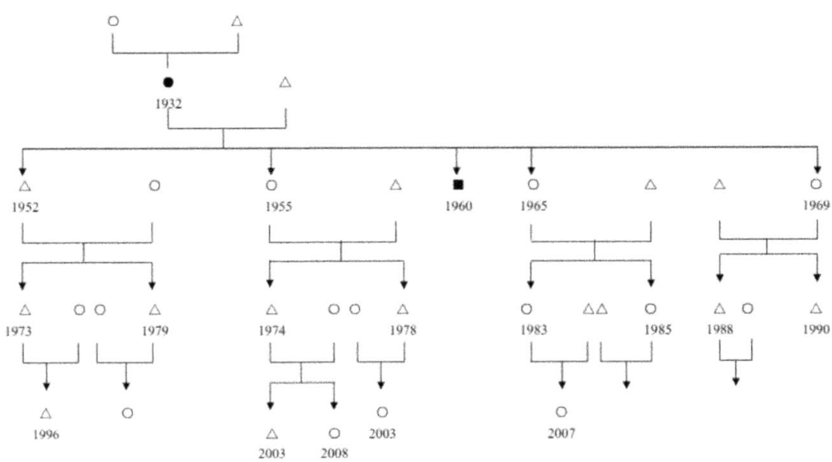

Figure A.15 Genogram for Yu Pengban's family
▲: male interviewee; ●: female interviewee;
△: male; ○: female;
■: male who died before turning 15; ★: female who died before turning 15;
□: a pregnancy with unknown sex of the fetus;
The sex of those born within each generation are listed in descending order of age, from left to right .
The sex of those born within each generation are listed in descending order of age, from left to right.

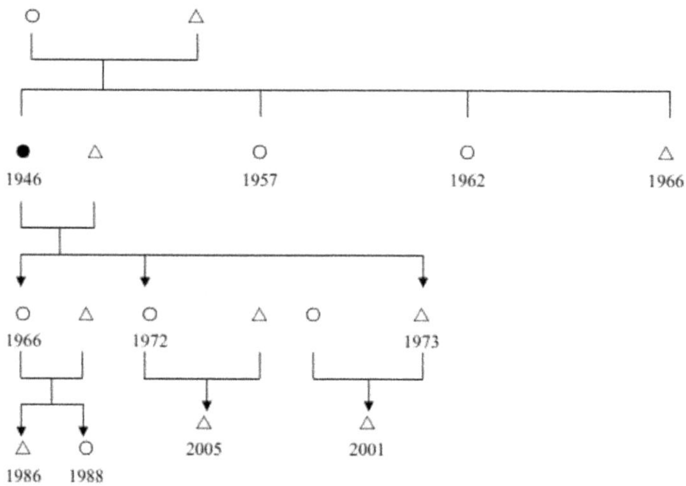

Figure A.16 **Genogram for Yu Nanlong's family**
▲: male interviewee; ●: female interviewee;
△: male; ○: female;
■: male who died before turning 15; ★: female who died before turning 15;
□: a pregnancy with unknown sex of the fetus;

The sex of those born within each generation are listed in descending order of age, from left to right.

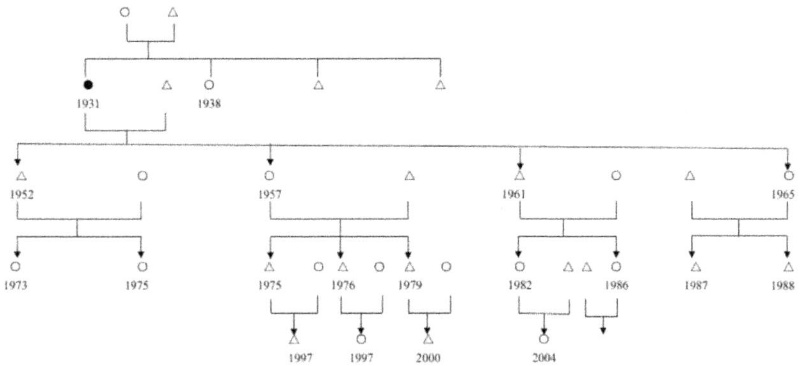

Figure A.17 **Genogram for Yu Yingbie's family**
▲: male interviewee; ●: female interviewee;
△: male; ○: female;
■: male who died before turning 15; ★: female who died before turning 15;
□: a pregnancy with unknown sex of the fetus;
The sex of those born within each generation are listed in descending order of age, from left to right.

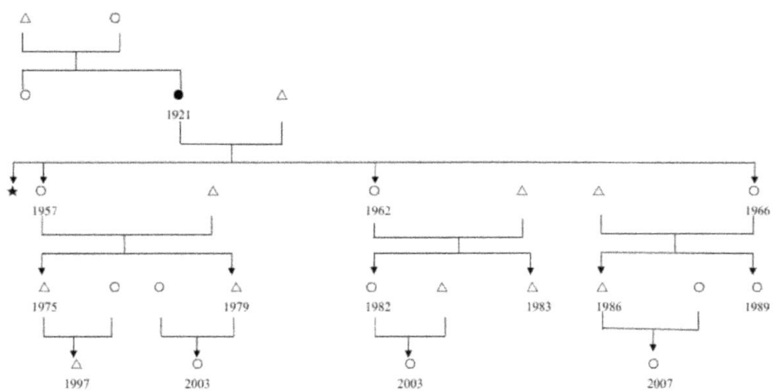

Figure A.18 **Genogram for Yu Bingbian's family**
▲: male interviewee; ●: female interviewee;
△: male; ○: female;
■: male who died before turning 15; ★: female who died before turning 15;
□: a pregnancy with unknown sex of the fetus;
The sex of those born within each generation are listed in descending order of age, from left to right.

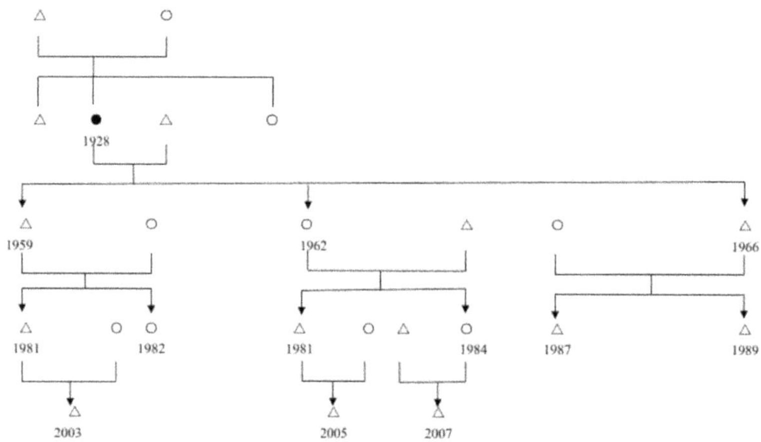

Figure A.19 **Genogram for Yu Ta's family**
▲: male interviewee; ●: female interviewee;
△: male; ○: female;
■: male who died before turning 15; ★: female who died before turning 15;
□: a pregnancy with unknown sex of the fetus;
The sex of those born within each generation are listed in descending order of age, from left to right.

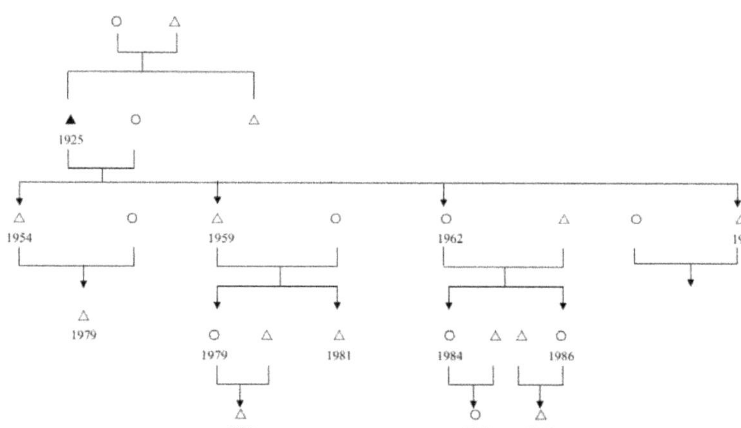

Figure A.20 **Genogram for Yan Xiangzai's family**
▲: male interviewee; ●: female interviewee;
△: male; ○: female;
■: male who died before turning 15; ★: female who died before turning 15;
□: a pregnancy with unknown sex of the fetus;
The sex of those born within each generation are listed in descending order of age, from left to right.

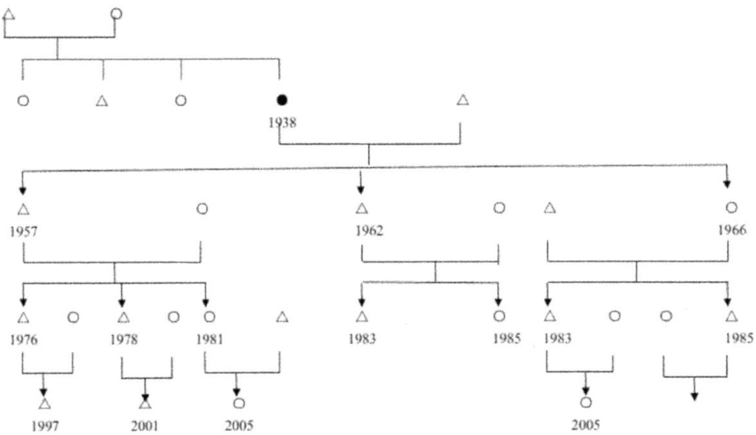

Figure A.21 **Genogram for Yu Lalun's family**
▲: male interviewee; ●: female interviewee;
△: male; ○: female;
■: male who died before turning 15; ★: female who died before turning 15;
□: a pregnancy with unknown sex of the fetus;
The sex of those born within each generation are listed in descending order of age, from left to right.

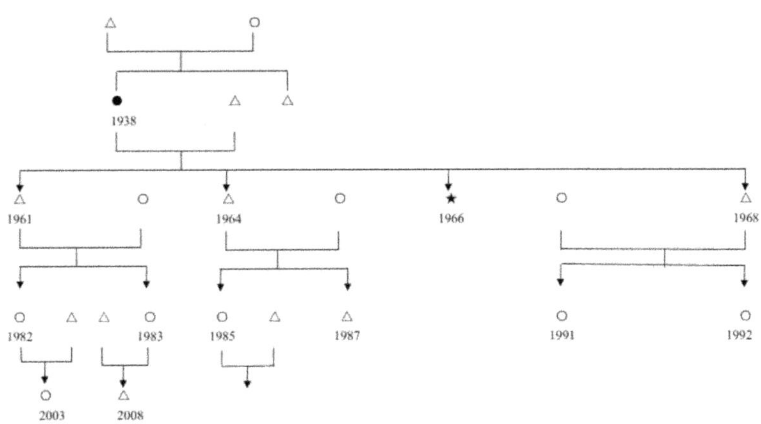

Figure A.22 **Genogram for Yu Wangsa's family**
▲: male interviewee; ●: female interviewee;
△: male; ○: female;
■: male who died before turning 15; ★: female who died before turning 15;
□: a pregnancy with unknown sex of the fetus;
The sex of those born within each generation are listed in descending order of age, from left to right.

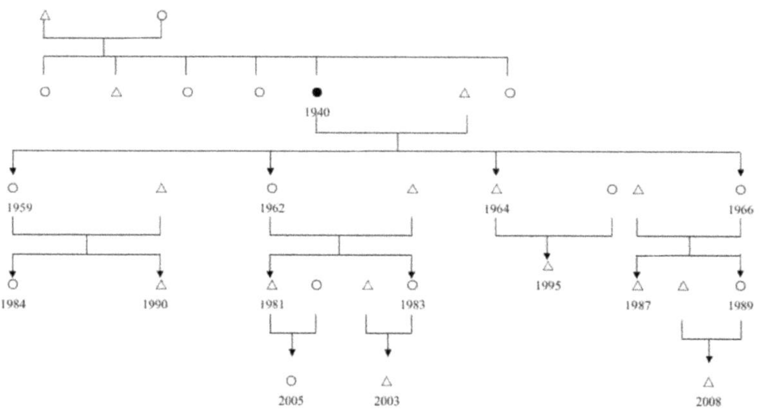

Figure A.23 **Genogram for Yu Taoda's family**
▲: male interviewee; ●: female interviewee;
△: male; ○: female;
■: male who died before turning 15; ★: female who died before turning 15;
□: a pregnancy with unknown sex of the fetus;
The sex of those born within each generation are listed in descending order of age, from left to right.

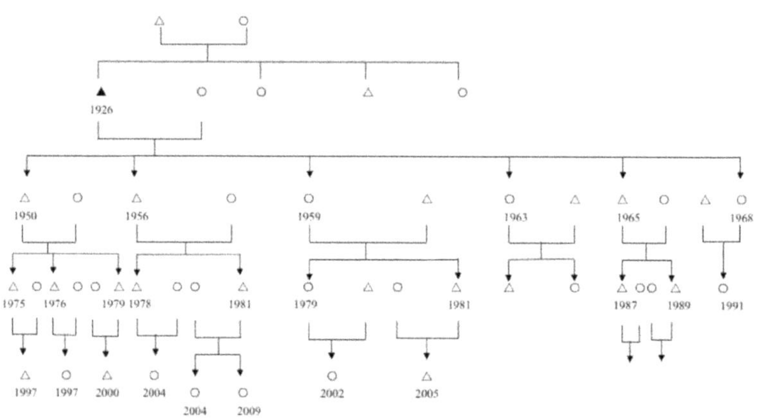

Figure A.24 **Genogram for Kang Nanbing's family**
▲: male interviewee; ●: female interviewee;
△: male; ○: female;
■: male who died before turning 15; ★: female who died before turning 15;
□: a pregnancy with unknown sex of the fetus;
The sex of those born within each generation are listed in descending order of age, from left to right.

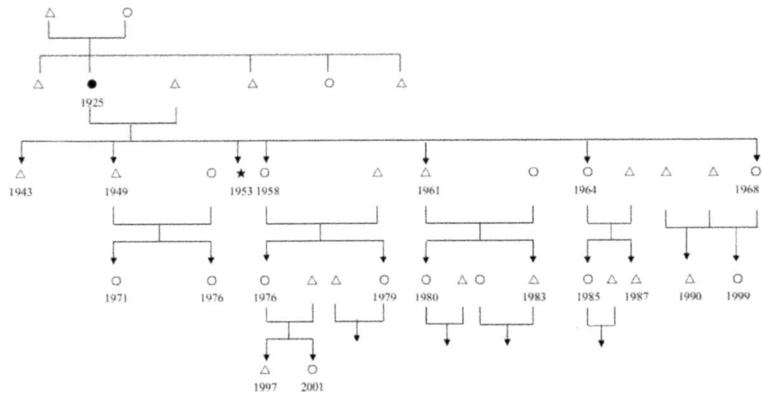

Figure A.25 **Genogram for Yu Zhuang's family**
▲: male interviewee; ●: female interviewee;
△: male; ○: female;
■: male who died before turning 15; ★: female who died before turning 15;
□: a pregnancy with unknown sex of the fetus;
The sex of those born within each generation are listed in descending order of age, from left to right.

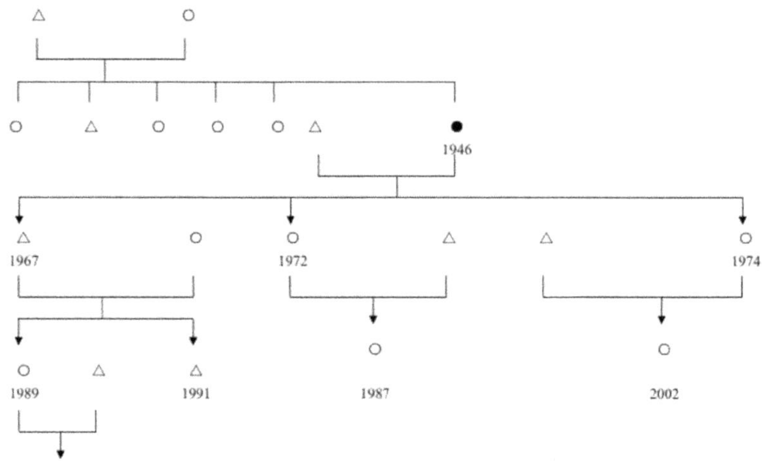

Figure A.26 **Genogram for Yu Yian's family**
▲: male interviewee; ●: female interviewee;
△: male; ○: female;
■: male who died before turning 15; ★: female who died before turning 15;
□: a pregnancy with unknown sex of the fetus;
The sex of those born within each generation are listed in descending order of age, from left to right.

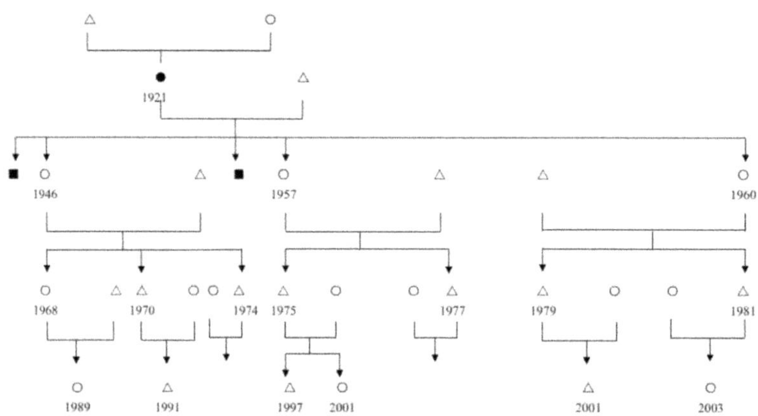

Figure A.27 **Genogram for Yu Lun's family**
▲: male interviewee; ●: female interviewee;
△: male; ○: female;
■: male who died before turning 15; ★: female who died before turning 15;
□: a pregnancy with unknown sex of the fetus;
The sex of those born within each generation are listed in descending order of age, from left to right.

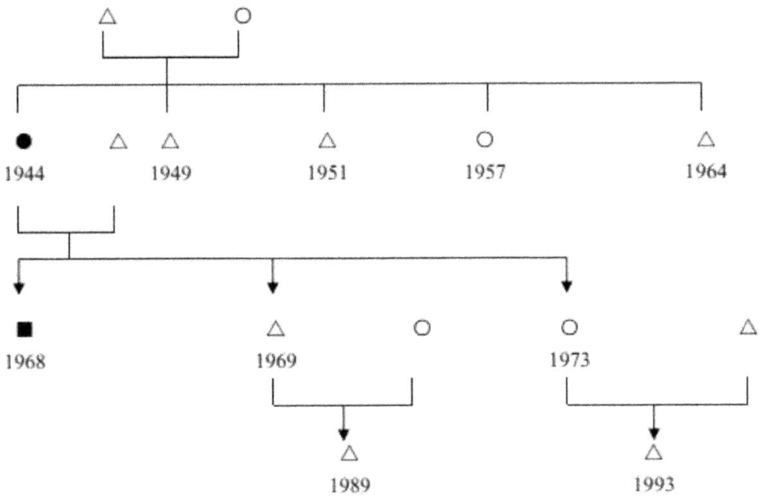

Figure A.28 **Genogram for Yu Shuailong's family**
▲: male interviewee; ●: female interviewee;
△: male; ○: female;
■: male who died before turning 15; ★: female who died before turning 15;
□: a pregnancy with unknown sex of the fetus;
The sex of those born within each generation are listed in descending order of age, from left to right.

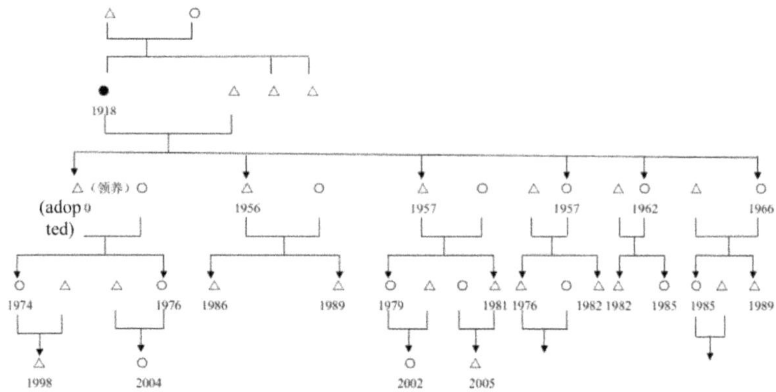

Figure A.29 **Genogram for Yu Lao's family**
▲: male interviewee; ●: female interviewee;
△: male; ○: female;
■: male who died before turning 15; ★: female who died before turning 15;
□: a pregnancy with unknown sex of the fetus;
The sex of those born within each generation are listed in descending order of age, from left to right.

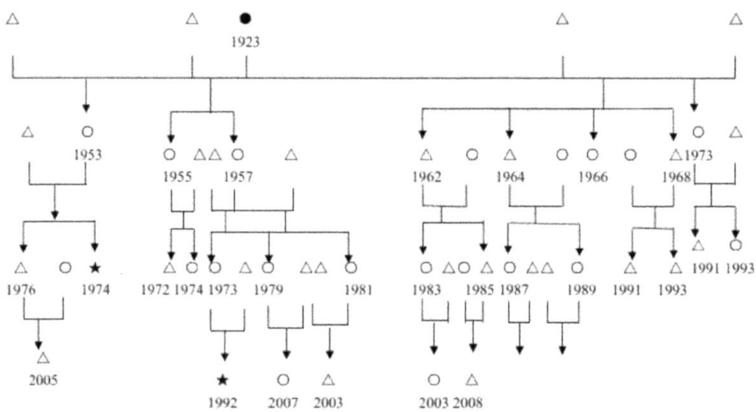

Figure A.30 **Genogram for Yu Hanxiang's family**
▲: male interviewee; ●: female interviewee;
△: male; ○: female;
■: male who died before turning 15; ★: female who died before turning 15;
□: a pregnancy with unknown sex of the fetus;
The sex of those born within each generation are listed in descending order of age, from left to right.

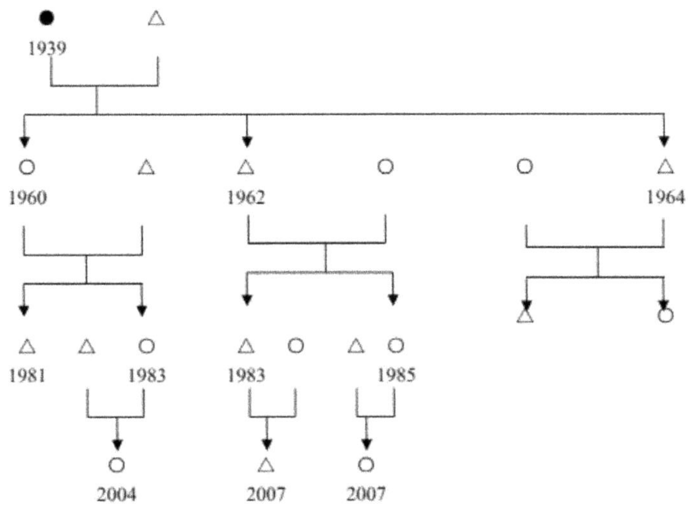

Figure A.31 **Genogram for Yu Yan's family**
▲: male interviewee; ●: female interviewee;
△: male; ○: female;
■: male who died before turning 15; ★: female who died before turning 15;
□: a pregnancy with unknown sex of the fetus;
The sex of those born within each generation are listed in descending order of age, from left to right.

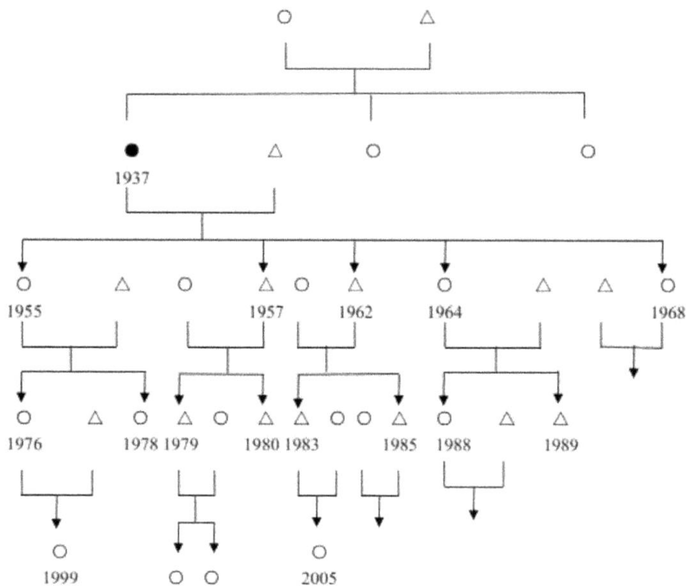

Figure A.32 **Genogram for Yu Han'er's family**
▲: male interviewee; ●: female interviewee;
△: male; ○: female;
■: male who died before turning 15; ★: female who died before turning 15;
□: a pregnancy with unknown sex of the fetus;
The sex of those born within each generation are listed in descending order of age, from left to right.

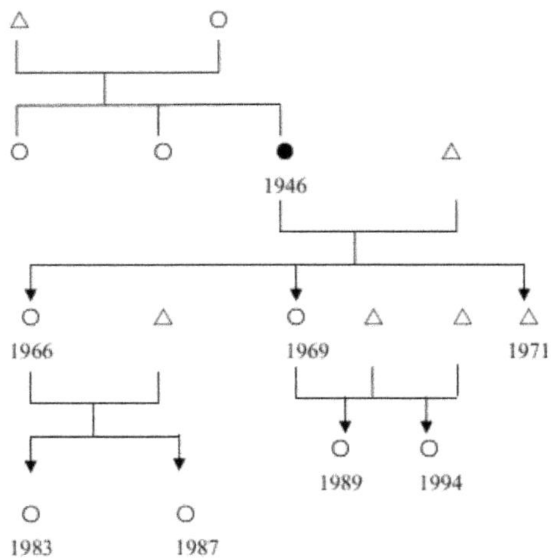

Figure A.33 **Genogram for Yu Lilong's family**
▲: male interviewee; ●: female interviewee;
△: male; ○: female;
■: male who died before turning 15; ★: female who died before turning 15;
□: a pregnancy with unknown sex of the fetus;
The sex of those born within each generation are listed in descending order of age, from left to right.

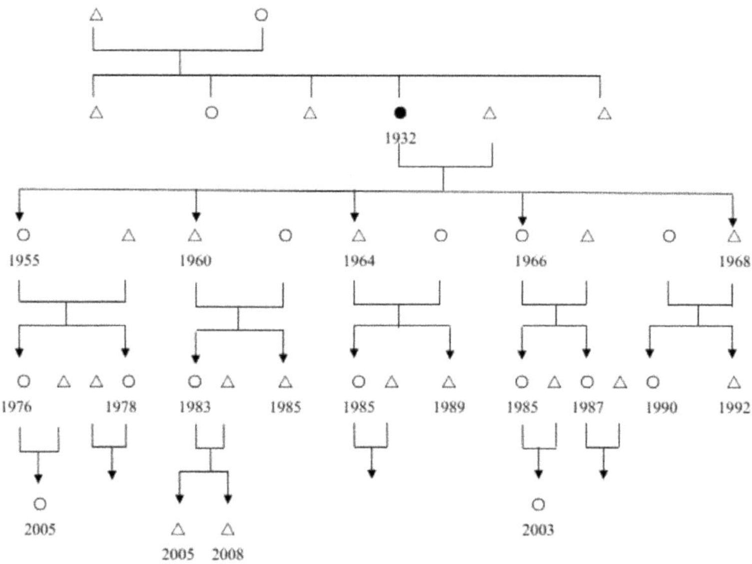

Figure A.34 **Genogram for Yu Jianxiang's family**
▲: male interviewee; ●: female interviewee;
△: male; ○: female;
■: male who died before turning 15; ★: female who died before turning 15;
□: a pregnancy with unknown sex of the fetus;
The sex of those born within each generation are listed in descending order of age, from left to right.

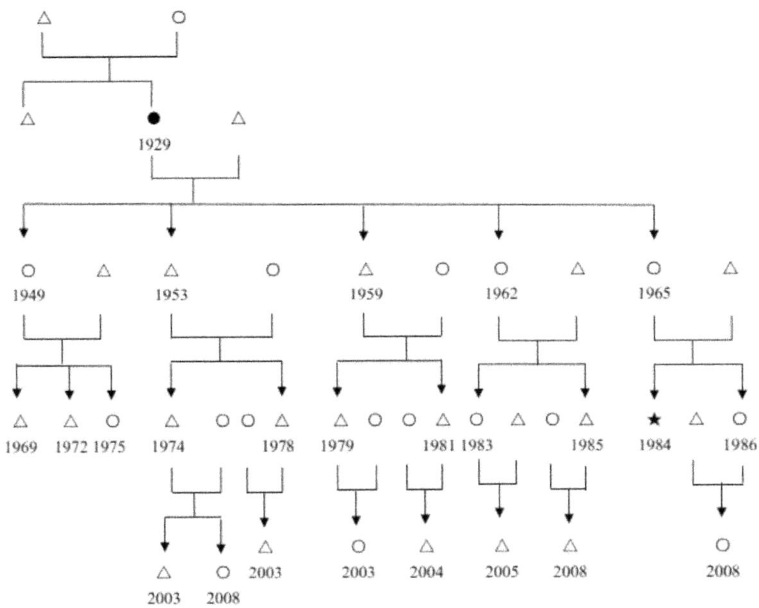

Figure A.35 **Genogram for Yu Ying's family**
▲: male interviewee; ●: female interviewee;
△: male; ○: female;
■: male who died before turning 15; ★: female who died before turning 15;
□: a pregnancy with unknown sex of the fetus;

The sex of those born within each generation are listed in descending order of age, from left to right.

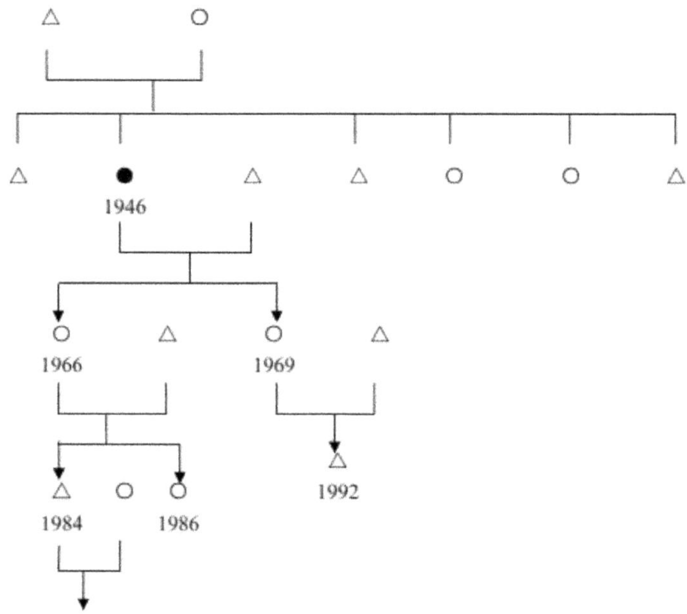

Figure A.36 **Genogram for Yu Ernan's family**
▲: male interviewee; ●: female interviewee;
△: male; ○: female;
■: male who died before turning 15; ★: female who died before turning 15;
□: a pregnancy with unknown sex of the fetus;
The sex of those born within each generation are listed in descending order of age, from left to right.

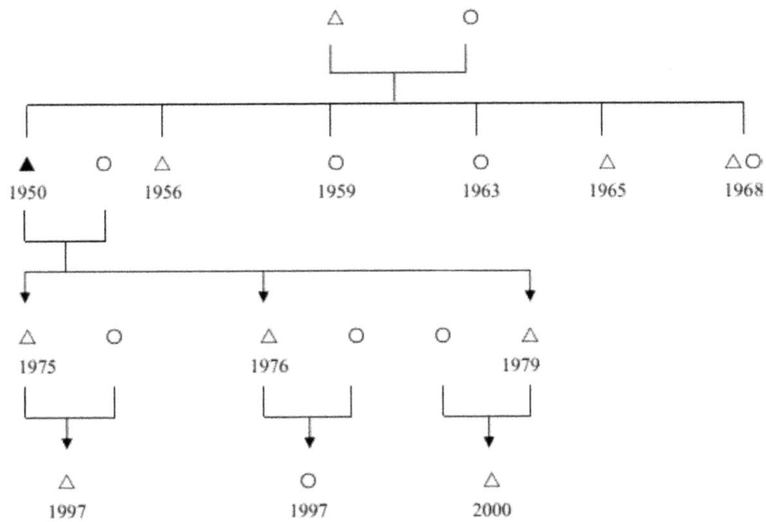

Figure A.37 **Genogram for Yan Wenxiang's family**
▲: male interviewee; ●: female interviewee;
△: male; ○: female;
■: male who died before turning 15; ★: female who died before turning 15;
□: a pregnancy with unknown sex of the fetus;
The sex of those born within each generation are listed in descending order of age, from left to right.

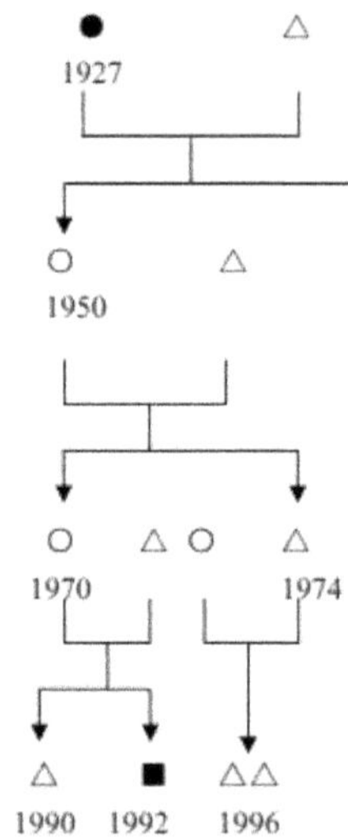

Figure A.38 **Genogram for Yan Dunhan's family**
▲: male interviewee; ●: female interviewee;
△: male; ○: female;
■: male who died before turning 15; ★: female who died before turning 15;
□: a pregnancy with unknown sex of the fetus;
The sex of those born within each generation are listed in descending order of age, from left to right.

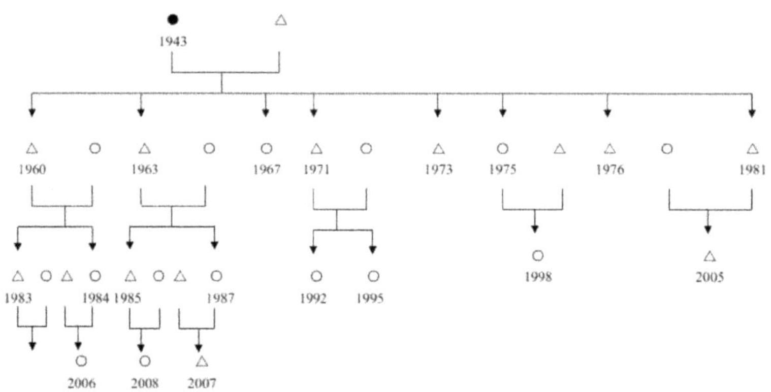

Figure A.39 **Genogram for Yan Hannan's family**
▲: male interviewee; ●: female interviewee;
△: male; ○: female;
■: male who died before turning 15; ★: female who died before turning 15;
□: a pregnancy with unknown sex of the fetus;
The sex of those born within each generation are listed in descending order of age, from left to right.

Village G in Mengzhe Township of Menghai County

General Information of the Village and Surveyed Households

In the southeastern of Mengzhe Township, Jingzhen Villagers' Committee was represented by eight natural villages: Jingmai, Jingdai-I, Jingdai-II, Manhai, Mansai, Manhelong, Manhui and Manyang. To the east of the National Highway No. 214 connecting Menghai County and Laku Ethnic Autonomous County, village G was administered by Jingzhen Villagers' Committee. As of April 2010, there had been 339 residents (162 males and 177 females) in 65 households in the village. Besides two Han villagers and one Bulang villager, all the rest were the Dai residents. By the time of the survey (April 2010), there had been 14 households meeting the survey criteria, making up 21.53% of the total.

The basic information of the surveyed households is listed below in Table A.6.

Records of the Reproductive Histories of the Surveyed Households Are Shown in the Following Table

Household No.: 6; Interviewee: Yu Duan; Figure A.40

Yu Duan was born on April 5, 1939. She was the fifth child in her family and had two brothers and two sisters. At 17 years old, she married a Bulang man two years older than her, had her first child at 19 years old (in February 1958) and her last child at 37 years old (1976). She gave birth to seven children all her life.

When asked about raising children, Yu Duan said that it was hard. With too many children and in a poor financial position, she had to work hard every day to support her family. Her first daughter gave birth to three girls, but the third girl died at an early age. So, Yu Duan gave her fifth son to her first daughter as her adopted child.

Parents' Generation:

Yu Duan's mother gave birth to five children, two males and three females. Sex of the children in descending order: M – M – F – F – F. Yu Duan was the youngest daughter in her family.

Table A.6: Basic Information of the Female Interviewees (Born in or before 1950) in Village G

Serial No.	Household No.	Name	Date of Birth	Time at First Marriage	Age at First Marriage (Years Old)	Current Marital Status	Time at Last Childbirth (Year)	Age at Last Childbirth (Years Old)	Contraception Methods
1	6	Yu Duan	1939.4.5	1956.2	17	First Marriage	1976	37	Tubal ligation
2	7	Yu Yingjiao	1931.9.12	1950.3	19	Remarriage	1971	40	Abortion-Induced Infertility
3	8	Yu Shuo	1938.6.5	1957.6	19	Widowhood	Lifetime Infertility		Toxic Birth[42]
4	13	Yi Yingkan	1942.4.28	1960.6	18	Restored Marriage	1980	38	Tubal ligation
5	14	Yu Xiangnuo	1948.4.16	1964.6	16	First Marriage	1970	28	Estrangement
6	15	Yu Wanjiao	1926.3.10	1945.5	19	Widowhood	1961	35	Tubal ligation
7	20	Yu Kan	1938.10.12	1957.2	19	Widowhood	1967	29	Tubal ligation
8	21	Yu Liu	1929.11.13	1949.2	20	Widowhood	1968	41	Toxic Birth

42 Toxic birth is a folkloric interpretation among the Dai people to the birth that will lead to infertility in the future.

9	22	Yu Yan	1947.8.13	1964.1	17	First Marriage	1968	21	Tubal ligation
10	34	Yu Shuai	1938.8.17	1960.4	22	First Marriage	1972	34	IUD
11	35	Yu Xiang	1949.4.6	1968.10	19	First Marriage	1972	33	Tubal ligation
12	36	Yu Xiangde	1937.4.11	1955.4	18	Remarriage	1971	34	Tubal ligation
13	42	Yu Yinger	1945.4.21	1961.2	16	Widowhood	1968	23	Tubal ligation
14	44	Yu Hansai	1947.6.1	1967.2	20	Remarriage	1973	26	Tubal ligation

Source: Field Survey Statistics by the Research Team.

Current Generation:

Yu Duan was born on April 5, 1939, got married in February 1956, and gave birth to seven children, three females and four males. Sex of the children in descending order: F (1958) – M (1962) – M (1963) – F (1968) – M (1970) – F (1973) – M (1976).

Children's Generation:

The first daughter gave birth to three children. Sex of the children in descending order: F (1979) – F (1981) – F. The youngest daughter died soon after being born.

The first son gave birth to two children. Sex of the children in descending order: M (1983) – M (1985).

The second son gave birth to two children. Sex of the children in descending order: F (1986) – F (1988).

The second daughter gave birth to two children. Sex of the children in descending order: M (1985) – M (1988).

The third son gave birth to one child, F (1994), received the only-child certificate.

The third daughter gave birth to two children. Sex of the children in descending order: M (1993) – F (1995).

The fourth son gave birth to two children. Sex of the children in descending order: M (1999) – F (2007).

Grandchildren's Generation:

The first daughter's first child gave birth to one child, M (2002).

The first daughter's second child gave birth to two children. Sex of the children in descending order: M (1996) – M (2006).

The first son's first child gave birth to two children. Sex of the children in descending order: F (2002) – M (2008).

The first son's second child were unmarried.

The second son's first child gave birth to one child, M (2006).

The second son's second child were unmarried.

The second daughter's first child gave birth to one child, M (2009).

The second daughter's second child had recently got engaged.

All the other grandchildren were unmarried.

Great-grandchildren's Generation:

Seven great-grandchildren, six males and one female.

On the issue of finding a partner, Yu Duan said: "Our parents would not accept a partner being unfamiliar with Buddhist customs as many activities in our Dai society are related to Buddhism. There are too many Buddhist festivals in a year, so it is not acceptable for us to date someone unfamiliar with Buddhist etiquette and customs. We learned these customs from childhood and developed a habit of practicing them. It surely doesn't work to live with a partner being clueless about these practices, for example, Religious Offerings, the Door-opening Festival, and the Door-closing Festival. Villagers would gossip about it."

As for financial support for elderly parents, Yu Duan said: "Previously, if there were many children in a family, the earlier-married siblings would move out to live separately, the youngest, either a boy or a girl, would leave behind and live with the parents. Nowadays, one can't afford to have many children. Everything is expensive. And the government has birth control policies. Generally speaking, the eldest child stays at home with parents and younger siblings set up their separate families. It feels like a complete reversal of the past."

Household No.: 7; Interviewee: Yu Yingjiao; Figure A.41

Yu Yingjiao's mother was the second child in her family, with one elder sister and two younger brothers. Both of the two brothers died young. Yu Yingjiao's mother became an orphan at six years old, had been adopted by relatives and worked as a babysitter when grown up.

Parents' Generation:

Yu Yingjiao's mother gave birth to six children. Sex of the children in descending order: M – M – F – F – F. Yu Yingjiao was the fourth of six siblings in her family. But all of them died in infancy except her eldest brother and herself: Her second brother died at 10, her third brother at 7, her eldest sister at 7, and her second sister died at 8. Later, her eldest brother also died fighting in Myanmar.

Current Generation:

Yu Yingjiao was born on September 12, 1931, married twice, and gave birth to eight children, four males and four females. Seven children survived, three males and four females.

She married her first husband in 1950 and gave birth to three children. Sex of the children in descending order: M (1951) – F (1953) – F (1955). When her husband went to Myanmar, she got divorced. She remarried in 1961 and gave birth to five children with her second husband. Sex of the children in descending order: M (1962) – M (1965) – F (1967) – M (1969) – F (1971).

Children's Generation:

The first son died of chickenpox at nine months old.

The first daughter went to Thailand with her ex-husband at 10 years old and gave birth to two children in Thailand. Sex of the children in descending order: F – M (1983).

The second daughter gave birth to two children. Sex of the children in descending order: M (1973) – M (1975), and now widowed.

The second son gave birth to two children. Sex of the children in descending order: F (1985) – F (1987).

The third son gave birth to two children. Sex of the children in descending order: F (1983) – F (1986).

The third daughter gave birth to two children. Sex of the children in descending order: M (1984) – F (1985).

The fourth son gave birth to two children. Sex of the children in descending order: M (1986) – F (1996). His wife underwent a tubal ligation surgery after giving birth to her second child in 1996.

The youngest daughter married twice, having no children with the first husband and giving birth to a girl with the second husband at 35 years old (2006).

Grandchildren's Generation:

The first daughter's first child died of drug abuse in Thailand.

The first daughter's second child, 27 years old, was in love.

The second daughter's first child gave birth to two children. Sex of the children in descending order: M (1993) – M (1996).

The second daughter's second child died at five years old (1980).

The second son's first child gave birth to two children. Sex of the children in descending order: M (1998) – M (2002).

The second son's second child gave birth to one child, F (2008).

The third son's two daughters were unmarried, working in other places and waiting for their father to come home.

The third daughter's first child gave birth to one child, M (2007), and was divorced.

The third daughter's second child was working in Shenzhen and in love.

The fourth son's first child got married in 2008 and still had no children.

Great-grandchildren's Generation:

Six great-grandchildren, five males and one female. The third grandson was a monk at this village temple.

Yu Yingjiao was very emotional about her childbearing. She said to us: "I have been very hard all my life for giving birth to babies. My fourth daughter was born in 1971, but I couldn't afford to raise her and had to give her to an infertile Han friend when the baby was just eight months old. Unfortunately, I was pregnant with the ninth child in 1973. At that time, I didn't want to have another child, but there was no other option. As the fetus grew up, both of us (husband and wife) were very worried. Surgical abortion was reported to be performed at People's Hospital of Menghai County. But the doctor said an induced abortion was the only option in late pregnancy, and such an operation might have negative impacts on the mother. After much thought, I decided to have an operation, and then I could be free of any worry (getting pregnant in the future) once and for all!"

The Han friend who had adopted her daughter was a very kind man, often having the child pay a visit to Yu Yingjiao. Now, the daughter was 39 years old and ran a flower shop in Mengzhe. She often came over to see Yu Yingjiao. While speaking of her, Yu Yingjiao was full of happiness.

Household No.: 8; Interviewee: Yu Shuo; Figure A.42

Grandparent Generation:

Yu Shuo's maternal grandmother gave birth to three children. Sex of the children in descending order: M – F – F. Her mother was the third child in her family.

Parents' Generation:

Yu Shuo's mother gave birth to three children, two males and one female. Sex of the children in descending order: M – M – F. The first son (Yu Shuo's eldest brother) died at five years old, the second son (Yu Shuo's second brother) died of stomachache at five months old and Yu Shuo was the youngest in the family. Since the birth of Yu Shuo, her mother had never got pregnant again as the toxic birth was described.

Current Generation:

Yu Shuo was born on June 5, 1938. She married her first husband at 19 years old (1957) and got divorced after a spontaneous abortion. Later, she married her second husband in 1968 but never got pregnant. "Yu Shuo got pregnant with a toxic birth, just as her mother did. Toxic birth is a folkloric interpretation among the Dai people to a birth that will lead to infertility in the future."

Children's Generation:

Yu Shuo had no children of her own all her life.

We asked: "Why didn't your second husband part with you as you didn't have any children?"

Smiling with relief, Yu Shuo replied: "He is also a remarried man. He had four boys and two girls with his ex-wife. He had told me all about it when we began to date. I had asked him: what if I can't get pregnant? He didn't care much about it. I married him because he was kind to me and didn't mind that I wouldn't have a baby." Yu Shuo's second husband passed away the year before last (2008). The first daughter of her second husband lived with her and other children of her second husband also often paid a visit to her. Though having no biological children of her own, Yu Shuo still lived a comfortable life and her second husband's children were very kind to her.

Household No.: 13; Interviewee: Yi Yingkan; Figure A.43

Yi Yingkan's mother, 88 years old (born in 1922), was kind and healthy. She had a poor memory and hearing, so we had to give up interviewing her directly. She got pregnant with 12 children with three husbands and gave birth to 10 children (suffering two abortions) all her life. She gave birth to her last child at 52 years old (1974), and Yi Yingkan was the child of her first husband. Yi Yingkan didn't know much about the siblings of her mother but that her mother was a stranger to this village. Elders in this village addressed her mother "Mitao Nan", which indicated that her mother was of aristocratic descent (i.e. having some relation with the Zhaopianling family in Xishuangbanna).

Though divorced from Yi Yingkan's father, Yi Yingkan's mother got along well with all the children of her three husbands. It happened to be the Door-opening Festival when we interviewed, and a major religious offering event was going on. All the children came to visit the old lady, joking and chatting with each other.

Parents' Generation:

Yi Yingkan's mother married three times and gave birth to 10 children all her life, five males and five females. Sex of the children in descending order: M (1940) – F (1942) – M (1944) – F (1945) – F (1947) – M

(1950) – F – M – M – F. Yi Yingkan was the second child in her family. The first son (Yi Yingkan's elder brother) died in 1978, the second daughter (Yi Yingkan's first younger sister) died at three years old (1948), and the third son (Yi Yingkan's second younger brother) died of fever at one year old (1952). The last four children were born about two years apart.

Current Generation:

Yi Yingkan was born on April 28, 1942. She had a checkered marriage experience: "marriage – divorce – remarriage – divorce – reunion" and also a rocky reproductive history: She was pregnant with seven children, suffering one natural abortion, giving birth to three females and three males. Two females and three males had grown up.

She married her first husband in 1960 and gave birth to three children. Sex of the children in descending order: F (1961) – F (1964) – M (1965). Her first daughter died soon after her birth and she was divorced. She married her second husband in 1967, getting pregnant four times, giving birth to two children and suffering one natural abortion. Sex of the children in descending order: F (1968) – M (1970) – M (1980). Yi Yingkan said: "It was a difficult time (the Cultural Revolution period). My second husband had relatives in Myanmar, so the whole family emigrated to live in Myanmar. There, I was expecting a baby but miscarried into the two-month pregnancy. After giving birth to my second son in 1970, I decided to have no baby any longer. However, I was unexpectedly pregnant once again in mid-1979 and gave birth to the third son in 1980, and went from Myanmar 15 days later for a surgical ligation in Thailand. That was the end of all trouble." Yi Yingkan was not yet into her 38 years old that year.

Children's Generation:

The second daughter gave birth to two children. Sex of the children in descending order: M (1980) – F (1983).

The first son gave birth to two children. Sex of the children in descending order: F (1985) – M (1986).

The third daughter got pregnant with three births and gave birth to two children (aborting one birth). Sex of the children in descending order: F (1986) – F (1989).

The second son gave birth to two children. Sex of the children in descending order: F (1990) – F (1992).

The third son gave birth to two children. Sex of the children in descending order: F (2003) – M (2009). His wife was planning to have an IUD operation and then to receive a tubal ligation surgery after their son was proven to be healthy.

Grandchildren's Generation:

The second daughter's first child gave birth to one child, F (2006).

The second daughter's second child was divorced and had no children. He had been to Malaysia and now was living in this village.

The first son's first child was a university student in Thailand, moonlighting in teaching Chinese and Thai. He wanted to pursue advanced study and were unmarried.

The first son's second child gave birth to one child, F (2009).

The third daughter's first child got married but still had no children.

The second son's first child got married two years ago (2008) and miscarried once. Now, she still had no children.

Great-grandchildren's Generation:

Two great-granddaughters.

Yi Yingkan had a very interesting marriage history. Her current husband was her first husband, and her second husband also moved back to the village from Myanmar, just living next door. While we were talking with Yi Yingkan's couple in her courtyard, her second husband (Myanmar husband) happened to pass by. Instead of avoiding her Myanmar husband, Yi Yingkan invited him to come over and talk with us, and he gladly accepted the invitation. Yi Yingkan said, "My first husband is very talented and used to be kind to me, but he didn't like to stay at home. He would read pattra-leaf scriptures at Buddhist temples, leaving two children behind to me, so I divorced him. The Myanmar husband is also very capable and treated me very well. I used to live comfortably in Myanmar. In 1985, I came back with my 5-year-old boy to see my mother, who had something wrong with her ear. My children (with my first husband) did not want me to go back to Myanmar, so they often had their father (Yi Yingkan's first and current husband) come over for dinner and chat. Nearly a month later, my Myanmar husband came over to this village to look for me and found that he (Yi Yingkan's first husband) often stayed at my mother's home. My Myanmar husband suspected that I was in love with him again and quarreled with me. My Myanmar husband went angrily back to Myanmar and divorced me. A few years later, when finding that my first husband was getting older and in poor health, I decided to reunite with him and take care of him (Yi Yingkan's first and current husband had mild amnesia)."

Throughout the interview, while Yi Yingkan recounted their shared past and their fleeting relationships, the two husbands listened, smiling and occasionally adding some historical facts. Now, when I thought of the three old men recounting their relationships in the yard, the word "harmony" would come across my mind.

Knowing that I was a teacher at Yunnan University, Yi Yingkan also told us about her granddaughter, who was still studying in Thailand. She said: "Having graduated from a normal school in Hunan, she went to Thailand for a master's degree. Her family could not afford her education, so her boyfriend (a Han lad from Hunan doing business in Jinghong) funded her education. She was about to graduate, but the school wished she would stay in Thailand. She also wanted to stay but felt sorry for her boyfriend. The Thai principal came over to this village twice to lobby the lad to part with her and promised to repay all the money. The other option is that a three-year holiday would be granted for her to settle her relationship with her boyfriend. If they couldn't get along well, she could still go back to Thailand." I asked, "Is that going to cause any trouble?" Yi Yingkan said: "No. Everything would be okay as long as they could achieve an agreement. If she does find a good job there, and the young man can also go over there to reunite with her." It could be seen that parents were very open to the marriage of their children.

As for the willingness of most women in the village to control their birth through a tubal ligation surgery, Yi Yingkan gave her explanation:

"The medication is unhealthy. The IUD is too troublesome, you have to change it every three years, and it might fall off when you do heavy work. So, ligation is the safest bet, and won't be affected by anything." (It was found in our interviews that the Dai couples often humorously deal with sexual issues, and never shied away from talking about the pleasure from their sex life).

Household No.: 14; Interviewee: Yu Xiangnuo; Figure A.44

Yu Xiangnuo's mother gave birth to six children all her life, but only three survived. Her father fled to Myanmar during the Cultural Revolution and never returned, and her mother never remarried until she died in 2003.

Parents' Generation:

Yu Xiangnuo's mother gave birth to six children. Three children survived. Sex of the children in descending order: F – F – F – M – M – M. Yu Xiangnuo was the second child in her family and her elder sister and first and second younger brothers all died in infancy.

Current Generation:

Yu Xiangnuo was born on April 16, 1948, got married in June 1964, and gave birth to four children all her life (only three children survived). Sex of the children in descending order: M – M (1965) – F (1966) – M (1970). Her first son died young.

Children's Generation:

The second son gave birth to two children. Sex of the children in descending order: M (1984) – F (1988).

The first daughter gave birth to two children. Sex of the children in descending order: F (1986) – F (1988). Later, she got divorced and remarried but had no additional children.

The third son gave birth to two children. Sex of the children in descending order: M (1992) – M (1994).

Grandchildren's Generation:

The second son's first child gave birth to one child, F (2007).

The second son's second child gave birth to one child, M (2009).

The first daughter's first child gave birth to one child, F (2007).

The first daughter's second child and Third son's children were unmarried.

Great-grandchildren's Generation:

Three great-grandchildren, one male and two females.

Household No.: 15; Interviewee: Yu Wanjiao; Figure A.45

Yu Wanjiao was the only girl in her family. Her mother gave birth to two children all her life: Yu Wanjiao and her elder brother. Since her birth, her mother could never get pregnant again. So, she was a child from what the Dai folklore described as a toxic birth (the birth that will lead to infertility in the future) and had a similar situation to that of Yu Shuo from Household No. 8 in this village. Yu Wanjiao's husband was the fourth of nine siblings in his family. Yu Wanjiao gave birth to eight children all her life, but only five children survived. Her first daughter was Yu Hansai from Household No. 44 in this village.

Yu Wanjiao had mixed feelings towards her reproductive experience and said: "It is really lucky to implement the birth control. Otherwise, I would have been dead long ago!" To clear our confusion with her comments, she continued: "It was so hard to give birth to these eight kids. Every time I suffered from hard labor from the fifth birth and was scared to death. I had told Botao (her husband) once that I would surely die from giving birth. When the fourth son was born (1961), I was tipped that: Go to Kunming and take an operation, and you won't have babies again! At that time, I didn't know it was a surgical ligation. But I didn't mind about what it was. I thought that as long as I could never be (pregnant) anymore, I would do it. Therefore, I asked Botao to take me to Menghai Hospital for the operation and had since become better-off. I am the first woman who has taken the surgical ligation (in the village) in Menghai County." Speaking of this, the old lady was very proud that she had set a good example for the popularization of national family planning in rural areas.

Parents' Generation:

Yu Wanjiao's mother gave birth to two children. Sex of the children in descending order: M – F. The boy died young and the girl was Yu Wanjiao. After his brother's death, Yu Wanjiao became the apple of his parents' eyes.

Current Generation:

Yu Wanjiao was born on March 10, 1926, got married in May 1945, and gave birth to eight children. Five children survived. Sex of the children in descending order: M (1946) – F (1947) – F (1949) – M (1952) – F (1958). F (1959) – M (1960) – M (1961). After giving birth to her youngest boy in 1961, she took the surgical ligation at the People's Hospital of Menghai County of her own accord, the first-ever case in the village. Her eldest boy and two last boys died young.

Children's Generation:

The first daughter was Yu Hansai from Household No. 44 in this village (her reproductive history is described below).

The second daughter gave birth to three children. Sex of the children in descending order: F (1969) – M (1970) – F (1973). She took ligation surgery after giving her third birth.

The second son gave birth to four children. Sex of the children in descending order: F (1974) – F (1979) – F (1981) – F (1984).

The third daughter gave birth to four children. Three children survived. Sex of the children in descending order: M – M (1975) – M (1978) – F (1982). The first son died young.

The fourth daughter gave birth to two children. Sex of the children in descending order: F (1980) – M (1981).

Grandchildren's Generation:

The second daughter's first child gave birth to two children. Sex of the children in descending order: F (1989) – F (1991).

The second daughter's second child gave birth to two children. Sex of the children in descending order: M (1990) – F (1993).

The second daughter's third child gave birth to one child, F (1995). She took the surgical ligation and received the only-child certificate.

The second son's first child gave birth to two children. Sex of the children in descending order: M (1995) – M (1997).

The second son's second child gave birth to two children. Sex of the children in descending order: M (1995) – M (1998).

The second son's third child gave birth to one child, M (2008).

The second son's fourth child gave birth to one child, M (2007). She took the surgical ligation and had a stepson from her husband.

The third daughter's first child gave birth to one child, M (2007). His wife took the surgical ligation and received the only-child certificate.

The third daughter's second child gave birth to two children. Sex of the children in descending order: M (1997) – M (2009). But the second boy died soon after his birth. The couple chose no to have additional children and received the only-child certificate.

The third daughter's third child gave birth to one child, M (2007).

The fourth daughter's first child gave birth to one child, F (2006). She migrated to the City of Xi'an.

The fourth daughter's second child gave birth to one child, M (2003).

Great-grandchildren's Generation:

The first daughter of the second daughter's first child gave birth to one child, M (2008).

The fourth Generation:

One great-grandson, born in 2008.

We spent three whole days in four sessions interviewing Yu Wanjiao's family, one of the largest clans in this village. It was a little surprise to us to find while sorting out the interview notes and recordings that the 84-year-old Yu Wanjiao had five children, 15 grandchildren (the oldest born in 1968 and the youngest born in 1984), and 22 great-grandchildren. Did they also embrace the fertility philosophy of "raising sons as support in advanced years" and "the more offspring, the more blessings"? With this question in mind, I paid a special visit to the old lady once again, talking with her about the Dai people's views on childbearing. She said: "Having too many kids is really a grueling thing. There was nothing we could do (to avoid pregnancy) before. Once you got it (meaning get pregnant), you would have to have it born. You couldn't imagine how hard it is to give birth to or take care of babies. That is just the reason why I jumped at the idea (sterilization operation) once I heard of it!" I asked: "Had the surgical ligation been performed already in Xishuangbanna as early as back in the 1970s?" She replied: "At that time we did not know of it. Even if we did know of it later, it was not the thing you could do as you wish." I continued: "Why is it like so? Family planning is a requirement from the government, isn't it?" The old man chuckled: "You don't know a thing or two about this matter. You'd better go to my eldest girl for some clues." During our later conversations with Yu Hansai about this topic, Yu Hansai gave me a detailed account of the whole story (as shown in our interview records with Yu Hansai).

Household No.: 20; Interviewee: Yu Kan; Figure A.46

Yu Kan, 72 years old, did not know much about her mother's siblings except for the talks that many people of the same generation as her mother, including many of her mother's relatives, fled their poor hometowns to Myanmar.

Parents' Generation:

Yu Kan's mother gave birth to six children. Four children survived. Sex of the children in descending order: F (1932) – M (1935) – F (1938) – F (1942) – F – M. Yu Kan was the second daughter in her family, and her youngest sister died at around one month old and her youngest brother died the second day after his birth.

Current Generation:

Yu Kan was born on October 12, 1938, got married in February 1957, got pregnant with six births, experienced one natural abortion and one induced abortion and gave birth to four children. Only Three children survived. Sex of the children in descending order: M (1959) – M (1962) – M (1964) – M (1967). Her fourth son died of hepatitis A at eight years old (1975).

Yu Kan always wanted to have a daughter and hoped her next child would be a girl. In the fifth month of her pregnancy with her sixth baby, she took the induced abortion of the male fetus and the surgical ligation at a Menghai Hospital. Yu Kan's husband died three years ago (2007).

Children's Generation:

The first son gave birth to three children. Sex of the children in descending order: F (1977) – F (1979) – M (1984).

The second son gave birth to two children. Sex of the children in descending order: M (1980) – F (1983). He died in 2008.

The third son gave birth to two children. Sex of the children in descending order: M (1988) – M (1991).

Grandchildren's Generation:

The first son's first child gave birth to two children, both males (they lived out of this village, so their exact ages were unknown and estimated to be respectively at 15 and 13 years old).

The first son's second child got pregnant twice and gave birth to one child, F (1996). She had one natural abortion, took the surgical ligation, and received the only-child certificate.

The first son's third child gave birth to one child, F (1999).

The second son's first child gave birth to one child, F (2006).

The second son's second child were unmarried.

The third son's first child gave birth to one child, M (2010). To be eligible for the marriage certificate, he changed the date of birth on the ID card to 1986.

Great-grandchildren's Generation:

Six great-grandchildren, three males and three females.

Speaking of her reproductive experience, Yu Kan showed up a strong desire for having a daughter and said: "In contrast with the Han majority, who prefer boys, we instead prefer girls as daughters can live with us in the future. Having had four boys, I wished that the fifth (fetus) would be a girl. In the fifth month of my pregnancy, I had a check-up at the hospital quietly through a relative, and found that it was also a boy. After a discussion with my husband, I decided to abort it. The doctor said to me: 'It (fetus) is too big to be aborted. You can only have an induced abortion, which may have negative impacts on your health. You'd better to keep it!' But I insisted on aborting it and taking the surgical ligation." Yu Kan turned 30 that year.

Yu Kan's second son married Yu Zhang, the first daughter of Yi Yingkan from Household No. 13 in this village. That is, their marriage was intermarriage in the village.

Household No.: 21; Interviewee: Yu Liu; Figure A.47

Yu Liu's maternal grandmother gave birth to six children. Three children survived. Sex of the children in descending order: M – F – F. Yu Liu's mother was the youngest daughter in her family.

Parents' Generation:

Yu Liu's mother gave birth to eight children. Four children survived. Sex of the children in descending order: M – F – M – F. Yu Liu was the youngest daughter in her family.

Current Generation:

Yu Liu was born on November 13, 1929, got married in February 1949, and gave birth to eight children, four males and four females. Six children survived, four females and two males. Sex of the children in descending order: F (1947) – M – M – F (1952) – M (1959) – F (1962) – F (1964) – M (1968). The first son died at one year old and the second son died at two years old.

Children's Generation:

The first daughter was born in 1947. She was Yu Yan from Household No. 22 in this village and one of our interviewees (her reproductive history is described below).

The second daughter gave birth to four children, two males and two females. Three children survived, two females and one male. Sex of the children in descending order: F (1969) – M (1970) – M – F (1975). Her second son died at seven months old and she also died of cancer at 41 years old (1997).

The third son and the fourth daughter of Yu Wanjiao from Household No. 15 in this village were a couple. They gave birth to two children. Sex of the children in descending order: F (1980) – M (1981).

The third daughter gave birth to three children, and the third birth were twin daughters. Only one birth survived. Sex of the children in descending order: M – M (1994) – F – F. The first son died at two years old and the twin daughters died at two months old.

The fourth daughter and the second son of Yu Xiangnuo from Household No. 14 in this village were a couple. She got pregnant with three births, aborted one birth, and gave birth to two children. Sex of the children in descending order: M (aborted) – M (1984) – F (1988).

The fourth son gave birth to three children and two births survived. Sex of the children in descending order: M – M (1988) – F (1990). The first child died two months after being born.

Grandchildren's Generation:

The second daughter's first child gave birth to two children. Sex of the children in descending order: M (1986) – F (1988).

The second daughter's second child gave birth to two children. One child survived, F (1992). The first child died from drowning at three years old.

The second daughter's third child gave birth to two children. Sex of the children in descending order: M (1992) – F (1995).

The third son's first child gave birth to one child, F (2006).

The third son's second child gave birth to one child, M (2003).

The third daughter's second child gave birth to one child, M (2006).

The fourth daughter's first child gave birth to one child, F (2007).

The fourth daughter's second child gave birth to one child, M (2009).

The fourth son's children were unmarried.

Great-grandchildren's Generation:

The son of the second daughter's first child gave birth to one child, M (2008).

The Daughter of the second daughter's first child gave birth to one child, M (2009).

The fourth Generation:

Two great-grandsons.

Yu Liu's clan saw more intermarriages than others in the village. Her first daughter Yu Yan lived in this village and her eldest son and fourth daughter both married the fellow villagers. Such intertwined kinship ties formed a powerful relationship network.

There was a framed picture of the twin boys on the wall of Yu Liu's home. When I asked about the twins, Yu Liu said: "They are kids of Yu Yan's second child (her second granddaughter). Behold, how good-looking they are! However, unfortunately, they didn't survive. If so, they would be more than 10 years old!"

Household No.: 22; Interviewee: Yu Yan; Figure A.48

Yu Yan was born on August 13, 1947 and the first daughter of Yu Liu from Household No. 21. We introduced her family starting with Current Generation. Yu Yan's husband died of a cerebral hemorrhage in 2008.

Current Generation:

Yu Yan got pregnant four times: She gave birth to three children and aborted one. Sex of the children in descending order: F (1962) – M (aborted) – F (1967) – M (1968). After giving birth to her fourth child, she did not get pregnant again, but still took the initiative to receive a tubal ligation surgery in 1975.

Children's Generation:

The first daughter gave birth to two children. Sex of the children in descending order: M (1978) – F (1985).

The second daughter gave birth to two children, and the second birth were twins. Sex of the children in descending order: F (1984) – M – M (1987). The twin boys died at more than two years old. After giving birth to the twins, she received a tubal ligation surgery. But later, the twins died, so she was left with only one daughter and received the only-child certificate as required by related policies.

The first son gave birth to two children. Sex of the children in descending order: M (1985) – F (1986) and his wife underwent a tubal ligation surgery after giving birth to the second children.

Grandchildren's Generation:

The first daughter's first child gave birth to two children. Sex of the children in descending order: M (2000) – M (2006) and his wife underwent a tubal ligation surgery after giving birth to the second child.

The first daughter's second child went to work first at the City of Lijiang after graduating from high school, and now worked in the City of Kunming and was just in a relationship.

The second daughter's first child gave birth to one child, M (2005).

The first son's first child married twice. He had no children from his first marriage. Now his second wife was in pregnancy.

The first son's second child, 14 years old, had been working outside this village after graduating from school, and now was back in the village. Yu Yan said it would be hard for her to find a husband in the village since she wasn't skilled at farming work.

Great-grandchildren's Generation:

Three great-grandsons.

Household No.: 34; Interviewee: Yu Shuai; Figure A.49

Yu Shuai's mother Yu En was the wife of a nobleman, namely the wife of a relative of Zhaopianling (local feudal ruler) in Xishuangbanna, and was therefore called Yu Nanshuai. The Chinese character "喃" indicates that she was of aristocratic descent. Yu En had four sisters and was the first child in the family.

Parents' Generation:

Yu Shuai's mother Yu En gave birth to nine children, four females and five males. Sex of the children in descending order: F – M – F- F – M – M – M – M – F. The first daughter died at 27 years old, the third daughter died at 40 years old, the second son died at 14 years old and the third son died at 17 years old. Yu Shuai was the third child and the second daughter in the family.

Current Generation:

Yu Shuai was born on August 17, 1938, got married in April 1960, and gave birth to three children, two females and one male. Sex of the children in descending order: F (1963) – M (1970) – F (1972). After giving birth to her youngest child at the age of 34, she used drug contraception and then IUD contraception until menopause at 52 years old.

Children's Generation:

The first daughter was married to Ganlanba in Jinghong, and gave birth to two children. Sex of the children in descending order: F (1985) – F (1987);

The first son gave birth to two children. Sex of the children in descending order: M (1988) – M (1990);

The second daughter gave birth to two children. Sex of the children in descending order: F (1991) – F (1993). The first daughter died three months after birth. She had a tubal ligation surgery in 1993 after having the second daughter and received the only-child certificate.

Grandchildren's Generation:

The first granddaughter gave birth to one child, M (2006);

The second granddaughter, 23 years old, worked away from home and were unmarried;

Two grandsons, 22 and 20 years old, both worked in farming fields and were unmarried.

Great-grandchildren's Generation:

One great grandson (2006).

Speaking about her experience with contraception, Yu Shuai jokingly said: "When the doctor asked me how I wanted to do, I said that to have a surgical ligation, it is going to cut it open (the skin), it hurts so much. So, the doctor recommended me take (contraceptive) medicines. Yet, taking medicines was troublesome and did harm to my stomach. Later, IUD (technology) was available. The doctor wouldn't give me any medicine. I had to ask my husband to take me to the prefecture hospital to do the IUD. While doing the IUD, it also hurt. I had never had the IUD replaced until it was removed finally."

Household No.: 35; Interviewee: Yu Xiang; Figure A.50

Yu Xiang's maternal grandmother gave birth to four children and two children survived. The first birth (a boy) and the third birth (a girl) both died young. Yu Xiang's mother was the first daughter in her family.

Parents' Generation:

Yu Xiang's mother gave birth to seven children. Six children survived. The twin boys in the first birth died soon after their birth. Sex of the children in descending order of the surviving children: M (1938) – F (1945) – F (1949) – M (1955) – F (1958) – F (1960). Yu Xiang was the second daughter in the family.

Current Generation:

Yu Xiang was born on April 6, 1949, got married in September 1968, and gave birth to three children. Sex of the children in descending order: F (1968) – F (1970) – M (1972). She had the tubal ligation surgery at 23 years old after having the third birth, one male.

Children's Generation:

The first daughter gave birth to two children. Sex of the children in descending order: M (1990) – M (1991).

The second daughter gave birth to two children. Sex of the children in descending order: M (1988) – M (1990).

The son gave birth to two children. Sex of the children in descending order: F (1991) – M (1992).

Grandchildren's Generation:

Six grandchildren all were unmarried.

The first daughter's first child was recently engaged.
The second daughter's first son worked at the sugar refinery of Jingzhen.
The son's daughter worked in Laos and was in a relationship.

Household No.: 36; Interviewee: Yu Xiangde; Figure A.51

Yu Xiangde's maternal grandmother gave birth to only one child and never got pregnant again, locally known as a toxic birth. Thus, Yu Xiangde's mother was the only daughter in the family.

Parents' Generation:

Yu Xiangde's mother gave birth to six children, three females and three males. Sex of the children in descending order: F – M – F – F – M – M. Yu Xiangde was the youngest daughter in the family, and the youngest boy in the family died from drowning at 31 years old.

Current Generation:

Yu Xiangde was born on April 11, 1937 and married twice. She married her first husband in April 1955 but had no children, and later married her second husband and gave birth to four children, two males and two females. Sex of the children in descending order: M (1965) – F (1967) – M (1969) – F (1971). The first son died at one year old of parotitis. She had the surgical ligation at 34 years old after giving birth to her youngest daughter.

Children's Generation:

The first daughter gave birth to two children. Sex of the children in descending order: F (1986) – F (1987).

The second son married twice but did not have children of his own for his intermittent epilepsy and poor health. After divorcing his first wife, he married a woman with children and had no children with his second wife anymore.

The second daughter gave birth to two children. Sex of the children in descending order: M (1989) – M (1993). She had the surgical ligation at 22 years old after having the second son, and hanged herself in 2001 over the shame of the stealing habit of her husband.

Grandchildren's Generation:

The first daughter's first child gave birth to two children. Sex of the children in descending order: F (2004) – F (2009).

The first daughter's second child was recently engaged.

The second daughter's two boys were both unmarried.

Great-grandchildren's Generation:

Two great granddaughters. One was six years old (born in 2004) and the other was one year old (born in 2009).

Yu Xiangde's second son suffered from genetic epilepsy as her husband also suffered from intermittent epilepsy.

Household No.: 42; Interviewee: Yu Yinger; Figure A.52

Yu Yinger didn't know much about the reproductive history of her maternal grandmother and had no much engagement with her maternal relatives.

Parents' Generation:

Yu Yinger's mother gave birth to eight children, four males and four females. Six children survived, three males and three females. Sex of the children in descending order: F – M – M – F – M – F. The third son and second daughter died young. Yu Yinger was the first child in the family.

Current Generation:

Yu Yingerw was born on April 21, 1945, got married in 1961, and got pregnant with five births. She gave birth to four children and aborted one birth. Three females and one male survived. Sex of the children in descending order: F (1962) – F (1965) – M (1967) – M (spontaneously aborted) – F (1968). She had the surgical ligation at 23 years old after having the youngest daughter and now was widowed.

Children's Generation:

The first daughter gave birth to three children and two births survived. Sex of the children in descending order: M (1983) – M (1985) – F – F (1987). The first boy died at one year old, and the third birth was twin girls.

The second daughter gave birth to three children and two children survived. Sex of the children in descending order: F (1983) – M – F (1986). The boy died two months after birth. She had the surgical ligation at 21 years old after having the younger daughter.

The first son gave birth to two children. Sex of the children in descending order: M (1985) – M (1988).

The youngest daughter gave birth to two children. Sex of the children in descending order: M (1987) – M (1989). She had the surgical ligation at 21 years old after having the younger son, who died at three years old.

Grandchildren's Generation:

The first daughter's first son gave birth to one child, F (2006), and now was divorced. The child lived with his former wife.

The first daughter's first boy twin: Yu Dashuang gave birth to one child, F (2007), and the second boy twin: Yu Xiaoshuang also gave birth to one child, F (2009).

The second daughter's first daughter gave birth to one child, F (2008), and the second daughter was unmarried and worked away from home.

The first son's first child gave birth to one child, M (2009), and the second child were unmarried.

The youngest daughter's son was married but still had no children.

Great-grandchildren's Generation:

Four great-granddaughters and one great-grandson.

As for the birth order for twins, according to the Dai customs: the baby born earlier is counted as the second one while the baby born later the first one and the explanation is that as the older would give precedence to the younger, so the younger is coming out earlier!

Household No.: 44; Interviewee: Yu Hansai; Figure A.53

Yu Hansai was the first daughter of Yu Wanjiao from Household No. 15 in this village, and the information of her parent generation was the same as in Household No. 15. We introduced her family starting with Current Generation.

Current Generation:

Yu Hansai was born on June 1, 1947, and married twice in her life. In 1962, she got married with her first husband and gave birth to two children. Sex of the children in descending order: M (1963) – M (1965). In 1966, she remarried her second husband and gave birth to three children. Sex of the children in descending order: M (1968) – M (1970) – F (1973).

Children's Generation:

The children from her previous marriage now lived with their father out of this village and their birth information was unknown.

The first son from her second marriage gave birth to two children. Sex of the children in descending order: M (1988) – F (1990).

The second son from her second marriage gave birth to two children. Sex of the children in descending order: F (1990) – F (1992).

The daughter from her second marriage got married twice. She gave birth to one child with her first husband, M (2000), and one child with her second husband, F (2007).

Grandchildren's Generation:

The first son's first child (Male) was married but still had no children, and the second child (Female) gave birth to one child, M (2009).

The second son's two daughters were unmarried.

Her youngest daughter's two children were still young.

Great-grandchildren's Generation:

One great-grandson (born in 2009).

When asked about her reproductive history, Yu Hansai told us about her experience of tubal ligation surgery: "After having a daughter in 1973, I wanted to receive a tubal ligation surgery, but the hospital said that the surgery was only for a mother with at least five children. But I finally managed to have the surgery based on false proof. The reason that I got the false proof was that being the attendance officer in the village, I was very busy and had no time to take care of additional kids."

Summary

Among the 14 households surveyed, the oldest interviewee was born on March 10, 1926 (84 years old) and the youngest on April 6, 1949 (61 years old).

The reproductive statistics by the age cohort (the 5-year interval) are shown in the following Tables A.7–A.10.

Statistics of Births and Surviving Births in Surveyed Households:

The Statistics of Intergenerational Births and Surviving Births of Surveyed Households:

Statistics of the Timespans and Proportions of Births in the Surveyed Households by Generational Cohort:

The retrospective Reproductive Statistics mentioned above showed that:

1. By April 2010, 14 female interviewees born in or before 1950 (60 years old or above) in village G had given birth to 67 children, each giving birth to 4.79 children on average; 57 children had survived till the age of 15 or above, with one household having 4.07 surviving children on average. The overall survival rate of the births was 85.07%.
2. The Reproductive Statistics by the 5-year interval showed, with a declining average age of the mothers, the average number of the children in a

Table A.7 (表 1.2.2 p. 236): Reproductive Statistics of the Female Interviewees by Generation (Born in or before 1950) in Village G

Households	Age Cohort (Year)	Number of Lifetime Births (Persons)			Births Surviving till the Age of 15 or above (Persons)			Average Births/ Household	Average Surviving Births/Household
		Total Births	M	F	Total Births	M	F		
4	1946–1950	15	9	6	14	8	6	3.75	3.5
2	1941–1945	10	4	6	9	4	5	5.0	4.5
5	1936–1940	18	11	7	16	9	7	3.6	3.2
1	1931–1935	8	4	4	7	3	4	8.0	7.0
2	1926–1930	16	8	8	11	3	8	8.0	5.5
In total: 14 Households		67	36	31	57	27	30	4.79	4.07

Source: Field Survey Statistics by the Research Team.

Table A.8: Births and Surviv of the Female Interviewees (Born in or before 1950) in Village G

Female interviewees		14 Interviewees (Households)			
Age of Female Interviewee		61–84 Years Old (1926–1949)			
Number of Lifetime Births	8 Births	3	Children Surviving till the Age of 15 or above	8 Surviving Births	0
	7 Births	1		7 Surviving Births	2
	6 Births	1		6 Surviving Births	1
	5 Births	1		5 Surviving Births	3
	4 Births	4		4 Surviving Births	2
	3 Births	3		3 Surviving Births	5
	2 Births	0		2 Surviving Births	0
	1 Birth	0		1 Surviving Birth	0
	0 Birth	1		0 Birth	1

Source: Field Survey Statistics by the Research Team.

household also went down, namely, younger mothers gave birth to fewer children.

3. The interviewees had throughout their lifetime given birth to 36 boys and 31 girls, with the boys slightly outnumbering the girls, and 27 boys and 30 girls had survived till the age of 15 or above, with the survival rate of the boys and the girls standing respectively at 75.00% and 96.77%; and the survival rate of the boys was slightly lower than that of the girls.
4. The interviewees who had given birth to four children throughout their lifetime made up the largest share of the total at 28.57%, and those who had three surviving births made up the largest share of the total at 35.71%.
5. The interviewees who had given birth to four or fewer children throughout their lifetime made up 57.14%, and those who had had four or fewer surviving births made up 57.14%.
6. The interviewees who had got married for the first time at 19 years old made up 35.71% of all, and the interviewees got married for the first time in the age range from 16 to 22 years old, at 18.5 years old on average.
7. The age at last childbirth (except for one who had never given birth) was between the ages of 21 and 41, at 32.46 years old on average.

Table A.9: Intergenerational Reproductive Statistics of Surveyed Households (Interviwees Born in or before 1950) in Village G (Table A1)

Generation	Households	Number of Lifetime Births (Persons)			Births Surviving till the Age of 15 or above (Persons)			Average Average Total Births per Household/Household	Average Average Total Surviving Births per Household/Household
		Total Births	M	F	Total Births	M	F		
Parent generation	12	74	36	38	53	23	30	6.17	4.41
Current Generation	14	67	36	31	57	27	30	4.79	4.07
Children's Generation	51	118	56	62	107	48	59	2.31	2.09
Grandchildren's Generation	49	64	37	27	62	35	27	1.31	1.27
Great-grandchildren's Generation	3	3	3	0	3	3	0	1.00	1.00

Source: Field Survey Statistics by the Research Team.

Table A.10: Reproductive Statistics of the Surveyed Households by Generational Cohort (Interviewees Born in or before 1950) in Village G (Table A.2)

Generation\Decade\ Percent (%)	1940s	1950s	1960s	1970s	1980s	1990s	2000s	Percent (%)
Current Generation	6.30	15.80	55.80	20.60	1.5			100.00
Children's Generation			1.80	12.85	57.80	22.02	5.53	100.00
Grandchildren's Generation					5.97	34.33	59.70	100.00

Source: Field Survey Statistics by the Research Team.

8. The interviewees (except for three who became infertile) of childbearing age took contraceptive measures. Nine had gone through surgical ligation and one had used the IUD, accounting for 90.91% of the total.
9. Each generation tends to have few births but more surviving ones on average. The survival rate of the births by Parents' Generation, Current Generation, Children's Generation, Grandchildren's Generation and Great-grandchildren's Generation was respectively 71.62%, 85.07%, 90.68%, 96.88% and 100%.
10. The reproductive lifespan for Current Generation (except for one having never given births) extended from the 1940s to the 1980s, but most of the births were from the 1950s to the 1960s, accounting for 76.40% of all the newborns in this period.
11. The reproductive lifespan for Children's Generation extended from the 1960s to the 2000s, but most of the births were from the 1980s to the 1990s, accounting for 79.82% of all the newborns in this period.
12. The reproductive lifespan for Grandchildren's Generation extended from the 1980s to the 2000s, but most of the births were in the 2000s.

Genograms

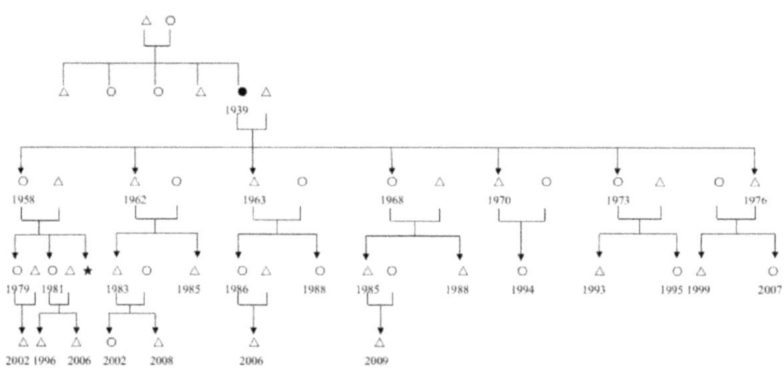

Figure A.40 **Genogram for Yu Duan's family**
▲: male interviewee; ●: female interviewee;
△: male; ○: female;
■: male who died before turning 15; ★: female who died before turning 15;
□: a pregnancy with unknown sex of the fetus;
The sex of those born within each generation are listed in descending order of age, from left to right.

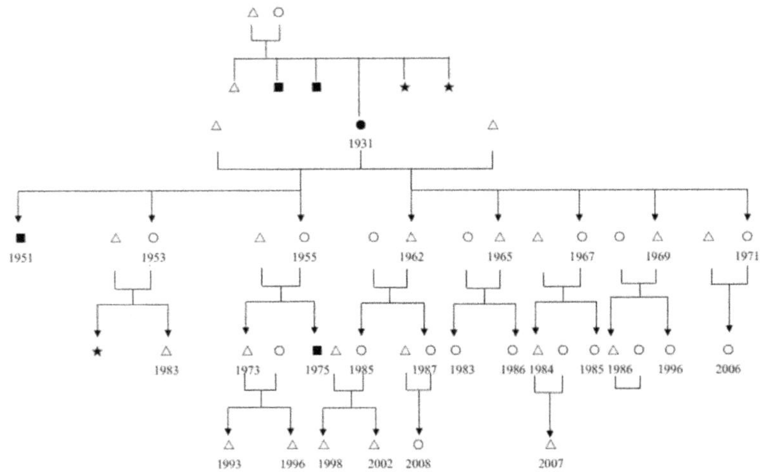

Figure A.41 **Genogram for Yu Yingjiao's family**
▲: male interviewee; ●: female interviewee;
△: male; ○: female;
■: male who died before turning 15; ★: female who died before turning 15;
□: a pregnancy with unknown sex of the fetus;
The sex of those born within each generation are listed in descending order of age, from left to right.

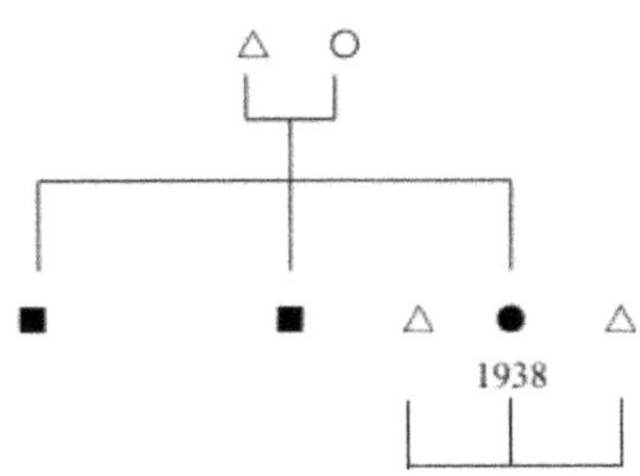

Figure A.42 **Genogram for Yu Shuo's family**
▲: male interviewee; ●: female interviewee;
△: male; ○: female;
■: male who died before turning 15; ★: female who died before turning 15;
□: a pregnancy with unknown sex of the fetus;
The sex of those born within each generation are listed in descending order of age, from left to right.

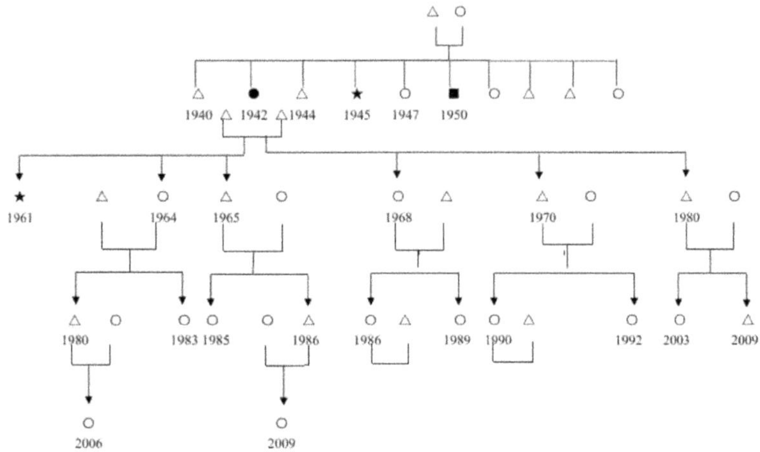

Figure A.43 **Genogram for Yi Yingkan's family**
▲: male interviewee; ●: female interviewee;
△: male; ○: female;
■: male who died before turning 15; ★: female who died before turning 15;
□: a pregnancy with unknown sex of the fetus;
The sex of those born within each generation are listed in descending order of age, from left to right.

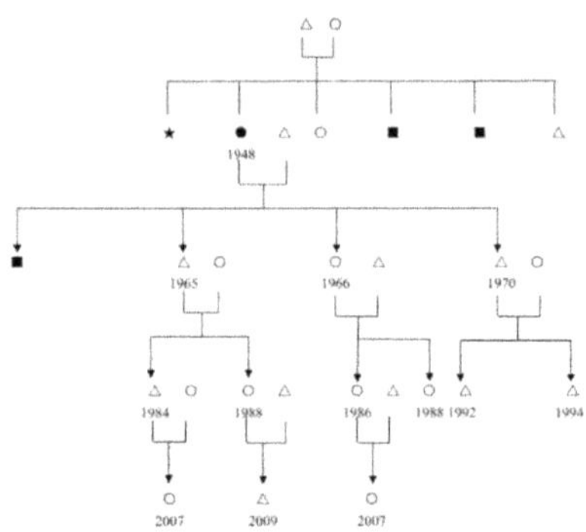

Figure A.44 **Genogram for Yu Xiangnuo's family**
▲: male interviewee; ●: female interviewee;
△: male; ○: female;
■: male who died before turning 15; ★: female who died before turning 15;
□: a pregnancy with unknown sex of the fetus;
The sex of those born within each generation are listed in descending order of age, from left to right.

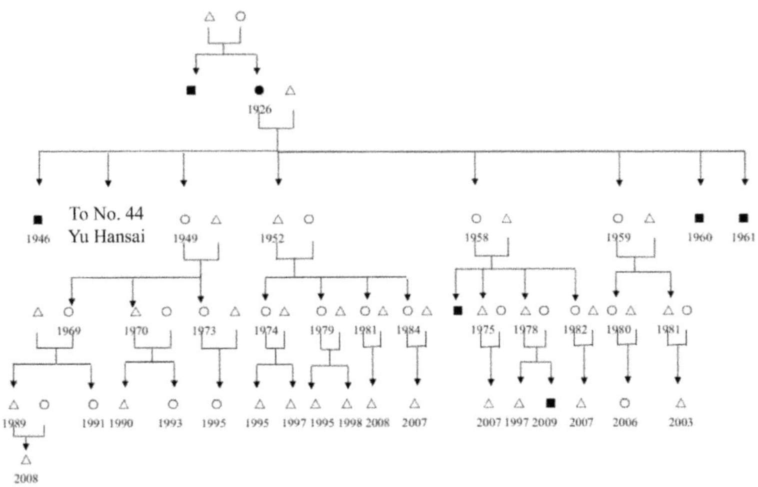

Figure A.45 **Genogram for Yu Wanjiao's family**
▲: male interviewee; ●: female interviewee;
△: male; ○: female;
■: male who died before turning 15; ★: female who died before turning 15;
□: a pregnancy with unknown sex of the fetus;

The sex of those born within each generation are listed in descending order of age, from left to right.

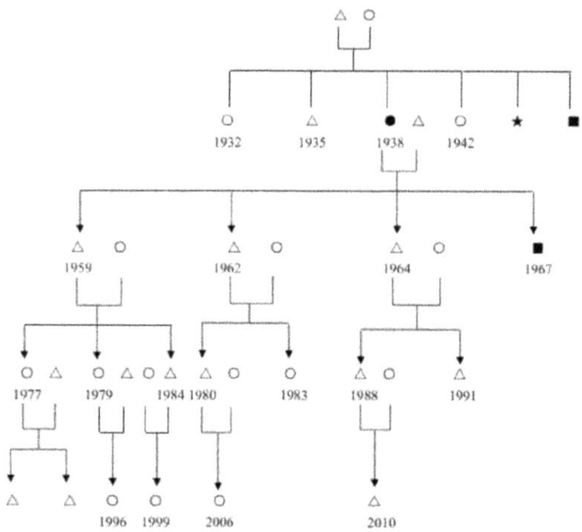

Figure A.46 **Genogram for Yu Kan's family**
▲: male interviewee; ●: female interviewee;
△: male; ○: female;
■: male who died before turning 15; ★: female who died before turning 15;
□: a pregnancy with unknown sex of the fetus;
The sex of those born within each generation are listed in descending order of age, from left to right.

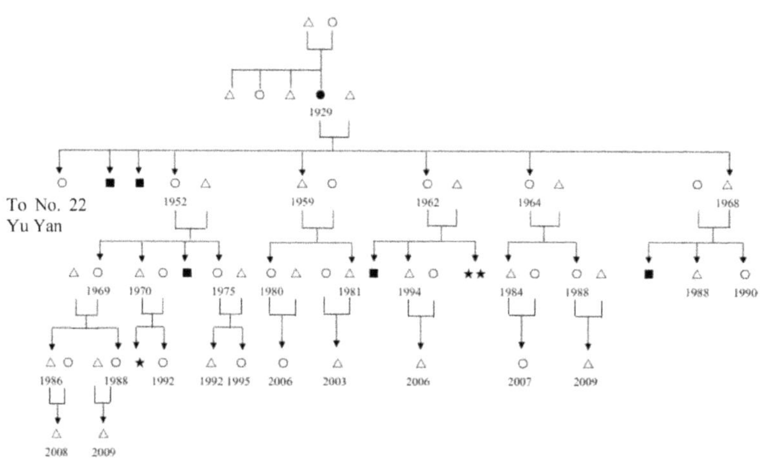

Figure A.47 **Genogram for Yu Liu's family**
▲: male interviewee; ●: female interviewee;
△: male; ○: female;
■: male who died before turning 15; ★: female who died before turning 15;
□: a pregnancy with unknown sex of the fetus;
The sex of those born within each generation are listed in descending order of age, from left to right.

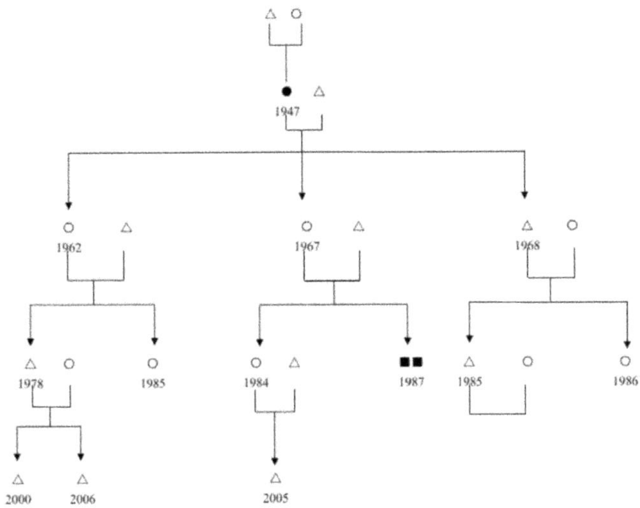

Figure A.48 **Genogram for Yu Yan's family**
▲: male interviewee; ●: female interviewee;
△: male; ○: female;
■: male who died before turning 15; ★: female who died before turning 15;
□: a pregnancy with unknown sex of the fetus;

The sex of those born within each generation are listed in descending order of age, from left to right.

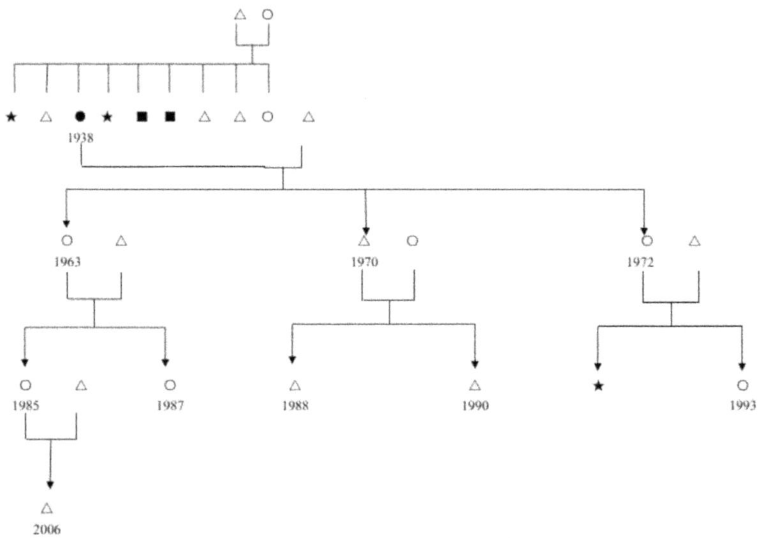

Figure A.49 **Genogram for Yu Shuai's family**
▲: male interviewee; ●: female interviewee;
△: male; ○: female;
■: male who died before turning 15; ★: female who died before turning 15;
□: a pregnancy with unknown sex of the fetus;
The sex of those born within each generation are listed in descending order of age, from left to right.

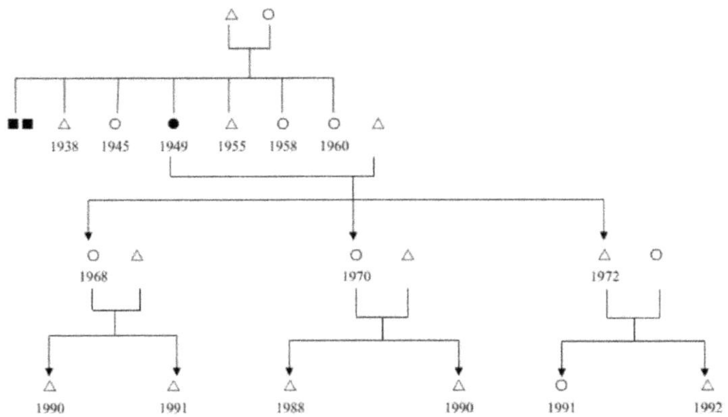

Figure A.50 **Genogram for Yu Xiang's family**
▲: male interviewee; ●: female interviewee;
△: male; ○: female;
■: male who died before turning 15; ★: female who died before turning 15;
□: a pregnancy with unknown sex of the fetus;
The sex of those born within each generation are listed in descending order of age, from left to right.

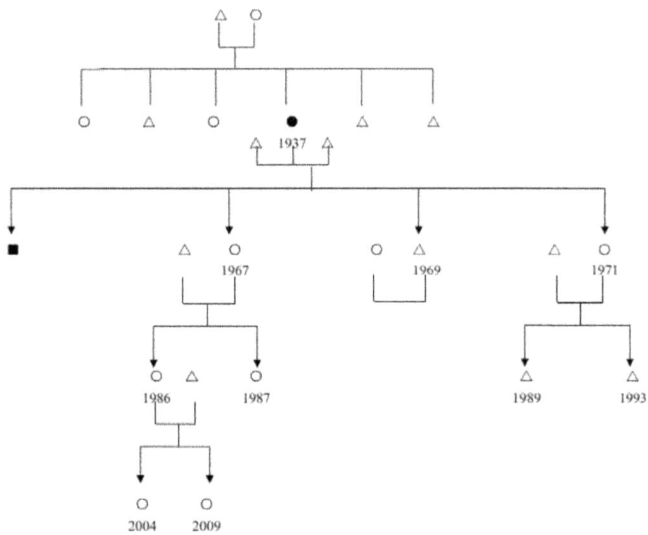

Figure A.51 **Genogram for Yu Xiangde's family**
▲: male interviewee; ●: female interviewee;
△: male; ○: female;
■: male who died before turning 15; ★: female who died before turning 15;
□: a pregnancy with unknown sex of the fetus;
The sex of those born within each generation are listed in descending order of age, from left to right.

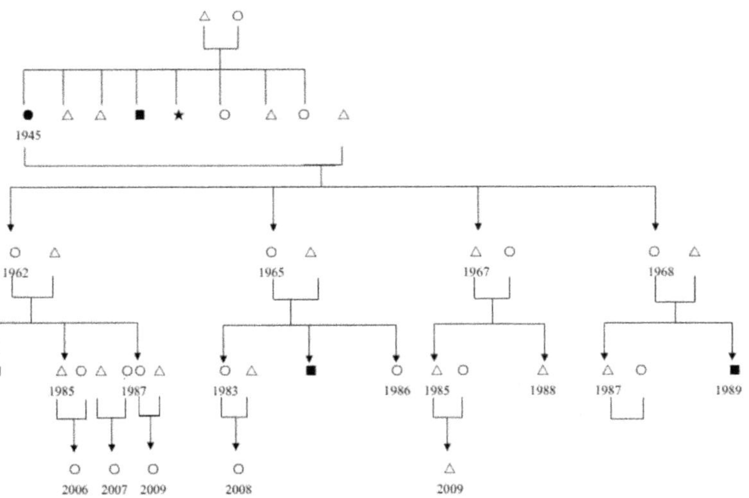

Figure A.52 **Genogram for Yu Yinger's family**
▲: male interviewee; ●: female interviewee;
△: male; ○: female;
■: male who died before turning 15; ★: female who died before turning 15;
□: a pregnancy with unknown sex of the fetus;
The sex of those born within each generation are listed in descending order of age, from left to right.

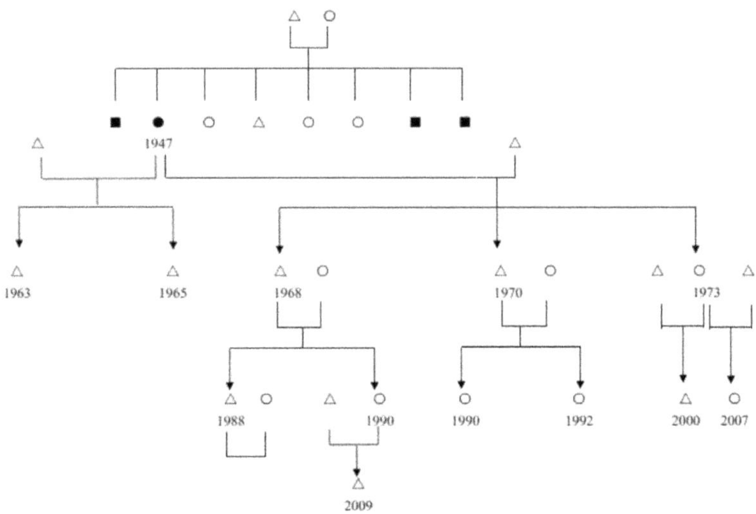

Figure A.53 **Genogram for Yu Hansai's family**
▲: male interviewee; ●: female interviewee;
△: male; ○: female;
■: male who died before turning 15; ★: female who died before turning 15;
□: a pregnancy with unknown sex of the fetus;
The sex of those born within each generation are listed in descending order of age, from left to right.

Village H in Mengpeng Township of Mengla County

General Information of the Village and Surveyed Households

In the southwest of Mengla County, Mengpeng Township is located approximately 34 kilometers away from the seat of the county government. Administered by Mengpeng Township and approximately seven kilometers away from the seat of the township government, village H was every inch an "authentic" Dai village. By October 2008, there had been 383 residents in 93 households (186 males and 197 females), and all the others (except for one Han matrilocal son-in-law in a household) were Dai.

When we surveyed in the village (in January 2009), 27 households met our survey criteria, accounting for 29.03% of the total. The basic information of the surveyed households is listed below in Table A.11:

Records of the Reproductive Histories of the Surveyed Households Are Shown in the Following Table

Household No.: 11; Interviewee: Yan Xiangyong; Figure A.54
Grandparent Generation:

Table A.11: Basic Information of the Interviewees (Born in or before 1950) in Village H

No.	Household No.	Name	Date of Birth	Number of Life-time Births	Surviving Births	Sex of children in descending order of birth
1	11	Yan Xiangyong	1941.7.6	2	2	M – F
2	13	Yi Yingjiao	1931.12.4	4	4	M – M – F – F
3	14	Yi Luo	1936.8.7	3	3	M – F – F
4	18	Yan Hanjiao	1947.7.2	3	3	M – F – M
5	21	Yu Ernan	1935.3.17	4	4	M – M – M – M
6	22	Nan La	1906.1.2	4	2	M – F – F – F
7	23	Yi Yingdi	1923.7.11	6	6	F – F – M – M – M – F
8	28	Yi Xiangshuai	1940.8.13	5	4	M – F – M – F – F
9	29	Yi Erwong	1931.4.9	4	3	F – M – F – M
10	31	Yan Honglong	1942.5.2	4	4	M – M – M – F
11	38	Yan Wenbing	1943.10.20	3	3	M – M – M
12	41	Yan Zaibao	1929.6.6	4	4	M – M – M – M
13	42	Yi Kangnan	1943.4.6	3	3	M – F – M-
14	43	Yi Jinzhang	1934.3.2	4	4	M – M – M – F
15	53	Yan Wenbang	1938.8.4	2	2	F – M
16	56	Yi Jianla	1949.11.3	3	3	F – F – F
17	57	Yi Nannen	1949.5.18	2	1	M – F

(Continued)

Table A.11: Continued

18	59	Yi Tila	1937.7.2	5	4	M – M – M – F – M
19	61	Yan Labing	1934.2.11	4	4	F – M – F – M
20	65	Yan Dila	1949.2.16	3	3	M – M – F
21	67	Yan Ruan	1936.1.3	5	5	F – M – F – F – M
22	69	Yan Ta	1944.6.4	2	2	M – F
23	74	Yan Lahong	1940.1.4	4	4	F – M – M – M
24	77	Yan Wenxing	1943.1.13	3	3	F – M – M
25	78	Yi Guangsao	1947.11.12	2	2	M – M
26	79	Yan Honghe	1944.6.9	2	2	M – F
27	81	Yi Guanghai	1950.7.3	2	2	F – F

Source: Field Survey Statistics by the Research Team.

Yan Xiangyong's maternal grandmother gave birth to six children, two males and four females. Sex of the children in descending order: F – F – F – M – F – M. Yan Xiangyong's mother was the youngest daughter in the family.

Parents' Generation:

Yan Xiangyong's mother gave birth to five children, two females and three males. Sex of the children in descending order: F – M- F (1937). M – M. Yan Xiangyong was the fifth child in the family, and his second sister was Yu Tila from Household No. 59 in this village.

Current Generation:

Yan Xiangyong was born on July 6, 1941, and her husband was born on April 8, 1943. The couple gave birth to two children. Sex of the children in descending order: M (1963) – F (1964).

Children's Generation:

The first son gave birth to two children. Sex of the children in descending order: F (1987) – M (1990).

The first daughter gave birth to two children. Sex of the children in descending order: M (1985) – F (1987).

Grandchildren's Generation:

The first son's first child gave birth to one child (male twins, 2008).

Great-grandchildren's Generation:

Two great-grandchildren, all males.

Household No.: 13; Interviewee: Yi Yingjiao; Figure A.55

Parents' Generation:

Yi Yingjiao's mother gave birth to four children. Sex of the children in descending order: F – M – M – F. She was the first daughter in the family and the youngest daughter was Yi Kangnan from Household No. 42 in this village.

Current Generation:

Yi Yingjiao was born on December 4, 1931, and her husband was born on May 9, 1930. The couple gave birth to four children. Sex of the children in descending order: M – M – F – F.

Children's Generation:

The first son gave birth to two children. Sex of the children in descending order: M – F.

The second son gave birth to one child, F.

The first daughter gave birth to three children. Sex of the children in descending order: M – M – M.

The second daughter gave birth to two children. Sex of the children in descending order: F – M.

Grandchildren's Generation:

The first son's first child gave birth to one child, M.

Great-grandchildren's Generation:

One great-grandchild, M.

Household No.: 14; Interviewee: Yi Luo; Figure A.56

Parents' Generation:

Yi Luo's mother gave only one birth. Yi Luo was the only daughter in the family and a native villager.

Current Generation:

Yi Luo was born on December 4, 1931 and gave birth to three children. Sex of the children in descending order: M – F – F.

Children's Generation:

The first son married twice but had no children all his life. His first wife had no children and his second wife had two children (one boy and one girl) with her former husband.

The first daughter gave birth to three children. Sex of the children in descending order: F – M – M.

The second daughter gave birth to two children. Sex of the children in descending order: M – F.

Grandchildren's Generation:

The first daughter's first child gave birth to two children. Sex of the children in descending order: M – M.

All the others were unmarried.

Great-grandchildren's Generation:

Two great-grandchildren, all males.

Household No.: 18; Interviewee: Yan Hanjiao; Figure A.57

Parents' Generation:

Yan Hanjiao's mother gave birth to six children. Sex of the children in descending order: M – M – M – F – F – F.

Yan Hanjiao was the first son in the family. His wife was the first daughter in the family and had five siblings. Sex of the children in descending order: F – F – F – M – M – M.

Current Generation:

Yan Hanjiao was born on July 2, 1947 and his wife was born on January 13, 1950. The couple gave birth to three children. Sex of the children in descending order: M (1969) – F – M (1975).

Children's Generation:

The first son gave birth to two children. Sex of the children in descending order: M – F.

The first daughter gave birth to two children. Sex of the children in descending order: M – M.

The second son gave birth to two children. Sex of the children in descending order: M – M.

Grandchildren's Generation:

Six grandchildren, five males and one female.

Household No.: 21; Interviewee: Yu Ernan; Figure A.58

Current Generation:

Yu Ernan was born on March 17, 1935, and gave birth to four children, all males. The first son died.

Children's Generation:

The first son gave birth to two children. Sex of the children in descending order: F – F.

The second son gave birth to two children. Sex of the children in descending order: M – F.

The third son gave birth to two children. Sex of the children in descending order: F – F.

The fourth son gave birth to two children. Sex of the children in descending order: M – M.

Grandchildren's Generation:

The first son's first child gave birth to one child, F.

The first son's second child gave birth to one child (fraternal twins). Sex of the children in descending order: M – F.

The second son's first child gave birth to one child, F.

The second son's second child were unmarried.

The third son's first child was married and pregnant.

The third son's second child and the fourth child's two boys all were unmarried.

Great-grandchildren's Generation:

Four great-grandchildren, one male and three females.

Household No.: 22; Interviewee: Nan La; Figure A.59

Current Generation:

Nan La was born on January 2, 1906 and gave birth to four children, one male and three females. Sex of the children in descending order: M – F – F – F and two births survived. The first son and second daughter died in infancy.

Children's Generation:

The first daughter gave birth to two children. Sex of the children in descending order: M – F.

The third daughter was the first daughter-in-law of Yu Ernan from Household No. 21 and gave birth to two children. Sex of the children in descending order: F – F.

Grandchildren's Generation:

The first daughter's first child gave birth to one child, F.

The third daughter's second child gave birth to one child, M.

The first daughter's second child (girl) and third daughter's first child (boy) were unmarried.

Great-grandchildren's Generation:

Two great-grandchildren, one male and one female.

Household No.: 23; Interviewee: Yi Yingdi; Figure A.60

Current Generation:

Yi Yingdi was born on July 11, 1923 and gave birth to six children. Sex of the children in descending order: F – F (1945) – M – M – M- F (1952).

Children's Generation:

The first daughter was married to Menghun village and her reproductive history was unknown.

The second daughter Yi Kanghan was the wife of Yan Honglong from Household No. 31 in this village, and gave birth to four children. Sex of the children in descending order: M – M – M – F.

The first son lived (as a matrilocal son-in-law) with his wife in Manjingman village and gave birth to two children. Sex of the children in descending order: M – F.

The reproductive history of the other children was unknown.

Grandchildren's Generation:

The second daughter's first child married the second daughter of Yan Xiangyong from Household No. 11 in this village and gave birth to two children. Sex of the children in descending order: M – F.

The second daughter's second child gave birth to two children. Sex of the children in descending order: F – F.

The second daughter's third child gave birth to two children. Sex of the children in descending order: F – F.

The second daughter's fourth child gave birth to two children. Sex of the children in descending order: M – F.

The first son's first child gave birth to two children. Sex of the children in descending order: F – M.

The first son's second child gave birth to two children. Sex of the children in descending order: M – F.

Great-grandchildren's Generation:

12 great-grandchildren, four males and eight females.

Household No.: 28; Interviewee: Yi Xiangshuai; Figure A.61

Parents' Generation:

Yi Xiangshuai's mother gave birth to four children. Sex of the children in descending order: F – F – M – F. Yi Xiangshuai was the youngest daughter in the family and her husband was the second of five siblings in his family. Sex of the children in descending order: M – F – M – M – F.

Current Generation:

Yi Xiangshuai was born on August 13, 1940 and her husband on June 9, 1933. The couple gave birth to five children. Sex of the children in descending order: M (1960) – F – M – F – F (1973). Four children survived, second son died in infancy. Yi Xiangshuai had the surgical ligation in 1975.

Children's Generation:

The first son gave birth to two children. Sex of the children in descending order: F (1983) – M (1986). One birth survived. The son died one month after his birth. The daughter-in-law had the surgical ligation after having the second son.

The first daughter gave birth to one child, M.

The second daughter gave birth to one child, F.

The third daughter gave birth to one child, F.

Grandchildren's Generation:

The first son's first child gave birth to one child, F (2004), and had the surgical ligation one month after giving birth.

The second daughter's child got married in 2007 and still had no children.

Great-grandchildren's Generation:

One great-grandchild, F.

Household No.: 29; Interviewee: Yi Erweng; Figure A.62

Current Generation:

Yi Erweng was born on April 9, 1931 and gave birth to four children, two males and two females. Sex of the children in descending order: F – M – F – M. Three children survived. The first daughter died young.

Children's Generation:

The first son gave birth to two children. Sex of the children in descending order: M – F.

The second daughter gave birth to two children. Sex of the children in descending order: M – F.

The youngest son gave birth to two children. Sex of the children in descending order: F – M.

Grandchildren's Generation:

The first son's first child gave birth to one child, M.

The first son's second child gave birth to one child, F.

The second daughter's first child gave birth to one child, M.

The second daughter's second child gave birth to one child, F.

The youngest son's children all were unmarried.

Great-grandchildren's Generation:

Four great-grandchildren, two males and two females.

Household No.: 31; Interviewee: Yan Honglong;

Parents' Generation:

Yan Honglong's mother gave birth to four children. Sex of the children in descending order: M – M – M – M. Yan Honglong was the youngest son in the family and his second brother was Yan Ruan from Household No. 67 in this village.

Current Generation:

Yan Honglong was born on May 4, 1942 and his wife Yu Kanghan was the second daughter of Yu Yingdi from Household No. 23 in this village. The reproductive history of the couple was introduced above.

Household No.: 38; Interviewee: Yan Wenbing; Figure A.63

Parents' Generation:

Yan Wenbing's mother gave birth to seven children, five males and two females. Sex of the children in descending order: M – M – M – F – M – M – F. Yan Wenbing was the first son in the family.

Current Generation:

Yan Wenbing was born on October 20, 1943 and his wife gave birth to three children, all males.

Children's Generation:

The first son gave birth to two children. Sex of the children in descending order: F – M.

The second son gave birth to two children. Sex of the children in descending order: F – F.

The third son gave birth to two children. Sex of the children in descending order: F – F.

Grandchildren's Generation:

The first son's first child gave birth to one child, M.

Great-grandchildren's Generation:

One great-grandchild, M.

Household No.: 41; Interviewee: Yan Zaibao; Figure A.64

Current Generation:

Yan Zaibao was born on June 6, 1929 and his wife Yu Liu on February 9, 1934. The couple gave birth to four children, all males.

Children's Generation:

The first son gave birth to two children. Sex of the children in descending order: M – F.

The second son gave birth to three children, all males.

The third son's wife was the second daughter of Yu Erweng from Household No. 29 in this village and gave birth to two children. Sex of the children in descending order: M – F.

The youngest son gave birth to two children, both females.

Grandchildren's Generation:

The first son's first child gave birth to two children, both females.

The first son's second child gave birth to two children, both females.

The second son's first child gave birth to one child, F.

The reproductive history of the second son's other two sons was unknown.

The third son's first child gave birth to one child, M.

The third son's second child gave birth to one child, F.

The reproductive history of the fourth son's two children was unknown.

Great-grandchildren's Generation:

Seven great-grandchildren, one male and six females.

Household No.: 42; Interviewee: Yi Kangnan; Figure A.65

Parents' Generation:

Yi Kangnan's mother gave birth to four children. Sex of the children in descending order: F – M – M – F. Yi Kangnan was the youngest daughter in the family and her elder sister was Yi Yingjiao from Household No. 13 in this village.

Current Generation:

Yi Kangnan was born on April 6, 1943 and gave birth to three children. Sex of the children in descending order: M – F – M.

Children's Generation:

The first son gave birth to two children, both females.

The first daughter gave birth to two children, both females.

The second son gave birth to two children. Sex of the children in descending order: M – F.

Grandchildren's Generation:

The reproductive history of the grandchildren was unknown.

Household No.: 43; Interviewee: Yi Jinzhang; Figure A.66

Current Generation:

Yi Jinzhang was born on March 2, 1934 and gave birth to four children. Sex of the children in descending order: M – M – M – F.

Children's Generation:

The first son gave birth to two children, both males.

The second son gave birth to two children. Sex of the children in descending order: M – F.

The third son gave birth to two children, both males.

The youngest daughter gave birth to two children, both females.

Grandchildren's Generation:

The first son's first child gave birth to two children, both females.

The first son's second child gave birth to one child, F.

The second son's first child gave birth to one child, M.

The second son's second child gave birth to one child, F.

Great-grandchildren's Generation:

Five great-grandchildren, one male and four females.

Household No.: 53; Interviewee: Yan Wenbang; Figure A.67

Parents' Generation:

Yan Wenbang's mother gave birth to four children, all males. Yan Wenbang was the third child in the family, his second elder brother (the second son in the family) was Yan Labing from Household No. 61 in this village, and his younger brother (the fourth son in the family) was Yan Lahong from Household No. 74 in this village.

Current Generation:

Yan Wenbang was born on August 4, 1938 and married twice. He gave birth to three children from the first marriage. Sex of the children in descending order: F – M – F. The first daughter died young and the other two children lived with his former wife. His second wife Yu Jin was born on

January 17, 1949 and the only child in her family. The couple gave birth to two children. Sex of the children in descending order: F – M.

Children's Generation:

The first daughter gave birth to two children, both males.

The first son gave birth to two children, both males.

Grandchildren's Generation:

The reproductive history of grandchildren was unknown.

Household No.: 56; Interviewee: Yi Jianla; Figure A.68

Parents' Generation:

Yi Jianla's mother gave birth to three children. Sex of the children in descending order: M – F – M. Her husband had three siblings. Sex of the children in descending order: M – M – F – M. Her husband was the second son in the family and his youngest brother died in infancy.

Current Generation:

Yi Jianla was born on November 3, 1949 and gave birth to three children, all females.

Children's Generation:

The first daughter gave birth to two children. Sex of the children in descending order: M – F.

The second daughter were unmarried.

The third daughter gave birth to one child, F.

Grandchildren's Generation:

The reproductive history of grandchildren was unknown.

Household No.: 57; Interviewee: Yi Nannen; Figure A.69

Parents' Generation:

Yi Nannen's mother gave birth to four children. Sex of the children in descending order: F – F – M – M. She was the first daughter in her family.

Current Generation:

Yi Nannen was born on May 18, 1949 and gave birth to two children. Sex of the children in descending order: M – F. One birth survived, M. The daughter died in infancy.

Children's Generation:

The son gave birth to two children. Sex of the children in descending order: M – F.

Grandchildren's Generation:

The reproductive history of grandchildren was unknown.

Household No.: 59; Interviewee: Yi Tila; Figure A.70

Yi Tila was the second elder sister of Yan Xiangyong from Household No. 11 in this village. The reproductive history of her mother is introduced above. Yi Tila's husband had four siblings. Sex of the children in descending order: M – F – F – M – M. Her husband was the second son in the family.

Current Generation:

Yi Tila was born on July 2, 1937 and gave birth to five children. Sex of the children in descending order: M – M – M – F – M. Four children survived. The youngest boy died young.

Children's Generation:

The first son gave birth to one child, F.

The second son gave birth to two children, both females.

The third son gave birth to two children, both males.

The youngest daughter gave birth to two children, both males.

Grandchildren's Generation:

The first son's daughter gave birth to one child, M.

The second son's first child gave birth to one child, F.

The second son's second child gave birth to one child, M.

All the other grandchildren were unmarried.

Household No.: 61; Interviewee: Yan Labing; Figure A.71

Yan Labing was the second elder brother of Yan Wenbang from Household No. 53 in this village, and the reproductive history of his mother is introduced above.

Current Generation:

Yan Labing was born on February 11, 1934 and gave birth to four children. Sex of the children in descending order: F – M – F – M.

Children's Generation:

The first daughter gave birth to one child, F.

The first son gave birth to one child, F.

The third daughter was the eldest daughter-in-law of Yu Kangnan from Household No. 42 in this village and gave birth to two children, both females.

The youngest son gave birth to two children. Sex of the children in descending order: M – F.

Grandchildren's Generation:

The first daughter's daughter gave birth to one child, F.

The first son's daughter gave birth to one child, M.

Household No.: 65; Interviewee: Yan Dila; Figure A.72

Parents' Generation:

Yan Dila's mother gave birth to three children. Sex of the children in descending order: M – F – M. He was the first son in the family.

Current Generation:

Yan Dila was born on February 16, 1949 and gave birth to three children. Sex of the children in descending order: M – M – F.

Children's Generation:

The first son gave birth to two children, both males.

The second son gave birth to one child, F.

The youngest daughter gave birth to two children. Sex of the children in descending order: F – M.

Household No.: 67; Interviewee: Yan Ruan; Figure A.73

Yan Ruan was the second elder brother of Yan Honglong from Household No. 31 in this village and the reproductive history of his mother is introduced above.

Current Generation:

Yan Ruan was born on January 3, 1936 and gave birth to five children. Sex of the children in descending order: F – M – F – F – M.

Children's Generation:

The first daughter gave birth to two children, both females. The second daughter died young.

The first son gave birth to two children. Sex of the children in descending order: F – M.

The second daughter gave birth to two children. Sex of the children in descending order: M – F.

The third daughter gave birth to two children. Sex of the children in descending order: F – M.

The youngest son gave birth to two children, both females.

Grandchildren's Generation:

The first daughter's child was married outside this village and her reproductive history was unknown.

The first son's first child gave birth to two children. Sex of the children in descending order: M – F.

The first son's second child gave birth to one child, M.

The second daughter's first child gave birth to one child, F.

The second daughter's second child gave birth to one child, F.

The third daughter's first child gave birth to one child, M.

All the other grandchildren were unmarried.

Great-grandchildren's Generation:

Four great-grandchildren, one male and three females.

Household No.: 69; Interviewee: Yan Ta; Figure A.74

Parents' Generation:

Yan Ta's mother gave birth to three children. Sex of the children in descending order: F – M – F. His wife had five siblings. Sex of the children in descending order: F – F – F – F – M – F. She was the third daughter in the family and her younger brother died in infancy.

Current Generation:

Yan Ta was born on June 4, 1944 and gave birth to two children. Sex of the children in descending order: M – F.

Children's Generation:

The son gave birth to two children. Sex of the children in descending order: M – M.

The daughter gave birth to two children, both females.

Household No.: 74; Interviewee: Yan Lahong; Figure A.75

Yan Lahong was the younger brother of Yan Wenbang from Household No. 53 in this village and the reproductive history of his mother is introduced above.

Current Generation:

Yan Lahong was born on January 4, 1940 and gave birth to four children. Sex of the children in descending order: F – M – M – M.

Children's Generation:

The first daughter gave birth to two children, both males.

The first son gave birth to two children, both males.

The second son gave birth to two children, both females.

The youngest son gave birth to one child, M.

Grandchildren's Generation:

The first daughter's first child gave birth to one child, F.

The first daughter's second child gave birth to one child, F.

All the other grandchildren were unmarried.

Great-grandchildren's Generation:

Two great-grandchildren, both girls.

Household No.: 77; Interviewee: Yan Wenxing; Figure A.76

Parents' Generation:

Yan Wenxing's mother gave birth to nine children. Sex of the children in descending order: M – F – M – F – F – M – M – F – M. Seven children survived. The first son and second daughter died in infancy. Yan Wenxing was the fourth son in the family. His wife was the first daughter in the family and had two siblings. Sex of the children in descending order: F – F – M.

Current Generation:

Yan Wenxing was born on January 13, 1943 and gave birth to three children. Sex of the children in descending order: F – M – M.

Children's Generation:

The first daughter gave birth to two children, both males.

The first son gave birth to two children, both females.

The youngest son married twice. He gave birth to one child from the first marriage, M, and also one birth from the second marriage, M.

The reproductive history of grandchildren was unknown.

Household No.: 78; Interviewee: Yi Guangsao; Figure A.77

Parents' Generation:

Yi Guangsao's mother gave birth to three children. Sex of the children in descending order: F – F – M. Yi Guangsao was the first daughter in the family.

Current Generation:

Yi Guangsao was born on November 12, 1947 and her husband Yanwen Jinle was born on February 3, 1949. The couple gave birth to two children, both males.

Children's Generation:

The first son gave birth to one child, M.

The second son gave birth to one child, F.

Household No.: 79; Interviewee: Yan Honghe; Figure A.78

Parents' Generation:

Yan Honghe's mother gave birth to four children. Sex of the children in descending order: M – M – F – M. Yan Honghe was the first son in the family.

Current Generation:

Yan Honghe was born on June 9, 1944 and his wife Yu Ying was born on February 3, 1949. The couple gave birth to two children. Sex of the children in descending order: M – F.

Children's Generation:

The son married twice. He gave birth to one child from the first marriage, M, and also one birth from the second marriage, M.

The daughter gave birth to two children. Sex of the children in descending order: M – F.

Household No.: 81; Interviewee: Yi Guanghai; Figure A.79

Parents' Generation:

Yi Guanghai's mother gave birth to five children. Sex of the children in descending order: M – F – M – M – F. Yi Guanghai was the second daughter in her family.

Current Generation:

Yi Guanghai was born on July 3, 1950 and gave birth to two children, both females.

Children's Generation:

The first daughter gave birth to two children, both females.

The second daughter gave birth to two children. Sex of the children in descending order: M – F.

Summary

Among the interviewees in the village, the oldest was born on January 2, 1906 (Nan La, 103 years old), and the youngest on July 3, 1950 (Yi Guanghai, 59 years old). The reproductive statistics by the age cohort (the 5-year interval) are shown in the following Tables A.12–A14.

Statistics of Births and Surviving Births in Surveyed Households by Generational Cohort:

Statistics of Births and Surviving Births in Surveyed Households by Generational Cohort:

The retrospective Reproductive Statistics mentioned above showed that:

1. By 2009 January, 27 interviewees born in or before 1950 (59 years old or above) in village H had given birth to 95 children, each giving birth to 3.52 children on average, and 88 children had survived till the age of 15 or above, with one household having 3.26 surviving children on average. The overall survival rate of the births was 92.63%.
2. The interviewees had throughout their lifetime given birth to 55 boys and 40 girls, with the boys slightly outnumbering the girls, and 52 boys and 36 girls had survived till the age of 15 or above, with the survival rate of the boys and the girls standing respectively at 94.55% and 90.00%; and the survival rate of the boys was slightly higher than that of the girls.
3. The interviewees had their births in the 2–6 range throughout their lifetime, with an interviewee having 3.51 births on average, and had surviving births in the 1–6 range;
4. The interviewees who had given birth to four children throughout their lifetime made up the largest share of the total at 33.33%, and those who had had four surviving birth made up the largest share of the total at 33.33%.

Table A.12: Reproductive Statistics of the Interviewees (Born in or before 1950) in Village H

Households	Age Cohort	Number of Lifetime Births (Persons)			Births Surviving till the Age of 15 or above (Persons)			Average Births/Household	Average Surviving Births/Household
		Total Births	M	F	Total Births	M	F		
6	1946–1950	15	7	8	14	7	7	2.5	2.33
7	1941–1945	19	13	6	19	13	6	2.71	2.71
6	1936–1940	24	13	11	22	11	11	4.00	3.67
5	1931–1935	20	13	7	19	13	6	4.00	3.80
1	1926–1930	4	4	0	4	4	0	4.00	4.00
1	1921–1925	6	3	3	6	3	3	6.00	6.00
0	1916–1920	——	——	——	——	——	——	——	——
	1911–1915	——	——	——	——	——	——	——	——
1	1906–1910	4	1	3	2	0	2	4	2
In total: 27 Households		**92**	**54**	**38**	**86**	**51**	**35**	**3.41**	**3.19**

Source: Field Survey Statistics by the Research Team.

Table A.13: Lifetime and Surviving Births of the Interviewees (Born in or before 1950) in Village H

Interviewees			27 Interviewees (Households)		
Age of Interviewee			50–103 Years Old		
Number of Lifetime Births	6 Births	1	Births Surviving till the Age of 15 or above (Persons)	6 Surviving Births	1
	5 Births	3		5 Surviving Births	1
	4 Births	9		4 Surviving Births	9
	3 Births	7		3 Surviving Births	8
	2 Births	7		2 Surviving Births	7
	1 Birth	0		1 Surviving Birth	1

Source: Field Survey Statistics by the Research Team.

5. The interviewees who had given birth to five or fewer children and four or fewer children respectively made up 96.30% and 85.19% of all, and those who had had five or fewer surviving births and four or fewer surviving births respectively made up 83.45% and 72.66% of all;
6. Each generation tends to have few births but more surviving ones on average. The survival rate of the births by Parents' Generation, Current Generation, Children's Generation and Grandchildren's Generation was respectively 97.26%, 92.63%, 98.51% and 100.00%.

Table A.14: Reproductive Statistics of Surveyed Households by Generational Cohort (Interviewees Born in or before 1950) in Village H

Generation	Households	Number of Lifetime Births (Persons)			Births Surviving till the Age of 15 or above (Persons)			Average Total Births per Household	Average Total Surviving Births per Household
		Total Births	M	F	Total Births	M	F		
Parents' Generation	17	73	43	30	71	42	29	4.29	4.18
Current Generation	27	95	55	40	88	52	36	3.52	3.26
Children's Generation	71	134	67	67	132	66	66	1.89	1.86
Grandchildren's Generation	41	54	22	32	54	22	32	1.32	1.32

Source: Field Survey Statistics by the Research Team.

Genograms

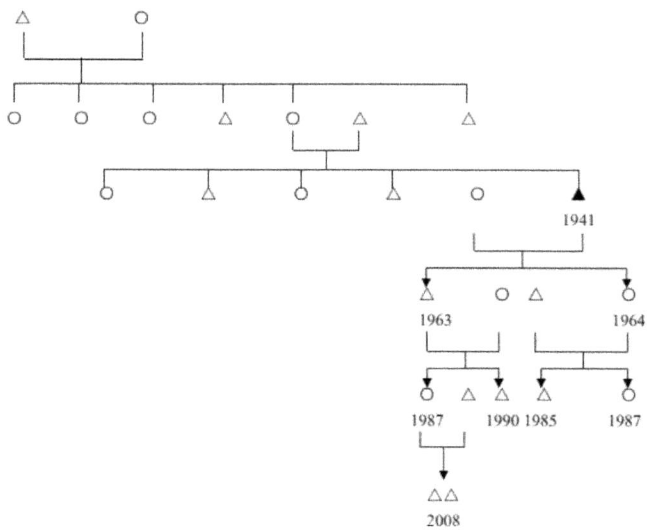

Figure A.54 Genogram for Yan Xiangyong's family
▲: male interviewee; ●: female interviewee;
△: male; ○: female;
■: male who died before turning 15; ★: female who died before turning 15;
□: a pregnancy with unknown sex of the fetus;

The sex of those born within each generation are listed in descending order of age, from left to right.

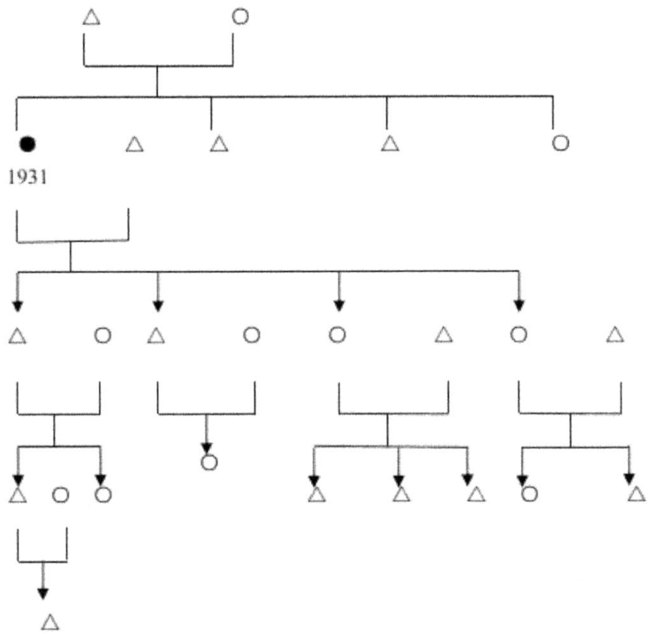

Figure A.55 **Genogram for Yi Yingjiao's family**
▲: male interviewee; ●: female interviewee;
△: male; ○: female;
■: male who died before turning 15; ★: female who died before turning 15;
□: a pregnancy with unknown sex of the fetus;
The sex of those born within each generation are listed in descending order of age, from left to right.

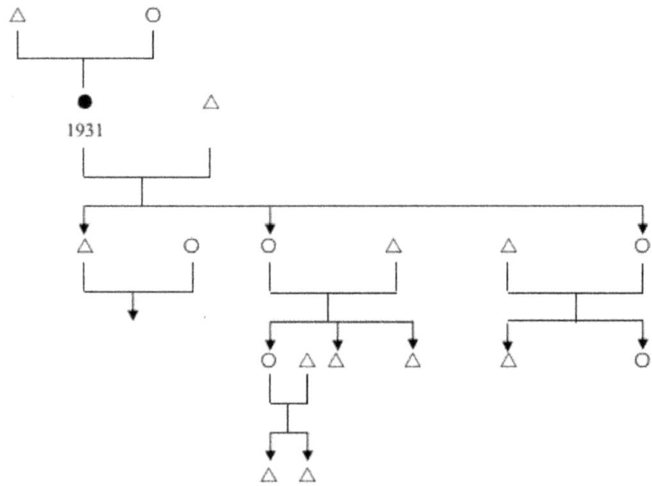

Figure A.56 **Genogram for Yi Luo's family**
▲: male interviewee; ●: female interviewee;
△: male; ○: female;
■: male who died before turning 15; ★: female who died before turning 15;
□: a pregnancy with unknown sex of the fetus;
The sex of those born within each generation are listed in descending order of age, from left to right.

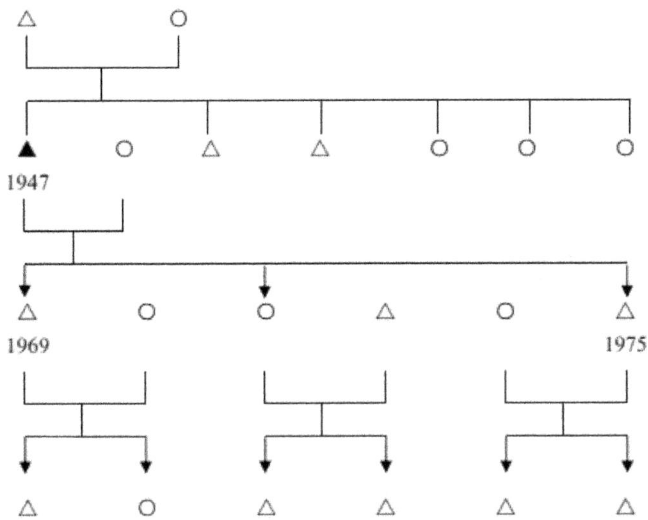

Figure A.57 **Genogram for Yan Hanjiao's family**
▲: male interviewee; ●: female interviewee;
△: male; ○: female;
■: male who died before turning 15; ★: female who died before turning 15;
□: a pregnancy with unknown sex of the fetus;

The sex of those born within each generation are listed in descending order of age, from left to right.

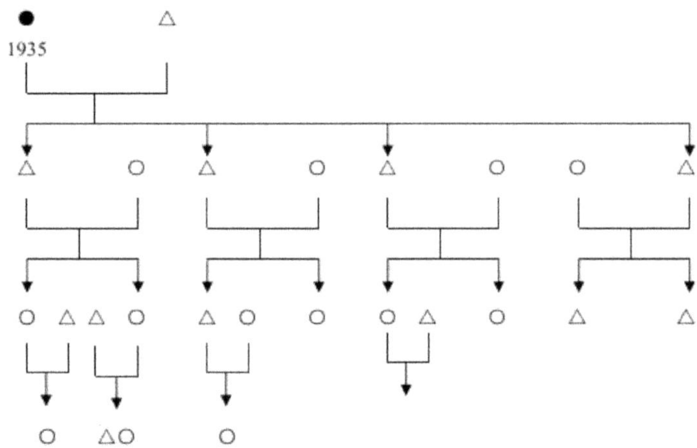

Figure A.58 **Genogram for Yu Ernan's family**
▲: male interviewee; ●: female interviewee;
△: male; ○: female;
■: male who died before turning 15; ★: female who died before turning 15;
□: a pregnancy with unknown sex of the fetus;

The sex of those born within each generation are listed in descending order of age, from left to right.

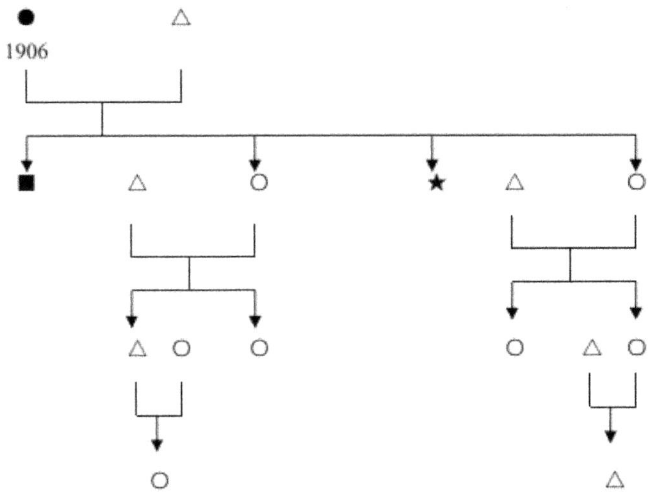

Figure A.59 **Genogram for Nan La's family**
▲: male interviewee; ●: female interviewee;
△: male; ○: female;
■: male who died before turning 15; ★: female who died before turning 15;
□: a pregnancy with unknown sex of the fetus;

The sex of those born within each generation are listed in descending order of age, from left to right.

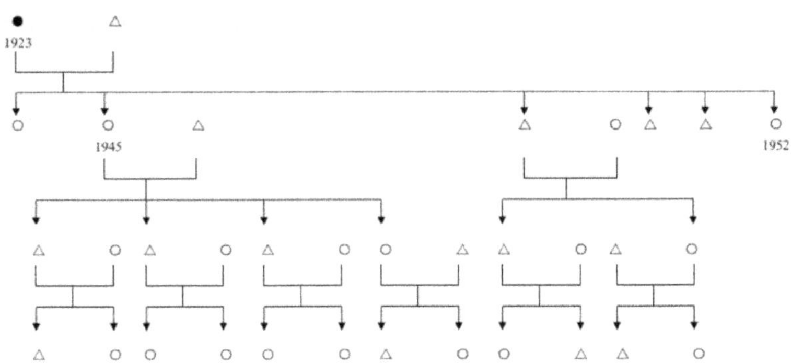

Figure A.60 **Genogram for Yi Yingde's family**
▲: male interviewee; ●: female interviewee;
△: male; ○: female;
■: male who died before turning 15; ★: female who died before turning 15;
□: a pregnancy with unknown sex of the fetus;

The sex of those born within each generation are listed in descending order of age, from left to right.

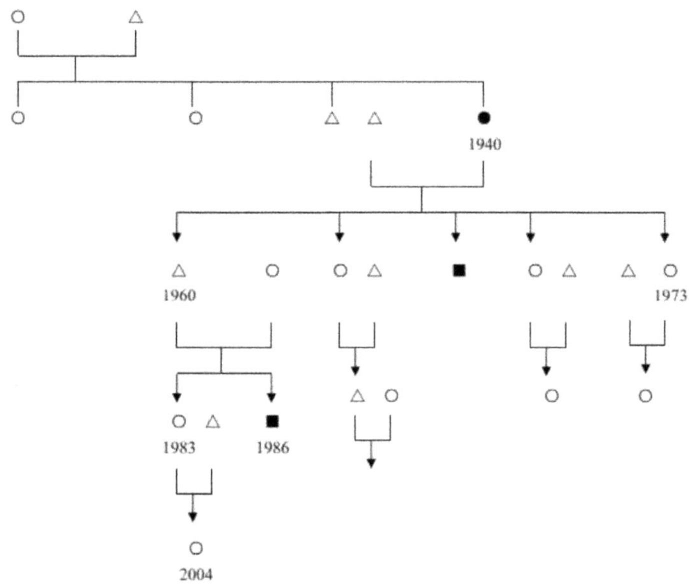

Figure A.61 **Genogram for Yi Xiangshuai's family**
▲: male interviewee; ●: female interviewee;
△: male; ○: female;
■: male who died before turning 15; ★: female who died before turning 15;
□: a pregnancy with unknown sex of the fetus;
The sex of those born within each generation are listed in descending order of age, from left to right.

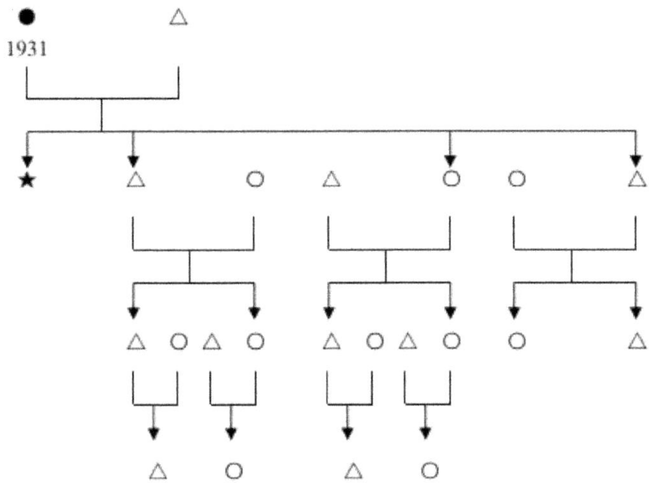

Figure A.62 **Genogram for Yi Erweng's family**

▲: male interviewee; ●: female interviewee;

△: male; ○: female;

■: male who died before turning 15; ★: female who died before turning 15;

□: a pregnancy with unknown sex of the fetus;

The sex of those born within each generation are listed in descending order of age, from left to right.

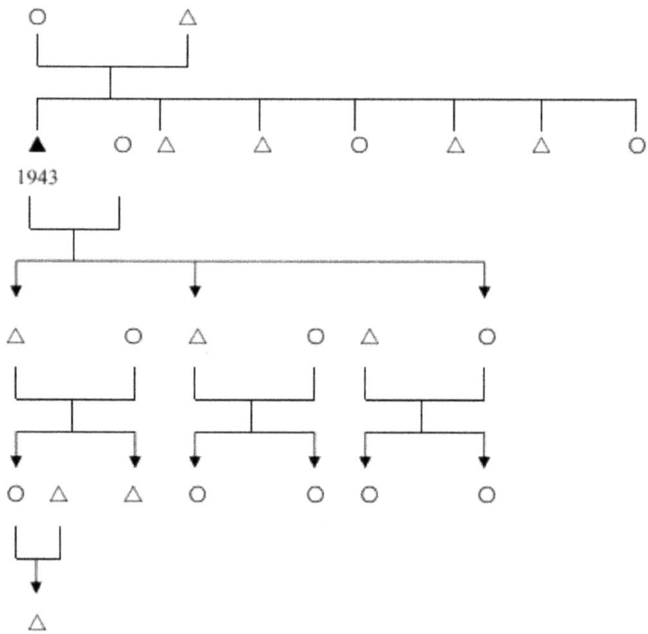

Figure A.63 **Genogram for Yan Wenbing's family**
▲: male interviewee; ●: female interviewee;
△: male; ○: female;
■: male who died before turning 15; ★: female who died before turning 15;
□: a pregnancy with unknown sex of the fetus;
The sex of those born within each generation are listed in descending order of age, from left to right.

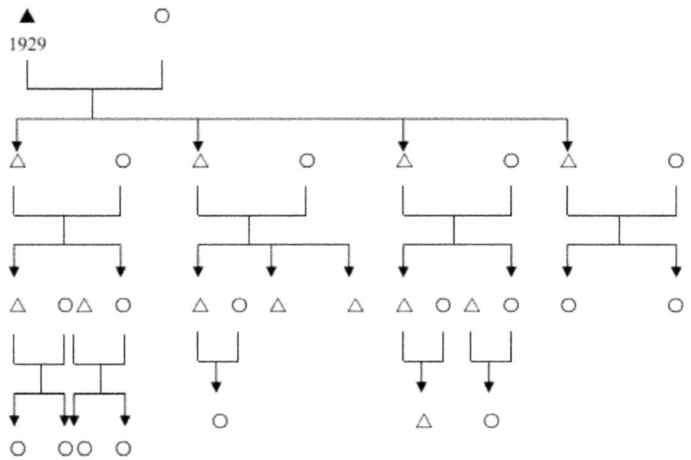

Figure A.64 **Genogram for Yan Zaibao's family**
▲: male interviewee; ●: female interviewee;
△: male; ○: female;
■: male who died before turning 15; ★: female who died before turning 15;
□: a pregnancy with unknown sex of the fetus;
The sex of those born within each generation are listed in descending order of age, from left to right.

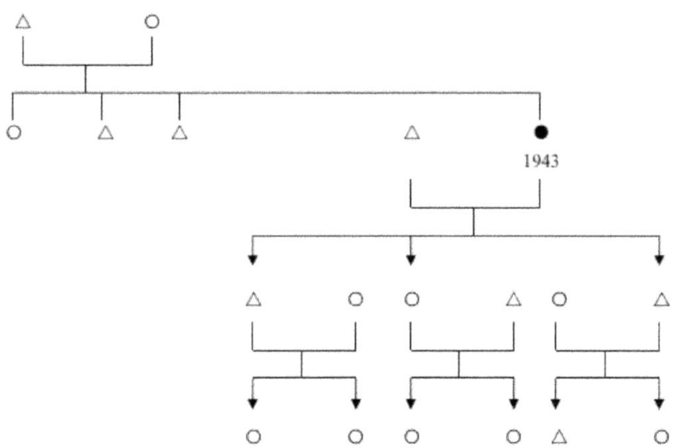

Figure A.65 **Genogram for Yi Kangnan's family**
▲: male interviewee; ●: female interviewee;
△: male; ○: female;
■: male who died before turning 15; ★: female who died before turning 15;
□: a pregnancy with unknown sex of the fetus;
The sex of those born within each generation are listed in descending order of age, from left to right.

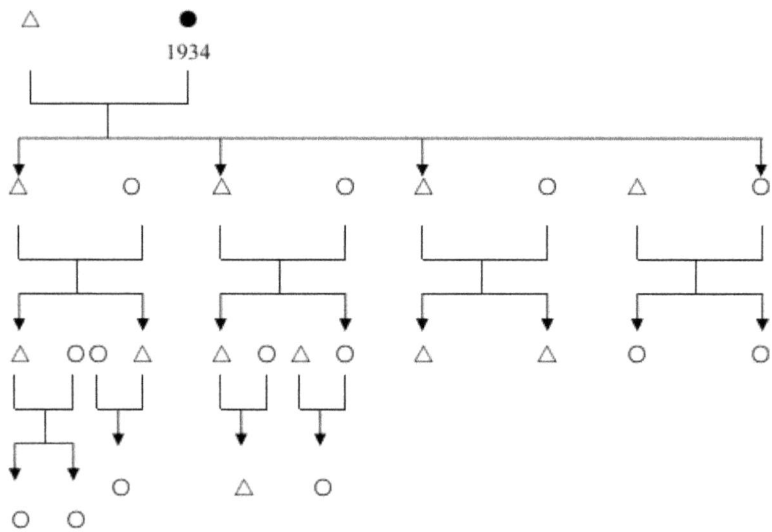

Figure A.66 **Genogram for Yi Jinzhang's family**
▲: male interviewee; ●: female interviewee;
△: male; ○: female;
■: male who died before turning 15; ★: female who died before turning 15;
□: a pregnancy with unknown sex of the fetus;
The sex of those born within each generation are listed in descending order of age, from left to right.

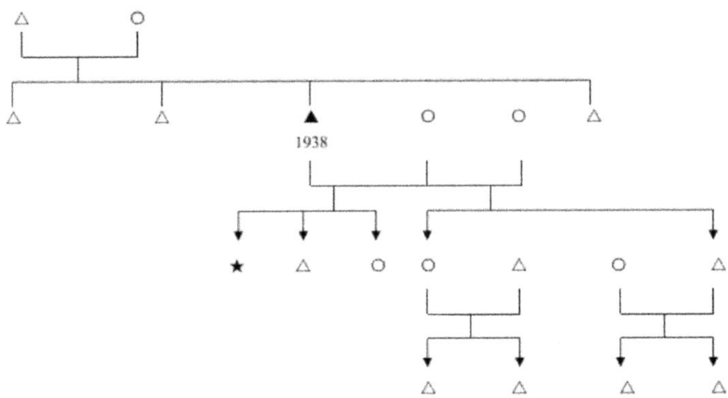

Figure A.67 **Genogram for Yan Wenbang's family**
▲: male interviewee; ●: female interviewee;
△: male; ○: female;
■: male who died before turning 15; ★: female who died before turning 15;
□: a pregnancy with unknown sex of the fetus;
The sex of those born within each generation are listed in descending order of age, from left to right.

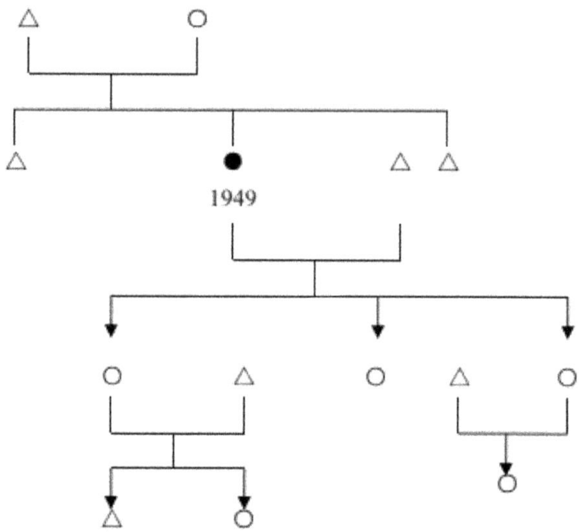

Figure A.68 **Genogram for Yi Jianla's family**
▲: male interviewee; ●: female interviewee;
△: male; ○: female;
■: male who died before turning 15; ★: female who died before turning 15;
□: a pregnancy with unknown sex of the fetus;

The sex of those born within each generation are listed in descending order of age, from left to right.

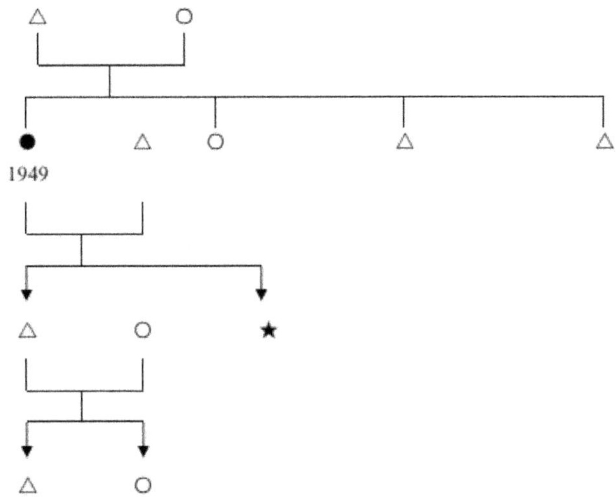

Figure A.69 **Genogram for Yi Nannen's family**
▲: male interviewee; ●: female interviewee;
△: male; ○: female;
■: male who died before turning 15; ★: female who died before turning 15;
□: a pregnancy with unknown sex of the fetus;

The sex of those born within each generation are listed in descending order of age, from left to right.

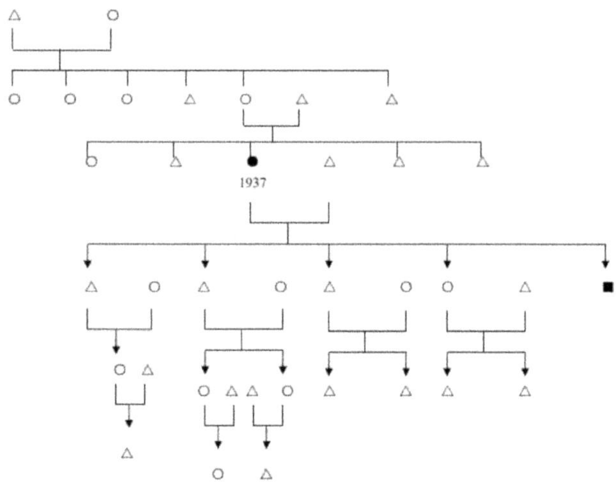

Figure A.70 **Genogram for Yi Tila's family**
▲: male interviewee; ●: female interviewee;
△: male; ○: female;
■: male who died before turning 15; ★: female who died before turning 15;
□: a pregnancy with unknown sex of the fetus;

The sex of those born within each generation are listed in descending order of age, from left to right.

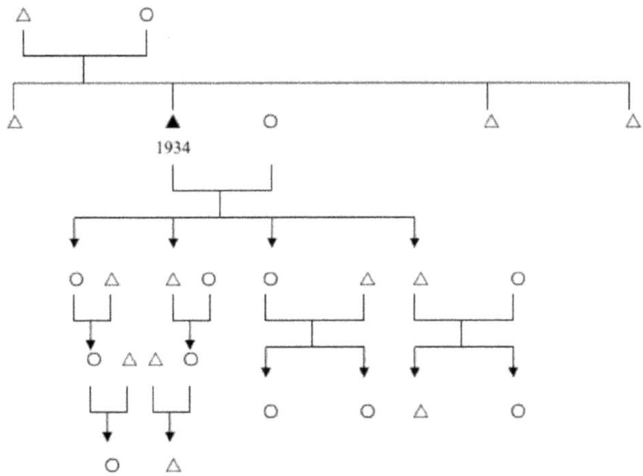

Figure A.71 **Genogram for Yan Labing's family**
▲: male interviewee; ●: female interviewee;
△: male; ○: female;
■: male who died before turning 15; ★: female who died before turning 15;
□: a pregnancy with unknown sex of the fetus;

The sex of those born within each generation are listed in descending order of age, from left to right.

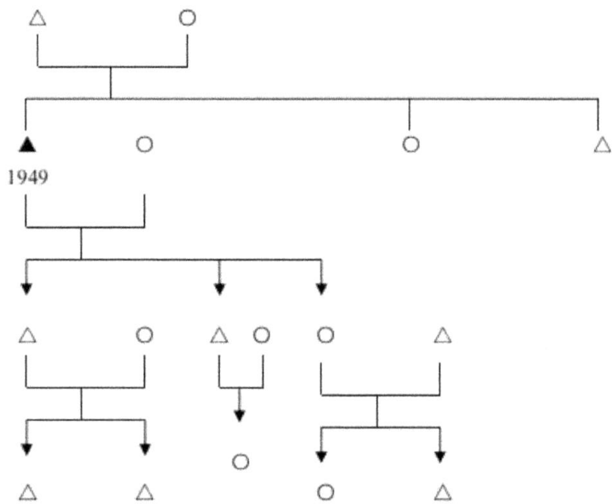

Figure A.72 **Genogram for Yan Dila's family**
▲: male interviewee; ●: female interviewee;
△: male; ○: female;
■: male who died before turning 15; ★: female who died before turning 15;
□: a pregnancy with unknown sex of the fetus;
The sex of those born within each generation are listed in descending order of age, from left to right.

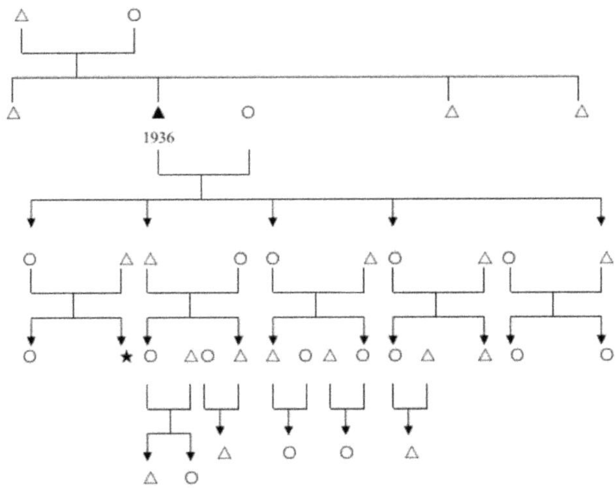

Figure A.73 **Genogram for Yan Ruan's family**
▲: male interviewee; ●: female interviewee;
△: male; ○: female;
■: male who died before turning 15; ★: female who died before turning 15;
□: a pregnancy with unknown sex of the fetus;

The sex of those born within each generation are listed in descending order of age, from left to right.

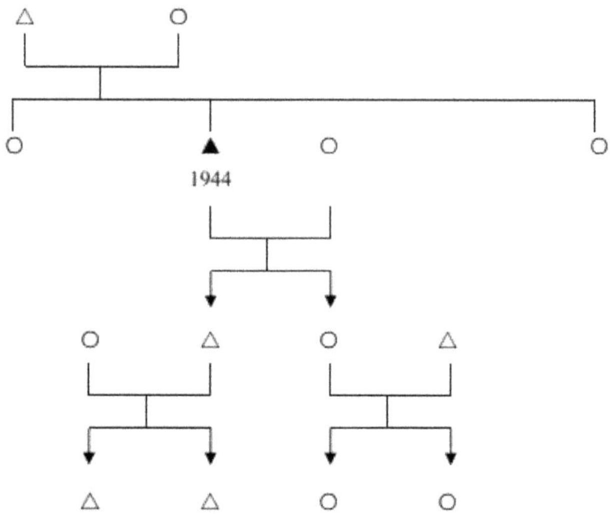

Figure A.74 **Genogram for Yan Ta's family**
▲: male interviewee; ●: female interviewee;
△: male; ○: female;
■: male who died before turning 15; ★: female who died before turning 15;
□: a pregnancy with unknown sex of the fetus;
The sex of those born within each generation are listed in descending order of age, from left to right.

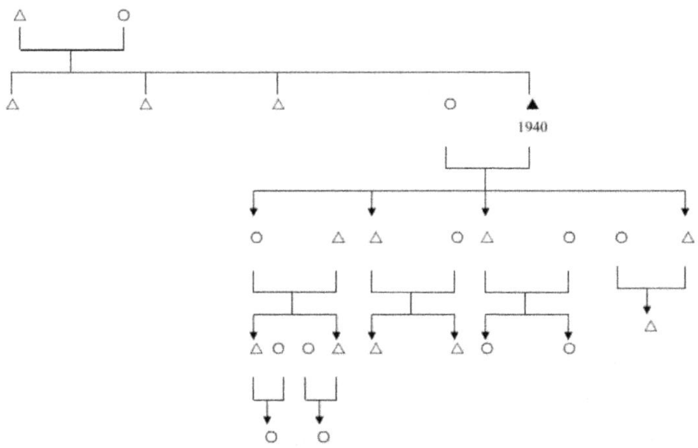

Figure A.75 **Genogram for Yan Lahong's family**
▲: male interviewee; ●: female interviewee;
△: male; ○: female;
■: male who died before turning 15; ★: female who died before turning 15;
□: a pregnancy with unknown sex of the fetus;
The sex of those born within each generation are listed in descending order of age, from left to right.

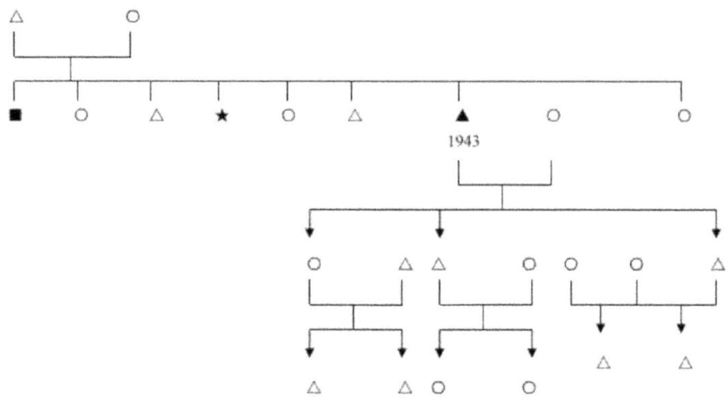

Figure A.76 **Genogram for Yan Wenxing's family**
▲: male interviewee; ●: female interviewee;
△: male; ○: female;
■: male who died before turning 15; ★: female who died before turning 15;
□: a pregnancy with unknown sex of the fetus;
The sex of those born within each generation are listed in descending order of age, from left to right.

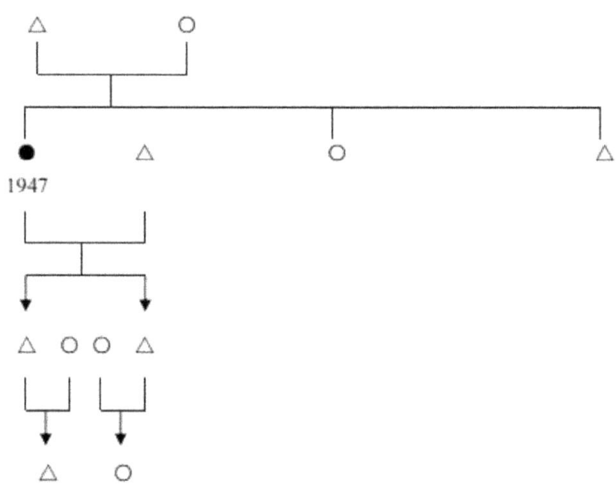

Figure A.77 **Genogram for Yi Guangsao's family**
▲: male interviewee; ●: female interviewee;
△: male; ○: female;
■: male who died before turning 15; ★: female who died before turning 15;
□: a pregnancy with unknown sex of the fetus;
The sex of those born within each generation are listed in descending order of age, from left to right.

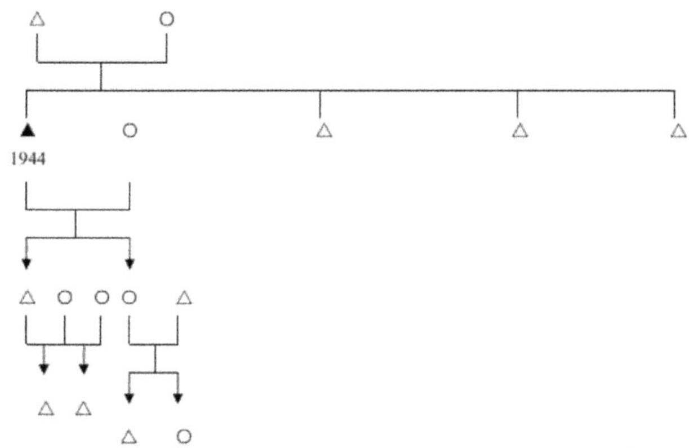

Figure A.78 **Genogram for Yan Honghe's family**
▲: male interviewee; ●: female interviewee;
△: male; ○: female;
■: male who died before turning 15; ★: female who died before turning 15;
□: a pregnancy with unknown sex of the fetus;
The sex of those born within each generation are listed in descending order of age, from left to right.

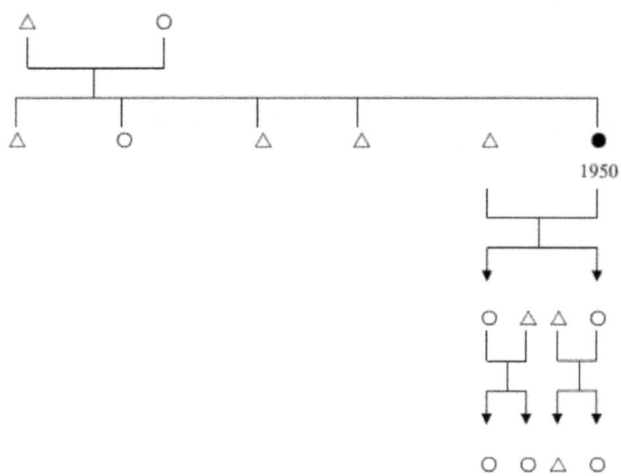

Figure A.79 **Genogram for Yi Guanghai's family**
▲: male interviewee; ●: female interviewee;
△: male; ○: female;
■: male who died before turning 15; ★: female who died before turning 15;
□: a pregnancy with unknown sex of the fetus;
The sex of those born within each generation are listed in descending order of age, from left to right.

Dehong Dai and Jingpo Autonomous Prefecture

Village N in Fengping Township of Luxi City

General Information of the Village and Surveyed Households

Being in the middle of the Mangshi Intermontane Basin and approximately 10 kilometers away from the seat of the municipal government of Mangshi, Fengping Township is cut through by the National Highway 320 and the Luxi-Yingjiang Expressway, and thus is the only route from Mangshi to Ruili and an important transportation hub in the City and even the entire Prefecture. It is composed of 11 villagers' committees, one neighborhood committee, 99 villagers' groups and 191 cooperatives, and its farming population accounts for 94.11% of the total population. The famous Fengping Pagoda on the National Highway 320 is located approximately 1.5 kilometers from the seat of the Township Government. Historical records show that the Pagoda was built more than 200 years ago and has the typical style of pagoda architecture in the later period of Theravada Buddhism.

In southern Fengping Township, village N is administered by the Villagers' Committee of Fengping, and is located approximately four kilometers away from the seat of the township government of Fengping. According to the statistics of the Villagers' Committee, as of December 2009, there had been 358 villagers in 74 households, including 180 males and 178 females. Except for eight Han and three Deang residents, all the others were the Dai ones.

When the investigation team surveyed in April 2010, 29 households met the survey criteria in the village, making up 39.19% of the total.

The basic information of the surveyed households is listed below in Table A.15.

Table A.15: Basic Information of the Interviewees (Born in or before 1950) in Village N

Serial No.	Household No.	Name	Date of Birth	Time at First Marriage	Number of Lifetime Births	Surviving Births	Time at Last Birth	Age at Last Birth (Years Old)	Sex of children in descending order of birth
1	3	Jiaomie Suowang	1921.10.8	1950.10	7	7	–	–	F – F – M – M – F – M – M
2	4	Xiangmie Yantuan'ao	1941.3.12	1961.10	4	3	1971	30	M – F – F – M
3	5	Caimie Xiangya	1936.11.24	1960.10	3	3	1966	30	F – M – M
4	7	Xianmie Pin	1934.8.10	1953.10	5	4	1967	33	F – F – F – F – M
5	8	Daomie Yanhanguo	1942.10	1961	3	3	1972	30	M – F – F
6	9	Jinmie Yanxiangzuo	1945	1961	4	4	1979	34	M – M – F – F
7	10	Daomie Yanfangbao	1940.8	1962.7	4	4	1973	33	M – M – M – M
8	13	Xiangmie Pin	1944.11	1965.10	4	4	1973	29	F – F – M – M

(Continued)

Table A.15: Continued

9	15	Xianmie Guobao	1949.12.12	1973	2	2	1981	32	M – M
10	16	Mie Yuefeng	1943.12	1964.10	4	4	1975	32	F – M – F – M
11	17	Yuemie Hanjin	1949.11.7	1970.	3	3	1975	26	F – F – F
12	18	Xiangmie Yuebaowang	1943.3.8	1969.10	4	4	1985	42	F – F – F – F
13	21	Xiangmie Wanpa	1942.10	1962.10	4	4	1973	31	F – M – F – F
14	22	Xiangmie Tuanhuang	1936.4	1958.10	4	4	1967	31	F – M – M – M
15	24	Jinmie Hannuo	1937.5	1955.12	6	5	1969	32	F – F – F – F-(F – F) – M
16	25	Jinmie Yanhantuan	1946.2	1966.1	4	4	1975	29	M – F – M – F
17	27	Mie Yuexiang	1941.10	1961.7	5	4	1973	32	M – F – M – F – M
18	33	Jinmie Yangtuanguo	1940.5	1960	4	3	–	–	M – M – F – F

19	36	Jinmie Yuebaowan	1950.7	1972.10	3	3	1978	28	F – F – F
20	40	Jiaomie Suoban	1942.10	1962	1	1	1983	41	M
21	44	Caibo Yanwan	1950.5	1970.1	5	4	–	–	M – F – M – M – F
22	47	Jiaomie Yuehansuo	1946.9	1965.10	2	2	1969	23	F – F
23	52	Daomie Xianghuang	1949.9	1975	1	1	1975	26	F
24	54	Jiaomie Yanhanya	1933.4	1954.11	5	4	1965	32	M – F – F – M – F
25	55	Xiangmie Yanxiangbao	1948.10.5	–	1	1	1968	20	M
26	57	Limie Gen'ao	1942.11	1962.10	5	5	1975	33	F – M – M – F – F
27	61	Daomie Yuehan'ao	1943.1.9	1961.11	6	6	1976	33	F – F – F – F – F – M
28	63	Daomie Yuepaguo	1948	1969	4	4	1976	28	F – F – F – M
29	67	Xiangmie Yuewangbao	1939	1957	6	6	1970	31	F – M – M – F – F – F

Source: Field Survey Statistics by the Research Team.

Records of the Reproductive Histories of the Surveyed Households Are Shown in the Following Table

Household No.: 3; Interviewee: Jiaomie Suowang; Figure A.80

Parents' Generation:

Jiaomie Suowang's mother gave birth to seven children, five females and two males. Seven births survived. Sex of the children in descending order: M – F – F – M- F – F – F. She was the youngest daughter in the family.

Current Generation:

Jiaomie Suowang was born on October 8, 1921, got married in October 1950, and gave birth to seven children, three females and four males. Seven births survived. Sex of the children in descending order: F – F – M – M – F – M – M.

Children's Generation:

The first daughter gave birth to three children, all males.

The second daughter gave birth to three children. Sex of the children in descending order: M – F – F.

The first son gave birth to three children. Sex of the children in descending order: M – F – F.

The second son gave birth to two children. Sex of the children in descending order: F – M.

The third daughter gave birth to one child, F.

The third son gave birth to two children. Sex of the children in descending order: M – F.

The fourth son married twice. He gave birth to two children with his first wife, all girls, and had no children with his second wife, who had a boy with her former husband.

Grandchildren's Generation:

The first daughter's first child gave birth to two children. Sex of the children in descending order: M – F.

The first daughter's second child was divorced and has no child.

The first daughter's third child gave birth to one child, F.

The second daughter's first child gave birth to one child, F.

The second daughter's second child and third child both were married and still had no children.

The first son's first child gave birth to one child, M.

The first son's second child and third child's two daughters all were married, and still had no children.

The second son's first child were unmarried.

The second son's second child was married, and still had no children.

The third daughter's child were unmarried.

The third son's two children also were unmarried.

The fourth son's first child (with his former wife) gave birth to one child, F.

All the other grandchildren were unmarried.

Great-grandchildren's Generation:

Six great-grandchildren, two males and four females.

Household No.: 4; Interviewee: Xiangmie Yantuanao; Figure A.81

Parents' Generation:

Xiangmie Yantuanao's mother gave birth to nine children, three females and six males. Sex of the children in descending order: F – F – F – M – M – M – M – M – M. Five children survived, two females and three males. Her second daughter, first son, second son and fifth son died in infancy. She was the first child in the family.

Current Generation:

Xiangmie Yantuanao was born on March 12, 1941, got married in October 1961, and gave birth to four children. Sex of the children in descending order: M (1962) – F (1964) – F (1967) – M (1971). The second daughter died in infancy.

Children's Generation:

The first son was married, had no children but adopted a girl, who was 16 years old now (2009).

The second daughter gave birth to two children. Sex of the children in descending order: F – F.

The second son gave birth to two children. Sex of the children in descending order: M – M.

Grandchildren's Generation:

The first son adopted a girl, who was now 16 years old and were unmarried.

The second daughter' two daughters were unmarried.

The second son's first child was 16 years old and the second child was still in kindergarten.

Household No.: 5; Interviewee: Caimie Xiangya; Figure A.82

Parents' Generation:

Caimei Xiangya's mother gave birth to six children. Six children survived, five females and one male. Sex of the children in descending order: F – F – M – F – F – F. She was the fourth child in her family.

Current Generation:

Caimei Xiangya was born on November 24, 1936, got married in October 1960, and gave birth to three children, one female and two males. Sex of the children in descending order: F (1962) – M (1964) – M (1966). She had the IUD operation after the third birth.

Children's Generation:

The first daughter gave birth to one child, F (1993).

The first son gave birth to two children. Sex of the children in descending order: F – M.

The second son gave birth to two children. Sex of the children in descending order: M – M.

Grandchildren's Generation:

Five grandchildren, two females and three males, were unmarried.

Caimei Xiangya was very busy at that time, working in a cooperative. She was already 30 years old when giving birth to the third baby. Being in a poor financial position back then, she couldn't afford more children and took the IUD birth control.

Household No.: 7; Interviewee: Xianmie Pin; Figure A.83

Parents' Generation:

Xianmei Pin's mother gave birth to nine children. Seven births survived, five males and two females. Sex of the children in descending order: M – F – M – M – F – M – M – M – F. The first son and first daughter died in infancy. She was the fifth child in the family.

Current Generation:

Xianmei Pin was born on August 10, 1934, got married in October 1953, and gave birth to five children. Four children survived. Sex of the children in descending order: F (1954) – F (1958) – F (1960) – F (1962) – M (1967). The third daughter died in infancy.

Children's Generation:

The first daughter gave birth to four children. Three children survived. Sex of the children in descending order: F – F (1980). M – F. The first daughter died at one year old.

The second daughter was married to Shandong in northeastern China and gave birth to one child, M.

The fourth daughter gave birth to two children. Sex of the children in descending order: F – M.

The youngest son gave birth to two children. Sex of the children in descending order: M – F.

Grandchildren's Generation:

The first daughter's second child gave birth to one child, M.

The first daughter's third child gave birth to one child, F.

The first daughter's fourth child gave birth to one child, F.

The second daughter's son gave birth to one child, M (2000).

The third daughter's children were all married and still had no children.

The youngest son's first child gave birth to two children. Sex of the children in descending order: M – F.

The youngest son's second child were unmarried.

Great-grandchildren's Generation:

Six great-grandchildren, three males and three females.

Household No.: 8; Interviewee: Daomie Yanhanguo; Figure A.84

Parents' Generation:

Daomie Yanhanguo's father married twice, giving birth to three children from his previous marriage and four children from his later marriage. Daomie Yanhanguo was the first child from her father's previous marriage.

Current Generation:

Daomie Yanhanguo was born in October 1942, and got married in 1961. Her husband married twice and she was the second wife of her husband. Her husband gave birth to four children from his previous marriage, one male and three females. Sex of the children in descending order: M – F – F – F. The youngest daughter died in infancy. She herself gave birth to three children, one male and two females. Sex of the children in descending order: M (1962) – F (1965) – F (1972).

Children's Generation:

The first son gave birth to one child, F.

The first daughter gave birth to two children. Sex of the children in descending order: M – F.

The second daughter gave birth to two children. Sex of the children in descending order: F – M.

Grandchildren's Generation:

Five grandchildren, three females and two males. The first daughter's first child was married but still had no children.

Household No.: 9; Interviewee: Jinmie Yanxiangzuo; Figure A.85

Parents' Generation:

Jinmie Yanxiangzuo's mother gave birth to 10 children, seven males and three females. Nine children survived. The first son died in infancy and Jinmei Yanxiangzuo was the second child in the family.

Current Generation:

Jinmie Yanxiangzuo was born in 1945 and gave birth to four children, two males and two females. Sex of the children in descending order: M (1962) – M (1969) – F (1974) – F (1979).

Children's Generation:

The first son gave birth to two children, all daughters.

The second son gave birth to one child, M.

The first daughter married twice. Her first husband was the son of her mother's younger brother and gave birth to one child, M. Later, she remarried a Han husband and gave birth to one child, F.

The second daughter gave birth to one child to twins, both daughters.

Grandchildren's Generation:

Seven grandchildren, two males and five females. All were unmarried.

Household No.: 10; Interviewee: Daomie Yanfangbao; Figure A.86

Grandparent Generation:

Daomei Yanfangbao's maternal grandmother gave birth to four children, one male and three females. Sex of the children in descending order: F – M – F – F. Daomie Yanfangbao's mother was the first daughter in her family.

Grandparent Generation:

Daomie Yanfangbao's mother gave birth to four children, three males and one female. Three children survived. Sex of the children in descending order: M – M – M – F. The first son died in infancy and Daomei Yanfangbao was the only daughter in the family.

Current Generation:

Daomie Yanfangbao was born in August 1940, got married in July 1962, and gave birth to four children, all males, respectively in 1962, 1964, 1967 and 1973.

Children's Generation:

The first son gave birth to one child, F (1988).

The second son gave birth to two children. Sex of the children in descending order: M (1986) – F (1988).

The third son gave birth to two children. Sex of the children in descending order: M (1990) – F (1994).

The fourth son gave birth to two children. Sex of the children in descending order: F (2000) – M (2007).

Grandchildren's Generation:

The second son's second child was married and gave birth to one child, F (2008).

All the other grandchildren were unmarried.

Great-grandchildren's Generation:

One great-grandchild, F (2008).

Household No.: 13; Interviewee: Xiangmie Pin; Figure A.87

Parents' Generation:

Xiangmie Pin's mother gave birth to seven children. Five children survived, one male and four females. She was the third child in her family.

Current Generation:

Xiangmie Pin was born in November 1944, got married in October 1965, and gave birth to four children, two males and two females. Sex of the children in descending order: F (1966) – F (1968) – M (1971) – M (1973).

Children's Generation:

The first daughter gave birth to two children, both males.

The second daughter gave birth to one child, F, and received the only-child certificate.
The first son gave birth to two children, both males (respectively in 1992 and 1996).
The second son gave birth to one child, F.

Grandchildren's Generation:
Six grandchildren, four males and two females, all were unmarried.

Household No.: 15; Interviewee: Xianmie Guobao; Figure A.88

Parents' Generation:
Xianmie Guobao's father married twice. He gave birth to three children with his first wife. Sex of the children in descending order: M – M – F. Later, he remarried and gave birth to three children with his second wife. Sex of the children in descending order: F – F – M. Xianmie Guobao was the first daughter of his second wife.

Current Generation:
Xianmie Guobao was born on December 12, 1949 and got married in 1973. She adopted a boy (born in 1972) before giving two births, both males (respectively in 1978 and 1981).

Children's Generation:
The first son gave birth to two children. Sex of the children in descending order: M (1996) – M (2001).
The second son gave birth to two children. Sex of the children in descending order: F (1995) – M (2004).
The third son was married but still given no birth.

Grandchildren's Generation:
Four grandchildren, three males and one female.

Household No.: 16; Interviewee: Mie Yuefeng (Fang Guiying); Figure A.89

Grandparent Generation:
Mie Yuefeng's grandmother gave birth to 14 children. Seven children survived, four males and three females.

Parents' Generation:
Mie Yuefeng's mother gave 15 births. Six children survived, four females and two males. She was the 12th child in the family.

Current Generation:

Mie Yuefeng was born in December 1943, got married in October 1964, and gave birth to four children. Sex of the children in descending order: F (1965) – M (1967) – F (1970) – M (1975).

Children's Generation:

The first daughter gave birth to two children. Sex of the children in descending order: M (1985) – F (1988).

The first son gave birth to two children. Sex of the children in descending order: F – M.

The second daughter gave birth to two children. Sex of the children in descending order: M – F.

The second son gave birth to one child, F.

Grandchildren's Generation:

The first daughter's first child gave birth to one child, M.

The first daughter's second child gave birth to one child, F.

All the other grandchildren were unmarried.

Great-grandchildren's Generation:

Two great-grandchildren, one male and one female.

Household No.: 17; Interviewee: Yuemie Hanjin; Figure A.90

Parents' Generation:

Yuemie Hanjin's mother gave birth to seven children, one male and six females. Sex of the children in descending order: F – M – F – F – F – F – F. Six children survived. She was the first daughter in the family and the first son died in infancy.

Current Generation:

Yuemie Hanjin was born on November 7, 1949, got married in 1970, and gave birth to three children, all females (respectively in 1970, 1973 and 1975).

Children's Generation:

The first daughter gave birth to two children. Sex of the children in descending order: M (1990) – F.

The second daughter gave birth to two children, both females.

The third daughter gave birth to one child, M.

Grandchildren's Generation:

Five grandchildren, two males and three females.

Household No.: 18; Interviewee: Xiangmie Yuebaowang; Figure A.91

Parents' Generation:

Xiangmie Yuebaowang's mother gave birth to five children. Sex of the children in descending order: F – F – M – M – F. She was the second child in the family.

Current Generation:

Xiangmie Yuebaowang was born on March 8, 1943, and got married in October 1969. Her husband married twice, giving one birth with his first wife, F (1971), and giving four births with her, all females (respectively in 1976, 1978, 1980 and 1985).

Children's Generation:

The first daughter gave birth to two children, both males.

The second daughter gave birth to one child, M, and received the only-child certificate.

The third daughter gave birth to one child, M, and received the only-child certificate.

The fourth daughter gave birth to two children. Sex of the children in descending order: M- F (2009).

Grandchildren's Generation:

Eight grandchildren, three females and five males.

Household No.: 21; Interviewee: Xiangmie Wanpa; Figure A.92

Parents' Generation:

Xiangmie Wanpa's mother gave birth to seven children. Three children survived. Sex of the children in descending order: F – M – M – F – F – F – F. After the first five births died in infancy, her mother decided to adopt a boy on the advice of a Buddha and later gave birth to two children, who both survived. Xiangmie Wanpa was the youngest daughter in the family.

Current Generation:

Xiangmie Wanpa was born in October 1942, got married in October 1962, and gave birth to four children, three females and one male. Sex of the children in descending order: F (1963) – M (1965) – F (1970) – F (1973).

Children's Generation:

The first daughter gave birth to two children, both males.

The first son gave birth to two children, both females. The first son died of illness.
The third daughter gave birth to two children. Sex of the children in descending order: M – F.
The youngest daughter gave birth to one child, M, and received the only-child certificate.

Grandchildren's Generation:
Seven grandchildren, three females and four males.

Household No.: 22; Interviewee: Xiangmie Tuanhuang; Figure A.93

Parents' Generation:
Xiangmie Tuanhuang's mother gave birth to two children and died with the second birth in the puerperal period.

Current Generation:
Xiangmie Tuanhuang was born in April 1936, got married in October 1958, and gave birth to four children, one female and three males. Sex of the children in descending order: F (1961) – M (1963) – M (1965) – M (1967).

Children's Generation:
The first daughter gave birth to two children, both males.
The first son gave birth to two children. Sex of the children in descending order: M – F.
The second son gave birth to one child, F, and received the only-child certificate.
The third son gave birth to two children, both females, decided not to have additional children and to be sterilized, and was awarded RMB 3,000 by the government for being a two-girl family.

Grandchildren's Generation:
Seven grandchildren. The first son's first child was married but still had no childrens. All the other grandchildren were unmarried.

Household No.: 24; Interviewee: Jinmie Hannuo; Figure A.94

Parents' Generation:
Jinmie Hannuo's mother gave birth to five children, four females and one male. Sex of the children in descending order: F – F – F – M – F. The

second daughter died at three years old and the youngest daughter died at five years old. Jinmie Hannuo was the first child in the family.

Current Generation:

Jinmie Hannuo was born in May 1937, got married in December 1955, and gave birth to six children, six females and one male. Sex of the children in descending order: F (1956) – F (1958) – F (1961) – F (1963) – F – F (1966) – M (1969). Five children survived. The twin daughters in the fifth birth died four days and nine days after their birth.

Children's Generation:

The first daughter gave birth to three children, two females and one male. Sex of the children in descending order: F – M – F.

The second daughter was 50 years old and in no mood to get married.

The third daughter gave birth to three children, two males and one female. Sex of the children in descending order: M – M – F.

The fourth daughter gave birth to two children, one male and one female. Sex of the children in descending order: M – F.

The youngest son gave birth to two children, both females, decided not to have additional children and to be sterilized, and was awarded RMB 3,000 by the government for being a two-girl family.

Grandchildren's Generation:

The first daughter's first child gave birth to one child, F.

The first daughter's second child gave birth to one child, F.

All the other grandchildren were unmarried.

Great-grandchildren's Generation:

Two great-grandchildren, all females.

Household No.: 25; Interviewee: Jinmie Yanhantuan; Figure A.95

Parents' Generation:

Jinmie Yanhantuan's mother married twice. She gave birth to five children from her first marriage, all males. Three children survived. The first and third sons both died in infancy. She gave birth to two children with her second husband, one male and one female. Sex of the children in descending order: M – F. Jinmei Yanhantuan was the youngest daughter of her mother to her second husband

Current Generation:

Jinmie Yanhantuan was born in February 1946, got married in January 1966, and gave birth to four children, two males and two females. Sex of the children in descending order: M (1966) – F (1969) – M (1972) – F (1975).

Children's Generation:

The first son gave birth to two children. Sex of the children in descending order: F (1987) – M.

The first daughter gave birth to three children, all males. The first son died in infancy.

The third son gave birth to two children, both females.

The youngest daughter gave birth to two children, both females.

Grandchildren's Generation:

The first son's first child gave birth to one child, F.

The first son's second child was married but still had no children.

The first daughter's second son gave birth to one child, F.

The first daughter's third son gave birth to one child, F.

The second son's first child was married but still had no children.

All the other grandchildren were unmarried.

Great-grandchildren's Generation:

Three great-grandchildren, all females.

Household No.: 27; Interviewee: Mie Yuexiang; Figure A.96

Parents' Generation:

Mie Yuexiang's mother gave 11 births. Seven births survived, four males and three females. Sex of the children in descending order: M – M – M – M- F- F – F. Mei Yuexiang was the youngest daughter in the family.

Current Generation:

Mie Yuexiang was born in October 1941, got married in July 1961, and gave birth to five children. Sex of the children in descending order: M (1962) – F (1965) – M (1968) – F (1970) – M (1973). Four children survived. The first son (1962) died in infancy.

Children's Generation:

The first daughter gave birth to two children, both females.

The second son gave birth to two children. Sex of the children in descending order: M – F.
The second daughter gave birth to two children, both males.
The third son married twice. He gave birth to one child with his first wife, M, and one birth with his second wife, M.

Grandchildren's Generation:
The first daughter's first child gave birth to one child, F.
The second daughter's first child gave birth to one child, M.
All the other grandchildren were unmarried.
Great-grandchildren's Generation:
Two great-grandchildren, one male and one female.

Household No.: 33; Interviewee: Jinmie Yangtuanguo; Figure A.97

Parents' Generation:
Jinmie Yangtuanguo's mother gave birth to two children and died with the second birth in the puerperal period. Her father remarried and gave birth to six children. Five children survived, four females and one male. Sex of the children in descending order: F – M – F – F – F. Jinmie Yangtuanguo was the first daughter of her father with his first wife.

Current Generation:
Jinmie Yangtuanguo was born in May 1940, got married in 1960, and gave birth to four children. Sex of the children in descending order: M (1961) – M – F – F. Three children survived. The second daughter died at four years old.

Children's Generation:
The first son gave birth to two children, both males.
The second son gave birth to two children, both females.
The first daughter gave birth to two children. Sex of the children in descending order: M – F.

Grandchildren's Generation:
The first son's first child was married but still had no children. All the other grandchildren were unmarried.

Household No.: 36; Interviewee: Jinmie Yuebaowan; Figure A.98

Parents' Generation:

Jinmie Yuebaowan's mother gave birth to 10 children, four males and six females. Sex of the children in descending order: M – M – M – F – M – F – F – F – F – F. The first son, third daughter and fourth daughter died in infancy. Jinmie Yuebaowan was the ninth child in the family. Later, her father divorced her mother, remarried his second wife and gave birth to one child, F.

Current Generation:

Jinmie Yuebaowan was born in July 1950, got married in October 1972, and gave birth to three children, all females (respectively in 1973, 1975 and 1978).

Children's Generation:

The first daughter gave birth to one child, one female, and received the only-child certificate.

The third daughter gave birth to two children, both males.

The third daughter gave birth to two children. Sex of the children in descending order: F – M.

Grandchildren's Generation:

Five grandchildren were all unmarried.

Household No.: 40; Interviewee: Jiaomie Suoban; Figure A.99

Parents' Generation:

Jiaomie Suoban's mother married twice. She and her first husband gave birth to six children, four females and two males. Sex of the children in descending order: F – F – F – M – M – F. Five children survived. The second daughter and second son both died in infancy. Later, she remarried her second husband and gave birth to one child, one male. Jiaomie Suoban was the youngest daughter of her mother with her first husband.

Current Generation:

Jiaomie Suoban was born in October 1942, got married in 1962, and gave birth to one child, M (1983).

Children's Generation:

Her daughter (adopted) gave birth to two children, both males.

Her son gave birth to two children. Sex of the children in descending order: F – M.

Grandchildren's Generation:

Two grandchildren, one male and one female, were unmarried.

Having not been pregnant for long, Jiaomie Suoban adopted a daughter (born in 1966) of her elder sister's nine children, and then got pregnant with her own child after 20 years of marriage (1982).

Household No.: 44; Interviewee: Caimie Yanwan; Figure A.100

Parents' Generation:

Caimie Yanwan's mother gave birth to six children, four males and two females. Five children survived. Sex of the children in descending order: M – F – M – M – F – M. The second daughter died in infancy and Caimie Yanwan was the third child in the family.

Current Generation:

Caimie Yanwan was born in May 1950, got married in January 1970, and gave birth to five children, three males and two females. Sex of the children in descending order: M (1970) – F (1972) – M (1974) – M (1977) – F. The third son died from a traffic accident at 20 years old and the youngest daughter died one month after her birth.

Children's Generation:

The first son gave birth to two children. Sex of the children in descending order: M – F.

The first daughter gave birth to three children. Sex of the children in descending order: F – M – F. the son died in infancy.

The second son gave birth to one child, F.

Grandchildren's Generation:

Five grandchildren, one male and four females, were unmarried.

Household No.: 47; Interviewee: Jiaomie Yuehansuo; Figure A.101

Parents' Generation:

Jiaomie Yuehansuo's mother gave birth to 10 children, five males and five females. The first five were all males, and the last five all girls. Five children survived. Only the second son out of the five boys survived and the first girl died in infancy. Jiaomie Yuehansuo was the youngest child in the family.

Current Generation:

Jiaomie Yuehansuo was born in September 1946, got married in October 1965, and gave birth to two children, F (1966) – F (1969).

Children's Generation:

The first daughter gave birth to three children. Sex of the children in descending order: F – F – M.

The second daughter gave birth to two children. Sex of the children in descending order: F – M.

Grandchildren's Generation:

The first daughter's first child gave birth to one child, M.

The first daughter's second child died from a traffic accident at 15 years old.

The first daughter's youngest son were unmarried.

The second daughter's first child gave birth to one child, F.

The second daughter's second child were unmarried.

Great-grandchildren's Generation:

Two great-grandchildren, one male and one female.

Household No.: 52; Interviewee: Daomie Xianghuang; Figure A.102

Parents' Generation:

Daomie Xianghuang's mother gave 12 births. Four children survived, two males and two females. Sex of the children in descending order: M – F – M – F. Daomei Xianghuang was the youngest child in the family.

Current Generation:

Daomie Xianghuang was born in September 1949, got married in 1975, and gave birth to one child, F (1975). She was married to Fapa and then came back with her daughter to this village. Now she received the only-child certificate.

Children's Generation:

Daughter gave birth to two children. Sex of the children in descending order: F (1995) – M (2002).

Grandchildren's Generation:

Two grandchildren were both underage.

Household No.: 54; Interviewee: Jiaomie Yanhanya; Figure A.103

Parents' Generation:

Jiaomie Yanhanya's mother gave birth to four children, three males and one female, and Jiaomie Yanhanya was the youngest in the family.

Current Generation:

Jiaomie Yanhanya was born in April 1933, got married in November 1954, and gave birth to five children, two males and three females. Sex of the children in descending order: M (1960) – F (1961) – F (1962) – M (1964) – F (1965). Four children survived. The youngest daughter died of illness three months after her birth.

Children's Generation:

The first son gave birth to two children. Sex of the children in descending order: M – F.

The first daughter gave birth to two children. Sex of the children in descending order: M – F.

The second daughter gave birth to two children, both females.

The second son gave birth to one child, M, and received the only-child certificate.

Grandchildren's Generation:

The first son's first child gave birth to one child, M.

The first daughter's second child gave birth to one child, M.

All the other grandchildren were unmarried.

Great-grandchildren's Generation:

Two great-grandchildren, all males. One was married but still had no children, and the other was unmarried.

Jiaomie Yanhanya was born in Myanmar. Her husband was from Nongmoben village and had been in Myanmar in the 1950s. She and her husband tied the knot in Myanmar and went back to this village when their youngest son was four years old (1969).

Household No.: 55; Interviewee: Xiangmie Yanxiangbao; Figure A.104

Parents' Generation:

Xiangmie Yanxiangbao's mother gave birth to seven children. Five children survived, two males and three females. Sex of the children in descending order: M – F – M – F – F. Xiangmie Yanxiangbao was the youngest in the family.

Current Generation:

Xiangmie Yanxiangbao was born on October 5, 1948 and gave birth to one child, M (1968).

Children's Generation:

Her son gave birth to two children. Sex of the children in descending order: M (1989) – F (1992).

Xiangmie Yanxiangbao never married. Her boyfriend cheated on her when she was pregnant, so she didn't marry him. Her former boyfriend (the father of the boy) gave the boy (born in 1968) RMB 55 every year as his living allowances for 10 years, and then was missing.

Household No.: 57; Interviewee: Limie Gen'ao; Figure A.105

Parents' Generation:

Limie Gen'ao's mother gave birth to 10 children. Sex of the children in descending order: M – F – M – F – F – M – M – M – F – F. Five children survived. The first son, second son, third son, second daughter and third daughter all died in infancy, and the fifth son suffered from mental illness. Limie Gen'ao was the first daughter in the family.

Current Generation:

Limie Gen'ao was born in November 1942, got married in October 1962, and gave birth to five children, three females and two males. Sex of the children in descending order: F (1963) – M (1965) – M (1969) – F (1972) – F (1975).

Children's Generation:

The first daughter gave birth to one child, F. She was a civil servant at the prefecture government and could only give birth to one child as required by related policies.

The first son gave birth to two children, both males.

The second son gave birth to one child, F. He worked at a prefecture-run cement mill and could only give birth to one child as required by related policies.

The second daughter gave birth to one child, F.

The youngest daughter gave birth to two children, both females. She decided on having no additional children and getting be sterilized and was awarded RMB 3,000 by the government for being a two-girl family.

Grandchildren's Generation:

The first son's first child gave birth to one child, F.

The second daughter's child gave birth to one child, M.

All the other grandchildren were unmarried.

Great-grandchildren's Generation:

Two great-grandchildren, one male and one female.

Household No.: 61; Interviewee: Daomie Yuehan'ao; Figure A.106

Parents' Generation:

Daomie Yuehan'ao's mother gave birth to 10 children, five males and five females. The first five births were all males and the last five births all girls. Seven births survived. The fourth son, first daughter and second daughter all died in infancy. Daomie Yuehan'ao was the third daughter in the family.

Current Generation:

Daomie Yuehan'ao was born on January 9, 1943, got married in November 1961, and gave birth to six children, five females and one male. Sex of the children in descending order: F (1962) – F (1965) – F (1968) – F (1970) – F (1973) – M (1976). She used the IUD contraception after giving birth to the youngest son.

Children's Generation:

The first daughter gave birth to three children and twins were born in the second birth. Sex of the children in descending order: F – F – F – M. The first child and a twin died soon after their birth.

The second daughter gave birth to two children. Sex of the children in descending order: F – M.

The third daughter gave birth to two children, both females.

The fourth daughter gave birth to two children, both females.

The fifth daughter gave birth to two children. Sex of the children in descending order: M – F.

The son gave birth to two children, both females.

Grandchildren's Generation:

12 grandchildren, nine females and three males. Except the first daughter's son, all the other grandchildren were unmarried.

Daomie Yuehan'ao's husband was a Han ethnic man, who insisted on having a boy. Therefore, she did not take contraceptive measures until the sixth child was a boy.

Household No.: 63; Interviewee: Daomie Yuepaguo; Figure A.107

Parents' Generation:

Daomie Yuepaguo's mother gave birth to 10 children, seven females and three males. Sex of the children in descending order: M – F – F – F – F – M – M – F – F – F. Nine children survived. The third son died in infancy. Daomie Yuepaguo was the second daughter in the family.

Current Generation:

Daomie Yuepaguo was born in 1948, got married in 1969, and gave birth to four children. Sex of the children in descending order: F (1970) – F (1973) – F (1975) – M (1976).

Children's Generation:

The first daughter gave birth to two children. Sex of the children in descending order: M – F.

The second daughter gave birth to two children, both females.

The third daughter was married but still had no children.

The youngest son gave birth to one child, F.

Grandchildren's Generation:

Five grandchildren, four females and one male.

Only after having a boy in the fourth birth did Daomie Yuepaguo decide not to have additional children as her grandpa wanted her to have a boy. The grandpa was a Dai man in Lujiang intermontane basin, insisting on her giving birth to or adopting a boy.

Household No.: 67; Interviewee: Xiangmie Yuewangbao; Figure A.108

Parents' Generation:

Xiangmie Yuewangbao's mother gave birth to six children, four females and two males. Sex of the children in descending order: F – M – M – F – F – F. Four children survived. The first daughter and second son died in infancy. Xiangmie Yuewangbao was the third daughter in the family.

Current Generation:

Xiangmie Yuewangbao was born in 1939 and gave birth to six children, four females and two males. Sex of the children in descending order: F (1958) – F (1961) – M (1963) – M (1966) – F (1967) – F (1970).

Children's Generation:

The first daughter gave birth to two children. Sex of the children in descending order: M – F.

The second daughter gave birth to two children. Sex of the children in descending order: F – M.

The first son gave birth to two children. Sex of the children in descending order: F – M.

The second son gave birth to two children, both males.

The third daughter gave birth to two children. Sex of the children in descending order: F – M.

The fourth daughter gave birth to two children, both males.

Grandchildren's Generation:

The first daughter's first child gave birth to one child, M.

The second daughter's second child was married but still had no children.

The first son's first child gave birth to one child, F.

The first son's second child gave birth to one child, F.

All the other grandchildren were unmarried.

Great-grandchildren's Generation:

Three great-grandchildren, one male and two females.

Summary

Among the 29 households surveyed, the oldest interviewee was born on October 8, 1921 (89 years old), and the youngest in July 1950 (60 years old).

The reproductive statistics by the age cohort (the 5-year interval) are shown in the following Tables A.16–A.19.

Statistics of Births and Surviving Births in Surveyed Households by Generational Cohort:

Statistics of Births and Surviving Births in Surveyed Households by generation:

Statistics of the Timespans and Proportions of Births in the Surveyed Households by Generational Cohort:

The retrospective Reproductive Statistics mentioned above showed that:

Table A.16: Reproductive Statistics of the Interviewees (born in or before 1950) in Village N

Households	Age Cohort	Number of Lifetime Births (Persons)			Births Surviving till the Age of 15 or above (Persons)			Average Births/Household	Average Surviving Births/Household
		Total Births	M	F	Total Births	M	F		
9	1946–1950	25	9	16	24	9	15	2.78	2.67
11	1941–1945	44	17	27	42	16	26	4.00	3.82
6	1936–1940	27	14	13	25	14	11	4.50	4.17
2	1931–1935	10	3	7	8	3	5	5.00	4.00
0	1926–1930	—	—	—	—	—	—	—	—
1	1921–1925	7	4	3	7	4	3	7	7
In total: 29 Households		113	47	66	106	46	60	3.90	3.66

Source: Field Survey Statistics by the Research Team.

Table A.17: Village N Female Interviewee (Born in or before 1950) Births and Surviving Births

Interviewees			29 Interviewees (Households)		
Age of Interviewee			60–89 Years Old (1921–1950)		
Number of Lifetime Births	7 Births	1	Births Surviving till the Age of 15 or above (Persons)	7 Surviving Births	1
	6 Births	3		6 Surviving Births	2
	5 Births	5		5 Surviving Births	2
	4 Births	11		4 Surviving Births	12
	3 Births	4		3 Surviving Births	6
	2 Births	2		2 Surviving Births	3
	1 Birth	3		1 Surviving Birth	3

Source: Field Survey Statistics by the Research Team.

Table A.18: Reproductive Statistics of Surveyed Households by Generational Cohort (Interviewees Born in or before 1950) in Village N (No. 1)

Generation	Households	Number of Lifetime Births (Persons)			Births Surviving till the Age of 15 or above (Persons)			Average Total Births per Household	Average Total Surviving Births per Household
		Total Births	M	F	Total Births	M	F		
Parents' Generation	29	194	89	105	140	59	81	6.69	4.83
Current Generation	29	115	48	67	107	47	60	3.97	3.67
Children's Generation	105	200	92	108	195	90	105	1.90	1.86
Grandchildren's Generation	29	31	12	19	31	12	19	1.07	1.07

Source: Field Survey Statistics by the Research Team.

Table A.19: Reproductive Statistics of Surveyed Households by Generational Cohort (Intervieweed Born in or before 1950) in Village N (No. 2)[①]

Generation\Decade\Percent (%)	1950s	1960s	1970s	1980s	1990s	2000s	Percent (%)
Current Generation	4.76	52.38	39.05	3.81	–	–	100.00
Children's Generation	–	–	–	36.67	40.00	23.33	100.00
Grandchildren's Generation	–	–	–	–	–	–	–

Source: Field Survey Statistics by the Research Team.

1. By 2010 April, 29 interviewees born in or before 1950 (59 years old or above) in village N had given birth to 113 children, each giving birth to 3.90 children on average, and had 106 children surviving the age of 15 or above, with one household having 3.66 surviving children on average. The overall survival rate of the births was 93.81%.
2. The interviewees had throughout their lifetime given birth to 47 boys and 66 girls, with the boys being slightly outnumbered by the girls, and 46 boys and 60 girls had survived till the age of 15 or above, with the survival rate of the boys and the girls standing respectively at 97.87% and 90.91% and the survival rate of the boys being slightly higher than that of the girls.
3. The interviewees had had their births in the 1–7 range throughout their lifetime, with one interviewee having 3.90 births on average, and had surviving births in the 1–7 range;
4. The interviewees got married for the first time in the age range from 16 to 29 years old (respectively Interviewee No. 9: Jinmie Yanxiangzuo and Interviewee No. 3: Jiaomie Suowang), and gave birth to their last child in the age range from 23 to 42 years old (respectively Interviewee No. 47: Jiaomie Yuehansuo, having her second birth and Interviewee No. 18: Xiangmie Yuebaowang, having her fourth birth), at 30.81 years old on average.
5. The interviewees had their last birth in the period from 1966 (Interviewee No. 5: Caimie Xiangya, having her third birth) to 1985 (Interviewee No. 18: Xiangmie Yuebaowang, having her fourth birth).
6. The interviewees who had given birth to four children throughout their lifetime made up the largest share of the total at 37.93% and those who had had four surviving births made up the largest share of the total at 41.38%.
7. The interviewees who had given birth to five or fewer children and four or fewer children respectively made up 86.21% and 68.97% of all, and those who had had five or fewer surviving births and four or fewer surviving births respectively made up 89.66% and 82.76% of all;

① Given the information of the birth time of most Grandchildren's Generation children was unavailable, so, this data item was statistically insignificant and omitted in our survey statistics

8. Each generation tends to have few births but more surviving ones on average. The survival rate of the births by Current Generation, Children's Generation and Grandchildren's Generation was respectively 92.44%, 97.89% and 100.00%.
9. The reproductive lifespan for Current Generation extended from the 1950s to the 1980s, but most of the births were from the 1950s to the 1960s, accounting for 91.43% of all the newborns in this period.
10. The period of time during which those of the Children's Generation extended from the 1970s to the 2000s, with most of the births taking place from the 1970s to the 1980s, accounting for 76.67% of all the newborns in this period.
11. The reproductive lifespan for Grandchildren's Generation extended from the 1980s to the 2000s, but most of the births were in the 2000s.
12. 29 interviewees had completed their lifetime childbirth behaviors by the end of 1980s, with seven, 16 and three interviewees respectively completing their lifetime childbirth behaviors in 1960s, 1970s and 1980s.

Genograms

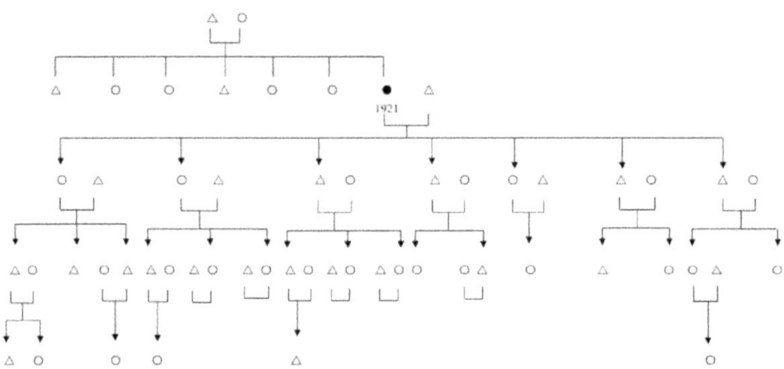

Figure A.80 **Genogram for Jiaomie Suowang's family**
▲: male interviewee; ●: female interviewee;
△: male; ○: female;
■: male who died before turning 15; ★: female who died before turning 15;
□: a pregnancy with unknown sex of the fetus;
The sex of those born within each generation are listed in descending order of age, from left to right.

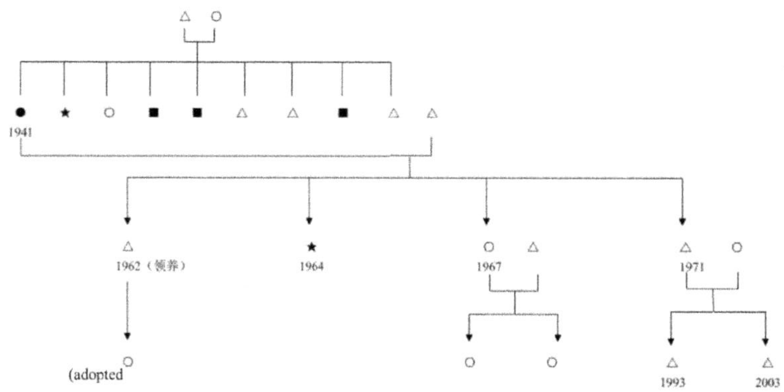

Figure A.81 **Genogram for Xiangmie Yantuanao's family**
▲: male interviewee; ●: female interviewee;
△: male; ○: female;
■: male who died before turning 15; ★: female who died before turning 15;
□: a pregnancy with unknown sex of the fetus;
The sex of those born within each generation are listed in descending order of age, from left to right.

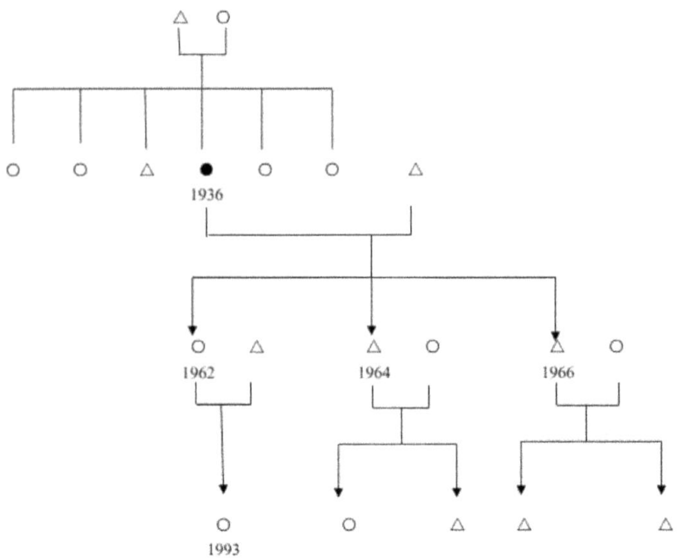

Figure A.82 **Genogram for Caimie Xiangya's family**
▲: male interviewee; ●: female interviewee;
△: male; ○: female;
■: male who died before turning 15; ★: female who died before turning 15;
□: a pregnancy with unknown sex of the fetus;
The sex of those born within each generation are listed in descending order of age, from left to right.

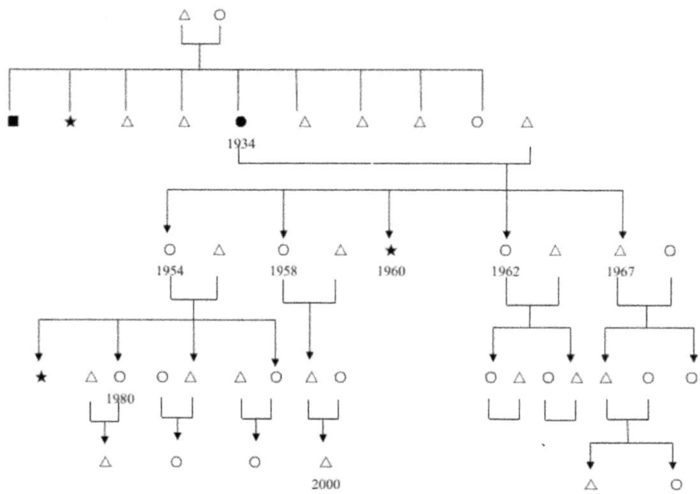

Figure A.83 **Genogram for Xianmie Pin's family**
▲: male interviewee; ●: female interviewee;
△: male; ○: female;
■: male who died before turning 15; ★: female who died before turning 15;
□: a pregnancy with unknown sex of the fetus;
The sex of those born within each generation are listed in descending order of age, from left to right.

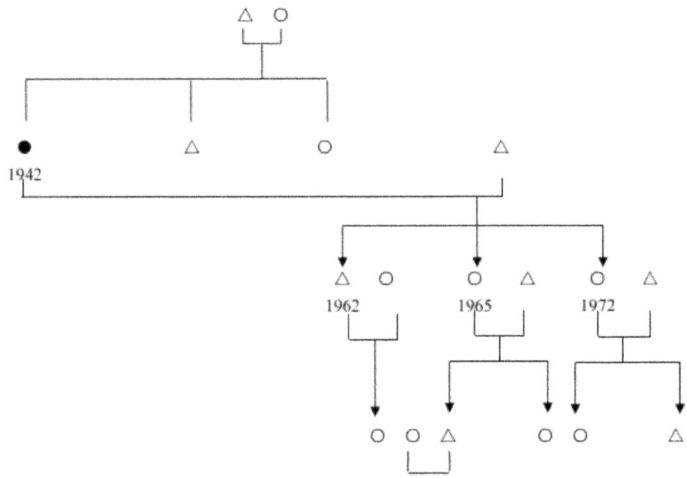

Figure A.84 **Genogram for Daomie Yanhanguo's family**
▲: male interviewee; ●: female interviewee;
△: male; ○: female;
■: male who died before turning 15; ★: female who died before turning 15;
□: a pregnancy with unknown sex of the fetus;

The sex of those born within each generation are listed in descending order of age, from left to right.

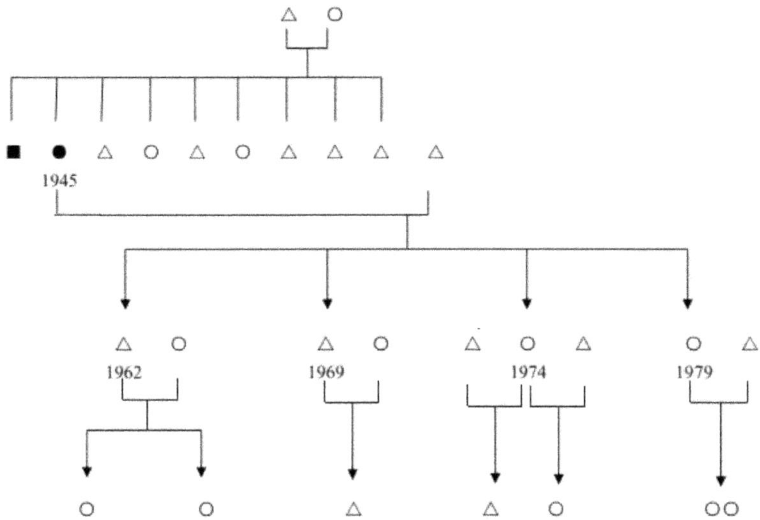

Figure A.85 **Genogram for Jinmie Yanxiangzuo's family**
▲: male interviewee; ●: female interviewee;
△: male; ○: female;
■: male who died before turning 15; ★: female who died before turning 15;
□: a pregnancy with unknown sex of the fetus;
The sex of those born within each generation are listed in descending order of age, from left to right.

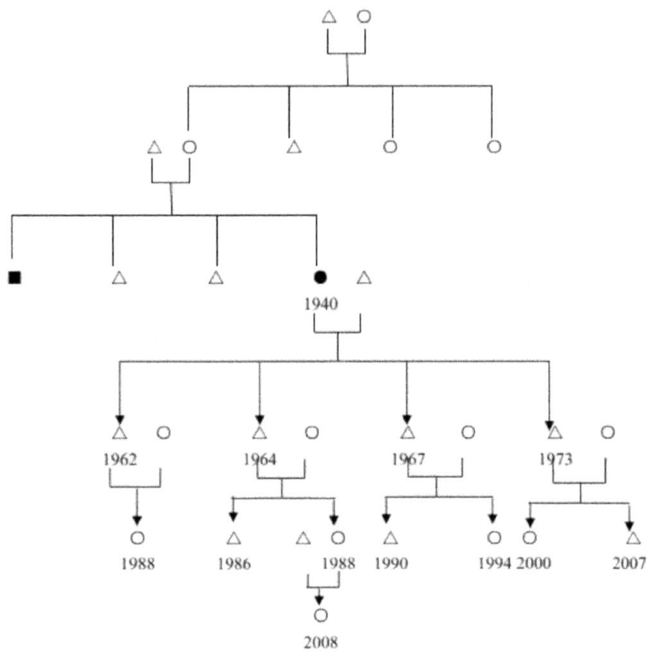

Figure A.86 **Genogram for Daomie Yanfangbao's family**
▲: male interviewee; ●: female interviewee;
△: male; ○: female;
■: male who died before turning 15; ★: female who died before turning 15;
□: a pregnancy with unknown sex of the fetus;
The sex of those born within each generation are listed in descending order of age, from left to right.

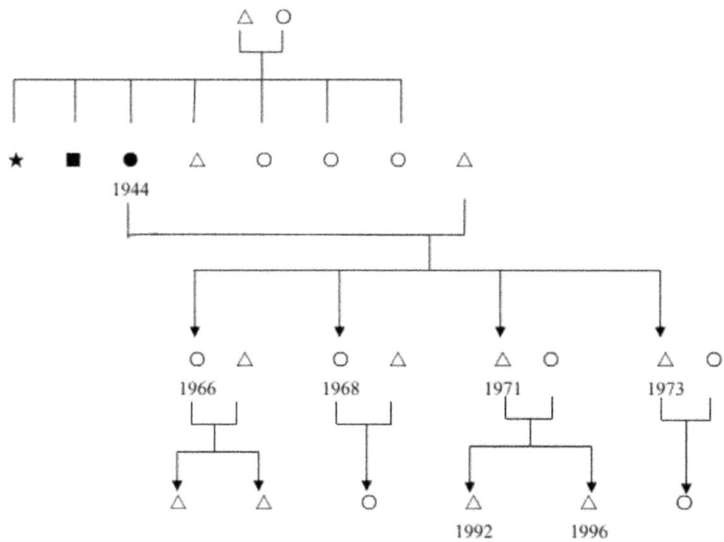

Figure A.87 **Genogram for Xiangmie Pin's family**
▲: male interviewee; ●: female interviewee;
△: male; ○: female;
■: male who died before turning 15; ★: female who died before turning 15;
□: a pregnancy with unknown sex of the fetus;
The sex of those born within each generation are listed in descending order of age, from left to right.

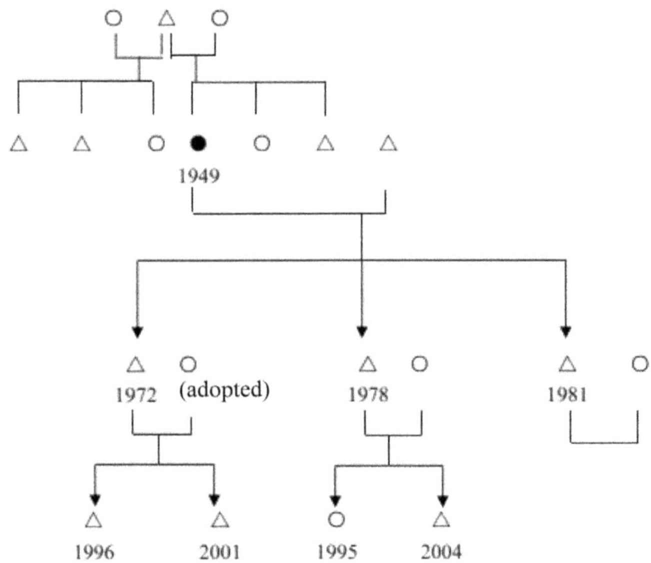

Figure A.88 **Genogram for Xianmie Guobao's family**
▲: male interviewee; ●: female interviewee;
△: male; ○: female;
■: male who died before turning 15; ★: female who died before turning 15;
□: a pregnancy with unknown sex of the fetus;
The sex of those born within each generation are listed in descending order of age, from left to right.

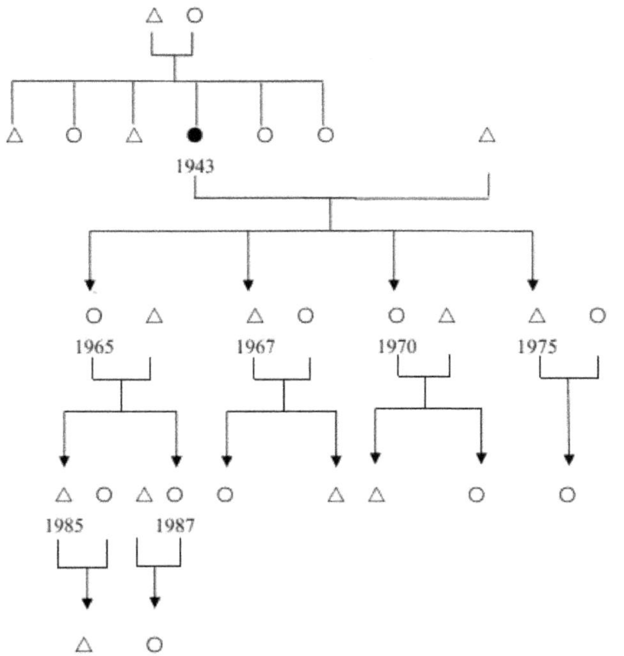

Figure A.89 **Genogram for Mie Yuefeng's family**
▲: male interviewee; ●: female interviewee;
△: male; ○: female;
■: male who died before turning 15; ★: female who died before turning 15;
□: a pregnancy with unknown sex of the fetus;
The sex of those born within each generation are listed in descending order of age, from left to right.

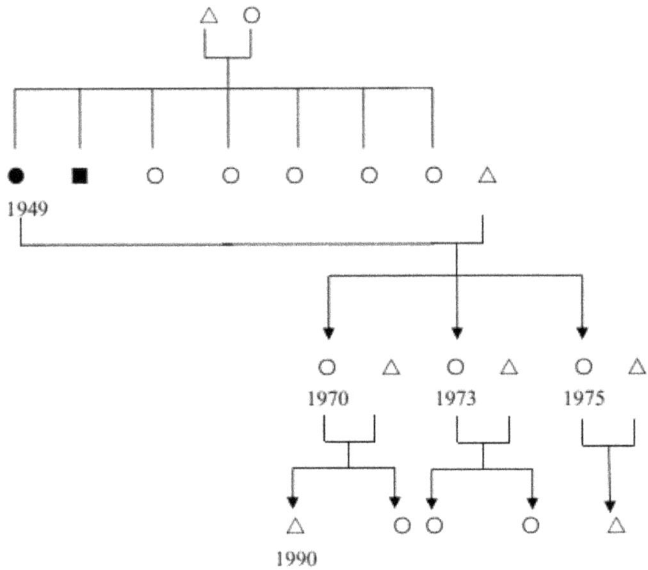

Figure A.90 **Genogram for Yuemie Hanjin's family**
▲: male interviewee; ●: female interviewee;
△: male; ○: female;
■: male who died before turning 15; ★: female who died before turning 15;
□: a pregnancy with unknown sex of the fetus;
The sex of those born within each generation are listed in descending order of age, from left to right.

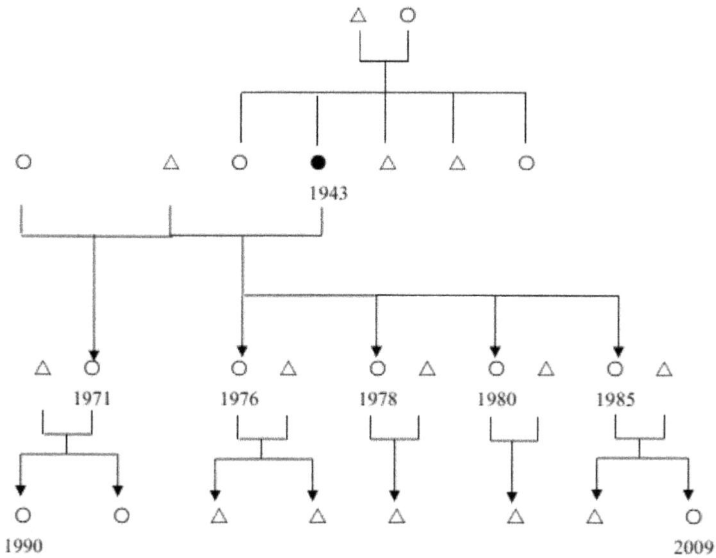

Figure A.91 **Genogram for Xiangmie Yuebaowang's family**
▲: male interviewee; ●: female interviewee;
△: male; ○: female;
■: male who died before turning 15; ★: female who died before turning 15;
□: a pregnancy with unknown sex of the fetus;

The sex of those born within each generation are listed in descending order of age, from left to right.

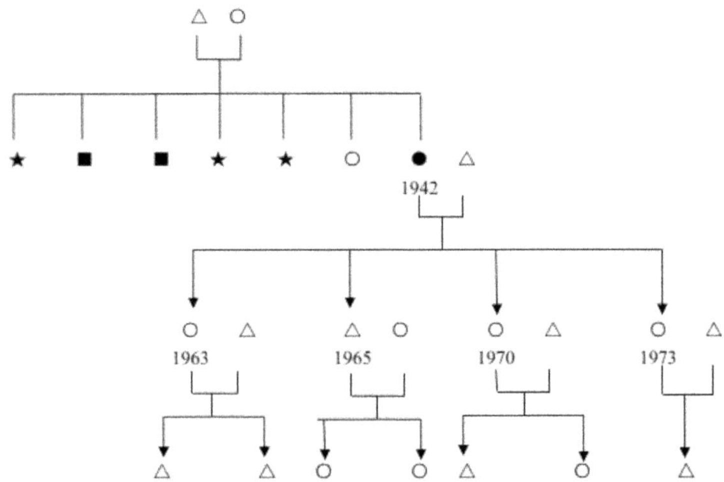

Figure A.92 **Genogram for Xiangmie Wanpa's family**
▲: male interviewee; ●: female interviewee;
△: male; ○: female;
■: male who died before turning 15; ★: female who died before turning 15;
□: a pregnancy with unknown sex of the fetus;
The sex of those born within each generation are listed in descending order of age, from left to right.

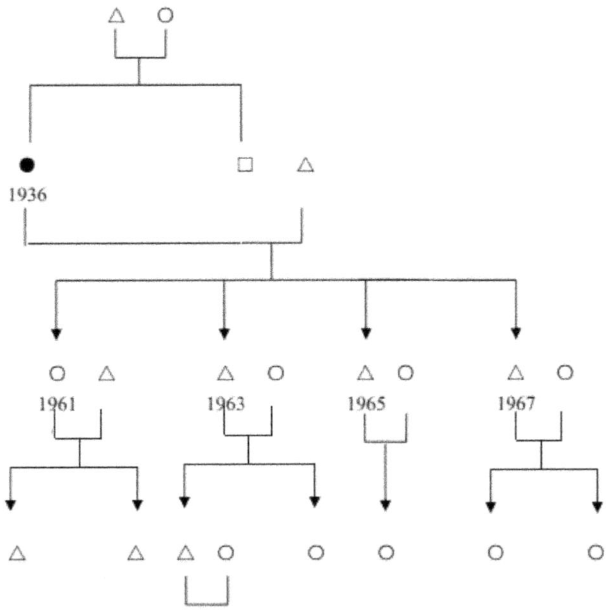

Figure A.93 **Genogram for Xiangmie Tuanhuang's family**
▲: male interviewee; ●: female interviewee;
△: male; ○: female;
■: male who died before turning 15; ★: female who died before turning 15;
□: a pregnancy with unknown sex of the fetus;
The sex of those born within each generation are listed in descending order of age, from left to right.

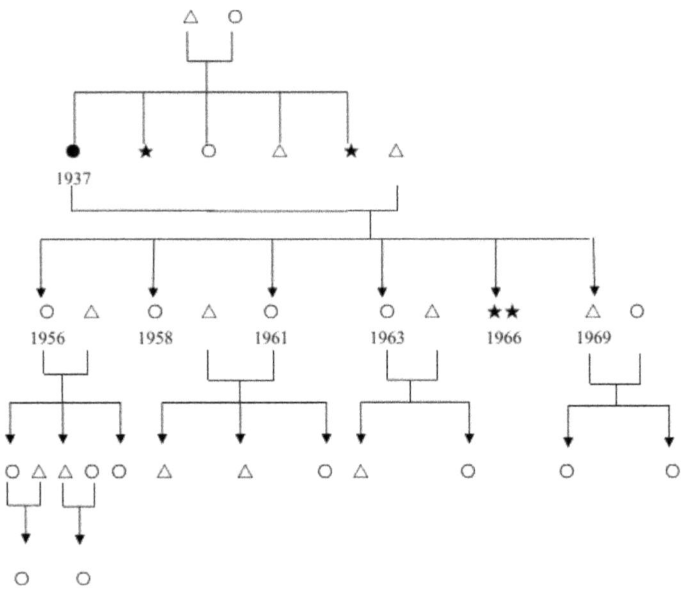

Figure A.94 **Genogram for Jinmie Hannuo's family**
▲: male interviewee; ●: female interviewee;
△: male; ○: female;
■: male who died before turning 15; ★: female who died before turning 15;
□: a pregnancy with unknown sex of the fetus;
The sex of those born within each generation are listed in descending order of age, from left to right.

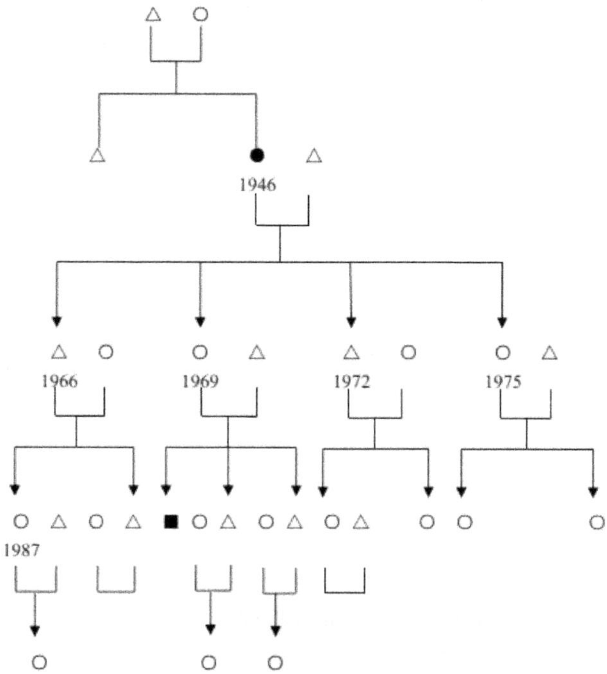

Figure A.95 **Genogram for Jinmie Yanhantuan's family**
▲: male interviewee; ●: female interviewee;
△: male; ○: female;
■: male who died before turning 15; ★: female who died before turning 15;
□: a pregnancy with unknown sex of the fetus;
The sex of those born within each generation are listed in descending order of age, from left to right.

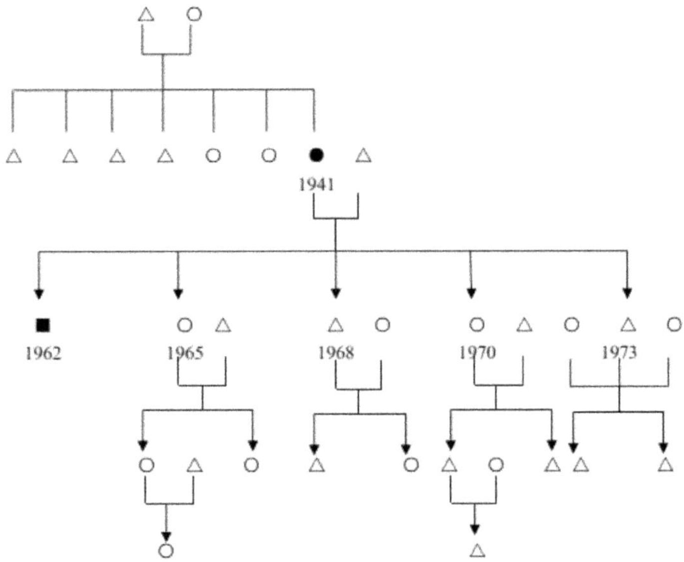

Figure A.96 **Genogram for Mie Yuexiang's family**
▲: male interviewee; ●: female interviewee;
△: male; ○: female;
■: male who died before turning 15; ★: female who died before turning 15;
□: a pregnancy with unknown sex of the fetus;
The sex of those born within each generation are listed in descending order of age, from left to right.

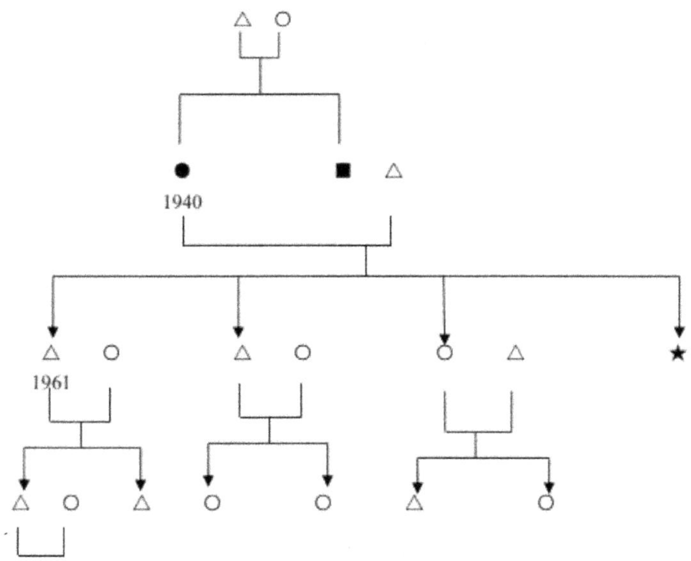

Figure A.97 **Genogram for Jinmie Yangtuanguo's family**
▲: male interviewee; ●: female interviewee;
△: male; ○: female;
■: male who died before turning 15; ★: female who died before turning 15;
□: a pregnancy with unknown sex of the fetus;
The sex of those born within each generation are listed in descending order of age, from left to right.

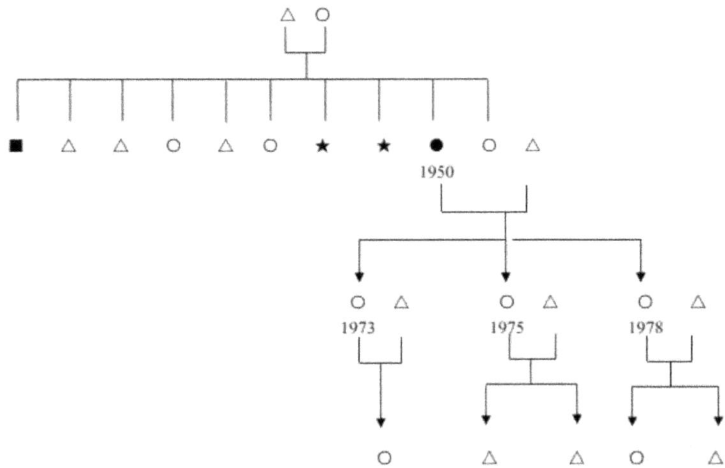

Figure A.98 **Genogram for Jinmie Yuebaowan's family**
▲: male interviewee; ●: female interviewee;
△: male; ○: female;
■: male who died before turning 15; ★: female who died before turning 15;
□: a pregnancy with unknown sex of the fetus;
The sex of those born within each generation are listed in descending order of age, from left to right.

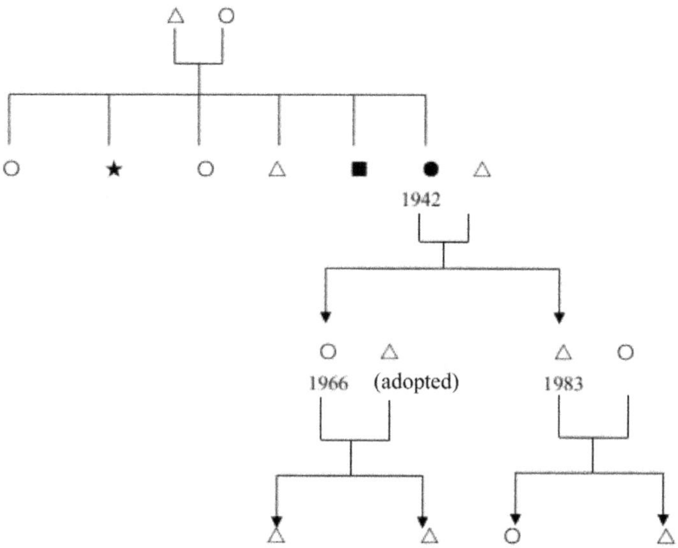

Figure A.99 **Genogram for Jiaomie Suoban's family**
▲: male interviewee; ●: female interviewee;
△: male; ○: female;
■: male who died before turning 15; ★: female who died before turning 15;
□: a pregnancy with unknown sex of the fetus;

The sex of those born within each generation are listed in descending order of age, from left to right.

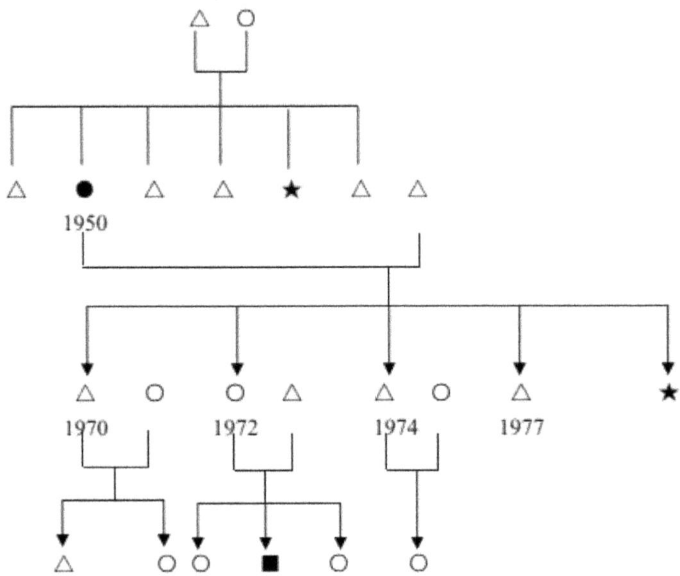

Figure A.100 **Genogram for Caimie Yanwan's family**

▲: male interviewee; ●: female interviewee;

△: male; ○: female;

■: male who died before turning 15; ★: female who died before turning 15;

□: a pregnancy with unknown sex of the fetus;

The sex of those born within each generation are listed in descending order of age, from left to right.

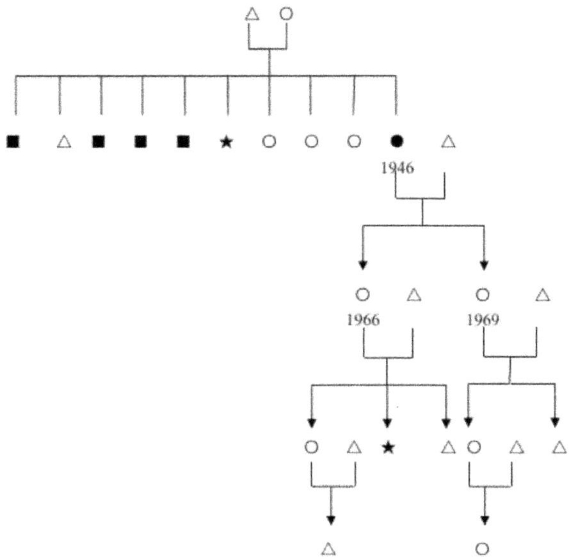

Figure A.101 **Genogram for Jiaomie Yuehansuo's family**
▲: male interviewee; ●: female interviewee;
△: male; ○: female;
■: male who died before turning 15; ★: female who died before turning 15;
□: a pregnancy with unknown sex of the fetus;

The sex of those born within each generation are listed in descending order of age, from left to right.

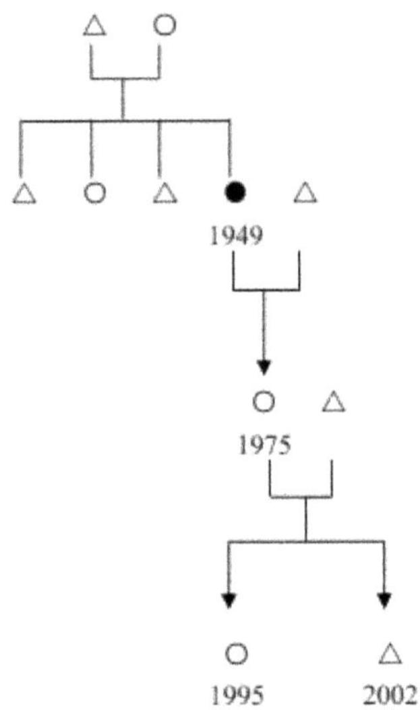

Figure A.102 **Genogram for Daomie Xianghuang's family**
▲: male interviewee; ●: female interviewee;
△: male; ○: female;
■: male who died before turning 15; ★: female who died before turning 15;
□: a pregnancy with unknown sex of the fetus;
The sex of those born within each generation are listed in descending order of age, from left to right.

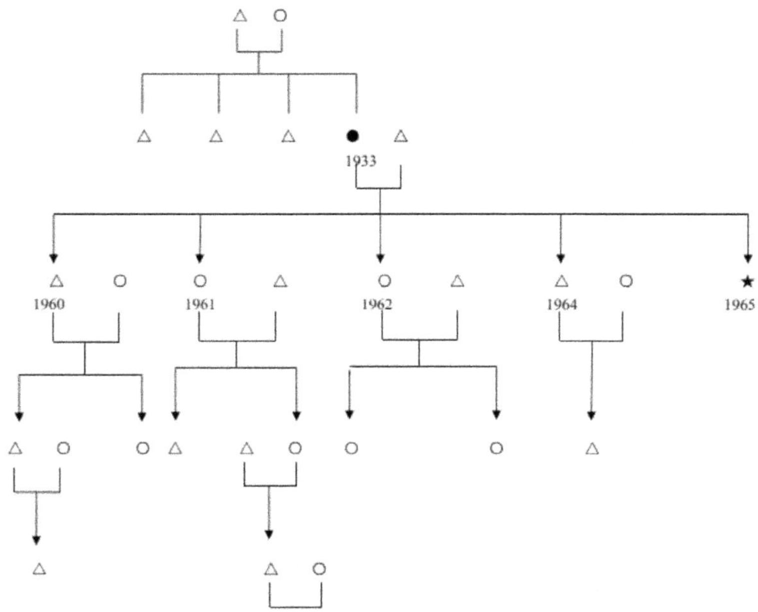

Figure A.103 **Genogram for Jiaomie Yanhanya's family**
▲: male interviewee; ●: female interviewee;
△: male; ○: female;
■: male who died before turning 15; ★: female who died before turning 15;
□: a pregnancy with unknown sex of the fetus;

The sex of those born within each generation are listed in descending order of age, from left to right.

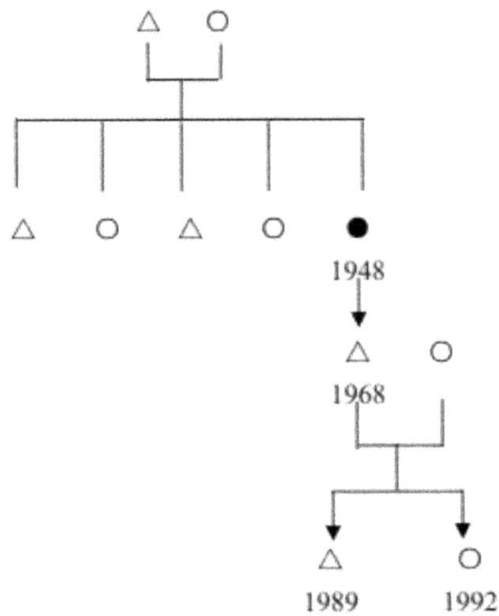

Figure A.104 **Genogram for Xiangmie Yanxiangbao's family**
▲: male interviewee; ●: female interviewee;
△: male; ○: female;
■: male who died before turning 15; ★: female who died before turning 15;
□: a pregnancy with unknown sex of the fetus;

The sex of those born within each generation are listed in descending order of age, from left to right.

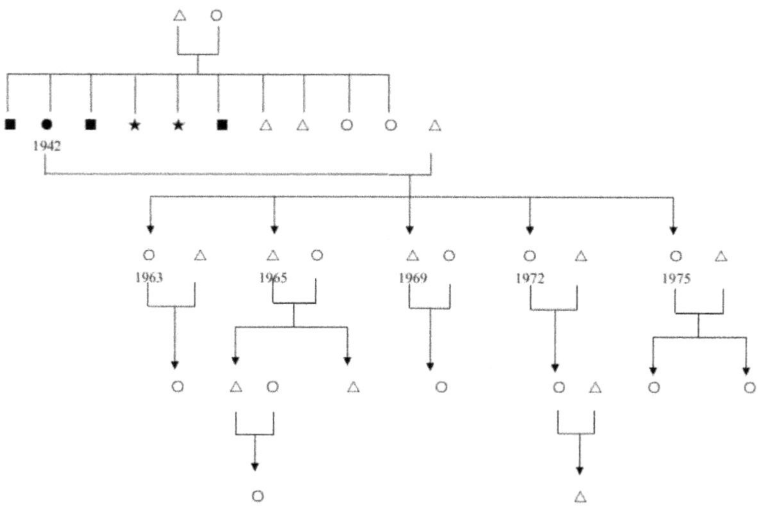

Figure A.105 **Genogram for Limie Gen'ao's family**
▲: male interviewee; ●: female interviewee;
△: male; ○: female;
■: male who died before turning 15; ★: female who died before turning 15;
□: a pregnancy with unknown sex of the fetus;
The sex of those born within each generation are listed in descending order of age, from left to right.

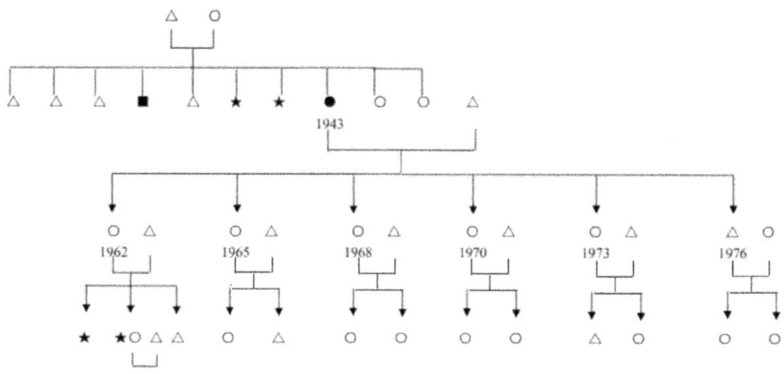

Figure A.106 **Genogram for Daomie Yuehan'ao's family**
▲: male interviewee; ●: female interviewee;
△: male; ○: female;
■: male who died before turning 15; ★: female who died before turning 15;
□: a pregnancy with unknown sex of the fetus;
The sex of those born within each generation are listed in descending order of age, from left to right.

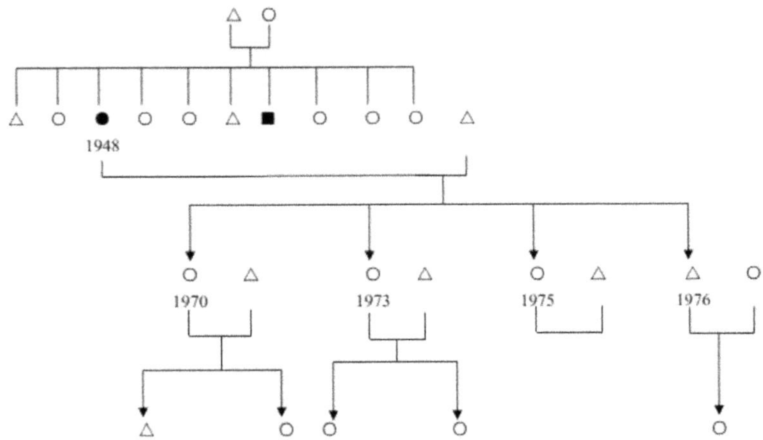

Figure A.107 **Genogram for Daomie Yuepaguo's family**
▲: male interviewee; ●: female interviewee;
△: male; ○: female;
■: male who died before turning 15; ★: female who died before turning 15;
□: a pregnancy with unknown sex of the fetus;
The sex of those born within each generation are listed in descending order of age, from left to right.

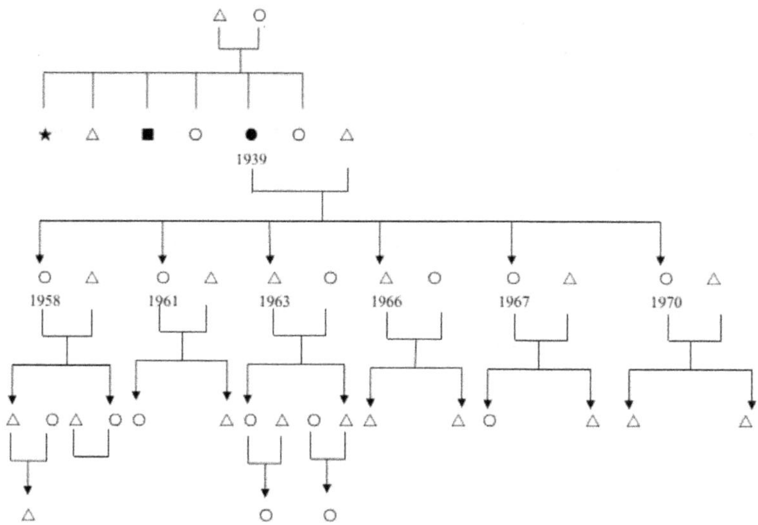

Figure A.108 **Genogram for Xiangmie Yuewangbao's family**
▲: male interviewee; ●: female interviewee;
△: male; ○: female;
■: male who died before turning 15; ★: female who died before turning 15;
□: a pregnancy with unknown sex of the fetus;

Village Z in Jiexiang Township of Ruili City

General Information of the Village and Surveyed Households

Situated in the southwest of Ruili City and surrounded by Huyu Township to the north, Longdao Township to the west and Myanmar to the south and southeast, Jiexiang Township is located approximately 20 kilometers away from the seat of government of Ruili City, and is cut through by the Gazhong-Leiyun Highway. It is composed of 13 villages, including Eluo, Longxiang and Hejie, and is a border town with close contact with Myanmar. village Z is in southwest Jiexiang Township and approximately six kilometers away from the seat of the township government. According to the statistics of the villagers' committee, as of December 2010, there were 714 residents (367 males and 347 females) in 163 households in the village. Except for 13 Han villagers, all the others were Dai. When the investigation team surveyed in the village in October 2011, there were 29 households (43 persons) meeting the survey criteria, making up 17.79% of the total households. The basic information of the surveyed households is listed below in the following Table A.20.

Records of the Reproductive Histories of the Surveyed Households Are Shown in the Following Table

Household No.: 2; Interviewee: Shuaien Miewang; Figure A.109

Current Generation:

Shuaien Miewan was born in 1946, got married in 1964, and had no children all the life. She adopted two children: one girl and one boy.

Children's Generation:

Her daughter gave birth to two children, both females (respectively in 1987 and 1990).

Her son gave birth to two children, both females (respectively in 1997 and 2000).

Grandchildren's Generation:

Her daughter's first child gave birth to one child, F (2009).

Her daughter's second child were unmarried and worked in the City of Ruili.

Her son's two children were both at school.

Unable to get pregnant for more than a year after marriage, Shuaien Meiwan adopted a girl in 1966 and a boy in 1973. The girl got married and lived separately, and the couple lived with the boy. Shuaien Miewan's husband passed away last year (2010).

Household No.: 5; Interviewee: Yue En; Figure A.110

Current Generation:

Yue En was born in 1936, married twice and gave birth to 11 children. Six children survived. She got married in 1952 and gave birth to six children with her first husband. Two children survived. Sex of the children in descending order: F (1953) – F – M – M – M (1960) – F. The first daughter and third son survived and all the others died in infancy. She got divorced in 1963 and remarried in 1964 and gave birth to five children with her second husband. Four children survived. Sex of the children in descending order: F (1964) – M (1967) – F (1970) – M (1973) – M (1975). The second son died within one year after birth.

Table A.20: Basic Information of the Interviewees (Born in or before 1950) in Village Z

Serial No.	Household No.	Name	Date of Birth	Age at First Marriage	Number of Lifetime Births	Surviving Births	Time at Last Birth	Age at Last Birth (Years Old)	Sex of children in descending order of birth
1	2	Shuaien Miewan	1946	18	0	2	–	–	F – M-
2	5	Yue En	1936	16	11	6	1975	39	F (F) (M) (M) M (F)F – M – F (M) – M
3	6	Yue Hantuan	1949	18	3	3	1978	29	M – M – M
4	8	Mei Hantuan	1947	18	7	7	1981	34	F – M – M – F – F – M – M
5	10	Moen Shuaimeng	1947	16	4	4	1971	24	M – M – F – F
6	12	Shuai Ensan	1950	30	2	2	–	–	F – F
7	14	Yue Enzhan	1937	17	10	10	1978	41	M – F – M – M – F – M – M – F – M – M
8	15	Xiang Henyan	1943	22	3	3	–	–	M – M – M
9	16	Shuai Enna	1941	20	1	2	1965	24	F – M
10	18	Mai Hanleng	1947	18	3	3	1973	26	F – F (M) – M
11	19	Mo Enshuai	1943	17	5	4	1975	32	F – F – F – F (M)
12	20	Han Shuai	1947	23	3	3	1978	31	F – F – F
13	21	Shuai Enpin	1949	17	4	4	1978	29	F – M – M – F
14	30	Shuai Henhan	1948	20	4	4	1978	30	M – M – F – M

(*Continued*)

Table A.20: Continued

15	43	Shuai Hanlun	1939	19	5	4	1971	32	(F)F – M – M – F
16	51	Mo Hanmen	1940	18	9	9	1977	37	M – F – M – M – M – F – F – M – M
17	60	Man Xianghuang	1941	19	6	4	1971	30	F – F (– F-) (– F-) – M – M
18	61	Ruiban Ruiliang	1951	–	0	0	–	–	–
19	62	Shuai Enlai	1947	16	9	9	1981	33	M – F – M – M – F – F – F – M – M
20	65	Ruiban	1946	18	4	4	1973	27	M – F – F – M
21	67	Yue Enman	1942	20	6	6	1973	31	F – M – M – M – M – M
22	68	Shuai Xiangbao	1941	17	7	6	1976	35	(F) M – F – M – F – F – F
23	69	Yu Hanwan	1929	18	9	8	1967	38	M (– F-) – M – F – F – F – F – M – M
24	70	Yuehan Xiangsha	1946	17	5	3	1966	20	(M) (M) – F – F – M
25	74	Mo Hanleng	1936	17	8	6	1967	31	(M) – M – M – M – F – M – F (M)
26	75	Yuehen Tuanwang	1927	19	10	8	1973	46	F – F – F (– F-) – F – F – M (M) – M – M
27	78	Shuai Xiangjing	1946	18	5	5	1976	28	F – M – F – F – F
28	90	Hanshuai Yanxin	1951	19	3	3	–	–	M – M – M
29	96	Yue Xiangyan	1948	19	4	4	1979	31	M – F – F – F

Source: Field Survey Statistics by the Research Team.

Children's Generation:

The first daughter got married in 1973 and gave birth to three children. Sex of the children in descending order: M (1974) – F (1976) – F (1978).

The second daughter died of illness at 15 years old (1993).

The third son gave birth to two children. Sex of the children in descending order: F (1982) – M (1985).

The fourth daughter (first daughter with her second husband) gave birth to two children, both males (respectively in 1989 and 1992).

The fourth son (first son with her second husband) gave birth to two children. Sex of the children in descending order: F (1994) – M (1998).

The fifth daughter (second daughter with her second husband) gave birth to two children. Sex of the children in descending order: M (1992) – F (1995).

The sixth son (third son with her second husband) were unmarried and worked away from this county.

Grandchildren's Generation:

The first daughter's first child gave birth to two children, both females (respectively in 2003 and 2007).

The first daughter's second child had never got pregnant and adopted a boy in 2011. Now, the boy wasn't yet one year old.

The third son's first child gave birth to two children. Sex of the children in descending order: F (2005) – M (2009).

The third son's second child gave birth to two children, both males (respectively in 2005 and 2011).

The fourth daughter's second child was married but still had no children.

All the other grandchildren were unmarried.

Great-grandchildren's Generation:

Seven great-grandchildren, four males and three females.

Household No.: 6; Interviewee: Yue Hantuan; Figure A.111

Current Generation:

Yue Hantuan was born in 1949, got married in 1967, and gave birth to three children, all males (respectively in 1971, 1975 and 1978).

Children's Generation:

The first son gave birth to two children. Sex of the children in descending order: M (1993) – F (1995). The daughter died a few months after birth.

The second son married a divorced woman with a daughter, who turned 16 years old this year. The second son gave birth to one child, M (2004).
The third son gave birth to one child, M (2006).

Grandchildren's Generation:
Four grandchildren, three males and one female, were unmarried.

Household No.: 8; Interviewee: Mei Hantuan; Figure A.112

Current Generation:
Mei Hantuan was born in 1947, got married in 1965, and gave birth to seven children. Seven births survived. Sex of the children in descending order: F (1966) – M (1968) – M (1970) – F (1973) – F (1977) – M (1979) – M (1981).

Children's Generation:
The first daughter was married to another village far away and her reproductive history was unknown
The first son gave birth to two children, both females (respectively in 1988 and 1990).
The second son was married and adopted a girl in 1988. Later, his wife got pregnant and gave birth to two children, both males (respectively in 1990 and 1993).
The second daughter was married to another village far away, and her reproductive history was unknown.
The third daughter gave birth to one child, M (1997), and the child was attending primary school.
The third son gave birth to two children. Sex of the children in descending order: M (1998) – F (2003).
The fourth son gave birth to one child, M (2008).

Grandchildren's Generation:
The first son's first child was married to another village far away, and her reproductive history was unknown.
The second son's first child was married but still had no children.
All the other grandchildren were unmarried.

Household No.: 10; Interviewee: Moen Shuaimeng; Figure A.113

Current Generation:

Moen Shuaimeng was born in 1947, got married in 1963 and gave birth to four children, all Four children survived. Sex of the children in descending order: M (1964) – M (1966) – F (1969) – F (1971).

Children's Generation:

The first son gave birth to two children. Sex of the children in descending order: F (1985) – M (1988).

The second son gave birth to two children. Sex of the children in descending order: M (1984) – F (1986).

The first daughter gave birth to one child, F (1994).

The second daughter gave birth to two children. Sex of the children in descending order: F (1991) – M (1995).

Grandchildren's Generation:

The first son's first child was married to another village far away, and her reproductive history was unknown.

The first son's second child gave birth to one child, M (2009).

The second son's first child gave birth to one child, M (2008).

The second son's second child gave birth to two children, both males (respectively in 2005 and 2010).

The first daughter's first child gave birth to one child, one male, who was now 17 years old (1994).

The second daughter's two children were unmarried. The first child worked outside this village, and the second child was attending junior middle school.

Great-grandchildren's Generation:

Four great-grandchildren, all males.

Household No.: 12; Interviewee: Shuai Ensan; Figure A.114

Current Generation:

Shuai Ensan was born in 1950, got married in 1980, and adopted a girl in 1984. Later, his wife gave birth to one child in 1989, a female.

Children's Generation:

The first daughter adopted a girl in 2005 and later gave birth to one child, M (2007).

The second daughter gave birth to one child, F (2011).

Grandchildren's Generation:

Three grandchildren, one male and two females. All were still young.

Household No.: 14; Interviewees: Yue Enzhan and Ruan Xianghen; Figure A.115

Current Generation:

Yue Enzhan was born in 1937, got married in 1954, and her husband was born in 1931. The couple gave birth to 10 children. 10 children survived. Sex of the children in descending order: M (1955) – F (1957) – M (1958) – M (1959) – F (1961) – M (1963) – M (1966) – F (1970) – M (1974) – M (1978).

Children's Generation:

The first son gave birth to four children. Sex of the children in descending order: F – M – M – F. The first child died young.

The first daughter gave birth to three children. Sex of the children in descending order: F – F – M.

The second son gave birth to two children. Sex of the children in descending order: M (1983) – F (1985).

The third son gave birth to two children, both males (respectively in 1980 and 1982).

The second daughter gave birth to two children, both males.

The fourth son gave birth to two children, both females (respectively in 1985 and 1987). The second child died in infancy.

The fifth son gave birth to two children. Sex of the children in descending order: M (1989) – F (1993).

The third daughter gave birth to two children, both males (respectively in 1995 and 1997). The first baby died soon and the third daughter received the only-child certificate.

The sixth son gave birth to two children, both males (respectively in 2006 and 2008).

Seventh son gave birth to two children. Sex of the children in descending order: F (2001) – M (2006).

Grandchildren's Generation:

The first son's second child gave birth to two children, both males.

The first son's third child was married and gave birth to one child, F. Later, he was divorced and his daughter lived with his former wife.

The first son's fourth child gave birth to one child, M (2011). She died soon after the child's birth.

The first daughter's first child gave birth to two children, both males (respectively in 1997 and 2000).

The first daughter's second child gave birth to two children. Sex of the children in descending order: M – F.

The first daughter's third child was recently married and still had no children.

The second son's first child gave birth to two children, both males. The first child died soon after birth.

The second son's second child gave birth to one child, F. She was divorced and her daughter lived with her former husband.

The third son's first child gave birth to two children. Sex of the children in descending order: M (2001) – F (2007).

The third son's second child gave birth to two children. Sex of the children in descending order: F (2005) – M (2010).

The second daughter's first child were unmarried.

The second daughter's second child gave birth to one child, F (2008).

The fourth son's first child gave birth to one child, M (2007).

The fifth son's two children were married but still had no children.

All the other grandchildren were unmarried.

Great-grandchildren's Generation:

16 great-grandchildren, 10 males and six females.

One of their 10 children lived in Myanmar, two lived outside this village and the remaining lived in this village. Their three children in Myanmar and outside this village would bring some gifts to visit them.

Household No.: 15; Interviewee: Xiang Henyan; Figure A.116

Current Generation:

Xiang Henyan was born in 1943, got married in 1965 and gave birth to three children, all males (respectively in 1967, 1970 and 1975).

Children's Generation:

The first son gave birth to two children, both males (respectively in 1987 and 1989).

The second son gave birth to two children. Sex of the children in descending order: M (1990) – F (1995).

The third son gave birth to one child, F (1994).

Grandchildren's Generation:

The first son's first child gave birth to one child, M (2011).

The first son's second child got married recently and still had no children.

All the other grandchildren were unmarried.

Household No.: 16; Interviewee: Shuai Enna; Figure A.117

Current Generation:

Shuai Enna was born in 1941, got married in 1961 and gave birth to one child, F (1965) and adopted one child, M (1975).

Children's Generation:

Daughter gave birth to three children. Sex of the children in descending order: M (1993) – F (1995) – F (1997).

Son gave birth to one child, F (1997), and received the only-child certificate.

Grandchildren's Generation:

Four grandchildren, one male and three females, all were unmarried.

Shuai Enna gave birth to her daughter in 1965. After divorce, she emigrated with her daughter back to this village, and adopted a boy in 1975. With her daughter married to Myanmar, she lived with her son. When asked of "why did you only give birth to one child and never get pregnant once again?" She answered: "I don't know why." I added: "Did you go to see a doctor?" she answered: "I already had a kid. I didn't go to see a doctor. It's fine if you have already had a child. There is no need to see a doctor. You won't be pregnant if you don't want to."

Household No.: 18; Interviewees: Mai Hanleng and Mai Hanyan; Figure A.118

Current Generation:

Mai Hanleng was born in 1947, got married in 1965 and her husband was born in 1945. The couple gave birth to three children. Sex of the children in descending order: F (1966) – F (1971) – M (1973). Their son died two days after birth, and they adopted one boy (born in June 1978) in 1979.

Children's Generation:

The first daughter gave birth to two children. Sex of the children in descending order: M (1992) – F (1995).

The second daughter gave birth to two children. Sex of the children in descending order: F (1991) – M (1995).

Their son gave birth to two children, both males (respectively in 1998 and 2003).

Grandchildren's Generation:

The first daughter's first child was married but still had no children.

The second daughter's first child was married but still had no children.

All the other grandchildren were unmarried.

Mai Hanleng underwent a tubal ligation surgery after giving birth to the third child, and the baby died two days later. When asked "If there were no ligation, would you want another child?" she replied: "No, I was very sad after the baby died. I didn't want to have another one." When asked "So why did you adopt another boy?" she replied: "This boy was a relative's baby. They have too many kids to raise them all. So, I adopted the boy."

Household No.: 19; Interviewees: Mo Enshuai and Mei Henyan; Figure A.119

Current Generation:

Mo Enshuai was born in 1943, got married in 1960 and her husband was born in 1941. The couple gave birth to five children. Four children survived. Sex of the children in descending order: F (1962) – F (1964) – F (1969) – F (1973) – M (1978). The boy died a few months after birth.

Children's Generation:

The first daughter gave birth to two children. Sex of the children in descending order: F (1984) – M (1987).

The second daughter married twice. She gave birth to one child with her first husband, M (1988). Later, she remarried and gave birth to one child with her second husband, F (2002).

The third daughter gave birth to two children. Sex of the children in descending order: F (1991) – M (1995).

The fourth daughter gave birth to two children, both males (respectively in 1997 and 2001).

Grandchildren's Generation:

The first daughter's first child gave birth to two children, both males (respectively in 2005 and 2010).

The first daughter's second child gave birth to one child, M (2008).

The second daughter's first child was married and had no children and was divorced.

The third daughter's first child gave birth to one child, M (2011).
All the other grandchildren were unmarried.

Great-grandchildren's Generation:
Four great-grandchildren, all males.

Household No.: 20; Interviewees: Han Shuai and Yuehan Yanleng; Figure A.120

Current Generation:
Han Shuai was born in 1947, got married in 1970, and her husband was born in 1945. The couple gave birth to three children, all females (respectively in 1972, 1975, and 1978).

Children's Generation:
The first daughter gave birth to two children. Sex of the children in descending order: F (1993) – M (2001).
The second daughter was married but still had no children.
The third daughter was married but still had no children.

Grandchildren's Generation:
Two grandchildren, one male and one female.
Han Shuai liked to read since childhood and was a local teacher after graduating from her junior high school. When asked why she didn't have a boy, she said, "Three kids are enough. For we Dai people, it doesn't matter if you have had a boy or a girl in the future, you just have to have children."
As for the issue of children's fertility, her view was: "(Though her second and third daughters were both in their 30s and had not given birth to any children, but) this kind of thing is up to the children themselves: If they want to have children, they will do it. And if they don't want it, yes, it also doesn't matter." When asked why her two daughters have not had any children after many years into their marriage, the second daughter replied: "I got married in 2004 (29 years old) and worked in the Municipal Disabled Persons' Federation. I was too busy at work and traveled a lot. So, I was in no mood to have children." The third daughter said: "I got married in 2003 (25 years old), and my husband is a man from Harbin. We have been working outside the village and didn't have time to have children. And we would have no time devoted to children even if we had them. We don't want to have our parents babysit for us. We don't want to bring troubles to them." When asked, "If you don't have children, what should you do

when you get old in the future?" The third daughter said: "I don't think so much now. I won't bother to worry about such a thing before I get old. Also, a friend working at the family planning office said that the government will take care of the elderly without children."

Household No.: 21; Interviewee: Shuai Enpin; Figure A.121

Current Generation:

Shuai Enpin was born in 1949, got married in 1966, and gave birth to four children. Sex of the children in descending order: F (1967) – M (1969) – M (1976) – F (1978).

Children's Generation:

The first daughter gave birth to two children. Sex of the children in descending order: F (1985) – M (1988).

The second son gave birth to two children, both females (respectively in 1993 and 1998).

The third son gave birth to two children. Sex of the children in descending order: F (1994) – M (1997). The couple adopted a boy in 1999 after their baby boy died.

The second daughter gave birth to two children. Sex of the children in descending order: M (1996) – F (2000).

Grandchildren's Generation:

The first daughter's first child gave birth to one child, M (2006).

The first daughter's second child was married but still had no children.

The first son's first child gave birth to one child, F (2011).

All the other grandchildren were unmarried.

Great-grandchildren's Generation:

Two great-grandchildren, one male and one female.

Household No.: 30; Interviewees: Shuai Henhan and Mo Hanyan; Figure A.122

Current Generation:

Shuai Henhan was born in 1948, got married in 1968, and gave birth to four children. Sex of the children in descending order: M (1970) – M (1974) – F (1976) – M (1978).

Children's Generation:

The first son gave birth to one child (twins), F (1997). The first son died in 1975.

The second son gave birth to one child, F (2006).

The first daughter gave birth to two children. Sex of the children in descending order: M (2004) – F (2009).

The third son gave birth to two children. Sex of the children in descending order: M – F. The third son died in 2010.

Grandchildren's Generation:

Seven grandchildren, two males and five females.

Household No.: 43; Interviewee: Shuai Hanlun; Figure A.123

Current Generation:

Shuai Hanlun was born in 1939, got married in 1958, and gave birth to five children. Four children survived. Sex of the children in descending order: F (1960) – F (1964) – M (1966) – M (1969) – F (1971). The first daughter died more than three months after birth.

Children's Generation:

The second daughter gave birth to two children. Sex of the children in descending order: F (1984) – M (1987).

The first son gave birth to two children. Sex of the children in descending order: M (1986) – F (1989).

The third son gave birth to two children. Sex of the children in descending order: M (1989) – F (1994).

The second daughter gave birth to one child, M (1993), and received the only-child certificate.

Grandchildren's Generation:

The second daughter's first child gave birth to one child, M (2008).

The second daughter's second child gave birth to one child, M (2011).

The first son's first child were unmarried and worked away from this county.

The first son's second child was married but still had no children.

All the other grandchildren were unmarried.

Great-grandchildren's Generation:

Two great-grandchildren, all males.

Recalling the experience of having a baby, Shuai Hanlun said: "It's too hard to have a baby, every time I get pregnant, my stomach hurts to death.

When pregnant with the fifth baby, I heard that some surgery (having people no longer get pregnant) may be performed in the city. I was very happy with the news. I went to have the surgery shortly after having the baby, and have since been a lot easier and relaxed!"

Household No.: 51; Interviewee: Mo Hanmen; Figure A.124

Current Generation:

Mo Hanmen was born in 1940, got married in 1958, and gave birth to nine children all her life. Nine children survived. Sex of the children in descending order: M (1960) – F (1962) – M (1963) – M (1965) – M (1967) – F (1970) – F (1972) – M (1975) – M (1977).

Children's Generation:

The first son married twice. He had no children with his first wife and adopted one girl. When they got divorced, his first wife took away the adopted girl. He later married his second wife and gave birth to two children with her. Sex of the children in descending order: M (1983) – F (1987).

The first daughter gave birth to two children, both females (respectively in 1983 and 1989).

The second son gave birth to two children. Sex of the children in descending order: F (1983) – M (1986).

The third son gave birth to two children. Sex of the children in descending order: F (1988) – M (1992).

The fourth son gave birth to two children, both males (respectively in 1990 and 1995).

The second daughter gave birth to one child, M (1992), and received the only-child certificate.

The third daughter was married and had no children, but her husband had two daughters (with his former wife) (1987 and 1989).

The fifth son gave birth to two children. Sex of the children in descending order: F (1996) – M (2001).

The sixth son gave birth to two children. Sex of the children in descending order: M (1999) – F (2005).

Grandchildren's Generation:

The first son's first child gave birth to one child, M (2007).

The first son's second child gave birth to one child, F (2009).

The first daughter's first child gave birth to one child, M (2007).
The first daughter's second child gave birth to one child, F (2009).
The second son's first child gave birth to one child, F (2008).
The second son's second child gave birth to one child, M (2006).
All the other grandchildren were unmarried.

Great-grandchildren's Generation:

Six great-grandchildren, three males and three females.

Mo Hanmen was very emotional with her pregnancy and childbirth and said that she had five children in 10 years, and it was very hard. She had always carried her kids with her while working in the farming fields, which was much tiring and harder than others. When asked why she had so many children, she said, "I like kids, so I gave birth to five children. In addition, I found it would be too tiring to have additional kids, but at that time, there was nothing you could do about it (birth control). I didn't have any other way (contraceptives). Indeed, it was said that drugs could do the trick, but that would also do damage to health. I wrote off drugs, so I had to continue to give birth to so many children. Later, it was said that the surgical ligation or an IUD may work. It was rumored that the ligation hurts (because the ligation is a knife surgery), (I) was nearly scared to death, so I (chose) an IUD and carried it for six years. However, the IUD method was rumored to be not very reliable either, so finally (1983), I decided to take the surgical ligation. Since the operation, I had been completely at ease!"

Household No.: 60; Interviewee: Man Xianghuang; Figure A.125

Current Generation:

Man Xianghuang was born in 1941, got married in 1960, and gave birth to six children. Four children survived. Sex of the children in descending order: F (1961) – F (1963) – F (1965) – F (1967) – M (1969) – M (1971). The third and fourth daughters both died a few days after birth.

Children's Generation:

The first daughter gave birth to four children. Sex of the children in descending order: M (1982) – M (1985) – F – M (1987). The girl died a few days after birth.

The second daughter gave birth to two children. Sex of the children in descending order: F (1984) – M (1988).

The first son gave birth to two children, both males (respectively in 1986 and 1988).

The second son gave birth to two children. Sex of the children in descending order: M (1992) – F (1996).

Grandchildren's Generation:

The first daughter's first child gave birth to two children, F – M. The boy died a few months after birth and he received the one-child certificate.

The first daughter's second child gave birth to one child, M (2008).

The first daughter's fourth child gave birth to one child, F (2007).

The second daughter's first child gave birth to one child, M (2007).

The second daughter's second child were unmarried.

The first son's first child married three times and had never given birth to any children all his life. He had no children with his first wife and got divorced, then married his second wife, who had a girl with her former husband, and got divorced, and finally married his third wife, who also had a girl with her former husband. Now, he lived with his third wife and the girl.

The first son's second child was newly married and still had no children.

All the other grandchildren were unmarried.

Great-grandchildren's Generation:

Three great-grandchildren, two males and one female.

Household No.: 61; Interviewee: Ruiban Ruiliang;

Current Generation:

Ruiban Ruiliang was born in 1951 and was unmarried all her life.

When asked "why have you been single?", she said: "I didn't look very good (she was fat). No man in this village would like me, so, I remained single. Actually, a lad had fallen in love with me, but he isn't a Dai man. I don't want to marry a man of other ethnic descents. As a result, I remain unmarried. Now, I am a leftover woman, and no man wants to marry me anymore." Yet, about this topic, she seemed to be open and hilarious, showing no hint of sadness and joking with us.

Household No.: 62; Interviewees: Shuai Enlai and Yue Xianger; Figure A.126

Current Generation:

Shuai Enlai was born in 1948 and got married in 1964. Her husband was born in 1945. The couple gave birth to nine children. Nine births survived. Sex of the children in descending order: M (1965) – F (1966) – M (1968) – M (1970) – F (1973) – F (1975) – F (1977) – M (1979) – M (1981).

Children's Generation:

The first son gave birth to two children, both males (respectively in 1988 and 1990).

The first daughter gave birth to three children. Sex of the children in descending order: F (1987) – F (1990) – M (1995).

The second son gave birth to two children, both males (respectively in 1990 and 1994).

The third son gave birth to two children. Sex of the children in descending order: M (1996) – F (2001). The son died in infancy.

The second daughter gave birth to one child, M (1996).

The third daughter gave birth to two children. Sex of the children in descending order: F (2000) – M (2006).

The fourth daughter gave birth to two children, both males (respectively in 2005 and 2009).

The fourth son was a monk (now, a Great Buddha).

The fifth son got married in 2011 and had not yet had any children.

Grandchildren's Generation:

The first son's first child gave birth to one child, F (2011).

The first daughter's first child gave birth to one child, F (2008).

All the other grandchildren were unmarried.

Great-grandchildren's Generation:

Two great-grandchildren, all females.

On why she had so many children, Shuai Enlai said: "The main reason is that my mother and grandmother wanted me to have more children. When ligation surgery was available in the 1970s, they all advised me not to have it. My mother had nine children, but only two of them survived, so she was wary that the same thing might happen to me. Therefore, she insisted that I should have more children." I asked: "Now, your children are all grown up and very healthy. Are you very happy with that? But it was very tiring to bring them up by yourself, wasn't it?" She replied: "Tiring. I was tired to death. You see, both of us (she and her husband) look so tired (looking older than they are)." She even joked in a witty way: "Later, they (her mother and grandmother) all were both surprised and confused by the survival of all my nine children, and had once asked me: 'How come all of your children managed to survive? Why?'" Seeing how hard she was – getting married late and having to work very hard to support a big family, her own children all claimed, "My mother learned from her mother, but we cannot learn from her. It's hard to give birth to so many children!" The eldest grandchildren – two grandsons and one granddaughter – were all in their 20s and had not dated. When asked why they had not dated, they all said they were in no hurry, and would wait until having had enough fun.

Household No.: 65; Interviewees: Ruiban and Yue Huangyi; Figure A.127

Current Generation:

Ruiban was born in 1947 and got married in 1963. Her husband Yue Huangyi was born in 1947. The couple gave birth to four children. Four children survived. Sex of the children in descending order: M (1965) – F (1969) – F (1971) – M (1973).

Children's Generation:

The first son gave birth to two children, both males (respectively in 1989 and 1991).

The first daughter gave birth to two children. Sex of the children in descending order: M (1988) – F (1991).

The second daughter gave birth to two children, both females (respectively in 1997 and 2000).

The second son gave birth to two children. Sex of the children in descending order: F (1996) – M (2000).

Grandchildren's Generation:

The first son's first child was married but still had no children.

The first daughter's first child and second child both were married but still had no children.

All the other grandchildren were unmarried.

Ruiban said she took the ligation surgery together with her friends. At that time, there was a sick old man and four kids to be taken care of in her family. It was very hard for her. She said, "I couldn't take a rest even back home from a hard day in the farming fields. I was so tired from housework every day. Completely exhausted. I was afraid of getting pregnant once again. Sometimes, I had to carry the kid with me while planting rice seedlings in the fields. It was really a grueling experience to have more kids!"

Household No.: 67; Interviewees: Yue Enman and Shuai Enyan; Figure A.128

Current Generation:

Yue Enman was born in 1942 and got married in 1962. Her husband Shuai Enyan was born in 1941. The couple gave birth to six children. Six children survived. Sex of the children in descending order: F (1964) – M (1966) – M (1968) – M (1970) – M (1972) – M (1974).

Children's Generation:

The first daughter gave birth to two children. Sex of the children in descending order: F (1985) – M (1991).

The first son gave birth to two children. Sex of the children in descending order: M (1985) – F (1988).

The second son gave birth to two children. Sex of the children in descending order: F (1985) – M (1989).

The third son gave birth to two children. Sex of the children in descending order: F (1991) – M (1995).

The fourth son gave birth to two children, both females (respectively in 1994 and 2000).

The fifth son gave birth to two children. Sex of the children in descending order: F (1997) – M (2001).

Grandchildren's Generation:

The first daughter's first child gave birth to one child, M (2006).

The first son's first child was married but still had no children.

The second son's first child gave birth to one child, M (2006).

The second son's second child was married but still had no children.

The third son's first child gave birth to one child, F (2008).

All the other grandchildren were unmarried.

Great-grandchildren's Generation:

Three great-grandchildren, two males and one female.

Yue Enman said that having heard of it (the contraception method), she went to have the tubal ligation surgery with her friends. After inquiring into her situation, the doctor urged her to keep the fetus: "Dear sister, you have only one girl, and all your other kids are boys. Why do you want to have surgery? Let the baby be born, it is another girl!" She replied: "No. I don't want to have another one!"

Household No.: 68; Interviewee: Shuai Xiangbao; Figure A.129

Current Generation:

Shuai Xiangbao was born in 1941, got married in 1958, and gave birth to seven children. Six children survived. Sex of the children in descending order: F (1959) – M (1961) – F (1967) – M (1970) – F (1972) – F (1974) – F (1976). The first daughter died of illness at eight years old.

Children's Generation:

The first son gave birth to three children. Sex of the children in descending order: F (1981) – F (1983) – M (1985).

The second daughter gave birth to two children. Sex of the children in descending order: F (1986) – M (1990).

The second son gave birth to two children. Sex of the children in descending order: M (1994) – F (1998).

The third daughter gave birth to two children, both males (respectively in 1994 and 1999).

The fourth daughter gave birth to two children, both males (respectively in 1991 and 2011).

The fifth daughter gave birth to two children, both females (respectively in 1999 and 2004).

Grandchildren's Generation:

The first son's first child gave birth to two children, both females (respectively in 2003 and 2008).

The first son's second child was married but still had no children.

The first son's third child gave birth to one child, F (2008).

The second daughter's first child gave birth to one child, M (2008).

The second daughter's second child was married but still had no children.

All the other grandchildren were unmarried.

Great-grandchildren's Generation:

Four great-grandchildren, one male and three females.

Household No.: 69; Interviewee: Yu Hanwang, Figure A.130

Current Generation:

Yu Hanwan was born in 1929, got married in 1947, and gave birth to nine children. Eight births survived. Sex of the children in descending order: M (1948) – F (1951) – M (1954) – F (1956) – F (1959) – F (1961) – F (1963) – M (1965) – M (1967). The first daughter died in infancy.

Children's Generation:

The first son was Yue Xiangyan from Household No. 96 in this village (his reproductive history is described below).

The second son gave birth to two children. Sex of the children in descending order: F (1983) – M (1994). He died 10 years ago (2001, 47 years old)

The second daughter gave birth to four children. Sex of the children in descending order: M – M (1981) – M- F (1984). The first son and third son died in infancy.

The third daughter gave birth to three children. Sex of the children in descending order: F (1978) – F (1981) – M (1984).

The fourth daughter gave birth to two children. Sex of the children in descending order: F (1983) – M (1985).

The fifth daughter gave birth to three children. Sex of the children in descending order: F (1979) – F (1984) – M (1987).

The third son gave birth to two children. Sex of the children in descending order: F (1987) – M (1990).

The fourth son gave birth to two children, both females (respectively in 1988 and 1991).

Grandchildren's Generation:

The second son's first child gave birth to two children, both males (respectively in 2005 and 2009).

The second son's second child were unmarried.

The second daughter's second child gave birth to two children, both females (respectively in 2005 and 2011).

The second daughter's fourth child gave birth to two children, both males (respectively in 2001 and 2006).

The third daughter's first child gave birth to one child, M (2007).

The third daughter's second child gave birth to one child, F (2005).

The third daughter's third child gave birth to one child, M (2007).
The fourth daughter's first child gave birth to one child, F (2007).
The fourth daughter's second child was married but still had no children.
The fifth daughter's first child was married but still had no children.
The fifth daughter's second child gave birth to one child, F (2005).
The fifth daughter's third child gave birth to one child, M (2011).
The third son's first child gave birth to one child, M (2009).
The third son's second child was married but still had no children.
The fourth son's two daughters were unmarried.

Great-grandchildren's Generation:

13 great-grandchildren, eight males and five females.

Household No.: 70; Interviewees: Yuehan Xiangsha and Gan Hansai; Figure A.131

Current Generation:

Yuehan Xiangsha was born in 1941 and got married in 1958. Her husband Gan Hansai was born in 1941. The couple gave birth to five children. Three children survived. Sex of the children in descending order: M (1959) – M (1960) – F (1962) – F (1964) – M (1966). The first son and second son both died within one year.

Children's Generation:

The first daughter gave birth to two children, both males (respectively in 1988 and 1991).

The second daughter married twice. She gave birth to two children with her first husband, all females (respectively in 1986 and 1994), and had no children with her second husband.

The third son gave birth to two children. Sex of the children in descending order: M (1986) – F (1989).

Grandchildren's Generation:

The first daughter's two sons were unmarried.

The second daughter's first child gave birth to two children. Sex of the children in descending order: F (2004) – M (2011).

The second daughter's second child were unmarried.

The third son's first child gave birth to one child, F (2008).

The third son's second child gave birth to one child, F (2011).

Great-grandchild generation:

Four great-grandchildren, one male and three females.

Household No.: 74; Interviewee: Mo Hanleng; Figure A.132

Current Generation:

Mo Hanleng was born in 1936 and got married in 1953. She gave birth to eight children and has brought up six births. Sex of the children in descending order: M (1954) – M (1955) – M (1957) – M (1959) – F (1961) – M (1963).

F (1965) – M (1967). The first and last sons died just a few months after being born.

Children's Generation:

The second son gave birth to four children. Sex of the children in descending order: M (1976) – M (1978) – M (1981) – F (1985). His first child died in infancy.

The third son was unmarried and had no children and adopted three children. Sex of the children in descending order: M (1978) – M (1981) – F (1985).

The second son turned deaf and died at 18 years old (1999).

The fourth son gave birth to two children. Sex of the children in descending order: F (1985) – M (1987).

The first daughter gave birth to two children. Sex of the children in descending order: M (1988) – F (1992).

The fifth son gave birth to two children, both males (respectively in 1987 and 1989).

The second daughter gave birth to two children, both males (respectively in 1988 and 1989).

Grandchildren's Generation:

The second son's second child gave birth to two children. Sex of the children in descending order: F (1999) – F (2005).

The second son's third child gave birth to two children. Sex of the children in descending order: F (2001) – M (2005).

The second son's fourth child gave birth to one child, F (2009).

The third son's first child gave birth to two children, both males (respectively in 1998 and 2004).

The third son's third child gave birth to one child, M (2005).

The fourth son's first child gave birth to one child, F (2007).

The fourth son's second child gave birth to one child, F (2007).
The first daughter's two children were married but still had no children.
The fifth son's first child gave birth to one child, M (2009).
The fifth son's second child were unmarried.
The second daughter's first child gave birth to one child, F (2009).
The second daughter's second child gave birth to one child, F (2011).

Great-grandchildren's Generation:
13 great-grandchildren, six males and seven females.

Household No.: 75; **Interviewee: Yuehen Tuanwang; Figure A.133**

Current Generation:
Yuehen Tuanwang was born in 1927, got married in 1946, and gave birth to 10 children. Eight births survived. Sex of the children in descending order: F (1947) – F (1949) – F (1952) – F (1954) – F (1957) – F (1959) – M (1962) – M (1964) – M (1965) – M (1973). The fourth daughter and second son died in infancy.

Children's Generation:
The first daughter was Han Shuai from Household No. 20 in this village (her reproductive history is described above).
The second daughter gave birth to three children. Sex of the children in descending order: M (1973) – F (1975) – M (1977).
The third daughter gave birth to two children, both females (respectively in 1974 and 1977), and adopted a child, M (1984).
The fifth daughter gave birth to two children, both males (respectively in 1980 and 1982).
The sixth daughter gave birth to two children, both males (respectively in 1982 and 1984).
The first son gave birth to three children. Sex of the children in descending order: F (1983) – M (1985) – F (1987).
The third son gave birth to two children. Sex of the children in descending order: M (1986) – F (1993).
The fourth son gave birth to two children. Sex of the children in descending order: M (1996) – F (2000).

Grandchildren's Generation:
The second daughter's first child gave birth to one child, M (1996), and his wife had a girl with her former husband (1993).

The second daughter's second child gave birth to two children, both females (respectively in 1996 and 1999).

The second daughter's third child gave birth to one child, M (2001).

The third daughter's first child had no children and adopted a boy (2005).

The third daughter's second child gave birth to two children. Sex of the children in descending order: F (1996) – M (2002).

The third daughter's third child gave birth to two children, both females (respectively in 2005 and 2009).

The fifth daughter's first child gave birth to two children. Sex of the children in descending order: M (2001) – F (2007).

The fifth daughter's second child gave birth to two children. Sex of the children in descending order: F (2005) – M (2009).

The sixth daughter's first child gave birth to two children, both females (respectively in 2005 and 2009).

The sixth daughter's second child were unmarried.

The first son's first child gave birth to one child, F (2007).

The first son's second child gave birth to one child, F (2007).

The first son's third child gave birth to one child, M (2011).

The third son's first child gave birth to one child, M (2011).

The third son's second child were unmarried and was working in another province.

The fourth son's two children are students.

Great-grandchildren's Generation:

20 great-grandchildren, eight males and 12 females.

Yuehen Tuanwang had poor hearing but remained healthy. Her first son said: "She can't stay idle, running around all day. She even came to help us dry up the millet, refusing to take a noon break. She hates to be idle."

Household No.: 78; Interviewees: Shuai Xiangjing and Xianghen Mengyi; Figure A.134

Current Generation:

Shuai Xiangjing was born in 1946 and got married in 1964. Her husband Xianghen Mengyi was born in 1948. The couple gave birth to five children. All Five children survived. Sex of the children in descending order: F (1965) – M (1967) – F (1970) – F (1974) – F (1976).

Children's Generation:

The first daughter gave birth to four children. Sex of the children in descending order: F (1985) – M (1987) – F (1989) – F (1991).

The first son gave birth to two children, both males (respectively in 1987 and 1989).

The second daughter gave birth to one child, M (1994), and received the only-child certificate.

The third daughter gave birth to one child, F (2000), and received the only-child certificate.

The fourth daughter gave birth to one child, F (2008).

Grandchildren's Generation:

The first daughter's first child gave birth to one child, M (2008).

The first daughter's second child and third child both were unmarried.

The first daughter's fourth child was married but still had no children.

The first son's first child gave birth to one child, F (2007). All the other grandchildren were unmarried.

Great-grandchildren's Generation:

Two great-grandchildren, one male and one female.

Shuai Xiangjing and her husband talked about their fertility experience: "At heart, we planned to have two children only. Having three children is well enough. But then, there was no way to do it (birth control), so we had the fourth child, and then, the fifth child. In the 1970s, I heard that there was a way to do it, so I without hesitation took the surgical ligation in the hospital after the fifth baby was born."

As for the children, Shuai Xiangjing said: "The children are also influenced by us. According to national regulations, both the third daughter and the fourth daughter could have had two children, but both of them didn't want to have another one anymore."

Household No.: 90; Interviewee: Hanshuai Yanxin; Figure A.135

Current Generation:

Hanshuai Yanxin was born in 1951, got married in 1970, and gave birth to three children, all males (respectively in 1971, 1973 and 1975).

Children's Generation:

The first son gave birth to two children, both males (respectively in 1992 and 1995).

The second son gave birth to two children. Sex of the children in descending order: M (1996) – F (1999).

The third son gave birth to two children. Sex of the children in descending order: F (2005) – M (2010).

Grandchildren's Generation:

Six grandchildren, four males and two females, were unmarried.

Household No.: 96; Interviewee: Yue Xiangyan; Figure A.136

Current Generation:

Yue Xiangyan was born in 1948, got married in 1967, and gave birth to four children, three females and one male. Sex of the children in descending order: M (1970) – F (1972) – F (1975) – F (1979). She took the surgical ligation after the fourth birth.

Children's Generation:

The first son gave birth to two children. Sex of the children in descending order: M (1994) – F (1998).

The first daughter gave birth to two children. Sex of the children in descending order: M (1991) – F (1993).

The third daughter gave birth to one child, F (2001).

The fourth daughter gave birth to one child, M (2003).

Grandchildren's Generation:

Six grandchildren, three females and three males, all were unmarried.

Summary

Among the 29 households surveyed, the oldest interviewee, Yuehen Tuanwang, was born in 1927 (84 years old) and the youngest, Hanshuai Yanxin and Ruiban Ruiliang, were born in 1951 (60 years old). The reproductive statistics by the age cohort (the 5-year interval) are shown in the following Tables A.21–A.24.

The statistics of births and surviving births in surveyed households by generational cohort:

The Statistics of Births and Surviving Births in Surveyed Households by Generational Cohort:

Table A.21: Reproductive Statistics of the Interviewees (Born in or before 1951) in Village Z

Households	Age Cohort	Number of Lifetime Births (Persons)			Births Surviving till the Age of 15 or above (Persons)			Average Births/ Household	Average Surviving Births/Household
		Total Births	M	F	Total Births	M	F		
2	1951–1955	3	3	0	3	3	0	1.50	1.50
14	1946–1950	57	27	30	54	24	30	4.07	3.86
6	1941–1945	28	13	15	24	12	12	4.67	4.00
5	1936–1940	43	27	16	35	22	13	8.60	7.00
0	1931–1935	—	—	—	—	—	—	—	—
2	1926–1930	19	8	11	16	7	9	9.50	8.00
In total: 29 Households		150	78	72	132	68	64	5.17	4.55

Source: Field Survey Statistics by the Research Team.

Table A.22: Village Z Interviewee (Born Before 1951) Births and Surviving Births

Interviewees		29 Interviewees (Households)			
Age of Interviewee		60–84 Years Old			
Number of Lifetime Births	11 Births	1	Births Surviving till the Age of 15 or above (Persons)	11 Surviving Births	0
	10 Births	2		10 Surviving Births	1
	9 Births	3		9 Surviving Births	2
	8 Births	1		8 Surviving Births	2
	7 Births	2		7 Surviving Births	1
	6 Births	2		6 Surviving Births	4
	5 Births	4		5 Surviving Births	1
	4 Births	5		4 Surviving Births	8
	3 Births	5		3 Surviving Births	5
	2 Births	1		2 Surviving Births	2
	1 Birth	1		1 Surviving Birth	1
	0 Birth	2		0 Surviving Birth	1

Source: Field Survey Statistics by the Research Team.

The Statistics of the Timespans and Proportions of Births in the Surveyed Households by Generational Cohort:

The retrospective Reproductive Statistics mentioned above showed that:

1. By October 2011, 29 interviewees born in or before 1951 (60 years old or above) in village Z had given birth to 154 children, each giving birth to 5.31 children on average, and had 136 children who had survived till the age of 15 or above, with one household having had 4.69 surviving children on average. The overall survival rate of the births was 88.31%.
2. The interviewees had throughout their lifetime given birth to 81 boys and 73 girls, with the boys being slightly outnumbered by the girls, and 71 boys and 65 girls had survived till the age of 15 or above, with the survival rate of the boys and the girls standing respectively at 87.65% and 89.04% and the survival rate of the boys being slightly lower than that of the girls.
3. The interviewees (except for one having never given births and another having never married) had their births in the 1–11 range throughout their lifetime, with each interviewee having 5.17 births on average, and had surviving births in the 1–10 range;

Table A.23: Reproductive Statistics of the Surveyed Households by Generational Cohort (Interviewees Born in or before 1950) in Village Z (No. 1)

Generation	Households	Number of Lifetime Births (Persons)			Births Surviving till the Age of 15 or above (Persons)			Average Total Births per Household	Average Total Surviving Births per Household
		Total Births	M	F	Total Births	M	F		
Current Generation	29	154	81	73	136	71	65	5.31	4.69
Children's Generation	128	258	140	118	247	134	113	2.02	1.93
Grandchildren's Generation	84	105	55	50	103	53	50	1.25	1.23

Source: Field Survey Statistics by the Research Team.

Table A.24: Generational Reproductive Statistics of the Households of the Interviewees (born in or before 1951) in Village Z(No. 2)

Generation\Decade\Percent (%)	**1940s**	**1950s**	**1960s**	**1970s**	**1980s**	**1990s**	**2000s**	**Percent** (%)
Current Generation	2.07	13.10	38.62	44.14	2.07			100.00
Children's Generation				6.57	38.52	38.52	16.39	100.00
Grandchildren's Generation						9.00	91.00	100.00

Source: Field Survey Statistics by the Research Team.

4. The interviewees got married for the first time in the age range from 16 to 30 years old (respectively Interviewee No. 5: Yue En and Interviewee No. 10: Moen Shuaimeng and Interviewee No. 12: Shuai Ensan), and had their last birth between the ages of 24 and 46 old (Interviewee No. 10: Moen Shuaimeng, having her fourth birth, Interviewee No. 16: Shuai Enna, having her second birth, and Interviewee No. 75: Yuehen Tuanwang, having her 10th birth), at 31.79 years old on average.
5. The time at their last childbirth of the interviewees was in the range from 1965 (Shuai Enna from Household No. 16, giving the second birth) to 1981 (Mei Hantuan from Household No. 8, having the seventh birth; Shuai Enlai from Household No. 62, having the ninth birth).
6. The interviewees who had given birth to three or four children made up the largest share of the total at 34.48% and those who had had four surviving births made up the largest share of the total at 27.59%.
7. The interviewees who had given birth to five or fewer children and four or fewer children respectively made up 62.07% and 48.28% of all, and those who had had five or fewer surviving births and four or fewer surviving births respectively made up 65.51% and 62.07% of all;
8. Each generation tends to have few births but more surviving ones on average. The survival rate of the births by Current Generation, Children's Generation and Grandchildren's Generation was respectively 88.31%, 95.74% and 98.10%.
9. The reproductive lifespan for Current Generation extended from the 1940s to the 1980s, but most of the births were from the 1950s to the 1960s, accounting for 82.76% of all the newborns in this period.
10. The reproductive lifespan for Children's Generation extended from the 1970s to the 2000s, but most of the births were from the 1980s to 1990s, accounting for 77.04% of all the newborns in this period.
11. The reproductive lifespan for Grandchildren's Generation extended from the 1990s to the 2000s, but most of the births were in the 2000s.
12. Except for one who had never been married and another who had never had any births, 27 interviewees had completed their lifetime childbirth behaviors by the end of 1980s, with four, 18 and two interviewees completing their lifetime childbirth behaviors respectively in 1960s, 1970s and 1980s.

Genograms

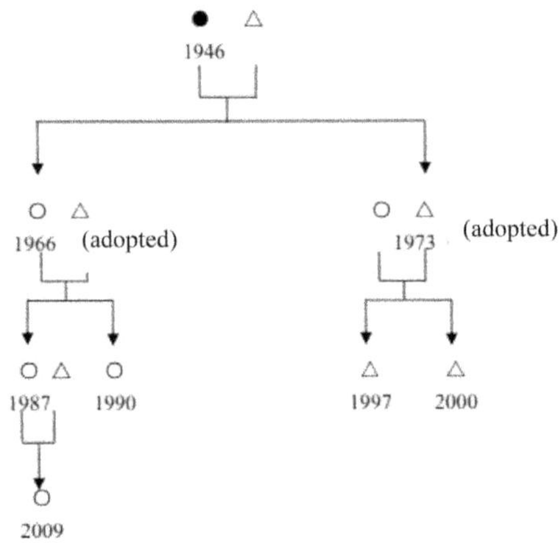

Figure A.109 **Genogram for Shuaien Miewang's family**
▲: male interviewee; ●: female interviewee;
△: male; ○: female;
■: male who died before turning 15; ★: female who died before turning 15;
□: a pregnancy with unknown sex of the fetus;

The sex of those born within each generation are listed in descending order of age, from left to right.

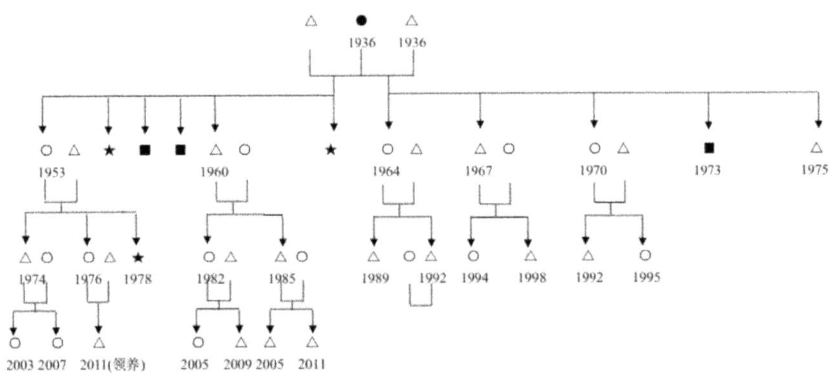

Figure A.110 Genogram for Yue En's family
▲: male interviewee; ●: female interviewee;
△: male; ○: female;
■: male who died before turning 15; ★: female who died before turning 15;
□: a pregnancy with unknown sex of the fetus;

The sex of those born within each generation are listed in descending order of age, from left to right.

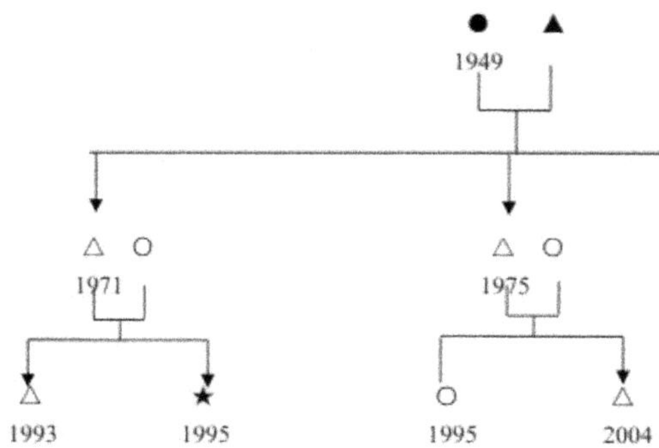

Figure A.111 **Genogram for Yue Hantuan's family**
▲: male interviewee; ●: female interviewee;
△: male; ○: female;
■: male who died before turning 15; ★: female who died before turning 15;
□: a pregnancy with unknown sex of the fetus;

The sex of those born within each generation are listed in descending order of age, from left to right.

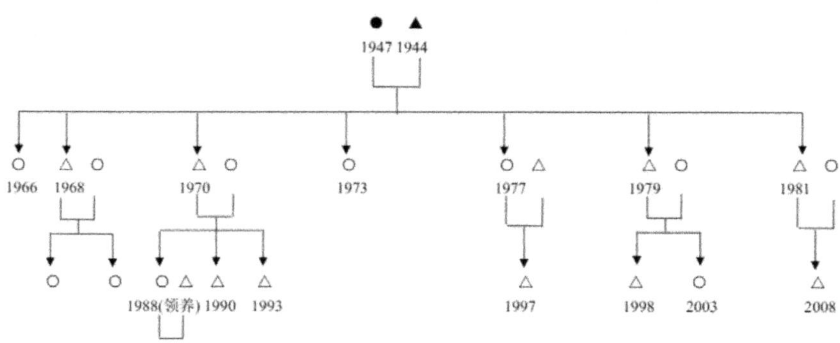

Figure A.112 Genogram for Mei Hantuan's family
▲: male interviewee; ●: female interviewee;
△: male; ○: female;
■: male who died before turning 15; ★: female who died before turning 15;
□: a pregnancy with unknown sex of the fetus;

The sex of those born within each generation are listed in descending order of age, from left to right.

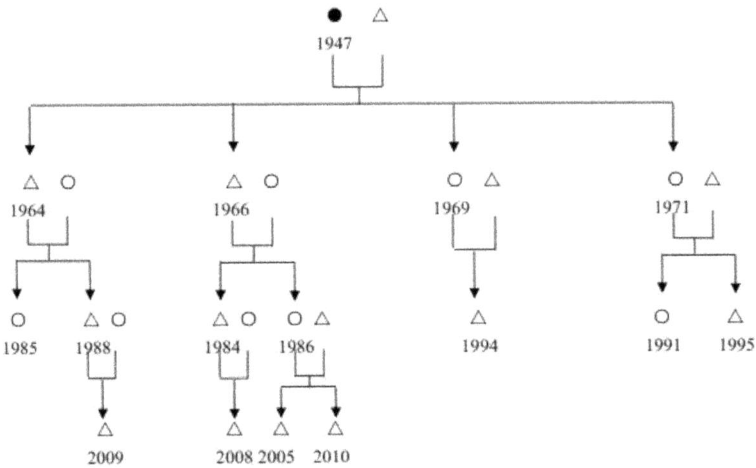

Figure A.113 **Genogram for Moen Shuaimeng's family**
▲: male interviewee; ●: female interviewee;
△: male; ○: female;
■: male who died before turning 15; ★: female who died before turning 15;
□: a pregnancy with unknown sex of the fetus;
The sex of those born within each generation are listed in descending order of age, from left to right.

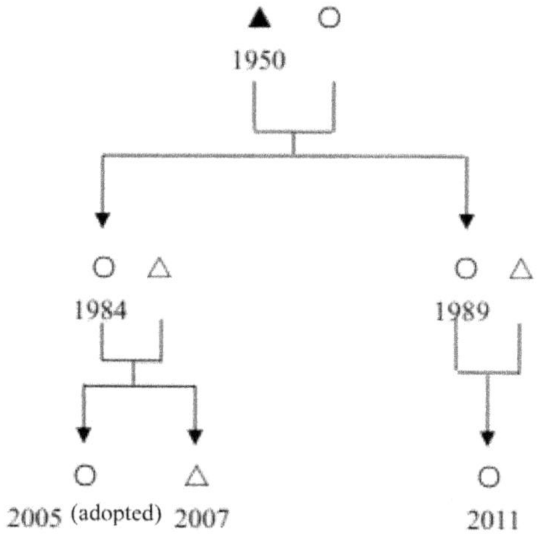

Figure A.114 **Genogram for Shuai Ensan's family**
▲: male interviewee; ●: female interviewee;
△: male; ○: female;
■: male who died before turning 15; ★: female who died before turning 15;
□: a pregnancy with unknown sex of the fetus;
The sex of those born within each generation are listed in descending order of age, from left to right.

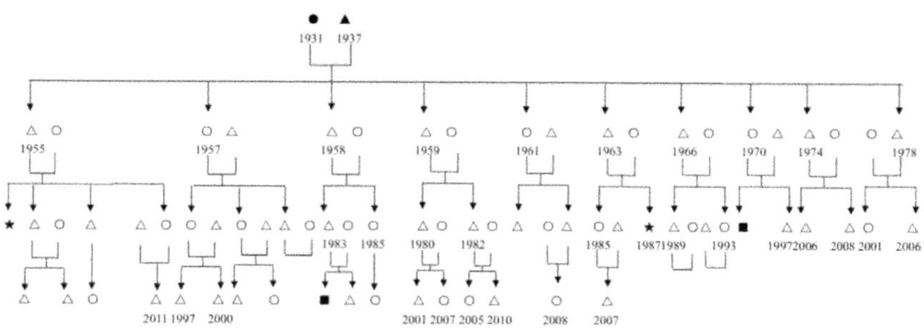

Figure A.115 **Genogram for Yue Enzhan's family**
▲: male interviewee; ●: female interviewee;
△: male; ○: female;
■: male who died before turning 15; ★: female who died before turning 15;
□: a pregnancy with unknown sex of the fetus;
The sex of those born within each generation are listed in descending order of age, from left to right.

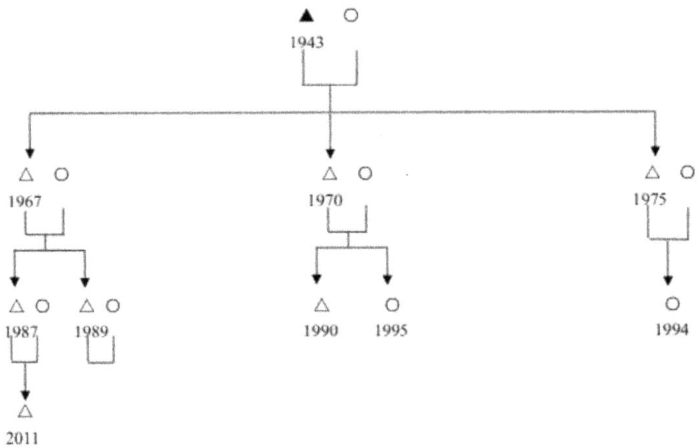

Figure A.116 **Genogram for Xiang Henyan's family**
▲: male interviewee; ●: female interviewee;
△: male; ○: female;
■: male who died before turning 15; ★: female who died before turning 15;
□: a pregnancy with unknown sex of the fetus;
The sex of those born within each generation are listed in descending order of age, from left to right.

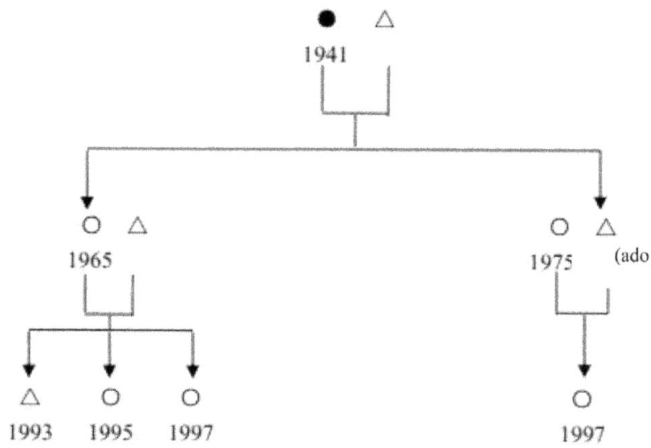

Figure A.117 **Genogram for Shuai Enna's family**
▲: male interviewee; ●: female interviewee;
△: male; ○: female;
■: male who died before turning 15; ★: female who died before turning 15;
□: a pregnancy with unknown sex of the fetus;
The sex of those born within each generation are listed in descending order of age, from left to right.

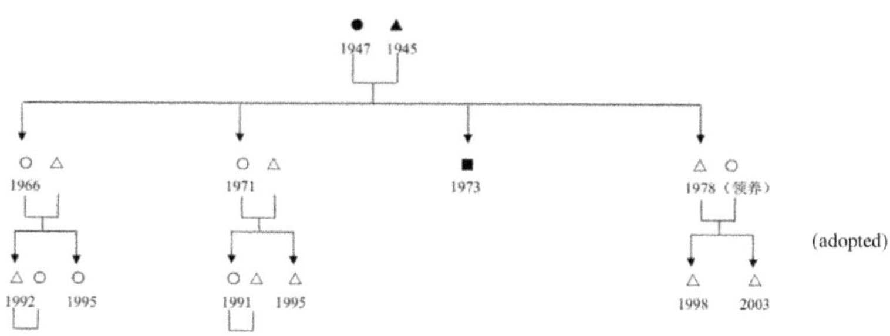

Figure A.118 **Genogram for Mai Hanleng's family**
▲: male interviewee; ●: female interviewee;
△: male; ○: female;
■: male who died before turning 15; ★: female who died before turning 15;
□: a pregnancy with unknown sex of the fetus;
The sex of those born within each generation are listed in descending order of age, from left to right.

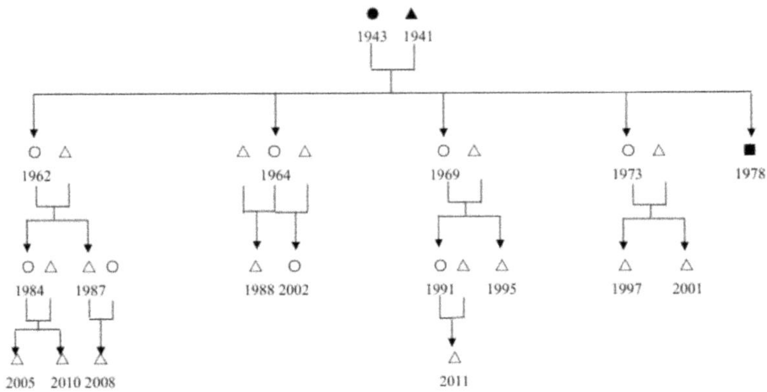

Figure A.119 **Genogram for Mo Enshuai's family**
▲: male interviewee; ●: female interviewee;
△: male; ○: female;
■: male who died before turning 15; ★: female who died before turning 15;
□: a pregnancy with unknown sex of the fetus;
The sex of those born within each generation are listed in descending order of age, from left to right.

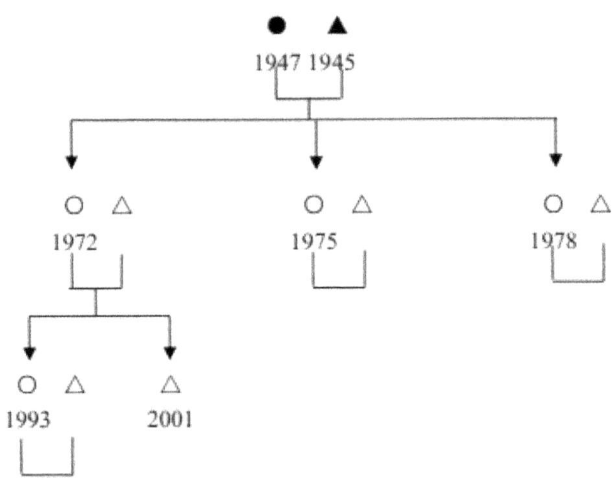

Figure A.120 **Genogram for Han Shuai's family**
▲: male interviewee; ●: female interviewee;
△: male; ○: female;
■: male who died before turning 15; ★: female who died before turning 15;
□: a pregnancy with unknown sex of the fetus;
The sex of those born within each generation are listed in descending order of age, from left to right.

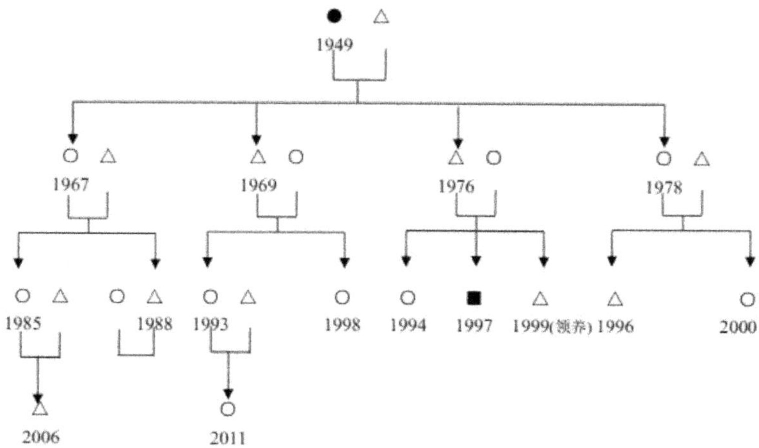

Figure A.121 **Genogram for Shuai Enpin's family**
▲: male interviewee; ●: female interviewee;
△: male; ○: female;
■: male who died before turning 15; ★: female who died before turning 15;
□: a pregnancy with unknown sex of the fetus;
The sex of those born within each generation are listed in descending order of age, from left to right.

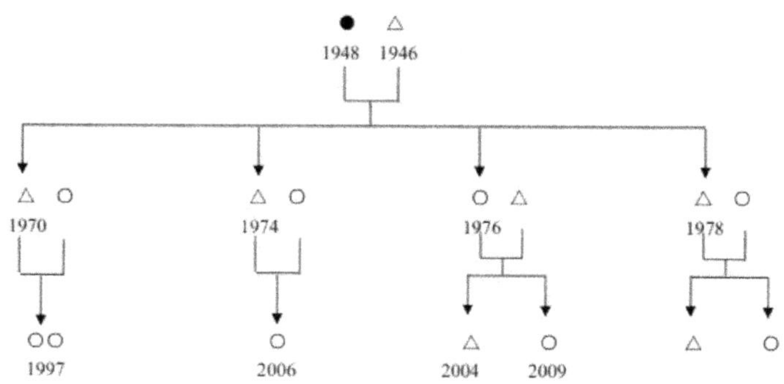

Figure A.122 **Genogram for Shuai Henhan's family**
▲: male interviewee; ●: female interviewee;
△: male; ○: female;
■: male who died before turning 15; ★: female who died before turning 15;
□: a pregnancy with unknown sex of the fetus;
The sex of those born within each generation are listed in descending order of age, from left to right.

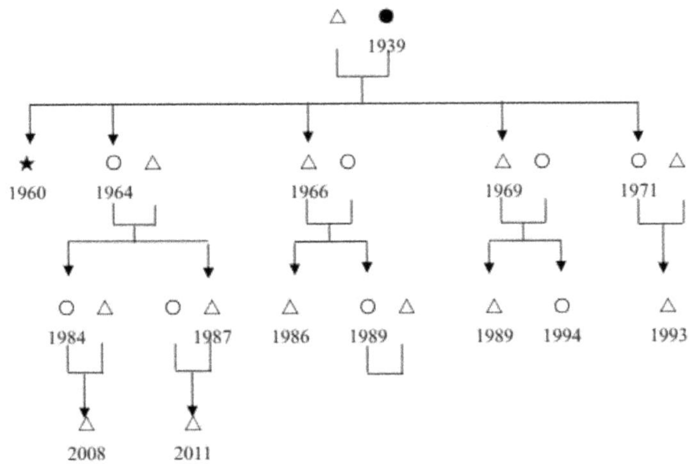

Figure A.123 **Genogram for Shuai Hanlun's family**
▲: male interviewee; ●: female interviewee;
△: male; ○: female;
■: male who died before turning 15; ★: female who died before turning 15;
□: a pregnancy with unknown sex of the fetus;
The sex of those born within each generation are listed in descending order of age, from left to right.

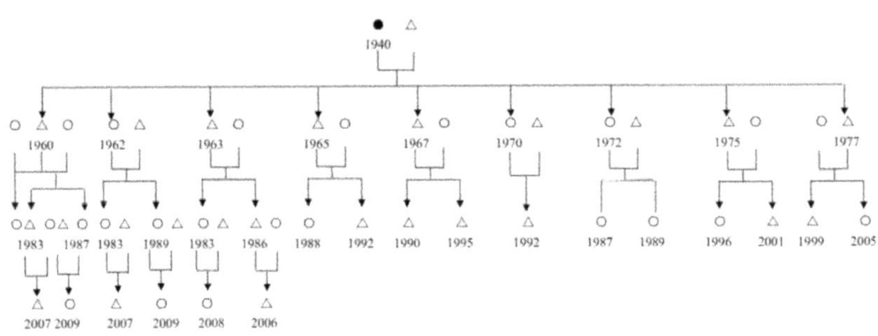

Figure A.124 **Genogram for Mo Hanmen's family**
▲: male interviewee; ●: female interviewee;
△: male; ○: female;
■: male who died before turning 15; ★: female who died before turning 15;
□: a pregnancy with unknown sex of the fetus;
The sex of those born within each generation are listed in descending order of age, from left to right.

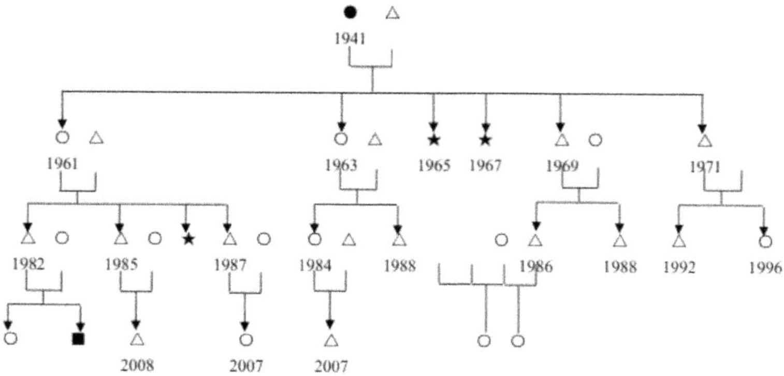

Figure A.125 **Genogram for Man Xianghuang's family**
▲: male interviewee; ●: female interviewee;
△: male; ○: female;
■: male who died before turning 15; ★: female who died before turning 15;
□: a pregnancy with unknown sex of the fetus;
The sex of those born within each generation are listed in descending order of age, from left to right.

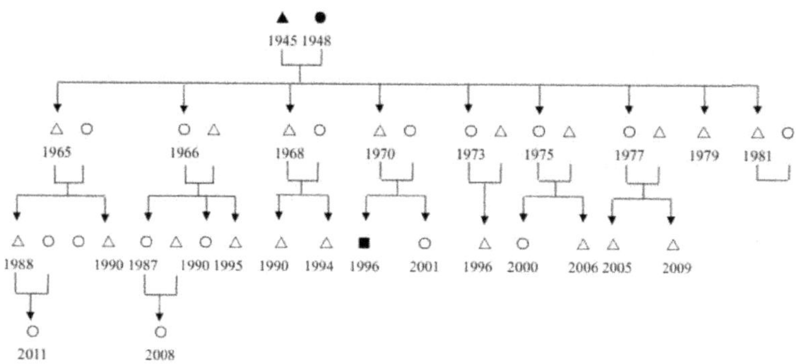

Figure A.126 **Genogram for Shuai Enlai's family**
▲: male interviewee; ●: female interviewee;
△: male; ○: female;
■: male who died before turning 15; ★: female who died before turning 15;
□: a pregnancy with unknown sex of the fetus;
The sex of those born within each generation are listed in descending order of age, from left to right.

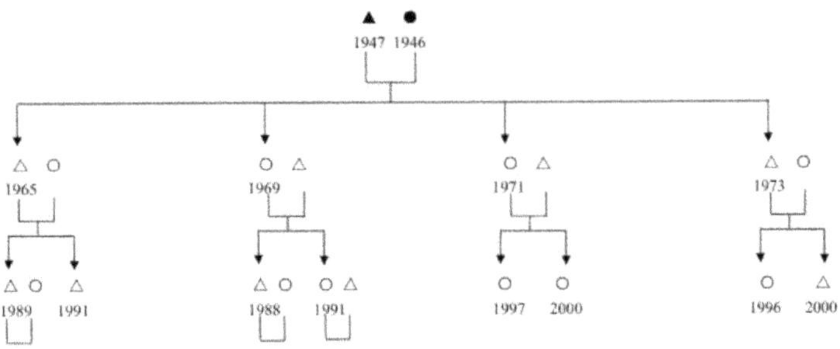

Figure A.127 **Genogram for Ruiban's family**
▲: male interviewee; ●: female interviewee;
△: male; ○: female;
■: male who died before turning 15; ★: female who died before turning 15;
□: a pregnancy with unknown sex of the fetus;
The sex of those born within each generation are listed in descending order of age, from left to right.

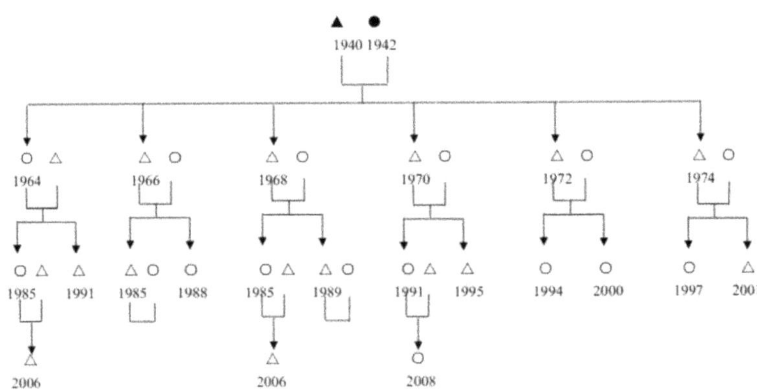

Figure A.128 **Genogram for Yue Enman's family**
▲: male interviewee; ●: female interviewee;
△: male; ○: female;
■: male who died before turning 15; ★: female who died before turning 15;
□: a pregnancy with unknown sex of the fetus;
The sex of those born within each generation are listed in descending order of age, from left to right.

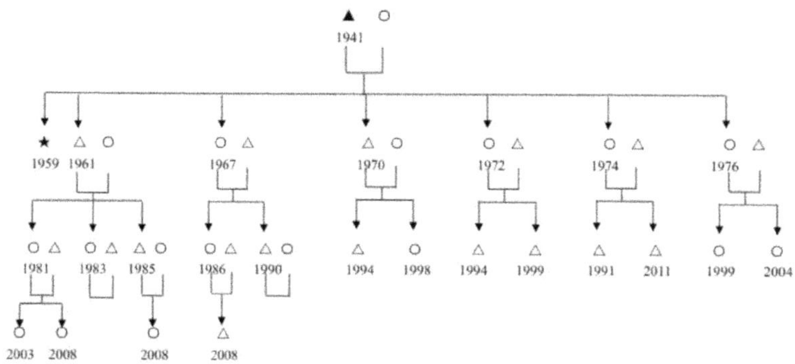

Figure A.129 **Genogram for Shuai Xiangbao's family**
▲: male interviewee; ●: female interviewee;
△: male; ○: female;
■: male who died before turning 15; ★: female who died before turning 15;
□: a pregnancy with unknown sex of the fetus;
The sex of those born within each generation are listed in descending order of age, from left to right.

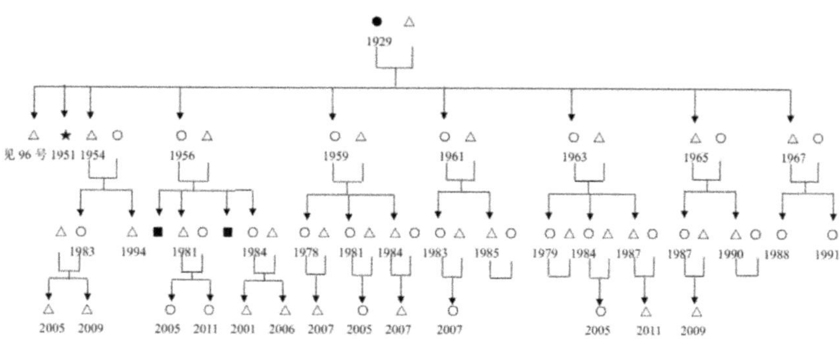

Figure A.130 **Genogram for Yu Hanwang's family**
▲: male interviewee; ●: female interviewee;
△: male; ○: female;
■: male who died before turning 15; ★: female who died before turning 15;
□: a pregnancy with unknown sex of the fetus;
The sex of those born within each generation are listed in descending order of age, from left to right.

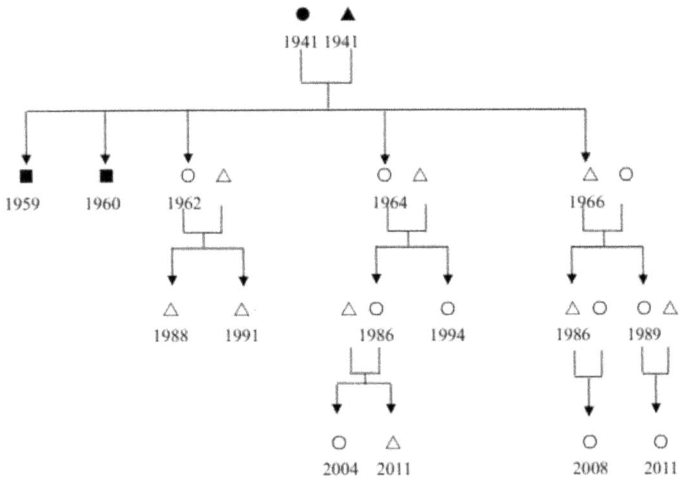

Figure A.131 **Genogram for Yuehan Xiangsha's family**
▲: male interviewee; ●: female interviewee;
△: male; ○: female;
■: male who died before turning 15; ★: female who died before turning 15;
□: a pregnancy with unknown sex of the fetus;
The sex of those born within each generation are listed in descending order of age, from left to right.

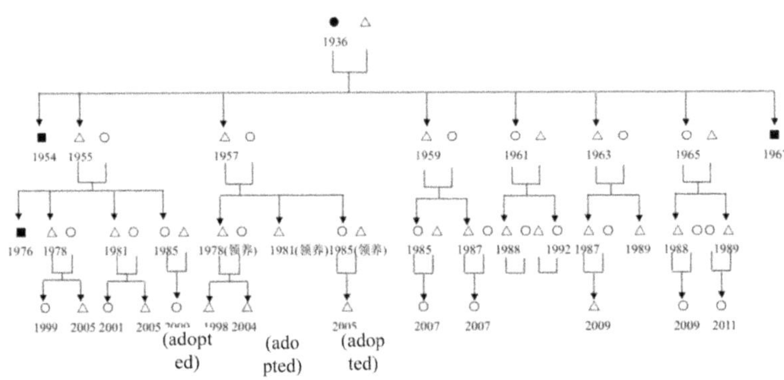

Figure A.132 **Genogram for Mo Hanleng's family**
▲: male interviewee; ●: female interviewee;
△: male; ○: female;
■: male who died before turning 15; ★: female who died before turning 15;
□: a pregnancy with unknown sex of the fetus;
The sex of those born within each generation are listed in descending order of age, from left to right.

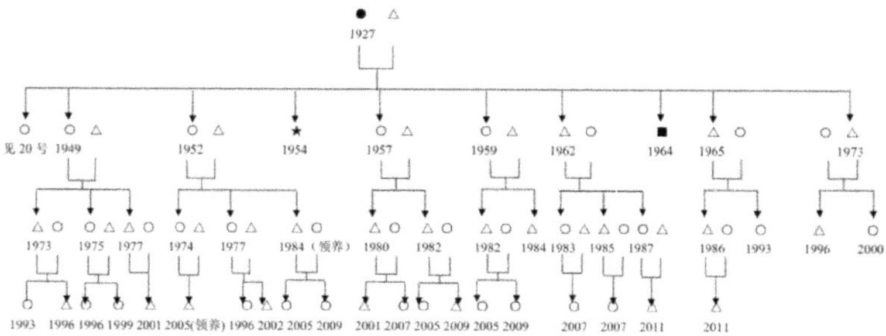

Figure A.133 **Genogram for Yuehen Tuanwang's family**
▲: male interviewee; ●: female interviewee;
△: male; ○: female;
■: male who died before turning 15; ★: female who died before turning 15;
□: a pregnancy with unknown sex of the fetus;

The sex of those born within each generation are listed in descending order of age, from left to right.

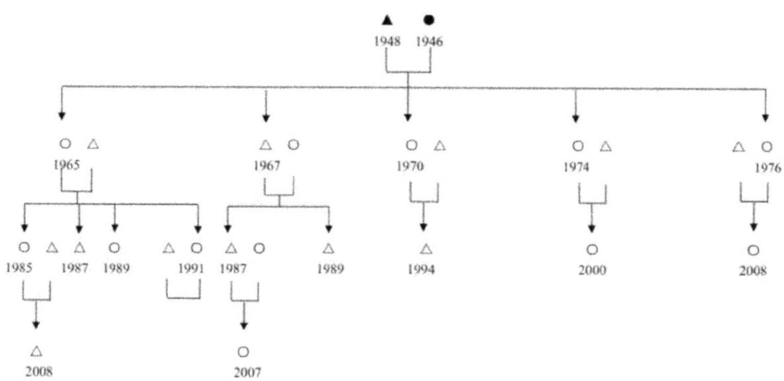

Figure A.134 **Genogram for Shuai Xiangjing's family**
▲: male interviewee; ●: female interviewee;
△: male; ○: female;
■: male who died before turning 15; ★: female who died before turning 15;
□: a pregnancy with unknown sex of the fetus;
The sex of those born within each generation are listed in descending order of age, from left to right.

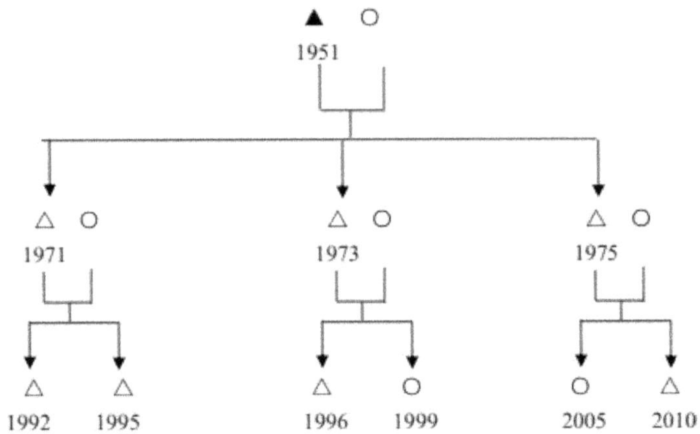

Figure A.135 **Genogram for Hanshuai Yanxin's family**
▲: male interviewee; ●: female interviewee;
△: male; ○: female;
■: male who died before turning 15; ★: female who died before turning 15;
□: a pregnancy with unknown sex of the fetus;
The sex of those born within each generation are listed in descending order of age, from left to right.

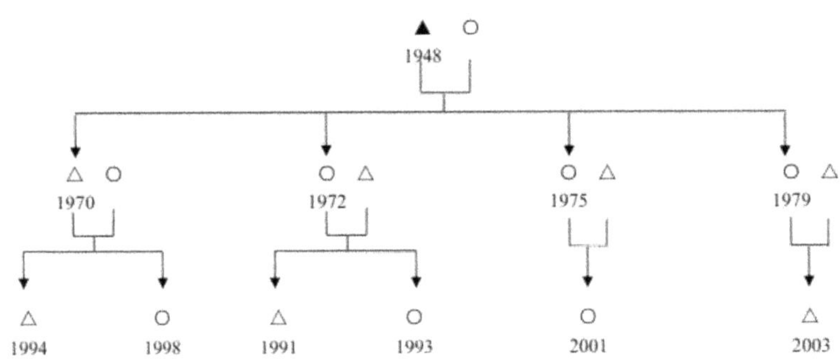

Figure A.136 **Genogram for Yue Xiangyan's family**
▲: male interviewee; ●: female interviewee;
△: male; ○: female;
■: male who died before turning 15; ★: female who died before turning 15;
□: a pregnancy with unknown sex of the fetus;
The sex of those born within each generation are listed in descending order of age, from left to right.

Summary

During the period from January to October 2011, the research team conducted a more comprehensive survey of reproductive histories in the Dai families in the five villages in the two prefectures based on the above survey design, and gained the primary data as in the following Tables A. 25-27:

The above statistics provided the following information:

1. By October 2011, 139 interviewees had given birth to 585 children, each giving birth to 4.21 children on average, and had 533 children who had survived till the age of 15 or above, with one household having had 3.83 surviving children on average. The overall survival rate of the births was 91.11%.
2. The interviewees had throughout their lifetime given birth to 301 boys and 284 girls, with the boys slightly outnumbering the girls, and 272 boys and 261 girls had survived till the age of 15 or above, with the survival rate of the boys and the girls standing respectively at 90.37% and 91.90% and the survival rate of the boys being slightly lower than that of the girls.
3. The interviewees (except for four who had never had any births) had had their births in the 1–11 range throughout their lifetime, and had surviving births in the 0–10 range;
4. The interviewees who had given birth to three or four children made up the largest share of the total at 48.92% and those who had had three or four surviving births made up the largest share of the total at 53.96%.
5. The interviewees who had given birth to five or fewer children and four or fewer children respectively made up 82.01% and 64.75% of all, and those who had had five or fewer surviving births and four or fewer surviving births respectively made up 83.45% and 72.66% of all;
6. The interviewees got married for the first time in the age range from 16 to 30 years old, at 19.57 years old on average, and had their last birth in the age range from 19 to 50 years old (respectively having the 1st birth and having the 8th births), at 31.93 years old on average.
7. The interviewees had their last birth in the period from 1950 (having the second birth) to 1985 (having the fourth birth).
8. Each generation tends to have few births but more surviving ones on average. The survival rate of the births by Current Generation, Children's

Table A.25: Reproductive Statistics of the Interviewees (Born in or before 1951) in the Five Villages

Households	Age Cohort	Number of Lifetime Births (Persons)			Births Surviving till the Age of 15 or above (Persons)			Average Births/ Household	Average Surviving Births/Household
		Total Births	M	F	Total Births	M	F		
2	1951–1955	3	3	0	3	3	0	1.50	1.50
40	1946–1950	130	61	69	124	57	67	3.25	3.10
29	1941–1945	115	57	58	107	54	53	3.97	3.69
32	1936–1940	153	88	65	136	78	58	4.78	4.25
13	1931–1935	60	31	29	54	28	26	4.62	4.15
11	1926–1930	63	34	29	54	28	26	5.73	4.91
10	1921–1925	51	23	28	47	21	26	5.10	4.70
1	1916–1920	6	3	3	6	3	3	6.00	6.00
0	1911–1915	——	——	——	——	——	——	——	——
1	1906–1910	4	1	3	2	0	2	4	2
In total: 139 Households		585	301	284	533	272	261	4.21	3.83

Source: Field Survey Statistics by the Research Team.

Table A.26: Reproductive Statistics of the Female Interviewees (Born in or before 1951) in the Five Villages

Age Cohort (At the Survey Time)		60–103 Years Old (1906–1951)			
Number of Lifetime Births	11 Births	1	Births Surviving till the Age of 15 or above (Persons)	11 Surviving Births	0
	10 Births	2		10 Surviving Births	1
	9 Births	3		9 Surviving Births	2
	8 Births	6		8 Surviving Births	4
	7 Births	5		7 Surviving Births	4
	6 Births	8		6 Surviving Births	10
	5 Births	24		5 Surviving Births	15
	4 Births	39		4 Surviving Births	40
	3 Births	29		3 Surviving Births	37
	2 Births	13		2 Surviving Births	16
	1 Birth	5		1 Surviving Birth	7
	0 Birth	4		0 Surviving Birth	3

Source: Field Survey Statistics by the Research Team.

Generation and Grandchildren's Generation was respectively 90.91%, 96.51% and 98.42%.

9. The reproductive lifespan for Current Generation extended from the 1940s to the 1980s, but most of the births were from the 1950s to the 1960s, accounting for 83.29% of all the newborns in this period.
10. The reproductive lifespan for Children's Generation extended from the 1970s to the 2000s, but most of the births were from the 1980s to 1990s, accounting for 78.38% of all the newborns in this period.
11. The reproductive lifespan for Grandchildren's Generation extended from the 1990s to the 2000s, but most of the births were in the 2000s.
12. The female interviewees (except for four ones who had never had any births) completed their lifetime childbirth behaviors, beginning at their first marriage and ending at their last birth, in a timeframe from one year (having one birth, female) to 27 years (having 10 births, four males and six females), in 12.36 years on average.

Table A.27: Reproductive Statistics of the Surveyed Households by Generational Cohort (Interviewees Born in or before 1951) in the Five Villages

Generation	Households	Number of Lifetime Births (Persons)			Births Surviving till the Age of 15 or above (Persons)			Average Total Births per Household	Average Total Surviving Births per Household
		Total Births	M	F	Total Births	M	F		
Parents' Generation	58/88	341	168	173	370	163	207	5.88	4.20
Current Generation	139	594	306	288	540	277	263	4.27	3.88
Children's Generation	494	973	494	479	939	474	465	1.97	1.90
Grandchildren's Generation	308	380	192	188	374	188	186	1.23	1.21
Great-grandchildren's Generation	3	3	3	0	3	3	0	1.00	1.00

Source: Field Survey Statistics by the Research Team.

References

Becker [The U.S.]. *The Family Economic Analysis* [M]. Translated by She Biping. Beijing: Huaxia Publishing House, 1987.

Becker [The U.S.]. *The Economic Analysis of Human Behaviors* [M]. Translated by Wang Yeyu and Chen Qi. Shanghai: Shanghai People's Publishing House, 1995.

Benedict [The U.S.]. *The Chrysanthemum and the Sword* [M]. Translated by Lyu Wanhe et al. Beijing: the Commercial Press, 2005.

Cao, Chengzhang. *Research on the Village Culture of the Dai Group* [M]. Beijing: China Minzu University Press, 2006.

Chen, Huixiong. *The Principle of Pleasure: An Analysis of Human Economic Behaviors* [M]. Beijing: Economic Sciences Press, 2003.

Chen, Qingde. *Resources Allocation and Institutional Change* [M]. Kunming: Yunnan University Press, 2001.

Chen, Zhen. Externality and Cultural Marginality of Peasants' Fertility Behavior [J]. *Population & Economics*, No. 1 (1998).

Chen, Xuguang, and Li Guangcan, ed. *An Introduction to the Population of Ethnic Minorities in Yunnan* [M]. Yunnan: Yunnan People's Publishing House, 1990.

China Population and Family Planning Commission. *The Proceedings of the National Symposium on Fertility Cultural Theory and Practice (Part I and Part II)* [C] Beijing: China Population Publishing House, 2003.

Compilation Committee of Local Chronicles of Dai Autonomous Prefecture of Xishuangbanna. *The Chronicles of Dai Autonomous Prefecture of Xishuangbanna*[M]. Beijing: Xinhua Publishing House, 2002.

Duan, Jixian *China Population Conditioning* [M]. Beijing: China Population Publishing House, 1999.

Durkheim [French]. *The Primary Forms of Religious Life* [M]. Translated by Lin Zengjin and Peng Shouyi. Beijing: China Minzu University Press, 1999.

Editorial Committee of Five Series of Books on Ethnic Issues. *A Survey of the Dai Ethnic Society and History (Xishuangbanna-Vol. 1–10)* [C]. Kunming: Yunnan People's Publishing House, 1983.

Editorial Committee of Five Series of Books on Ethnic Issues. *A Comprehensive Survey of the Dai Ethnic Society in Xishuangbanna-Vol. 2*[C]. Kunming: The Nationalities Publishing House of Yunnan, 1984.

Editorial Committee of Five Series of Books on Ethnic Issues. *A Comprehensive Survey of the Dai Ethnic Society in Xishuangbanna-Vol.1*[C]. Kunming: The Nationalities Publishing House of Yunnan, 1984.

Editorial Committee of Five Series of Books on Ethnic Issues. *A Brief History of the Dai Ethnic Group* [M]. Kunming: Yunnan People's Publishing House, 1985.

Fang, Tie. *Traditional Culture and Reproductive Health*[C]. Beijing: China Social Sciences Press, 1997.

Fei, Xiaotong. *Reproduction Institutions in Rural China* [M]. Beijing: Peking University Press, 1998.

Fei, Xiaotong. *The Economy of Jiang Village – Fertility of Chinese Farmers* [M]. Beijing: the Commercial Press, 2001.

Fei, Xiaotong. "Cultural Consciousness amid the Social Changes in China over the Recent Century and Globalization" [J]. *Journal of Xiamen University*, 4 (2005).

Fei, Xiaotong, and Zhang Zhiyi. *Three Villages in Yunnan* [M]. Beijing: Social Sciences Academic Press, 2006.

Foucault, Michel [French]. *The History of Sexuality* [M]. Translated by She Biping. Shanghai: Shanghai People's Publishing House, 2005.

Gao, Fayuan. *Survey on Ethnic Villages in Yunnan·Dai Ethnic Group in Mangang Village, Mengzhe Township, Menghai County* [M]. Kunming: Yunnan University Press, 2001.

Gao, Lishi. *The History and Culture of the Dai Ethnic People in Xishuangbanna* [M]. Kunming: The Nationalities Publishing House of Yunnan, 1992.

Gao, Lishi. *Selected Works on the Dai Ethnic Group by Gao LaShip* [M]. Kunming: The Nationalities Publishing House of Yunnan, 2006.

Gu, Baochang. *Sociodemographic Perspective* [M]. Beijing: the Commercial Press, 1992.

Guo, Liangyun. *Buddhas and Primitive Buddhist Thoughts* [M]. Beijing: China Social Sciences Press, 1997.

Harris, Ian. *Buddhism and Politics in 21th Century Asia*, Continuum Publishing, NY, 2001.

Harris, Marvin [French]. *Cannibals and Kings: The Origins of Cultures* [M]. Translated by She Biping. Beijing: Huaxia Publishing House, 1987.

Hayek [The U.K.]. *The Fatal Conceit* [M]. Translated by Feng Keli. Beijing: China Social Sciences Press, 2000.

Hu, Shaohua. *The Records of the Dai Ethnic Customs* [M]. Beijing: China Social Sciences Press, 1999.

Jiang, Yingliang. *The Cultural Life of the Dai Ethnic Group* [M]. Shanghai: Zhonghua Book Company, 1950.

Jiang, Yingliang. *The Economic Life of the Dai Group* [M]. Guangzhou: Tsinghua Press, 1950.

Jiang, Yingliang. *The History of the Dai Ethnic Group* [M]. Chengdu: The Nationalities Publishing House of Sichuan, 1983.

Ke, Wugang, and Shi Manfei [German]. *The Institutional Economics* [M]. Translated by Han Zhaohua. Beijing: the Commercial Press, 2004.

Li, Fuyi. *The Annals of 12 Bannas* [M]. Taiwan: Chiang Kai-shek Publishing Company, 1955.

Li, Jianmin. "China's Fertility Revolution" [J]. *Population Research*, 1 (2009).

Li, Jingneng. *Research on Population and Economy in Current China* [M]. Beijing: China Population Publishing House, 1998.

Li, Jingneng. *New Selection of Population Theories* [M]. Beijing: China Population Publishing House, 2001.

Li, Yinhe. *Procreation and Village Cultures* [M]. Beijing: China Social Sciences Press, 1994.

Li, Zhongqing, and Wang Feng [The U.S.]. *One Fourth of Human Beings: Thomas Malthus's Myth and the Realities in China (1700–2000)* [M]. Translated Chen Wei and Yao Yuan. Beijing: Joint Publishing Press, 2000.

Lin, Fang ed. *Human Potential and Value* [M]. Beijing: Huaxia Publishing House, 1987.

Liu, Ye, Trans. *Maslow's Wisdom* [M]. Beijing: China Film Press, 2005.

Liu, Zhi. *Research on the Cross-boundary Ethnic Development in China and Southeast Asia* [M]. Beijing: The Ethnic Publishing House, 2007.

Luo, Chun et al., "Comparative Research on Women's Fertility Rates and Patterns of Ethnic Groups in Yunnan" [J].*Journal of Yunnan Nationalities University*, 6 (2004).

Lyu, Zhaohe. *Institutional Changes and Population Development* [M]. Beijing: China Social Sciences Press, 1999.

Lyu, Zhaohe et al. "Analysis of the Fertility Behavior and Rational Choices in Ethnic Minority Villages in China" [J]. *Ethno-National Studies*, 1 (2005).

Ma, Chongwei. "The Protection of Tradition and Invention" [J]. *Journal of Yunnan University*, 2 (2005).

Ma, Yao. *A Collection of Academic Treatises by Ma Yao* [M]. Kunming: Yunnan People's Publishing House, 1998.

Malthus, Thomas [The UK]. *An Essay on the Principle of Population* [M]. Translated by Zhu Yang. Hu Qilin and Zhu Hezhong. Beijing: the Commercial Press, 1992.

Maslow [The U.S.]. *Realize the Value of Life* [M]. Translated by Feng Huaping. Hohhot: People's Publishing House of Inner Mongolia, 2002.

Maslow [The U.S.]. *Self-Actualizing Man* [M]. Translated by Xu Jinsheng and Liu Feng. Beijing: Joint Publishing Press, 1987.

Marx, Engels [German]. *Selected Works of Mark and Engels*: Vol.-I [M]. Beijing: People's Publishing House, 1995.

Malinowski [The U.K.]. *The Sexual Life of Savages* [M]. Translated by He Yong. Beijing: China Knowledge Press, 1998.

Malinowski [The U.K.]. *A Scientific Theory of Culture and Other Essays* [M]. Translated by Fei Xiaotong. Beijing: Huaxia Publishing House, 2002.

Max, Weber [German]. *Confucianism and Taoism* [M]. Translated by Wang Rongfen. Beijing: the Commercial Press, 1995.

Max, Weber [German]. *Chinese Religions: Religions and the World* [M]. Translated by Kang Le and Jian Huimei. Guilin: Guangxi Normal University Press, 2004.

Max, Weber [German]. *Soziologische Grundbegriffe* [M]. Translated by Gu Zhonghua. Guilin: Guangxi Normal University Press, 2005.

Morris [The U.K.]. *Anthropology of Religion* [M]. Translated by Zhou Guoli. Beijing: China Today Publishing House, 1992.

Peng, Peiyun, ed. *Encyclopedia of Family Planning in China* [M]. Beijing: China Population Publishing House, 1997.

Radcliffe-Brown [The U.K.]. *Structure and Function in Primitive Society* [M]. Translated by Pan Jiao and Wang Xianhai. Beijing: China Minzu University Press, 1999.

Schmidt [The U.S.]. *Under the Influence: How Christianity Transformed Civilization* [M]. Translated by Wang Xiaodan and Zhao Wei. Beijing: Peking University Press, 2004.

Smith, Bardwell L. *Tradition and Change in Theravada Buddhism*, Contributions to *Asia Studies*, Vol. 4. Leiden: E.J.Brill, 1973.

Song, Enchang. *Collected Works of Research on Ethnic Minorities in Yunnan*[C]. Kunming: Yunnan People's Publishing House, 1986.

Song, Jian. "Population Dynamics in the Information Age" [J]. *Xinhua Digest*, 10 (2007).

Song, Lidao, *Sacred and Secular- Religions and Politics in South Buddhist Countries* [M]. Beijing: China Religious Culture Publisher, 2000.

Song, Lidao. *Tradition and Modernity: the Changing World of Southern Buddhism* [M]. Beijing: China Social Sciences Press, 2002.

Tan, Leshan, *Theravada Buddhism and the Dai Village Economy* [M]. Translated by Zhao Xiaoniu. Kunming: Yunnan University Press, 2005.

Tian, Xueyuan, ed. *The Ethnic Populations in China* [M]. Beijing: China Population Publishing House, 2005.

Tian, Xueyuan et al. *Research on Fertility Cultures* [M]. Beijing: China Modern Economic Publishing House, 2006.

Tong, Xin. Population Sociology [M]. Beijing: Peking University Press, 2000.

Tong, Shaoyu, and Chen Yongsen. *Research on Intermontane Basins in Yunnan* [M]. Kunming: Yunnan University Press, 2007.

Trevor, Ling. *Buddhism Trends in Southeast Asia.* Singapore: Institute of Southeast Asian Studies, 1996.

Wang, Yizhi, and Yang Shiguang. *On the Pattra leaf Culture* [M]. Kunming: Yunnan People's Publishing House, 1990.

Westermarck [Finland]. *The History of Human Marriage* (Vol. I-III) [M]. Translated by Li Shan and Li Yifu. Beijing: the Commercial Press, 2002.

Xia, Jianzhong. *Theories of Cultural Anthropology* [M]. Beijing: China Renmin University Press, 1997.

Xie, Shizhong, and Dai Le. *Ethnic Groups in Xishuangbanna* [M]. Taiwan: Department of Culture and Publication, *Independent Evening News*, 1993.

Xu, Yafei et al. *Economic Perspectives on Ethnic Groups and Religions* [M]. Kunming: Yunnan People's Publishing House, 1991.

Yang, Zhuhui. *Research on the Fertility Cultures of Ethnic Groups in Southwest China* [M]. Beijing: China Minzu University Press, 2006.

Yao, Hesheng, *The Folklore of Shui Clan of the Dai Ethnic Group* [M]. Kunming: Yunnan People's Publishing House, 2003.

Yuan, Yongxi, ed. *China's Population (General Introduction)* [M]. Beijing: Chinese Financial & Economic Publishing House, 1991.

Zhang, Tianlu, ed. *The Evolution of the Chinese Ethnic Populations* [M]. Beijing: China Ocean Press, 1993.

Zhang, Weiqing, ed. *Readings on Coordinated Efforts in Solving Population Issues* [M]. Beijing: China Population Publishing House, 2007.

Zhao, Shilin, and Wu Qionghua. *The Annals of the Dai Ethnic Culture* [M]. Kunming: The Nationalities Publishing House of Yunnan, 1997.

Zheng, Weidong. *Transformations and Fertility Cultures in Village Societies* [M]. Shanghai: Shanghai People's Publishing House, 2007.

Zhu, Depu. *Dai Ethnic Spirits Worship Catalog Record* [M]. Kunming: The Nationalities Publishing House of Yunnan, 1996.

www.ingramcontent.com/pod-product-compliance
Ingram Content Group UK Ltd.
Pitfield, Milton Keynes, MK11 3LW, UK
UKHW021835100926
8556IPUK00004B/358

9 781433 181474